STREET ATLAS
East Sussex

First published in 1998

George Philip Ltd, a division of
Octopus Publishing Group Ltd
2–4 Heron Quays, London E14 4JP

Second colour edition 2001
First impression 2001

ISBN 0-540-07970-7
ISBN 0-540-07971-5

© George Philip Ltd 2001

This product includes mapping data licensed
from Ordnance Survey®, with the permission of
the Controller of Her Majesty's Stationery Office.
© Crown copyright 2001. All rights reserved.
Licence number 100011710

Printed and bound in Spain
by Cayfosa-Quebecor

Contents

III Key to map symbols

IV Key to map pages

VI Route planning

VIII Administrative and Postcode boundaries

1 Street maps at 3½ inches to 1 mile

189 Street map of Brighton city centre
at 7 inches to 1 mile

190 Town maps of Chichester and Crawley

191 Town maps of Horsham and Worthing

192 Index of towns and villages

193 Index of streets, hospitals, industrial estates, railway
stations, schools, shopping centres and universities

Digital Data

The exceptionally high-quality mapping found in this atlas is available as digital data in TIFF
format, which is easily convertible to other bit mapped (raster) image formats.

The index is also available in digital form as a standard database table. It contains all the details
found in the printed index together with the National Grid reference for the map square in which
each entry is named and feature codes for places of interest in eight categories such as education
and health.

For further information and to discuss your requirements, please contact Philip's on
020 7531 8440 or george.philip@philips-maps.co.uk

	Motorway with junction number		Railway station
	Primary route – dual/single carriageway		Private railway station
	A road – dual/single carriageway		Bus, coach station
	B road – dual/single carriageway		Ambulance station
	Minor road – dual/single carriageway		Coastguard station
	Other minor road – dual/single carriageway		Fire station
	Road under construction		Police station
	Pedestrianised area		Accident and Emergency entrance to hospital
DY7	Postcode boundaries	H	Hospital
	County and unitary authority boundaries	+	Place of worship
	Railway	i	Information Centre (open all year)
	Tramway, miniature railway	P	Parking
	Rural track, private road or narrow road in urban area	P&R	Park and Ride
	Gate or obstruction to traffic (restrictions may not apply at all times or to all vehicles)	PO	Post Office
	Path, bridleway, byway open to all traffic, road used as a public path		Camping site
	The representation in this atlas of a road, track or path is no evidence of the existence right of way		Caravan site
			Golf course
160			Picnic site
84	Adjoining page indicators	Prim Sch	Important buildings, schools, colleges, universities and hospitals
189	The map area within the pink band is shown at a larger scale on the page indicated by the red block and arrow	River Medway	Water name
			Stream
			River or canal – minor and major
			Water
			Tidal water
			Woods
			Houses
		House	Non-Roman antiquity
		VILLA	Roman antiquity

Allot Gdns	Allotments	Meml	Memorial
Acad	Academy	Mon	Monument
Cemy	Cemetery	Mus	Museum
C Ctr	Civic Centre	Obsy	Observatory
CH	Club House	Pal	Royal Palace
Coll	College	PH	Public House
Crem	Crematorium	Recn Gd	Recreation Ground
Ent	Enterprise	Resr	Reservoir
Ex H	Exhibition Hall	Ret Pk	Retail Park
Ind Est	Industrial Estate	Sch	School
Inst	Institute	Sh Ctr	Shopping Centre
Ct	Law Court	TH	Town Hall/House
L Ctr	Leisure Centre	Trad Est	Trading Estate
LC	Level Crossing	Univ	University
Liby	Library	Wks	Works
Mkt	Market	YH	Youth Hostel

■ The dark grey border on the inside edge of some pages indicates that the mapping does not continue onto the adjacent page

■ The small numbers around the edges of the maps identify the 1 kilometre National Grid lines

The scale of the maps is 5.52 cm to 1 km
3½ inches to 1 mile 1: 18103

| 0 | ¼ | ½ | ¾ | 1 mile |
| 0 | 250 m | 500 m | 750 m | 1 kilometre |

The scale of the maps on pages numbered in red is 11.04 cm to 1 km 7 inches to 1 mile 1: 9051.4

| 0 | 220 yards | 440 yards | 660 yards | ½ mile |
| 0 | 125 m | 250 m | 375 m | ½ kilometre |

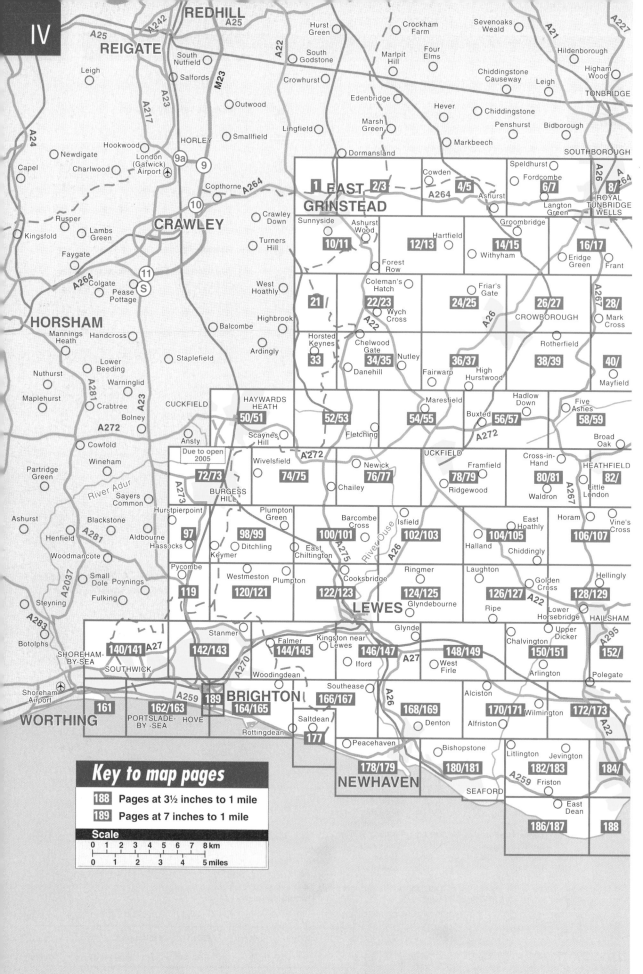

IV

REDHILL

REIGATE

Key to map pages

| 188 | Pages at 3½ inches to 1 mile |
| 189 | Pages at 7 inches to 1 mile |

Scale

0 1 2 3 4 5 6 7 8 km

0 1 2 3 4 5 miles

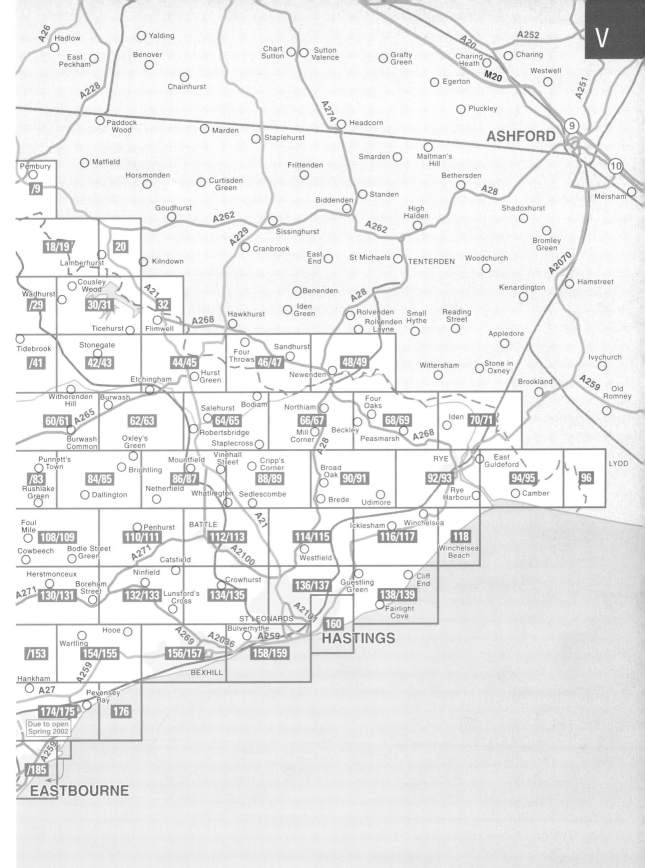

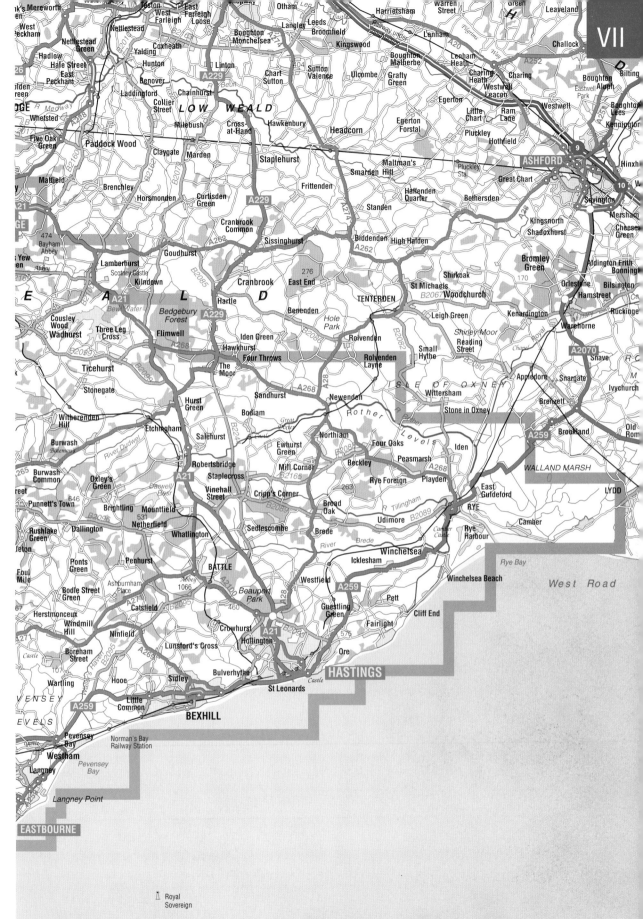

Major administrative and Postcode boundaries

County and unitary authority boundaries
District boundaries
Postcode boundaries
Area covered by this atlas

Scale

| 0 | 5 | 10 | 15 km |

| 0 | 5 | 10 miles |

Surrey

West Sussex

Kent

East Sussex

Wealden

Rother

Hastings

Lewes

Eastbourne

City of Brighton & Hove

RH7
RH19
East Grinstead
Forest Row
RH18
Haywards Heath
RH16
RH17
Burgess Hill
RH15
Pycombe
BN45
Keymer
BN6

TN11
TN2
TN1
TN4
Royal Tunbridge Wells
TN3
Groombridge
TN8
Cowden
TN7
Hartfield
Nutley
Horsted Keynes
RH17
Newick
TN22
Uckfield

TN12
Lamberhurst
TN5
Wadhurst
TN6
Crowborough
TN20
Mayfield
TN19
Burwash
TN17

TN18
Newenden
Sandhurst
TN32
Salehurst
Northiam
TN30
TN31
Rye
TN29
Camber
Winchelsea
TN36
TN35
Broad Oak
Pett
Baldslow
TN34
TN37
TN38
Hastings
St Leonards

Heathfield
TN21
Rushlake Green
East Hoathly
BN8
Ringmer
BN7
Lewes
TN33
Battle
BN27
Hailsham
BN26
Lower Willingdon
Alfriston
TN39
Pebsham
TN40
Bexhill
BN24
Pevensey Bay
BN22
Langney
BN23
BN21
Eastbourne
BN20
East Dean
BN25
Seaford

BN1
BN41
Portslade-by-Sea
Southwick
BN43
Shoreham-by-Sea
BN3
Brighton
BN2
Woodingdean
Patcham
BN42
Hove
BN9
Newhaven
BN10
Peacehaven

TQ TR
TV

TQ
TV

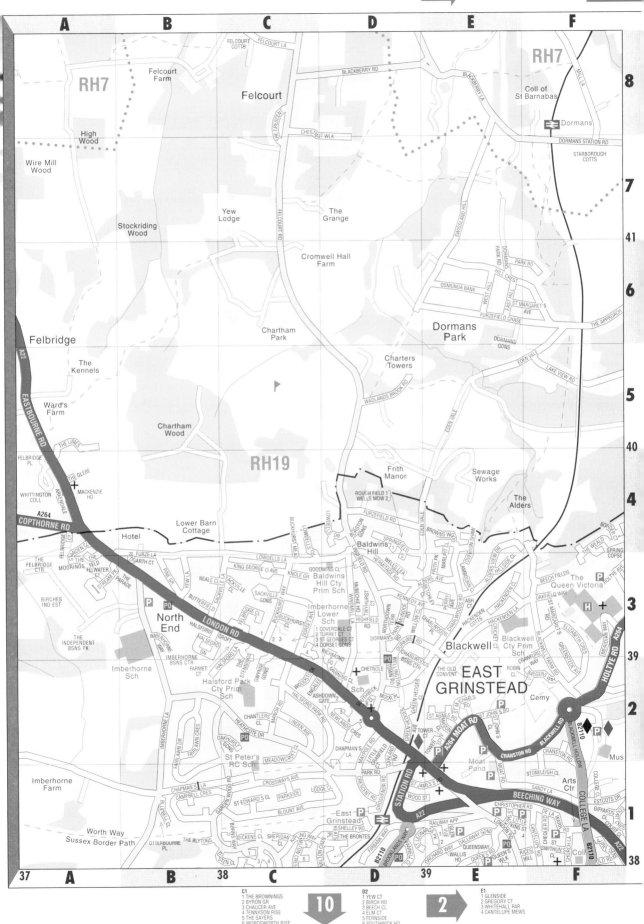

C1
1 THE BROWNINGS
2 BYRON GR
3 CHAUCER AVE
4 TENNYSON RISE
5 THE SAYERS
6 WORDSWORTH RISE

D2
1 YEW CT
2 BIRCH HO
3 BEECH CL
4 ELM CT
5 FERNSIDE
6 SOUTHWICK HO

E1
1 GLENSIDE
2 GREGORY CT
3 WHITEHALL PAR
4 CANTELUPE MEWS

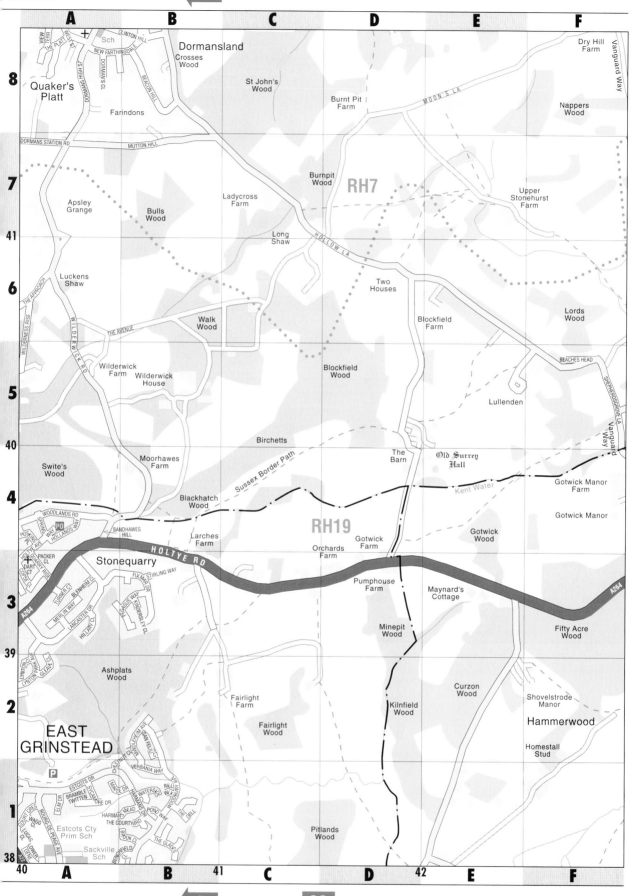

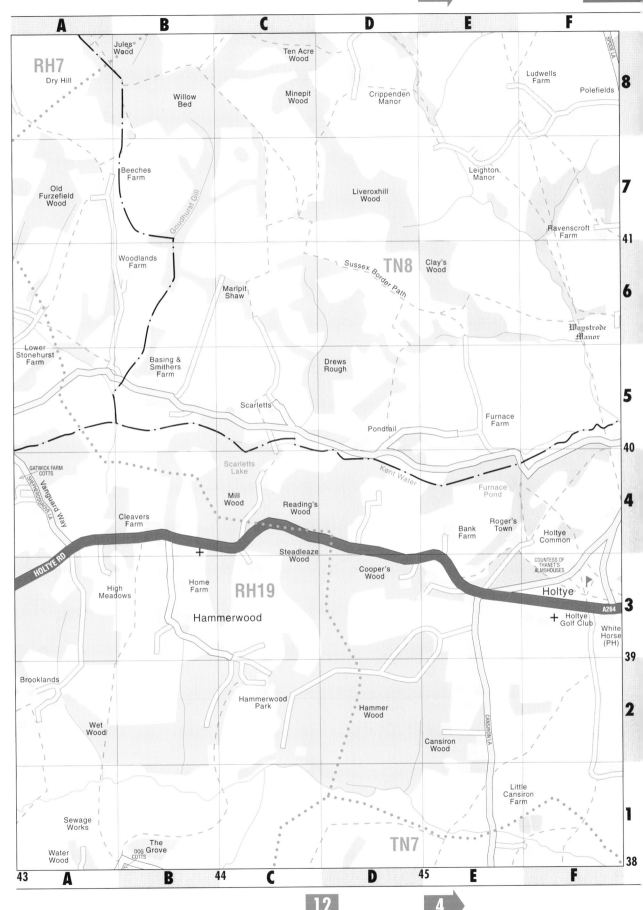

A   B   C   D   E   F

RH7
Dry Hill
Jules Wood

Ten Acre Wood

Ludwells Farm
Polefields

8

Willow Bed

Minepit Wood

Crippenden Manor

Beeches Farm

Leighton Manor

7

Old Furzefield Wood

Liveroxhill Wood

Ravenscroft Farm

41

Goudhurst Gill

Woodlands Farm

Sussex Border Path

TN8

Clay's Wood

6

Marlpit Shaw

Lower Stonehurst Farm

Basing & Smithers Farm

Drews Rough

5

Scarletts

Pondtail

Furnace Farm

40

Gatwick Farm Cotts

Scarletts Lake

Kent Water

Furnace Pond

4

Vanguard Way

SHEPHERDSGROVE LA

Mill Wood

Reading's Wood

Cleavers Farm

Bank Farm

Roger's Town

Holtye Common

Steadleaze Wood

Cooper's Wood

COUNTESS OF THANET'S ALMSHOUSES

HOLTYE RD

High Meadows

Home Farm

RH19

Hammerwood

Holtye

A264

3

Holtye Golf Club

White Horse (PH)

39

Brooklands

Hammerwood Park

Hammer Wood

CANSIRON LA

Wet Wood

Cansiron Wood

2

Little Cansiron Farm

Sewage Works

The Grove

DOG COTTS

TN7

1

Water Wood

38

43   A   B   44   C   D   45   E   F

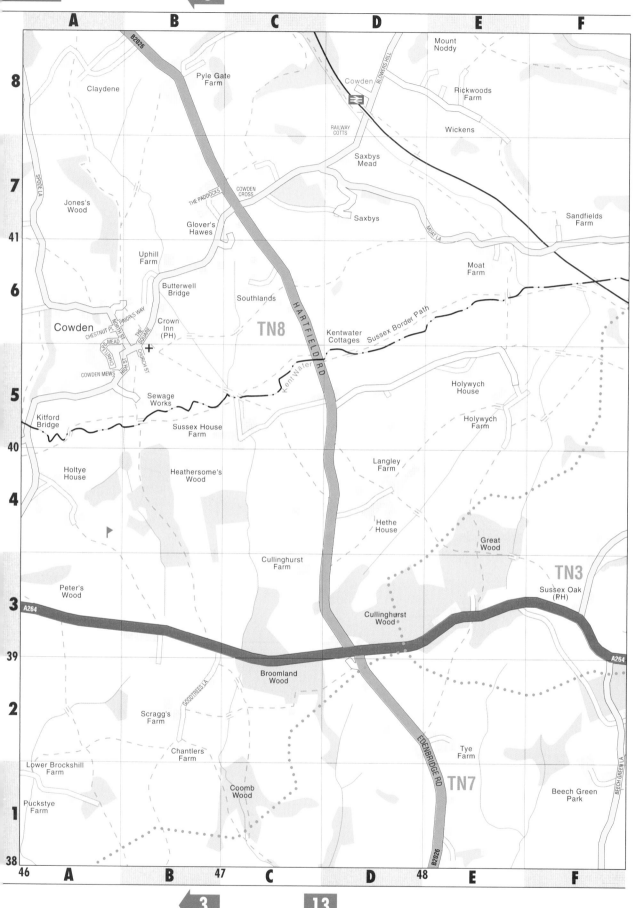

A B C D E F

8

Claydene

Pyle Gate
Farm

Mount
Noddy

Cowden

Rickwoods
Farm

RAILWAY
COTTS

Wickens

7

Jones's
Wood

THE PADDOCKS

COWDEN
CROSS

Saxbys
Mead

Sandfields
Farm

41

Glover's
Hawes

Saxbys

MOAT LA

Uphill
Farm

Moat
Farm

6

Butterwell
Bridge

Southlands

HARTFIELD RD

Cowden

PRIOR'S WAY

Crown Inn
(PH)

Kentwater
Cottages

Sussex Border Path

TN8

CHESTNUT PL

NORTH ST

THE SQUARE

CHARLES MEAD

HIGH ST

CHURCH ST

COWDEN MEWS

Holywych
House

Kent Water

5

Sewage
Works

Holywych
Farm

Kitford
Bridge

Sussex House
Farm

40

Holtye
House

Heathersome's
Wood

Langley
Farm

4

Hethe
House

Cullinghurst
Farm

Great
Wood

TN3

Peter's
Wood

Sussex Oak
(PH)

3

A264

Cullinghurst
Wood

39

GOODTREES LA

Broomland
Wood

EDENBRIDGE RD

A264

2

Scragg's
Farm

Chantlers
Farm

Tye
Farm

BEECH GREEN LA

Lower Brockshill
Farm

Coomb
Wood

TN7

Beech Green
Park

Puckstye
Farm

1

B2026

38

46 A B 47 C D 48 E F

SPODE LA

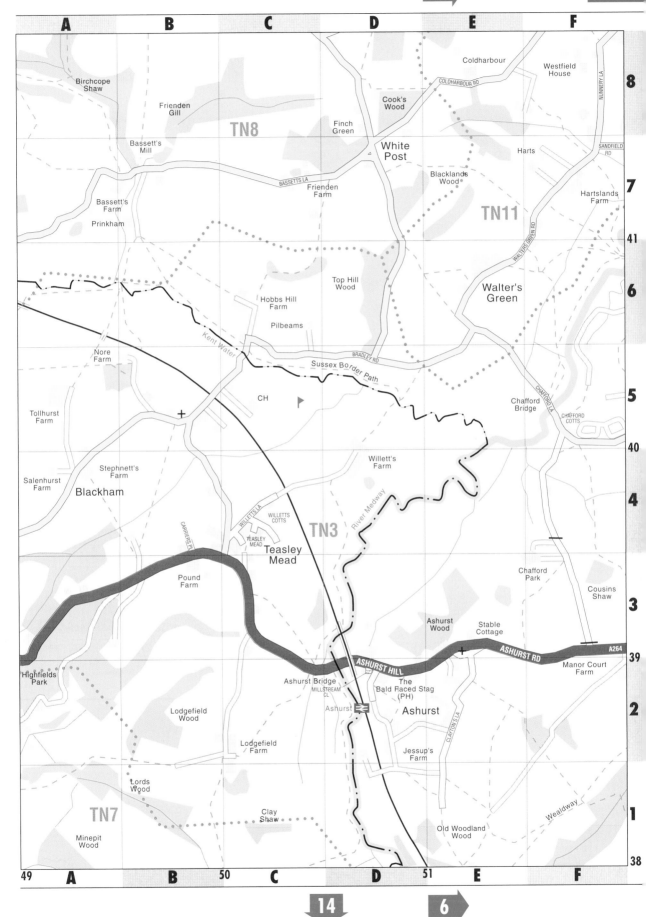

A B C D E F

8

Birchcope
Shaw

Coldharbour

Westfield
House

NUNNERY LA

Frienden
Gill

COLDHARBOUR RD

TN8

Cook's
Wood

Finch
Green

Harts

SANDFIELD
RD

Bassett's
Mill

White
Post

7

BASSETTS LA

Frienden
Farm

Blacklands
Wood

Hartslands
Farm

TN11

41

Bassett's
Farm

Prinkham

WALTERS GREEN RD

6

Nore
Farm

Top Hill
Wood

Walter's
Green

Kent Water

Hobbs Hill
Farm

Pilbeams

BRADLEY RD

Sussex Border Path

CHAFFORD LA

5

Tollhurst
Farm

CH

Chafford
Bridge

CHAFFORD
COTTS

40

Salenhurst
Farm

Stephnett's
Farm

Willett's
Farm

River Medway

Blackham

4

CARRIERS PL

WILLETTS LA

WILLETTS
COTTS

TN3

Chafford
Park

Cousins
Shaw

TEASLEY
MEAD

Teasley
Mead

Pound
Farm

3

Ashurst
Wood

Stable
Cottage

Highfields
Park

ASHURST HILL

ASHURST RD

A264

Manor Court
Farm

39

Ashurst Bridge

MILLSTREAM
CL

The
Bald Faced Stag
(PH)

CLAYTON'S LA

2

Lodgefield
Wood

Ashurst

Ashurst

Lodgefield
Farm

Jessup's
Farm

Lords
Wood

Wealdway

TN7

Clay
Shaw

Old Woodland
Wood

1

Minepit
Wood

38

5

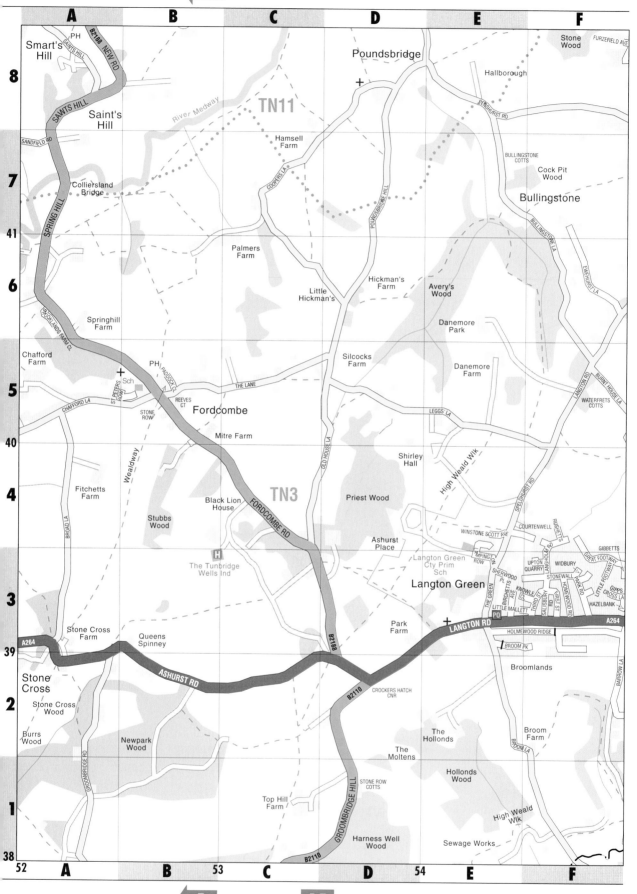

5

15

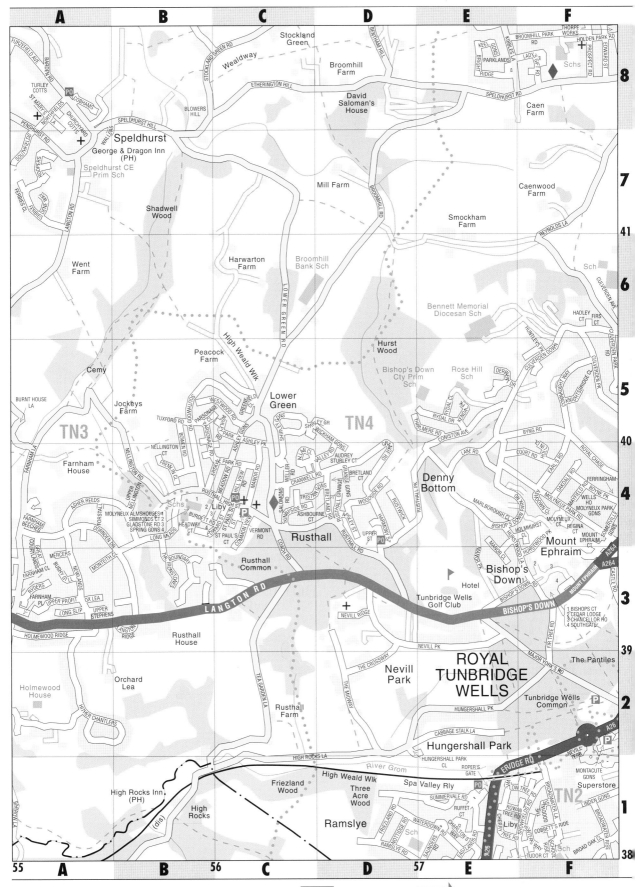

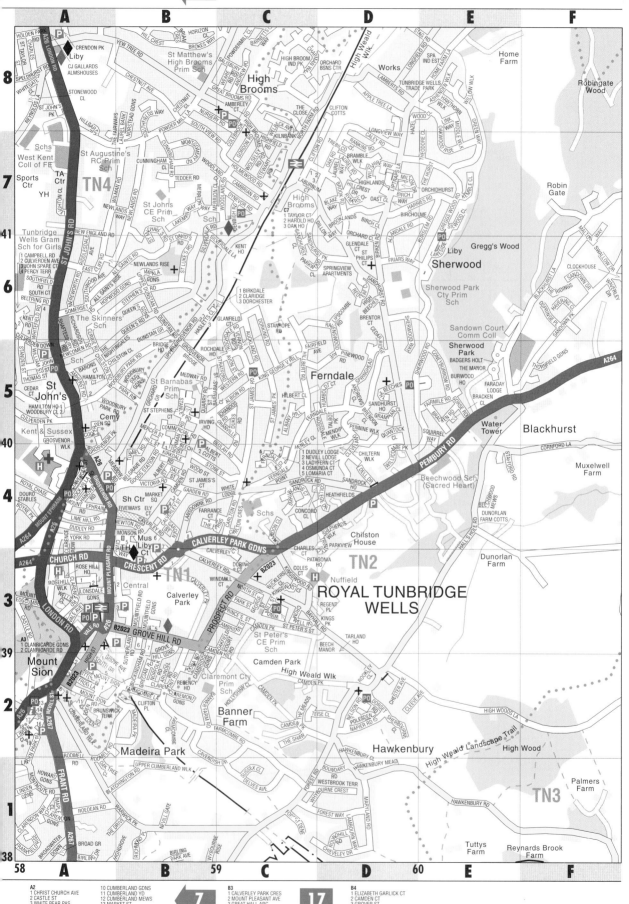

A2
1 CHRIST CHURCH AVE
2 CASTLE ST
3 WHITE BEAR PAS
4 WARWICK RD
5 BELGROVE
6 SPENCER MEWS
7 BERKELEY RD
8 CHAPEL PL
9 BEDFORD TERR

10 CUMBERLAND GDNS
11 CUMBERLAND YD
12 CUMBERLAND MEWS
13 MARKET ST
14 MARKET PL
15 COACH & HORSES PAS
16 SUSSEX MEWS
17 THE PANTILES
18 UNION SQ
19 REGENCY HALL

B3
1 CALVERLEY PARK CRES
2 MOUNT PLEASANT AVE
3 GREAT HALL ARC
4 MOUNTFIELD CT
5 THE MEWS
6 MEADOW HILL RD
7 GUILDFORD RD

B4
1 ELIZABETH GARLICK CT
2 CAMDEN CT
3 GROVER ST
4 SPENCER'S WAY
5 MONSON WAY
6 CADOGAN GDNS
7 CATHERINE PL
8 LANSDOWNE SQ

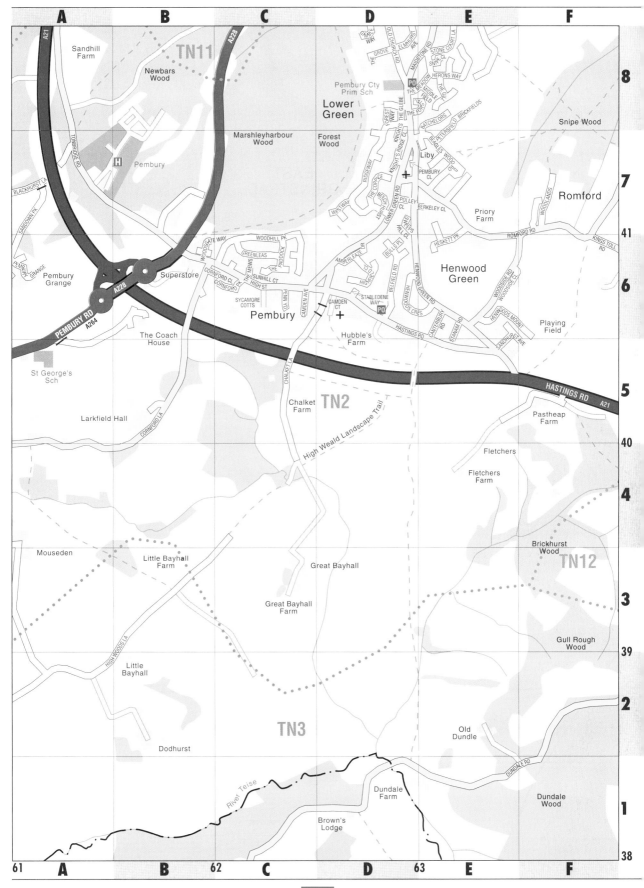

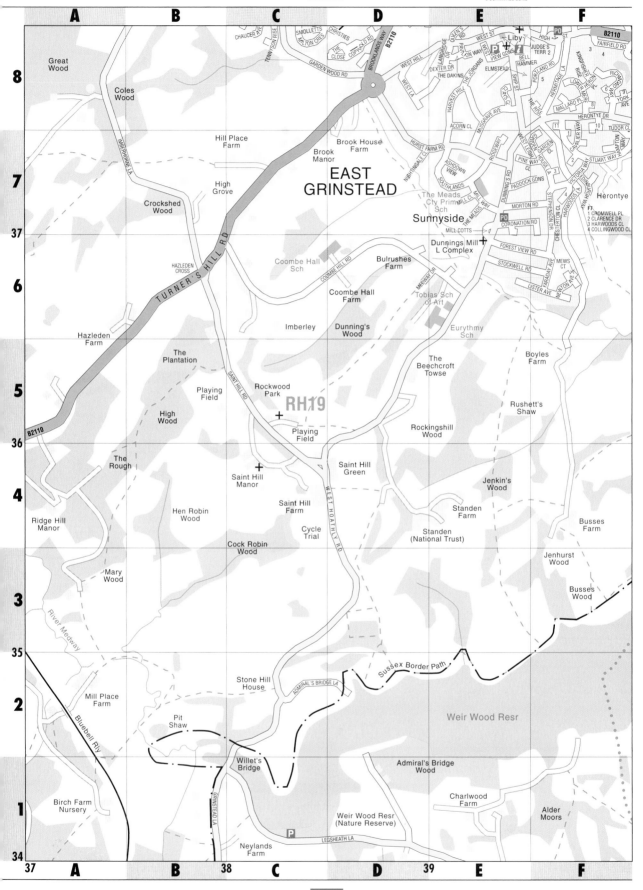

F8
1 MIDDLE ROW
2 FOREST LODGE
3 SACKVILLE CT
4 GREAT HOUSE CT
5 PORTLAND HO
6 CORNWALL GDNS
7 NORMANDY CL
8 WILLOW MEAD
9 KINGS COPSE
10 REGAL DR
11 BECKETT WAY

Great Wood

Coles Wood

Hill Place Farm

High Grove

Brook Manor

Brook House Farm

EAST GRINSTEAD

Sunnyside

Crockshed Wood

HAZLEDEN CROSS

TURNER'S HILL RD

IMBERHORNE LA

Hazleden Farm

The Plantation

Playing Field

Rockwood Park

RH19

Coombe Hall Sch

COOMBE HILL RD

Bulrushes Farm

Coombe Hall Farm

Imberley

Dunning's Wood

SAINT HILL RD

High Wood

Playing Field

Saint Hill Manor

Saint Hill Farm

Saint Hill Green

The Beechcroft Towse

Tobias Sch of Art

Eurythmy Sch

Boyles Farm

Rushett's Shaw

Rockingshill Wood

B2110

The Rough

Hen Robin Wood

WEST HOATHLY RD

Cycle Trial

Standen Farm

Jenkin's Wood

Busses Farm

Ridge Hill Manor

Cock Robin Wood

Standen (National Trust)

Jenhurst Wood

Mary Wood

Busses Wood

River Medway

Sussex Border Path

Weir Wood Resr

Stone Hill House

ADMIRAL'S BRIDGE LA

Mill Place Farm

Bluebell Rly

Pit Shaw

Willet's Bridge

Admiral's Bridge Wood

Charlwood Farm

Alder Moors

Birch Farm Nursery

GRINSTEAD LA

Weir Wood Resr (Nature Reserve)

Neylands Farm

LEGSHEATH LA

Herontye

F7
1 CROMWELL PL
2 CLARENCE DR
3 HARWOODS CL
4 COLLINGWOOD CL

B2110

FAIRFIELD RD

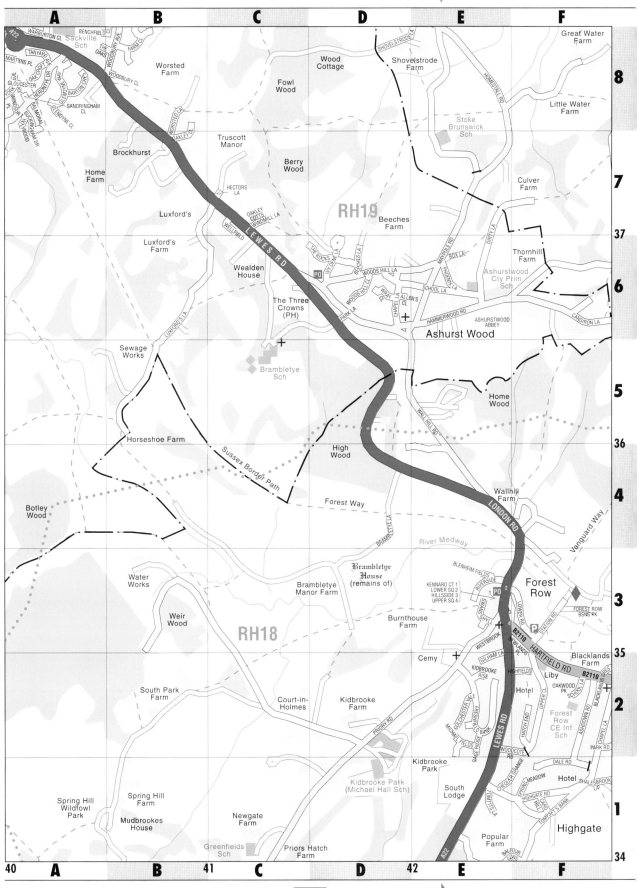

A B C D E F

8

Vanguard Way

Owlett's Farm

CANSIRON LA

Church Wood

Acre Wood

Great Cansiron Farm

BUTCHERFIELD LA

7

Thornhill

Great Surries

Great Surries Farm

RH19

Roughfield Wood

37

Little Surries

Pollard Wood

Paupersdale Wood

Marlpit Shaw

6

Grove Farm

Little Surries Farm

High Weald Landscape Trial

North Clays

Vanguard Way

CANSIRON LA

St Ives Farm West

5

Mast

Highams Wood

Collingsbush Wood

Wick Wood

36

TN7

4

Pixton Hill Farm

Ashdown Farm

Ashdown House

Lower Parrock

3

Emerson Coll

RH18

River Medway

Alder Shaw

Sussex Border Path

Sewage Works

35

Blacklands Cres

Medway Dr

Medway View

Stonedene Cl

Forest Way

Upper Parrock Farm

PARROCK LA

Gassonsfield Wood

B2110

Park Cres

Stonepark Dr

HARTFIELD RD

Lines Farm

Upper Parrock

2

Chapel La

Forest Row

Broadstone

London Cl

Post Horn La

Forest Rd

Park Rd

Primrose La

Ryst Wood Rd

Rystwood Farm

Vanguard Way

Little Parrock

Little Parrock Farm

Paternoster Wood

1

Shalesbrook La

Shalesbrook

CH

Quabrook

B2110

CAT ST

B2110

34

43 A B 44 C D 45 E F

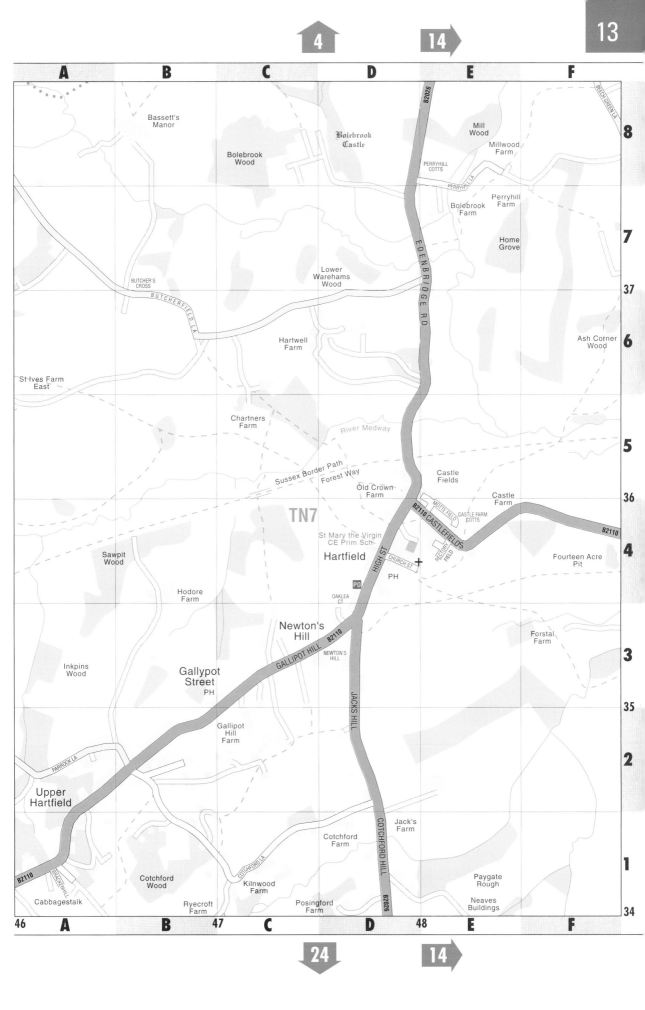

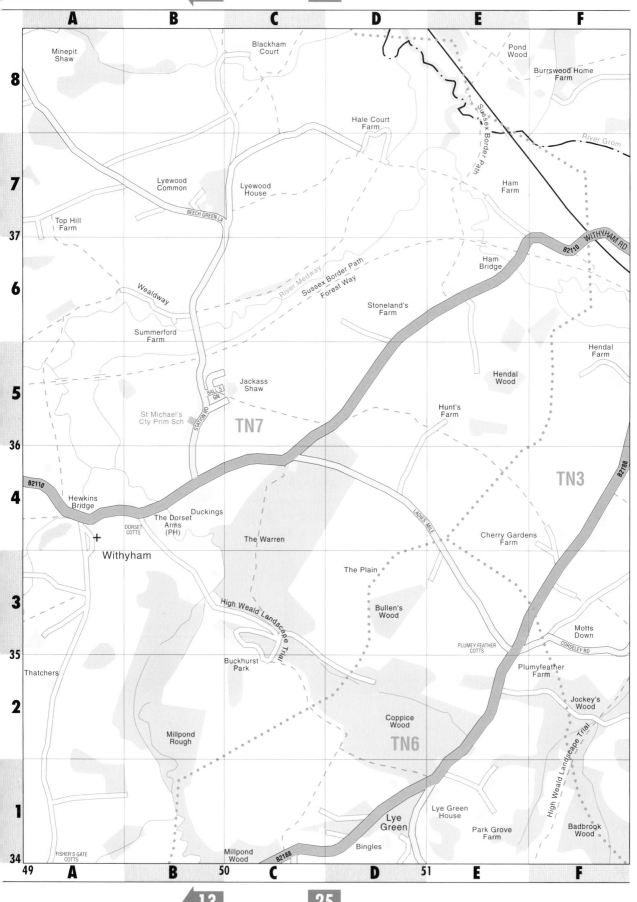

A **B** **C** **D** **E** **F**

8

Minepit
Shaw

Blackham
Court

Pond
Wood

Burrswood Home
Farm

Hale Court
Farm

Sussex Border Path

River Grom

7

Lyewood
Common

Lyewood
House

Ham
Farm

BEECH GREEN LA

37

Top Hill
Farm

WITHYHAM RD

B2110

6

Wealdway

River Medway

Sussex Border Path

Forest Way

Ham
Bridge

Summerford
Farm

Stoneland's
Farm

Hendal
Farm

BALL'S GN

Jackass
Shaw

Hendal
Wood

5

STATION RD

St Michael's
Cty Prim Sch

TN7

Hunt's
Farm

36

TN3

B2188

4

B2110

Hewkins
Bridge

Duckings

Ladies Mile

Cherry Gardens
Farm

DORSET
COTTS

The Dorset
Arms
(PH)

The Warren

Withyham

The Plain

3

High Weald Landscape Trail

Bullen's
Wood

Motts
Down

CORSELEY RD

PLUMEY FEATHER
COTTS

35

Thatchers

Buckhurst
Park

Plumyfeather
Farm

2

Jockey's
Wood

Millpond
Rough

Coppice
Wood

TN6

High Weald Landscape Trail

1

Lye Green
House

Park Grove
Farm

Badbrook
Wood

Lye
Green

34

FISHER'S GATE
COTTS

Millpond
Wood

B2188

Bingles

49 **A** **B** 50 **C** **D** 51 **E** **F**

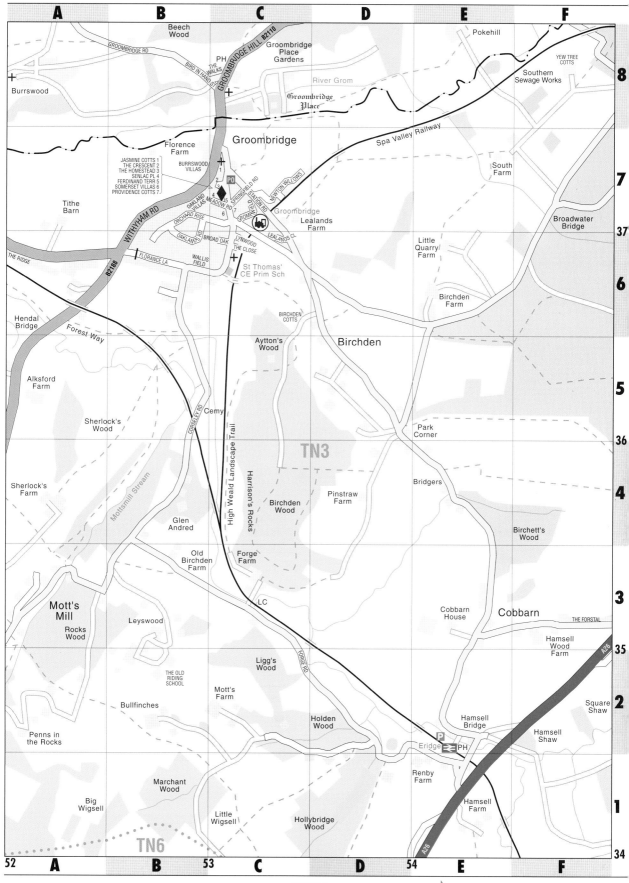

A **B** **C** **D** **E** **F**

Spa Valley Rly

TN4

Ramslye
Wood

RAMSLYE RD
EASTLANDS CL

SCOTTS
WAY
SHOWFIELDS RD
STUART CL
SURREY CL
FURNIVAL
BROADCROFT

ERIDGE RD
A26

Ramslye
Farm

Sch

8

Ramslye
Cotts

Strawberry
Hill

BROADMEAD
LINEDA DR
ESSEX CL
GLENMORE PK
BROADWATER

ST GEORGE'S
PK

KENTISH GDNS
BROADWATER
CT

1 LEICESTER DR
2 DEVONSHIRE CL
3 BROADMEAD AVE

Ruffet
Wood

BROADWATER DOWN

STRAWBERRY CL
HARGATE CL

BARNFIELD

ST MARK'S RD

HARESCROFT

The
Firs

**Broadwater
Down**

TN2

7

Broadwater
Forest

Spratsbrook
Farm

Strawberry Hill
Farm

37

Broadwater
Lodge

Sprat's Brook

Hargate
Forest

6

Firtree
Plantation

The
Warren

The
Roundabouts

BUNNY LA

Bohemia

5

Whitehill
Wood

36

Eridge
Rocks

TN3

Warren
Farm

The Nevill
Crest & Gun
(PH)

4

WARREN FARM LA

Eridge
Park

Eridge
Park

**Eridge
Green**

3

Crown
House

A26

Mill
Wood

35

Keepers
Cottages

Steel
Bridge

High Weald Landscape Trail

2

Steel Bridge
Farm

Forge
Wood

Eridge
Old Park

1

Bushy
Wood

Great Robbins
Shaw

Bushy
Shaw

34

55 **A** **B** **56** **C** **D** **57** **E** **F**

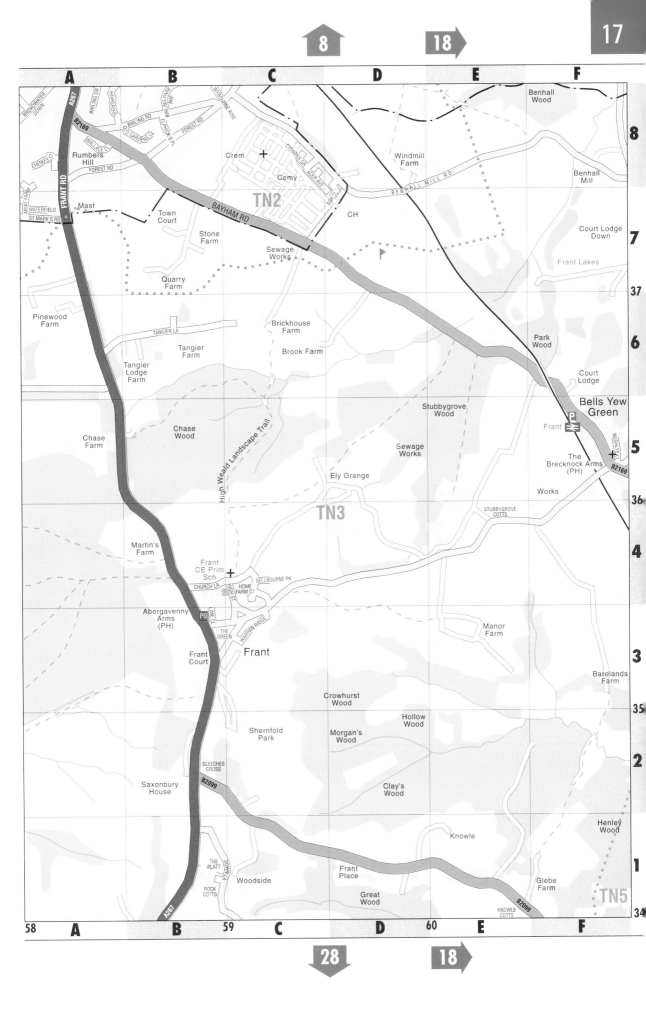

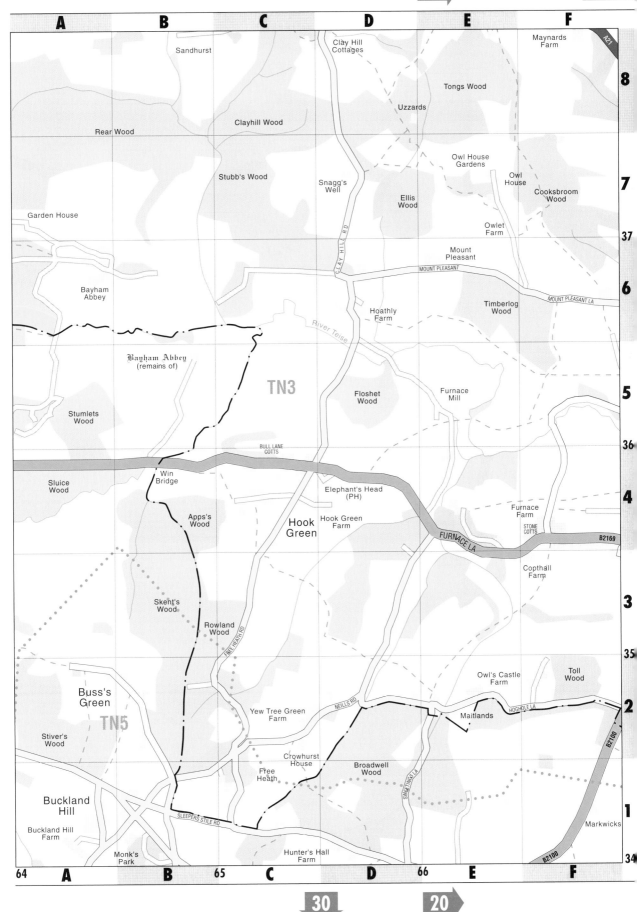

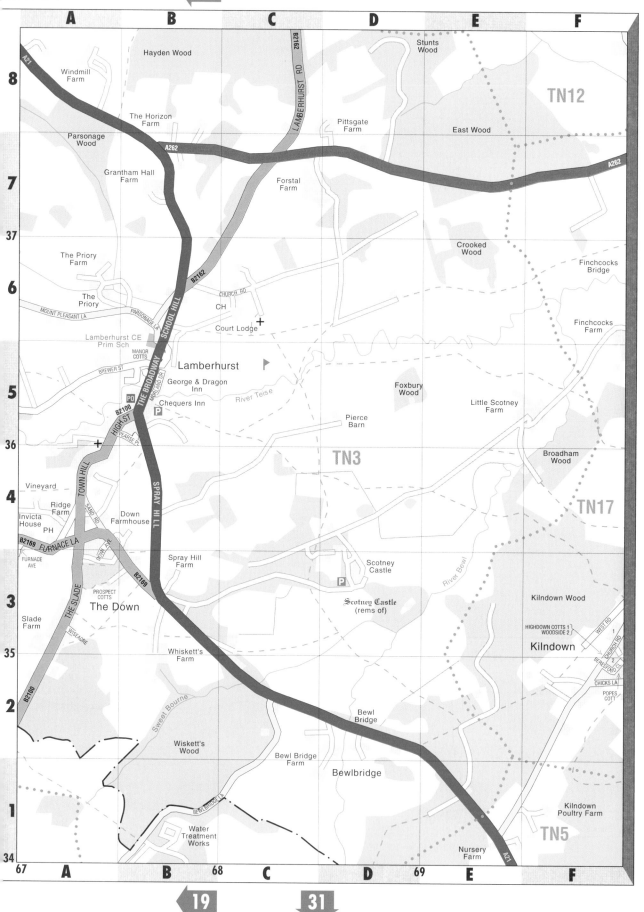

A B C D E F

8

TN12

Hayden Wood

Stunts Wood

Windmill Farm

East Wood

The Horizon Farm

Pittsgate Farm

A262

Parsonage Wood

LAMBERHURST RD

B2162

7

Grantham Hall Farm

Forstal Farm

A262

37

6

The Priory Farm

Crooked Wood

Finchcocks Bridge

The Priory

CHURCH RD

Finchcocks Farm

MOUNT PLEASANT LA

PARSONAGE LA

CH

SCHOOL HILL

B2162

Court Lodge

Lamberhurst CE Prim Sch

MANOR COTTS

Lamberhurst

BREWER ST

THE BROADWAY

George & Dragon Inn

Foxbury Wood

River Teise

Little Scotney Farm

5

PO

MORLAND DR

Chequers Inn

P

B2100

Pierce Barn

Broadham Wood

HIGH ST

PEARSE PL

36

TN3

TN17

Vineyard

TOWN HILL

4

Ridge Farm

SAND RD

Down Farmhouse

Invicta House

PH

DOWN AVE

SPRAY HILL

B2169

FURNACE LA

Spray Hill Farm

Scotney Castle

River Bewl

Kilndown Wood

FURNACE AVE

P

HIGHDOWN COTTS 1
WOODSIDE 2

WEST RD

3

PROSPECT COTTS

B2169

Scotney Castle (rems of)

Kilndown

CHURCH RD

THE SLADE

The Down

BERESFORD CL

WISEACRE

Slade Farm

35

Whiskett's Farm

CHICKS LA

POPES COTT

2

B2100

Sweet Bourne

Bewl Bridge

Bewl Bridge

Wiskett's Wood

Bewl Bridge Farm

Bewlbridge

Kilndown Poultry Farm

1

BEWLBRIDGE LA

Water Treatment Works

Nursery Farm

A21

TN5

34

67 A B 68 C 69 D E F

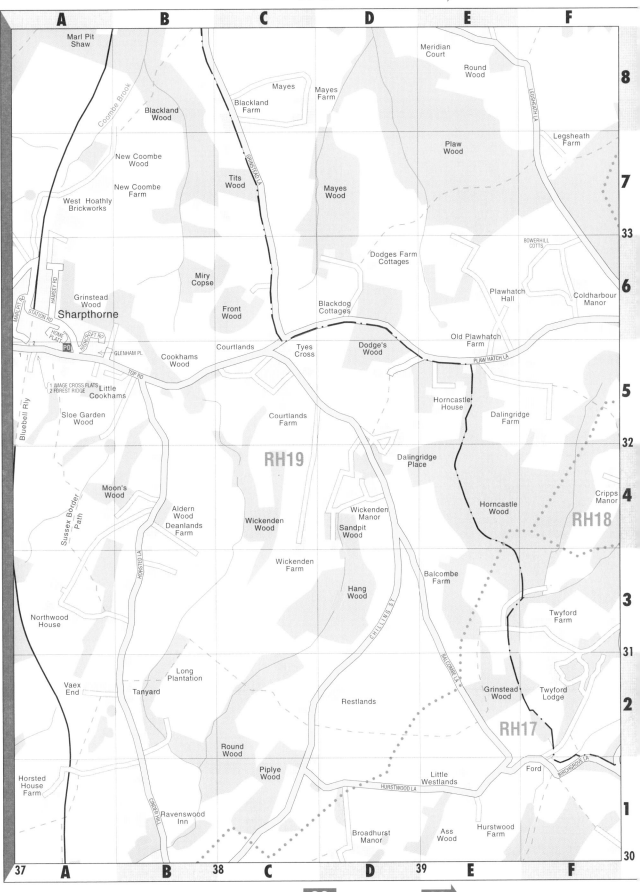

10 **22**

A B C D E F

8

Marl Pit
Shaw

Meridian
Court

Round
Wood

Mayes

Mayes
Farm

Blackland
Wood

Blackland
Farm

Coombe Brook

Plaw
Wood

LEGSHEATH LA

Legsheath
Farm

New Coombe
Wood

7

Tits
Wood

GRINSTEAD LA

Mayes
Wood

New Coombe
Farm

West Hoathly
Brickworks

33

BOWERHILL
COTTS

Dodges Farm
Cottages

6

Miry
Copse

Plawhatch
Hall

Coldharbour
Manor

MARL PIT RD

HAMSEY RD

Grinstead
Wood

Front
Wood

Blackdog
Cottages

Sharpthorne

STATION RD

RICROFT RD

HOME
PLATT

PO

Courtlands

Tyes
Cross

Dodge's
Wood

Old Plawhatch
Farm

PLAW HATCH LA

2

GLENHAM PL

Cookhams
Wood

TOP RD

Horncastle
House

5

1 IMAGE CROSS FLATS
2 FOREST RIDGE

Little
Cookhams

Dalingridge
Farm

Bluebell Rly

Sloe Garden
Wood

32

Courtlands
Farm

Dalingridge
Place

Cripps
Manor

4

Moon's
Wood

RH19

Horncastle
Wood

RH18

Sussex Border Path

Aldern
Wood

HORSTED LA

Wickenden
Wood

Wickenden
Manor

Deanlands
Farm

Sandpit
Wood

Wickenden
Farm

CHILLING ST

Balcombe
Farm

3

Northwood
House

Hang
Wood

Twyford
Farm

BALCOMBE LA

31

Long
Plantation

Vaex
End

Tanyard

Restlands

Grinstead
Wood

Twyford
Lodge

2

Round
Wood

RH17

Horsted
House
Farm

Piplye
Wood

Little
Westlands

Ford

BIRCHGROVE LA

CINDER HILL

HURSTWOOD LA

1

Ravenswood
Inn

Broadhurst
Manor

Ass
Wood

Hurstwood
Farm

30

37 A 38 B C 39 D E F

33 **22**

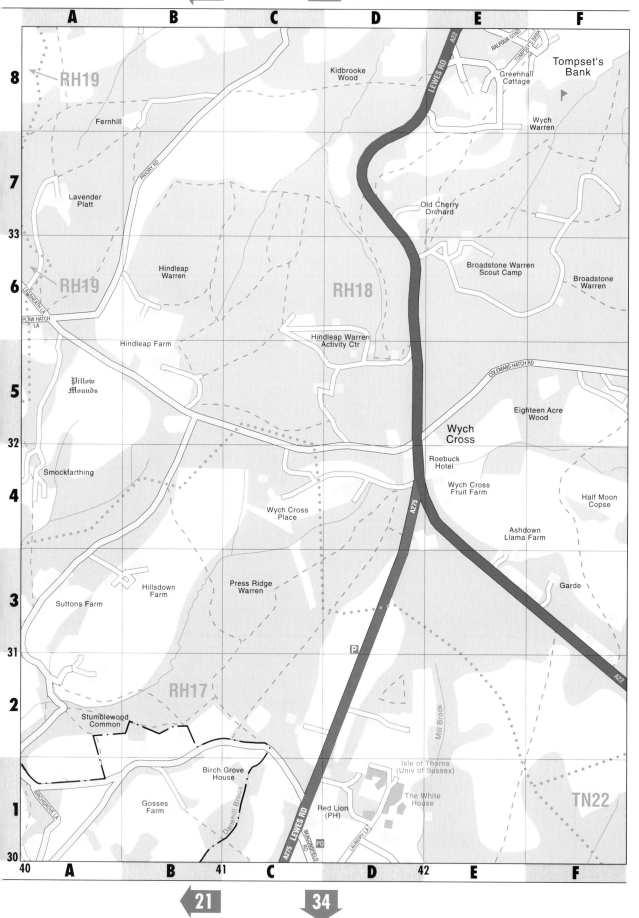

23
13

A B C D E F

8

Fincham
Farm

Buckhurst
Farm

B2026

Tile Barn
Farm

Marsh
Green

Neaves
Farm

7

Hart's
Farm

Posingford
Wood

Chuck
Hatch

Pimp Barn
Cottages

33

Podlea Flock
Farm

Jumper's
Town

Five Hundred
Rough

Five Hundred
Acre Wood

6

Spring
Farm

Lone Oak
Hall

B2188

The
Rough

Wren's
Warren

5

Fagot Stack
Corner

TN7

32

Gills
Lap

Wood
Eaves

4

Kidd's Hill
Farm

KIDD'S HILL

Vanguard Way

Wealdway

3

Tile
Lodge

TN6

Jack
Daw

Heasman's
Lodge
Farm

31

Black
Hill

Greenwood
Gate

2

Deerswood
Farm

The
Orchard

Lodge

TN22

King's
Standing

The
Nursery

1

B2188

The Old Mill
House

B2026

30

46 A B 47 C D 48 E F

23
36

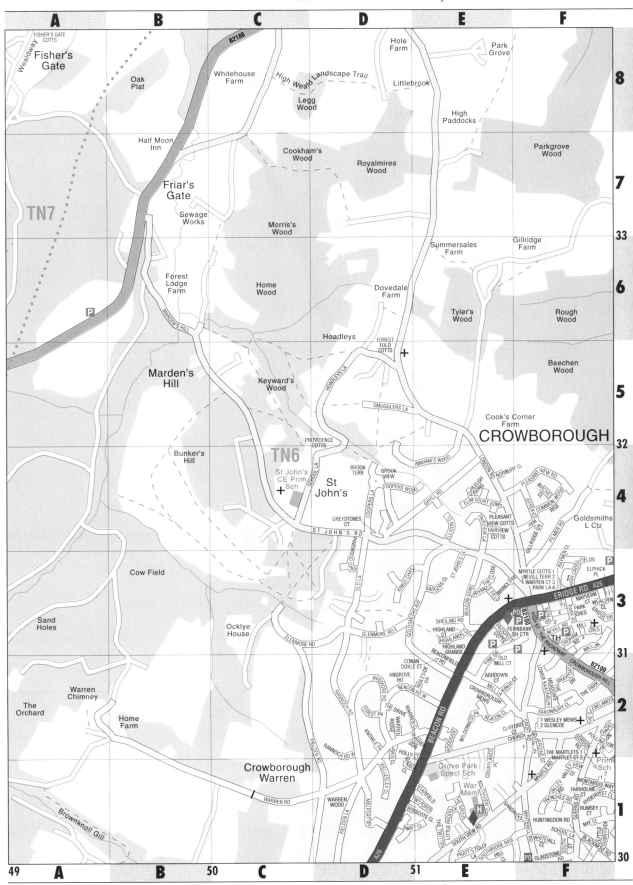

A **B** **C** **D** **E** **F**

FISHER'S GATE COTTS
Fisher's Gate
Oak Plat

B2188
Whitehouse Farm
High Weald Landscape Trail
Legg Wood
Cookham's Wood
Royalmires Wood

Hole Farm
Park Grove
Littlebrook
High Paddocks
Parkgrove Wood

8

Half Moon Inn
Friar's Gate
Sewage Works

Summersales Farm
Gillridge Farm

7

33

Forest Lodge Farm
Morris's Wood
Home Wood
Dovedale Farm
Tyler's Wood
Rough Wood

6

TN7

Marden's Hill
Keyward's Wood
Hoadleys
FOREST FOLD COTTS
Beechen Wood

5

SMUGGLERS LA
Cook's Corner Farm
CROWBOROUGH

32

Bunker's Hill
TN6
PROVIDENCE COTTS
St John's CE Prim Sch
St John's
BROOK TERR
BROOK VIEW
COOPERS WOOD
INNHAM'S WOOD
NORBURY CL
PLEASANT VIEW RD

4

Cow Field
GREYSTONES CT
COOPERS LA
ST JOHN'S RD
GHYLL RD
ELIM COURT GDNS
PLEASANT VIEW COTTS
FAIRVIEW COTTS
COMMON WOOD
Goldsmiths L Ctr

Sand Holes
OLD LA
KING'S CHASE
BADGERS CL
ST JOHN'S CL
BEACON GDNS
BRYAN'S FIELD
THE CLOSE
BRIMOL CTS
MYRTLE COTTS 1
NEVILL TERR 2
WARREN CT 3
PARK LA 4
FIELDS
ELPHICK PL
P

3

Ocklye House
GLENMORE RD
GLENMORE RD E
GOLDSMITHS AVE
SHEILING RD
HIGHLAND CT
HIGHLANDS
HIGHLAND GRANGE
BEACONFIELD
ERIDGE RD A26
PO
FERNBANK SH CTR
B2100
MAYVERN CT
WEALDEN CL
ERIDGE DR
TH
CROMAR
MILL CRES
MILL OR

31

CONAN DOYLE CT
ANGROVE HO
INGLEDENE
BEACON RD W
PINE OR OLD MILL CT
ASHDOWN CT
MILL LA
KINGS CT
Crowborough Mews
CROWBOROUGH HILL
The Park
B2100
SAXONBURY CL
THE MEADOWS
LOWER SAXONBURY
GRAYCASTLE DR
THE GLEBELANDS

2

Warren Chimney
The Orchard
Home Farm
RANNOCH RD
FOREST PK
THE DRIVE
WARREN RIDGE
AVIEMORE RD
RANNOCH RD W
KNOWLE DR
VINS CL
HOLLY CT
GRANGE
WARREN GDN
WILDERNESS PK
BEACON CL
CLIFFORD RD
CHURCH RD
1 WESLEY MEWS
2 GLENCOE
THE MARTLETS 1
MARTLET CT 2
Prim Sch
GORDON RD
POLLINGTON
CAPEL
VALLEY VIEW
MONTARGIS WAY

Crowborough Warren
WARREN RD
FELDEN RD
MELFORT RD
WELLESLEY CL
Grove Park Specl Sch
War Mem
H
COURT LANDS PL
STARFIELD
TWYFORDS
WINSCOTE RD
SWIFT CL
LITTLE PADDOCK
THE TWITTEN
SOUTHVIEW RD
THE GROVE
FAIRHOLME CT
HYDEHURST CT
TRENCHES RD
RUMSEY CT
NYE CL
HUNTINGDON RD
SCHOOL LA
BLACKNESS RD
QUEENS RD
SUNNYSIDE
LITTLE BLACKNESS RD

1

Brownknoll Gill
WARREN WOOD
A26
BEACON RD
PRATT'S FOLLY LA
SOUTHRIDGE RISE
HILL CL
GLADSTONE
WHITEHILL RD
WHITEHILL
PO

30

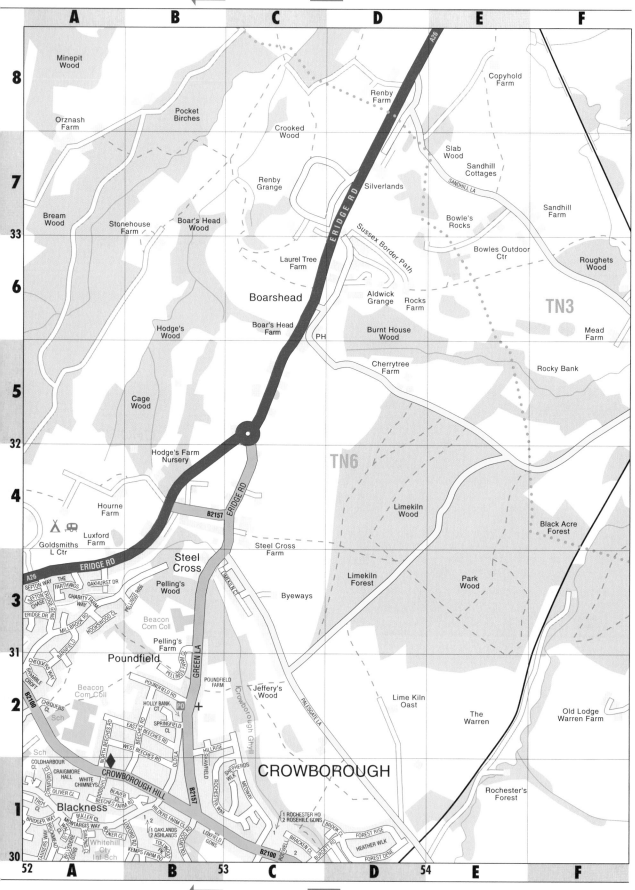

A B C D E F

8

Hamsell Manor

Danegate

Sham Farm

Long Wood

Rocks Wood

Rowland Wood

Stonewall Ghyll

Stonewall

Spring Wood

7

Stitches Farm

TN3

Sussex Border Path

Saxonbury Wood

Saxonbury Hill

33

Marchant's Wood

Whitehouse Farm

Great Danegate

Ashets

6

Hoth Farm

BLACKDON HILL

Redgate Mill Farm

Lords Wood

Green Hedges Farm

Blackdon Hill Farm

Card's Wood

Entryhill Wood

Towsers Lodge Farm

5

Newhouse Farm

BRICKYARD LA

32

Sewage Works

The Cants

Hoth Wood

Entry Hill

4

Stone House Farm

Forest Farm

Hornshurst Wood

The Gill

Little Millhole Wood

Big Millhole Wood

TN6

Lodge Farm

3

Greenhouse Farm

Markhouse Farm

B2100

Town Row Green Farm

31

ERIDGE LA

Orphanage Wood

Heathfield Hall

2

Cemy

Town Row

Chant Lane Farm

DOUGLAS RD

STATION CL

ASHLEY RD

Ashley Farm

Medway Farm

Bletchingley Wood

CATT'S HILL

Highgate Farm

CHANT LA

St Deny's Lodge

PO

CATT'S CORNER COTTS

1

Biddenden Farm

STATION RD

NEW RD

PH

BAINDEN CL

VENTREE LA

HOSMERS FIELD RD

BLETCHINGLYE LA

Bletchinglye Farm

HIGHGATE FLATS

B2100

30

55 A B 56 C D 57 E F

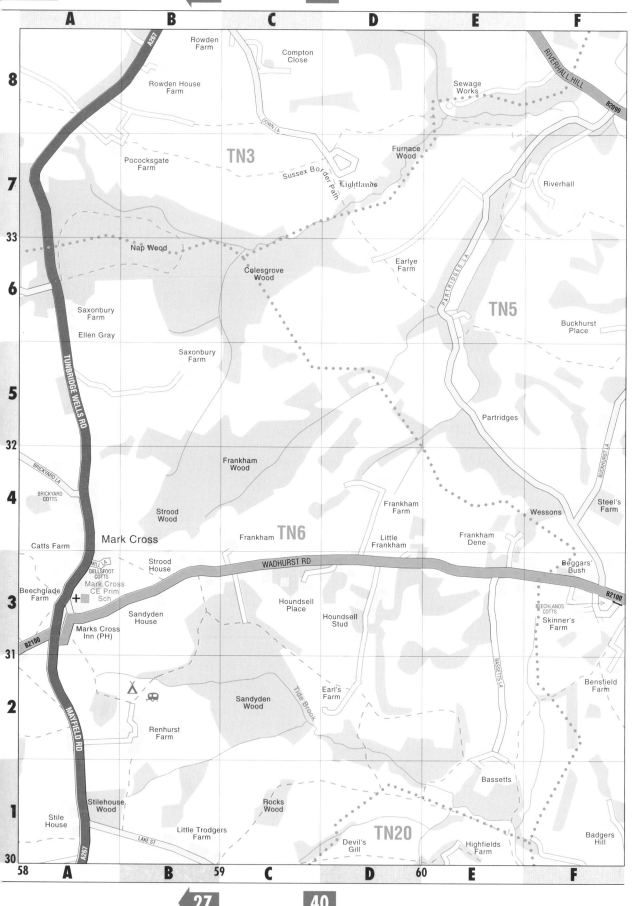

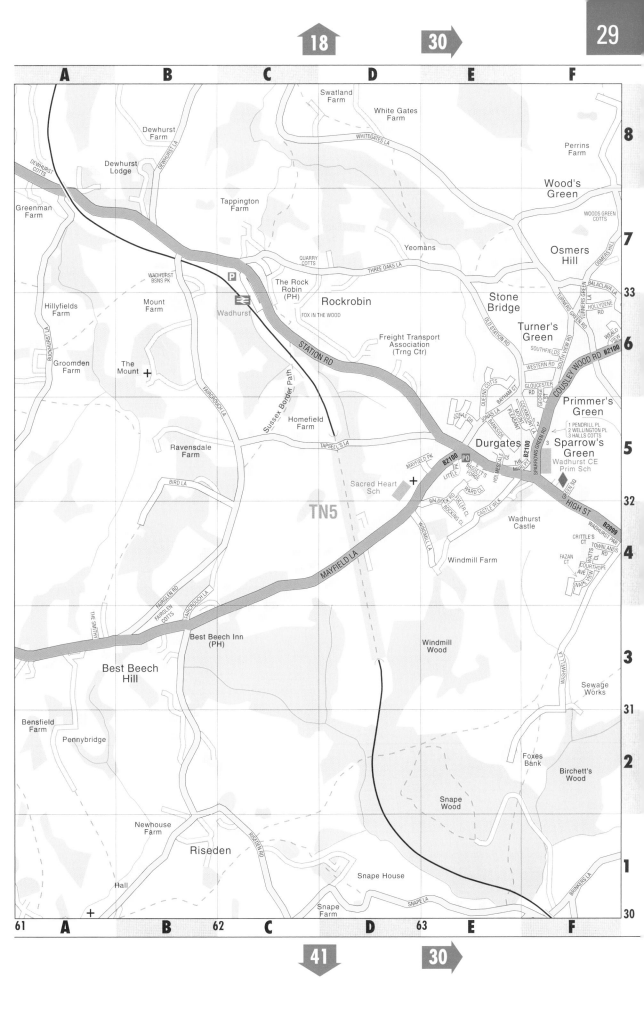

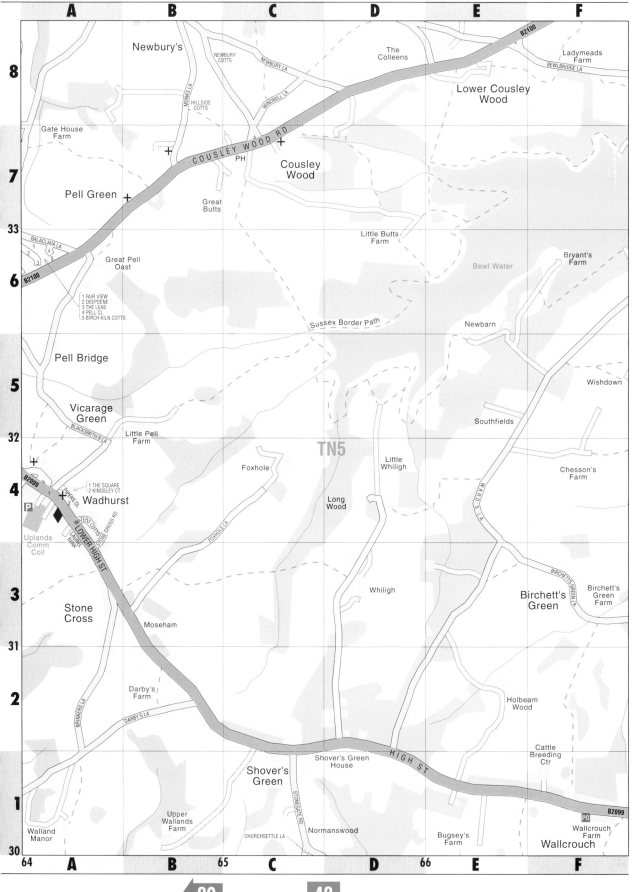

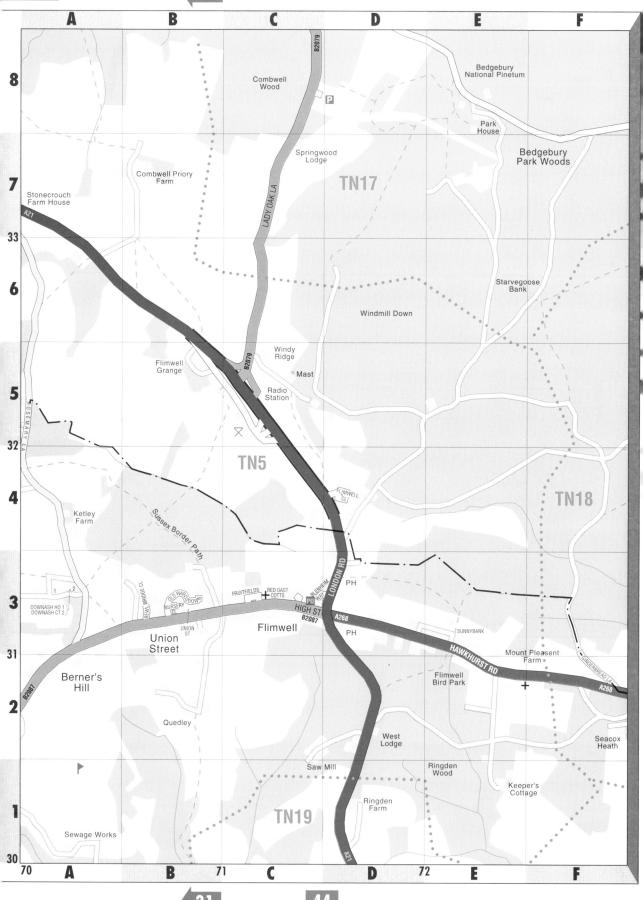

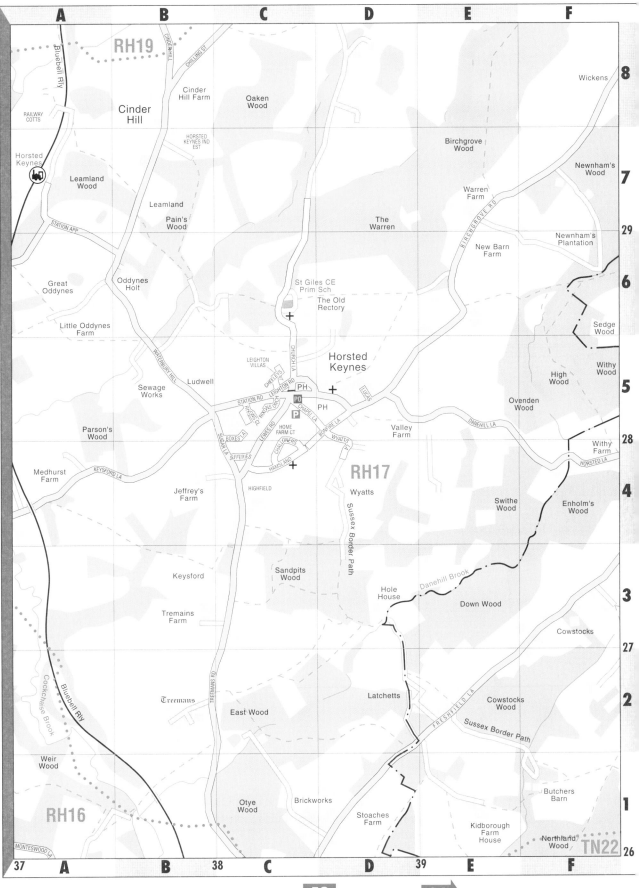

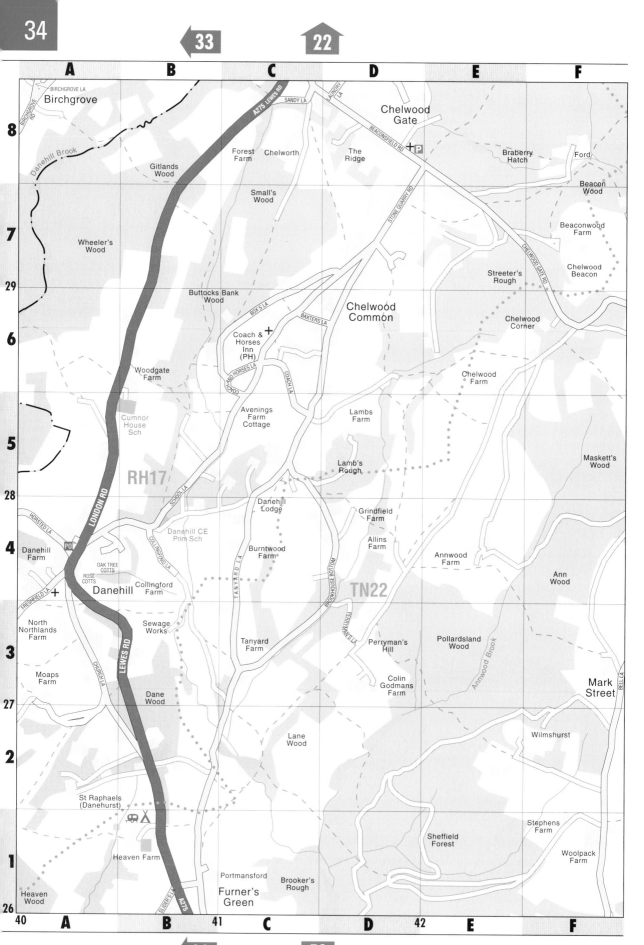

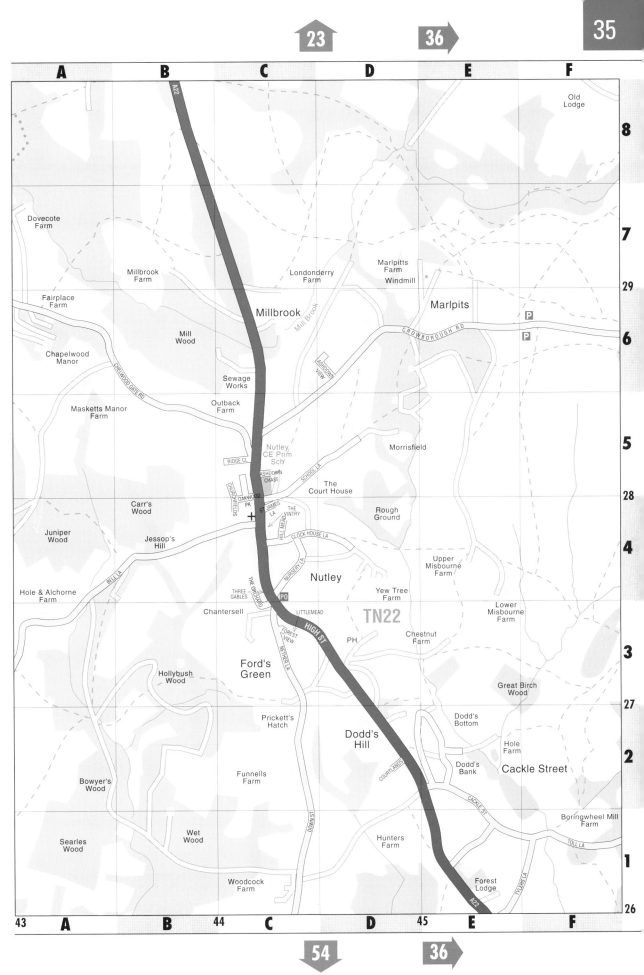

23
36

A   B   C   D   E   F

8

7

29

6

Old Lodge

Dovecote Farm

Millbrook Farm

Fairplace Farm

Londonderry Farm

Marlpitts Farm
Windmill

Marlpits

Mill Wood

A22

Mill Brook

CROWBOROUGH RD

P
P

Chapelwood Manor

CHELWOOD GATE RD

Sewage Works

ASHDOWN VIEW

Masketts Manor Farm

Outback Farm

Nutley CE Prim Sch

Morrisfield

5

RIDGE CL

SCHOOL LA

ASHDOWN CHASE

The Court House

28

Carr's Wood

CHURCHFIELDS

OAKWOOD PK

ST JAMES LA

THE VINTRY

HILL MEAD

Rough Ground

4

Juniper Wood

Jessop's Hill

CLOCK HOUSE LA

NURSERY LA

Nutley

Upper Misbourne Farm

BELL LA

Hole & Alchorne Farm

THREE GABLES

THE ORCHARD

PO

LITTLEMEAD

Yew Tree Farm

Lower Misbourne Farm

Chantersell

FOREST VIEW

NETHER LA

HIGH ST

TN22

PH

Chestnut Farm

3

Hollybush Wood

Ford's Green

Great Birch Wood

27

Prickett's Hatch

Dodd's Bottom

Dodd's Hill

COURTLANDS

Dodd's Bank

Hole Farm

Cackle Street

2

Bowyer's Wood

Funnells Farm

DOWN ST

CACKLE ST

Boringwheel Mill Farm

TOLL LA

Searles Wood

Wet Wood

Hunters Farm

TYLERS LA

1

Woodcock Farm

Forest Lodge

A22

26

43   A   B   44   C   D   45   E   F

54
36

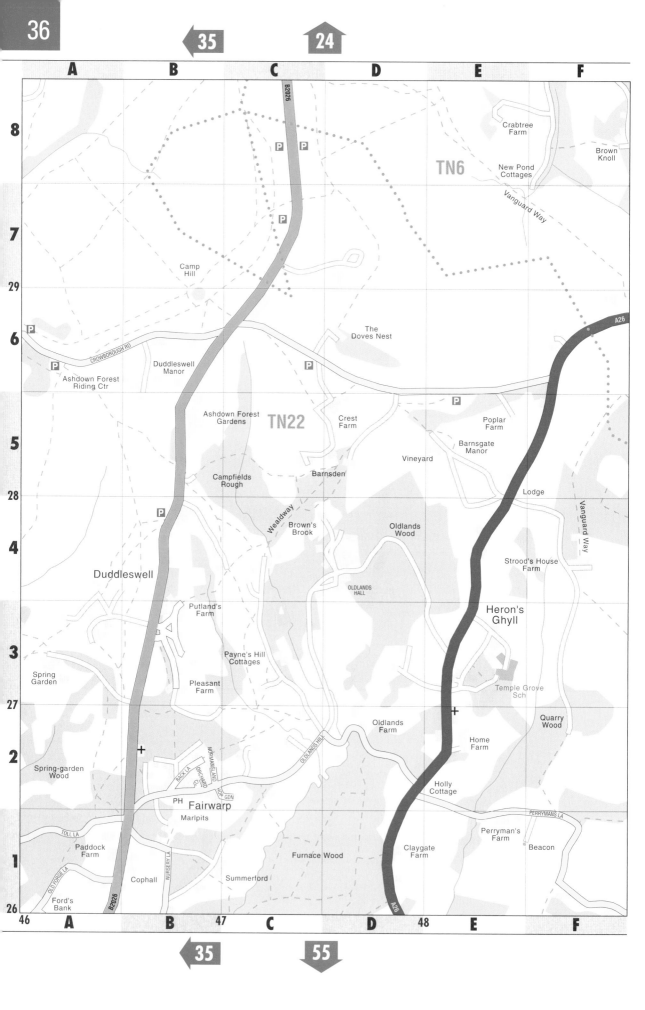

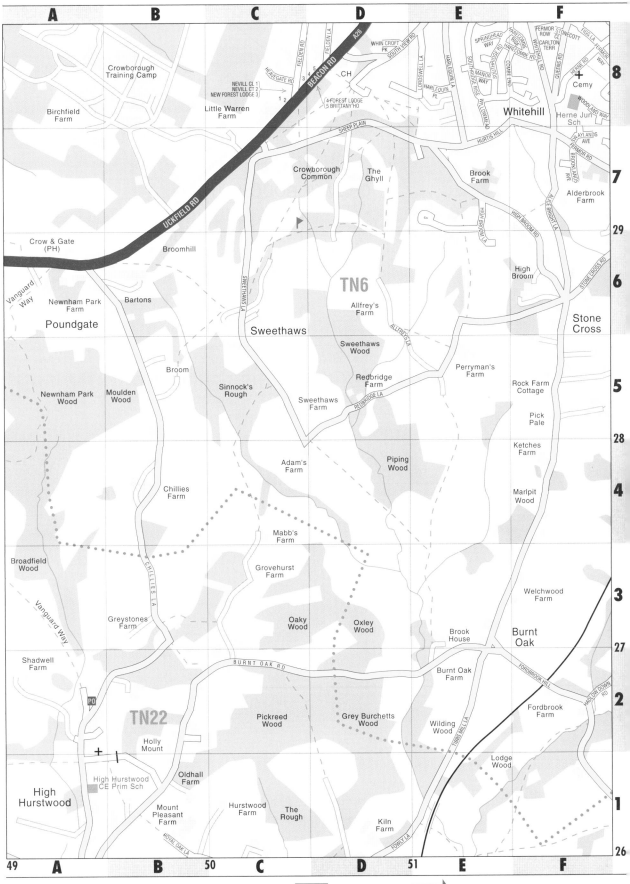

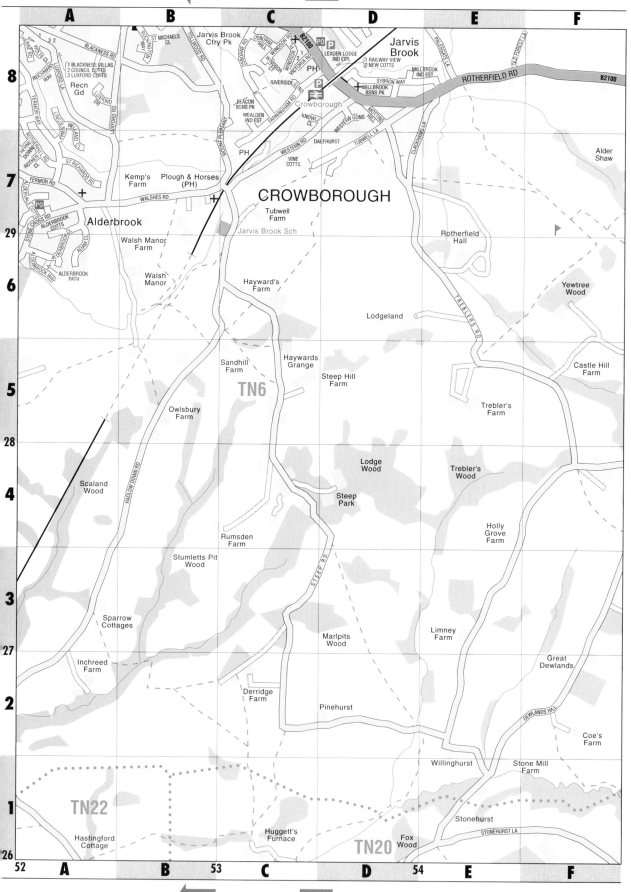

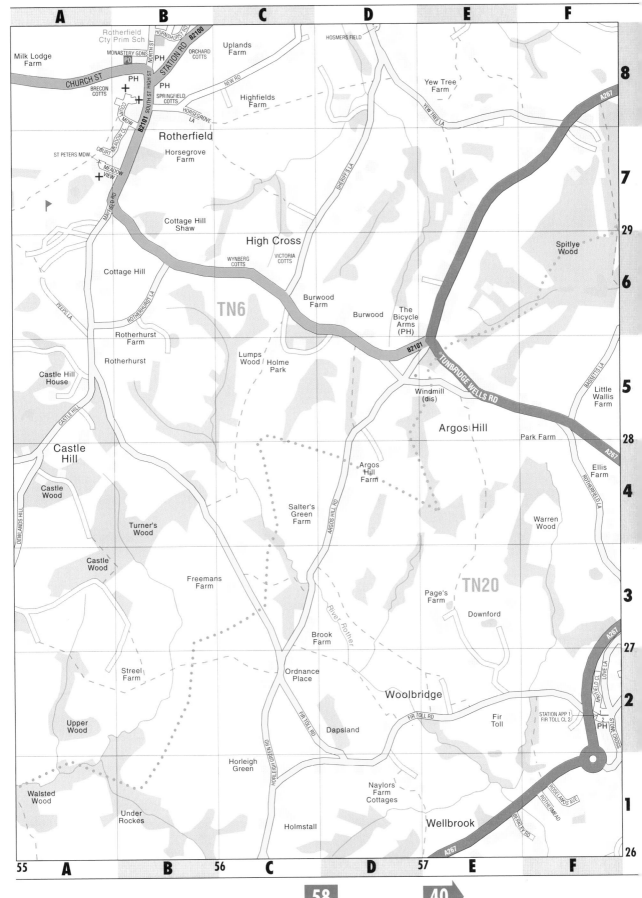

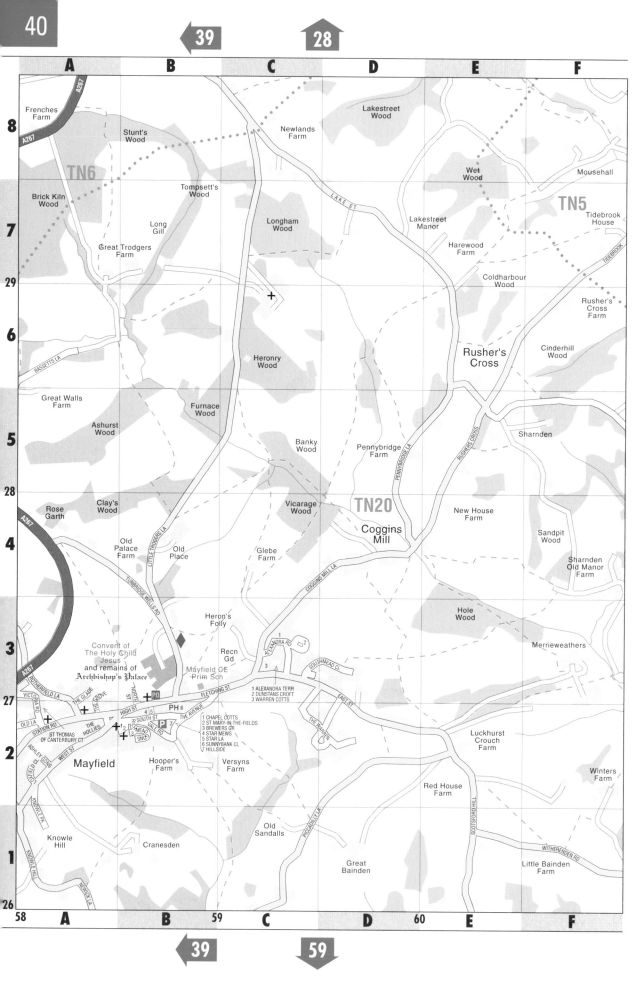

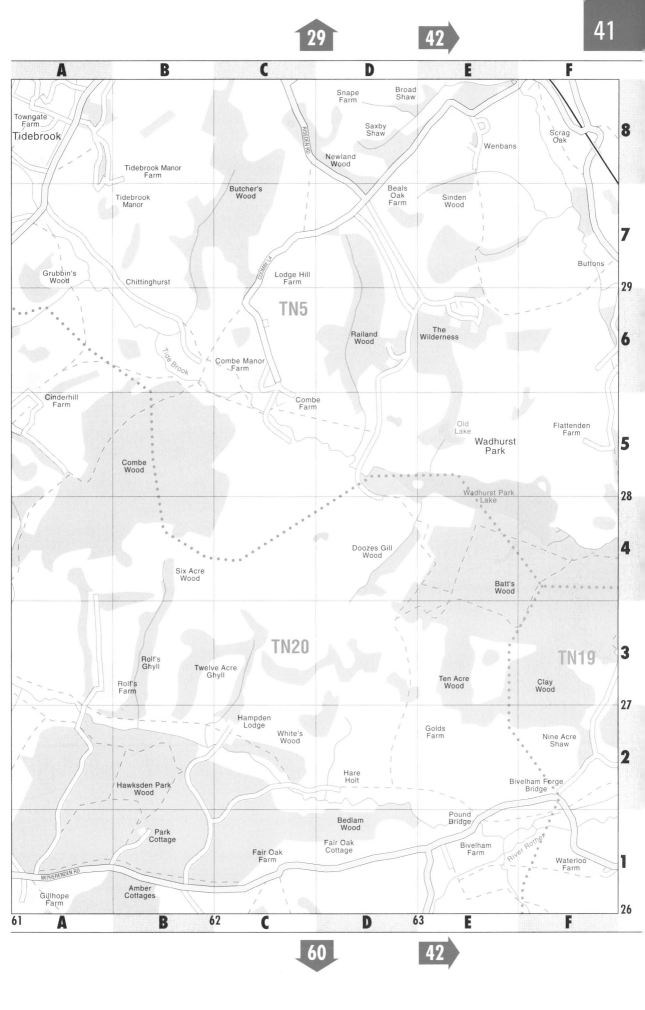

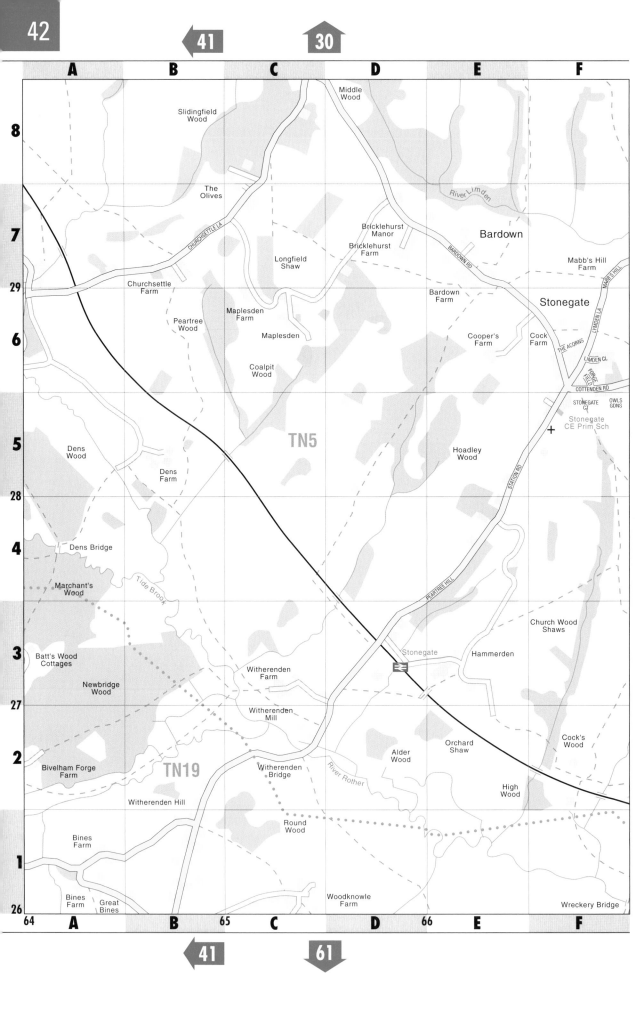

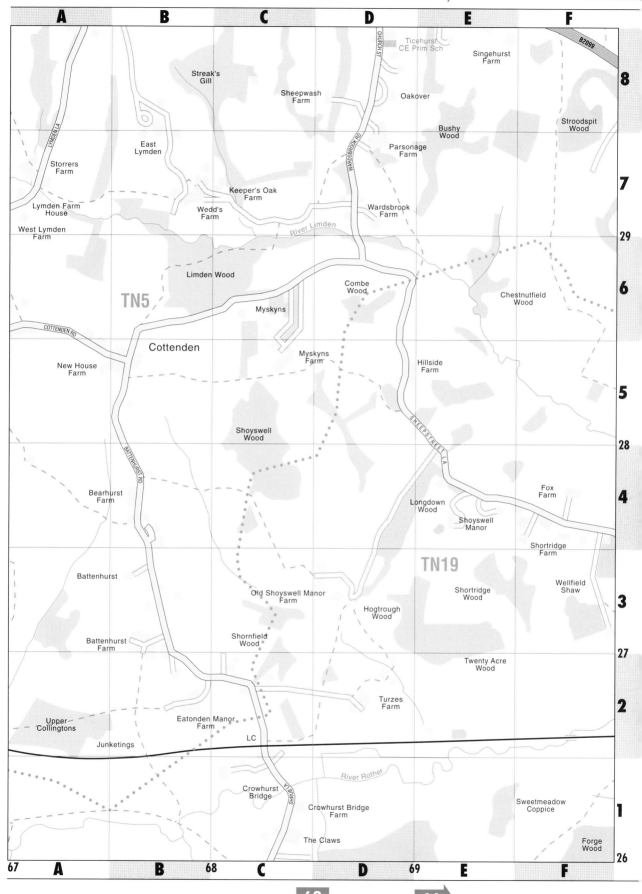

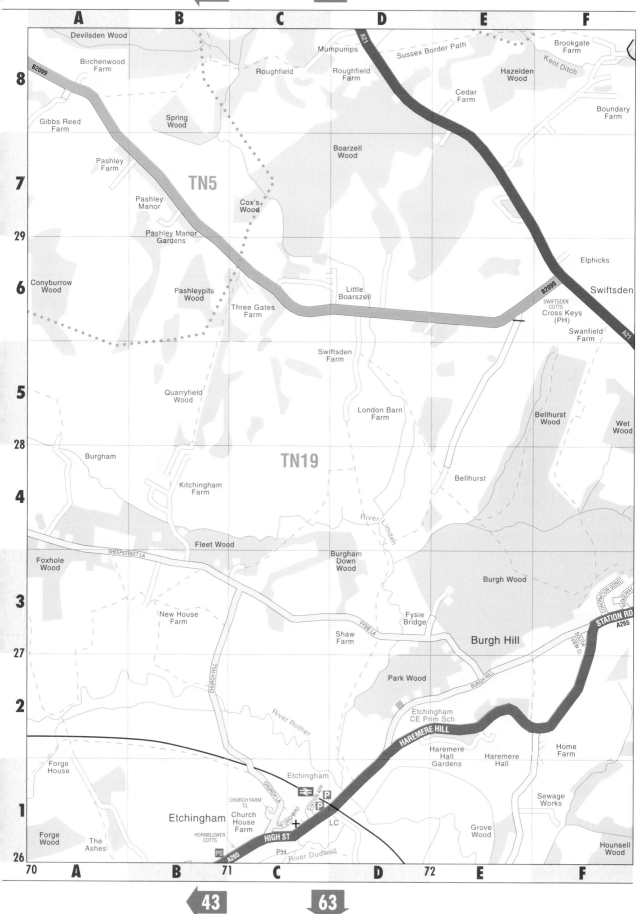

A   B   C   D   E   F

8

B2099

Devilsden Wood

Birchenwood Farm

Gibbs Reed Farm

Pashley Farm

TN5

7

Spring Wood

Roughfield

Mumpumps

Roughfield Farm

Sussex Border Path

Cedar Farm

Hazelden Wood

Brookgate Farm

Kent Ditch

A21

Boundary Farm

Boarzell Wood

29

Pashley Manor

Pashley Manor Gardens

Cox's Wood

6

Conyburrow Wood

Pashleypits Wood

Three Gates Farm

Little Boarszell

Swiftsden Farm

SWIFTSDEN COTTS
Cross Keys (PH)

Elphicks

Swiftsden

B2099

Swanfield Farm

A21

5

Quarryfield Wood

London Barn Farm

Bellhurst Wood

Wet Wood

28

Burgham

Kitchingham Farm

TN19

Bellhurst

4

Fleet Wood

SHEEPSTREET LA

River Limden

Foxhole Wood

Burgham Down Wood

Burgh Wood

STATION RD
A265

3

New House Farm

CHURCH HILL

Shaw Farm

FYSIE LA

Fysie Bridge

Burgh Hill

SOUTH VIEW CL

27

River Rother

Park Wood

BURGH HILL

2

HAREMERE HILL

Etchingham CE Prim Sch

Haremere Hall Gardens

Haremere Hall

Home Farm

Forge House

CHURCH LA

Etchingham

CHURCH FARM CL

THE ORCHARD

STATION APP

P

P

LC

Sewage Works

1

Etchingham

Church House Farm

Grove Wood

Hounsell Wood

Forge Wood

The Ashes

HORNBLOWER COTTS

PO

A265

HIGH ST

PH

River Dudwell

26

70   A   71   B   C   72   D   E   F

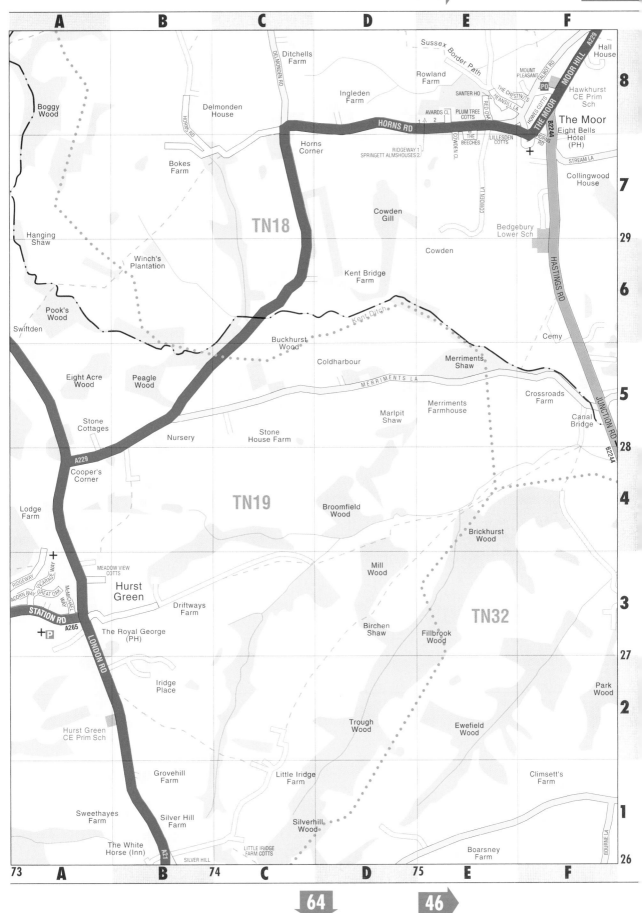

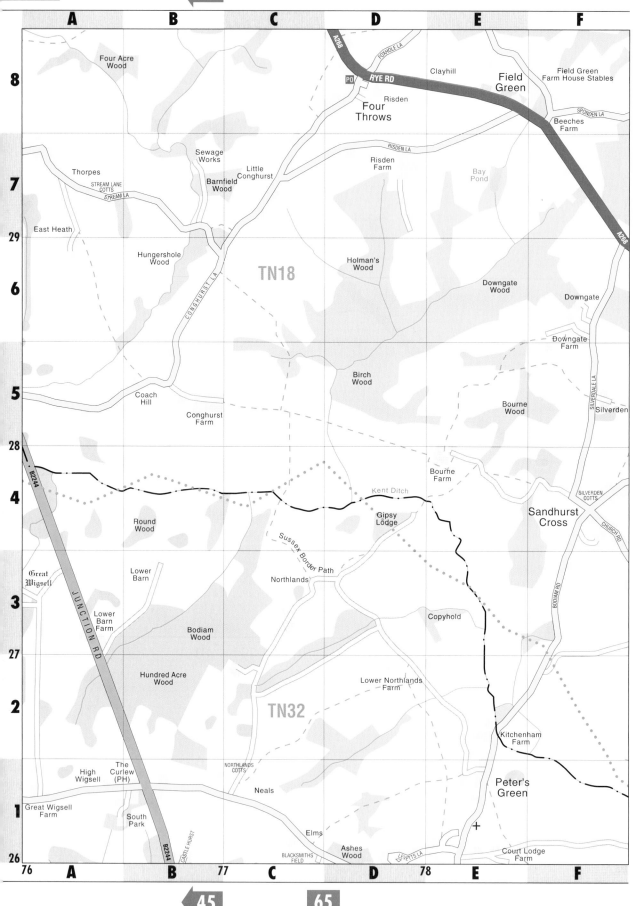

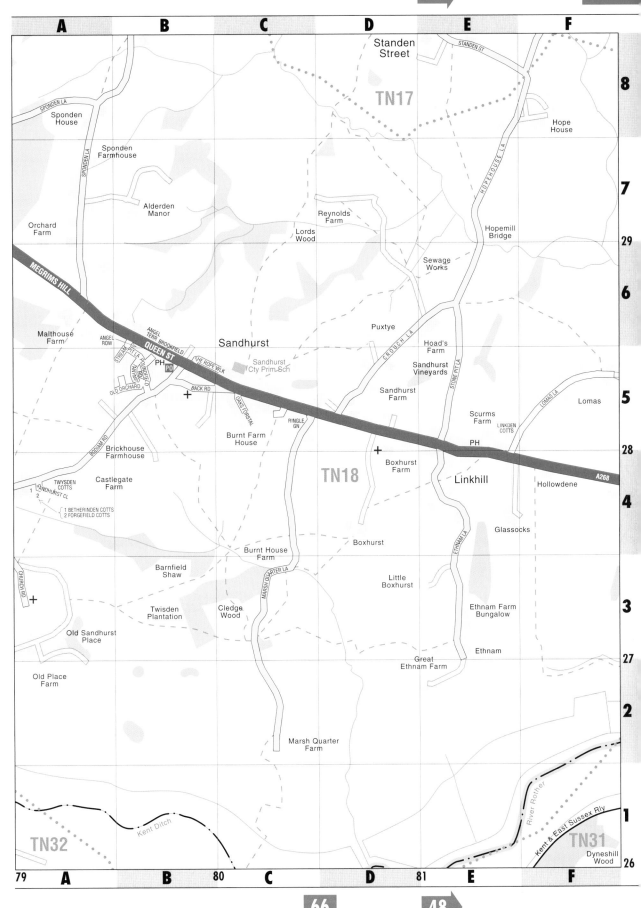

48

A   B   C   D   E   F

8

7

29

6

5

28

4

27

3

2

1

26

Standen Street

TN17

Hope House

Sponden House

SPONDEN LA

Sponden Farmhouse

Alderden Manor

Orchard Farm

Reynolds Farm

Lords Wood

HOPEHOUSE LA

Hopemill Bridge

Sewage Works

MEGRIMS HILL

Malthouse Farm

ANGEL TERR BROOKFIELD
ANGEL ROW
QUEEN ST
STREAM PIT LA
POUNDFIELD
TANYARD
OLD ORCHARD
PH PO

Sandhurst

THE ROPE WLK

Sandhurst Cty Prim Sch

BACK RD

Puxtye

Hoad's Farm

CROUCH LA

Sandhurst Vineyards

STONE PIT LA

Lomas

LOMAS LA

Scurms Farm

LINKDEN COTTS

PH

A268

RODIAM RD

Brickhouse Farmhouse

OAKSTON STL

RINGLE GN

Burnt Farm House

Sandhurst Farm

Boxhurst Farm

Linkhill

Hollowdene

TN18

Twysden Cotts
SANDHURST CL
1 BETHERINDEN COTTS
2 FORGEFIELD COTTS

Castlegate Farm

Glassocks

ETHNAM LA

Boxhurst

Little Boxhurst

Ethnam Farm Bungalow

CHURCH RD

Barnfield Shaw

Twisden Plantation

Cledge Wood

MARSH QUARTER LA

Burnt House Farm

Old Sandhurst Place

Ethnam

Great Ethnam Farm

Old Place Farm

Marsh Quarter Farm

River Rother

Kent & East Sussex Rly

TN31

Dyneshill Wood

TN32

Kent Ditch

79   A   B   80   C   D   81   E   F

66   48

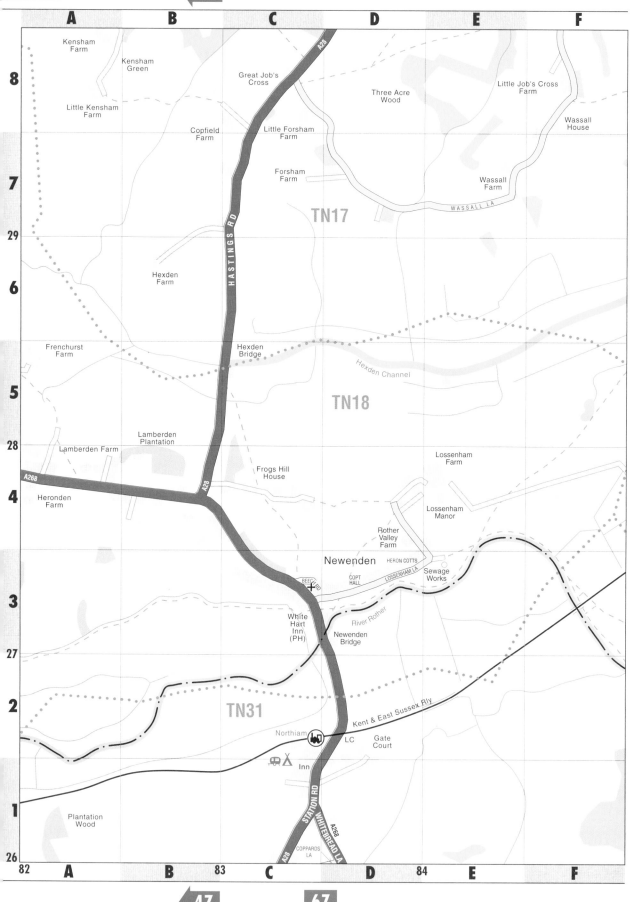

A   B   C   D   E   F

8

Kensham
Farm

Kensham
Green

Great Job's
Cross

Three Acre
Wood

Little Job's Cross
Farm

Little Kensham
Farm

Copfield
Farm

Little Forsham
Farm

Wassall
House

7

Forsham
Farm

Wassall
Farm

WASSALL LA

TN17

29

HASTINGS RD

Hexden
Farm

6

Frenchurst
Farm

Hexden
Bridge

Hexden Channel

5

TN18

Lamberden
Plantation

28

Lamberden Farm

Frogs Hill
House

Lossenham
Farm

A268

4

Heronden
Farm

A28

Lossenham
Manor

Rother
Valley
Farm

Newenden

HERON COTTS

Sewage
Works

COPT
HALL

LOSSENHAM LA

BEEC RD

3

White
Hart
Inn
(PH)

River Rother

Newenden
Bridge

27

2

TN31

Kent & East Sussex Rly

Northiam

LC

Gate
Court

Inn

1

Plantation
Wood

STATION RD

WHITEBREAD LA

A268

26

COPPARDS
LA

A28

82   A   B   83   C   D   84   E   F

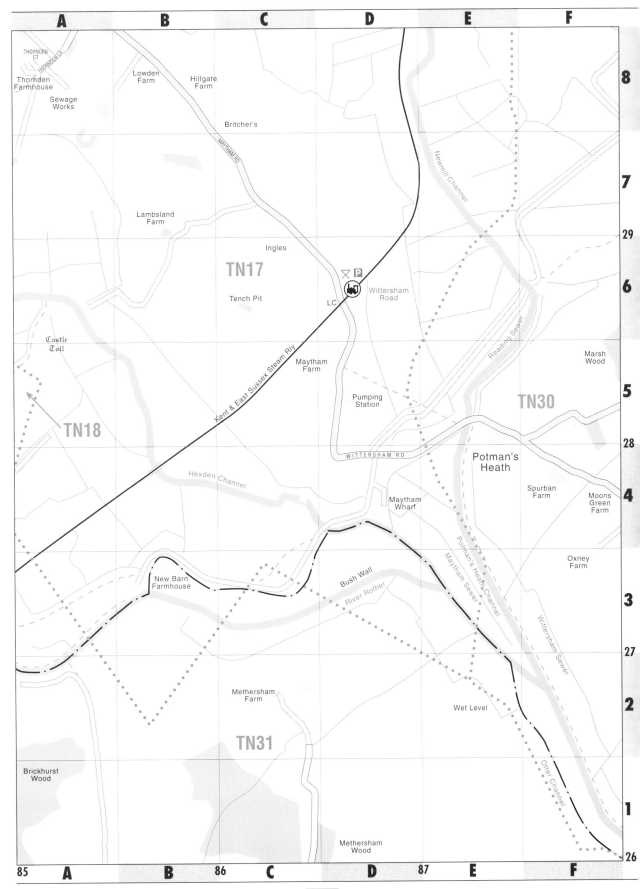

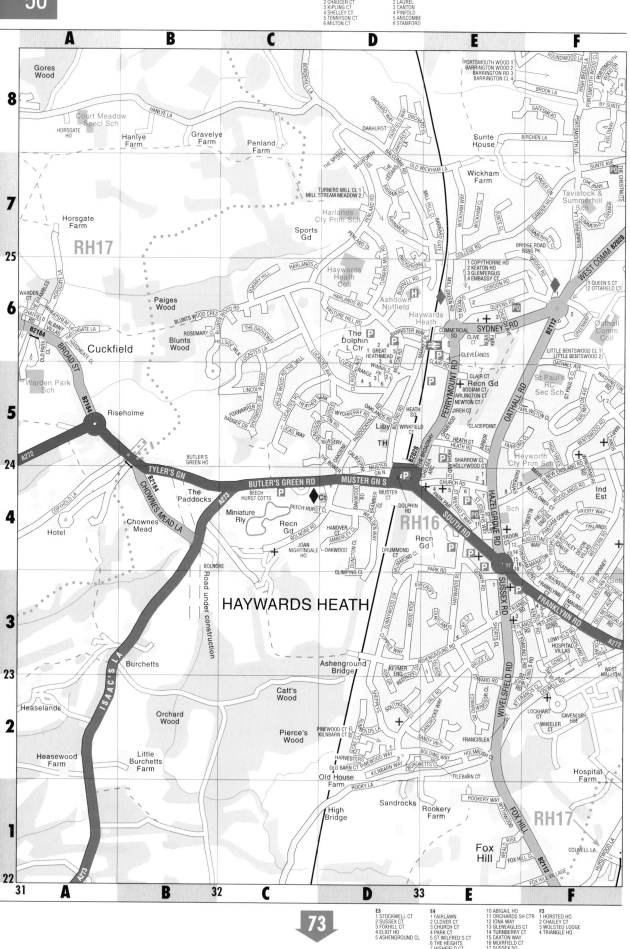

D5
1 BYRON CT
2 CHAUCER CT
3 KIPLING CT
4 SHELLEY CT
5 TENNYSON CT
6 MILTON CT

D6
1 WILTON
2 LAUREL
3 CANTON
4 PINFOLD
5 ANSCOMBE
6 STAMFORD

E3
1 STOCKWELL CT
2 SUSSEX CT
3 FOXHILL CT
4 ELIOT HO
5 ASHENGROUND CL

E4
1 FAIRLAWN
2 CLOVER CT
3 CHURCH CT
4 PARK CT
5 ST WILFRED'S CT
6 THE HEIGHTS
7 HIGHFIELD CT
8 HAZELGROVE GDNS
9 HEATH CL

10 ABIGAIL HO
11 ORCHARDS SH CTR
12 IONA WAY
13 GLENEAGLES CT
14 TURNBERRY CT
15 CAXTON WAY
16 MUIRFIELD CT
17 SUSSEX SQ
18 CARNOUSTIE CT

F3
1 HORSTED HO
2 CHAILEY CT
3 WOLSTED LODGE
4 TRIANGLE HO

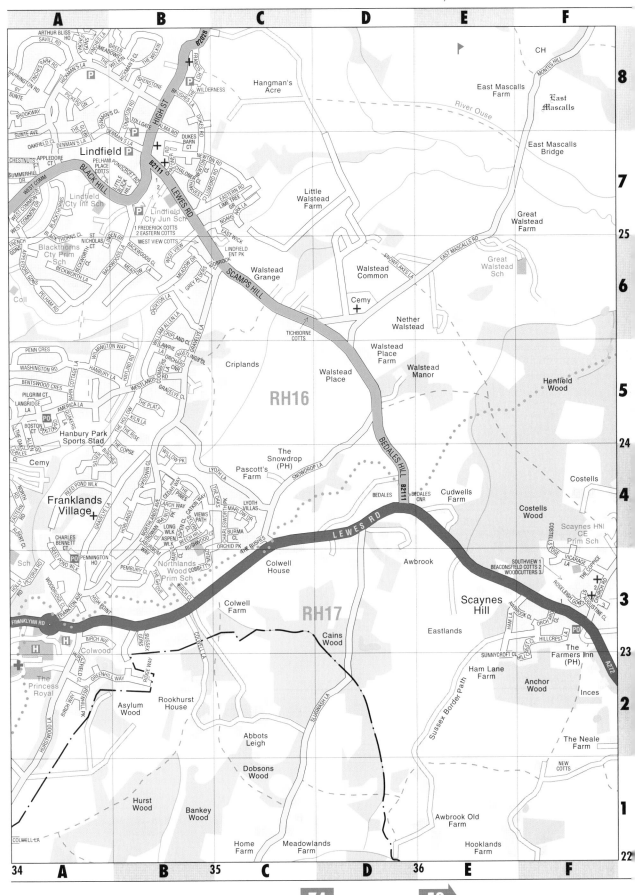

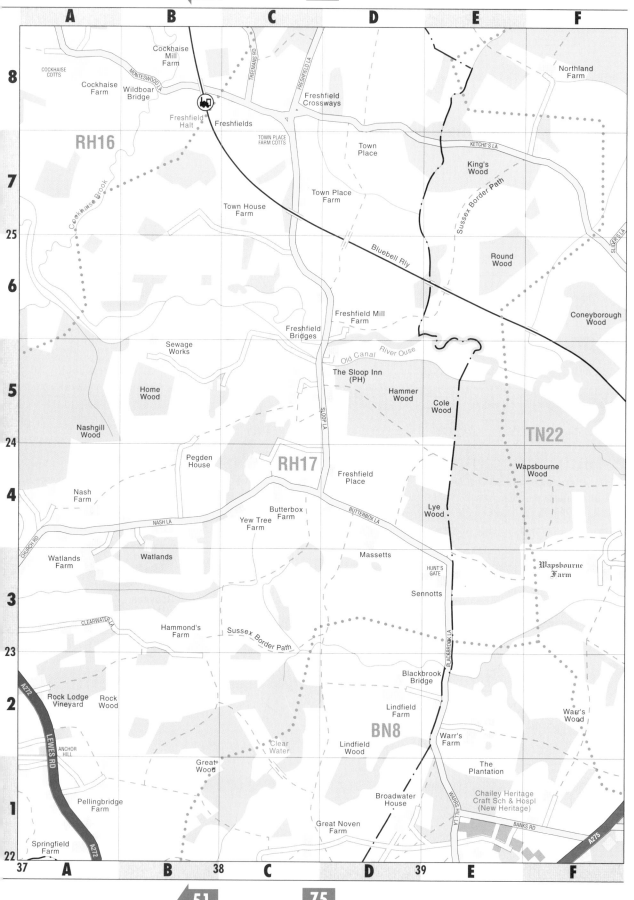

A   **B**   **C**   **D**   **E**   **F**

8

COCKHAISE COTTS

Cockhaise Mill Farm

Cockhaise Farm

MONTESWOOD LA

Wildboar Bridge

Cockhaise Mill Farm

Freshfield Halt

Freshfields

TREEMANS RD

FRESHFIELD LA

Freshfield Crossways

Northland Farm

RH16

7

Cockhaise Brook

Town House Farm

TOWN PLACE FARM COTTS

Town Place

Town Place Farm

King's Wood

KETCHE'S LA

Sussex Border Path

SLIDERS LA

25

Bluebell Rly

Round Wood

6

Coneyborough Wood

Freshfield Mill Farm

Freshfield Bridges

Sewage Works

Old Canal

River Ouse

The Sloop Inn (PH)

Hammer Wood

Cole Wood

5

Home Wood

Nashgill Wood

SLOOP LA

24

Pegden House

RH17

Freshfield Place

Wapsbourne Wood

TN22

Nash Farm

Butterbox Farm

Yew Tree Farm

BUTTERBOX LA

Lye Wood

4

NASH LA

Watlands Farm

Watlands

Massetts

HUNT'S GATE

Wapsbourne Farm

3

CLEARWATER LA

Hammond's Farm

Sussex Border Path

Sennotts

BLACKBROOK LA

23

Blackbrook Bridge

Warr's Wood

A272

Rock Lodge Vineyard

Rock Wood

Lindfield Farm

BN8

Warr's Farm

2

LEWES RD

ANCHOR HILL

Clear Water

Lindfield Wood

The Plantation

Great Wood

Broadwater House

WARRS HILL LA

Chailey Heritage Craft Sch & Hospl (New Heritage)

1

Pellingbridge Farm

BANKS RD

A275

Springfield Farm

A272

Great Noven Farm

22

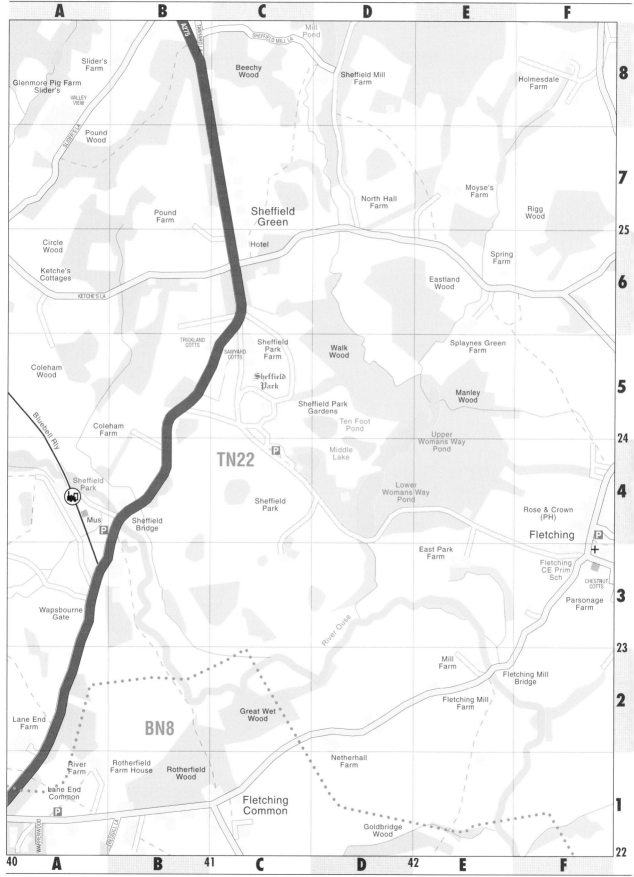

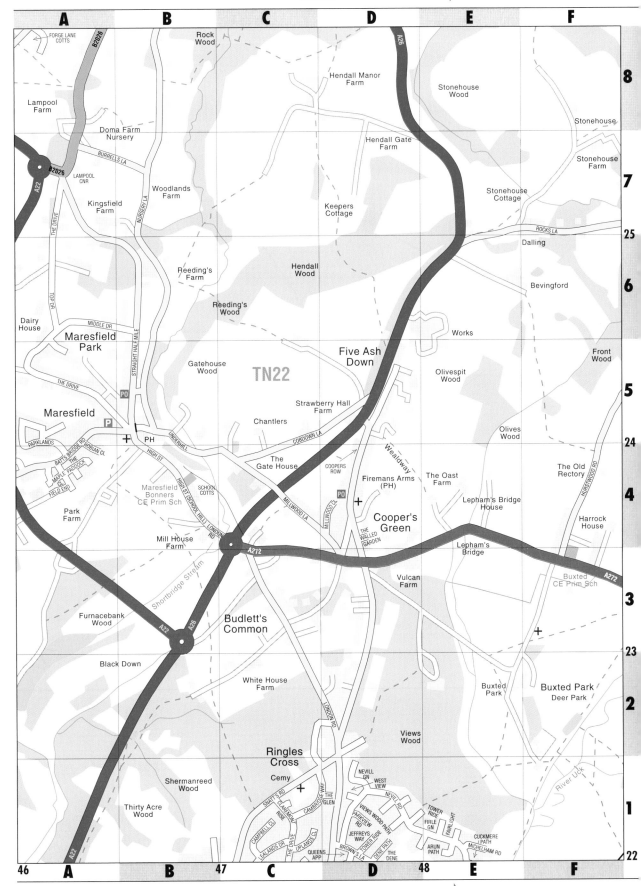

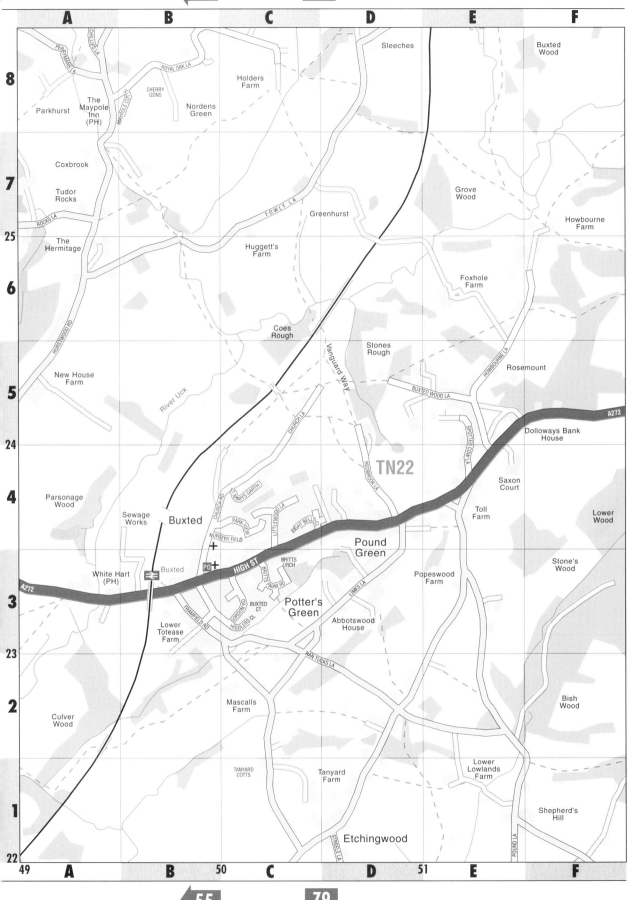

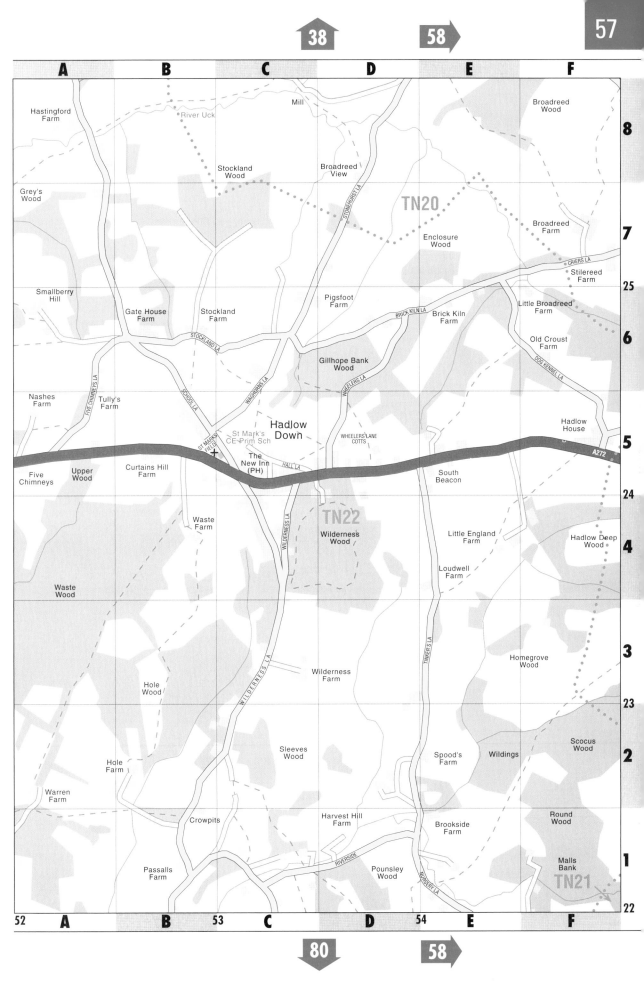

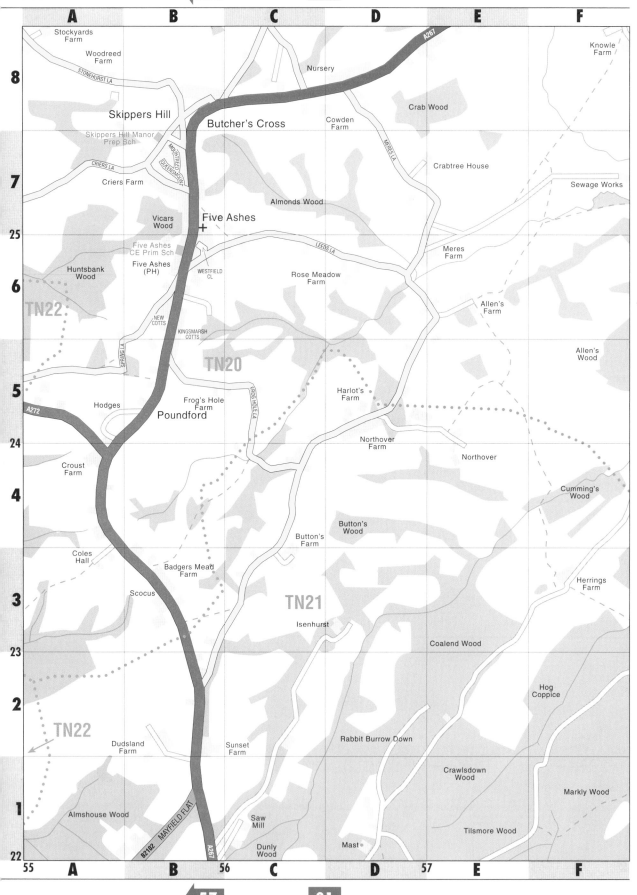

Stockyards Farm
Woodreed Farm
STONEHURST LA
Skippers Hill
Butcher's Cross
Skippers Hill Manor Prep Sch
MOUNT FIELD DRIVE
QUEENSMOUNT
CRIERS LA
Criers Farm
Vicars Wood
Five Ashes
Five Ashes CE Prim Sch
Five Ashes (PH)
WESTFIELD CL
Huntsbank Wood
TN22
NEW COTTS
SPRING LA
KINGSMARSH COTTS
TN20
Hodges
Frog's Hole Farm
Poundford
FROG HOLE LA
A272
Croust Farm
Coles Hall
Scocus
Badgers Mead Farm
TN22
Dudsland Farm
Sunset Farm
B2102
MAYFIELD FLAT
A267
Almshouse Wood
Saw Mill
Dunly Wood

Nursery
A267
Crab Wood
Cowden Farm
MERES LA
Crabtree House
Sewage Works
Almonds Wood
LEEDS LA
Meres Farm
Rose Meadow Farm
Allen's Farm
Allen's Wood
Harlot's Farm
Northover Farm
Northover
Cumming's Wood
Button's Wood
Button's Farm
Herrings Farm
TN21
Isenhurst
Coalend Wood
Hog Coppice
Rabbit Burrow Down
Crawlsdown Wood
Markly Wood
Tilsmore Wood
Mast
Knowle Farm

8 7 25 6 5 24 4 3 23 2 1 22

A | B | C | D | E | F

8

Great Calem
Wood

Little Calem
Wood

Froghole
Farm

Turk's
Bridge

River Rother

Froghole
Bridge

TN20

Turk's
Farm

Holmshurst
Manor Farm

7

Great Broadhurst
Farm

Little Broadhurst
Farm

Oaken
Wood

25

Coxdown
Farm

6

Little
Stonehurst
Farm

Lakedown
Farm

Great
Stonehurst
Farm

Great
Bigknowle
Farm

Ashen
Wood

Nursements
Farm

Shovels
Wood

Limberlost
Farm

Marlpit
Shaw

Climshurst
Wood

5

Pottens Mill
Farm

Taylor's
Farm

Knowle
Farm

Broadhurst

Blackdown
Wood

24

Corner
Farm

TN21

Foxhole
Wood

TN19

4

PAINE'S CNR

Foxhole
Farm

Oakdown
Farm

Baltham
Wood

Little Park
Farm

Doel's
Farm

A265

WEST END
COTTS

3

Barklye
Farm

Burralands

Mill House
Farm

STOKES
COTTS

THE
MARTLETS

Black Sand
Wood

Holban's
Farm

23

Swife
Wood

Cedar Swiffe
Farm

Kingsdown
Farm

Swiffes
Farm

Home
Farm

Poundsford

2

Spinney
Farm House

Poundsford
Farm

A265

Tottingworth
Park

Oak Hall

Milkhurst
Wood

Applebrook
Farm

Stonehole
Wood

1

Limekiln
Wood

22

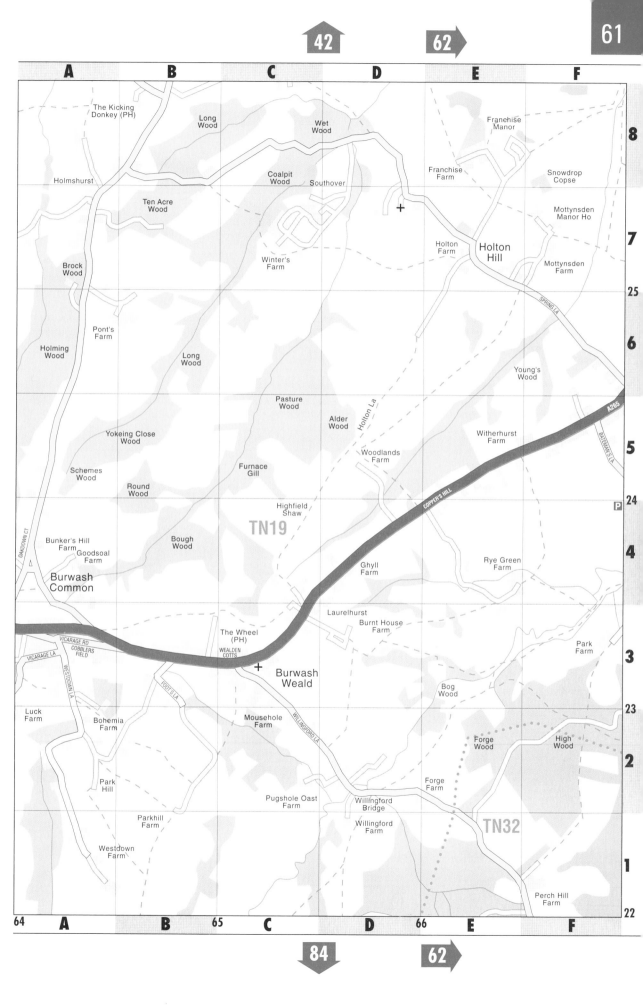

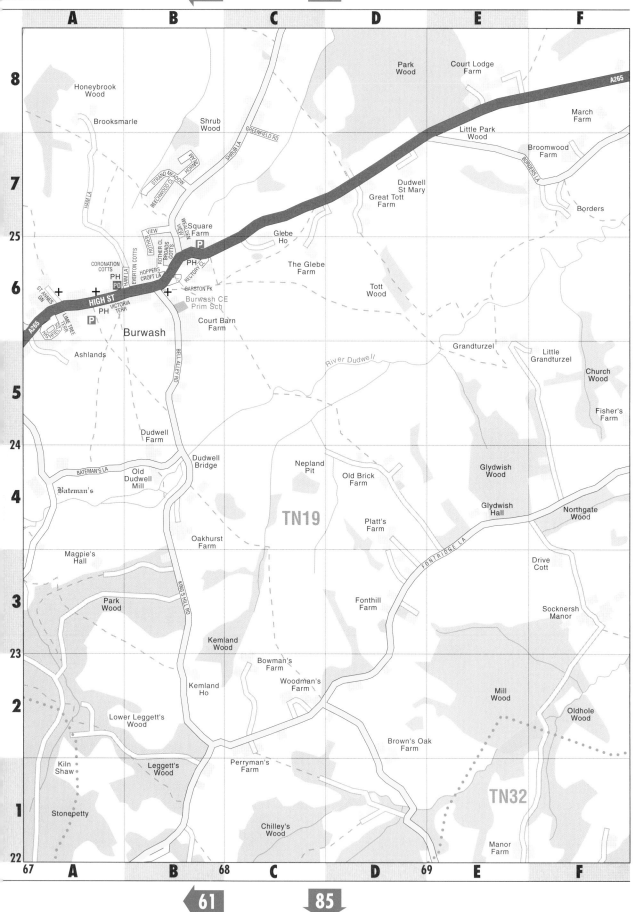

A B C D E F

8

Honeybrook Wood

Brooksmarle

Shrub Wood

Park Wood

Court Lodge Farm

A265

March Farm

7

HAM LA

STRAND MEADOW

HORNS

BEECHWOOD CL

Shrub Wood

GREENFIELD RD

SHRUB LA

Little Park Wood

Dudwell St Mary

Great Tott Farm

Broomwood Farm

BORDERS LA

Borders

25

VIEW

ROTHER CL

WEALDEN VIEW

Square Farm

P

Glebe Ho

6

ST ANNES GN

A265

LIME TREE TERR

SCHOOL HILL

CORONATION COTTS

PH PO

EVERTON COTTS

HAM LA

HOPPERS CROFT LA

ROTHER CL

BROADS COTTS

P

PH

PH

RECTORY CL

VICTORIA TERR

GARSTON PK

Burwash CE Prim Sch

Court Barn Farm

The Glebe Farm

Tott Wood

Grandturzel

Little Grandturzel

Church Wood

Burwash

Ashlands

River Dudwell

Fisher's Farm

5

24

Dudwell Farm

BATEMAN'S LA

Old Dudwell Mill

Bateman's

Dudwell Bridge

Nepland Pit

Old Brick Farm

Glydwish Wood

Glydwish Hall

Northgate Wood

4

TN19

Oakhurst Farm

Platt's Farm

FONTRIDGE LA

Drive Cott

Magpie's Hall

KING'S HILL RD

Park Wood

Fonthill Farm

Socknersh Manor

3

23

Kemland Wood

Bowman's Farm

Woodman's Farm

Mill Wood

Oldhole Wood

2

Lower Leggett's Wood

Kemland Ho

Brown's Oak Farm

Kiln Shaw

Leggett's Wood

Perryman's Farm

TN32

Manor Farm

1

Stonepetty

Chilley's Wood

22

67 A 68 B C 68 D 69 E F

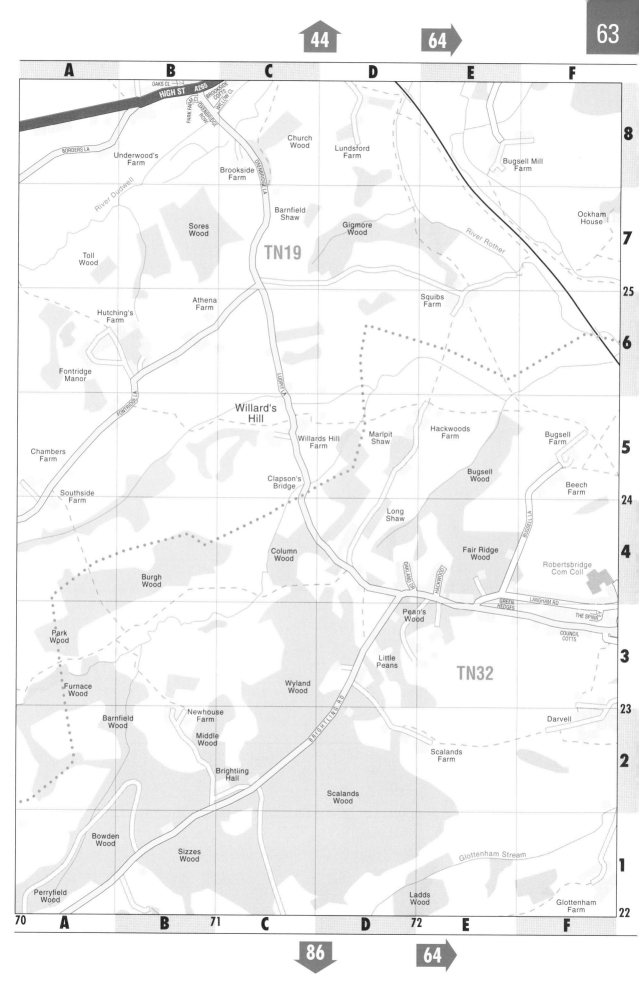

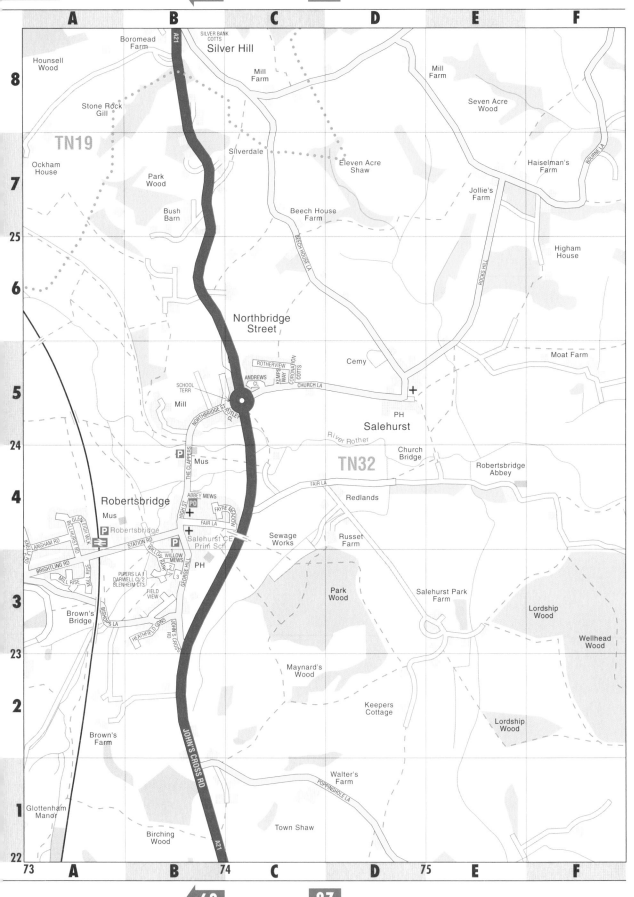

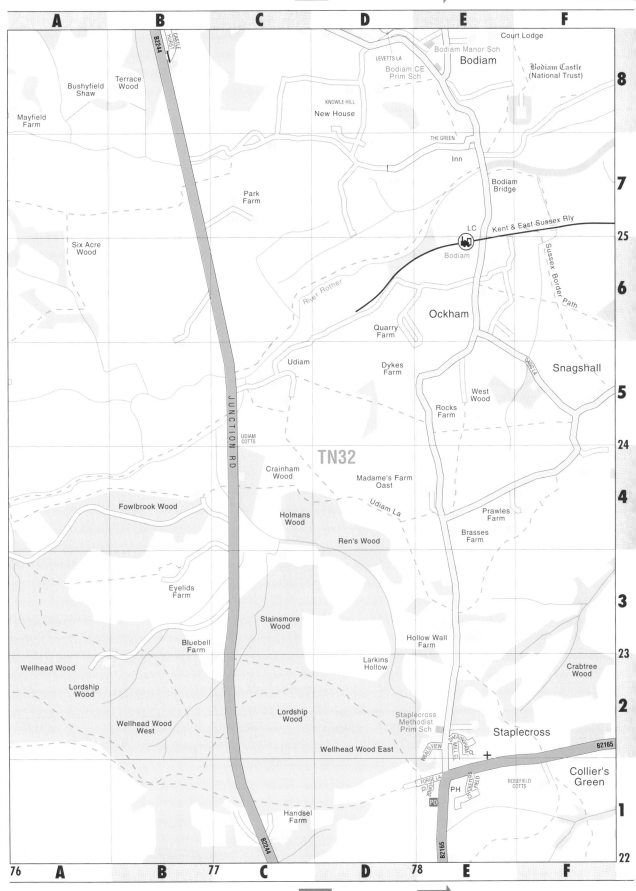

A B C D E F

B2244
CASTLE HURST

Bushyfield Shaw
Terrace Wood
Mayfield Farm

Court Lodge
Bodiam Manor Sch
LEVETTS LA
Bodiam CE Prim Sch
Bodiam
Bodiam Castle (National Trust)

8

KNOWLE HILL
New House

THE GREEN
Inn

Bodiam Bridge

7

Park Farm

Kent & East Sussex Rly

LC
Bodiam

25

Six Acre Wood

River Rother

Sussex Border Path

6

Quarry Farm

Ockham

Snagshall

Udiam

Dykes Farm

DAIG LA

5

West Wood

Rocks Farm

UDIAM COTTS

24

TN32

Crainham Wood

Madame's Farm Oast

4

Fowlbrook Wood

Udiam La

Prawles Farm

Holmans Wood

Brasses Farm

Ren's Wood

Eyelids Farm

3

Stainsmore Wood

Hollow Wall Farm

23

Bluebell Farm

Wellhead Wood

Larkins Hollow

Crabtree Wood

Lordship Wood

2

Wellhead Wood West

Lordship Wood

Staplecross Methodist Prim Sch

Staplecross

B2165

Wellhead Wood East

WEALD VIEW
SHERINGHAM
MILL CL

Collier's Green

+

FORGE LA
FORGE
PO
PH
CRYKETTERS FIELD
ROSEFIELD COTTS

1

Handsel Farm

B2244

B2165

22

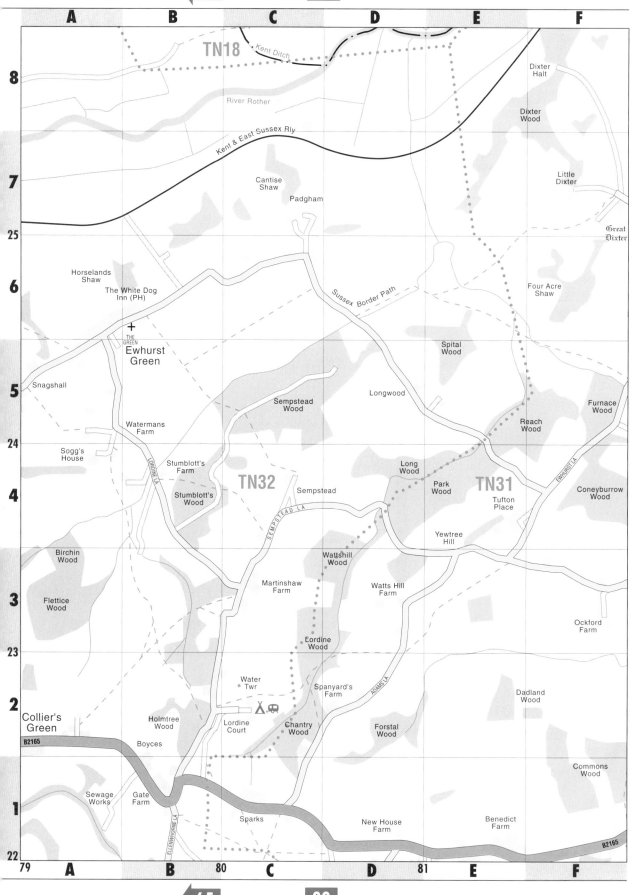

A B C D E F

TN18

Kent Ditch

8

River Rother

Kent & East Sussex Rly

7

Cantise Shaw

Padgham

Dixter Halt

Dixter Wood

Little Dixter

Great Dixter

25

Horselands Shaw

The White Dog Inn (PH)

THE GREEN

Ewhurst Green

6

Sussex Border Path

Spital Wood

Four Acre Shaw

Snagshall

5

Watermans Farm

Sempstead Wood

Longwood

Reach Wood

Furnace Wood

Sogg's House

24

Stumblott's Farm

Stumblott's Wood

LORDINE LA

TN32

Sempstead

SEMPSTEAD LA

Long Wood

Park Wood

TN31

Tufton Place

Coneyburrow Wood

EWHURST LA

4

Birchin Wood

Martinshaw Farm

Wattshill Wood

Watts Hill Farm

Yewtree Hill

Flettice Wood

3

Lordine Wood

Ockford Farm

23

Water Twr

Spanyard's Farm

ADAMS LA

Dadland Wood

2

Collier's Green

Holmtree Wood

Lordine Court

Chantry Wood

Forstal Wood

B2165

Boyces

Commons Wood

Sewage Works

Gate Farm

1

Sparks

New House Farm

Benedict Farm

B2165

22

79 A B 80 C D 81 E F

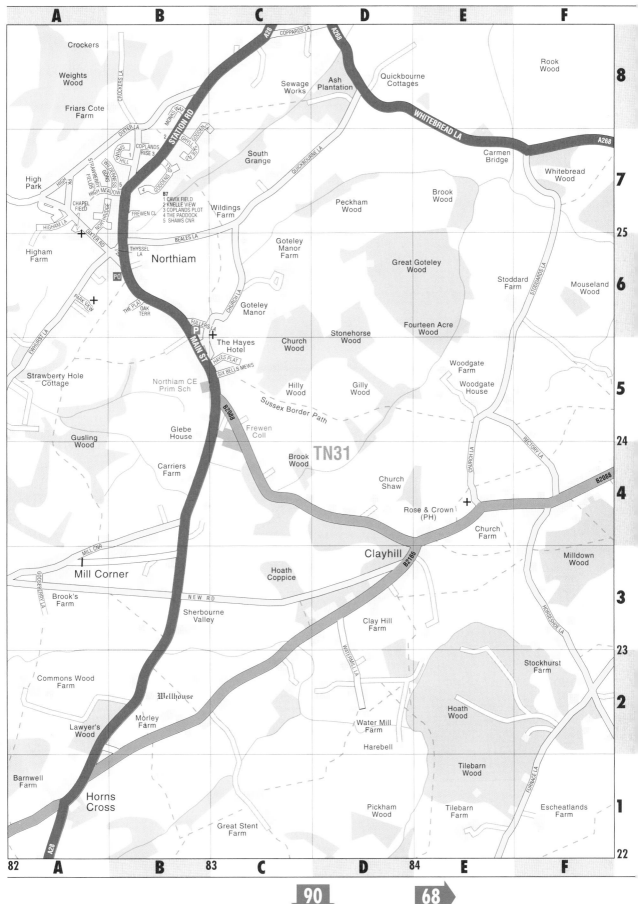

67
49

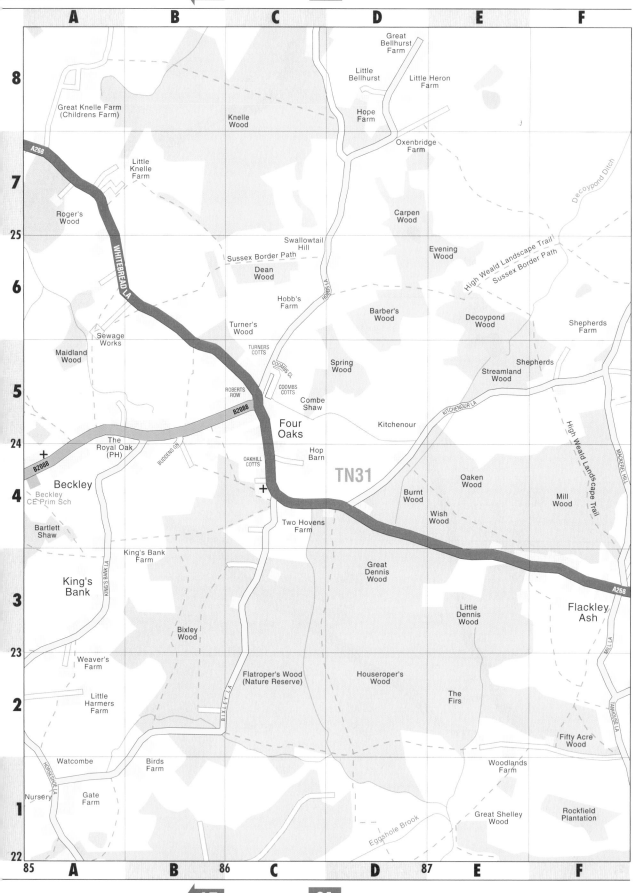

67
91

Blackwall
Bridge

TN30

River Rother

Sussex Border Path

Kitchenham

Corkwood
Farm

New House
Farm

Baron's
Grange

Moat Farm

Forstals
Farmhouse

Moat

TN31

Willow
Beds

Flackley Ash
Farmhouse

Cock
Wood

Old House
Farm

Iden
Wood

Brabands
Wood

Flackley Ash
Hotel

COLDHARBOUR LA

RECTORY LA

READERS LA

Coldharbour

Malthouse
Wood

MALTHOUSE LA

King's
Wood

PO

The
Cock Horse
Inn
(PH)

Pioneer
Nurseries

TANHOUSE LA

Tanhouse

Peasmarsh +

MALTHOUSE LA

THE MALTHOUSE
BSNS PK

THE MALTINGS

THE OLD HOP

RYE RD

A268

Brabands

FARLEYS WAY

MAIN ST

BRICKFIELD

Stream
Farm

Cock
Wood

SCHOOL LA

PARK VIEW

GDN FARM
GDNS

ORCHARD WAY

Rumples
Motel

Rye
Foreign

TANHOUSE LA

Peasmarsh
CE Prim
Sch

Horse & Cart
Inn
(PH)

Morfey
Wood

Lea
Farm

DEW LA

Van's
Gill

High Weald Landscape Trail

Corner
Wood

CHURCH LA

Peasmarsh
Park

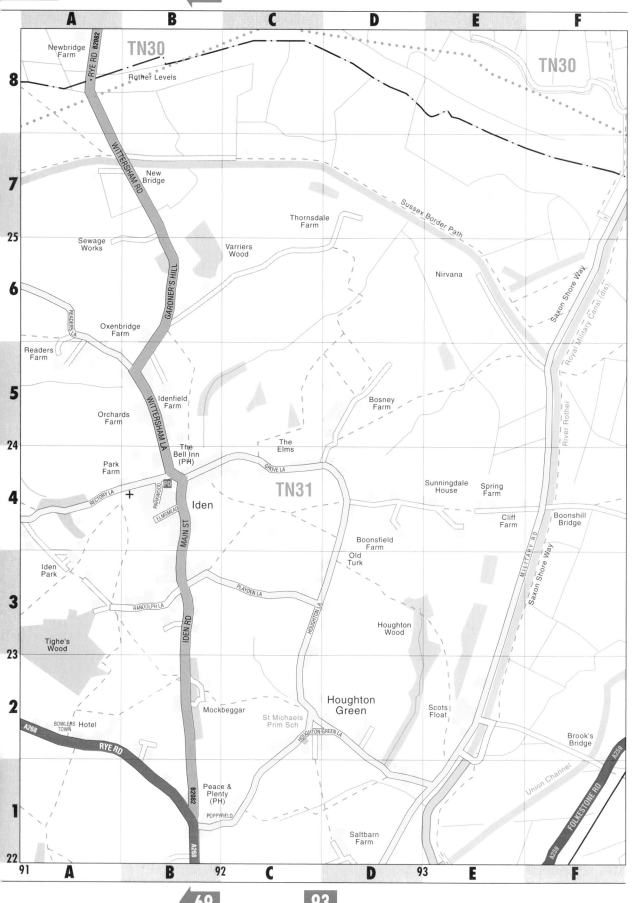

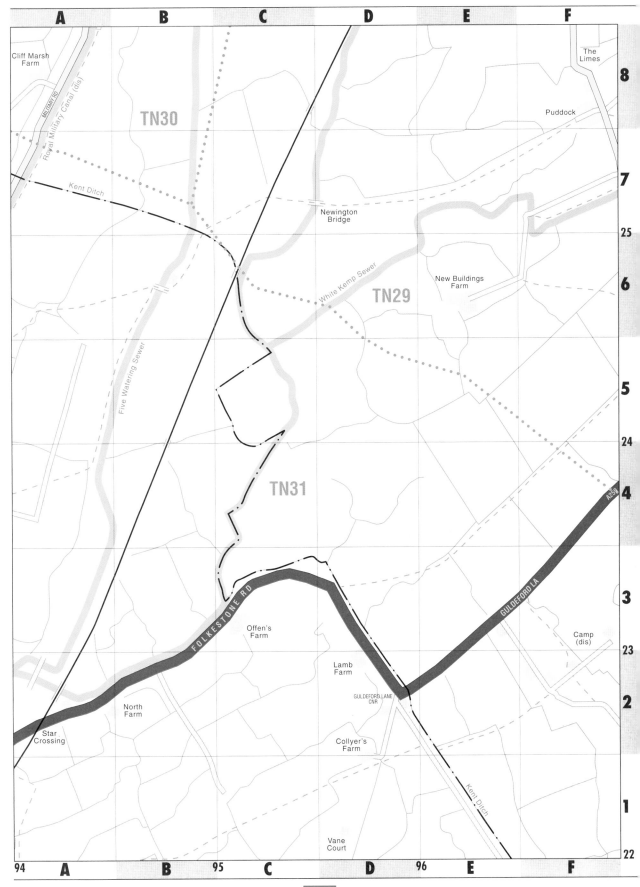

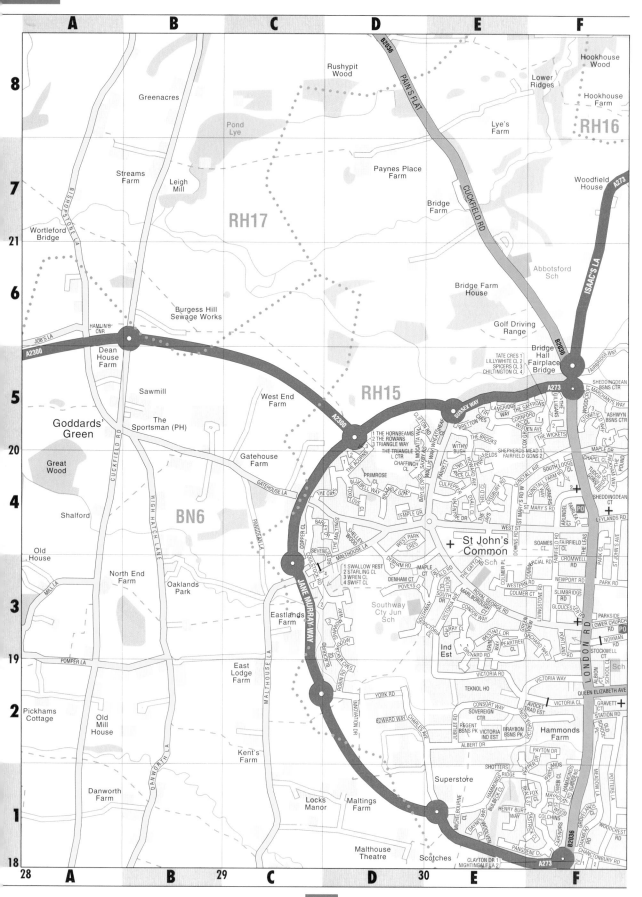

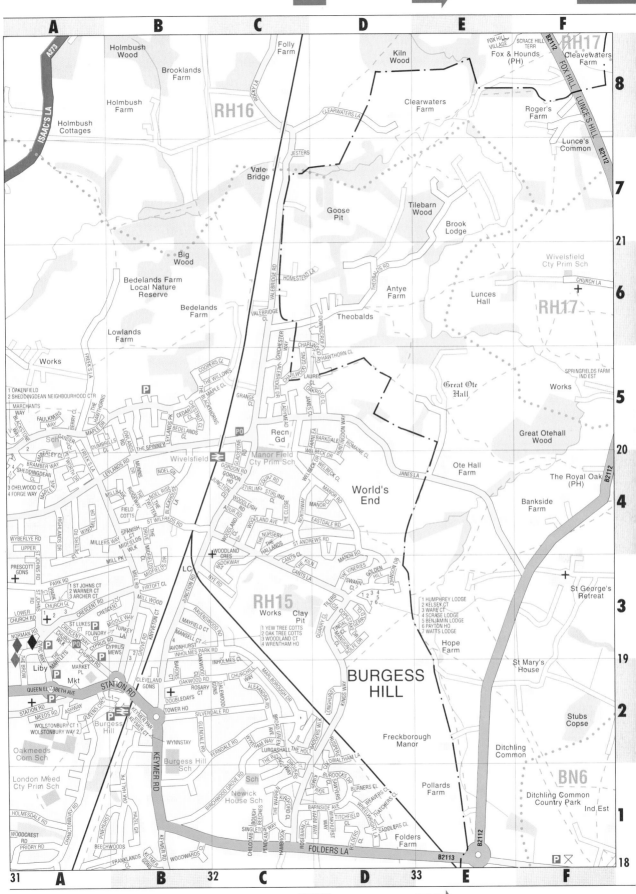

73

51

A B C D E F

8

RH16

Ham
Bridge

Ham
Wood

7

Tylevel
Wood

Sussex Border Path

Ham La

Wilderness
Wood

Holford
Manor

B2112

Fatting
Hovel

Strood
Wood

21

LUNCE'S HILL

More
House

SLUGWASH LA

Townings
Place

Wivelsfield
Hall

Hole
Farm

Wivelsden
Farm

Newhouse
Wood

6

CHURCH LA

RH17

Strood
Farm

Roseland
Wood

BLACKMORES

Mann's
Farm

Roselands

Newhouse
Farm

B2112

Diamond
Cotts

TANNERS FIELD

PEPPER HALL
COTTS

Wivelsfield

Longridge

5

BALDINGS
COTTS

GREEN RD

Fanners

Cock Inn
(PH)

STROOD GATE

NORTH COMMON RD

Sedgebrook
Wood

BALDINGS
COTTS

Recn
Gd

P

FARNCOMBE CL

20

GREEN PARK CNR

GREEN LA

PO

COPPARDS CL

BN8

Locksfrood
Farm

EASTERN RD

FAIRPLACE

ALLWOOD CRES

DOWNSVIEW RD

4

Coldharbour
Farm

Wivelsfield
Green

SOUTH RD

Grassy
Wood

Longridge
Wood

Purchase
Wood

Woodlands
Farm

3

RH15

Cemy

Sussex Border Path

West
Wood

Lashmar
Wood

HUNDRED ACRE LA

19

Melbourne
Farm

Heath
Farm

2

Park
Farm

Cottage
Wood

Plumpton
Wood

St Helena
Farm

Beresford
Manor

1

Ind
Est

BN6

North America
Farm

Hunt's
Wood

BN7

PLUMPTON
CROSSWAYS

The Plough Inn
(PH)

Shaw
Farm

18

POTTERY
COTTS

34 A B 35 C D 36 E F

73

99

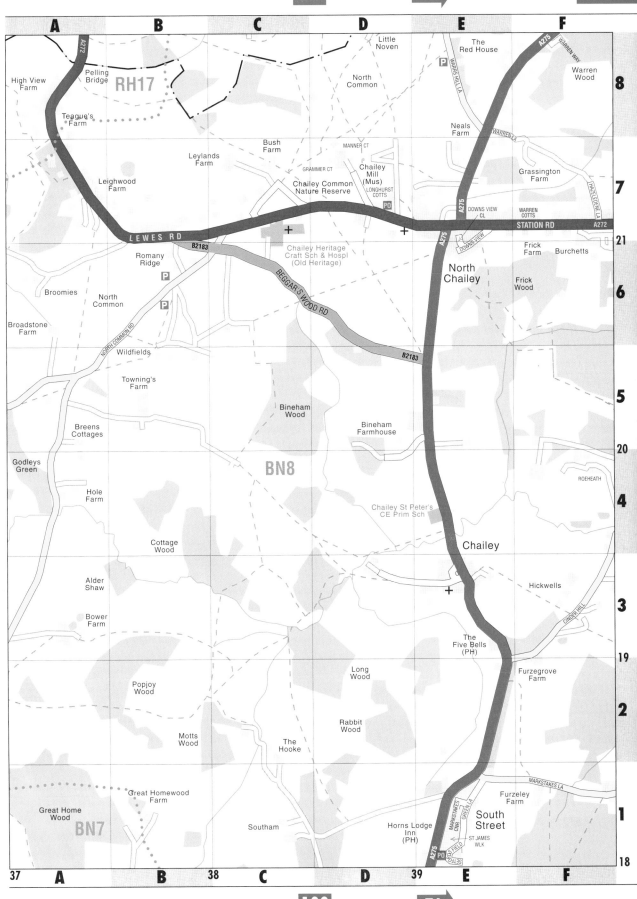

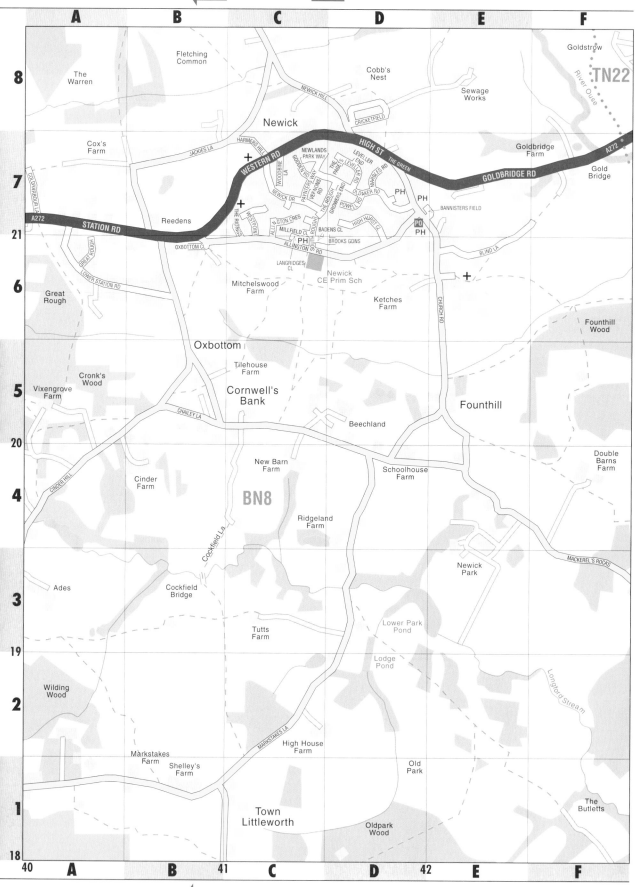

A B C D E F

8 The Warren
Fletching Common
Cobb's Nest
Sewage Works
Goldstrow
TN22

River Ouse

Newick
Newick Hill

Cox's Farm
Jackies La
HARMERS HILL
High St
The Green
Goldbridge Farm
Goldbridge Rd
A272
Gold Bridge

7 Western Rd
Newlands Park Way
Woodbine La
Golden Rd Way
Paynters Way
The Rough
Levellers
Leveller End
Marples Rd
Oldaker Rd
Powell
PH
PH
Bannisters Field

21 A272 Station Rd
Reedens
The Richness
Westpoint
Newick Dr
Allington Cres
Millfield Cl
Allington
South Rough
Groomers End
Badens Cl
Brooks Gdns
High Hurst Cl
Langridges Cl
PO
PH
Blind La

6 Great Rough
Lower Station Rd
Great Rough
Mitchelswood Farm
Newick CE Prim Sch
Ketches Farm
Founthill Wood

5 Vixengrove Farm
Cronk's Wood
Oxbottom
Tilehouse Farm
Cornwell's Bank
Chailey La
Beechland
Founthill
Double Barns Farm

20 Cinder Hill
Cinder Farm
New Barn Farm
Schoolhouse Farm

4 BN8
Ridgeland Farm
Cockfield La
Mackerel's Rocks
Newick Park

3 Ades
Cockfield Bridge
Tutts Farm
Lower Park Pond
Longford Stream

19 Wilding Wood
Lodge Pond

2 Markstakes La
High House Farm
Old Park

1 Markstakes Farm
Shelley's Farm
Town Littleworth
Oldpark Wood
The Butletts

18
40 A B 41 C D 42 E F

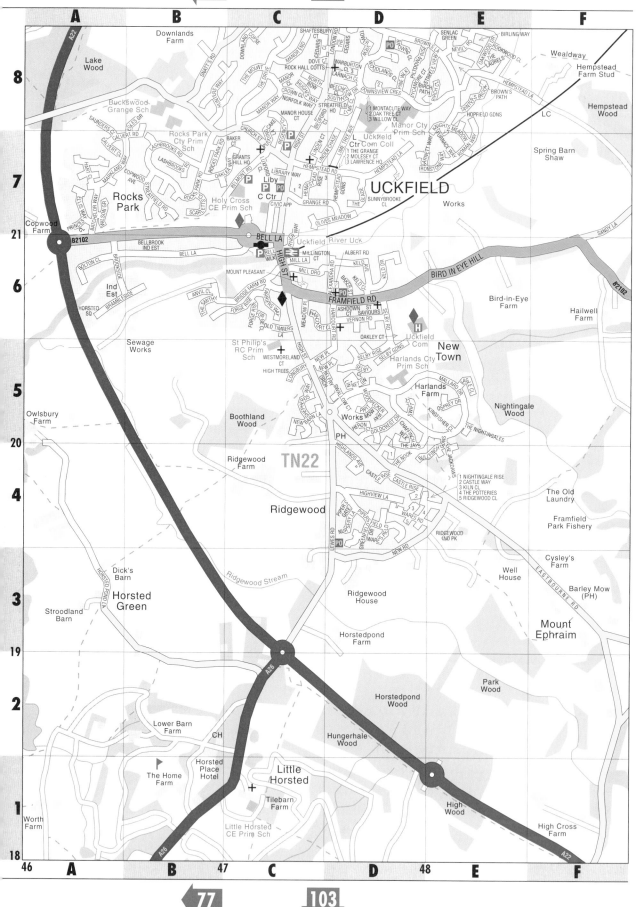

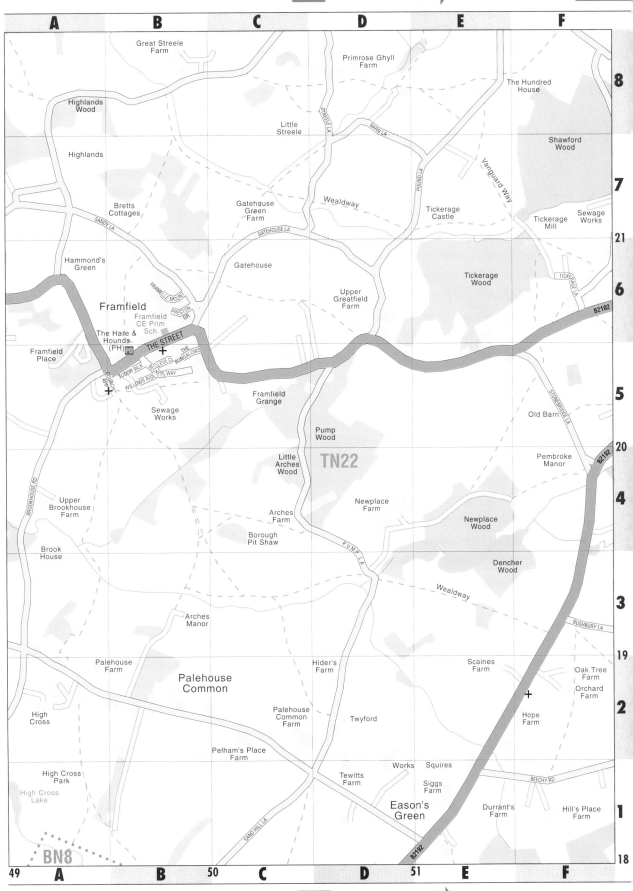

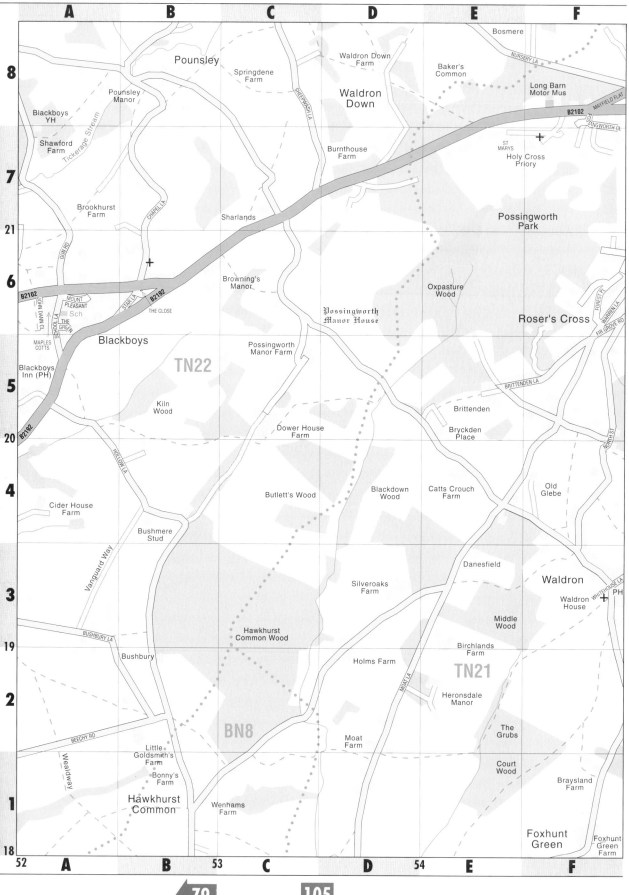

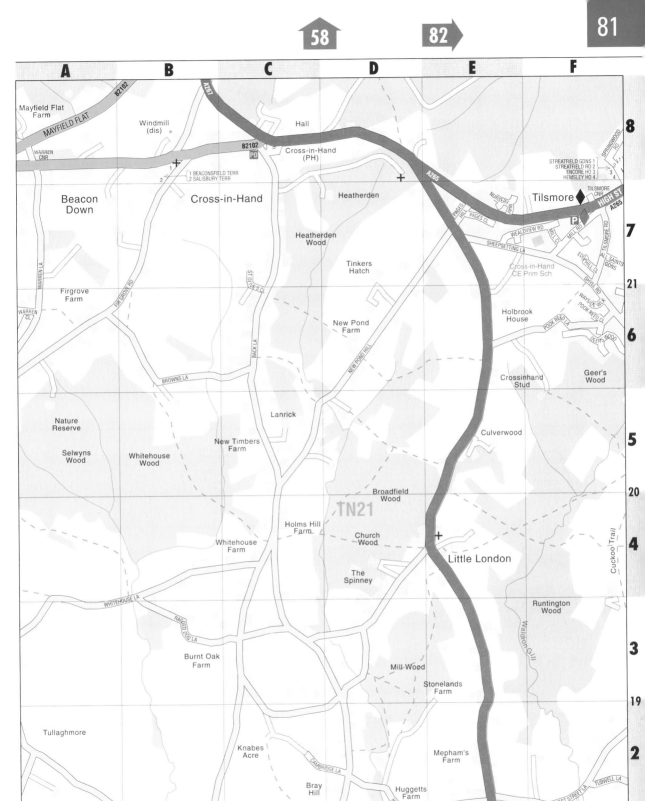

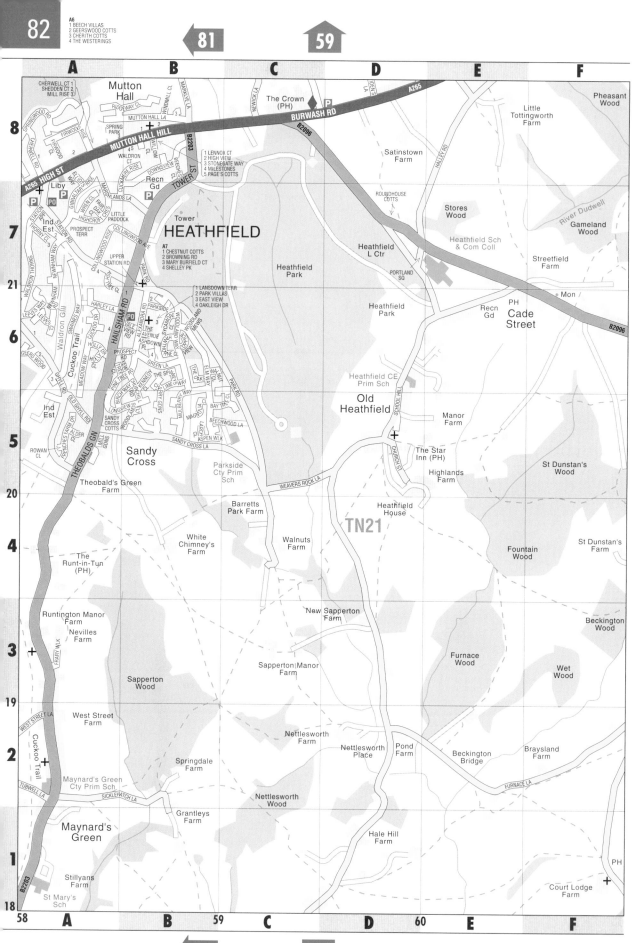

81
59

A   B   C   D   E   F

8
Mutton Hall

CHERWELL CT 1
SHEDDEN CT 2
MILL RISE 3

RIDGEWAY CL
WINDMILL CL
MARKWICK LA
NEWICK LA

The Crown (PH)

BURWASH RD

A265

Pheasant Wood

Little Tottingworth Farm

SPRINGWOOD RD
CHERWELL RD
FIRWOOD RISE

SPRING PARK
MUTTON HALL LA

MUTTON HALL HILL

B2203

B2096

Satinstown Farm

HALLEY RD

River Dudwell

WALDRON CT
DOWNSVIEW
BEECHES
TOWER ST

1 LENNOX CT
2 HIGH VIEW
3 STONEGATE WAY
4 MILESTONES
5 PAGE'S COTTS

ROUNDHOUSE COTTS

Stores Wood

Gameland Wood

A265 HIGH ST

Liby
PO

Recn Gd

Tower
HEATHFIELD

Heathfield L Ctr

Heathfield Sch & Com Coll

Streetfield Farm

7

Ind Est

MARYLANDS LA
HIGHCROFT
PROSPECT TERR
UPPER STATION RD
COLLINGWOOD AVE
PARK RD

A7
1 CHESTNUT COTTS
2 BROWNING RD
3 MARY BURFIELD CT
4 SHELLEY PK

Heathfield Park

PORTLAND SQ

Recn Gd

PH

Cade Street

Mon

B2096

21

COLLINGWOOD RISE
TREE CL

1 LANSDOWN TERR
2 PARK VILLAS
3 EAST VIEW
4 OAKLEIGH DR

6

Waldron Gill
Cuckoo Trail

GEERS WOOD
MEADOW WAY
OLD BRYLE RD
HAILSHAM RD
HARLEY LA
CUCKOO DR
HOLLY DR
THE AVENUE
ASHDOWN PL
PINE TREE PL
GREEN LA
SYCAMORE
THE SPUR
PARKSIDE
WOODLAND MEWS

ELM WAY
WALNUT WAY
WAY
LIME WAY
BAY TRE
MAGNOL

Heathfield Park

Heathfield CE Prim Sch

Old Heathfield

SCHOOL HILL

Manor Farm

5

ROWAN CL

FRENCHES FARM
ALDER
THEOBALDS GN
MILL

SANDY CROSS COTTS

BIRCHWAY
KENNEDY
LONGVIEW
LARCH
ASPEN WLK

SANDY CROSS LA
BEECHWOOD LA

Sandy Cross

Parkside Cty Prim Sch

WEAVERS ROCK LA

CHURCH ST

The Star Inn (PH)

Highlands Farm

St Dunstan's Wood

20

Theobald's Green Farm

Barretts Park Farm

Heathfield House

TN21

St Dunstan's Farm

4

The Runt-in-Tun (PH)

White Chimney's Farm

Walnuts Farm

Fountain Wood

3

FRARY WLK

WEST STREET LA

Runtington Manor Farm

Nevilles Farm

Sapperton Wood

New Sapperton Farm

Sapperton Manor Farm

Furnace Wood

Wet Wood

Beckington Wood

19

West Street Farm

2

Cuckoo Trail

TUBWELL LA

Maynard's Green Cty Prim Sch

SICKLEHATCH LA

Springdale Farm

Grantleys Farm

Nettlesworth Farm

Nettlesworth Place

Pond Farm

Beckington Bridge

FURNACE LA

Braysland Farm

1

Maynard's Green

Stillyans Farm

St Mary's Sch

Nettlesworth Wood

Hale Hill Farm

PH

Court Lodge Farm

B2203

18

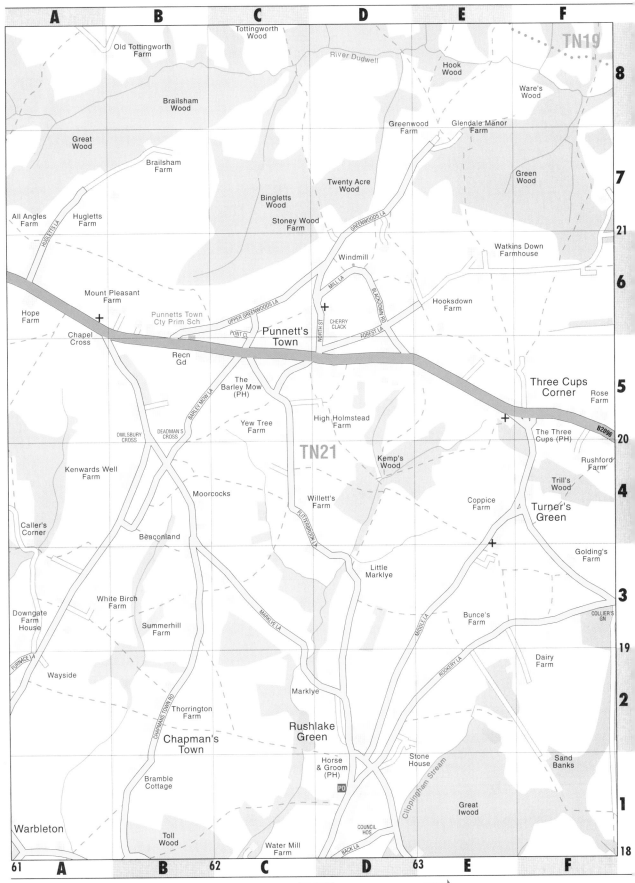

A B C D E F

8

TN19

River Dudwell

Blackbrooks

Coombe Wood

Glazier's Forge Farm

Little Worge Farm

Stonehouse

7

Little Poundsford Farm

TN32

Long Wood

Sugarloaf Wood

Great Worge

21

6

Dallington Forest

Forge Wood

Upper Plantation

Brightling Down

Lower Plantation

5

Highlands Farm

Cox's Mill

Buckholt Farm

20

Rigford Farm

B2096

Oakside

Willingford Stream

TN21

Hook's Farm House

4

Millars Farm

Earl's Down

Brooklands

Upper Brooklands Farm

Carrick's Hill

Brooklands Farm

Graylings

Wyatts Farm

PO

B2096

Rabbetts Farm

The Swan Inn (PH)

3

Alms Wood

Dallington CE Prim Sch

Wood's Corner

Northfleet Farm

Old Castle

Dallington

19

New Castle Farm

Acelands Farm

SOUTH LA

High Wood

Highwood Gill

2

Hoad's Wood

HOADSWOOD CROSS

Uplands Farm

Stream Farm

Oaklands Farm

Clayton Gill

TN33

1

GROVELEY LA

Grovelye Farm

Cripps Farm

Parkfields Farm

HERRING'S RD

Herring's Farm

18

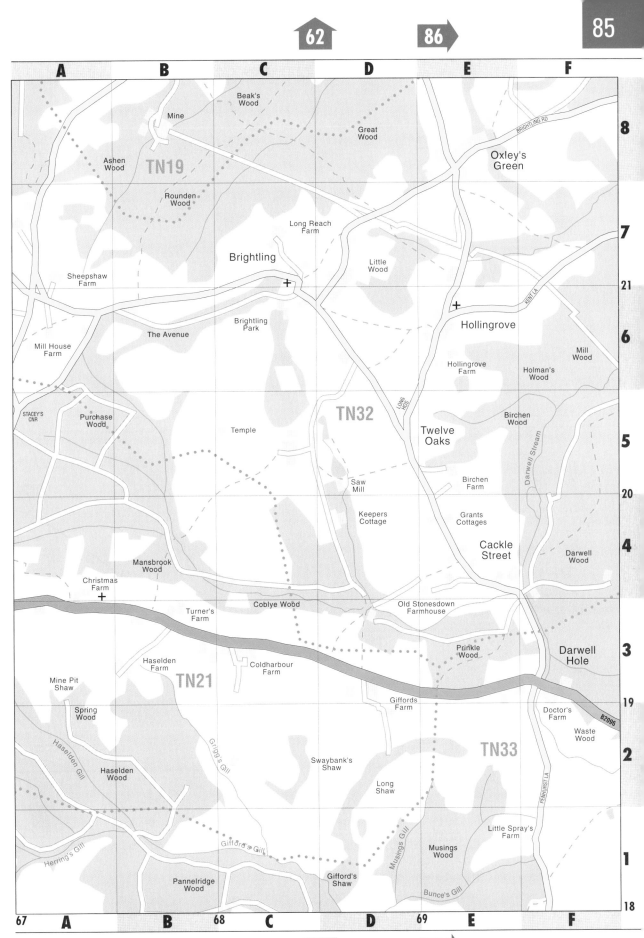

A   B   C   D   E   F

8

Beak's
Wood

Mine

Great
Wood

Brightling Rd

Oxley's
Green

Ashen
Wood

TN19

Rounden
Wood

7

Long Reach
Farm

Brightling

Little
Wood

21

Sheepshaw
Farm

+

KENT LA

6

Mill House
Farm

The Avenue

Brightling
Park

Hollingrove

+

Mill
Wood

Hollingrove
Farm

Holman's
Wood

STACEY'S
CNR

Purchase
Wood

Temple

TN32

LONG HOS

Twelve
Oaks

Birchen
Wood

Darwell Stream

5

Saw
Mill

Birchen
Farm

20

Keepers
Cottage

Grants
Cottages

Cackle
Street

Darwell
Wood

4

Mansbrook
Wood

Christmas
Farm
+

Turner's
Farm

Coblye Wood

Old Stonesdown
Farmhouse

Darwell
Hole

3

Mine Pit
Shaw

Haselden
Farm

TN21

Coldharbour
Farm

Prinkle
Wood

Doctor's
Farm

B2096

19

Spring
Wood

Giffords
Farm

Waste
Wood

Haselden Gill

Haselden
Wood

Griggs Gill

Swaybank's
Shaw

TN33

Little Spray's
Farm

PENHURST LA

2

Long
Shaw

Herring's Gill

Musings Gill

Musings
Wood

1

Pannelridge
Wood

Gifford's Gill

Gifford's
Shaw

Bunce's Gill

18

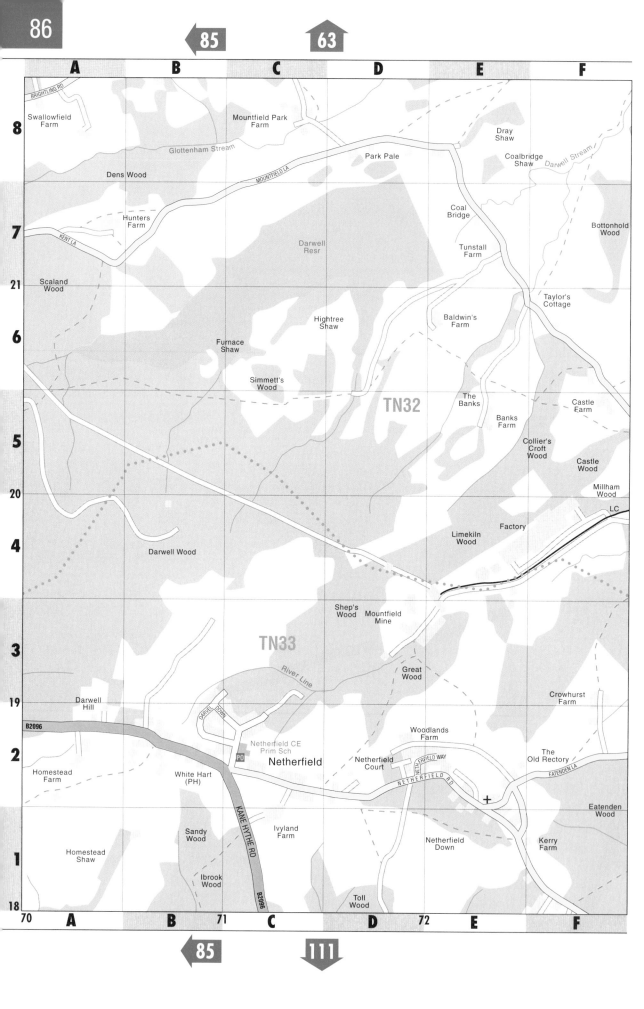

A B C D E F

Clean's Wood

Walter's
Wood

Oakey
Wood

Starven
Wood

8

Lee Bank
Farm

Newpond
Farm

High Hurst
Wood

POPPINGHOLE LA

John's Cross Inn
(PH)

Poppinghole
Farm

Barnes
Farm

7

Bottonhold Brook

A21

Temple
Wood

BARRACKS
COTTS

John's
Cross

JOHN'S CROSS RD

Fern
Wood

Mountfield &
Whatlington CE
Prim Sch

21

Spring
Wood

Mountfield
Court

TN32

A2100

Vinehall
Street

6

New House
Farm

Couchman
Wood

VINEHALL RD

Vinehall
(Prep Sch for Boys)

Vinehall
Farm

B2089

5

Mountfield

CHURCH RD

Hoath
Farm

MOUNTFIELD
VILLAS

NEW CUT

Springlands
Farm

Tunnel

HOATH HILL

Hoath
Wood

MOUNTFIELD
VILLAS

Millham
LC

Lot's
Wood

Riverhall
Bridge

SOLOMON'S LA

River Line

Line
Wood

A21

20

LC

LC

4

Lower Hucksteep
Wood

LONDON RD

Maddomswood
Farm

Crowhurst
Wood

Battle
Wood

Upper Hucksteep
Wood

EATENDEN LA

Footway
Wood

Spring
Wood

Duke's
Wood

Maddoms
Wood

3

19

Brickhouse
Wood

Burnt Oak
Wood

Wood's
Place

2

Goldspur
Wood

Archer
Wood

Woodsdale
Farm

TN33

Cottage
Wood

Mill
Farm

Burnthouse
Wood

Adderley
Lodge

A2100

Eastlands
Farm

WHATLINGTON RD

1

18

73 A B 74 C D 75 E F

A B C D E F

8

Andrew's Gill

B2244

Upper Morgay Wood

B2165

Wattlehill

Badland Wood

Strawberry Hill Farm

Poppinghole La

Badland Shaw

The Beacon

Beacon La

Miles Farm

7

Cripp's Corner

Swaile's Green

Wimbletott's Wood

B2165

B2089

The White Hart (PH)

Catts Green Farm

Ellenkorne La

21

Orchard Farm

Compass's La

B2089

6

Hooks Beech

Barne's Wood

TN32

Greenden Wood

Streetfield Wood

Vinehall Forest

P

Footland Farm

Sedlescombe Vineyard

Mill

Thorp's Wood

5

B2089

Forest Wlk

Footland Wood

Junction Rd

Park La

20

B2090

Dorrells Farm

Beech Farm House

4

A21

Great Sanders Ho

Austford Wood

Coombe Wood

Beech Farm Rd

Hurst Wood

PO

Woodmans Green

Hancox Farm

TN33

Killingan Wood

Hurst La

3

Royal Oak Inn (PH)

Woodmans Oak

Churchland La

Hurst House

19

Whatlington Rd

Riccards La

Stream La

Durhamford Manor

2

Spilsted Farm

Highfield

Riccards Farm

Leeford Cotts

Plovers Mead

Balcombe Gn

Eaton Wlk

The Street

Orchard Way

Gorselands

Conqueror Terr

1

Whatlington

Leeford Farm

River Line

Park Shaw

Streetlands

Brede La

Blacklands

East View Terr

Sedlescombe

A21

Meadowside

P

PH

Roselands

B2244

Sedlescombe CE Prim Sch

Sewage Works

18

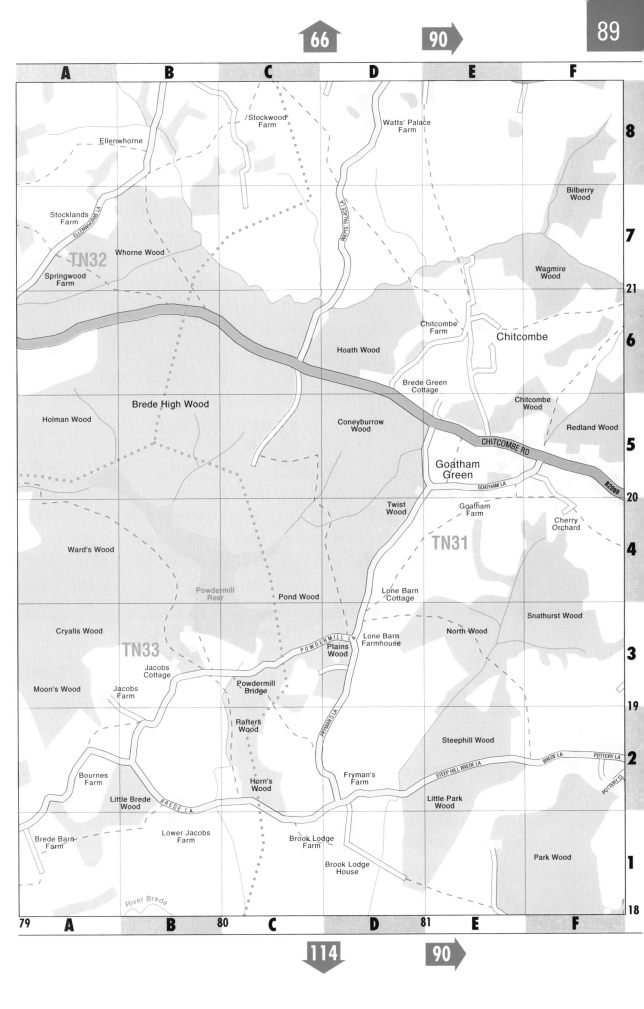

A B C D E F

8

Stockwood
Farm

Watts' Palace
Farm

Ellenwhorne

Bilberry
Wood

7

Stocklands
Farm

ELLENWHORNE LA

Whorne Wood

TN32

WATTS PALACE LA

Wagmire
Wood

Springwood
Farm

21

Chitcombe
Farm

Chitcombe

6

Hoath Wood

Brede Green
Cottage

Brede High Wood

Chitcombe
Wood

Holman Wood

Coneyburrow
Wood

Redland Wood

5

CHITCOMBE RD

Goatham
Green

GOATHAM LA

B2089

20

Twist
Wood

Goatham
Farm

Ward's Wood

TN31

Cherry
Orchard

4

Powdermill
Resr

Pond Wood

Lone Barn
Cottage

Cryalls Wood

North Wood

Snathurst Wood

POWDERMILL LA

Lone Barn
Farmhouse

19

TN33

Jacobs
Cottage

Plains
Wood

3

Moon's Wood

Jacobs
Farm

Powdermill
Bridge

FRYMAN'S LA

Steephill Wood

BREDE LA

POTTERY LA

2

Rafters
Wood

Bournes
Farm

STEEP HILL BREDE LA

POTTERY CL

Little Brede
Wood

BREDE LA

Horn's
Wood

Fryman's
Farm

Little Park
Wood

Brede Barn
Farm

Lower Jacobs
Farm

Brook Lodge
Farm

Park Wood

1

Brook Lodge
House

River Brede

18

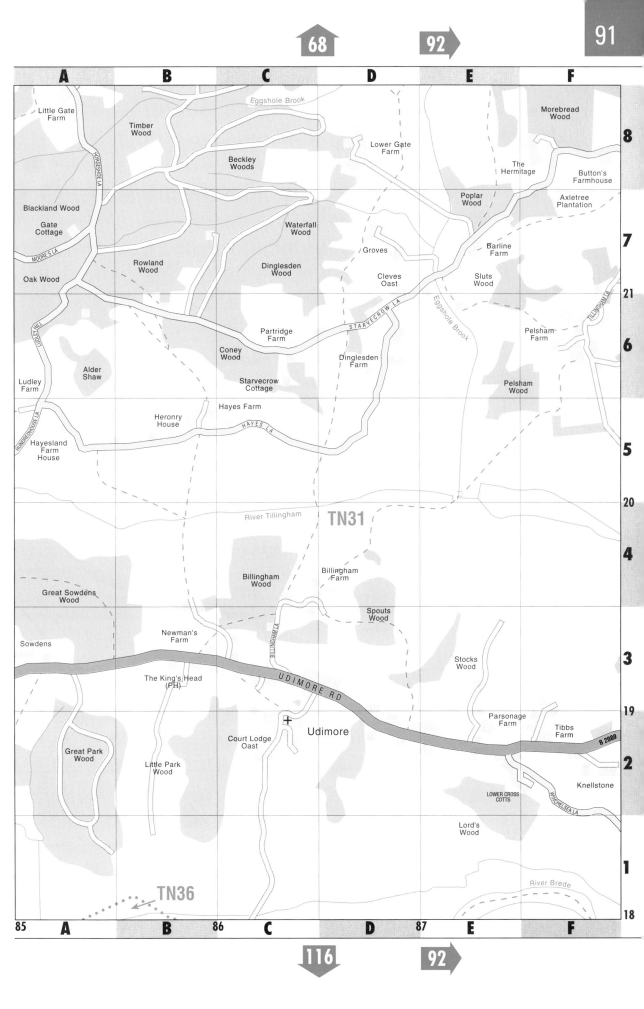

68
92

A   B   C   D   E   F

Eggshole Brook

Little Gate
Farm

Timber
Wood

Morebread
Wood

Beckley
Woods

Lower Gate
Farm

The
Hermitage

Button's
Farmhouse

Blackland Wood

Poplar
Wood

Axletree
Plantation

Gate
Cottage

Waterfall
Wood

Groves

Barline
Farm

MOORE'S LA

Rowland
Wood

Dinglesden
Wood

Cleves
Oast

Sluts
Wood

Oak Wood

21

TILLINGHAM LA

Starvecrow La

Eggshole Brook

Pelsham
Farm

7

LUDLEY HILL

Partridge
Farm

Coney
Wood

Dinglesden
Farm

6

Ludley
Farm

Alder
Shaw

Starvecrow
Cottage

Pelsham
Wood

HUNDREDHOUSE LA

Hayes Farm

Heronry
House

HAYES LA

Hayesland
Farm
House

5

River Tillingham

TN31

20

Great Sowdens
Wood

Billingham
Wood

Billingham
Farm

4

Spouts
Wood

Newman's
Farm

BILLINGHAM LA

Sowdens

Stocks
Wood

3

The King's Head
(PH)

UDIMORE RD

Parsonage
Farm

Tibbs
Farm

19

B 2089

Court Lodge
Oast

Udimore

Great Park
Wood

Little Park
Wood

Knellstone

2

LOWER CROSS
COTTS

WINCHELSEA LA

Lord's
Wood

1

TN36

River Brede

18

85   A   B   86   C   D   87   E   F

116
92

91
69

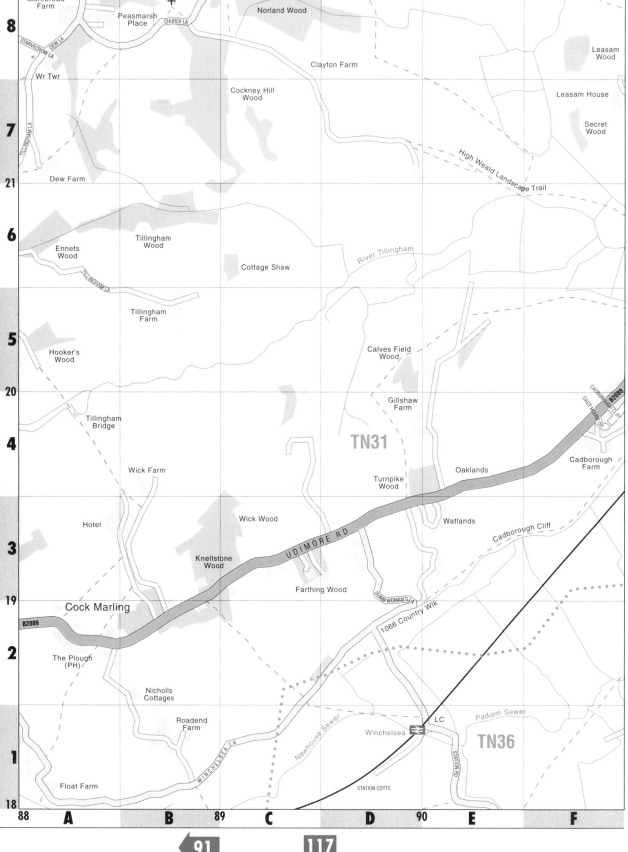

91
117

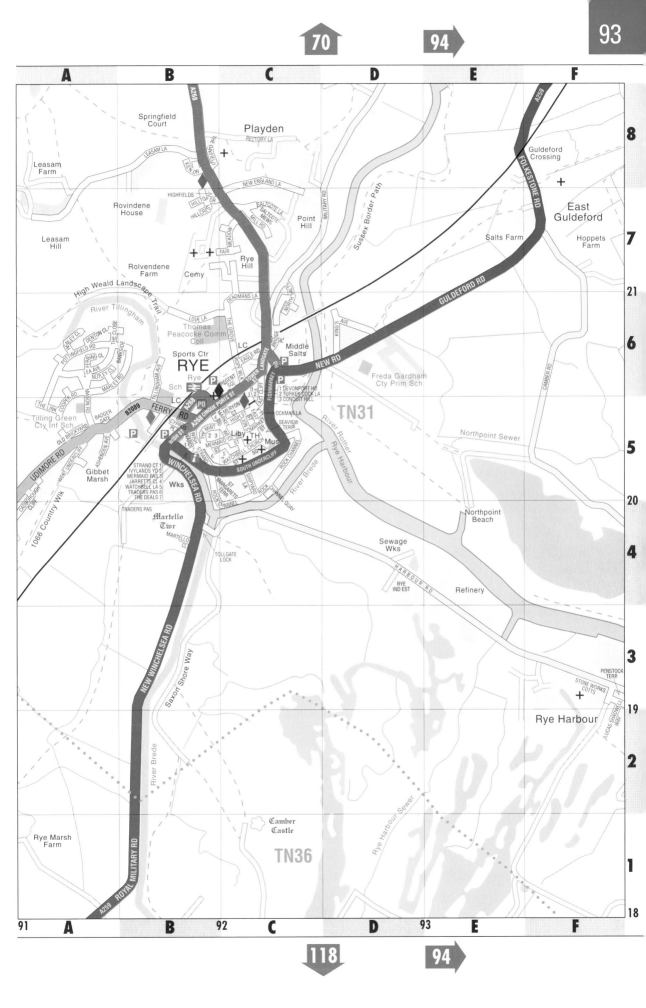

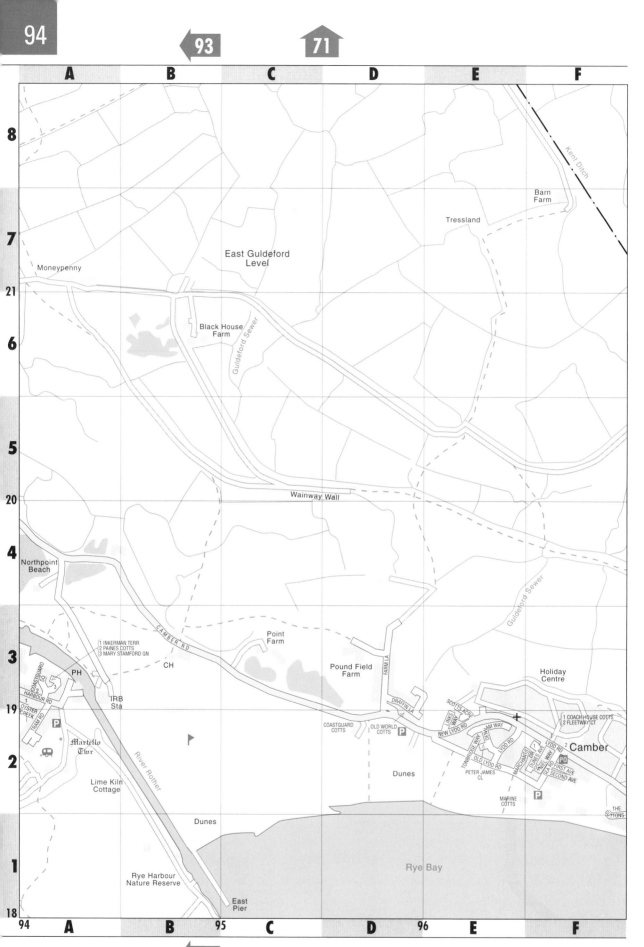

93
71

A　B　C　D　E　F

8

93

71

Barn
Farm

Kent Ditch

Tressland

7

East Guldeford
Level

Moneypenny

21

Black House
Farm

Guldeford Sewer

6

5

20

Wainway Wall

Guldeford Sewer

4

Northpoint
Beach

CAMBER RD

Point
Farm

3

1 INKERMAN TERR
2 PAINES COTTS
3 MARY STAMFORD GN

CH

Pound Field
Farm

FARM LA

Holiday
Centre

PH

19

COASTGUARD
SQ

HARBOUR RD

IRB
Sta

DRAFFIN LA

SCOTTS ACRE

LINKS
WAY

1 COACH HOUSE COTTS
2 FLEETWAY CT

OYSTER
CREEK

TRAM RD

P

COASTGUARD
COTTS

OLD WORLD
COTTS

P

NEW LYDD RD

LYDD RD

DRAM WAY

Camber

PO

Martello
Twr

River Rother

Lime Kiln
Cottage

2

TONBRIDGE WAY

OLD LYDD RD

PETER JAMES
CL

MARCIANS CL

LYDD RD

DUNES AVE

DANIEL WAY

SEA RD

CAMBER WAY

LYDD RD

FIRST AVE

SECOND AVE

Dunes

MARINE
COTTS

P

THE
SUTTONS

Dunes

Rye Harbour
Nature Reserve

Rye Bay

1

East
Pier

18

93

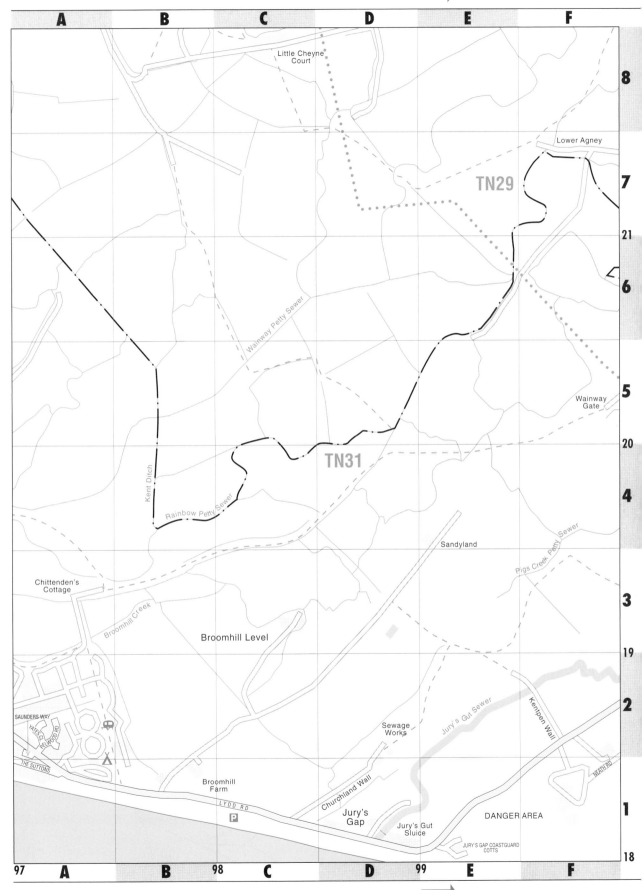

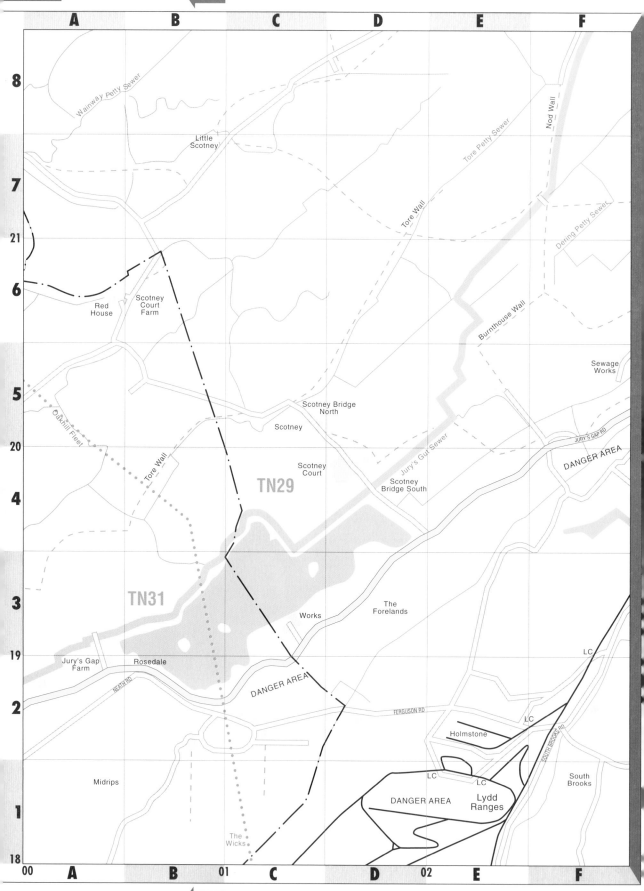

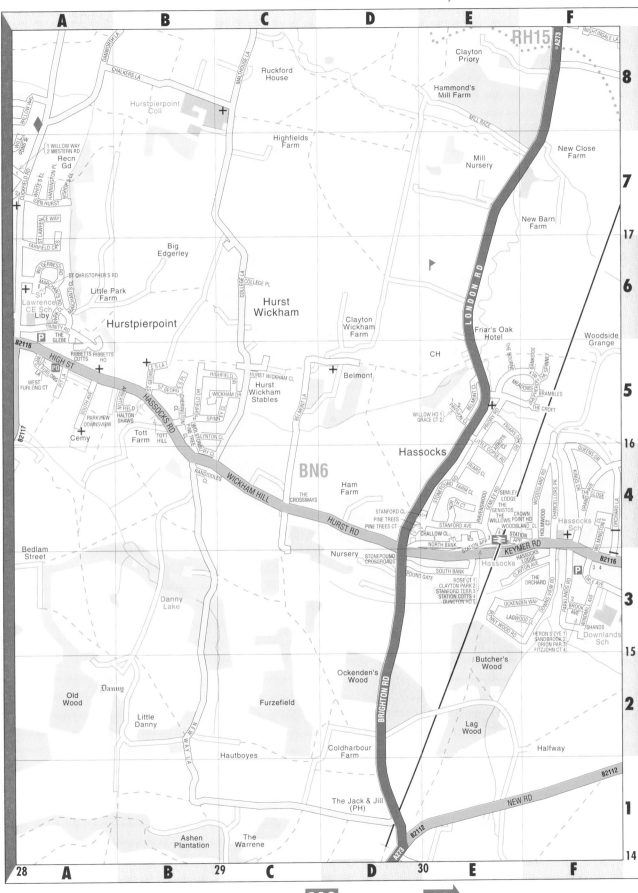

RH15

A273

Nightingale La

Clayton Priory

Hammond's Mill Farm

Mill Race

New Close Farm

8

Ruckford House

Mill Nursery

7

Chalkers La

Danworth La

Malthouse La

Highfields Farm

London Rd

New Barn Farm

17

Hurstpierpoint Coll

1 Willow Way
2 Western Rd

Recn Gd

Willow Way

Cuckfield Rd

White's Pl

Hannington Pl

Bishop's Sq

Iden Hurst

College La

College Pl

Friar's Oak Hotel

Woodside Grange

6

St Lawrence Way

Fairfield Ct

Big Edgerley

Hurst Wickham

CH

The Bourne

Bankside

Prophet's Spinney

Brambles

The Croft

Meadows

5

Wilderness Rd

Merchants Cl

Little Park Farm

St Christopher's Rd

Clayton Wickham Farm

Belmont

St Georg

St Georg's La

Highfield Dr

Wickham Dr

Hurst Wickham Cl

Hurst Wickham Stables

Belmont La

WILLOW HO 1
GRACE CT 2

PAVILION CL

Belmont Cl

Friars Oak Rd

Priory Rd

Little Copse Rd

16

St Lawrence CE Sch

Liby

Hurstpierpoint

Trinity Rd

THE GLEBE

P

RIBBETTS COTTS

RIBBETTS HO

Cherington Cl

Highfield Cl

Spinney

Lynton Cl

Hassocks

Friars Cl

Abbots

Ravenswood

Sealey Rd

Semley Rd

The Spinney

4

B2116

HIGH ST

PO

WEST FURLONG CT

FURLONG LA

PIT LA

SOUTH AVE

Parkview

Downsview

HASSOCKS RD

ABERDEEN RD

FIELD

HALTON SHAWS

Tott Farm

TOTT HILL

PINE TREE

RANDIDDLES CL

WICKHAM HILL

BN6

THE CROSSWAYS

Ham Farm

STONEPOUND FARM CL

NURZ

THE CT

CL

SEMLEY LODGE

THE GENISTOS

CROWN POINT HO

THE WILLOWS

WOODSLAND CL

Woodsland Rd

Chancellors Pk

Holmwood Rd

Queens Dr

Kings Dr

GRAND AVE

Orchard La

THE CLOSE

Wilmington Cl

Hassocks Sch

B2117

Cemy

HURST RD

STANFORD CL
PINE TREES
PINE TREES CT

STANFORD AVE

CHALLOW CL

NORTH BANK

STATION APP

STATION APP

Keymer Rd

B2116

3 4

B2116

Bedlam Street

Nursery

STONEPOUND CROSSROADS

POUND GATE

SOUTH BANK

ROSE CT 1
CLAYTON PARK 2
STANFORD TERR 3
STATION COTTS 4
DUNCTON HO 5

Hassocks

HASSOCKS LODGE

CLAYTON AVE

THE ORCHARD

P

DALE AVE

Downs View Rd

Parklands Rd

Windmill Ave

BROOK AVE

3

Danny Lake

OCKENDEN WAY

LAGWOOD

NW WOOD RD

HERON'S TYE 1
SANDBROOK 2
ORION PAR 3
FITZJOHN CT 4.

SHANDS

Downlands Sch

15

Ockenden's Wood

Butcher's Wood

Old Wood

Danny

Furzefield

Brighton Rd

Lag Wood

Halfway

2

Little Danny

NEW WAY LA

Coldharbour Farm

B2112

NEW RD

B2112

1

Hautboyes

The Jack & Jill (PH)

Ashen Plantation

The Warrene

A273

A273

14

28

29

30

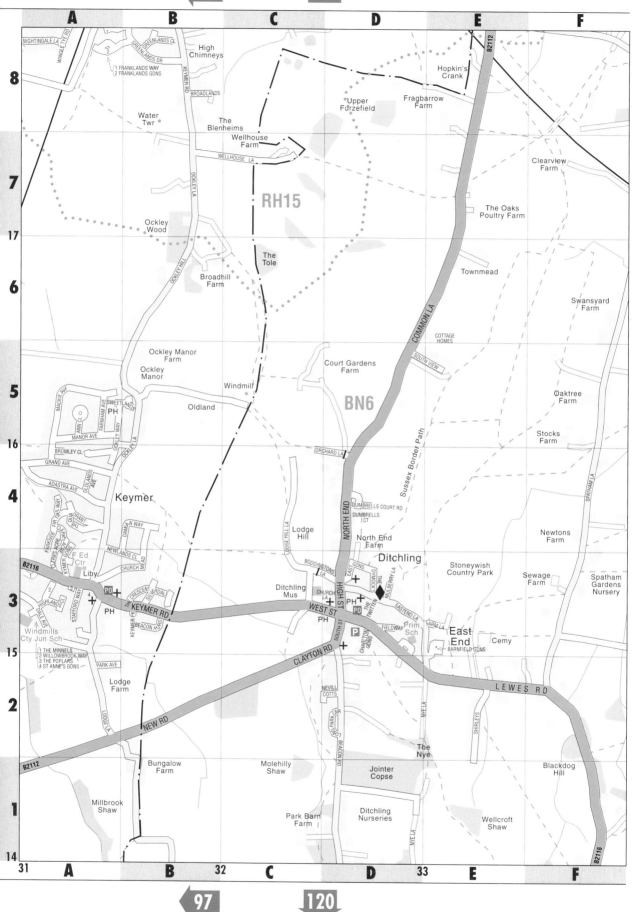

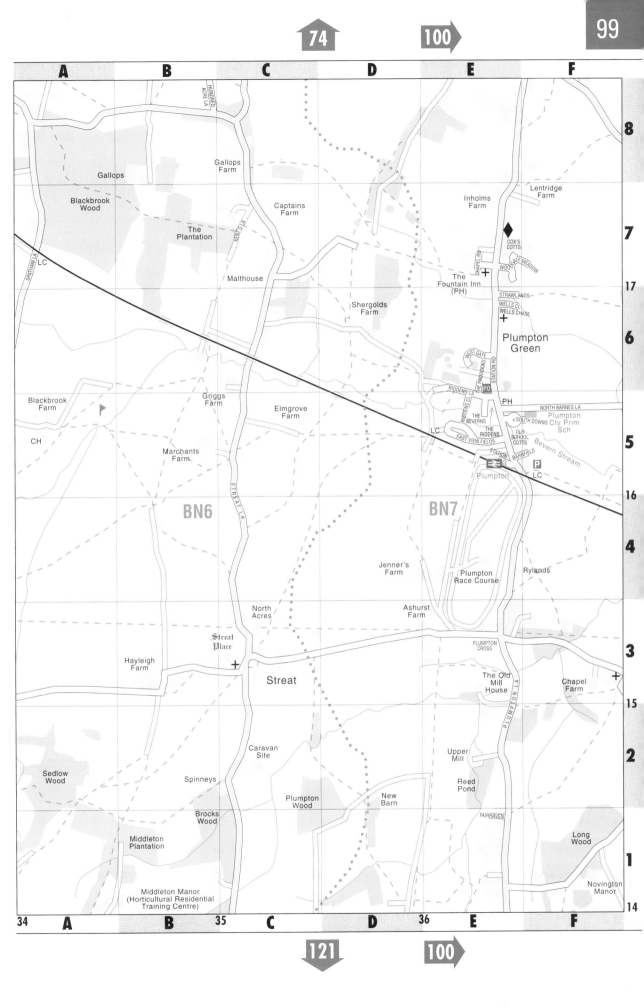

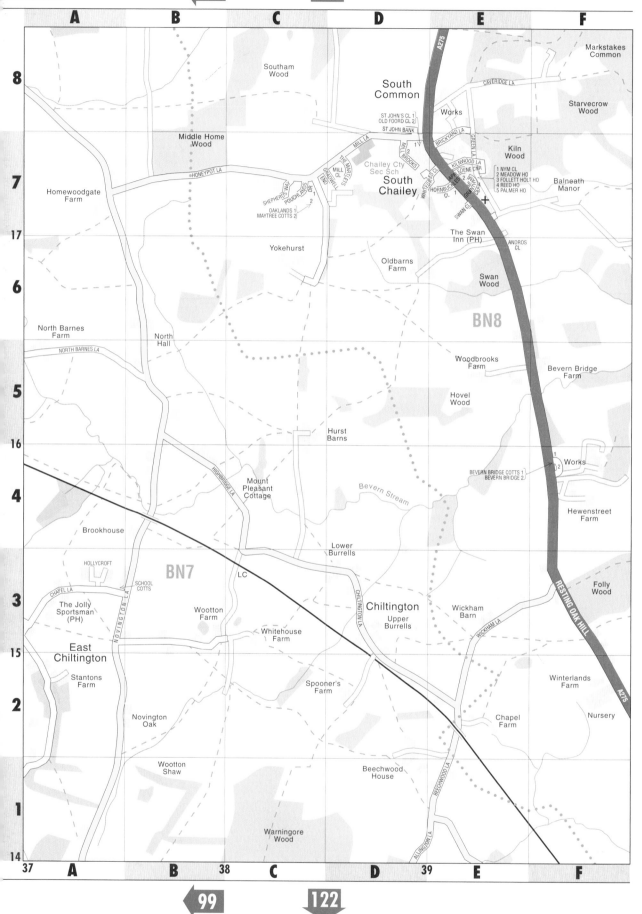

A B C D E F

8

Grantham's Rough

Balneath La

Oldpark Wood

Spithurst

Spithurst House

Church Farm

Balneath Wood

Nursery

7

Down View Farm

Slutsgarden Wood

Oaktree Farm

Mount Pleasant

Harelands Farm

Balneath Barn

Burtenshaw Farm

17

Holman's Bridge

Knowlands Wood

BYE-LAW COTTS

SPITHURST RD

6

Holman's Bridge Farm

Sewage Works

Knowlands Farm

MOUNT PLEASANT

Scobell's Farm

DALLAS LA

CLAY CORNER

Bevern Stream

BOAST LA

BN8

Laine Pit

DEANS MEADOW

5

Beachy Wood

Birdshole La

Sewell's Farm

Sewage Works

THE WILLOWS

Clapper's Bridge

16

Barcombe CE Prim Sch

SCHOOL FIELD

DENNIS MEAD

Red Bridge

Bird's Hole

Hillside Nursery

SCHOOL PATH

SCHOOL HILL

GRANTHAM PARK

Barcombe Place

P

4

Gallybird Hall

PH

P

Barcombe Cross

Handlye Farm

BRIDGELANDS

THE GRANGE

HIGH ST

GRANGE RD

MUNSTER GN

OAKTREE

MONGER'S MEAD

BARCOMBE MILLS RD

Half Yard Farm

Blunt's Wood

POUND CNR

Mongers Farm

1 GLADSTONE BLDGS
2 WEALD CL
3 MUNSTER COTTS

Camoys Court Farm

DEADMANTREE HILL

Camoys Court

CRINK HILL

3

Curds Farm

Shelley's Folly

15

Nursery

MILL LA

The Anglers Rest (PH)

BARCOMBE MILLS RD

Over's Farm

Packham's Brow

CHAPPELL RD

Sewage Works

River Ouse

2

Conyboro

Croft Ham

Barcombe

Culver Farm

RESTING OAK HILL

The Rainbow (PH)

Court House

1

Cooksbridge Farm

The Wilderness

Avery's

The Wilderness

A275

14

40 A B 41 C D 42 E F

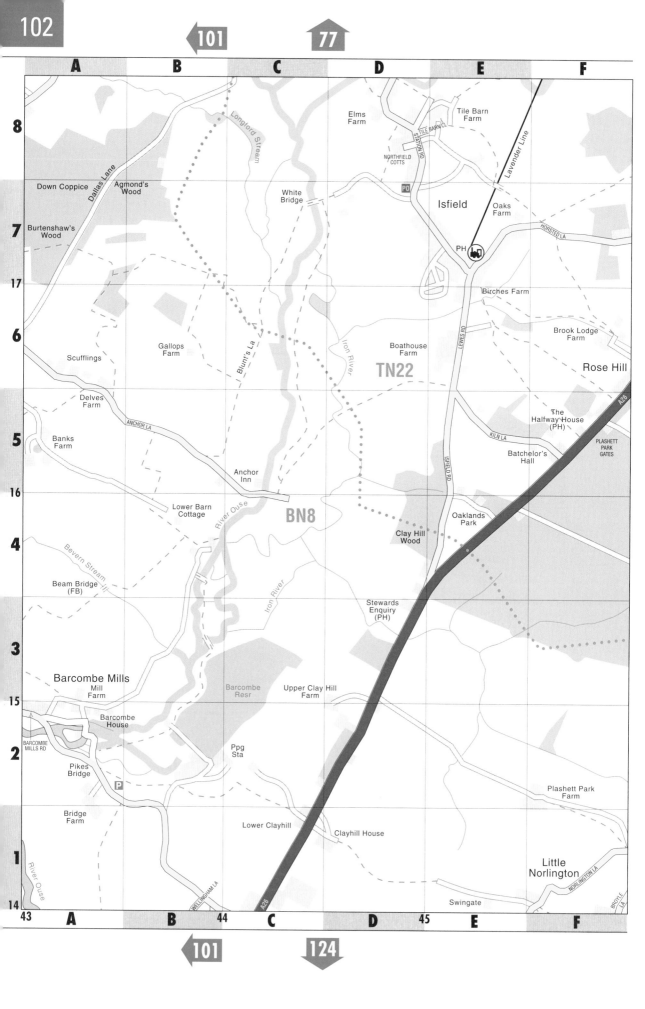

101
77

A   B   C   D   E   F

8

Down Coppice
Dallas Lane
Agmond's Wood
Longford Stream
White Bridge
Elms Farm
Tile Barn Farm
Tile Barn Cl
Station Rd
Northfield Cotts
PO
Isfield
Oaks Farm
Lavender Line

7

Burtenshaw's Wood
Horsted La
PH
Birches Farm

17

6

Scufflings
Gallops Farm
Blunt's La
Iron River
Boathouse Farm
TN22
Lewes Rd
Brook Lodge Farm
Rose Hill

5

Delves Farm
ANCHOR LA
Banks Farm
Anchor Inn
The Halfway House (PH)
KILN LA
Batchelor's Hall
Isfield Rd
A26
Plashett Park Gates

16

Lower Barn Cottage
River Ouse
BN8
Clay Hill Wood
Oaklands Park

4

Bevern Stream
Beam Bridge (FB)
Iron River
Stewards Enquiry (PH)

3

Barcombe Mills
Mill Farm
Barcombe Resr
Upper Clay Hill Farm

15

Barcombe House
Barcombe Mills Rd
Ppg Sta

2

Pikes Bridge
P
Plashett Park Farm

Bridge Farm
Lower Clayhill
Clayhill House
Little Norlington
Norlington La
Broyle La

1

River Ouse
Wellingham La
A26
Swingate

14

43   A   B   44   C   D   45   E   F

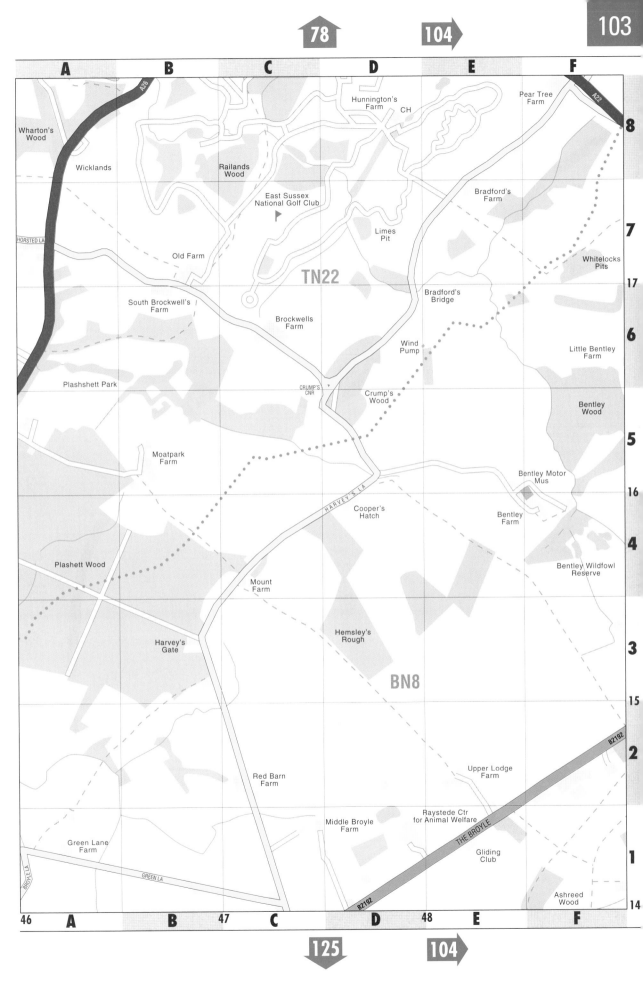

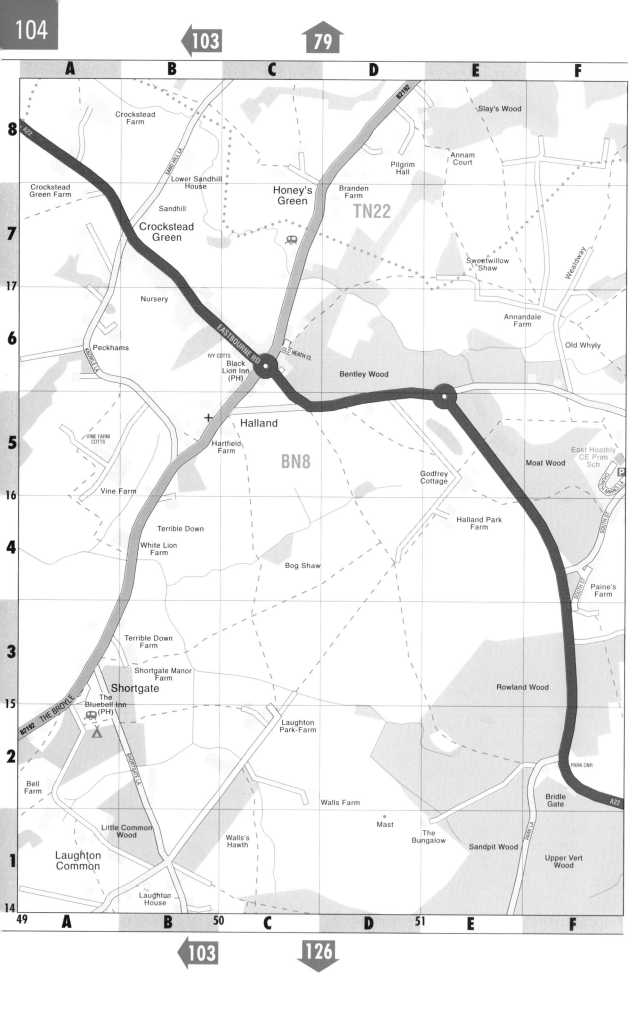

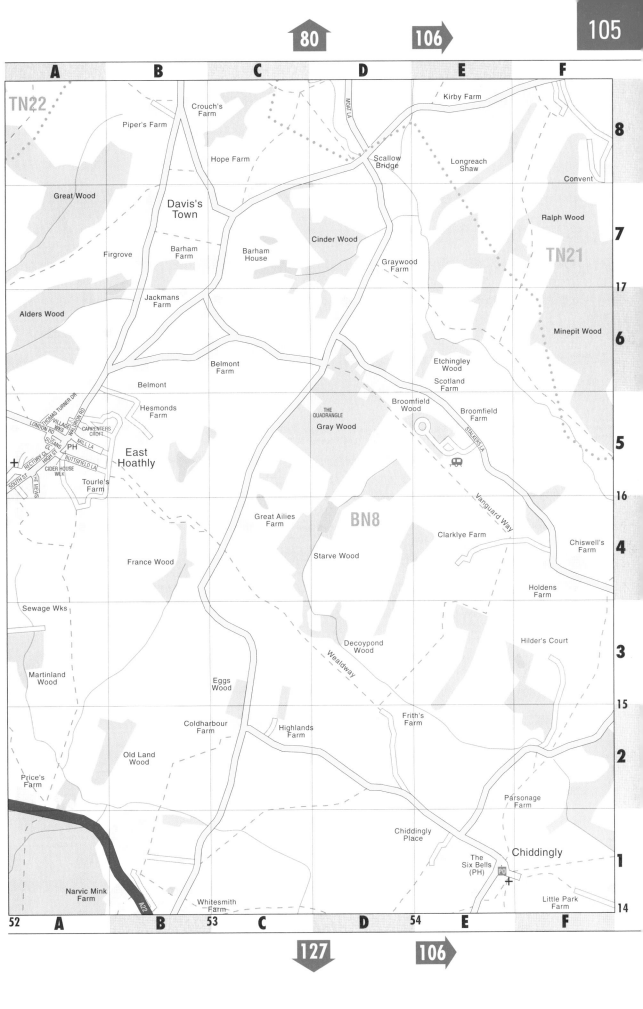

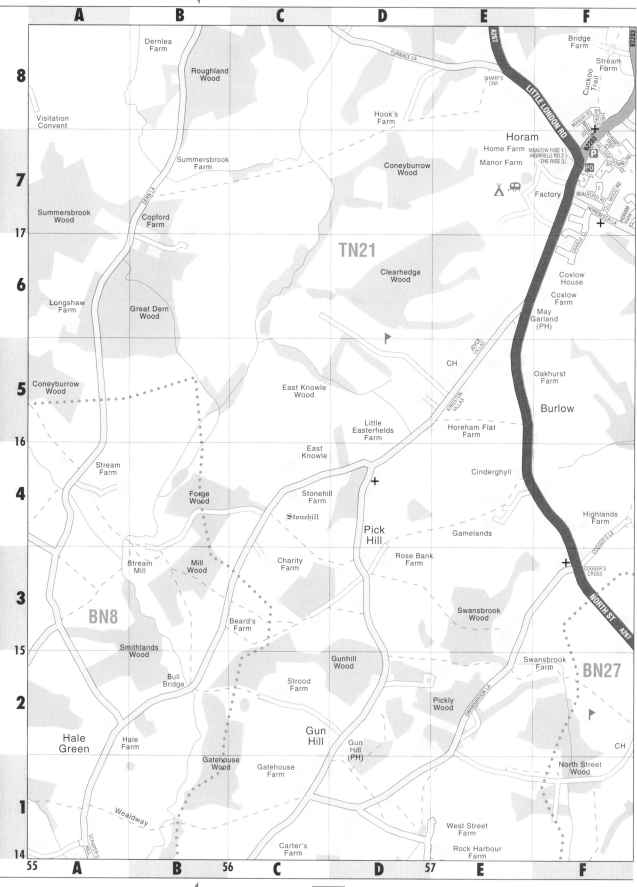

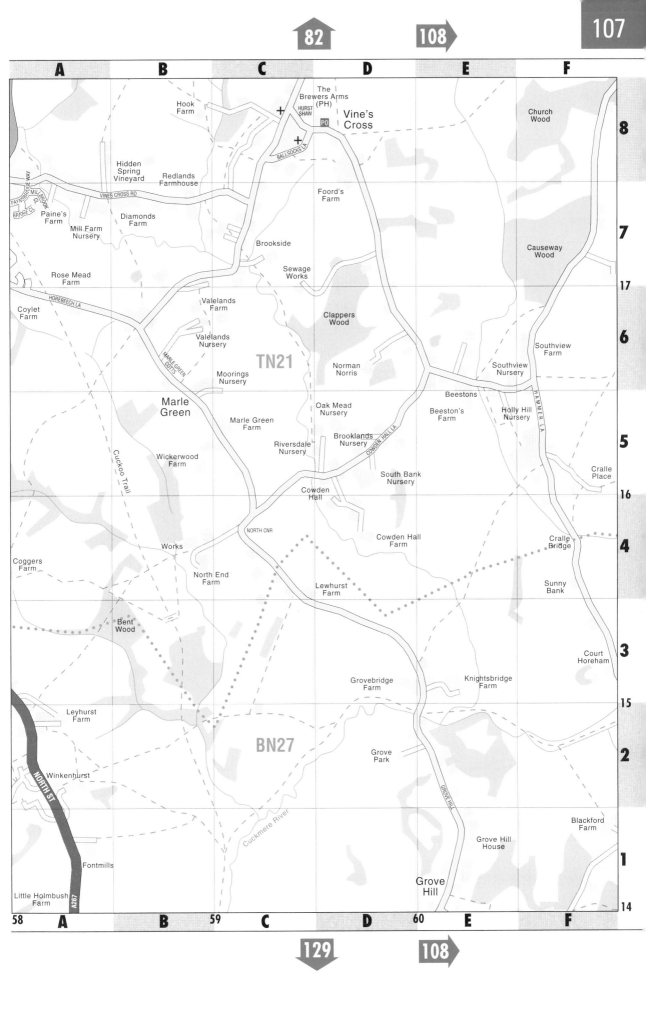

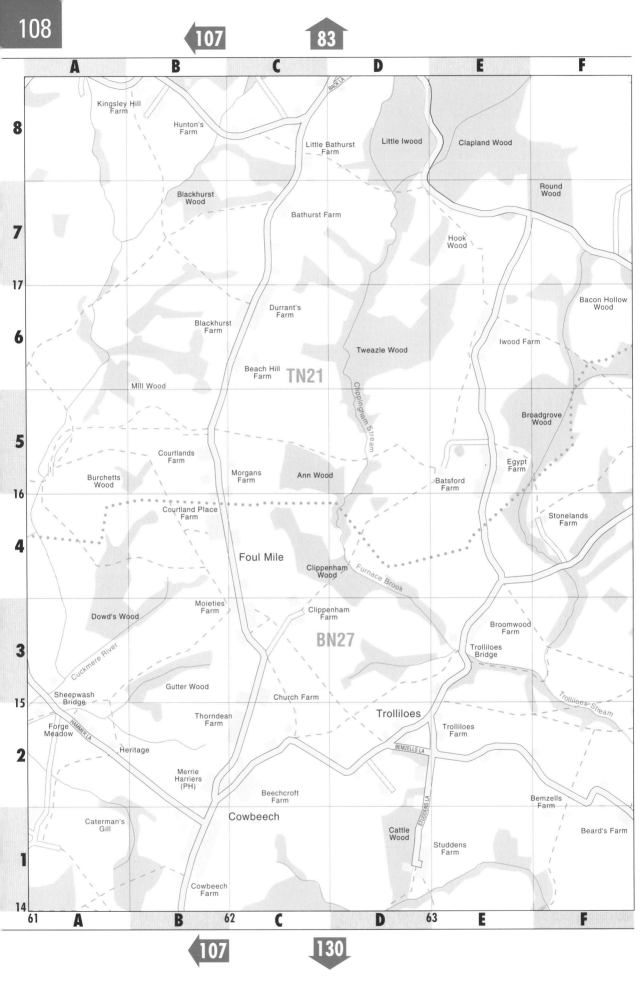

107
83

A   B   C   D   E   F

8

Kingsley Hill
Farm

Hunton's
Farm

Little Bathurst
Farm

Little Iwood

Clapland Wood

Round
Wood

Blackhurst
Wood

Bathurst Farm

7

Hook
Wood

Bacon Hollow
Wood

17

Durrant's
Farm

6

Blackhurst
Farm

Tweazle Wood

Iwood Farm

Beach Hill
Farm

TN21

Mill Wood

Broadgrove
Wood

5

Courtlands
Farm

Morgans
Farm

Ann Wood

Batsford
Farm

Egypt
Farm

Burchetts
Wood

16

Courtland Place
Farm

Stonelands
Farm

4

Foul Mile

Clippenham
Wood

Furnace Brook

Moieties
Farm

Clippenham
Farm

Broomwood
Farm

Dowd's Wood

BN27

Trolliloes
Bridge

3

Cuckmere River

Gutter Wood

Church Farm

15

Sheepwash
Bridge

Trolliloes
Stream

Thorndean
Farm

Trolliloes

Trolliloes
Farm

Forge
Meadow

Heritage

BEMZELLS LA

2

Merrie
Harriers
(PH)

Bemzells
Farm

Beechcroft
Farm

Caterman's
Gill

Cowbeech

Cattle
Wood

Beard's Farm

STUDDENS LA

Studdens
Farm

1

Cowbeech
Farm

14

61   A   B   62   C   D   63   E   F

107
130

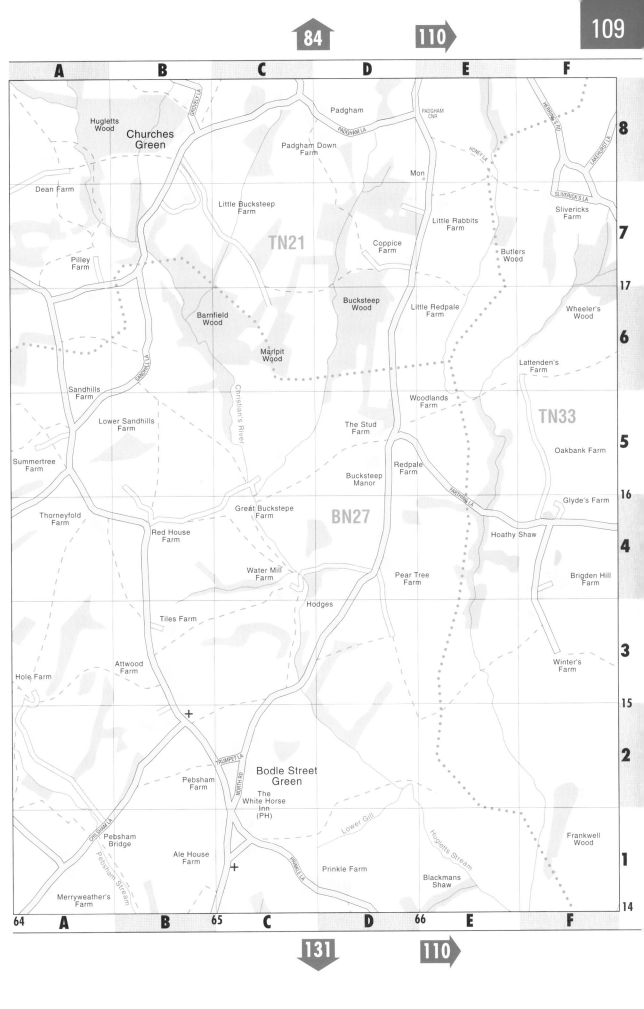

109
85

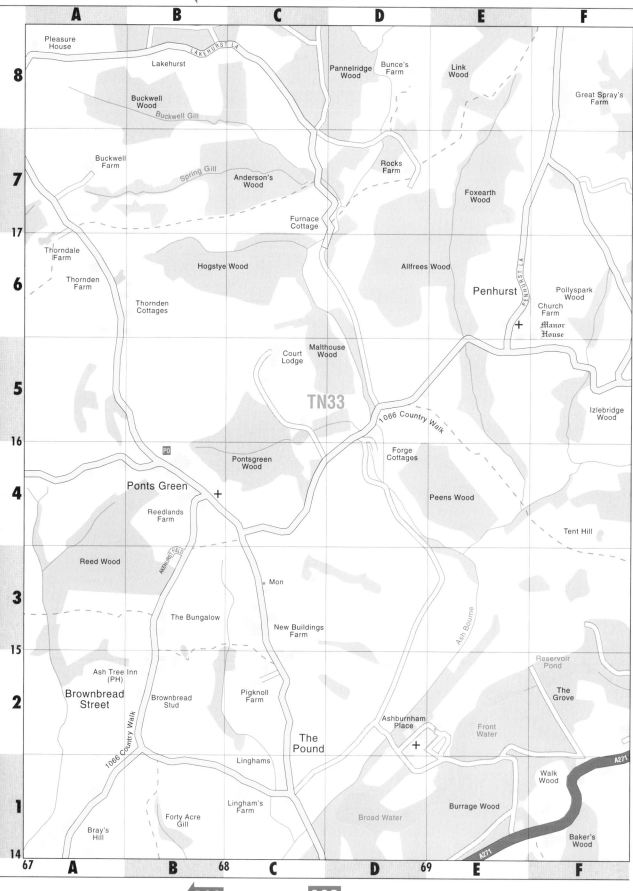

109
132

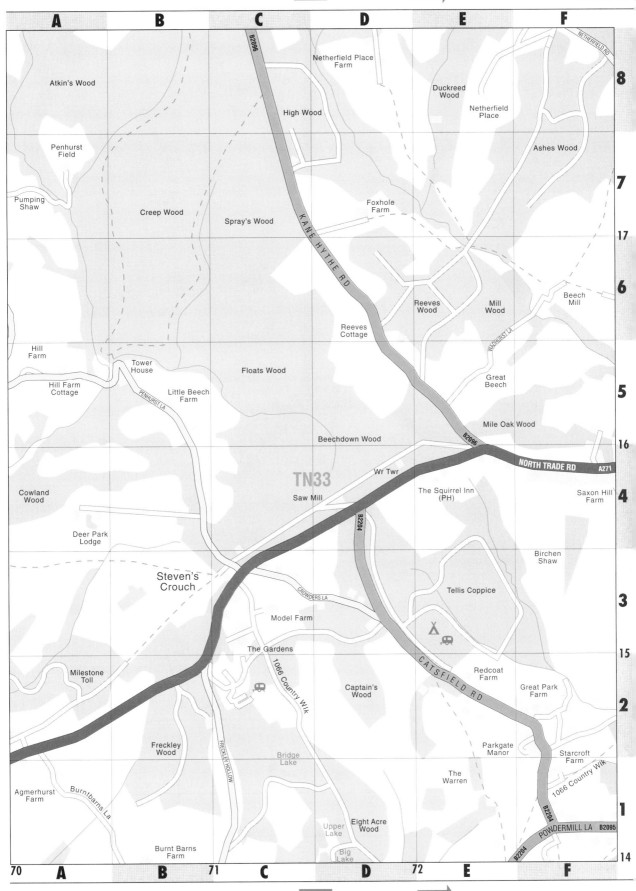

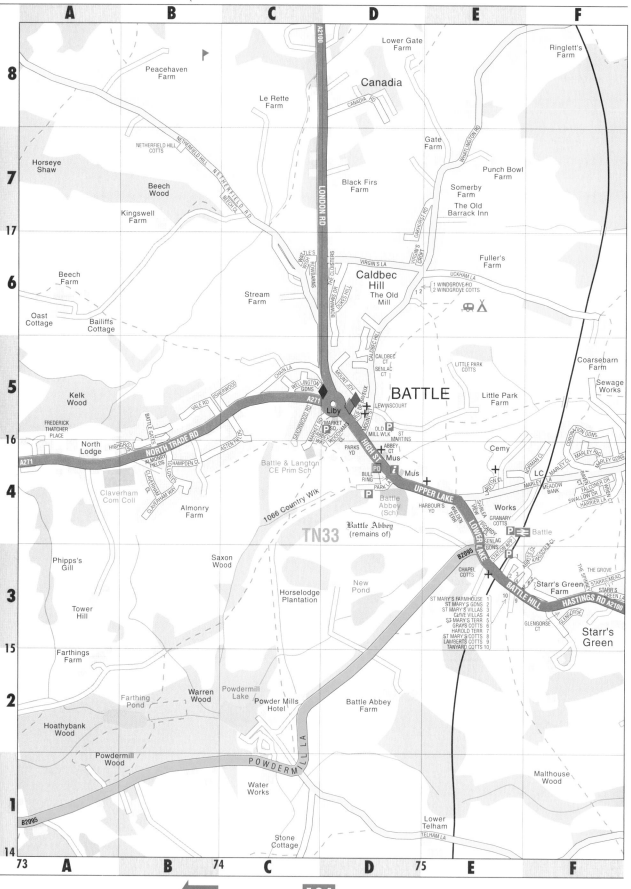

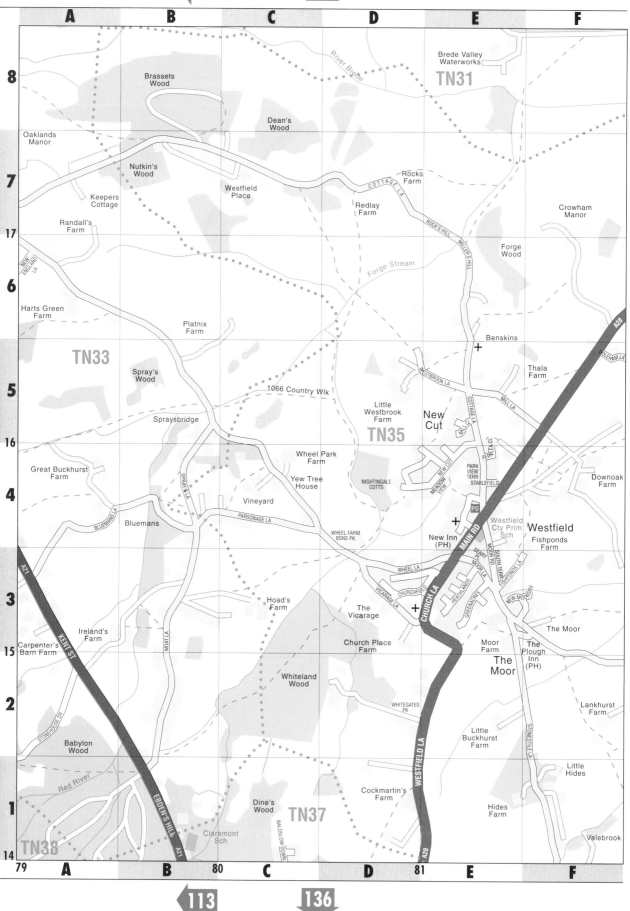

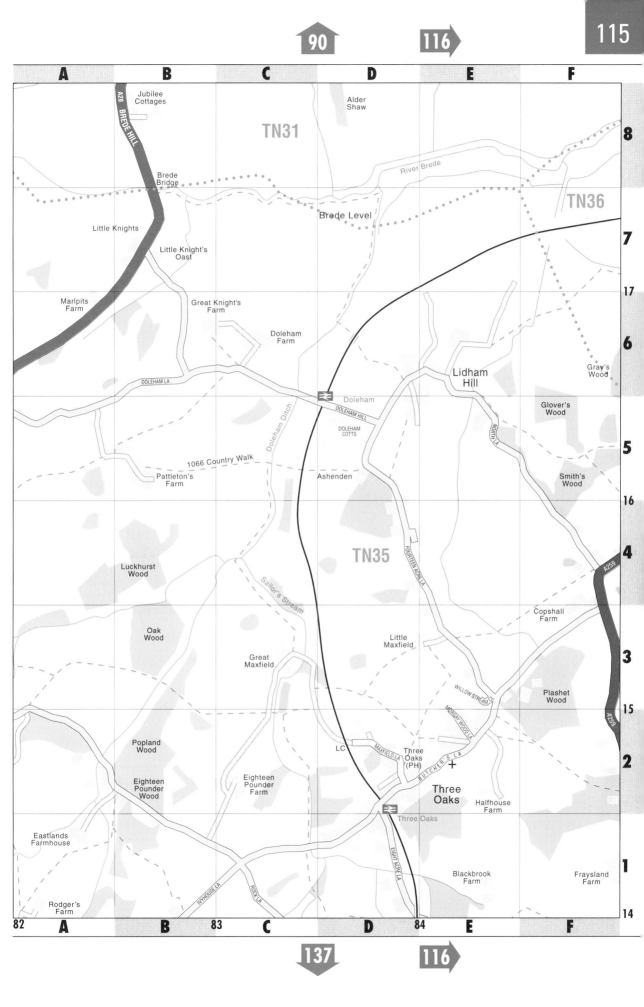

115 91

A B C D E F

8

River Brede

Brede Level

TN31

LC

7

Lower
Snailham

Snailham
Wood

17

Snaylham
Farm

Brook
Farm

1066 Country Wlk

6

Pond
Wood

Broad
Street

TN36

Icklesham

The
Queen's Head Inn
(PH)

FIVE VILLAGES
HO

Icklesham
CE Prim
Sch

PARSONAGE LA

OAST HOUSE FIELD

Toke
Farm

HIGH FORDS CL

PLAYING FIELD

LITTLE FIELD

BURNT OAK

MANOR CL

OAST
HOUSE
RD

A259

WORKHOUSE LA

5

Three
Corner
Wood

Broad
Street
Wood

MAIN RD

LITTLE SHERWOOD
IND PK

Robin Hood
(PH)

BREDE VALLEY
VIEW

COLDHURST GDN

HIGH FORDS
FIELD

1 2

PO

1 SEAVIEW COTTS
2 SEAVIEW TERR

WELLPLACE
COTTS

LAUREL LA

Stocks
Farm

16

THORN
COTTS

Croft
Wood

Bench
Wood

Roughters

Place
Farm

Knockbridge

Knockbridge
Farm

4

A259

Guestling
Thorn

Scrag
Oak

Little Pannel
Farm

3

Kitchen
Wood

WATERMILL LA

Pannel Sewer

TN35

15

Broomham
Sch

Pickham
Mill

Pannel
Wood

Factory
Wood

2

A259

Pickham
Farm

Burnt
Wood

PANNEL LA

Church
Farm

CHURCH LA

P

Guestling
Wood

Pett
Wood

THE
GLEBE

1

WINCHELSEA RD

A259

Pound
Farm

Nature
Reserve

Fairlight
Wood

French Court
Farm

PETT RD

ELMS LA

THE OAK FIELD

14

85 A 86 B C 87 D E F

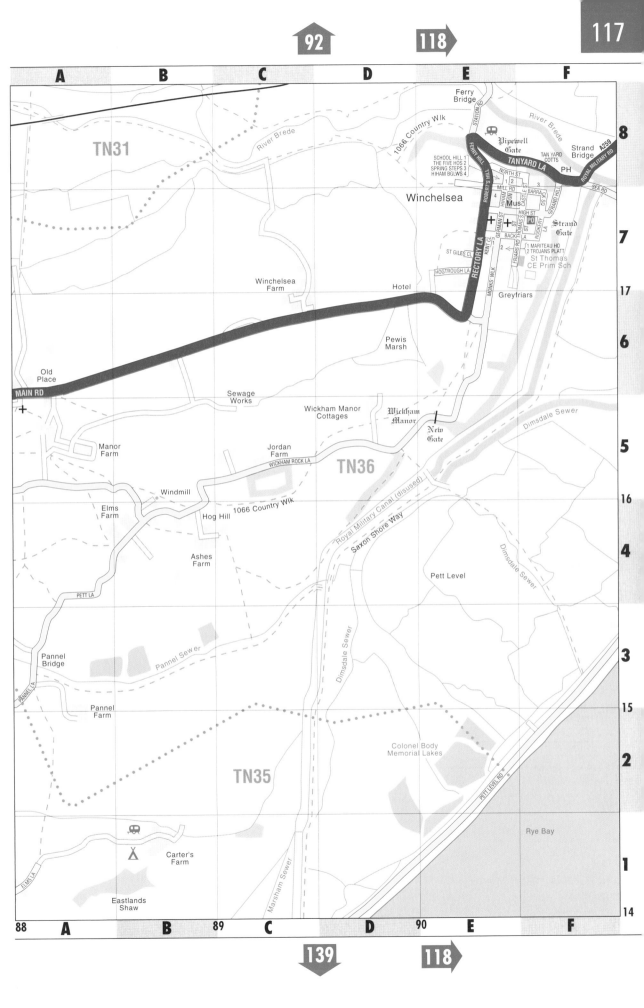

92
118
139
118

A B C D E F

8 7 17 6 5 16 4 3 15 2 1 14

TN31

River Brede

Ferry Bridge

1066 Country Wlk

Pipewell Gate

STATION RD

River Brede

Strand Bridge

A259

TANYARD LA

TAN YARD COTTS

ROYAL MILITARY RD

SCHOOL HILL 1
THE FIVE HOS 2
SPRING STEPS 3
HIHAM BGLWS 4

FERRY HILL

ROBERT'S HILL

NORTH ST

HIHAM RD

MILL RD

CASTLE ST

BARRA-
CK SQ

STRAND HILL

PH

Winchelsea

1 2
GN
HIGH ST

3

4

Mus

SEA RD

RECTORY LA

GERMAN ST

KENT CL

Strand
Gate

ST GILES CL

BACK LA

FRIARS RD

THOMAS ST

ROOKERY LA

HOGTROUGH LA

MONKS WLK

PO

1 MARITEAU HO
2 TROJANS PLATT

St Thomas
CE Prim Sch

Winchelsea
Farm

Hotel

Greyfriars

Pewis
Marsh

Old
Place

MAIN RD

Sewage
Works

Wickham Manor
Cottages

Wickham
Manor

New
Gate

Dimsdale Sewer

Manor
Farm

Jordan
Farm

WICKHAM ROCK LA

TN36

Royal Military Canal (disused)

Saxon Shore Way

Dimsdale Sewer

Windmill

Elms
Farm

Hog Hill

1066 Country Wlk

Pett Level

Ashes
Farm

PETT LA

Dimsdale Sewer

Pannel
Bridge

Pannel Sewer

PANNEL LA

Pannel
Farm

TN35

Colonel Body
Memorial Lakes

PETT LEVEL RD

ELMS LA

Carter's
Farm

Rye Bay

Marsham Sewer

Eastlands
Shaw

88 A B 89 C D 90 E F

117

93

A B C D E F

8

A259 ROYAL MILITARY RD

Sewage Wks

Nook Beach

TN31

River Brede Farm

Saxon Shore Way

The Nook

River Brede

Castle Farm

Nature Reserve

TN36

7

SUTTONS IND PK

SEA RD

OLD RIVER WAY

Watch House

Nook Drain

17

WINDMILL WAY

GREYFRIARS PL

MORLAIS PL

WINDMILL CT

MORLAIS RIDGE

HARBOUR FARM

6

The Ship (PH)

WILLOW LA

HARBOUR LA

HARBOUR BARN

Dimsdale Sewer

THE RIDGE

PO

5

Winchelsea Beach

SMEATONS LA

DOGS HILL RD

DONALD WAY

VICTORIA WAY

WINDSOR WAY

VUE GRIS NEZ

16

Dogs Hill

PETT LEVEL RD

4

Rye Bay

3

15

2

1

14

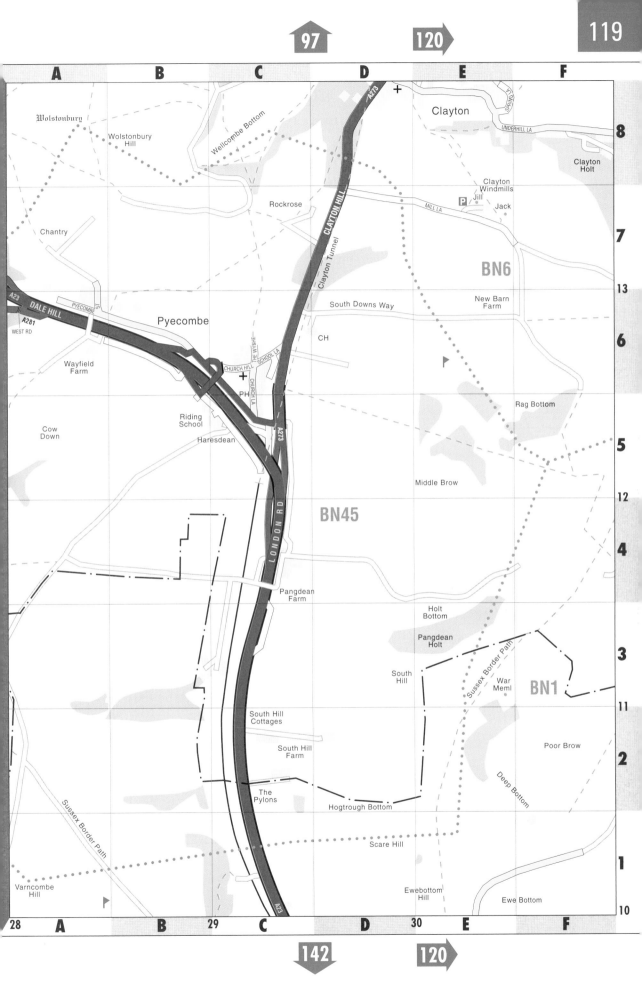

A   B   C   D   E   F

8

Whitelands

Lodge La

Coombe
Bottom

Burnhouse Bostall

Underhill La

Beacon Rd

Nye La

Westmeston
Place

B2116

Lewes Rd

Saillards

Downview
Westmeston

The Street

B2116

Westmeston
Farm

Wick
Farm

Ditchling Bostall

Westmeston
Bostall

7

Clayton
Holt

Ditchling Beacon
Nature Reserve

South Downs Way

Sussex Border Path

Burnhouse Bostall

Ditchling
Beacon

13

BN6

P

Middleton Bostall

Home Bottom

Home Brow

6

Dencher
Bottom

Hogtrough
Bottom

Big Bottom

5

Heathy
Brow

12

North Bottom

4

Highpark
Corner

Ditchling Rd

High Park
Farm

White Thorn

Lower
Standean

Doddlis
Plantation

Highpark
Wood

BN1

3

Wonderhill
Plantation

Green
Broom

11

New Barn

Moon's
Bottom

Mid-down
House

Piddingworth
Plantation

Millbank
Wood

2

Granny's
Belt

Alpha Cottage

Beta
Cottage

Flint Heap

1

Tegdown
Hill

Upper Lodge
Wood

Limekiln
Wood

10

31   A   B   32   C   D   33   E   F

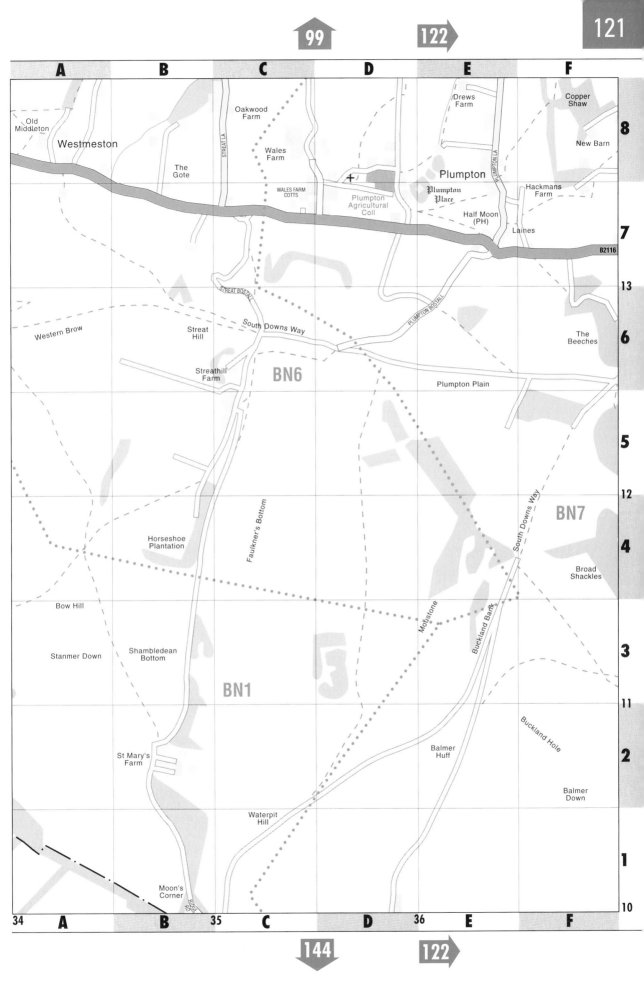

99
122

A B C D E F

8

Old Middleton

Drews Farm

Copper Shaw

New Barn

Westmeston

Oakwood Farm

Wales Farm

Plumpton

The Gote

Plumpton Place

Hackmans Farm

WALES FARM COTTS

Plumpton Agricultural Coll

Half Moon (PH)

Laines

7

B2116

13

Western Brow

STREAT BOSTALL

South Downs Way

PLUMPTON BOSTALL

The Beeches

6

Streat Hill

Streathill Farm

BN6

Plumpton Plain

5

12

Faulkner's Bottom

South Downs Way

BN7

4

Horseshoe Plantation

Broad Shackles

Bow Hill

Molstone

Buckland Bank

Stanmer Down

Shambledean Bottom

3

BN1

11

Buckland Hole

St Mary's Farm

Balmer Huff

2

Balmer Down

Waterpit Hill

1

Moon's Corner

RIDGE RD

10

34 A B 35 C D 36 E F

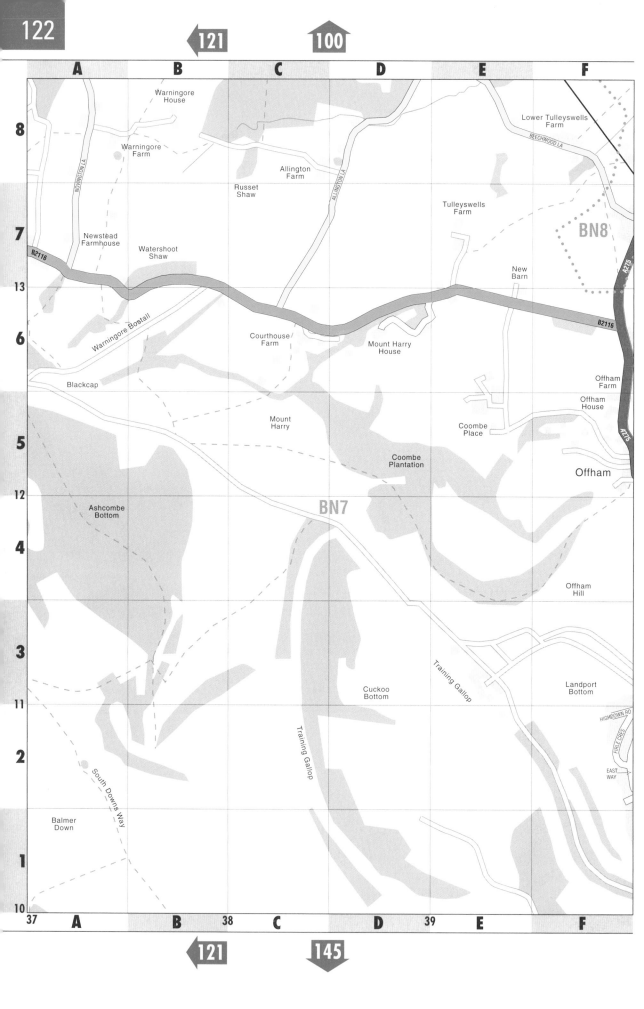

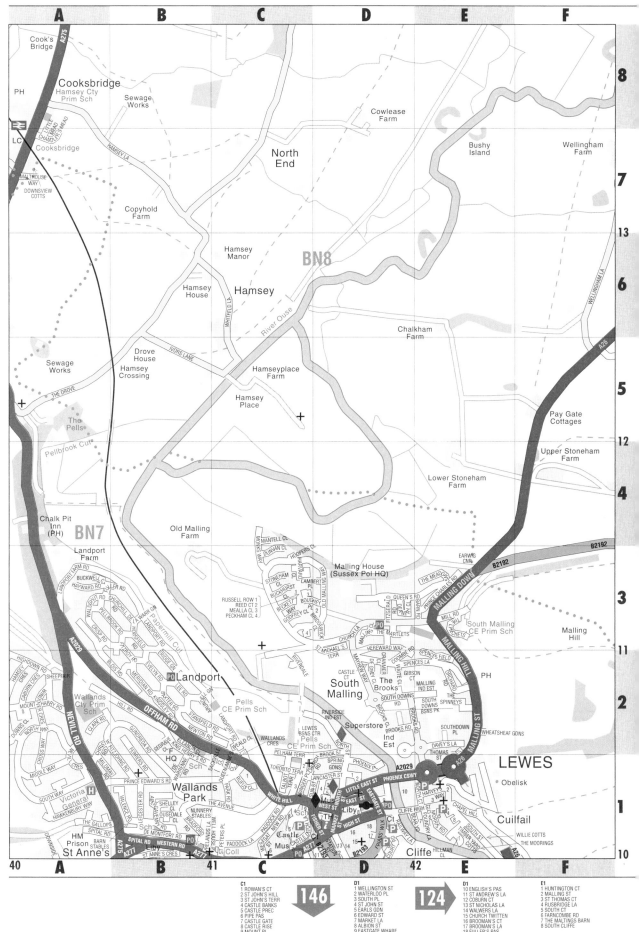

C1
1 ROWAN'S CT
2 ST JOHN'S HILL
3 ST JOHN'S TERR
4 CASTLE BANKS
5 CASTLE PREC
6 PIPE PAS
7 CASTLE GATE
8 CASTLE RISE
9 MOUNT PL

146

D1
1 WELLINGTON ST
2 WATERLOO PL
3 SOUTH PL
4 ST JOHN ST
5 EARLS GDN
6 EDWARD ST
7 MARKET LA
8 ALBION ST
9 EASTGATE WHARF

124

D1
10 ENGLISH'S PAS
11 ST ANDREW'S LA
12 COBURN CT
13 ST NICHOLAS LA
14 WALWERS LA
15 CHURCH TWITTEN
16 BROOMAN'S CT
17 BROOMAN'S LA
18 FULLER'S PAS

E1
1 HUNTINGTON CT
2 MALLING ST
3 ST THOMAS CT
4 RUSBRIDGE LA
5 SOUTH CT
6 FARNCOMBE RD
7 THE MALTINGS BARN
8 SOUTH CLIFFE

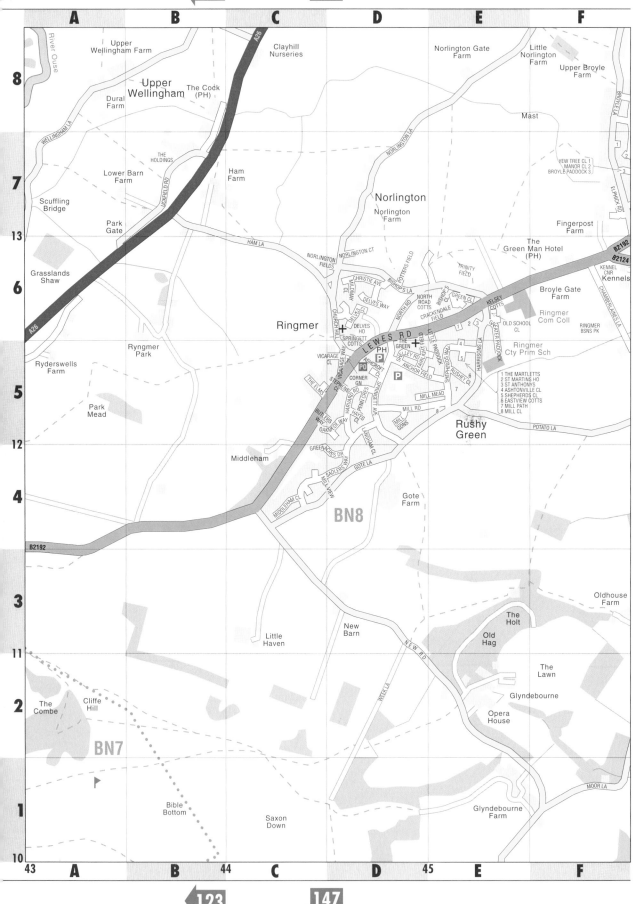

A B C D E F

8

River Ouse

Upper Wellingham Farm

Clayhill Nurseries

Norlington Gate Farm

Little Norlington Farm

Upper Broyle Farm

Upper Wellingham

The Cock (PH)

Dural Farm

Mast

7

Wellingham La

The Holdings

Lower Barn Farm

Ham Farm

Uckfield Rd

Norlington La

Norlington

Yew Tree Cl 1
Manor Cl 2
Broyle Paddock 3

Elphick Rd

Scuffling Bridge

Norlington Farm

Fingerpost Farm

13

Ham La

Park Gate

Norlington Ct

Norlington Fields

The Green Man Hotel (PH)

B2192
B2124

6

A26

Grasslands Shaw

Christie Ave

Bishop's La

Potters Field

Trinity Field

Broyle Gate Farm

Kennel Cnr Kennels

Delves Way

North Road Cotts

Green Cl

Bishop's Cl

Kelsey Cotts

Ringmer Com Coll

Chamberlains La

Ringmer

Church Hill

North Rd

Crackendale Field

Old School Cl

Ringmer Bsns Pk

Delves Ho

Springett Cotts

Lewes Rd

The Green

Slater Paddock

Ringmer Cty Prim Sch

Ryngmer Park

Vicarage Cl

PH

PO

Harrisons La

1 The Martletts
2 St Martins Ho
3 St Anthonys
4 Ashtonville Cl
5 Shepherds Cl
6 Eastview Cotts
7 Mill Path
8 Mill Cl

Ryderswells Farm

The Elms

Corner Gn

Anchor Field

Shepherds Way

Rushey Cl

5

Stephens Cl

Harvard Rd

Penny Bridges

Springett Ave

Little Paddock

Fairlight Rd

Selney Rd

Mill Mead

Park Mead

Butlers Way

Hayes Cl

Mill Gdns

Mill Rd

Potato La

12

Oaktree Way

Langham Cl

Greenacres Dr

Sadlers Way

Gote La

Rushy Green

Middleham

Mill View

Middleham Cl

Gote Farm

4

BN8

B2192

3

Oldhouse Farm

The Holt

Old Hag

Little Haven

New Barn

New Rd

Glyndebourne

The Lawn

11

Week La

2

The Combe

Cliffe Hill

Opera House

BN7

Moor La

1

Bible Bottom

Saxon Down

Glyndebourne Farm

10

43 A B 44 C D 45 E F

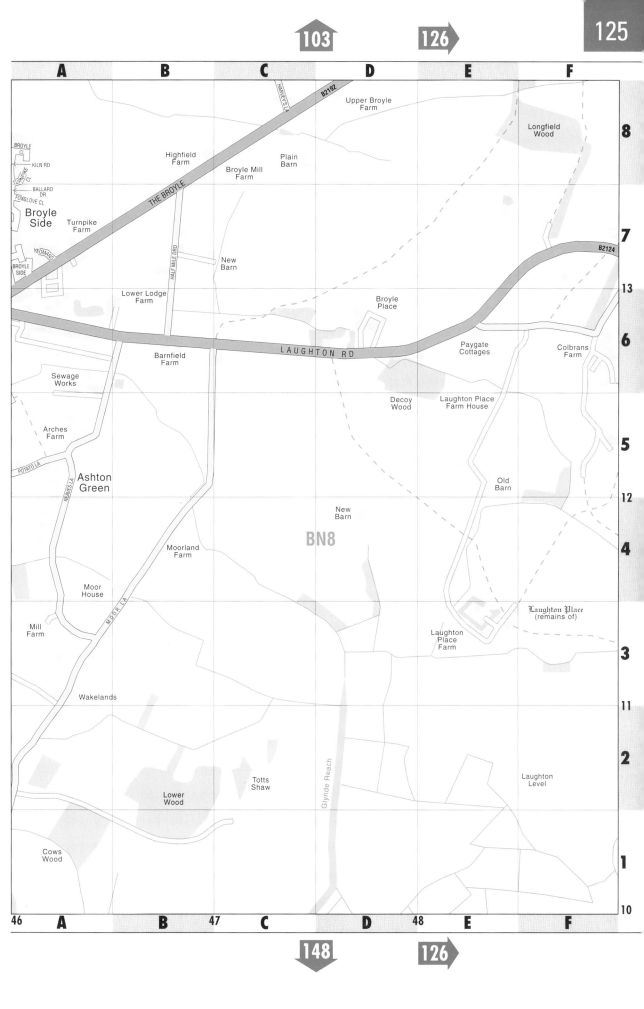

A B C D E F

8
7
13
6

5
12
4

3
11
2

1
10

46 47 48

HARVEY'S LA
B2192
Upper Broyle Farm
Longfield Wood

BROYLE CL
KILN RD
TURNPIKE CL
BALLARD DR
FOXGLOVE CL
Broyle Side
YEOMANS
BROYLE SIDE
Turnpike Farm
THE BROYLE
Highfield Farm
Broyle Mill Farm
Plain Barn

B2124

Half Mile Dro
New Barn
Lower Lodge Farm
Broyle Place

LAUGHTON RD
Barnfield Farm
Paygate Cottages
Colbrans Farm

Sewage Works
Decoy Wood
Laughton Place Farm House

Arches Farm
POTATO LA
Ashton Green
NEAVES LA
Old Barn

New Barn
BN8

Moorland Farm
Laughton Place (remains of)

MOOR LA
Moor House
Laughton Place Farm

Mill Farm
Laughton Place Farm

Wakelands

Totts Shaw
Glynde Reach
Laughton Level

Lower Wood

Cows Wood

← 125

104

A **B** **C** **D** **E** **F**

8

Brickhurst Wood

Laughton Common Wood

Lower Vert Wood

Laughton Lodge

BRICKHURST LA

SHORTGATE LA

Brickhurst Farm

Saw Mill

Averys Oak Farm

Wood Bungalows

The Roebuck (PH)

7

Laughton Manor

ELM COTTS

ELM CL

POUND LA

PARK LA

Helouan Farm

Queeake

B2124

LAUGHTON RD

13

Home Farm

Bowen Wood

Laughton

Laughton Cty Prim Sch

Bowen Farm

6

Coopers Farm

B2124

Black Shaw

Stone Cross Farm

+

5

CHURCH LA

New House Farm

Marchants Farm

Milward's Farm

Church Farm

Harben's Farm

12

BN8

4

Cleaver's Farm

Little Stream Farm

Muslins Pit

Airfield

3

Cleggett's Farm

Mill Farm

11

MARK CROSS

RIPE LA

2

Curl's Farm

Fowler's Barn

1

Lamb Inn (PH)

BN27

Ripe

PO

CHANNERS LA

10

49 **A** **B** 50 **C** **D** 51 **E** **F**

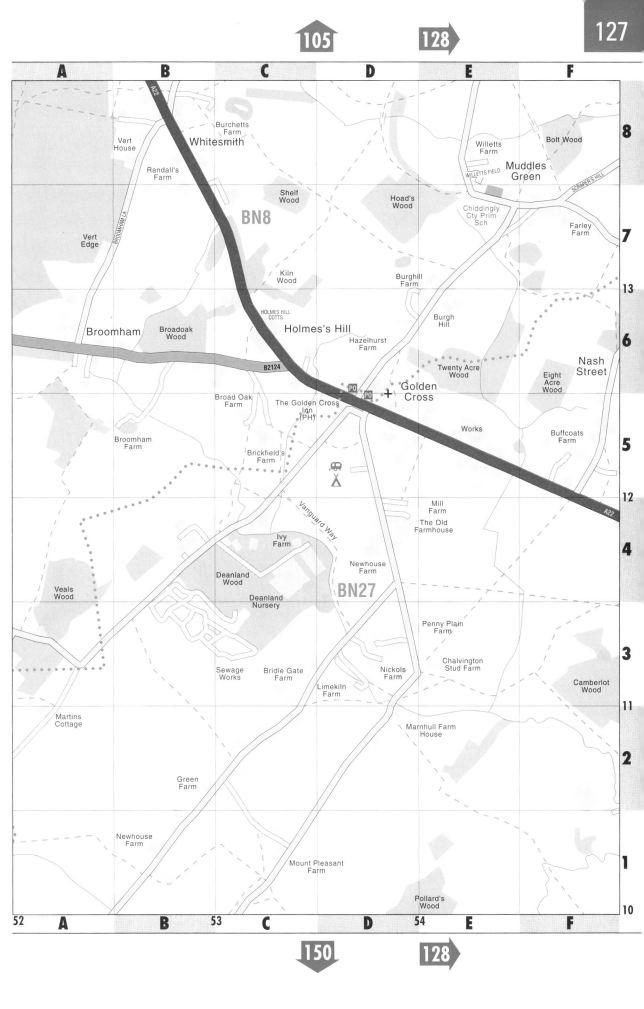

105
128

A B C D E F

8

Vert
House

Burchetts
Farm

Whitesmith

Willetts
Farm

Bolt Wood

Muddles
Green

Randall's
Farm

Shelf
Wood

Hoad's
Wood

BN8

Chiddingly
Cty Prim
Sch

WILLETTS FIELD

SCRAPER'S HILL

Farley
Farm

7

Vert
Edge

Kiln
Wood

Burghill
Farm

13

HOLMES HILL
COTTS

Holmes's Hill

Burgh
Hill

Broomham

Broadoak
Wood

Hazelhurst
Farm

Nash
Street

6

Broad Oak
Farm

B2124

Twenty Acre
Wood

Eight
Acre
Wood

PO
PO

Golden
Cross

Broomham
Farm

The Golden Cross
Inn (PH)

Works

Buffcoats
Farm

5

Brickfield's
Farm

Mill
Farm

12

Vanguard Way

The Old
Farmhouse

Veals
Wood

Ivy
Farm

Newhouse
Farm

BN27

4

Deanland
Wood

Deanland
Nursery

Penny Plain
Farm

3

Sewage
Works

Bridle Gate
Farm

Nickols
Farm

Chalvington
Stud Farm

Camberlot
Wood

Martins
Cottage

Limekiln
Farm

11

Marnhull Farm
House

2

Green
Farm

Newhouse
Farm

1

Mount Pleasant
Farm

Pollard's
Wood

10

52 A 53 B C 54 D E F

A   B   C   D   E   F

Park Bridge

BN8

Scrapper's Hill Farm

Thunder's Hill

Pekes House

Hamly Bridge

Hawthbush Farm

TN21

Popp's Farm

World's End Farm

Wealdway

Westenden Wood

Pekes Farm

Nash Street Farm

Leabridge Farm

Nash Street

Perryland Farm

Boggy Wood

Broad Farm

Marigolds Farm

Hackhurst Farm

HACKHURST LA

B2104

Hellingly Cty Prim Sch

HACKHURST LA IND EST

BN27

Cemy

NORTH ST

A22

Blackbarn Farm

NORTHFIELDS BSNS PK

THE CROFT

HACKHURST LA

CALDICOTT'S LA

Caldicott's Wood

Caldicotts Farm

White House

B2104

PO

Nursery

Camberlot Wood

Camberlot Farm

The Mount

MANSERS LA

LOWER DICKER

Lower Dicker

Knight's Farm

Coldharbour Farm

POTTERIES COTTS

A261

i

BROOKLANDS TERR

A271

P

The King's Head (PH)

Lower Horsebridge

A271

Camberlot Wood

CAMBERLOT RD

Field House

Hatches Farm

Boship Farm Hotel

Cuckmere River

Clover Farm

COLDHARBOUR RD

The Nurseries

Wealdway

Welbury Farm

STROMA GDNS

Malvern House

Plenties Farm

Starnash

Bourne Farm

Hempstead Farm

HEMPSTEAD LA

Woodside Farm

Chicheley Farm

A22

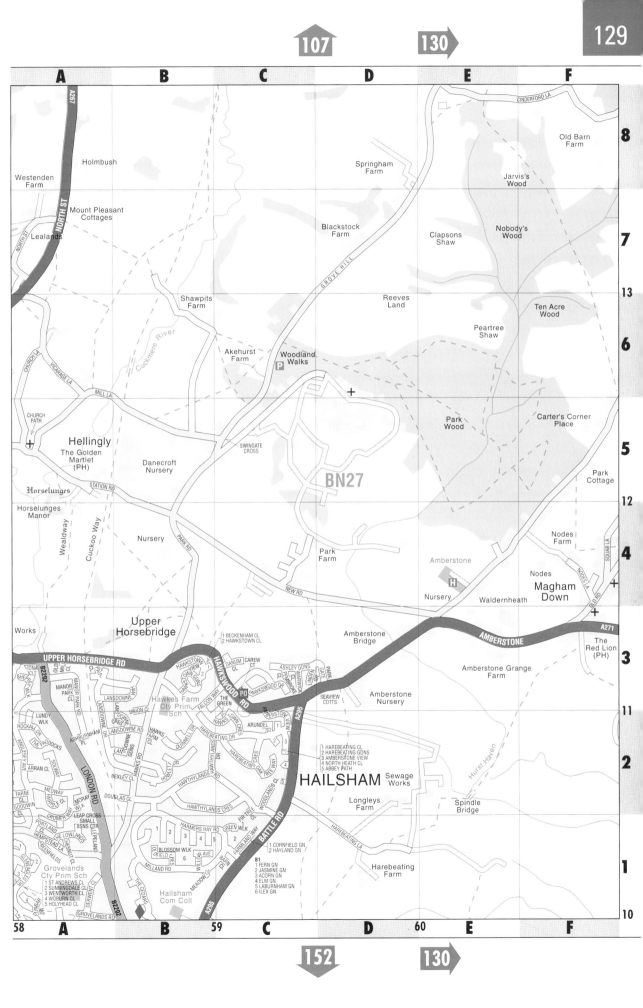

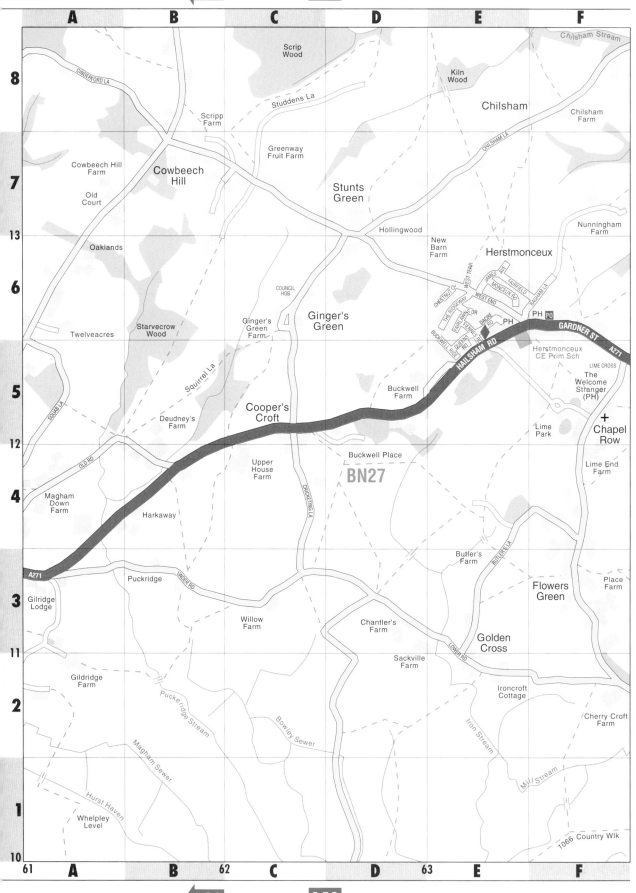

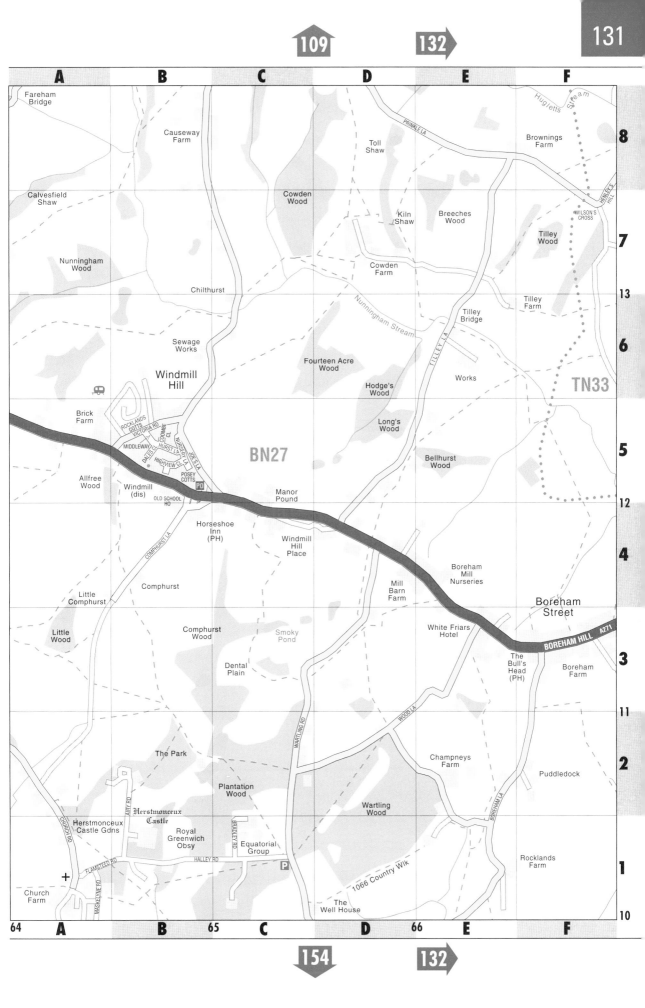

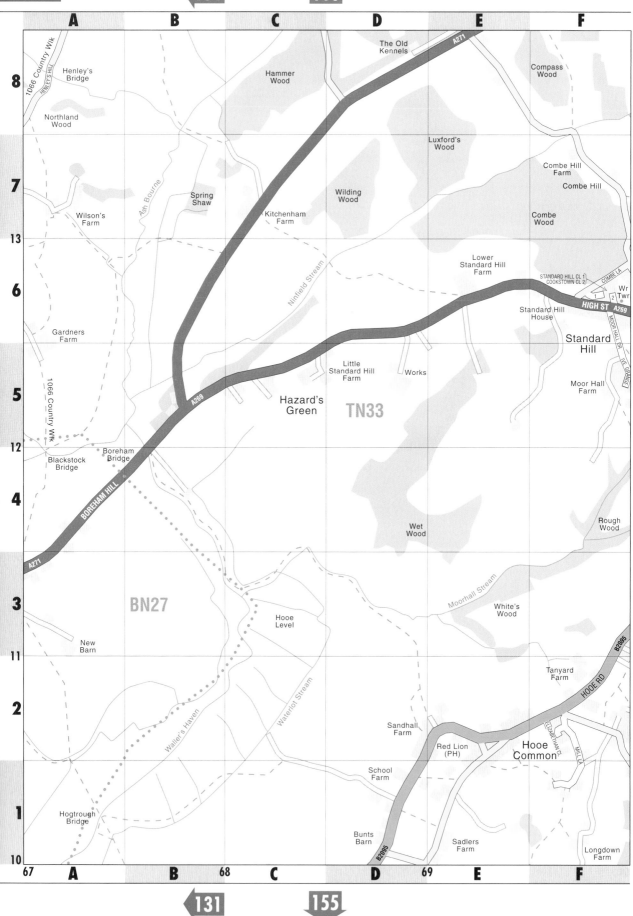

| A | B | C | D | E | F |

8 Henley's Bridge · Hammer Wood · The Old Kennels · A271 · Compass Wood
1066 Country Wlk · Henley's Hill
Northland Wood

7 Wilson's Farm · Ash Bourne · Spring Shaw · Kitchenham Farm · Wilding Wood · Luxford's Wood · Combe Hill Farm · Combe Hill · Combe Wood
13
6 Lower Standard Hill Farm · STANDARD HILL CL 1 · COOKSTOWN CL 2 · Wr Twr · HIGH ST · A269 · COMBE LA
Ninfield Stream · Standard Hill House · MOOR HALL DR · THE GRANGE
5 Gardners Farm · A269 · Little Standard Hill Farm · Works · Standard Hill · Moor Hall Farm
1066 Country Wlk · Hazard's Green · TN33
12 Blackstock Bridge · Boreham Bridge
4 BOREHAM HILL · Wet Wood · Rough Wood
A271
3 BN27 · New Barn · Hooe Level · Moorhall Stream · White's Wood · B2095
11 Tanyard Farm · HOOE RD
2 Waller's Haven · Waterlot Stream · Sandhall Farm · Red Lion (PH) · Hooe Common · ELIZABETHAN CL · MILL LA
School Farm
1 Hogtrough Bridge · Bunts Barn · Sadlers Farm · Longdown Farm
10 B2095

| 67 | A | B | 68 | C | D | 69 | E | F |

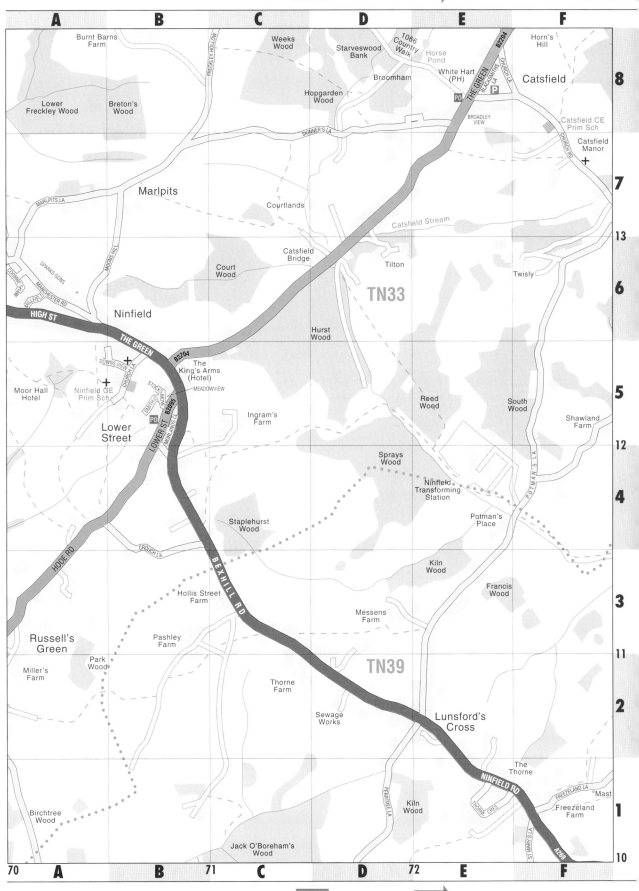

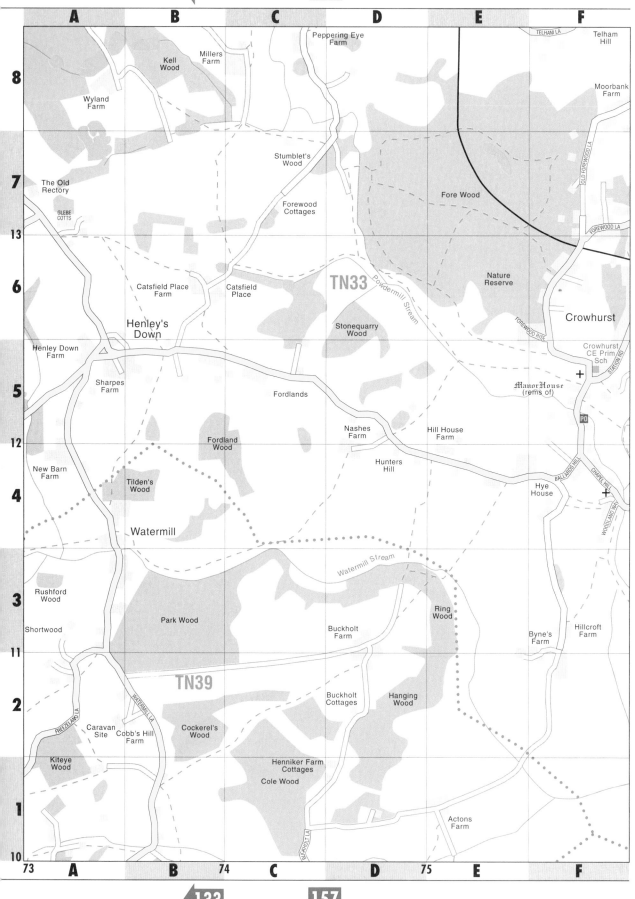

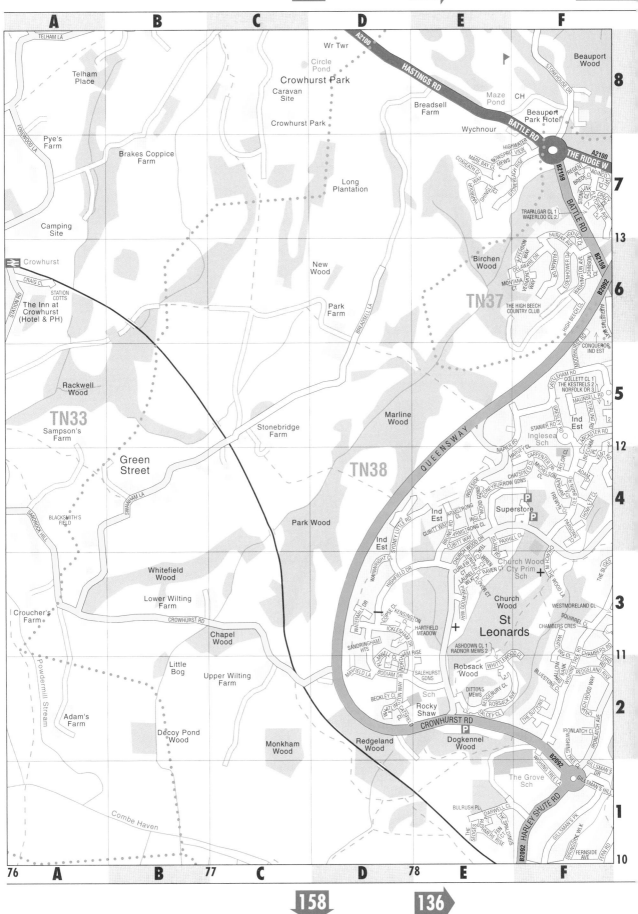

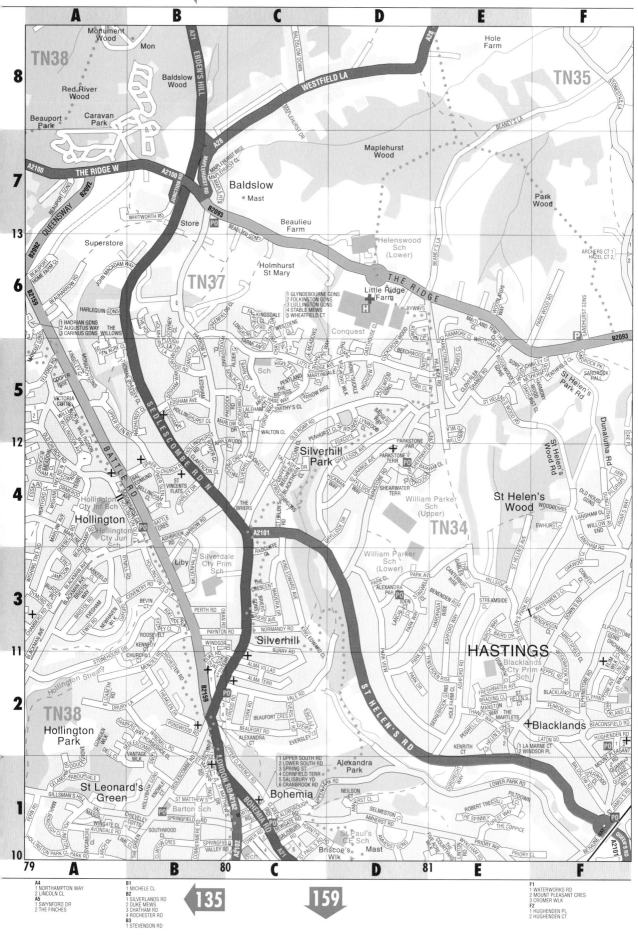

A4
1 NORTHAMPTON WAY
2 LINCOLN CL
A5
1 SWYNFORD DR
2 THE FINCHES

B1
1 MICHELE CL
B2
1 SILVERLANDS RD
2 DUKE MEWS
3 CHATHAM RD
4 ROCHESTER RD
B3
1 STEVENSON RD

F1
1 WATERWORKS RD
2 MOUNT PLEASANT CRES
3 CROMER WLK
F2
1 HUGHENDEN PL
2 HUGHENDEN CT

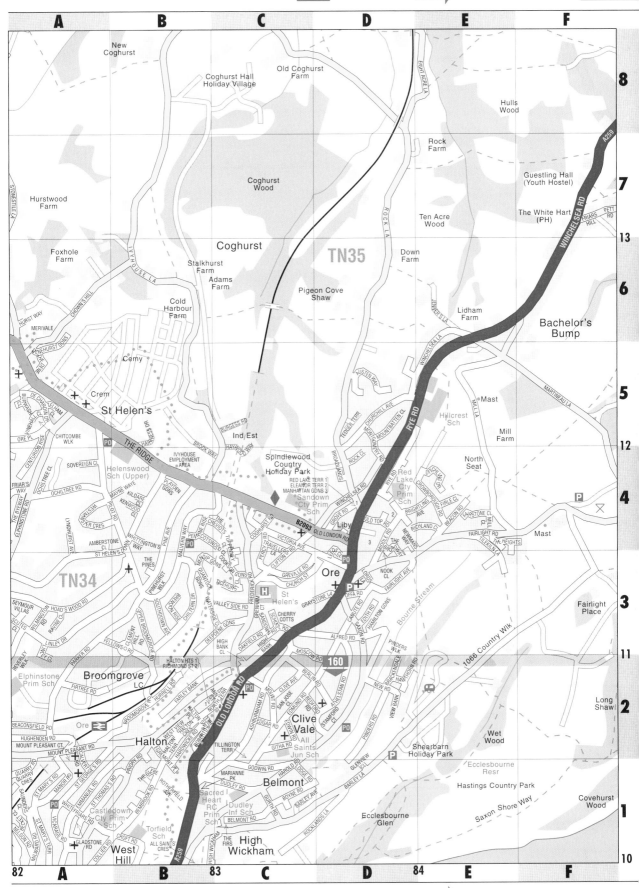

137
116

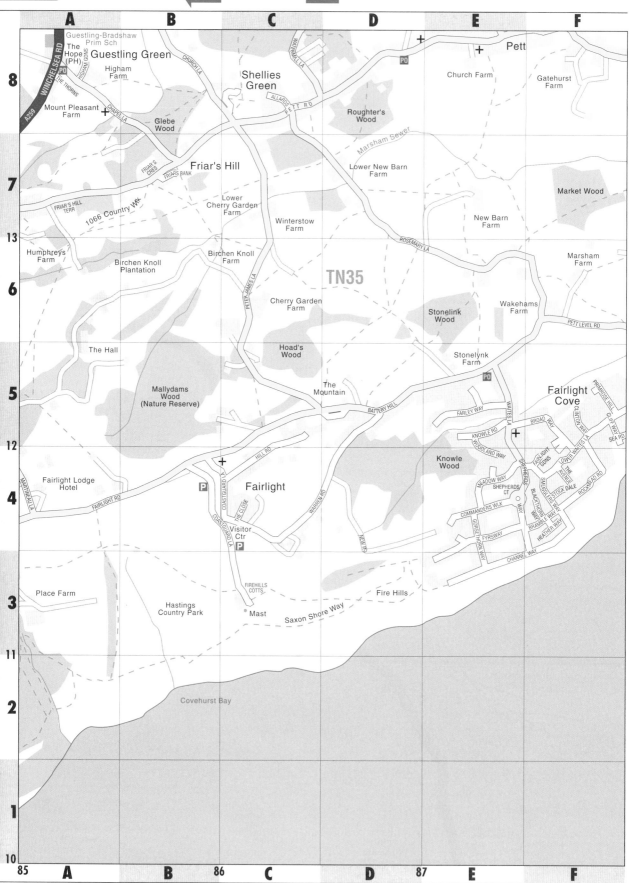

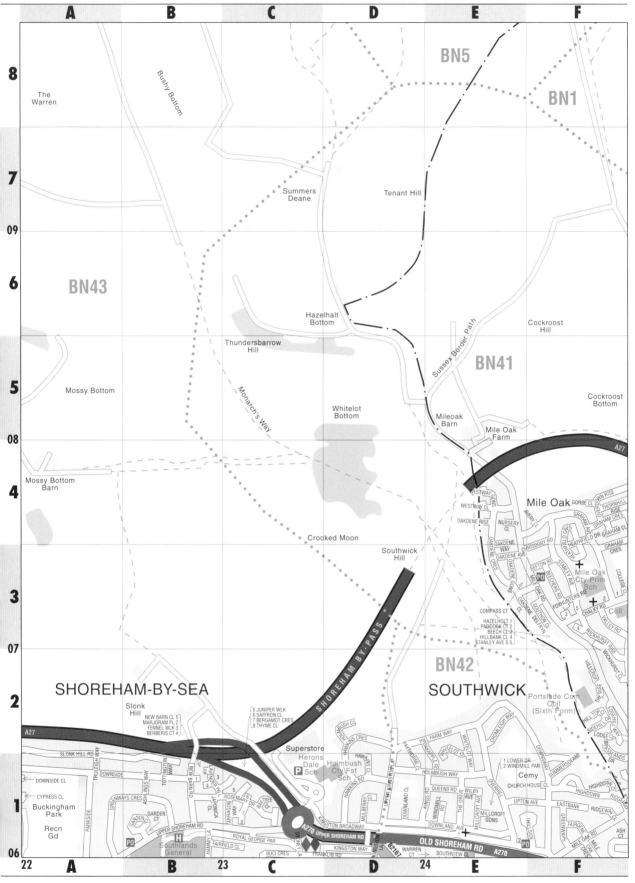

A   B   C   D   E   F

BN5

BN1

The Warren

Bushy Bottom

Summers Deane

Tenant Hill

BN43

Hazelhalt Bottom

Cockroost Hill

Thundersbarrow Hill

BN41

Sussex Border Path

Mossy Bottom

Monarch's Way

Whitelot Bottom

Mileoak Barn

Cockroost Bottom

Mile Oak Farm

Mossy Bottom Barn

WESTWAY GDNS

Mile Oak

GORSE CL WIN RISE

THORNHILL RISE

WESTWAY CL

GRAHAM AVE

HEATHFIELD DR GRAHAM CL

OAKDENE RISE

NURSERY CL

CHRISDORY RD

GRAHAM CRES

Crooked Moon

OAKDENE WAY

OAKDENE AVE

OAKDENE CRES

SEFTON RD

STANLEY AVE

BEECHERS RD

MILE OAK RD

Mile Oak Cty Prim Sch

Southwick Hill

OAKDENE GDNS

FORHUNTERS RD

CHALKY RD

VALLEY CL

Coll

COMPASS CT

SOUTHDN

HAZELHOLT 1

PADDOCK CT 2

BEECH CL 3

HILLBANK CL 4

STANLEY AVE S 5

OAKDENE DELL RTN

WICKHURST RISE

SHOREHAM BY-PASS

BN42

HILLCROFT

WIGMORE RD

SHOREHAM-BY-SEA

SOUTHWICK

Portslade Com Coll (Sixth Form)

HILL TOP

LONGHILL WAY

LODGE WAY

BRASSLANDS DR

Slonk Hill

5 JUNIPER WLK

6 SAFFRON CL

7 BERGAMOT CRES

8 THYME CL

NEW BARN CL 1

MARJORAM PL 2

FENNEL WLK 3

BERBERIS CT 4

A27

SLONK HILL RD

TRULEIGH WAY

DOWNSIDE

TOTTINGTON WAY

NEW BARN RD

LAVENDER HILL

Superstore

Herons Dale Sch

BUSH CL

HAWKINS CRES

HILL FARM WAY

CROMLEIGH WAY

HAWK CL

Holmbush Cty Fst Sch

PAYTHORNE CL

WHYTELOT WAY

WHITELOT WAY

HOLMBUSH WAY

1 LOWER DR

2 WINDMILL PAR

Cemy

CHURCH HOUSE CL

HIGHDOWN

ASHLINGS WAY

GREENWAYS CRES

GARDEN CT

ROSEMARY DR

JAPONICA CL

TARRAGON CL

TREE CL

HAWKINS LA

HAWKINS RD

MULBERRY CL

DOWNLAND CL

KINGS RD

QUEENS RD

WINDMILL RD

THE DRIVE

WILBY AVE

MILLCROFT RD

OVENHILL

SUMMERSDEANE

MILLCROFT GDNS

UPTON AVE

EASTBANK

RIDGEWAY

GREENWAYS

FAIRCROFT

HIGHDOWN

MILE OAK RD

ASH CL

Buckingham Park Recn Gd

DOWNSIDE CL

CYPRESS CL

PARKSIDE

EDEN

UPPER SHOREHAM RD

PO

HAMBLA

FAIRFIELD CL

ROYAL GEORGE PAR

BUCI CRES

STONEY LA

KINGSTON BROADWAY

KINGSTON WAY

FRANKLIN RD

WARREN CT

B2167

SOUTHVIEW CL

OLD SHOREHAM RD

A270

UPPER SHOREHAM RD

A270

KINGSTON LA

DOWNLAND AVE

PO

MILE OAK RD

Southlands General

H

22   A   23   B   C   D   24   E   F

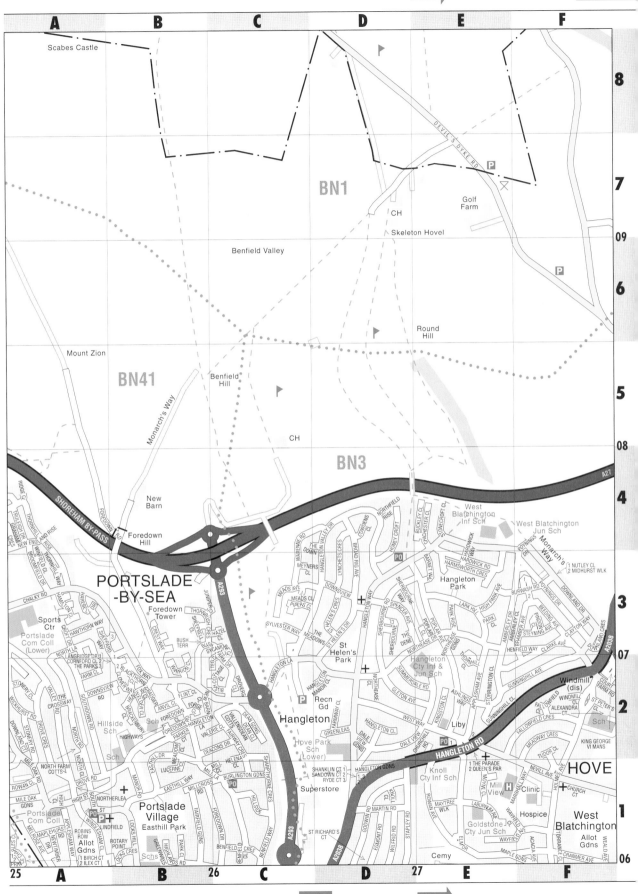

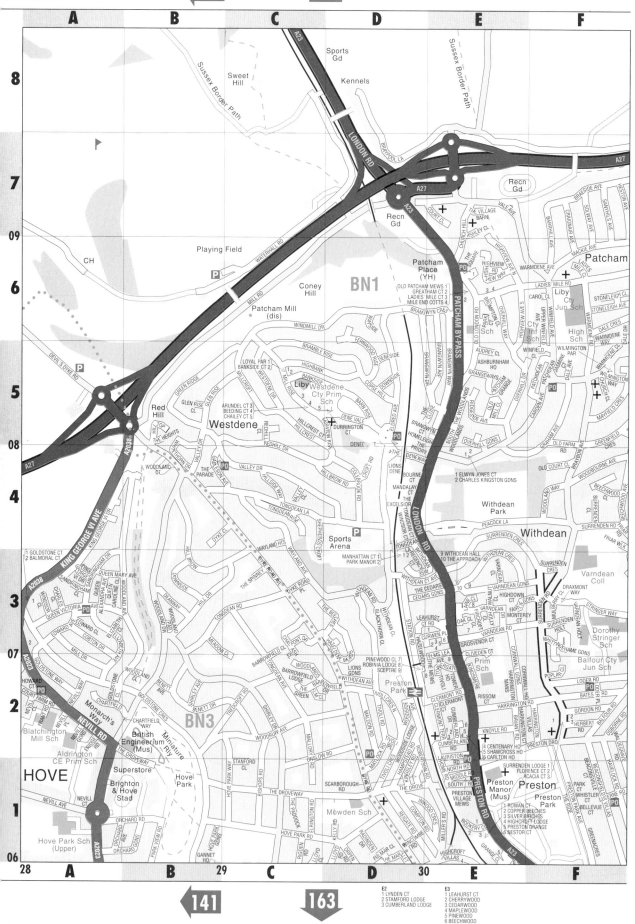

E2
1 LYNDEN CT
2 STAMFORD LODGE
3 CUMBERLAND LODGE

E3
1 LEAHURST CT
2 CHERRYWOOD
3 CEDARWOOD
4 MAPLEWOOD
5 PINEWOOD
6 BEECHWOOD
7 WITHDEAN CT
8 WELLINGTONIA CL

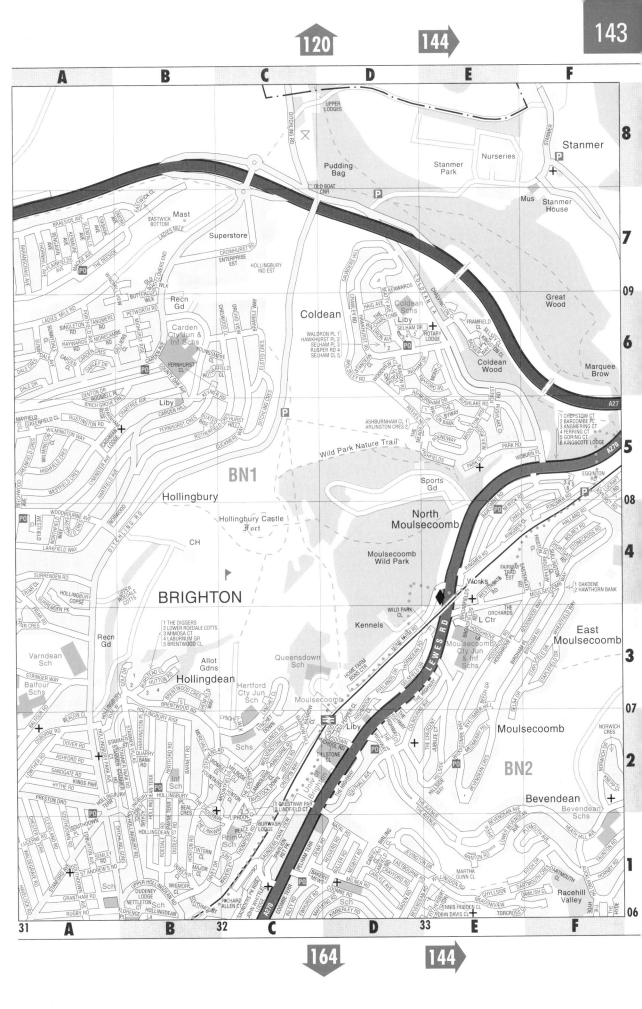

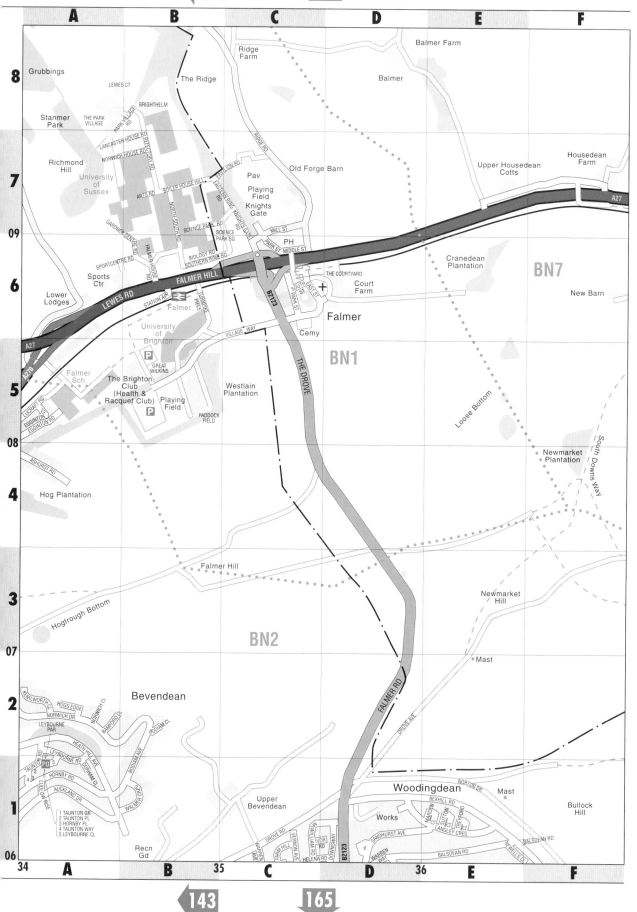

A B C D E F

8 Grubbings

Ridge
Farm

Balmer Farm

The Ridge

Balmer

LEWES CT

BRIGHTHELM

Stanmer
Park

THE PARK
VILLAGE

PARK VILLAGE RD

Housedean
Farm

Richmond
Hill

LANCASTER HOUSE RD

RECTORY RD

PAVILION RD

Upper Housedean
Cotts

Old Forge Barn

A27

7 University
of
Sussex

NORWICH HOUSE RD

BOILER HOUSE HILL

EASTERN RING RD

RIDGE RD

Pav

Playing
Field

ARTS RD

NORTH SOUTH RD

Knights
Gate

KNIGHTS GATE

09 GARDNER CENTRE RD

SCIENCE PARK RD

SCIENCE
PARK SQ

MILL ST

PH

Cranedean
Plantation

BN7

SPORTCENTRE RD

FALMER HOUSE

BIOLOGY RD

SOUTHERN RING RD

PARK ST

MIDDLE ST

Sports
Ctr

6 Lower
Lodges

LEWES RD

FALMER HILL

STATION APP

TURNPIKE
PIECE

Falmer

SOUTH
ST

NORTH EAST ST

THE COURTYARD

Court
Farm

New Barn

Falmer

B2123

South Park St

University of
Brighton

VILLAGE WAY

Cemy

BN1

5 FALMER
Sch

A27(T)

P

GREAT
WILKINS

THE DROVE

A27(T)

The Brighton
Club
(Health &
Racquet Club)

P

Playing
Field

Westlain
Plantation

Loose Bottom

LUDLAY RD

EGGINTON CL

EGGINTON RD

PADDOCK
FIELD

08 Newmarket
Plantation

South Downs Way

ASHURST RD

4 Hog Plantation

Falmer Hill

Newmarket
Hill

3 Hogtrough Bottom

07 BN2

Mast

2 KENILWORTH CT

HOGS EDGE

NORWICH DR

BAMFORD CL

Bevendean

BODIAM CL

FALMER RD

DROVE AVE

LEYBOURNE
PAR

HEATH HILL AVE

LEYBOURNE RD

DURHAM CL

BODIAM AVE

NORTON DR

Mast

TAUNTON RD

PO 5

HORNBY RD

WALMER CRES

Woodingdean

Bullock
Hill

1 LUDLOW RISE

AUCKLAND DR

1 TAUNTON GR
2 TAUNTON PL
3 HORNBY PL
4 TAUNTON WAY
5 LEYBOURNE CL

Upper
Bevendean

Works

BEXHILL RD

MARDEN CL

SUTTON CL

TREYFORD CL

LANGLEY CRES

BALSDEAN RD

DROVE RD

MCWILLIAM RD

VERNON AVE

HELENA RD

IVOR RD

DOWNSWAY

B2123

SANDHURST AVE

NEWELLS CL

06 Recn
Gd

FARM HILL

WARREN AVE

WARREN
WAY

BALSDEAN RD

34 A B 35 C D 36 E F

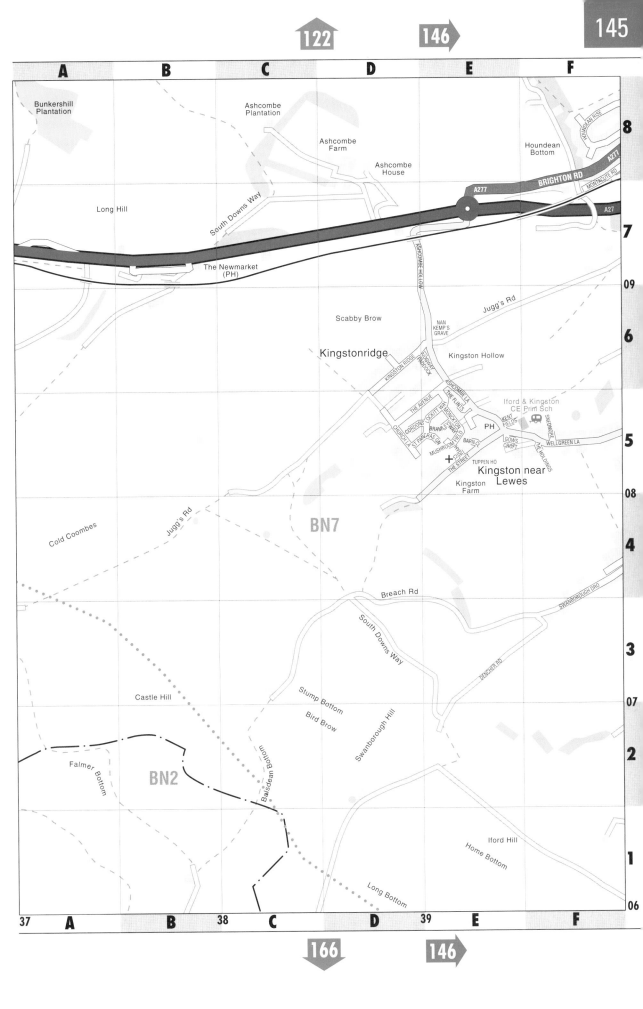

A B C D E F

Bunkershill
Plantation

Ashcombe
Plantation

Ashcombe
Farm

Ashcombe
House

Houndean
Bottom

8

HOUNDEAN RISE

A277

BRIGHTON RD

MONTAGUTE RD

Long Hill

South Downs Way

A277

A27

7

The Newmarket
(PH)

09

Scabby Brow

ASHCOMBE HOLLOW

Jugg's Rd

NAN
KEMP'S
GRAVE

6

Kingstonridge

BRIDWAY
PADDOCK

Kingston Hollow

KINGSTON RIDGE

ASHCOMBE LA

THE FLINTS

Iford & Kingston
CE Prim Sch

KENT
FIELDS

SNEDMORE

THE AVENUE

CORDDONS

LOCKITT WAY

MONCKTON

BRAMLEY

SWAN MEAD

PH

GOWS
CROFT

WELLGREEN LA

THE HOLDINGS

5

CHURCH LA

ST PANCRAS GN

BARN CL

MUSHROOM FIELD

THE STREET

TUPPEN HO

Kingston near
Lewes

Kingston
Farm

08

Cold Coombes

Jugg's Rd

BN7

4

Breach Rd

SWANBOROUGH DRO

South Downs Way

DENCHER RD

3

Castle Hill

Stump Bottom

Bird Brow

Swanborough Hill

07

Falmer Bottom

BN2

Balsdean Bottom

2

Iford Hill

Home Bottom

1

Long Bottom

06

145
123

C8
1 ST SWITHUN'S LA
2 BULL LA
3 STEWARDS INN LA
4 ST MARTIN'S LA
5 ELM GR
6 ST SWITHUN'S TERR

7 PRIORY FLATS
8 FAIRHOLME
9 MANOR TERR
10 SOUTHOVER MANOR HO
11 MONKS LA
12 VERRALL'S WLK
13 ANNE'S PATH

A B C D E F

SOUTHDOWN AVE
HOUNDEAN
DOWNSIDE
BRIGHTON RD
WARREN DR
BISHOPS DR
A271
Liby
Cty Hall
St Anne's Sch
CHURCH
HIGH ST
A277
Sch
Sch
P
B2193
Lewes Tertiary Coll
CH
LODGE
BARN HATS
WARREN CL
1 CLEVEDOWN
2 BARONS WLK
Cemy
ROTTEN ROW
GRANGE CT
GRANGE RD
ANTIOCH ST
KEERE
SOUTHOVER RD
GARDEN ST
PINWELL RD
COURT RD
STATION RD
Lewes
MONTACUTE RD
DOWN RD
BARONS CL
DELAWARE RD
DALE RD
BERKELEY ROW
WINTERBOURNE HOLLOW
WINTERBOURNE LA
BELL LA
WILLYFIELD
ST PANCRAS RD
ST PANCRAS GDNS
DUMBRELL CT 1
GREENE CT 2
BARBER CT 3
THE COURSE 4
CLEVE TERR 5
Mus
Schs
ST JAMES
EASTPORT LA
WHITEGATE RD
B2193
PO
P
Coll
L Ctr
MOUNTFIELD RD
CLIFFE IND EST
8
VALLEY RD
WINTERBOURNE LA
JUGGS CL
MORLEY CL
B2193
SOUTHOVER HIGH ST
CLUNY ST
13 11
PRIORY ST
CRES
MOUNT ST
COCKSHUT RD
PO
1 LANSDOWN PL
2 TANNERS BROOK
3 DORSET RD
4 PRIORY HO
5 PRIORY CT
6 ROYAL SUSSEX CT
Coll
Priory Sch
HAM LA

Southover
The Cockshut
Sewage Works
Southerham Farm
A27
JUGGS RD
A26
A27
7
LEWES
GRANDOWN
KINGSTON RD

09
Spring Barn Farm
Rise Farm
River Ouse
BN8

6
Upper Rise

WELLGREEN LA
Swanborough Fishing Lake
Celery Sewer
5
Sewage Works
THE DROVEWAY
Rise Barn

08
BN7
NORTON WALL
The Brooks
Lower Rise

4
Swanborough Manor
SWANBOROUGH DRO
SWANBOROUGH HOLLOW
Celery Sewer

Iford Farm
SUTTON WALL
3
Iford
Iford Farm
SUTTON COTTS

07
NORTHEASE WALL

2
Northease Manor
WHITEWAYS COTTS
Sewage Works

1
Northease Farm
WHITE WAY
Rodmell
BARLEY FIELD COTTS
Monk's House
Rodmell CE Prim Sch
South Farm
Front Hill
MARTENS FIELD

06
40 A B 41 C D 42 E F

145
167

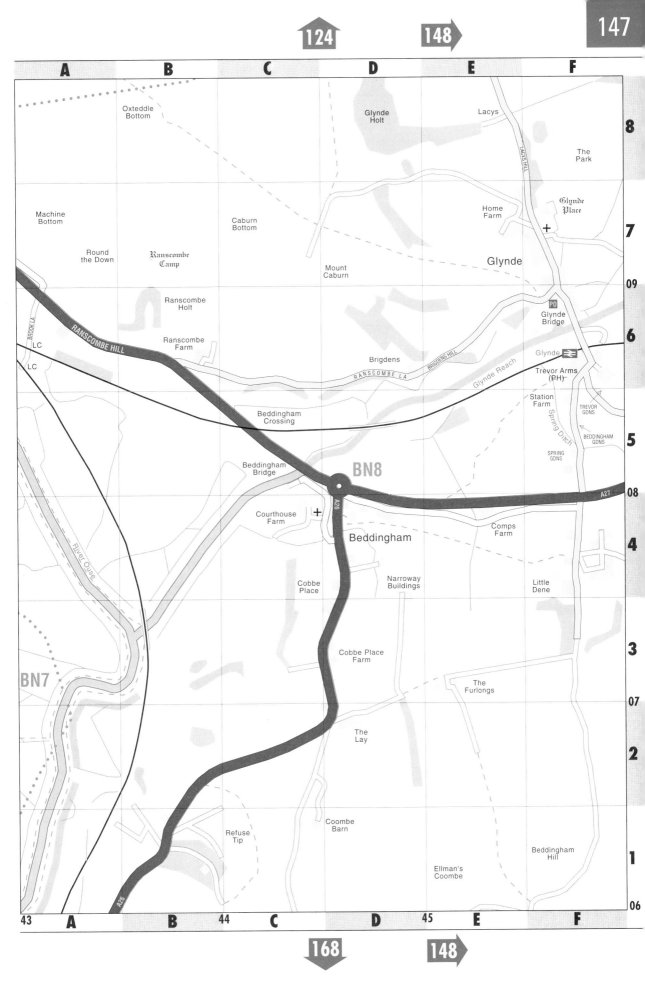

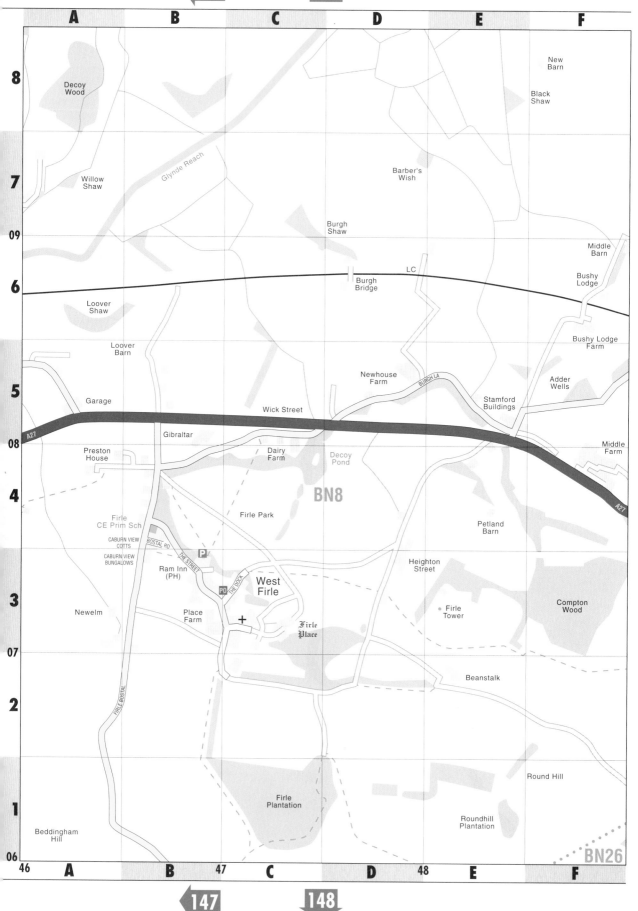

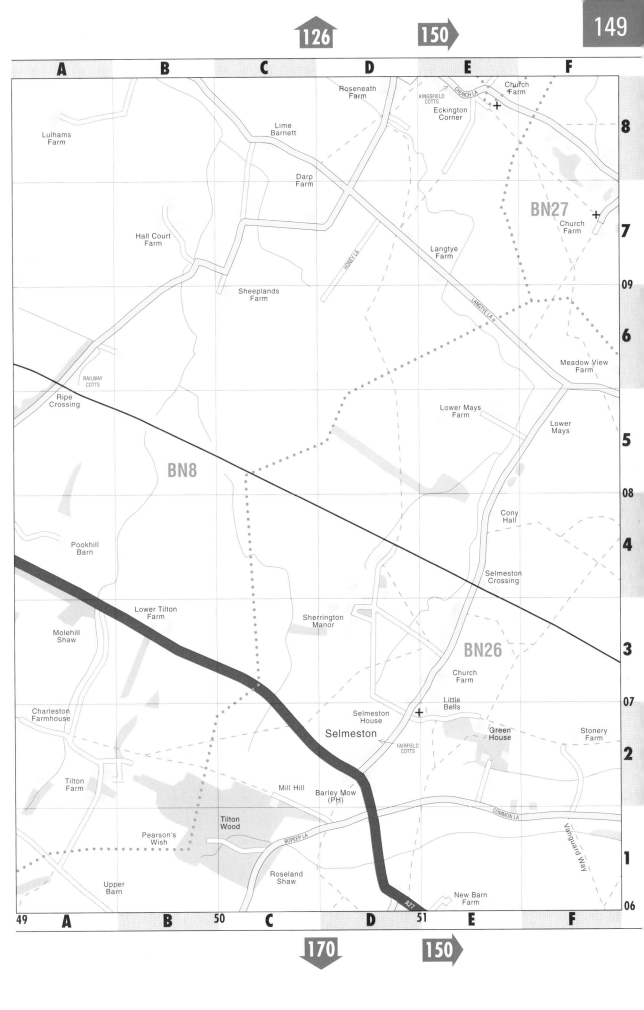

A **B** **C** **D** **E** **F**

8

Yew Tree
(PH)

Selmeston
Croft

Clifton
Farm

Yew
Farm

The Plough
(PH)

BN27

Diplocks
Farm

High
Barn

7

Chalvington

Lower Claverham
Farm

Park
Wood

Vanguard Way

09

Claverham
Manor

Parkwood
Farm

Bungalow
Farm

Wickstreet
Farm

6

Wickstreet

Lower Claverham
House

Batbrooks
Farm House

Sessingham
Farm

5

Batbrook
Cottages

08

Cobb
Court

BN26

Raylands
Farm

TYE HILL RD

4

Ludlay
Coppice

Cuckmere River

Wealdway

Arlington

Vanguard Way

Ludlay

Arlington
Resr

The Yew Tree
Inn (PH)

3

Ludlay
Farm

+

Copyhold
Cottages

Wilbees
Farm

07

PRINCES
FIELD

DOWNSWAY

Polhill's
Farm

Stapley's

2

Berwick
Inn (PH)

Berwick

LC

Garage

Chilverbridge
House

Works

Endlewick
Cottages

Chilver Bridge
Farm

Endlewick
Farm

1

COMMON LA

Moors
Hill

06

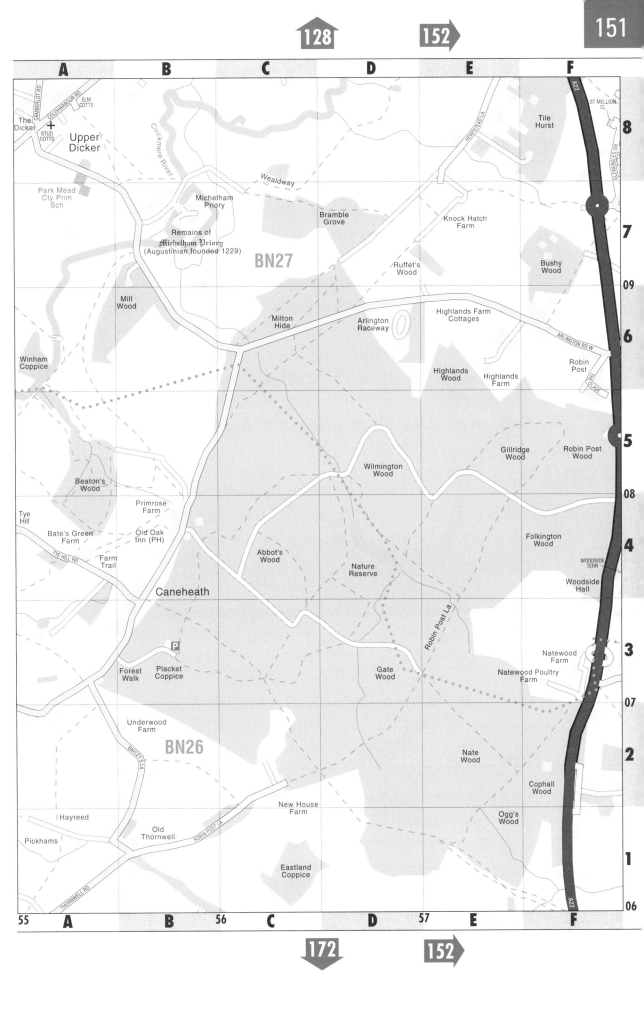

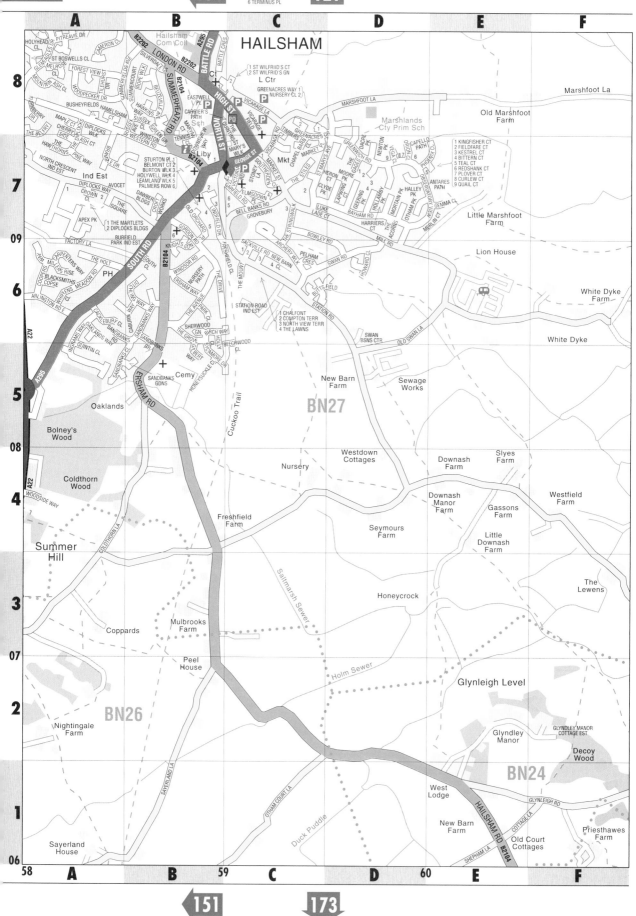

151
129

C7
1 MARKET SQ
2 ELIZABETH CT
3 SOUTHDOWN CT
4 ASHFORD CL
5 COBDEN PL
6 TERMINUS PL

C7
7 DEER PADDOCK LA

HAILSHAM

BN27

BN26

BN24

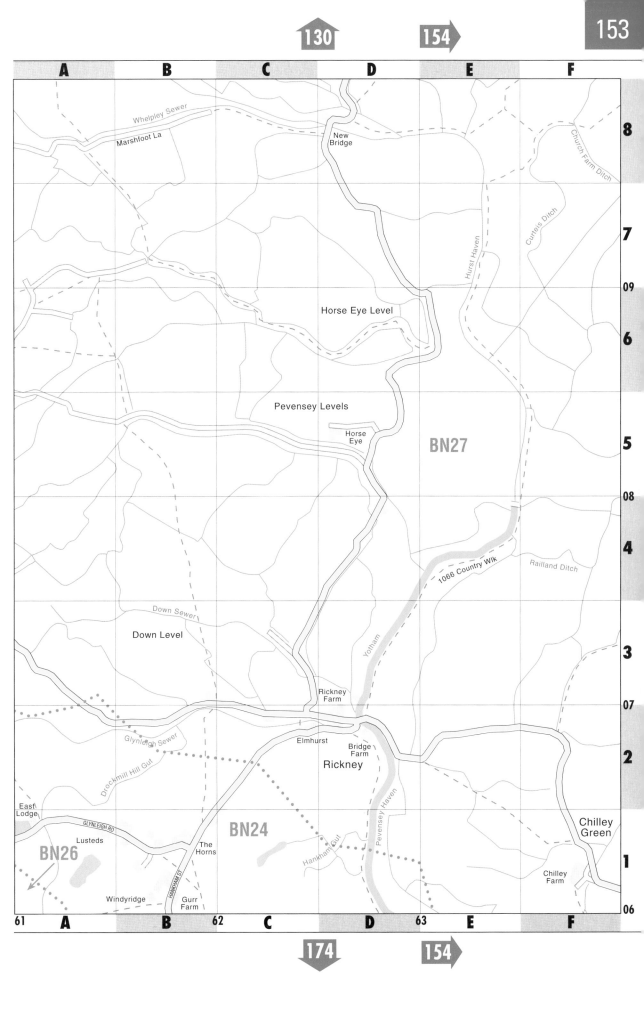

← 153
131

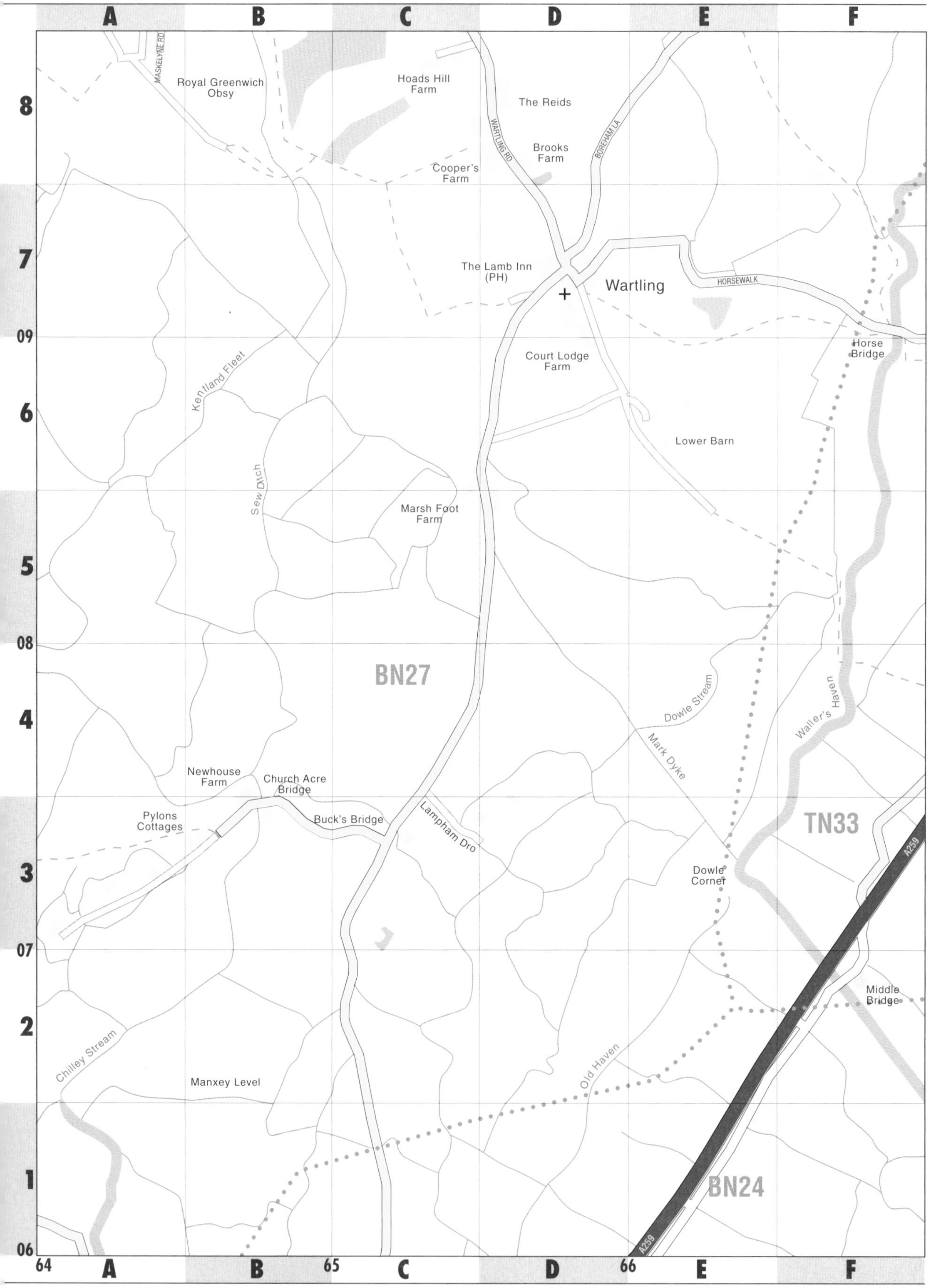

A   **B**   **C**   **D**   **E**   **F**

8

MASKELYNE RD

Royal Greenwich
Obsy

Hoads Hill
Farm

The Reids

Brooks
Farm

WARTLING RD

BOREHAM LA

Cooper's
Farm

7

The Lamb Inn
(PH)

Wartling

HORSEWALK

09

Horse
Bridge

Kentland Fleet

Court Lodge
Farm

6

Lower Barn

Sew Ditch

Marsh Foot
Farm

5

08

BN27

Dowle Stream

Waller's Haven

4

Mark Dyke

TN33

A259

Newhouse
Farm

Church Acre
Bridge

Pylons
Cottages

Buck's Bridge

Lampham Dro

Dowle
Corner

3

07

Middle
Bridge

2

Chilley Stream

Manxey Level

Old Haven

A259

1

BN24

06

64   **A**   **B**   65   **C**   **D**   66   **E**   **F**

← 153
175

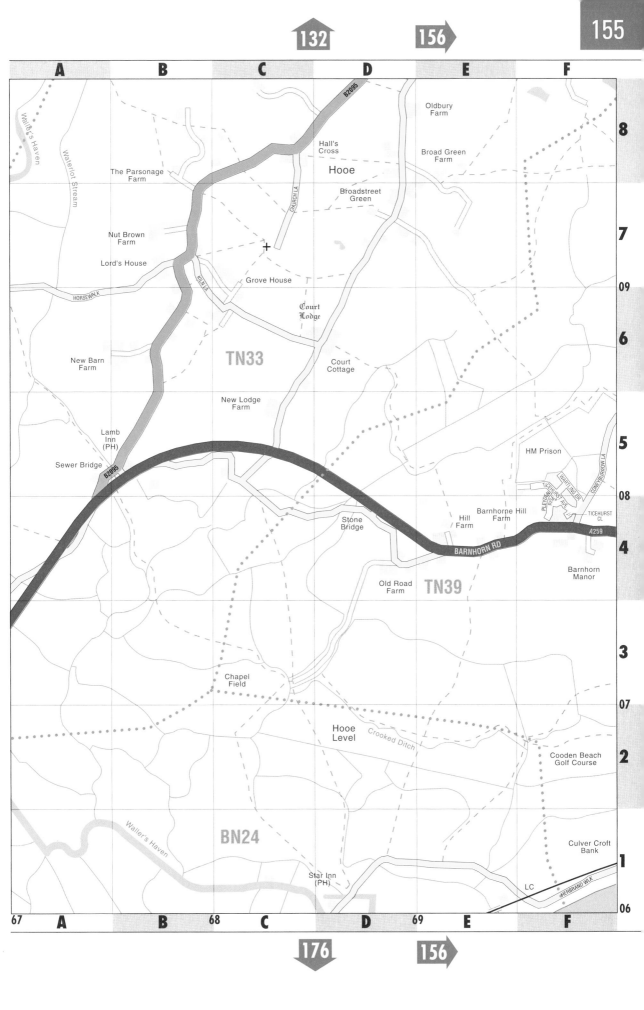

A B C D E F

8
7
09
6
5
08
4
3
07
2
1
06

Waller's Haven
Waterlot Stream

B2095

Oldbury Farm

The Parsonage Farm

Hall's Cross

Broad Green Farm

Hooe

Broadstreet Green

CHURCH LA

Nut Brown Farm

Lord's House

HORSEWALK

Grove House

KILN LA

Court Lodge

TN33

New Barn Farm

Court Cottage

New Lodge Farm

HM Prison

Lamb Inn (PH)

CONEYBURROW LA

WARTLING DR

TICEHURST RISE
PLEYDENHURST AVE

Sewer Bridge

B2095

TICEHURST CL

Barnhorne Hill Farm

Hill Farm

A259

Stone Bridge

BARNHORN RD

Barnhorn Manor

Old Road Farm

TN39

Chapel Field

Hooe Level

Crooked Ditch

Cooden Beach Golf Course

Waller's Haven

BN24

Culver Croft Bank

Star Inn (PH)

LC

HERBRAND WLK

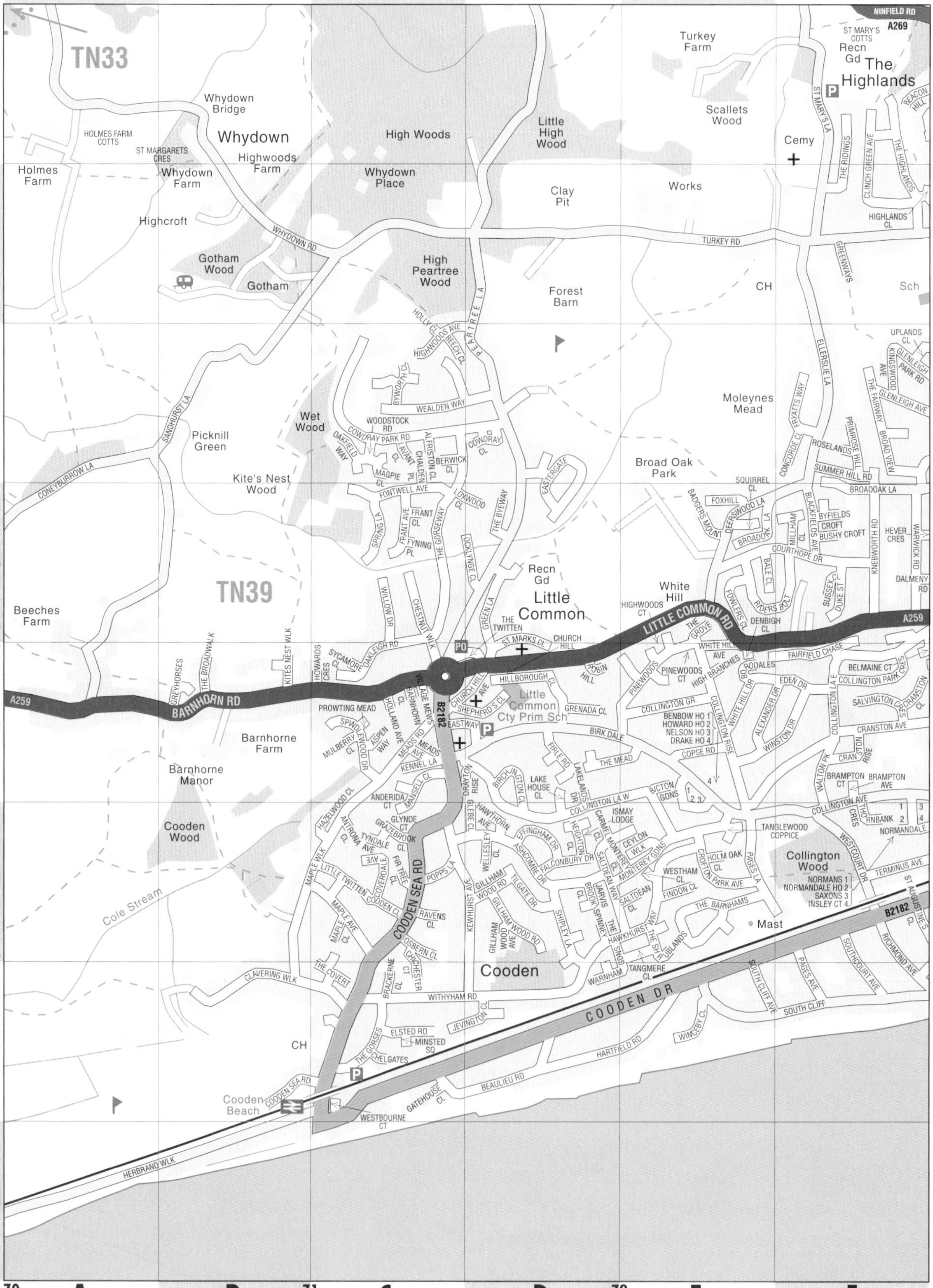

155
133
A B C D E F
8 7 6 5 4 3 2 1
09 08 07 06
70 71 72
TN33
TN39
Whydown Bridge
Whydown
Holmes Farm Cotts
St Margarets Cres
Whydown Farm
Highwoods Farm
Holmes Farm
Highcroft
High Woods
Whydown Place
Little High Wood
Clay Pit
Turkey Farm
Scallets Wood
Works
Cemy
St Mary's Cotts
Recn Gd
The Highlands
Ninfield Rd
A269
Whydown Rd
Turkey Rd
Gotham Wood
Gotham
High Peartree Wood
Forest Barn
CH
Sch
Peartree La
Holly Cl
Highwoods Ave
Beech Cl
Bynworth Cl
Wealden Way
Woodstock Rd
Cowdray Park Rd
Oakfield Way
Lavant Cl
Chalden Pl
Alfriston Cl
Berwick Cl
Cowdray Cl
Magpie Cl
Fontwell Ave
Loxwood Cl
Spring La
Frant Ave
Frant Cl
Fyning Pl
The Gorseway
Ocklynge Cl
The Byeway
Eastergate
Wet Wood
Picknill Green
Kite's Nest Wood
Sandhurst La
Coneyburrow La
Moleynes Mead
Fryatts Way
Concorde Cl
Roselands
Ellerslie La
Broad Oak Park
Squirrel Cl
Foxhill
Badgers Mount
Deerswood La
Broadoak La
Millham Cl
Blackfields Ave
Byfields Croft
Bushy Croft
Courthope Dr
Summer Hill Rd
Broadoak La
Primrose Hill
Kingswood Ave
The Fairway
Broad View
Glenleigh Ave
Glenleigh Park Rd
Uplands Cl
Greenways
Highlands Cl
Clinch Green Ave
The Ridings
The Highlands
St Mary's La
Beacon Hill
Hever Cres
Knebworth Rd
Warwick Rd
Dalmeny Rd
Sussex Cl
Duke St
Bale Cl
Ryders Bolt
Fowlers Cl
Denbigh Cl
White Hill
Highwoods Ct
Recn Gd
Little Common
The Twitten
Church Hill
St Marks Cl
Little Common Rd
A259
The Grove
White Hill Ave
High Branches
Rodales
Fairfield Chase
Belmaine Ct
Collington Park Cres
Cranston Cl
Salvington Cres
Cranston Ave
Cranston Rise
Walton Pk
Brampton Ct
Brampton Ave
Collington Ave
Thornbank
Normandale
Westcourt Dr
Terminus Ave
Collington Wood
Normans 1
Normandale Ho 2
Saxons 3
Insley Ct 4
St Augustines Cl
B2182
Southcourt Ave
Richmond Ave
Pages Ave
South Cliff Ave
South Cliff
Beeches Farm
Willow Dr
Chestnut Wlk
Green La
Barnhorn Rd
Greyhorses
The Broadwalk
Kites Nest Wlk
Howards Cres
Sycamore Cl
Oakleigh Rd
PO
Hillborough Cl
Robin Hill
Pinewoods
Pinewoods Ct
Eden Dr
Collington Gr
Benbow Ho 1
Howard Ho 2
Nelson Ho 3
Drake Ho 4
Copse Rd
Collington Rise
White Hill Dr
Alexander Dr
Winston Dr
Collington La E
Prowting Mead
Village Mews
Barnhorn
Holland Ave
Spindlewood Dr
Aspen Way
Mulberry Cl
Meads Rd
Meads Ave
Kennel La
B2182
Church Hill Ave
Shepherd's Cl
Little Common Cty Prim Sch
Eastway
Grenada Cl
Birk Dale
The Mead
Firle Rd
Lakelands Dr
Lake House Cl
Birchington Cl
Drayton Rise
Collington La W
Bicton Gdns
Ismay Lodge
Tanglewood Coppice
Barnhorne Farm
Barnhorne Manor
Cooden Wood
Hazelwood Cl
Anderida Ct
Mansell Cl
Glynde Ct
Antrona Cl
Grazebrook Cl
Tyndale Ave
Fir Tree Cl
Coverdale Ave
Hawthorn Ave
Glebe Cl
Effingham Dr
Ashcombe Dr
Heighton Cl
Carmel Cl
Monterey Cl
Ceylon Wlk
Monterey Gdns
Westham Cl
Crofton Park Ave
Holm Oak Cl
Pages La
Falconbury Dr
Saltdean Way
Saltdean Cl
Findon Cl
The Barnhams
Mast
Maple Wlk
Little Twitten
Cooden Cl
Cooden Sea Rd
Popps La
Ravens Cl
Kewhurst Ave
Wellesley Cl
Gillham Wood Rd
Tilgate Dr
Brook Cl
Spinney
Jarvis
The Hawkhurst Way
Shipley La
The Ship
Ublands
Gillham Wood Ave
Gillham Wood Rd
Osbern Cl
Chichester Ct
Chester Cl
Brackerne Cl
Cooden
Sings
Warnham
Tangmere Cl
Cole Stream
Maple Ave
Maple Cl
The Covert
Clavering Wlk
Withyham Rd
Jevington Cl
Cooden Dr
Wingeby Cl
Hartfield Rd
Elsted Rd
Minsted Sq
The Gorses
Chelgates
CH
Cooden Sea Rd
Cooden Beach
Gatehouse Cl
Beaulieu Rd
Westbourne Ct
Herbrand Wlk

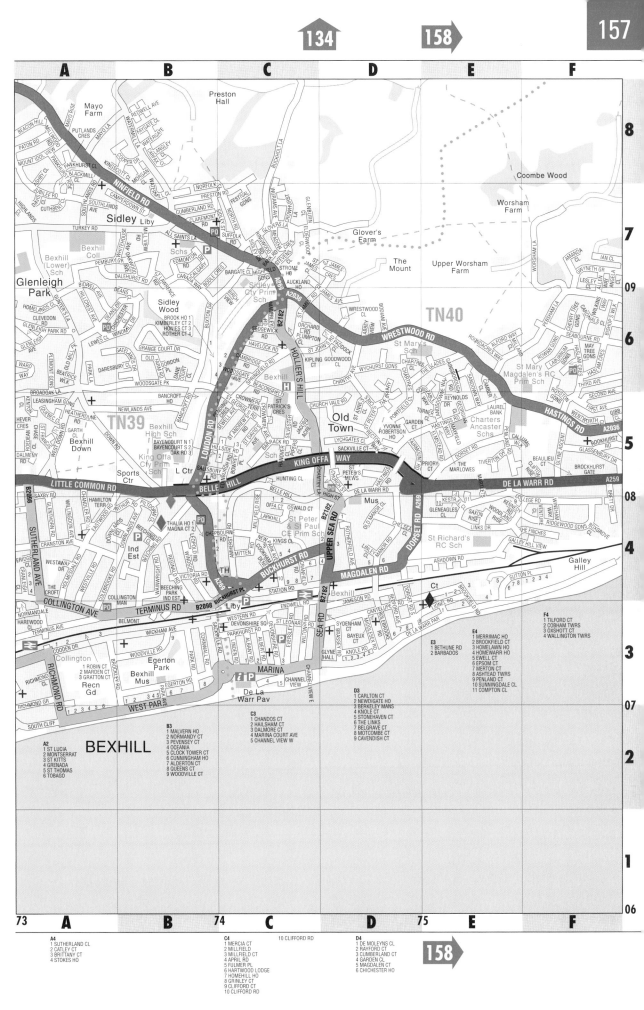

157
135

A **B** **C** **D** **E** **F**

8

Nature Reserve

FERNSIDE AVE

GEORGIAN WICK

FIELD WAY

HERON CL
MAGPIE CL
FIELD WAY
WARREN CL
BUNTING CL

KITE CL

West
St Leonards
Cty Prim
Sch

GANTON PL

THE LINKS
FERN RD
THE DORRIE

LYTHAM CL

REEDSWOOD RD

ASTEN

HARLEY SHUTE RD

Saxon
Mount Sch

CARNOUSTIE CL

WENTWORTH WAY

MUIRFIELD CL

MUIRFIELD WY
SANDWICH

TURNBERRY CL

7

Pebsham
Wood

Combe Haven

TN38

Harley
Shute

WILLIAM RD

EDINBURGH RD

Filsham
Valley Sch

SUNNINGDALE DR

GLEAGLES DR

FILSHAM VALLEY

BIRKHILL WAY

COLLINGWOOD DR

TN40

Refuse Tip

CONQUEROR RD

West
St Leonards

FILSHAM RD

ST VINCENT'S

West
St Leonards

LAUREL

1 IAN CL
2 GWYNETH GR
3 CHRISTINE CL

Pebsham
Farm

HARLEY WAY

LOVAT
MEAD

West St Leonards
Prim Sch

St Vincent's
Sch

09

TOP CROSS RD

Pebsham
La

Playing Fields

CLIFF CT

B2092

KEYMER CL

ST SAVIOUR'S RD

FINLEY
CT

WEST HILL RD

BUCKHOLT AVE

PEBSHAM DR

FILSHAM DR

ARNBURY RD

RAILWAY COTTS

GROSVENOR CRES

6

PENHURST DR

DIANA CL

SILVA CL

Nursery

Pebsham

Bulverhythe

BEXHILL RD

CLIFTONVILLE
WAY

BULVERHYTHE RD

TA
Ctr

SEASIDE

WILTON
HO

GROSVENOR GDNS

SEA RD

A259

GAVIN AVE

ASTOR CL

MISTLEY CL

LONG AVE

CLIFTONVILLE RD

1 SEASIDE WAY
2 KEATS CL
3 WEST HILL MEWS
4 FLORIDA CT

SEABOURNE RD

WANNOCK CL

DALLINGTON CL

West Marina

LULLINGTON CL

THAKEHAM CL

KINVER CL

MARTYNS WAY

BRIDGE WAY

BARN CL

GLYNE DR

CLAXTON RD

AIRLIGHT

HURSTWOOD RD

ABBEY DR

HYTHE AVE

PO

5

A2036

Schs

HASTINGS RD

A2036

Glyne
Gap

BELLEIGH AVE

FIRST AVE

GIBB CL

GRAND AVE

SCHOOL PL

YORK RD

GLOUCESTER AVE

KENT CL

LEWIS AVE

PENN LA

A259
DE LA WARR RD

08

RAVENSIDE
RET & L PK

4

3

07

2

1

06

76 **A** 77 **B** **C** 78 **D** **E** **F**

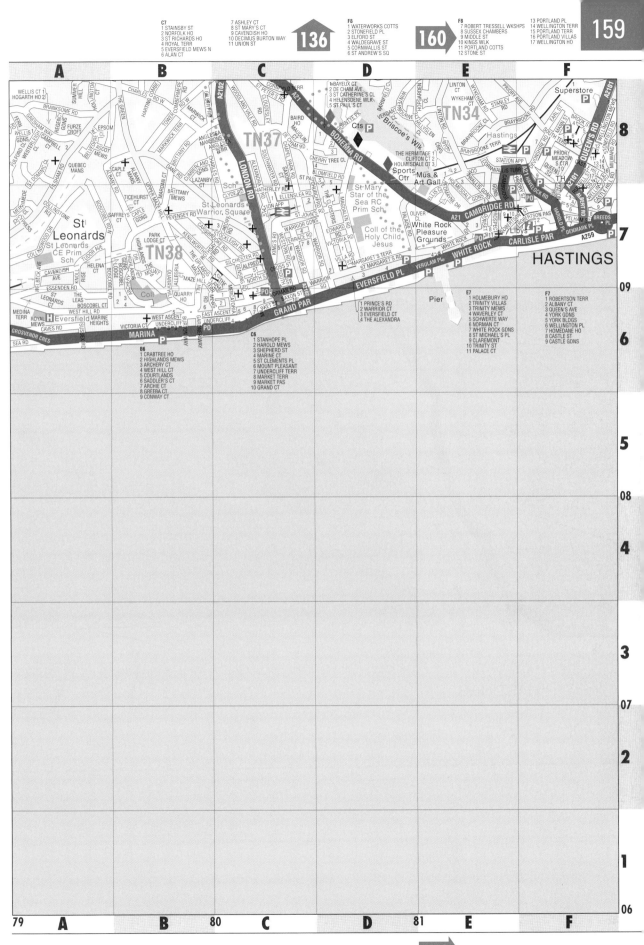

C7
1 STAINSBY ST
2 NORFOLK HO
3 ST RICHARDS HO
4 ROYAL TERR
5 EVERSFIELD MEWS N
6 ALAN CT

7 ASHLEY CT
8 ST MARY'S CT
9 CAVENDISH HO
10 DECIMUS BURTON WAY
11 UNION ST

136

F8
1 WATERWORKS COTTS
2 STONEFIELD PL
3 ELFORD ST
4 WALDEGRAVE ST
5 CORNWALLIS SQ
6 ST ANDREW'S SQ

160

F8
7 ROBERT TRESSELL WKSHPS
8 SUSSEX CHAMBERS
9 MIDDLE ST
10 KINGS WLK
11 PORTLAND COTTS
12 STONE ST

13 PORTLAND PL
14 WELLINGTON TERR
15 PORTLAND TERR
16 PORTLAND VILLAS
17 WELLINGTON HO

HASTINGS

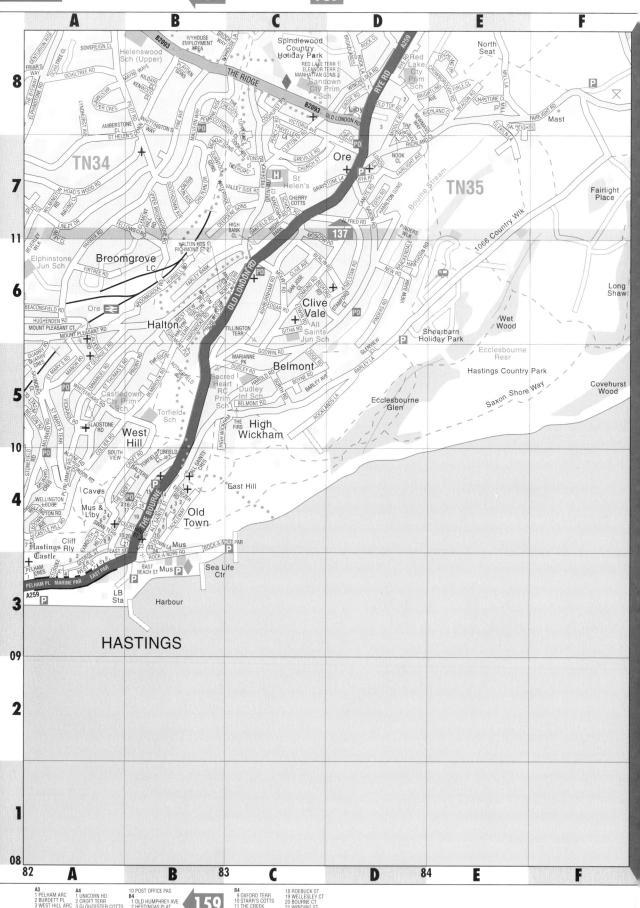

HASTINGS

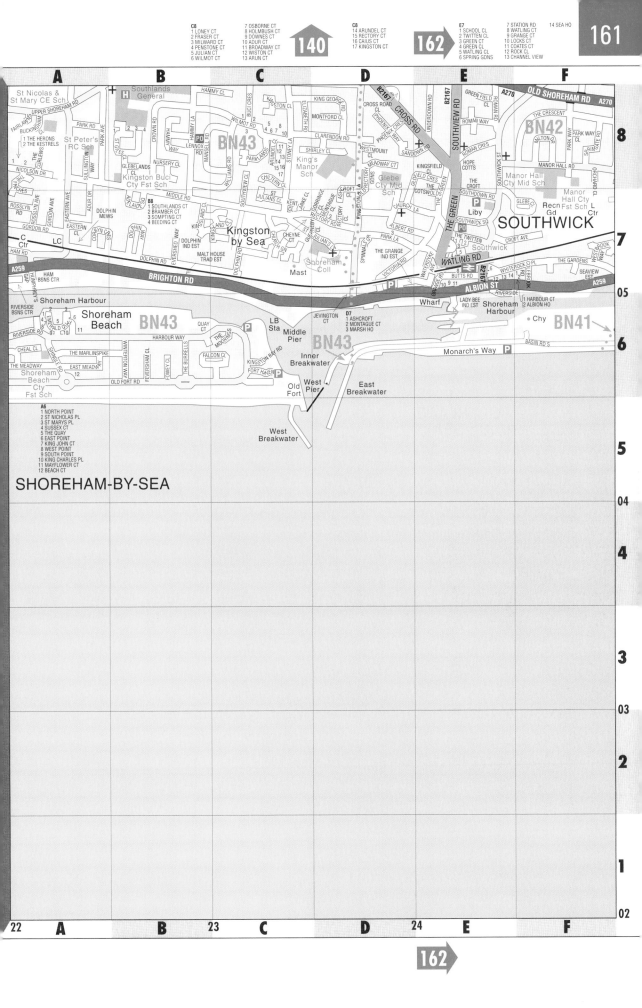

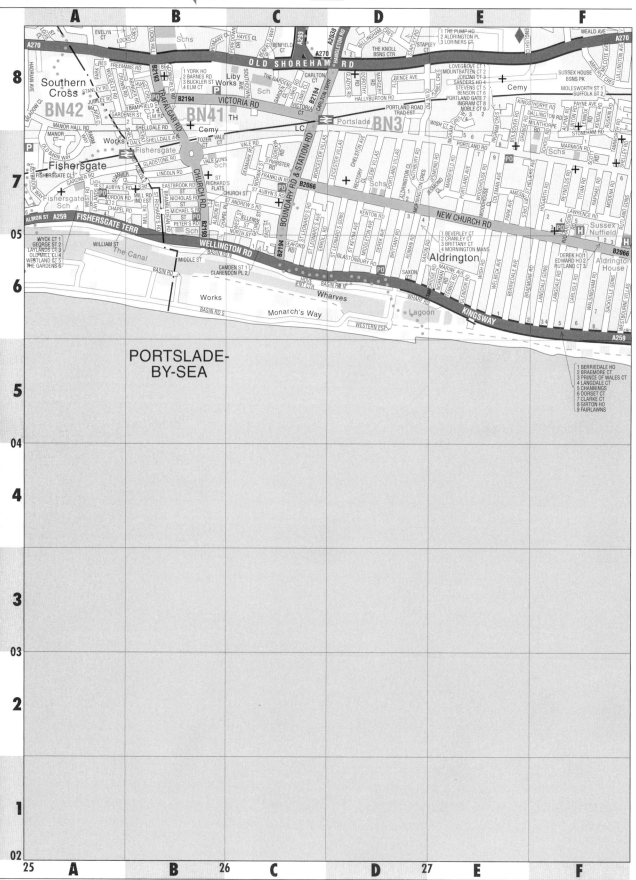

F7
1 MAINSTONE RD
2 EVEREST HO
3 ST PHILIPS MEWS
4 LION MEWS
5 RICHARDSON CT
6 STRATTON CT

PORTSLADE-
BY-SEA

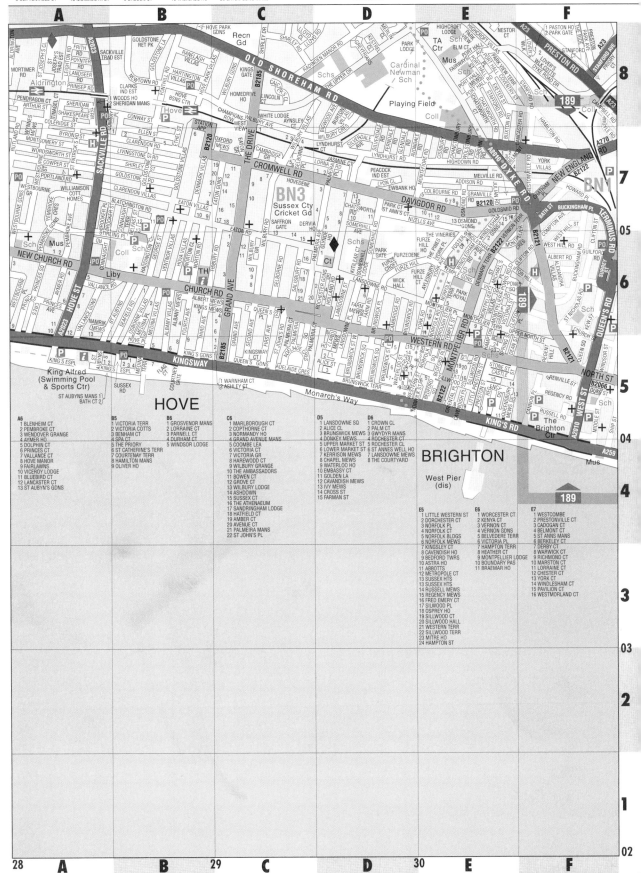

142 → **164**

B7
1 CONWAY CT
2 CLARENDON HO
3 ELLEN HO
4 GOLDSTONE HO
5 LIVINGSTONE HO
6 CLIFTONVILLE CT
7 STEYNING CT
8 BRAMBER CT
9 EATON CT
10 GRANVILLE CT
11 HADDINGTON ST
12 MALVERN ST
13 MONMOUTH ST

C7
1 DEVONSHIRE CT
2 CORNWALL CT
3 SOMERSET CT
4 JANESTON CT
5 STIRLING CT
6 BRECON CT
7 ELIZABETH CT
8 PHILIP CT
9 BALTIMORE CT
10 DRIVE LODGE
11 EATON MANOR
12 VERIC
13 VALVERDE HO
14 VALENTINE CT
15 HEREFORD CT
16 GAINSBOROUGH HO
17 EATON GATE
18 CHARIS CT
19 EATON HALL
20 EATON GDNS MANS

C7
21 VANBRUGH CT

D7
1 COWDRAY CT
2 GOODWOOD CT
3 CROMWELL CT
4 WILLOW CT

D7
5 KINSALE CT
6 PALMEIRA HO
7 BELL MEAD
8 AMBER CT
9 CONISTON CT
10 SOMERHILL CT
11 BERESFORD CT
12 PARHAM HO
13 PETWORTH HO

A6
1 BLENHEIM CT
2 PEMBROKE CT
3 WENDOVER GRANGE
4 AYMER HO
5 DOLPHIN CT
6 PRINCES CT
7 VALLANCE CT
8 HOVE MANOR
9 FAIRLAWNS
10 VICEROY LODGE
11 BLUEBIRD CT
12 LANCASTER CT
13 ST AUBYN'S GDNS

B5
1 VICTORIA TERR
2 VICTORIA COTTS
3 BENHAM CT
4 SPA CT
5 THE PRIORY
6 ST CATHERINE'S TERR
7 COURTENAY TERR
8 HAMILTON MANS
9 OLIVER HO

B6
1 GROSVENOR MANS
2 LORRAINE CT
3 PARNELL CT
4 DURHAM CT
5 WINDSOR LODGE

C6
1 MARLBOROUGH CT
2 COPTHORNE CT
3 NORMANDY HO
4 GRAND AVENUE MANS
5 COOMBE LEA
6 VICTORIA CT
7 VICTORIA GR
8 HAREWODD CT
9 WILBURY GRANGE
10 THE AMBASSADORS
11 BOWEN CT
12 GROVE CT
13 WILBURY LODGE
14 ASHDOWN
15 SUSSEX CT
16 THE ATHENAEUM
17 SANDRINGHAM LODGE
18 HATFIELD CT
19 AMBER CT
20 AVENUE CT
21 PALMEIRA MANS
22 ST JOHN'S PL

D5
1 LANSDOWNE SQ
2 ALICE CL
3 BRUNSWICK MEWS
4 DONKEY MEWS
5 UPPER MARKET ST
6 LOWER MARKET ST
7 KERRISON MEWS
8 CHAPEL MEWS
9 WATERLOO HO
10 EMBASSY CT
11 GOLDEN LA
12 CAVANDISH MEWS
13 IVY MEWS
14 CROSS ST
15 FARMAN ST

D6
1 CROWN CL
2 PALM CT
3 GWYDYR MANS
4 ROCHESTER CT
5 ROCHESTER CL
6 ST ANNES WELL HO
7 LANSDOWNE MEWS
8 THE COURTYARD

E5
1 LITTLE WESTERN ST
2 DORCHESTER CT
3 NORFOLK PL
4 NORFOLK CT
5 NORFOLK BLDGS
6 NORFOLK MEWS
7 KINGSLEY CT
8 CAVENDISH HO
9 BEDFORD TWRS
10 ASTRA HO
11 ABBOTTS
12 METROPOLE CT
13 SUSSEX HTS
13 SUSSEX HTS
14 RUSSELL MEWS
15 REGENCY MEWS
16 FRED EMERY CT
17 SILWOOD PL
18 OSPREY HO
19 SILLWOOD CT
20 SILLWOOD HALL
21 WESTERN TERR
22 SILLWOOD TERR
23 MITRE HO
24 HAMPTON ST

E6
1 WORCESTER CT
2 KENYA CT
3 VERNON CT
4 VERNON GDNS
5 BELVEDERE TERR
6 VICTORIA PL
7 HAMPTON TERR
8 HEATHER CT
9 MONTPELLIER LODGE
10 BOUNDARY PAS
11 BRAEMAR HO

E7
1 WESTCOMBE
2 PRESTONVILLE CT
3 CADOGAN CT
4 BELMONT CT
5 ST ANNS MANS
6 BERKELEY CT
7 DERBY CT
8 WARWICK CT
9 RICHMOND CT
10 MARSTON CT
11 LORRAINE CT
12 CHESTER CT
13 YORK CT
14 WINDLESHAM CT
15 PAVILION CT
16 WESTMORLAND CT

164 → For full street detail of the highlighted area see page 189.

B8
1 ST SAVIOURS CT
2 ROUND HILL RD
3 ROUND HILL ST
4 DITCHLING CT
5 MAYO CT
6 CENTENARY IND EST

7 ASHDOWN RD
8 EDINBURGH RD

C5
1 LAKE VIEW
2 HILARY LODGE
3 THE GRAPERIES
4 SLOANE CT

◀ 163

C5
1 PATCHING LODGE
6 JACQUELINE DU PRE CT
7 EVELYN GLENNIE CT
8 CELLO CT
C6
1 FINSBURY LODGE

▲ 143

C6
2 HIGHDEN
3 WESTMOUNT
4 CROWN HILL
5 SYDNEY TIDY HO
6 ATTREE CT
7 CARN CT

C7
1 AINSWORTH HO
2 BARCLAY HO
3 NAPIER HO
4 JOHNSON BANK
5 UPPER WELLINGTON RD
6 ST MARTIN'S FLATS
7 CORONATION ST
8 NORMANTON ST

C8
1 FREEHOLD TERR
2 SAUNDERS PARK HO
3 STANLEY CT

8 BARN FIELD GDNS
9 WINDERMERE CT
10 STONEHURST RD

4 FREEHOLD TERR
5 SAUNDERS PARK HO
6 STANLEY CT

4 INVERNESS RD
5 ABERDEEN RD
6 LEWIS CT
7 PEVENSEY RD
8 FAIRLIGHT PL
9 ST LEONARD'S RD
10 OLD VIADUCT CT

11 SHANKLIN CT
12 NEWMARKET TERR

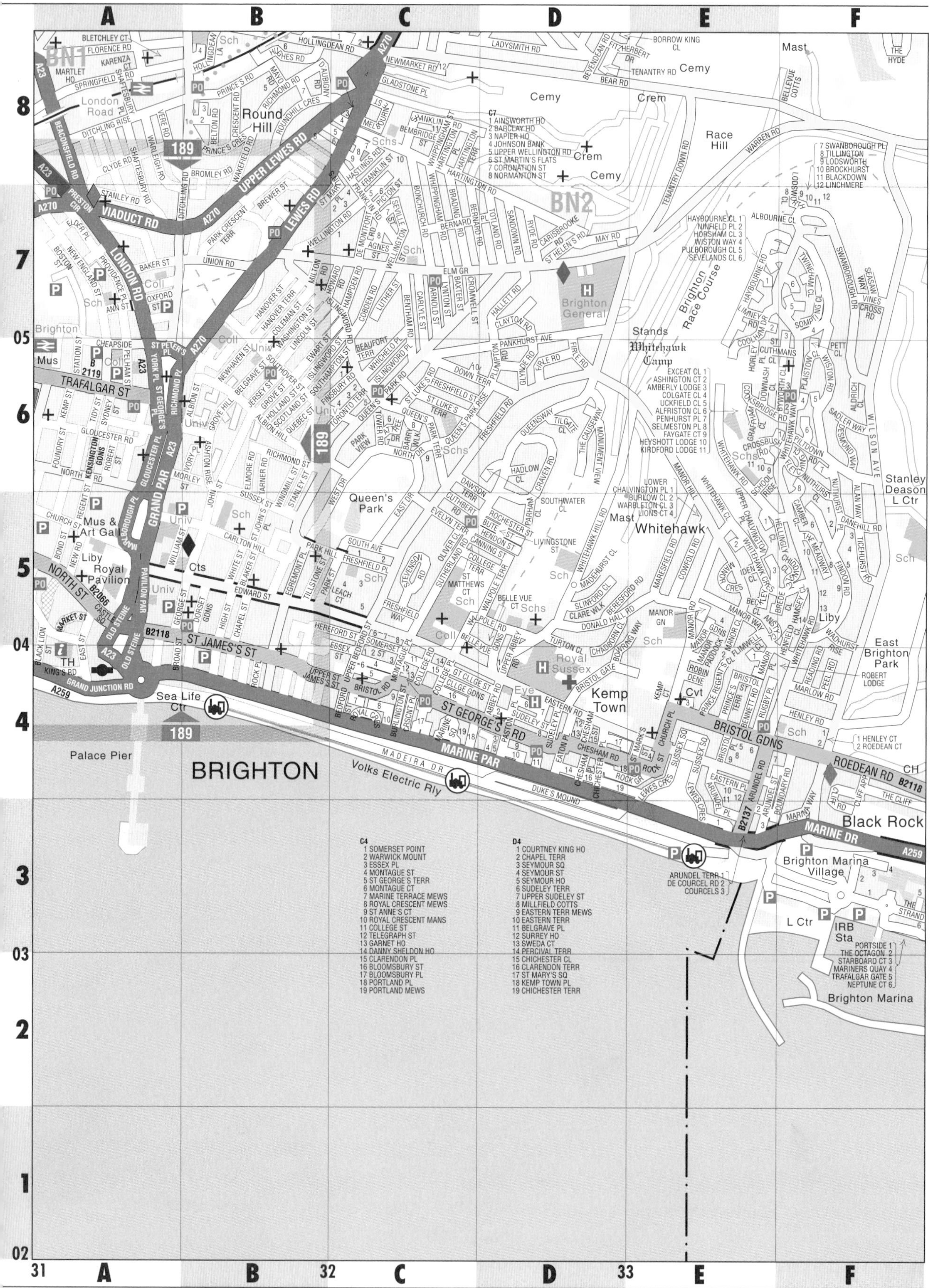

7 SWANBOROUGH PL
8 TILLINGTON
9 LODSWORTH
10 BROCKHURST
11 BLACKDOWN
12 LINCHMERE

C4
1 SOMERSET POINT
2 WARWICK MOUNT
3 ESSEX PL
4 MONTAGUE ST
5 ST GEORGE'S TERR
6 MONTAGUE CL
7 MARINE TERRACE MEWS
8 ROYAL CRESCENT MEWS
9 ST ANNE'S CT
10 ROYAL CRESCENT MANS
11 COLLEGE ST
12 TELEGRAPH ST
13 GARNET HO
14 DANNY SHELDON HO
15 CLARENDON PL
16 BLOOMSBURY ST
17 BLOOMSBURY PL
18 PORTLAND PL
19 PORTLAND MEWS

D4
1 COURTNEY KING HO
2 CHAPEL TERR
3 SEYMOUR SQ
4 SEYMOUR ST
5 SEYMOUR HO
6 SUDELEY TERR
7 UPPER SUDELEY ST
8 MILLFIELD COTTS
9 EASTERN TERR MEWS
10 EASTERN TERR
11 BELGRAVE PL
12 SURREY HO
13 SWEDA CT
14 PERCIVAL TERR
15 CHICHESTER CL
16 CLARENDON TERR
17 ST MARY'S SQ
18 KEMP TOWN PL
19 CHICHESTER TERR

ARUNDEL TERR 1
DE COURCEL RD 2
COURCELS 3

PORTSIDE 1
THE OCTAGON 2
STARBOARD CT 3
MARINERS QUAY 4
TRAFALGAR GATE 5
NEPTUNE CT 6

Map area labels (as printed):

BN1, BN2, Round Hill, Brighton, Palace Pier, BRIGHTON, Sea Life Ctr, Queen's Park, Whitehawk, Whitehawk Camp, Brighton Race Course, Race Hill, Kemp Town, Black Rock, Brighton Marina, Brighton Marina Village, East Brighton Park, Royal Pavilion, Mus & Art Gall, Stanley Deason L Ctr, Volks Electric Rly, Madeira Dr, Marine Par, Marine Dr, Royal Sussex, Brighton General

For full street detail of the highlighted area see page 189.

◀ 163

E4
1 PLAYDEN CL
2 PRINCE REGENT'S CT
3 BRISTOL MEWS
4 SUSSEX MEWS
5 RUGBY CT
6 ARUNDEL CT
7 BELL TOWER IND EST
8 HOLLINGBOURNE CT
9 LANGHURST

10 ARUNDEL MEWS
11 KEMPTOWN MEWS
12 LEWES MEWS

F5
1 SANDERSTEAD
2 KINGSFOLD
3 BYLANDS
4 GRINSTEAD MOUNT
5 LANCING CT
6 HURSTWOOD
7 COTSWOLD PL
8 WELLSBOURNE
9 SOUTH LODGE

10 LICHFIELD CT
11 FRAMFIELD
12 RYECROFT
13 WESTHAM
14 WALTER MAY HO

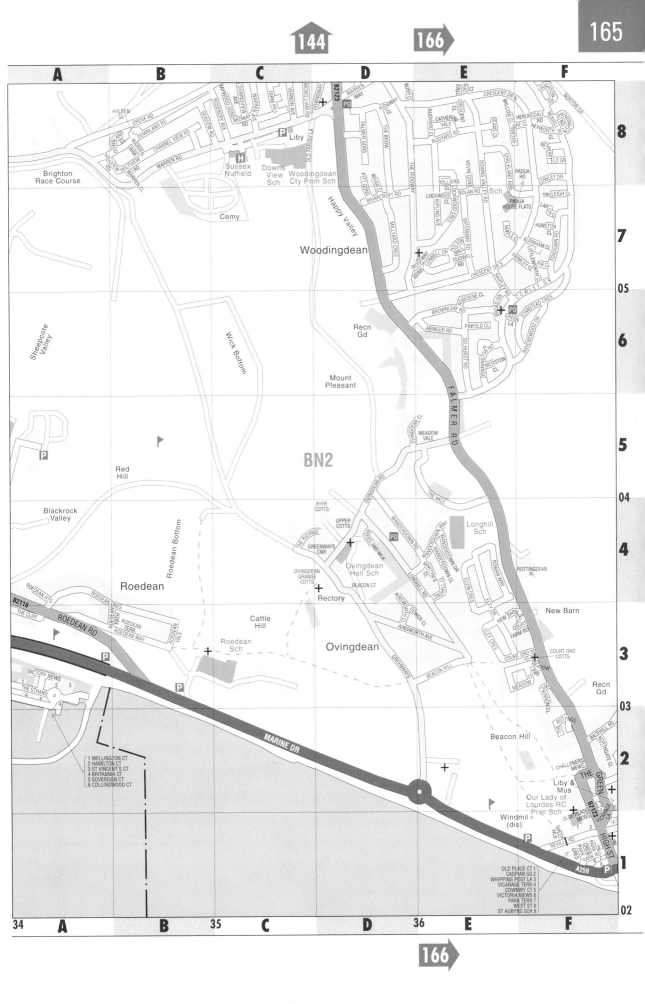

8

HYLDEN CL
BANWOOD GDNS
DOWNSVIEW AVE
WARREN HILL
FARM HILL
VERNON AVE
McWILLIAM RD
DOWNSWAY
B2123
WARREN WAY
RIDGWAY
BUSH CL
CRESCENT DR N
HERONSDALE RD
LAUGHTON RD
BEXHILL RD
NORTON DR
HEYWORTH CL
NEHERFIELD GN

ROSEBERY AVE
DOWNLAND RD
SEAVIEW RD
PO
Liby
FALMER GDNS
THE BROW
CATHERINE VALE
CRESCENT CL
WILLOW CL
DEANS CL
LOVE CL
CHALK CL
PADUA HO
COWLEY DR
NEHERFIELD GN

DROVE RD
CHANNEL VIEW RD
MIDWAY RD
H
Sussex
Nuffield
Downs
View
Sch
Woodingdean
Cty Prim Sch
PITT GDNS
BRIARCROFT RD
THE RIDGWAY
RUDYARD CL
RUDYARD RD
KEVIN GDNS
DOWNS VALLEY RD
LOCKWOOD CRES
NOLAN RD
VILLIERS
Sch
TRULEIGH CL

DOWNLAND
WARREN
RISE
HOLTVIEW RD
HILLVIEW RD
WARREN CL
WARREN RD
Cemy
Happy Valley
LOCKWOOD CL
KIPLING AVE
BATEMANS RD
CHALKLAND RI
PADUA HOUSE FLATS
LARCH CL
HUNSTON CL
BURNHAM RD
WOODLEA RD

7

Woodingdean
RIDGWAY
GDNS
CONNELL DR
WOLTON RD
DUDWELL RD
MAPLE CL
CRESCENT DR S
PRIMLEY CL
FIR CL
LITTLEWORTH CL
05

Sheepcote
Valley
Wick Bottom
BROWNLEAF RD
RESEDENE CL
SHIRLEY RD
COWLEY DR
GREEN LA
PO
STANSTEAD CRES
RAVENSWOOD DR

BN2
ABINGER RD
PINFOLD CL
DOWNS CL
MERSTON CL
6

Red
Hill
Mount
Pleasant
SELHURST RD
RD

Blackrock
Valley
BYRE
COTTS
OVINGDEAN RD
MAGPIE CL
MEADOW VALE
FALMER RD
5

Roedean Bottom
UPPER
COTTS
THE RIDINGS
GREENWAYS
CNR
WANDERDOWN WAY
THE VALE
04

Roedean
OVINGDEAN
GRANGE
COTTS
WOODLAND WLK
PO
WANDERDOWN RD
WANDERDOWN DR
WANDERDOWN CL
Longhill
Sch
ROTTINGDEAN PL
4

B2118
ROEDEAN HTS
THE CLIFF
ROEDEAN CRES
BURDEAN
PATH
ROEDEAN
TERR
ROEDEAN WAY
ROEDEAN VALE
Rectory
BEACON CT
MARTIN'S
LONGHILL RD
ROWAN WAY
ELVIN CRES
NEW BARN RD
New Barn

Cattle
Hill
Roedean
Sch
Ovingdean
AINSWORTH CL
TOWER RD
AINSWORTH AVE
GREENWAYS
ELY DR
ELY CRES
NEW BARN
COURT
FARM RD
COURT ORD RD
Court Ord
Cotts
3

ROEDEAN RD
P
P
BEACON HILL RD
MEADOW
Recn
Gd
03

VICTORY MEWS
THE STRAND
1 2 3
6 5 4
P
MARINE DR
1 WELLINGTON CT
2 HAMILTON CT
3 ST VINCENT'S CT
4 BRITANNIA CT
5 SOVEREIGN CT
6 COLLINGWOOD CT
Beacon Hill
RIDINGS
BAZEHILL RD
NOTTINGATE CL
CHALLONERS
MEWS
2

Liby &
Mus
Our Lady of
Lourdes RC
Prim Sch
OLDE PLACE MEWS
THE GREEN
VICARAGE
B2123
HIGH ST

Windmil
(dis)
P
NEVILL RD
SWEET WLK
A259
P

OLD PLACE CT 1
CASPIAN SQ 2
WHIPPING POST LA 3
VICARAGE TERR 4
COWNWY CT 5
VICTORIA MEWS 6
PARK TERR 7
WEST ST 8
ST AUBYNS SCH 9
1

02

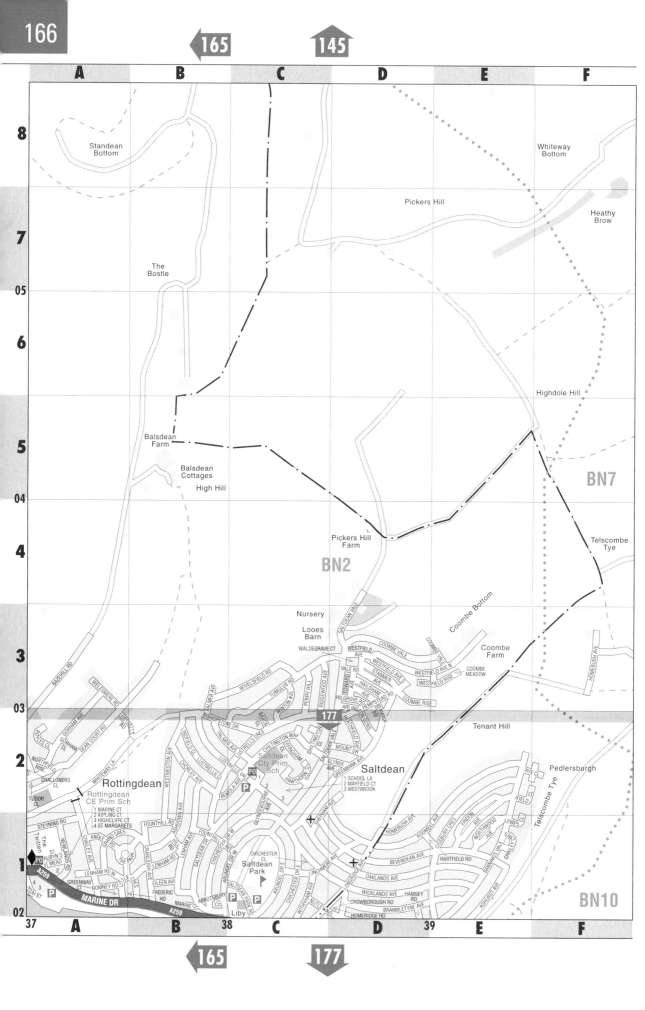

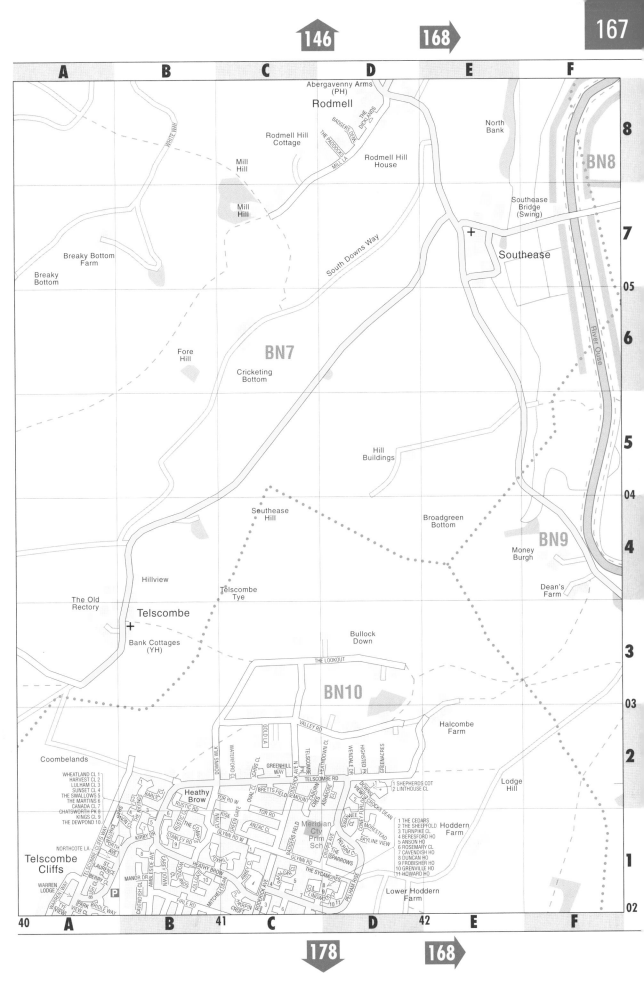

146
168

A B C D E F

8

BN8

Abergavenny Arms
(PH)
Rodmell

North
Bank

Rodmell Hill
Cottage

WHITE WAY

THE DICKLANDS

BADGERS DENE

THE PADDOCKS

MILL LA

Mill
Hill

Rodmell Hill House

Southease
Bridge
(Swing)

7

Mill
Hill

+

Southease

Breaky Bottom
Farm

South Downs Way

05

Breaky
Bottom

6

BN7

River Ouse

Fore
Hill

Cricketing
Bottom

5

Hill
Buildings

04

Southease
Hill

Broadgreen
Bottom

BN9

4

Hillview

Telscombe
Tye

Money
Burgh

The Old
Rectory

Telscombe

Dean's
Farm

+

Bank Cottages
(YH)

Bullock
Down

3

THE LOOKOUT

03

BN10

Coombelands

VALLEY RD

GOLD LA

Halcombe
Farm

Lodge
Hill

WHEATLAND CL 1
HARVEST CL 2
LULHAM CL 3
SUNSET CL 4
THE SWALLOWS 5
THE MARTINS 6
CANADA CL 7
CHATSWORTH PK 8
KINGS CL 9
THE DEWPOND 10

DOWN VIEW SNWOD

WATERFORD CL

JOHNS CL

TELSCOMBE RD

HEATHDOWN CL

WENDALE DR

HIGHSTED

GREENACRES

2

Heathy
Brow

GREENHILL
WAY

BRETTS FIELD

RODMOUNT

TELSCOMBE RD

ASHMORE CL

SAUBURN

CRES

SWANMEE

DOWNS
VIEW

CROCKS DEAN

1 SHEPHERDS COT
2 LINTHOUSE CL

BARLE CL

RUSTIC RD

THE COMPANY

TOR RD W

RISE

GREEN GATE

TOR RD

ANZAC CL

BADGERS FIELD

GLYNN RD W

RODERICK AVE N

CONEY FURLONG

MORESTEAD

SKYLINE VIEW

1 THE CEDARS
2 THE SHEEPFOLD
3 TURNPIKE CL
4 BERESFORD HO
5 ANSON HO
6 ROSEMARY CL
7 CAVENDISH HO
8 DUNCAN HO
9 FROBISHER HO
10 GRENVILLE HO
11 HOWARD HO

Hoddern
Farm

NORTHCOTE LA

RAYMOND CL

KIRBY DR

STANLEY RD

THE COMPANY

GLYNN RD

ABBEY CL

PELHAM RISE

CRIPPS AVE

THE
SPARROWS

DOWN CL

Meridian
Cty
Prim
Sch

Telscombe
Cliffs

ST
LAURENCE

BERRY CL

MANOR DR

AMBLESIDE AVE

HEATHY BROW

SOUTHDOWN

TOXHILL

GLYNN RD

THE SYCAMORES

CLINGWOS

PELHAM RISE

Lower Hoddern
Farm

WARREN
LODGE

WARREN WAY

TYE
VIEW

PARK
VIEW CL

BLIST CL

BISHOPSTONE

CAVENDISH CL

BRIDLE WAY

COLDEAN

MITCHELDEAN

FIRLE RD

RODERICK AVE

PIRPIN
CROFT

GAR

P

02

40 A B 41 C D 42 E F

167
147

A26

LC

Southease

Itford Farm

Itford Hill

White Lion Pond

Red Lion Pond

Mast

Radio Sta

America Farm

South Downs Way

BN8

Well Bottom

Baydean

Baydean Bottom

Cow Wish Bottom

Itford Bottom

Muggery Pope

Stock Cottages

Durham Farm

Manor Farm

BN9

Court Farm

Tarring Neville

Page's New Barn

LC

Works

New Barn

Rodmell HO

DOWNS VILLAS

South Heighton Farm

Piddinghoe

Royal Oak (PH)

River Ouse

Court Farm CL

BROOKSIDE

E2
1 SOUTH VIEW
2 ORCHARD MEWS
3 GUINNESS TRUST BGLWS

South Heighton

HARFIELD CL

ST LEONARDS

THE CLOSE

CANTERCROW HILL

WELLINGTON RD

ST LEONARDS CL

HEIGHTON RD

BRANDS CL

PORT VW

HAMPDEN GDNS

The Wish

PORTLAND TERR 1
FIRLE TERR 2
WEST VIEW TERR 3
MARTELLO CT 4
COTTAGE CL 5.

1 CEDARWELL CL
2 SHEPHERDS CL

BN9

DENTON RISE

ROOKERY CL

LEWES RD

PARK DRIVE

VICARAGE CL

HILL RISE

Denton

HEIGHTON CRES

EDWARD CL

BEACH CL

ACACIA RD

THE GROVE

RECTORY CL

DENTON RD

Mount Pleasant

Nore Down

Brookside Farm

LEWES RD

ST MARTINS CL

TARRING CL

POND CL

YEAST CL

HIPOMELL

NEW RD

DENTON DR

Denton Cty Prim Sch

KING'S AVE

FAIRHOLME RD

CREST RD

SEAVIEW RD

PALMERSTON RD

HOWEY CL

CLAREMONT RD

ARUNDEL RD

MOUNT RD

FALAISE RD

Cemy

PIDDINGHOE MEAD

NORTH QUAY RD

ESTATE RD

A26

B2109

NEW RD

Mus

Paradise Family L Pk

GUINNESS CT

AVIS RD

AVIS CL

AVIS WAY

Ind Est

AVIS PAR

AVIS RD

B2109

BERESFORD RD

HOLMDALE RD

43

44

45

167
179

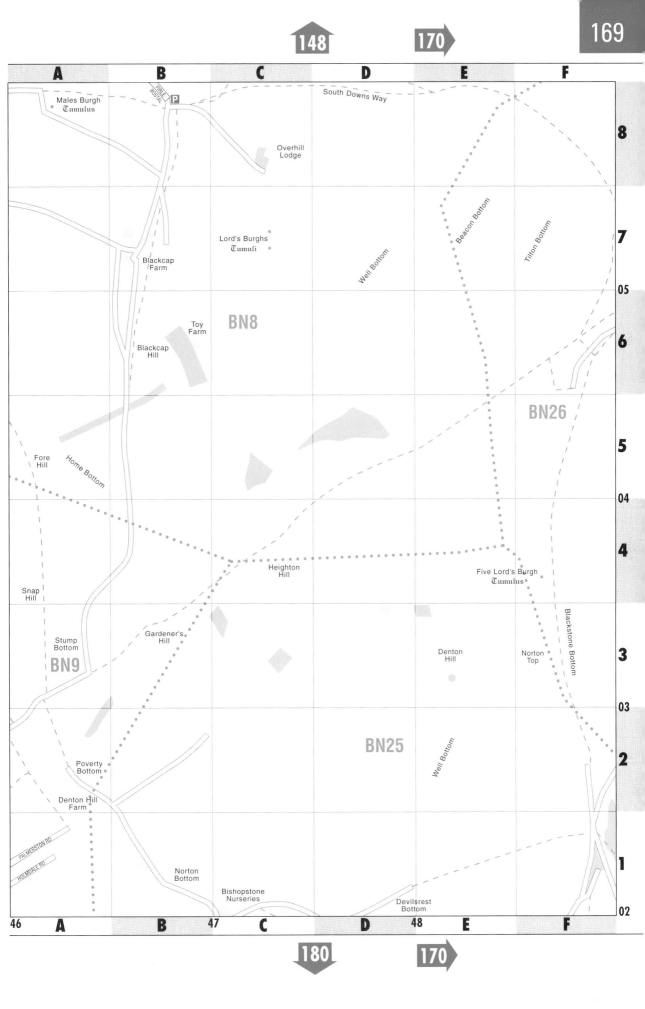

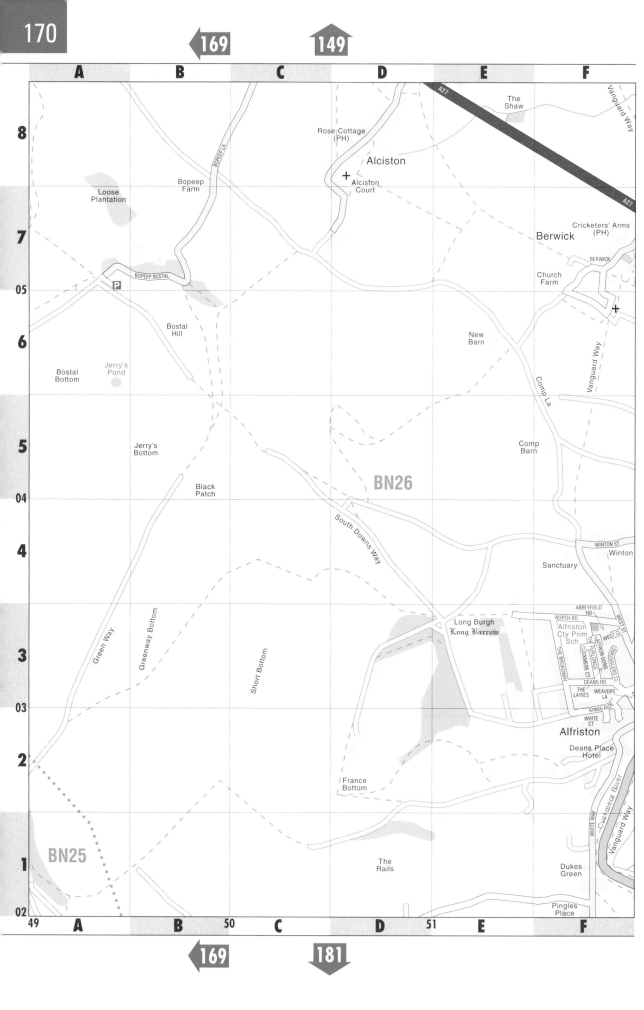

A B C D E F

8

Rose Cottage (PH)

The Shaw

Vanguard Way

A27

Alciston

+ Alciston Court

Berwick

Cricketers' Arms (PH)

BERWICK

Bopeep Farm

Loose Plantation

7

Church Farm

BOPEEP LA

05

P

BOPEEP BOSTAL

Vanguard Way

6

Bostal Hill

New Barn

Vanguard Way

Jerry's Pond

Bostal Bottom

Comp La

5

Jerry's Bottom

Comp Barn

BN26

04

Black Patch

South Downs Way

WINTON ST

Winton

4

Sanctuary

ABBEYFIELD HO

NORTH RD

WEST ST

Long Burgh Long Barrow

Alfriston Cty Prim Sch

SAFFRON GDNS

WEST CT

THE FURLONGS

CUCKMERE CT

SMUGGLERS CT

THE BROADWAY

3

Green Way

Greenway Bottom

Short Bottom

DEANS RD

THE LAINES

WEAVERS LA

03

KINGS RIDE

WHITE CT

Alfriston

Deans Place Hotel

2

France Bottom

Cuckmere River

WHITE WAY

Vanguard Way

1

BN25

The Rails

Dukes Green

Pingles Place

02

49

A B 50 C D 51 E F

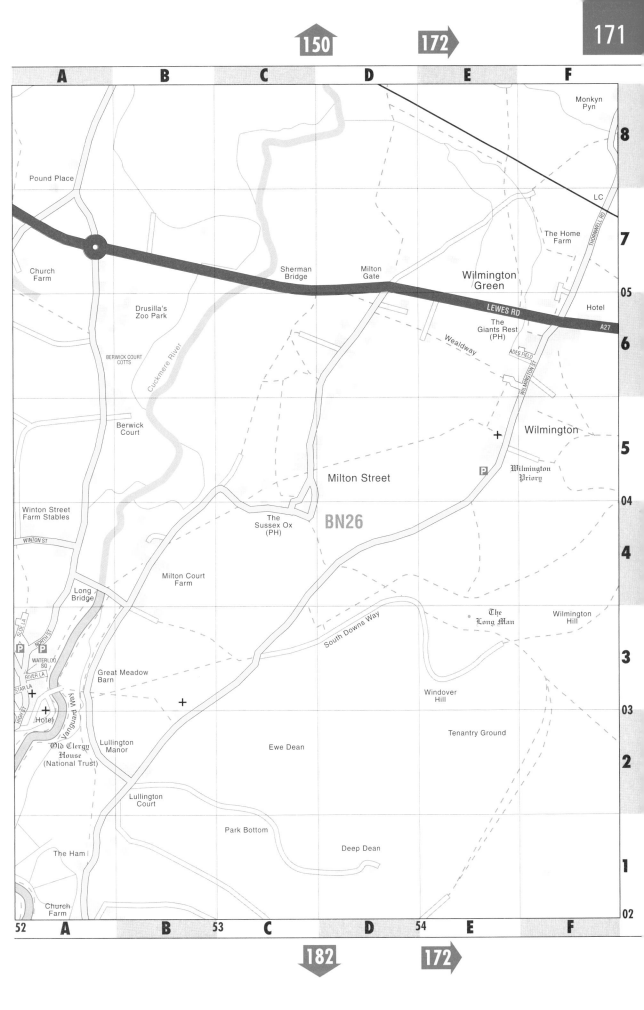

171
151

A   B   C   D   E   F

8

THORNWELL RD
Warren
Farm
Monkyn
Pyn
Hide
Farm
Cophall
Farm
Cop Hall
Road under
construction

BAY TREE LA
A22

7

Newbarn
Farm
Wootton
Manor
POLEGATE BY-PASS
A27 HAILSHAM RD
HAVERLAND RD
GUARDIAN
ST LEONARDS
TERR
BROOKSIDE AVE
VICTORIA
DIPLOCK RD
CT
DROUET
BROOK ST
GOSFORD WAY

05

GRAND PAR 1
THE BERNHARD BARON COTTAGE HOMES 2

A27

6

A27
LEWES RD
The Flint
House
Farm
A27
OLD DR
SOUTHDOWN CT
A22
HYPERION AVE
BAHRAM RD
SUNSTAR LA
GOLDEN MILLER LA
GAINSBOROUGH LA
BROWN JACK AVE
REYNOLDSTOWN LA
The Stud
Farm
HILARY CL
SNO
BARONS WAY
BERNHARD

The
Rough
Puddingham
Wood
Folkington
Manor Farm
NORTHFIELD
Recn
Gd
WANNOCK DR

5

The
Links
Wannock
Coppice
SOUTHFIELD
GROSVENOR CL
WANNOCK RD
ASHLANDS WAY
THE MILLING

04

The
Holt
Folkington
Manor
MAYFAIR CT
PADDOCK GDNS
LANCING WAY
MILLSTREAM
GDNS
FARMLANDS
AVE
PO

4

Folkington
BN26
Wannock
Willingdon
Sch
CORRAL GDNS
MILL LA
GLEN CL
BROAD RD
BRIDAL CL

MILL GDNS
MORTIMER GDNS
MILL WAY
BROADWATER
MEWS
MILL WAY
HONEY SYN CL
WANNOCK GDNS
WANNOCK AVE
WANNOCK LA
THE PARAGON

3

Folkington Bottom
Cranedown Bottom
Crane
Down
Filching
GLEN COTTS
FILCHING CT
THE GROVE
Middle Brow
MAVEARING DOWN

03

Folkington
Hill
Ash
Farm
Filching Manor
Motor Mus
JEVINGTON RD
Wealdway
Dean
Wood
Hanging
Hill
Willingdon
Links

2

Hill
Barn
Teddard's
Bottom
South Downs Way
Helling Down
BN20
The Combe
1066 Country Wlk

1

Hayward's
Bottom
Jevington Holt
Wealdway

Holt
Brow
Holt
Bottom
GREEN LA
Combe
Hill

02

55   A   B   56   C   D   57   E   F

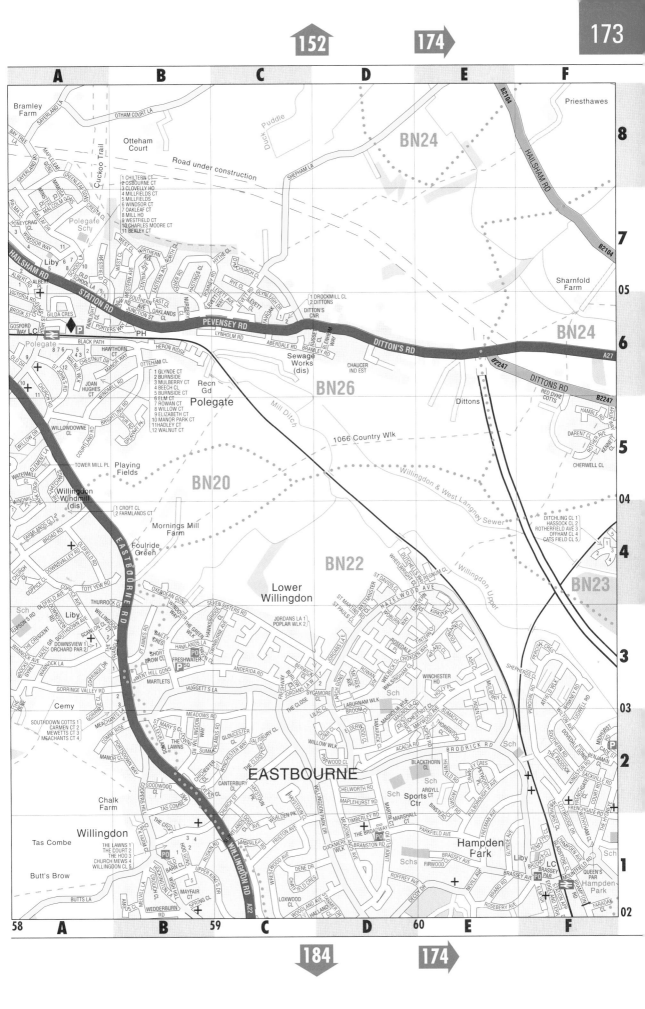

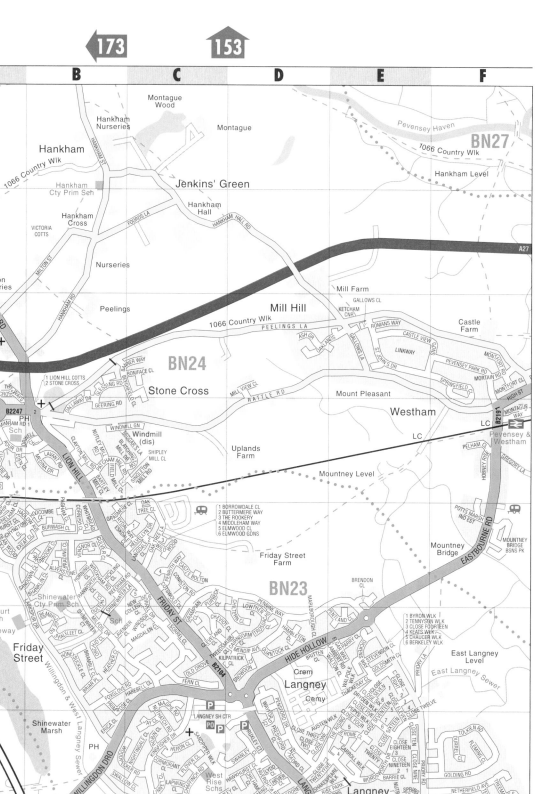

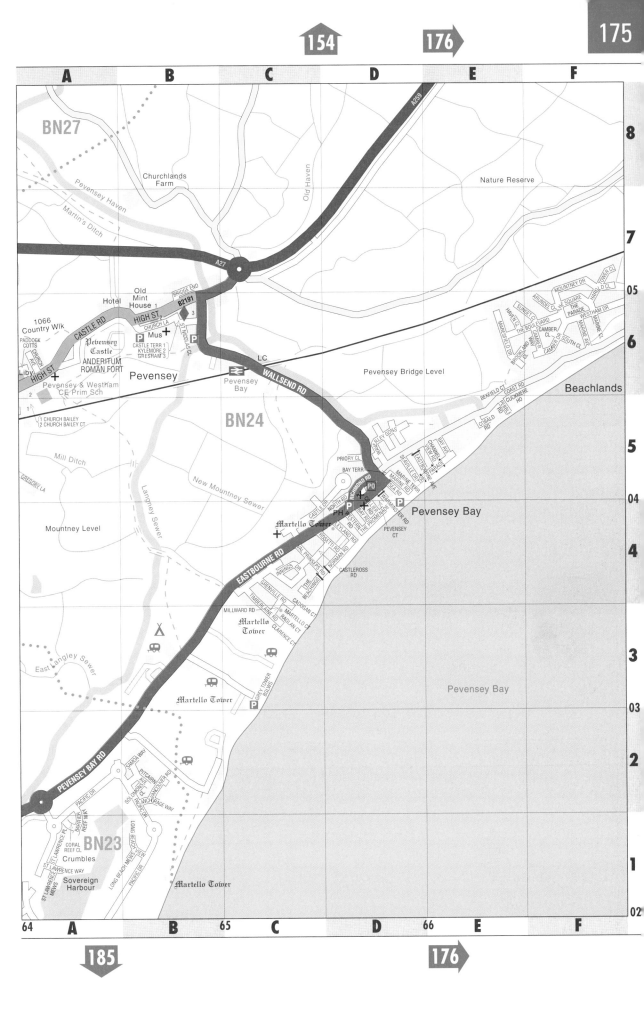

154

176

185

176

175
155

| | A | B | C | D | E | F |

8

Normans' Bay

Rockhouse Bank

LC

COASTGUARD CL

BN24

Normans' Bay

1 COASTGUARD COTTS
2 ST JAMES

7

COAST RD

BAY COTTS

Martello Tower

05

WESTHAM DR

6

Pevensey Bay

5

04

4

3

03

2

1

02

67

68

69

Weenham Stream

Waller's Haven

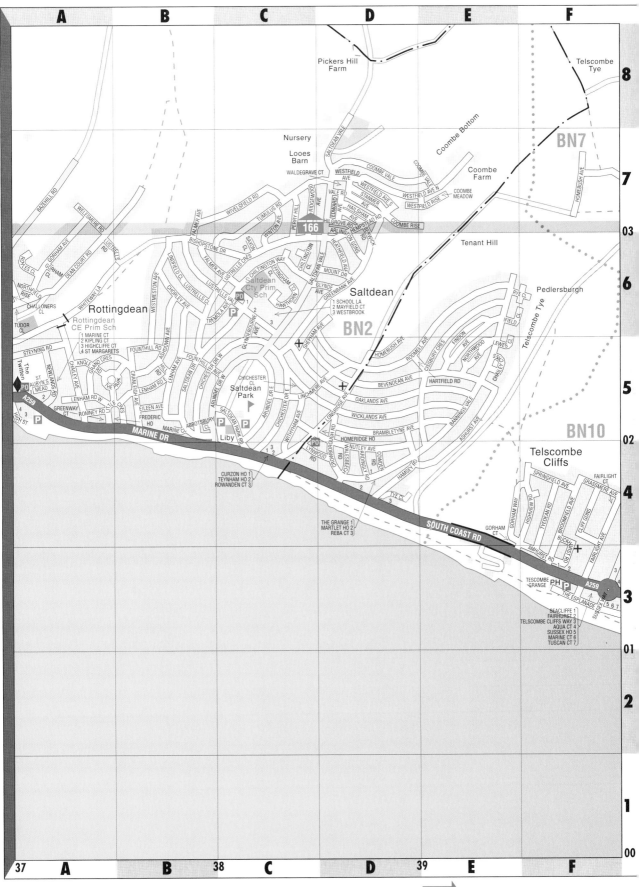

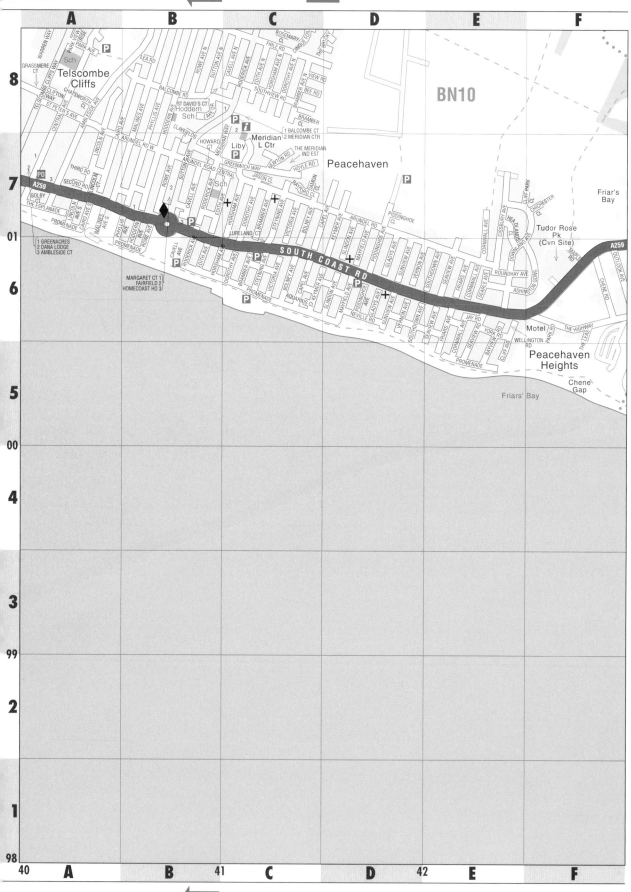

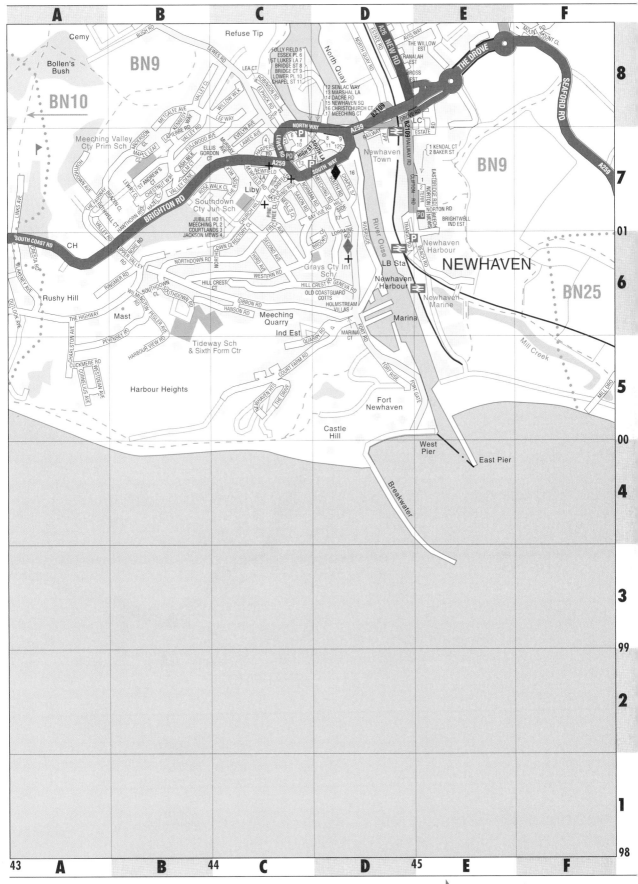

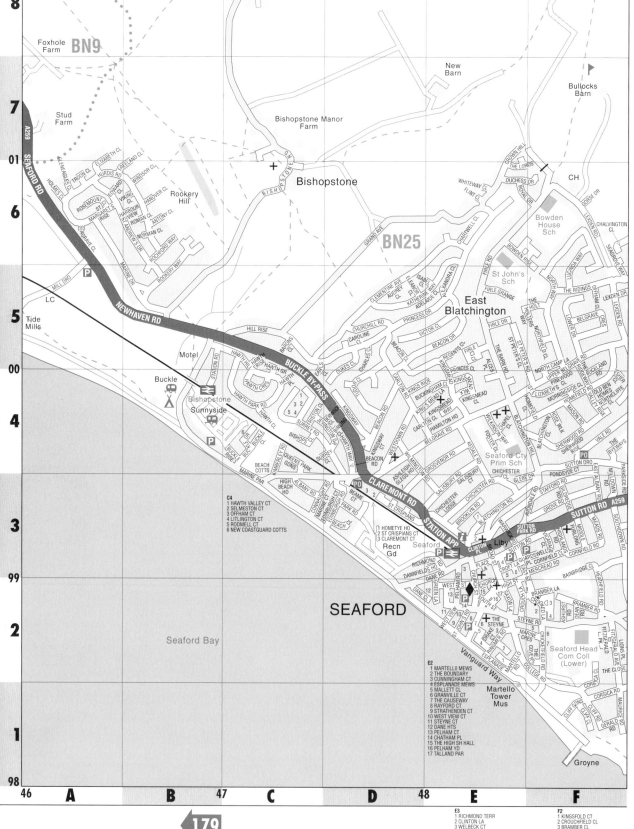

Norton

Norton Farm

Beacon Hill

Blackstone Barn

Foxhole Farm

BN9

New Barn

Bullocks Barn

Stud Farm

Bishopstone Manor Farm

CH

A259

SEAFORD RD

Bishopstone

Crown Hill

THE LORDS

DUCHESS DR

WHITEWAY CL

FLINT CL

ROYAL DR

GORSE DR

BN25

Bowden House Sch

CHALVINGTON CL

SEAFORD CL

MILL DRO

LC

Tide Mills

NEWHAVEN RD

MARINE DR

HILL RISE

East Blatchington

St John's Sch

FIRLE GRANGE

THE RIDINGS

OFFHAM CL

LEXDEN DR

Motel

BUCKLE BY-PASS

STATION RD

HAWTH HILL

HAWTH CRES

HAWTH PARK RD

HAWTH CL

St PETER'S CL

St ELIZABETH'S

NORTH CAMP LA

UPPER BELGRAVE RD

PINEWOOD

MORNINGSIDE CL

HOMEFIELD RD

OLD BEN HOMES

NORTHCLIFFE

Buckle

Bishopstone

Sunnyside

BUCKLE RISE

BISHOPS

KINGSWAY

BEACON RD

KINGS RIDE

BUCKINGHAM CL

KINGSMEAD

KINGSMEAD CL

CARLTON CL

HAMILTON HO

BELGRAVE RD

CHAPEL

WILKINSON WAY

FOSTER CL

BLATCHINGTON HILL

ROSE WLK

SHERWOOD

SHERWOOD RISE

VALE RD

THE BYEWAYS

SUTTON DRO

PO

C4
1 HAWTH VALLEY CT
2 SELMESTON CT
3 OFFHAM CT
4 LITLINGTON CT
5 RODMELL CT
6 NEW COASTGUARD COTTS

CLAREMONT RD

STATION APP

CHICHESTER LODGE

SALISBURY RD

CHICHESTER RD

BLATCHINGTON RD

STAFFORD RD

PONDSYDE CT

SUTTON RD A259

SUTTON PARK RD

MILLBERG

HIGHLANDS

MEADS RD

SOUTHDOWN RD

BEACH COTTS

HIGH BEACH HO

QUEENS PARK GDNS

KIMBERLEY RD

SURREY RD

BEACH

St CRISPIANS

1 HOMETYE HO
2 St CRISPIANS CT
3 CLAREMONT CT

Seaford

Recn Gd

Liby

BROAD ST

CROFT LA

GUARDSWELL PL

CORNFIELD CL

CORNFIELD RD

BAINBRIDGE CL

HEATHFIELD RD

RICHMOND

DANNFIELDS HO

DANE RD

GREEN LA

WEST ST

CHURCH LA

SAXON LA

STEYNE RD

BRAMBER LA

BRAMBER RD

BRAMBER RD

99

SEAFORD

Seaford Bay

WEST VIEW

PELHAM

CHURCH

PELHAM PL

THE STEYNE

MARINE CRES

ESPLANADE

STEYNE RD

CRICKETFIELD RD

THE COVE

COLLEGE RD

Seaford Head Com Coll (Lower)

FITZGERALD PK

THE CLOSE

LIONS PL

FITZGERALD RD

Vanguard Way

Martello Tower Mus

MAURICE RD

CLIFF GDNS

CLIFF CL

CORSICA RD

GERALD RD

Groyne

E2
1 MARTELLO MEWS
2 THE BOUNDARY
3 CUNNINGHAM CT
4 ESPLANADE MEWS
5 MALLETT CL
6 GRANVILLE CT
7 THE CAUSEWAY
8 RAYFORD CT
9 STRATHENDEN CT
10 WEST VIEW CT
11 STEYNE CT
12 DANE HTS
13 PELHAM CT
14 CHATHAM PL
15 THE HIGH SH HALL
16 PELHAM YD
17 TALLAND PAR

E3
1 RICHMOND TERR
2 CLINTON LA
3 WELBECK CT
4 SUTTON CROFT LA
5 FITZGERALD HO
6 CROFT CT

F2
1 KINGSFOLD CT
2 CROUCHFIELD CL
3 BRAMBER CL
4 STEYNE CL
5 SEA COTTS
6 CRICKETFIELD CT
7 WAVERLY CT

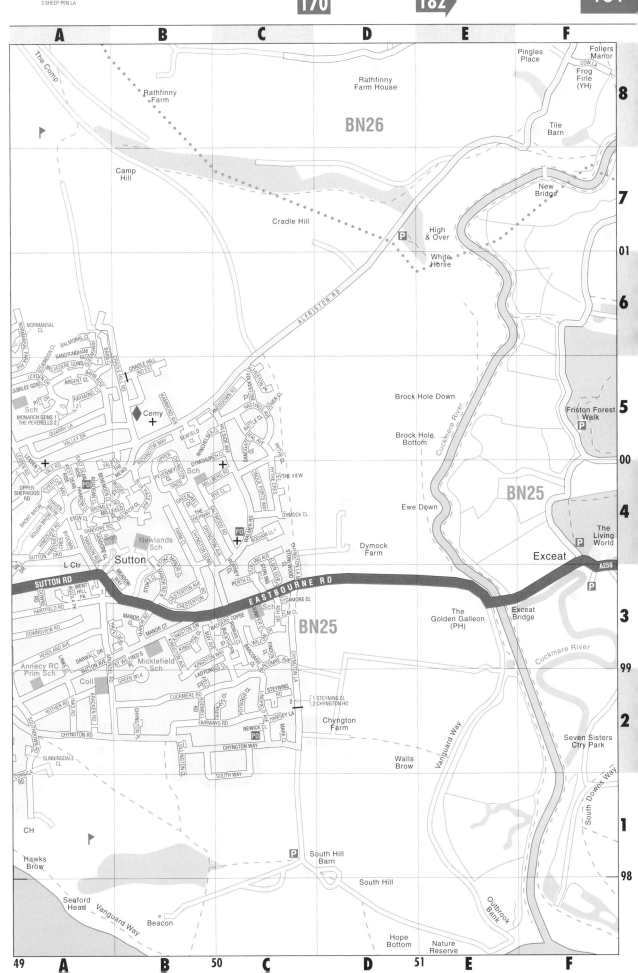

181
171

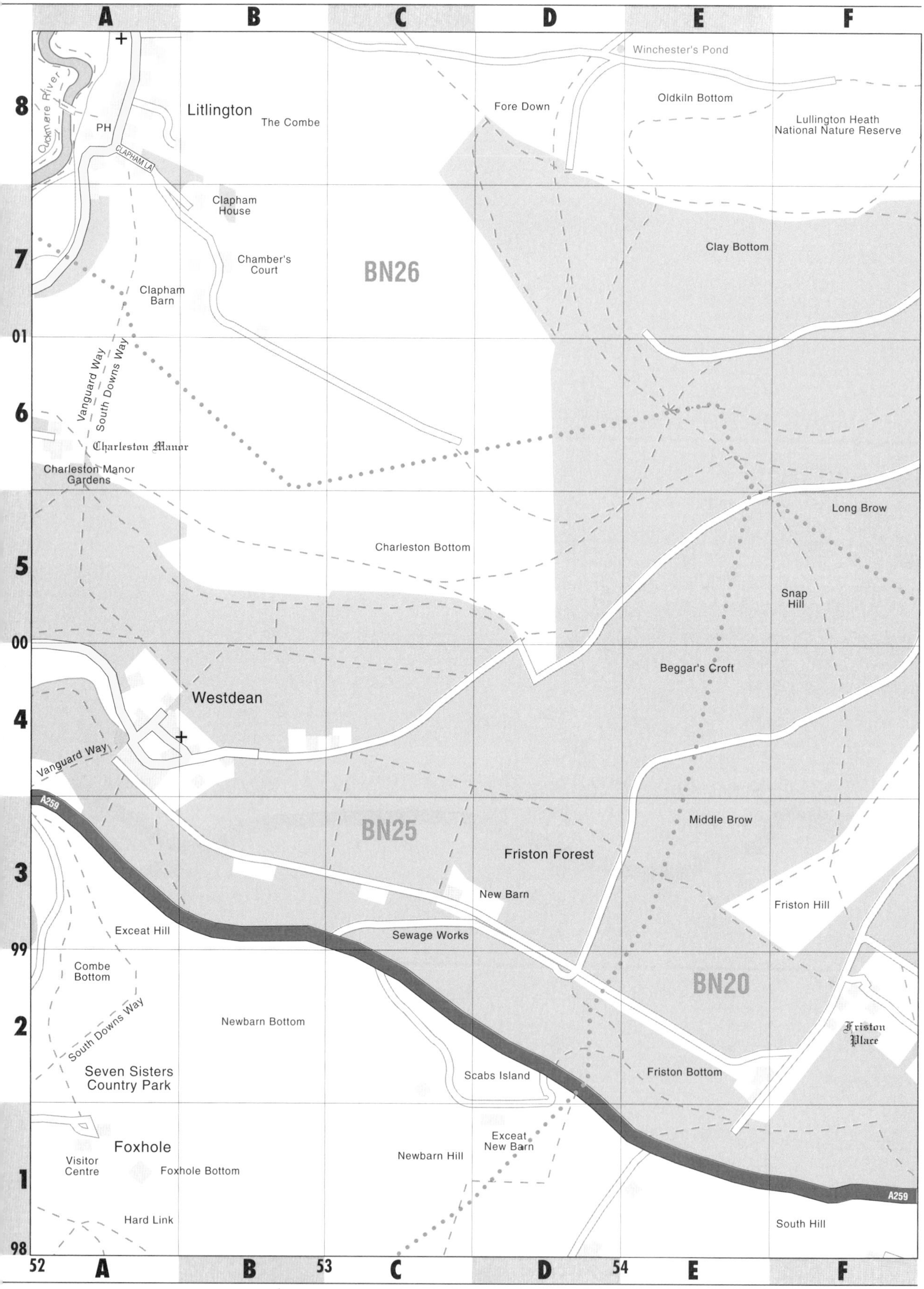
A
B
C
D
E
F
8
7
01
6
5
00
4
3
99
2
1
98
52
53
54
Winchester's Pond
Oldkiln Bottom
Fore Down
Lullington Heath
National Nature Reserve
Litlington
The Combe
PH
Cuckmere River
CLAPHAM LA
Clapham
House
Chamber's
Court
BN26
Clay Bottom
Clapham
Barn
Vanguard Way
South Downs Way
Charleston Manor
Charleston Manor
Gardens
Long Brow
Charleston Bottom
Snap
Hill
Beggar's Croft
Westdean
Vanguard Way
A259
BN25
Middle Brow
Friston Forest
New Barn
Friston Hill
Exceat Hill
Sewage Works
Combe
Bottom
BN20
Newbarn Bottom
South Downs Way
Friston
Place
Seven Sisters
Country Park
Scabs Island
Friston Bottom
Foxhole
Exceat
New Barn
Newbarn Hill
Visitor
Centre
Foxhole Bottom
A259
Hard Link
South Hill

181
186

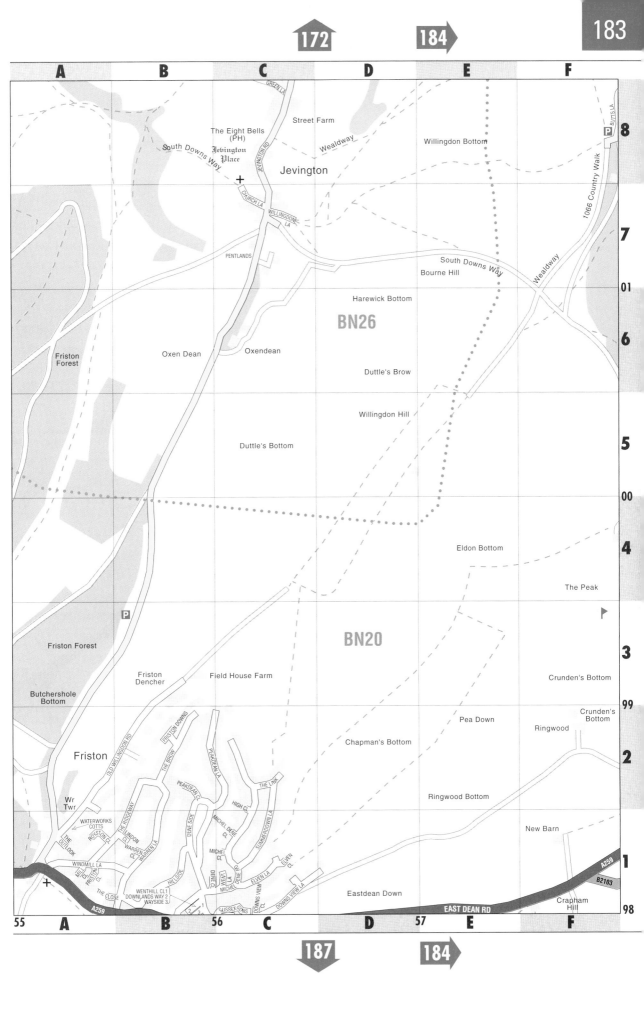

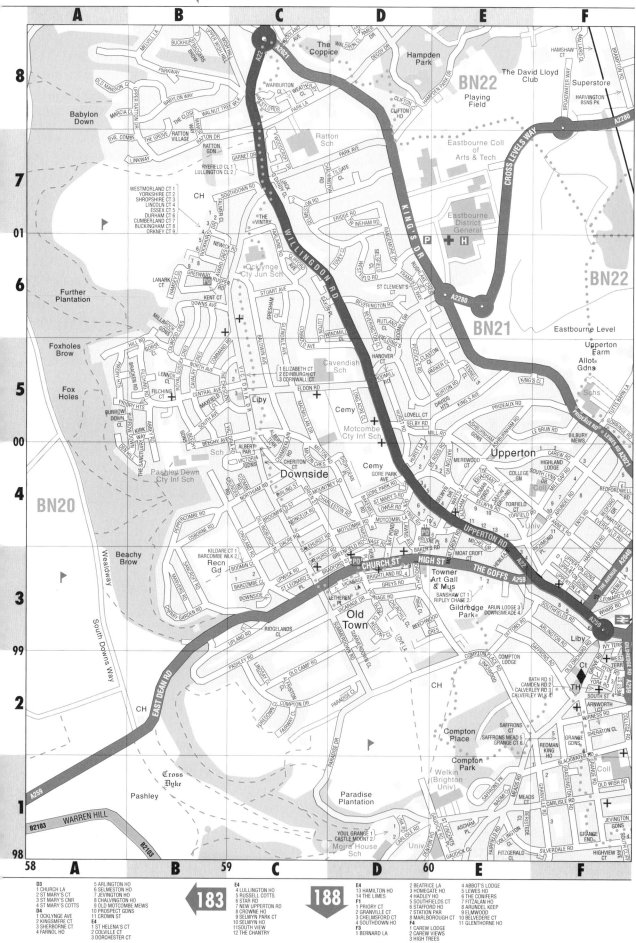

183
173

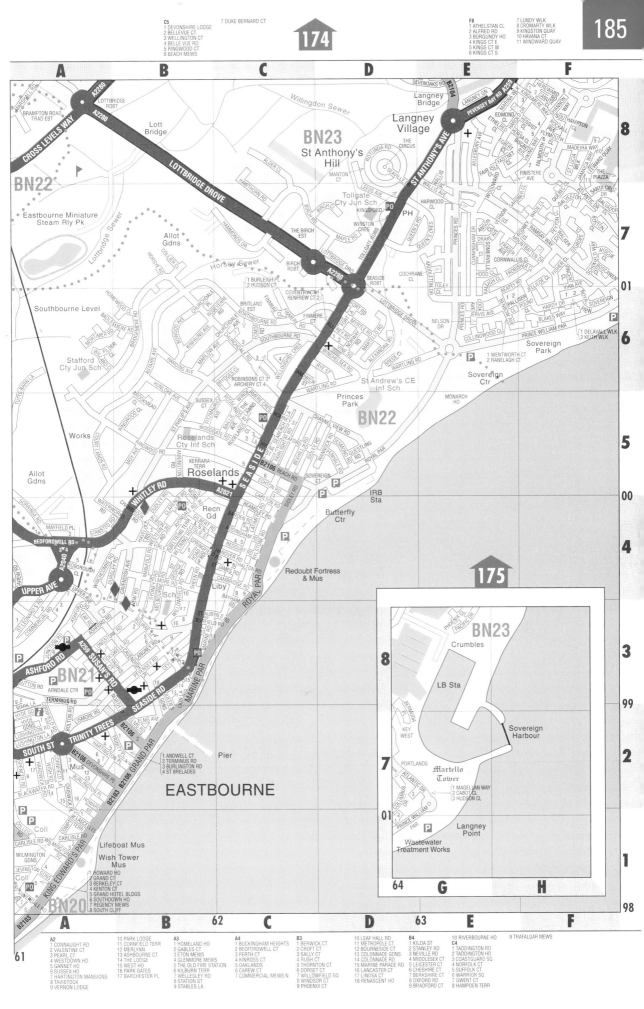

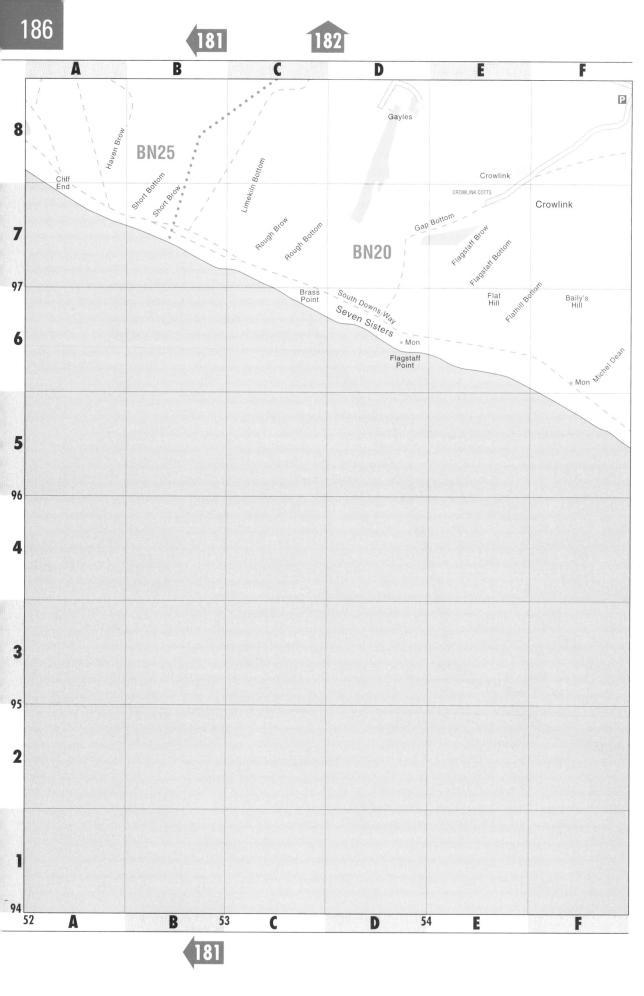

Gayles

BN25

Haven Brow

Cliff End

Short Bottom

Short Brow

Limekiln Bottom

Crowlink

CROWLINK COTTS

Crowlink

Rough Brow

Rough Bottom

Gap Bottom

BN20

Flagstaff Brow

Flagstaff Bottom

Flathill Bottom

Baily's Hill

Brass Point

South Downs Way

Seven Sisters

Flat Hill

Mon

Flagstaff Point

Mon Michel Dean

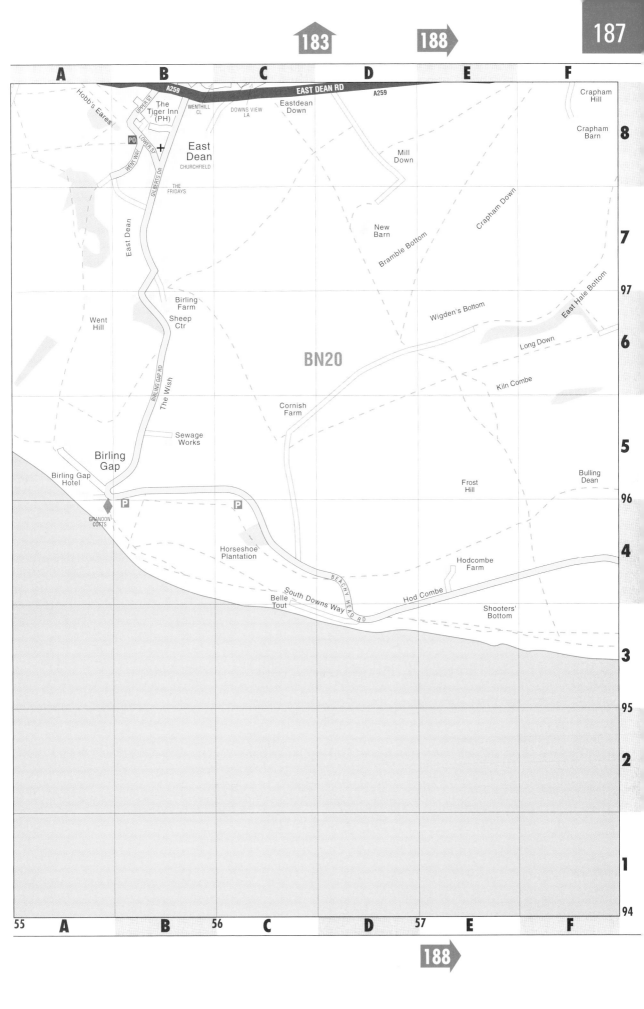

A B C D E F

EAST DEAN RD
A259
A259

Crapham Hill

Hobb's Eares

The Tiger Inn (PH)

WENTHILL CL

DOWNS VIEW LA

Eastdean Down

Crapham Barn

8

PO

East Dean

CHURCHFIELD

Mill Down

East Dean

THE FRIDAYS

New Barn

Crapham Down

7

Bramble Bottom

97

Birling Farm

Went Hill

Sheep Ctr

Wigden's Bottom

East Hale Bottom

Long Down

6

BN20

Kiln Combe

The Wish

Cornish Farm

Sewage Works

5

Birling Gap

Frost Hill

Bulling Dean

Birling Gap Hotel

96

P

P

GRANDOON COTTS

Horseshoe Plantation

Hodcombe Farm

4

South Downs Way

BEACHY HEAD RD

Hod Combe

Belle Tout

Shooters' Bottom

3

95

2

1

94

55 A B 56 C D 57 E F

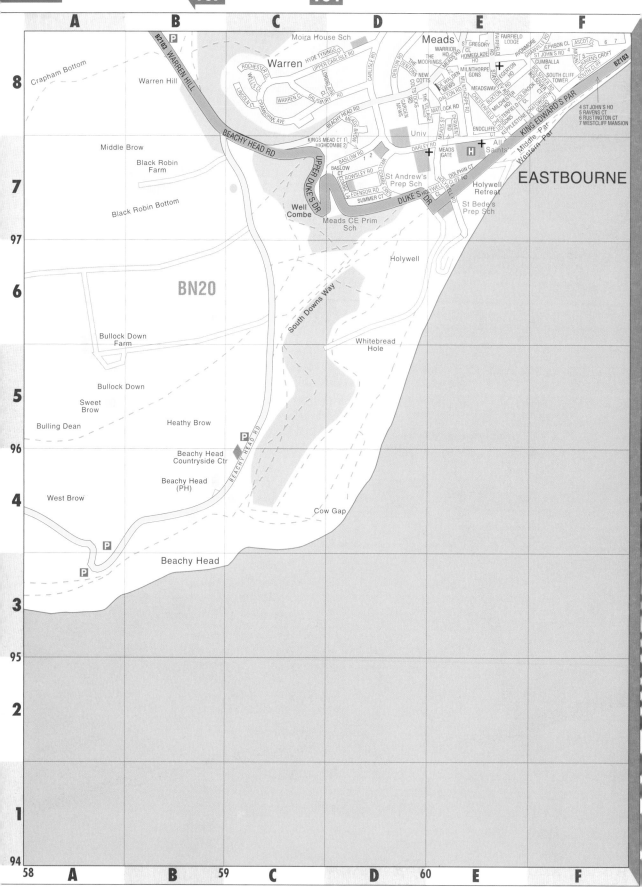

A B C D E F

8

7

97

6

5

96

4

3

95

2

1

94

Crapham Bottom

Warren Hill

Middle Brow

Black Robin Farm

Black Robin Bottom

BN20

Bullock Down Farm

Bullock Down

Sweet Brow

Bulling Dean

Heathy Brow

Beachy Head Countryside Ctr

Beachy Head (PH)

West Brow

Beachy Head

Moira House Sch

Warren

ROCHESTER CL
WELLS CL
LINCOLN CT
WARREN CL
CRANBORNE AVE
SALISBURY RD

HYDE TYNINGS CL
UPPER CARLISLE RD
UPPER LORDALAINE
LORDALAINE CL

CARLISLE RD
DENTON RD
COLSTOCKS RD
THE DENTONS
NEW COTTS
GARDEN MEWS
THE VILLAGE

Meads
WARRIOR HO
THE MOORINGS
DE WALDEN MEWS
DALTON RD
MATLOCK RD

St GREGORY CL
HOMEGLADE HO
MILNTHORPE GDNS
MEADSWAY
MILNTHORPE RD

FAIRFIELD LODGE
FAIRFIELD RD
AVONMORE
ST JOHN'S RD
EGERTON RD
STAVELEY RD

ASCOT CL
6 7
GRANVILLE RD
JEPHSON CL
CUMBALLA
SOUTH CLIFF TOWER
CRAVENS CROFT
B2103

EASTBOURNE

BEACHY HEAD RD

UPPER DUKE'S DR

KINGS MEAD CT
HIGHCOMBE 2
BASLOW RD
BASLOW CT
COMBE RD
ROWSLEY RD
EDENSOR RD
SUMMER CT

Univ

DARLEY RD

Well Combe

Meads CE Prim Sch

St Andrew's Prep Sch

DUKE'S DR

MEADS GATE

DOLPHIN CT
CLIFF RD

All Saints

Holywell Retreat

St Bede's Prep Sch

HOLYWELL RD

KING EDWARD'S PAR

Middle Par

Western Par

4 ST JOHN'S HO
5 RAVENS CT
6 RUSTINGTON CT
7 WESTCLIFF MANSION

Holywell

South Downs Way

Whitebread Hole

Cow Gap

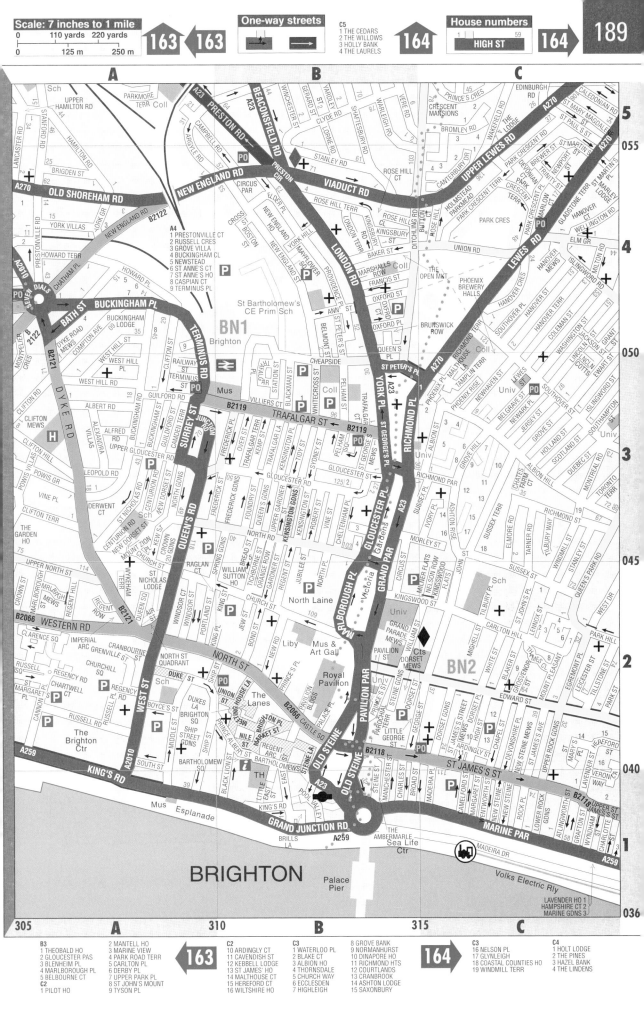

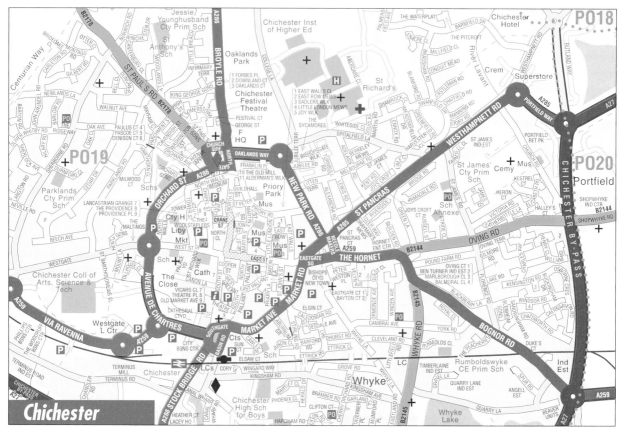

Chichester

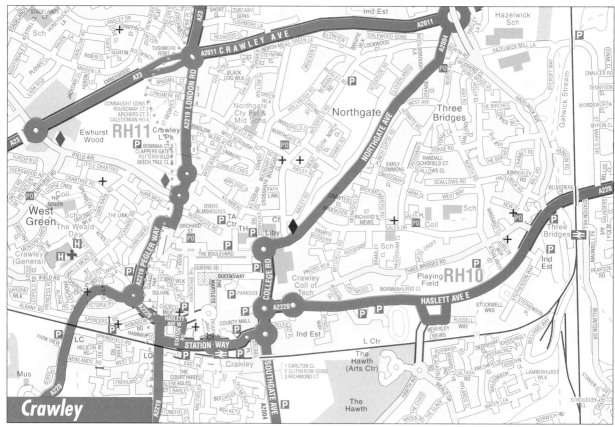

Crawley

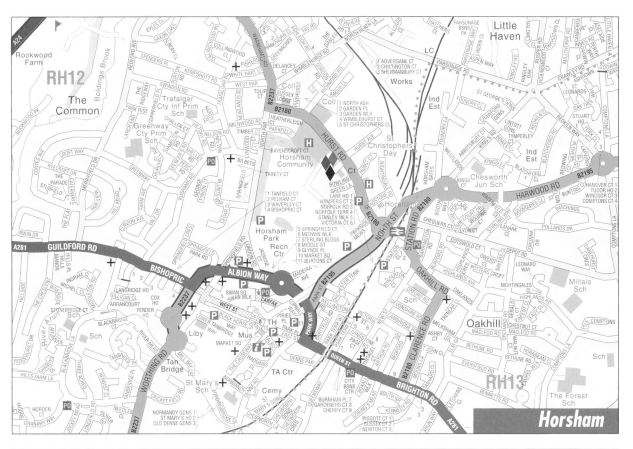

Horsham

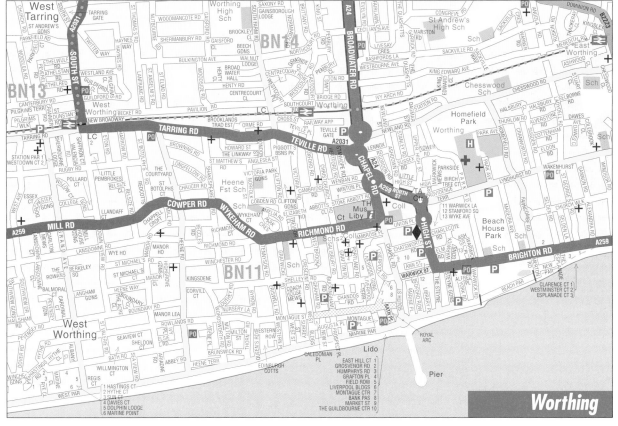

Worthing

Index

Street names are listed alphabetically and show the locality, the Postcode District, the page number and a reference to the square in which the name falls on the map page

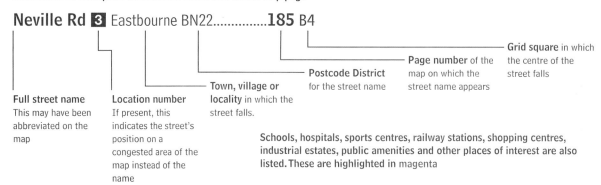

Full street name
This may have been abbreviated on the map

Location number
If present, this indicates the street's position on a congested area of the map instead of the name

Town, village or locality in which the street falls.

Postcode District for the street name

Page number of the map on which the street name appears

Grid square in which the centre of the street falls

Schools, hospitals, sports centres, railway stations, shopping centres, industrial estates, public amenities and other places of interest are also listed. These are highlighted in magenta

Abbreviations used in the index

App **Approach**	Cl **Close**	Espl **Esplanade**	N **North**	S **South**
Arc **Arcade**	Comm **Common**	Est **Estate**	Orch **Orchard**	Sq **Square**
Ave **Avenue**	Cnr **Corner**	Gdns **Gardens**	Par **Parade**	Strs **Stairs**
Bvd **Boulevard**	Cotts **Cottages**	Gn **Green**	Pk **Park**	Stps **Steps**
Bldgs **Buildings**	Ct **Court**	Gr **Grove**	Pas **Passage**	St **Street, Saint**
Bsns Pk **Business Park**	Ctyd **Courtyard**	Hts **Heights**	Pl **Place**	Terr **Terrace**
Bsns Ctr **Business Centre**	Cres **Crescent**	Ind Est **Industrial**	Prec **Precinct**	Trad **Trading Est**
Bglws **Bungalows**	Dr **Drive**	**Estate**	Prom **Promenade**	Wlk **Walk**
Cswy **Causeway**	Dro **Drove**	Intc **Interchange**	Ret Pk **Retail Park**	W **West**
Ctr **Centre**	E **East**	Junc **Junction**	Rd **Road**	Yd **Yard**
Cir **Circus**	Emb **Embankment**	La **Lane**	Rdbt **Roundabout**	

Town and village index

Alfriston 170 F2	Crowhurst 134 F6	Holtye 3 F3	Peacehaven Heights ... 178 F5	Steel Cross 26 B3
Argos Hill 39 E5	Crowlink 186 F7	Hooe 155 D8	Peasmarsh 69 B2	Stone Cross 6 A2
Ashton Green 125 A5	Cuckfield 50 A6	Hooe Common 132 F2	Pembury 9 C6	Stone Cross 174 C6
Ashurst Wood 11 E6	Danehill 34 A4	Hook Green 19 C4	Pett 138 E8	Stonecrouch 31 F6
Barcombe 101 E2	Ditchling 98 D3	Horam 106 E7	Pevensey 175 B6	Stonegate 42 F6
Barcombe Cross 101 E4	Dodd's Hill 35 D2	Horsted Keynes 33 D5	Pevensey Bay 175 D5	Telscombe 167 B3
Battle 112 D5	Dormans Park 1 E6	Hove 163 B5	Piddinghoe 168 A2	Telscombe Cliffs 167 A1
Beachlands 175 F6	Dormansland 2 B8	Hurst Green 45 B3	Plumpton Green 99 E6	The Moor 45 F8
Beachy Head 188 B3	Durgates 29 E5	Hurst Wickham 97 C6	Polegate 173 B5	Ticehurst 31 E2
Beacon Down 81 A7	East Chiltington 100 A3	Hurstpierpoint 97 B6	Portslade Village 141 B1	Town Row 27 C2
Beckley 68 A4	East Dean 187 B8	Icklesham 116 E6	Portslade-by-Sea 162 B5	Turner's Green 29 F6
Beckley Furnace 90 D7	East Grinstead 1 E2	Iden 70 B4	Potman's Heath 49 E4	Uckfield 78 D7
Beddingham 147 D4	East Hoathly 105 B5	Isfield 102 E7	Poundfield 26 B2	Union Street 32 B3
Bells Yew Green 17 F5	Eastbourne 185 B2	Jevington 183 C8	Poundgate 37 A6	Upper Wellingham 124 B8
Berner's Hill 32 A2	Etchingham 44 B1	John's Cross 87 C7	Poundsbridge 6 D8	Wadhurst 30 A4
Berwick 170 F7	Ewhurst Green 66 B5	Keymer 98 B4	Punnett's Town 83 C5	Waldron 80 C7
Bevendean 144 B2	Fairlight 138 C4	Kilndown 20 F3	Pyecombe 119 B6	Waldron Down 80 D8
Bewlbridge 20 D1	Fairlight Cove 138 F5	Kingston near Lewes .. 145 E5	Ringmer 124 C6	Wannock 172 A5
Bexhill 157 A2	Fairwarp 36 B2	Lamberhurst 20 B5	Ripe 126 D1	Warbleton 83 A1
Blackboys 80 A5	Falmer 144 D6	Langton Green 6 E3	Robertsbridge 64 A4	Wartling 154 D7
Blackness 26 A1	Felbridge 1 A6	Laughton 126 C6	Rockrobin 29 D6	Watermill 134 B4
Boarshead 26 C6	Felcourt 1 C8	Lewes 123 E1	Rodmell 167 D8	Wellbrook 39 E1
Bodiam 65 E8	Five Ashes 58 B7	Lidham Hill 115 E6	Romford 9 F7	West Firle 148 C3
Bodle Street Green 109 C2	Flackley Ash 68 F3	Lindfield 51 A7	Roser's Cross 80 F6	Westfield 114 F4
Brighton 189 B1	Fletching 53 F4	Linkhill 47 E4	Rotherfield 39 B7	Westham 174 E5
Brighton 164 B4	Flimwell 32 C3	Lions Green 81 B1	Rottingdean 177 A6	Westmeston 120 F8
Broad Oak 59 F1	Flowers Green 130 F3	Lower Cousley Wood 30 E8	Royal Tunbridge Wells ... 8 D3	Whatlington 88 A1
Broad Oak 90 C4	Fordcombe 6 B5	Lower Dicker 128 D3	Rushlake Green 83 D2	White Post 5 D7
Broyle Side 125 A7	Forest Row 11 F3	Lower Horsebridge 128 F3	Rusthall 7 C4	Whitehill 37 F8
Burgess Hill 73 D2	Four Throws 46 D8	Lower Street 133 B5	Rye 93 B6	Whitesmith 127 B8
Burwash 62 B6	Framefield 79 B6	Lower Willingdon 173 C4	Rye Foreign 69 E1	Willingdon 173 B1
Burwash Common 61 A4	Frant 17 C3	Magham Down 129 F4	Rye Harbour 93 F2	Winchelsea 117 C2
Buxted 56 B4	Friston 183 A2	Maresfield 55 A5	St John's Common 72 E4	Winchelsea Beach 118 A5
Cackle Street 90 A2	Ginger's Green 130 C6	Maresfield Park 55 A6	St Leonards 159 A7	Windmill Hill 131 B6
Cade Street 82 E6	Glynde 147 E7	Mark Cross 28 A4	Saint's Hill 6 A8	Withyham 14 A3
Camber 94 F2	Goatham Green 89 E5	Marlpits 35 E6	Saltdean 177 D6	Wivelsfield 74 B5
Catsfield 133 F8	Goddards' Green 72 A5	Mayfield 40 A2	Sandhurst 47 C6	Wivelsfield Green 74 C4
Chailey 75 E4	Golden Cross 130 E3	Maynard's Green 82 A1	Sandhurst Cross 46 F4	Wood's Corner 84 F3
Chapman's Town 83 B2	Green Street 135 B4	Mill Corner 67 A3	Scaynes Hill 51 E3	Woodingdean 165 D7
Chelwood Common 34 D6	Groombridge 15 C7	Mount Pleasant 101 F6	Seaford 180 D2	Woolbridge 39 E2
Chelwood Gate 34 D8	Grove Hill 107 E1	Mountfield 87 A5	Sedlescombe 88 D1	
Churches Green 109 B8	Guestling Green 138 A8	Newbury's 30 B8	Selmeston 149 D2	
Cinder Hill 33 B8	Hadlow Down 57 C6	Newenden 48 D3	Sharpthorne 21 A6	
Clayhill 67 D3	Hailsham 152 C8	Newhaven 179 E6	Shellies Green 138 C8	
Clayton 119 E8	Halland 104 C5	Newick 76 C8	Shoreham-by-Sea 161 A5	
Cobbarn 15 E3	Hankham 174 B8	Ninfield 133 B6	Shortgate 104 A3	
Cock Marling 92 A2	Hartfield 13 D4	Normans' Bay 176 D8	South Chailey 100 D7	
Coggins Mill 40 D4	Hassocks 97 E4	North Chailey 75 E6	South Heighton 168 E2	
Coleman's Hatch 23 E7	Hastings 159 F7	Northbridge Street 64 C6	South Street 75 E1	
Cooksbridge 123 A8	Haywards Heath 50 C3	Northiam 67 B6	Southwick 161 F7	
Cousley Wood 30 C7	Heathfield 82 B7	Nutley 35 C4	Sparrow's Green 29 F5	
Cowden 4 A4	Hellingly 129 A5	Offham 122 F5	Speldhurst 7 B5	
Cripp's Corner 88 D7	Herstmonceux 130 E6	Old Heathfield 82 D5	Standard Hill 132 F6	
Cross-in-Hand 81 C7	High Cross 39 C6	Ovingdean 165 D3	Standen Street 47 D8	
Crowborough 26 C1	High Hurstwood 37 A1	Peacehaven 178 D7	Staplecross 65 E2	

A

Abberton Field BN6 .....97 B5
Abbey Cl BN10 .....167 C1
Abbey Ct TN33 .....112 D4
Abbey Dr TN38 .....158 B5
Abbey Mews TN32 .....64 B4
Abbey Path BN27 .....129 C2
Abbey Rd Brighton BN2 .....164 D4
  Eastbourne BN20 .....184 B5
Abbey View TN40 .....157 D6
Abbey Way TN33 .....112 D5
Abbeyfield Ho BN26 .....170 F3
Abbot's Lodge **4** BN21 .....184 F4
Abbots Cl Battle TN33 .....112 F3
  Hassocks BN6 .....97 E4
Abbotsbury Cl BN2 .....177 B5
Abbotsfield Cl TN34 .....136 F3
Abbotsford Sch RH15 .....72 E6
Abbotts **11** BN1 .....163 E5
Aberdale Rd BN26 .....173 C6
Aberdeen Rd **5** BN2 .....164 C8
Abergavenny Rd BN27 .....123 B1
Abigail Ho **10** RH16 .....50 E4
Abinger Pl BN7 .....123 C1
Abinger Rd
  Portslade-by-Sea BN41 .....162 B8
  Woodingdean BN2 .....165 E6
Acacia Ave BN3 .....141 F1
Acacia Ct BN1 .....142 F2
Acacia Rd
  Eastbourne BN22 .....173 D2
  Newhaven BN9 .....168 E2
Acer Ave TN2 .....17 C8
Acorn Cl
  East Grinstead RH19 .....10 E8
  St Leonards TN37 .....136 C4
Acorn Gn **3** BN27 .....129 B1
Acorn Way TN19 .....45 A3
Acorns The
  Burgess Hill RH15 .....72 D4
  Hailsham BN27 .....152 D7
  Stonegate TN5 .....42 F6
Acre Cl RH16 .....50 D2
Acres Rise TN5 .....31 E1
Adam Cl Crowborough TN6 .....38 A6
  St Leonards TN38 .....135 F4
Adams Cl BN1 .....143 B2
Adams La TN31 .....66 D2
Adastra Ave BN6 .....98 A4
Addingham Rd BN22 .....185 C4
Addington Cl TN38 .....158 F7
Addison Rd BN1, BN3 .....163 E7
Adelaide Cl BN25 .....180 E5
Adelaide Cres BN3 .....163 C5
Adelaide Rd TN38 .....136 B3
Adelaide Sq BN43 .....161 B7
Ades Field TN37 .....171 F6
Admiral's Bridge La RH19 .....10 C2
Adur Ct **10** BN43 .....161 C8
Adur Dr
  Shoreham-by-Sea BN43 .....161 A7
  Stone Cross BN24 .....174 A5
Adur Rd RH15 .....73 C4
Agincourt Cl TN37 .....135 F7
Agnes St BN2 .....164 C7
Ainsworth Ave BN2 .....165 D3
Ainsworth Cl BN2 .....165 D3
Ainsworth Ho **1** BN2 .....164 C7
Air St BN1 .....189 A2
Airy Rd BN27 .....131 B2
Akehurst Field TN33 .....110 B3
Alan Ct **6** TN37 .....159 C7
Alan Way BN2 .....164 F5
Albany Ct **2** TN34 .....159 F7
Albany Hill TN2 .....8 C5
Albany Mans TN38 .....159 B8
Albany Mews BN3 .....163 B6
Albany Rd Bexhill TN40 .....157 C4
  Seaford BN25 .....180 C3
  St Leonards TN38 .....159 B7
Albany Villas
  Cuckfield RH17 .....50 A6
  Hove BN3 .....163 B6
Albert Cl RH16 .....51 A4
Albert Cotts TN1 .....8 B4
Albert Dr RH15 .....72 E2
Albert Mews BN3 .....163 C6
Albert Par BN21 .....184 C4
Albert Pl BN26 .....173 A7
Albert Rd Bexhill TN40 .....157 C3
  Brighton BN1 .....189 A3
  Hastings TN34 .....159 F7
  Polegate BN26 .....173 A7
  Southwick BN42 .....161 D7
  Uckfield TN22 .....78 D6
Albert St TN1 .....8 B4
Albert Terr BN21 .....184 C5
Albion Ct TN15 .....72 F2
Albion Hill BN2 .....189 C3
Albion Ho **3** Brighton BN2 .....189 C3
  Southwick BN42 .....161 F7
Albion La **4** TN34 .....160 A3
Albion Rd
  Eastbourne BN22 .....185 B4
  Royal Tunbridge Wells TN1 .....8 B5
Albion St Brighton BN2 .....189 C3
  8 Lewes BN7 .....123 D1
  Portslade-by-Sea BN41 .....162 B7
  Southwick BN42 .....161 E7
Albourne Cl Brighton BN2 .....164 F7
  St Leonards TN38 .....158 F8
Alces Pl BN25 .....180 E5
Aldborough Rd TN37 .....136 C1
Alder Cl Eastbourne BN23 .....185 C8
  Heathfield TN21 .....82 A5
  St Leonards TN37 .....136 C5

Alderbrook Cl TN6 .....38 A6
Alderbrook Cotts TN6 .....38 A7
Alderbrook Path TN6 .....38 A6
Alderbrook Way TN6 .....38 A6
Alders Ave RH19 .....1 E3
Alders View Dr RH19 .....1 E3
Alderton Ct **7** TN39 .....157 B3
Aldervale Cotts TN6 .....38 A7
Aldrich Cl BN2 .....164 F6
Aldrington Ave BN3 .....163 A8
Aldrington CE Fst Sch
  BN3 .....162 F7
Aldrington CE Prim Sch
  BN3 .....142 A2
Aldrington Cl BN3 .....162 D7
Aldrington House (Hospl)
  BN3 .....162 F6
Aldrington Pl BN3 .....162 D8
Aldrington Sta BN3 .....163 A8
Alexander Dr TN39 .....156 E4
Alexandra Cl BN25 .....180 E5
Alexandra Ct Hove BN3 .....141 F3
  St Leonards TN37 .....136 C2
Alexandra Par TN34 .....136 D3
Alexandra Rd
  Burgess Hill RH15 .....73 C2
  Eastbourne BN22 .....185 D6
  Heathfield TN21 .....82 B6
  Mayfield TN20 .....40 C3
  St Leonards TN37 .....159 C8
  Uckfield TN22 .....78 D6
Alexandra Terr TN20 .....40 C3
Alexandra The TN37 .....159 D7
Alexandra Villas BN1 .....189 A3
Alford Way TN40 .....157 E6
Alfray Rd TN40 .....158 A5
Alfred Brighton BN1 .....189 A3
  2 Eastbourne BN23 .....185 E8
  Hastings TN35 .....137 D3
Alfred St TN38 .....159 C7
Alfriston Cl Bexhill TN39 .....156 C6
  Brighton BN2 .....164 F6
  Eastbourne BN20 .....184 C2
Alfriston Cty Prim Sch
  BN26 .....170 F4
Alfriston Pk BN25 .....181 C5
Alfriston Rd BN25, BN26 .....181 D6
Alice Bright La TN6 .....37 F7
Alice Cl **2** BN3 .....163 D5
Alice St BN3 .....163 D5
All Saints CE Prim Sch
  TN39 .....157 B7
All Saints Gdns TN21 .....81 F7
All Saints Jun Sch TN35 .....160 C6
All Saints La TN39 .....157 B7
All Saints Rd TN4 .....8 B6
All Saints Rise TN4 .....8 A6
All Saints' Cres TN5 .....160 B4
All Saints' Hospl BN20 .....188 E7
All Saints' St TN34 .....160 B4
Allan Cl TN4 .....7 C4
Allandale Rd TN2 .....8 D7
Allards TN35 .....138 C8
Allegria Ct TN38 .....159 B7
Allen Rd RH16 .....51 A4
Allen Way TN40 .....157 F7
Allen's Cl RH19 .....11 D6
Allfrey Rd BN22 .....185 D6
Allfreys La TN6 .....37 D6
Allington Cres BN8 .....76 C7
Allington La BN7 .....122 D7
Allington Rd BN8 .....76 C6
Allwood Cres RH17 .....74 C4
Alma Rd RH16 .....51 B8
Alma Terr TN37 .....136 C2
Alma Villas TN37 .....136 C2
Almonry Fields TN33 .....112 B4
Alpine Rd Hastings TN34 .....160 A4
  Hove BN3 .....162 F8
Alverstone Cl BN23 .....174 B4
Amanda Cl TN40 .....157 F7
Ambassadors The **10**
  BN3 .....163 C6
Amber Ct **13** Hove BN3 .....163 C6
  8 Hove BN3 .....163 D7
Amberleaze Dr TN2 .....9 D6
Amberley Cl
  Burgess Hill RH15 .....73 A4
  Haywards Heath RH16 .....50 D4
  Hove BN3 .....141 E3
Amberley Ct TN4 .....8 C8
Amberley Dr BN3 .....141 E3
Amberley Lodge BN2 .....189 B4
Amberley Rd BN22 .....173 C5
Amberly Lodge BN2 .....164 F6
Ambermarle The BN2 .....189 B1
Amberstone BN27 .....129 C3
Amberstone Ct TN34 .....137 A4
Amberstone Hospl BN27 .....129 E4
Amberstone View BN27 .....129 C2
Ambleside Ave BN10 .....178 A8
Ambleside Ct BN10 .....178 A7
America La RH16 .....51 A5
Amesbury Cres BN3 .....162 C2
Amherst Cl TN34 .....136 D1
Amherst Cres BN3 .....162 F8
Amherst Gdns TN34 .....136 D1
Amherst Rd Bexhill TN40 .....157 C4
  Hastings TN34 .....136 D1
  Royal Tunbridge Wells TN4 .....8 A5
Amhurst Rd BN10 .....177 F3
Anchor Field BN6 .....124 D5
Anchor Hill RH17 .....52 A2
Anchor La BN8 .....102 B5
Anchorage Way BN23 .....175 B2
Anderida Ct TN39 .....156 C4
Anderida Rd BN22 .....173 C3
Anderson Rd BN9 .....179 B7

Andrew Rd TN4 .....8 C8
Andrews Cl
  Northborough Street TN32 .....64 C5
  Royal Tunbridge Wells TN2 .....8 D5
Andros Cl BN8 .....100 E6
Andwell Ct BN21 .....185 B2
Angel Row TN18 .....47 B5
Angel Terr TN18 .....47 B6
Angela Cl TN40 .....157 F7
Anglesea Mans TN38 .....159 B8
Anglesea Terr
  TN37, TN38 .....159 C8
Anglesey Ave BN27 .....129 A2
Angmering Ct BN1 .....143 F5
Angrove Ho TN6 .....25 C7
Angus Cl BN20 .....173 B1
Anjou Ct BN23 .....174 F1
Ann Cl BN6 .....98 A5
Ann St Brighton BN1 .....189 B4
  Hastings TN34 .....160 C6
Anne's Path **18** BN7 .....146 C8
Annecy RC Prim Sch
  BN25 .....181 A2
Annington Rd BN22 .....185 B5
Anscombe **5** RH16 .....50 D6
Anson Cl BN23 .....185 E7
Anson Ho BN10 .....167 C1
Ansty Ct BN2 .....164 E5
Antares Path BN27 .....152 E7
Antioch St BN7 .....146 C8
Antony Cl BN25 .....180 B6
Antrim Ct BN23 .....174 D1
Antrona Ct TN39 .....156 C3
Anvil Cl
  Portslade-by-Sea BN41 .....141 B2
  Uckfield TN22 .....78 B6
Anvil Ct TN37 .....136 C5
Anzac Cl BN10 .....167 C1
Apex Pk BN27 .....152 A7
Apple Tree La TN2 .....8 D8
Appledene Cnr BN8 .....100 C4
Appledore Cl BN23 .....174 D2
Appledore Ct RH16 .....51 A7
Appledore Gdns RH16 .....51 A6
Appledore Rd BN2 .....143 F4
Applesham Ave BN3 .....141 E2
Applesham Way BN41 .....141 A1
Applewood Cl TN37 .....136 B5
Approach The
  Brighton BN1 .....142 E3
  Dormans Park RH19 .....1 F6
April Pl **4** TN40 .....157 C4
Apsley St TN4 .....7 D4
Aqua Ct BN10 .....177 F3
Aquarius Cl BN10 .....178 C6
Aquila Pk BN25 .....181 A3
Arbor Ct RH16 .....50 E5
Arbourvale TN38 .....136 A1
Archer Ct TN35 .....136 F6
Archery Ct
  Eastbourne BN22 .....185 C6
  3 St Leonards TN38 .....159 B6
Archery Rd TN38 .....159 B7
Archery Wlk BN27 .....152 C6
Archie Ct **7** TN38 .....159 B6
Ardingly Ct **10** BN2 .....189 C2
Ardingly Rd BN2 .....177 D4
Ardingly St BN2 .....189 C2
Argent Cl BN25 .....181 A5
Argos Hill Rd TN20,TN6 .....39 D4
Argyle Rd BN1 .....189 A5
Argyll Ct BN22 .....173 E2
Arkendale RH19 .....1 A4
Arkwright Rd BN23 .....174 A1
Arlington Cres BN1 .....143 E5
Arlington Ct RH16 .....50 E5
Arlington Gdns BN2 .....177 D6
Arlington Ho **5** BN2 .....184 D4
Arlington Rd BN21 .....184 F3
Arlington Rd E BN27 .....152 A6
Arlington Rd W BN27 .....151 F6
Arlington Resr BN26 .....150 C3
Armstrong Cl TN38 .....135 E4
Arnbury Mews TN38 .....158 E6
Arndale Ctr BN21 .....185 A3
Arnold St BN2 .....164 C7
Arnside Rd TN38 .....158 E6
Arnworth Ct BN21 .....184 F2
Arran Cl BN27 .....129 A2
Arthur Bliss Ho RH16 .....51 A8
Arthur Rd TN39 .....157 B4
Arthur St BN3 .....163 A8
Arts Rd BN1 .....144 B7
Arun Ct **13** BN43 .....161 C8
Arun Lodge BN21 .....184 E3
Arun Path TN22 .....55 E1
Arun Way BN24 .....173 F5
Arundel Cl
  Beachlands BN24 .....175 F6
  Hailsham BN27 .....129 C2
  Shoreham-by-Sea BN43 .....161 C8
Arundel Ct
  6 Brighton BN2 .....164 E4
  Burgess Hill RH15 .....72 F4
  Hove BN3 .....142 C5
  14 Shoreham-by-Sea BN43 .....146 E8
Arundel Dr E BN2 .....177 C5
Arundel Dr W BN2 .....177 C5
Arundel Keep **8** BN21 .....184 F4
Arundel Mews **10** BN2 .....164 E4
Arundel Pl BN2 .....164 E4
Arundel Rd Brighton BN2 .....164 E4
  Eastbourne BN21 .....184 F4
  Newhaven BN9 .....168 F1
  Peacehaven BN10 .....178 D7
  Royal Tunbridge Wells TN1 .....8 B2
  Seaford BN25 .....181 A3

Arundel Rd W BN10 .....178 B7
Arundel Road Central
  BN10 .....178 B7
Arundel St BN2 .....164 E5
Arundel Terr BN2 .....164 E5
Arundell Gn BN7 .....123 B2
Ascham Pl BN21 .....184 E1
Ascot Cl BN20 .....188 F8
Ascot Mews TN38 .....159 A8
Ash Cl Eastbourne BN22 .....173 E3
  Hove BN3 .....142 C3
  Royal Tunbridge Wells TN2 .....8 E7
Ash Ct East Grinstead RH19 .....1 C4
  Hailsham BN27 .....152 A7
  Southwick BN42 .....140 F1
Ash Dr BN25 .....181 C3
Ash Gr
  Haywards Heath RH16 .....50 D2
  Westham BN24 .....174 D6
Ash Tree Cl TN21 .....82 A7
Ash Wlk BN9 .....179 B7
Ashbourne Ct
  13 Eastbourne BN21 .....185 A2
  Rusthall TN4 .....7 D4
Ashbrook Rd TN37 .....136 B4
Ashburnham Cl BN1 .....143 E5
Ashburnham Dr BN1 .....143 E5
Ashburnham Gdns BN1 .....184 E5
Ashburnham Ho BN1 .....142 E5
Ashburnham Pl BN27 .....129 A2
Ashburnham Rd
  Eastbourne BN21 .....184 E5
  Hastings TN35 .....160 C6
Ashby Cl BN39 .....157 A8
Ashcombe Dr TN39 .....156 D3
Ashcombe Hollow BN7 .....145 D7
Ashcombe La BN7 .....145 E5
Ashcroft **1** BN43 .....161 D7
Ashcroft Cl Ringmer BN8 .....124 D5
  Shoreham-by-Sea BN43 .....161 D8
Ashdown **14** BN3 .....163 C6
Ashdown Ave BN2 .....177 B5
Ashdown Chase TN22 .....35 C5
Ashdown Cl
  Forest Row RH18 .....12 A2
  Haywards Heath RH16 .....51 B4
  Royal Tunbridge Wells TN4 .....7 F4
  St Leonards TN38 .....135 E2
Ashdown Ct
  Crowborough TN6 .....25 C2
  Uckfield TN22 .....78 D6
Ashdown Forest
  Riding Ctr TN22 .....36 B6
Ashdown Forest Visitors
  Information Ctr RH18 .....23 A5
Ashdown Gate RH19 .....1 D2
Ashdown Llama Farm
  RH18 .....22 C4
Ashdown Nuffield Hospl
  RH16 .....50 D6
Ashdown Pl TN21 .....82 B6
Ashdown Rd Bexhill TN40 .....157 E4
  7 Brighton BN2 .....164 B8
  Forest Row RH18 .....11 D7
Ashdown View
  East Grinstead RH19 .....10 E7
  Nutley TN22 .....35 D6
Ashenden Ave TN31 .....93 A5
Ashenden Wlk TN2 .....8 E7
Ashenground **6** RH16 .....50 D7
Ashenground Rd RH16 .....50 D8
Asher Reeds TN3 .....7 A4
Ashford Cl **4** BN27 .....152 C7
Ashford Rd Brighton BN1 .....143 A2
  Eastbourne BN21 .....185 A3
  Hastings TN34 .....136 D2
Ashford Sq BN21 .....185 A3
Ashford Way TN34 .....136 E3
Ashgate Rd BN23 .....174 E2
Ashington Ct BN2 .....164 F6
Ashington Gdns BN10 .....178 F6
Ashington Rd BN22 .....174 A1
Ashlands TN6 .....26 B1
Ashleigh Gdns TN6 .....25 E4
Ashleigh Glegg Ho BN25 .....180 D4
Ashley Cl BN1 .....142 E7
Ashley Ct Hove BN3 .....163 C5
  7 St Leonards TN37 .....159 C7
Ashley Gdns
  Hailsham BN27 .....129 C3
  Mayfield TN20 .....40 A2
  Rusthall TN4 .....7 C5
Ashley Park Cl TN4 .....7 C5
Ashley Pk TN4 .....7 C5
Ashley Rd TN6 .....27 D1
Ashlings Way Hove BN3 .....141 E2
  Shoreham-by-Sea BN43 .....140 B1
Ashmore Cl BN10 .....167 D2
Ashstead Twrs **8** TN40 .....157 E4
Ashton Lodge **14** BN2 .....189 C3
Ashton Rise BN2 .....189 C3
Ashtonville Cl BN8 .....124 E5
Ashurst Ave BN2 .....177 C5
Ashurst Hill TN3 .....5 D2
Ashurst Rd Brighton BN2 .....143 F5
  Seaford BN25 .....180 F2
  Stone Cross TN3 .....6 B2
Ashurst Sta TN3 .....5 D2
Ashurstwood Abbey RH19 .....11 E6
Ashurstwood Cty Prim Sch
  RH19 .....11 E6
Ashway TN15 .....73 A2
Ashwyn Bsns Ctr RH15 .....72 F5
Aspen Cl RH16 .....51 B4
Aspen Rd BN22 .....173 E2
Aspen Way TN39 .....156 C6
Aspen Wlk
  Haywards Heath RH16 .....51 B4

Aspen Wlk *continued*
  Heathfield TN21 .....82 B5
Astaire Ave BN22 .....185 B6
Asten Cl TN38 .....158 E7
Asten Fields TN33 .....112 C4
Astra Ho **10** BN1 .....163 E5
Atfield Wlk BN22 .....173 C5
Athelstan Cl **1** BN23 .....185 F8
Athelstan Rd TN7 .....8 C5
Athenaeum The **16** BN3 .....163 C6
Atlantic Dr BN23 .....185 F7
Atlingworth St BN2 .....189 C1
Attree Ct **6** BN2 .....164 C6
Attree Dr BN2 .....164 C6
Auckland Dr BN2 .....143 F1
Auckland Ho TN40 .....157 C7
Auckland Rd TN1 .....8 C5
Audrey Cl Brighton BN1 .....142 E5
Audrey Sturley Ct TN4 .....7 D4
Augustines Way RH16 .....50 F4
Augustus Way TN37 .....135 F6
Austen Cl RH19 .....1 B1
Austen Way TN35 .....137 D5
Austen Wlk BN23 .....174 D2
Avard Cres BN23 .....184 B6
Avards Cl TN18 .....45 E8
Avenue Ct **20** BN3 .....163 C6
Avenue La BN21 .....184 F3
Avenue The Brighton BN2 .....143 E1
  Dormansland RH19 .....2 B6
  Eastbourne BN21 .....184 F3
  Fairlight Cove TN35 .....138 F4
  Hailsham BN27 .....152 B6
  Heathfield TN21 .....82 B6
  Horam TN21 .....106 F8
  Kingston near Lewes BN7 .....145 D5
  Lewes BN7 .....123 C1
  Mayfield TN20 .....40 B2
Avery Cl BN41 .....140 F4
Aviemore Rd TN6 .....25 D2
Avis Cl BN9 .....168 E1
Avis Par BN9 .....168 E1
Avis Rd BN9 .....168 E1
Avis Way BN9 .....168 E1
Avocet BN27 .....152 A7
Avocet Trad Est RH15 .....72 F2
Avon St TN1 .....8 C5
Avondale Rd
  Eastbourne BN22 .....185 B4
  Hove BN3 .....163 D7
  Seaford BN25 .....180 F3
  St Leonards TN38 .....136 A1
Avonhurst RH15 .....73 B3
Avonmore BN20 .....188 E8
Awbrook Cl RH17 .....51 E3
Aylesbury BN3 .....163 E6
Aylesbury Ave BN23 .....185 E8
Aymer Ho **4** BN3 .....163 A6
Aymer Rd BN3 .....163 A6
Aynsley Ct BN3 .....163 C8
Ayscue Cl BN23 .....185 F7

B

Babylon Way BN20 .....184 B8
Back La Cross-in-Hand TN21 .....81 C6
  Fairwarp TN22 .....36 B2
  Rushlake Green TN21 .....83 D1
  Winchelsea TN36 .....117 E7
Back Rd TN18 .....47 B5
Backwoods Cl RH16 .....51 B6
Backwoods La RH16 .....51 B6
Baden Rd BN2 .....143 D1
Badens Cl BN8 .....76 C6
Badger Dr BN41 .....141 B2
Badger Dr RH16 .....50 C5
Badger Gate TN31 .....93 A3
Badger Way BN1 .....143 E6
Badgers Brow BN20 .....184 B8
Badgers Cl TN6 .....25 E3
Badgers Copse BN25 .....181 C3
Badgers Dene BN7 .....167 D8
Badgers Field BN10 .....167 C1
Badgers Holt TN2 .....8 E5
Badgers Mount TN39 .....156 E5
Badgers Way
  East Grinstead RH19 .....1 F2
  Hastings TN34 .....136 D5
Badgers Wlk RH15 .....73 D2
Badlesmere Rd BN22 .....185 B6
Bagham La BN27 .....130 F6
Bahram Rd BN26 .....172 F6
Bailey Cres BN22 .....173 B3
Baillie Ave BN22 .....185 C5
Bainbridge Cl BN25 .....180 F3
Bainden Cl TN6 .....27 D1
Baird Dr TN34 .....136 E3
Baird Ho TN37 .....159 C8
Baker Ct TN22 .....78 C7
Baker St
  Brighton BN1, BN2 .....189 B4
  Newhaven BN9 .....179 E7
  Uckfield TN22 .....78 D6
Baker's Rd BN21 .....184 D3
Bakery Mews BN1 .....143 C1
Bakewell Rd BN21 .....184 D4
Bal Edmund TN37 .....136 B4
Balaclava La TN5 .....30 A6
Balcombe Cl BN10 .....178 C8
Balcombe Gn TN33 .....88 E1
Balcombe La RH17, RH19 .....21 E1
Balcombe Rd
  Haywards Heath RH16 .....50 D7

Balcombe Rd continued
Peacehaven BN10 ....**178** B8
Baldings Cotts RH17 ....**74** B5
Baldock Rd TN5 ....**29** E4
Baldslow Down TN37 ...**136** C8
Baldslow Rd TN34 ......**136** F1
Baldwin Ave BN21 ......**184** C5
Baldwins Hill Cty Prim Sch
RH19 ....**1** D3
Bale Cl TN39 ....**156** E5
Balfour Cty Inf Sch BN1 .143 A3
Balfour Cty Jun Sch BN1 143 A3
Balfour Gdns RH18 ......**11** E1
Balfour Rd BN1 ....**143** B2
Ball's Gn TN7 ....**14** B5
Ballard Dr BN8 ....**125** A7
Ballards Hill TN33 ....**134** F4
Ballsocks La TN21 ....**107** C8
Balmoral RH19 ....**11** A8
Balmoral Cl BN25 ....**181** A6
Balmoral Ct BN3 ....**142** A3
Balsdean Rd BN2 ......**144** F1
Baltimore Ct 8 BN3 ......**163** C7
Bamford Cl BN2 ....**144** A2
Bampfield St BN41 ......**162** B8
Bancroft Ho BN39 ......**157** B5
Bancroft Rd TN39 ......**157** B5
Bank Rd TN39 ....**157** C7
Banks Rd BN8 ....**52** F1
Bankside Brighton BN1 ..**142** C5
Hassocks BN6 ....**97** F5
Rye TN31 ....**93** B6
Sparrow's Green TN5 ....**29** C5
Bankside Ct BN1 ....**142** C5
Banner Farm Rd TN2 ....**8** B2
Banner Way BN24 ......**174** C6
Bannings Vale BN2 .....**177** E5
Bannister Way RH16 ....**50** D6
Bannisters Field TN38 ...**76** D7
Baranscraig Ave BN1 ...**143** A7
Barbados 2 TN40 ......**157** E3
Barber Ct BN7 ....**146** B8
Barchester 17 BN21 ...**185** A2
Barclay Ho 2 BN2 .....**164** C7
Barcombe Ave BN25 ....**181** C3
Barcombe CE Prim Sch
BN8 ....**101** D5
Barcombe Cl
Eastbourne BN20 ......**184** C3
Seaford BN25 ....**181** C4
Barcombe Mills Rd BN8 .**101** E4
Barcombe Pl BN1 ....**143** F5
Barcombe Rd BN1 ......**143** E4
Barcombe Wlk BN20 ....**184** C3
Barden Rd
Eastbourne BN22 ......**185** C4
Speldhurst TN3 ....**7** A8
Bardown Rd TN5 ....**42** E7
Bargate Cl BN39 ....**157** C7
Barham TN34 ....**136** D4
Barkdale RH15 ....**73** D5
Barkham Manor Vineyard
TN22 ....**77** B8
Barley Ave TN35 ....**160** C5
Barley Cl BN10 ....**167** B2
Barley Dr RH15 ....**72** D4
Barley Field Cotts BN7 ..**146** D1
Barley La TN35 ....**160** D5
Barley Mow La TN21 ....**83** B5
Barming Cl BN23 ......**174** D2
Barn Cl Hailsham BN27 .**129** C1
Kingston near Lewes BN7 .**145** E5
Seaford BN25 ....**181** A6
Stone Cross BN24 ......**174** A6
Barn Cottage La RH16 ..**51** A5
Barn Cotts 2 BN25 ....**181** A3
Barn Ct TN37 ....**136** C5
Barn Field Cotts 8 BN2 .**164** C6
Barn Hatch Cl BN7 .....**146** A8
Barn La TN22 ....**79** D8
Barn Rd BN7 ....**123** E3
Barn Rise Brighton BN1 ..**142** D5
Seaford BN25 ....**181** A5
Barn Stables BN7 ......**123** B1
Barnard Gate RH16 ....**50** E7
Barnes Rd BN41 ....**162** B8
Barnet Way BN3 ....**141** E3
Barnett Rd BN1 ....**143** B2
Barnett Way TN22 ......**78** D7
Barnetts Way TN4 ......**8** C8
Barnfield Crowborough TN6 .26 A3
Plumpton Green BN7 ....**99** E5
Royal Tunbridge Wells TN2 ..16 F7
Barnfield Cl TN34 ......**159** D8
Barnfield Gdns BN6 ....**98** E3
Barnham Cl BN22 ......**174** A2
Barnhams The TN39 ....**156** E3
Barnhorn Cl TN39 ......**156** C4
Barnhorn Rd TN39 .....**156** B4
Barnmead RH16 ....**50** D7
Barnsgate Manor Vineyard
TN22 ....**36** E5
Barnside Ave RH15 .....**73** D1
Barons Cl BN25 ....**180** C5
Barons Ct Burgess Hill RH15 73 B2
Royal Tunbridge Wells TN4 ..8 A5
Barons Down Rd BN7 ...**146** A8
Barons Way BN26 ......**172** F5
Barrack Rd TN40 ......**157** C5
Barrack Sq TN36 ......**117** F7
Barracks Cotts TN32 ....**87** C7
Barrhill Ave BN1 ....**142** F7
Barrie Cl BN23 ....**174** E2
Barrier Reef Way BN23 .**175** A1

Barrington Cl RH16 .....**50** F8
Barrington Rd RH16 ....**51** A8
Barrington Wood RH16 .**50** F8
Barrow Cl BN1 ....**143** C2
Barrow Hill BN1 ....**143** C2
Barrow La TN3 ....**6** F1
Barrow Rise TN37 ......**136** C5
Barrowcliff Cl BN3 .....**142** C3
Barrowfield Dr BN3 ....**142** C2
Barrowfield Lodge BN3 .**142** C2
Barry Wlk BN2 ....**164** C6
Bartholomew Sq BN1 ..**189** B2
Bartholomews BN1 .....**189** B2
Bartley Mill Cl BN24 ....**174** B5
Barton Cres RH19 ......**11** A8
Barton Sch TN38 ......**136** B1
Basin Rd N BN41 ......**162** B6
Basin Rd S BN3, BN41 ..**162** B6
Baslow Ct BN20 ....**188** D7
Baslow Rd BN20 ......**188** D7
Bassett's Forge TN5 ....**29** C6
Bassetts La Argos Hill TN20 .39 F5
Mark Cross TN6 ....**28** E2
White Post TN8, TN11 ...**5** C7
Batchelor Way BN1 ....**189** B2
Batchelors TN22 ....**9** E8
Bateman's TN19 ....**62** A4
Bateman's La TN19 .....**62** A4
Batemans Rd BN2 .....**165** E7
Bates Rd BN1 ....**142** F2
Bath Ct BN3 ....**163** A5
Bath Rd BN21 ....**184** F2
Bath St BN1 ....**189** A4
Bathford Cl BN23 .....**174** D2
Battenhurst Rd TN5 ....**43** B4
Battery Hill TN35 ......**138** D5
Battle & Langton
CE Prim Sch TN33 .....**112** C4
Battle Abbey TN33 .....**112** D4
Battle Abbey (Sch) TN33 .112 D4
Battle Cl BN25 ....**181** C5
Battle Cres Hailsham BN27 152 B8
St Leonards TN37 ......**136** B4
Battle Gates TN33 .....**112** B5
Battle Hill TN33 ......**112** E3
Battle Rd Hailsham BN27 .**129** C1
St Leonards TN37 ......**136** A4
Battle Sta TN33 ....**112** E4
Batts Bridge Rd TN22 ...**55** A4
Bavant Rd BN1 ....**142** E2
Baxter Rd BN7 ....**123** B2
Baxter St BN2 ....**164** C7
Baxters La RH17 ....**34** C6
Bay Ave BN24 ....**175** E5
Bay Cotts BN24 ....**176** C7
Bay Pond Rd BN21 ....**184** D4
Bay Rd BN24 ....**175** D4
Bay Terr BN24 ....**175** D5
Bay Tree Cl Heathfield TN21 .82 C5
Shoreham-by-Sea BN43 ..**140** C1
Bay Tree La BN26 .....**172** F8
Bay Vue Rd BN9 ......**179** D7
Bayencourt N TN40 ....**157** C5
Bayencourt S TN40 ....**157** C5
Bayeux Ct Bexhill TN40 .**157** D3
St Leonards TN37 ......**159** D8
Bayhall Rd TN2 ....**8** C3
Bayham Abbey TN3 ....**19** B5
Bayham Ct TN5 ....**29** E6
Bayham Rd
Eastbourne BN22 ......**185** C4
Hailsham BN27 ....**152** D7
Royal Tunbridge
Wells TN2,TN3 ....**17** C7
Bayley's La TN35 ......**151** B2
Baylis Cres RH15 ......**72** D4
Bayview Rd BN10 .....**178** E5
Baywood Gdns BN2 ...**165** C8
Bazehill Rd BN2 ......**165** F2
Beach Cl BN25 ....**180** D3
Beach Cotts BN25 .....**180** C4
Beach Ct 10 BN43 .....**161** A6
Beach Mews 6 BN22 ..**185** C5
Beach Rd
Eastbourne BN22 ......**185** C5
Newhaven BN9 ....**179** E6
Beachings The BN24 ...**175** C4
Beachy Head
Countryside Ctr BN20 ..**188** B4
Beachy Head Rd
Beachy Head BN20 ....**188** C4
Eastbourne BN20 ......**188** D8
Beacon Bsns Pk TN6 ...**38** C8
Beacon Cl Brighton BN1 .**143** A2
Crowborough TN6 .....**25** C1
Seaford BN25 ....**180** D5
Beacon Com Coll
Crowborough TN6 .....**26** A2
Crowborough TN6 .....**26** B3
Beacon Ct BN2 ....**165** D4
Beacon Dr BN25 ......**180** E5
Beacon Gdns TN6 .....**25** E3
Beacon Hill Bexhill TN39 .**157** A8
Dormansland RH7 .....**2** B8
Ovingdean BN2 ....**165** E3
Beacon Hurst BN6 ....**98** B3
Beacon La TN32 ......**88** E7
Beacon Rd
Crowborough TN6 .....**25** E2
Ditchling BN6 ....**98** D2
Hastings TN35 ....**137** E4
Seaford BN25 ....**180** D4
Beacon Rd W TN6 .....**25** D2
Beaconfield Ho TN6 ....**25** E2
Beaconsfield Cotts RH17 .51 F3
Beaconsfield Rd
Bexhill TN40 ....**157** C6
Brighton TN1 ....**164** A8

Beaconsfield Rd continued
Chelwood Gate RH17 ...**34** D3
Hastings TN34 ....**136** F2
Portslade-by-Sea BN41 ..**162** B8
Beaconsfield Terr TN21 ..**81** B8
Beaconsfield Villas BN1 .**142** F1
Beaconsville Ct BN1 ....**142** F1
Beagles Wood Rd TN2 ..**9** E7
Beal Cres BN1 ....**143** B2
Beale St RH15 ....**72** F1
Beales La TN31 ....**67** B6
Beame Ct BN25 ....**180** D3
Beamsley Rd BN22 ....**185** C4
Beaney's La TN34,TN35 ..**136** E6
Bear Rd BN2 ....**164** D8
Bear Yd BN7 ....**123** D1
Beatrice La 2 BN21 ....**184** F3
Beatrice Wlk TN39 .....**157** A6
Beatty Ave BN1 ....**143** D6
Beatty Rd BN23 ....**185** E7
Beauchamp Rd TN38 ..**136** A4
Beauford Rd TN21 .....**106** F7
Beaufort Cres TN37 ....**136** C2
Beaufort Rd TN37 .....**136** C2
Beaufort Terr BN2 .....**164** C6
Beauharrow Rd TN37 ..**136** A6
Beaulieu Ct TN40 .....**157** F5
Beaulieu Dr BN24 .....**174** A5
Beaulieu Gdns TN37 ...**136** C6
Beaulieu Rd TN39 .....**156** D2
Beauport Gdns TN37 ...**136** A4
Beauport Home Farm Cl
TN37 ....**136** A6
Beaver Cl TN6 ....**26** A1
Beckenham Cl BN27 ...**129** B3
Becket Cl TN34 ....**160** A5
Beckets Way TN22 ....**79** B5
Beckett Way
  11 East Grinstead RH19 ...**10** F8
Lewes BN7 ....**123** C3
Beckley CE Prim Sch
TN31 ....**68** A4
Beckley Cl Brighton BN2 .**164** C5
St Leonards TN38 .....**135** D2
Beckworth Cl RH16 ....**51** A5
Beckworth La RH16 ....**51** A6
Bedales RH17 ....**51** D4
Bedales Cnr RH17 .....**51** C5
Bedales Hill RH16,RH17 ..**51** D4
Beddingham Gdns BN8 .**147** F5
Bedelands Cl RH15 ....**73** B5
Bedelands Farm Local
Nature Reserve RH15 ...**73** B6
Bedford Ave TN40 .....**157** D3
Bedford Cl TN22 ......**78** C8
Bedford Gr BN21 ......**184** F4
Bedford Pl BN1 ....**163** B5
Bedford Rd TN35 ......**160** C6
Bedford Sq BN1 ....**163** B5
Bedford St BN2 ....**164** C4
Bedford Terr 9 TN1 ...**8** A2
Bedford Twrs 9 BN1 ...**163** B5
Bedfordwell Ct 2 BN22 .**185** A4
Bedfordwell Rd BN22 ...**185** A4
Bedgebury Cl TN38 ....**135** E2
Bedgebury Lower Sch
TN18 ....**45** F7
Bedgebury National
Pinetum TN17 ....**32** E8
Bee Rd BN10 ....**178** C8
Beech Cl Battle TN33 ...**112** C7
Bexhill TN39 ....**156** C6
  3 East Grinstead RH19 ...**1** D2
Portslade-by-Sea BN41 ..**140** F3
Beech Ct BN26 ....**173** A6
Beech Farm Rd TN33 ...**88** D3
Beech Fields RH19 .....**1** F3
Beech Gr BN2 ....**143** E3
Beech Green La TN7 ...**14** B7
Beech Hill RH16 ......**51** B4
Beech House La
TN19,TN32 ....**64** C6
Beech Hurst TN2 ......**9** D7
Beech Hurst Cl RH16 ...**50** C4
Beech Hurst Cotts RH16 .50 C4
Beech Manor TN2 .....**8** D3
Beech Mews BN9 .....**179** E7
Beech Rd TN18 ....**48** C3
Beech St TN1 ....**8** A4
Beech Villas 1 TN21 ...**82** A6
Beecham Pl TN38 .....**135** F4
Beechers Rd BN41 ....**140** F3
Beeches Cl
Heathfield TN21 ......**82** B8
Uckfield TN22 ....**78** D8
Beeches Farm Rd TN6 ..**26** A1
Beeches Head RH19 ...**2** F5
Beeches La RH19 .....**11** D6
Beeches Rd BN2 ......**26** B2
Beeches The
Brighton BN1 ....**142** D3
Royal Tunbridge Wells TN2 ..8 D5
The Moor TN18 ....**45** E7
Beechfield Cl BN24 ....**174** B6
Beeching Cl TN39 .....**157** B4
Beeching Park Ind Est
TN39 ....**157** B4
Beeching Rd TN39 ....**157** B4
Beeching Way RH19 ...**1** E1
Beechlands Cotts TN5 ..**28** F3
Beechwood 6 BN1 ....**142** E3
Beechwood Ave BN1 ...**142** F4
Beechwood Cl
Brighton BN1 ....**142** F4
Burwash TN19 ....**62** B7
Hailsham BN27 ....**152** C5
Beechwood Cres BN20 .**184** D3
Beechwood Gdns TN37 .136 D5

Beechwood La
Cooksbridge BN7, BN8 ..**122** F8
Heathfield TN21 ......**82** B5
Beechwood Mews TN2 ..**8** E4
Beechwood Sch
(Sacred Heart) TN2 .....**8** E4
Beechwoods RH15 ....**73** A1
Beechy Ave BN20 .....**184** B5
Beechy Gdns BN20 ....**184** B5
Beechy Rd TN22 ......**80** A2
Beeding Ave BN3 .....**141** F3
Beeding Cl Hove BN3 ..**142** C5
  4 Shoreham-by-Sea BN43 .161 B8
Beggar's La TN14 .....**122** F8
Beggar's Wood Rd BN8 .**75** C6
Belbourne Ct 5 BN1 ..**189** B3
Belbourne St 5 BN1 ..**189** B3
Belfast St BN3 ....**163** B7
Belfield Rd TN2 ....**9** D6
Belfry Orch TN22 .....**78** D5
Belfry The BN27 ......**152** A8
Belgrave Cres BN25 ...**180** F5
Belgrave Ct 7 TN40 ...**157** D3
Belgrave Pl 11 BN2 ...**164** D4
Belgrave Rd
Royal Tunbridge Wells TN1 ..8 B4
Seaford BN25 ....**180** E4
Belgrave St BN2 ......**189** C3
Belgrove 5 TN1 ......**8** A2
Bell Alley Rd TN19 ....**62** B5
Bell Banks Rd BN27 ...**152** C7
Bell Hammer RH19 ....**10** E8
Bell La Lewes BN7 .....**146** B8
Nutley TN22 ....**35** A4
Uckfield TN22 ....**78** B6
Uckfield TN22 ....**78** C6
Bell Mead 7 BN3 .....**163** D7
Bell Tower Ind Est 7
BN2 ....**164** E4
Bell Wlk TN22 ....**78** C6
Bellbrook Ind Est TN22 ..**78** B6
Bexhill TN40 ....**157** C5
Belle Hill Bexhill TN40 ..**157** B5
Belle Vue Ct TN40 .....**157** C5
Belle Vue Rd 4 BN22 ..**185** C5
Bellevue Cotts BN2 ....**164** F8
Bellevue Ct Brighton BN1 .142 F1
  2 Eastbourne BN22 .....**185** C5
Bellevue Gdns BN2 ....**164** D4
Bellhurst Rd TN32 .....**64** A4
Bellingham Cl TN37 ...**136** B4
Bellingham Cres BN3 ..**162** D8
Belmaine Ct BN39 .....**156** F4
Belmont Bexhill TN39 ..**157** B3
Brighton BN1, BN3 .....**163** E7
Belmont Cl BN6 ......**97** E5
Belmont Ct
  4 Brighton BN1 ......**163** E7
Hailsham BN27 ....**152** B7
Belmont La BN6 ......**97** C5
Belmont Rd
Hastings TN35 ....**160** C5
Uckfield TN22 ....**78** C7
Belmont St BN1 ......**189** B3
Belmore Rd BN21 .....**185** B4
Belton Rd BN2 ....**164** B8
Beltring Rd
Eastbourne BN22 ......**185** B4
Royal Tunbridge Wells TN4 ..8 A6
Beltring Terr BN21 ....**185** B4
Belvedere Ct 11 BN21 ..**184** F4
Belvedere Gdns
Crowborough TN6 .....**26** A1
Seaford BN25 ....**181** A5
Belvedere Pk TN38 ....**159** A8
Belvedere Terr 5 BN1 .**163** E6
Bembridge Rd BN23 ...**174** B3
Bembridge St BN2 ....**164** C8
Bembrook Rd TN34 ....**160** B5
Bemzells La BN27 .....**108** D2
Benbow Ave BN25 ....**185** E6
Benbow Ho TN39 .....**156** E4
Benchfield Cl RH19 ....**2** B1
Bending Cres TN40 ....**157** C5
Benenden Cl BN25 ....**181** A4
Benenden Rise TN34 ..**136** E3
Benett Ave BN3 ......**142** B2
Benett Dr BN3 ....**142** B2
Benfield Cl BN41 .....**141** C1
Benfield Cres BN41 ...**141** C1
Benfield Rd BN41 .....**162** C8
Benfield Cty Jun Sch
BN41 ....**162** C8
Benfield Way BN41 ...**141** C1
Bengairn Ave BN1 ....**143** A7
Benhall Mill Rd TN2,TN3 ..17 D8
Benham Ct 3 BN3 ....**163** B5
Benjamin Cl BN22 ....**173** F2
Benjamin Lodge RH15 .**73** D3
Bennett Meml
Diocesan Sch TN4 ....**7** E6
Bennett Rd BN2 ......**164** E4
Benson Ct BN3 ....**162** E7
Bentham Hill TN3 .....**7** D8
Bentham Rd BN2 .....**164** C7
Bentley Motor Mus BN8 .103 F1
Bentley Wildfowl Reserve
BN8 ....**103** F4
Bentswood Cres RH16 .**51** A5
Bentswood Rd RH16 ..**50** F5
Berberis Ct BN3 ......**140** B1
Beresford Cl TN17 ....**20** F2
Beresford Ct 11 BN3 ..**163** D7
Beresford Ho BN10 ...**167** C1
Beresford Rd
Brighton BN2 ....**164** D5
Newhaven BN9 ....**168** E1
Bergamot Cres BN43 ..**140** C1
Beristede Cl BN20 ....**184** E1

Berkeley Cl TN2 ......**9** E7
Berkeley Ct 6 BN3 ...**163** E7
Berkeley Mans 3 TN40 .157 F3
Berkeley Row BN7 ....**146** A8
Berkeley Wlk BN23 ...**174** E3
Berkley Rd TN20 .....**39** E1
Berkshire Ct 7 BN22 .**185** B4
Berlin TN35 ....**160** C6
Bermuda Pl BN23 .....**185** E6
Bernard La 1 BN21 ...184 F3
Bernard Pl BN2 ....**164** C7
Bernard Rd BN2 ......**164** C7
Bernhard Baron Cottage
Homes The BN26 ......**172** F6
Bernhard Gdns BN26 ..**172** F5
Berriedale Ave BN3 ...**162** E6
Berriedale Ho BN3 ....**162** E6
Berry Cl Burgess Hill RH15 .73 A5
Telscombe Cliffs BN10 ..**167** A1
Berwick BN26 ....**170** F7
Berwick Cl Bexhill TN39 .156 C6
Lower Willingdon BN22 ..**173** C3
Seaford BN25 ....**180** D4
Berwick Court Cotts
BN26 ....**171** A6
Berwick Ct 1 BN21 ..**185** B3
Berwick Rd BN2 ......**166** D3
Berwick Sta BN26 ....**150** B2
Betchley Cl RH19 .....**1** E3
Betherinden Cotts TN18 ..47 A4
Bethune Rd 1 TN40 ..**157** C3
Bethune Way TN34 ...**136** F1
Beulah Rd TN1 ....**8** C4
Beuzeville Ave BN27 ..**152** B8
Bevendean Ave BN2 ..**177** D5
Bevendean Cres BN2 ..**143** E2
Bevendean Prim Sch
BN2 ....**143** F1
Bevendean Rd BN2 ...**143** D1
Beverington Cl BN21 ..**184** D6
Beverington Rd BN21 ..**184** D6
Beverley Ct BN3 ......**162** D7
Beverley Wlk TN34 ...**160** A6
Bevern Bridge BN8 ...**100** F4
Bevern Bridge Cotts BN8 100 F4
Beverns The BN7 .....**99** E5
Bevin Ct TN38 ....**136** B3
Bewl Bridge Cl TN5 ...**32** B3
Bewl Water TN5 ......**31** C6
Bewl Water Visitors Ctr
TN5 ....**31** C6
Bewlbridge La
Bewlbridge TN3, TN5 ...**20** B1
Lower Cousley Wood TN5 ..30 F8
Bexfield Ct BN24 .....**175** E6
Bexhill (Lower) Sch
TN39 ....**157** A7
Bexhill Coll TN39 .....**157** A7
Bexhill High Sch TN39 .**157** B5
Bexhill Hospl TN40 ...**157** C5
Bexhill Mus TN39 ....**157** B3
Bexhill Rd
Eastbourne BN22 ......**185** C5
Lower Street TN33, TN39 .**133** C3
St Leonards TN33, TN40 .**158** D6
Woodingdean BN2 ....**144** E1
Bexhill Sta TN40 .....**157** C4
Bexleigh Ave TN38 ...**158** C5
Bexley Cl BN27 ......**129** B2
Bexley Ct BN26 ......**173** A7
Bicton Gdns TN39 ....**156** E4
Biddenden Cl BN23 ...**174** D2
Bidwell Ave TN39 ....**157** A7
Bigwood Ave BN1 ....**163** D8
Bilbury Mews BN21 ...**184** F5
Billingham La TN31 ...**91** C3
Binstead Cl BN22 ....**173** E1
Biology Rd BN1 ......**144** B6
Birch Ave RH17 ......**51** A5
Birch Cl Eastbourne BN23 .185 D7
Haywards Heath RH17 ...**51** B3
Royal Tunbridge Wells TN2 ..8 D7
Uckfield TN22 ....**78** E8
Birch Ct BN42 ....**141** A1
Birch Est The BN23 ...**185** C7
Birch Grove Cres BN1 .**143** A5
Birch Ho 2 RH19 ....**1** D2
Birch Kiln Cotts TN5 ..**30** A6
Birch Path TN22 .....**78** D8
Birch Rd BN23 ....**185** C7
Birch Rdbt BN23 .....**185** C7
Birch View TN39 .....**157** C6
Birch Way Hailsham BN27 .152 B6
Hastings TN34 ....**136** D4
Haywards Heath RH17 ...**51** A2
Heathfield TN21 ......**82** A5
Royal Tunbridge Wells TN2 ..8 D7
Birchden Cotts TN3 ...**15** C6
Birchen La RH16 .....**50** F8
Birches TN6 ....**25** F4
Birches Ind Est RH19 ..**1** A3
Birchetts Ave TN3 ....**6** E3
Birchetts Green La TN5 .**31** A2
Birchgrove La RH17 ...**22** A1
Birchgrove Rd RH17 ..**33** C3
Birchington Cl TN39 ..**156** C6
Bircholme TN6 ....**8** D7
Birchwood Grove
Cty Prim Sch RH15 ....**73** C1
Birchwood Grove Rd
RH15 ....**73** C1
Bird in Eye Hill TN22 ..**78** C6
Bird in Hand St TN3 ..**15** B8
Bird La TN5 ....**29** E5
Birdham Pl BN2 ......**143** C3
Birdham Rd BN2 .....**143** C3
Birk Dale TN39 ......**156** D4

Birkdale TN1 . . . . .8 B6
Birken Rd TN2 . . . . .8 D6
Birling Cl Brighton BN2 . .143 D1
  Seaford BN25 . . . . .180 D4
Birling Dr TN2 . . . . .8 A1
Birling Gap Rd BN20 . . . .187 B6
Birling Park Ave TN2 . . .17 B8
Birling Rd TN2 . . . . .17 B8
Birling St BN21 . . . . .184 C4
Birling Way TN22 . . . . . . .78 E8
Biscay Ave BN3 . . . . .185 F8
Bishop Bell CE Sch BN23 174 E1
Bishop's Cl
  Hurstpierpoint BN6 . . . . .97 A7
  Ringmer BN8 . . . . .124 E6
Bishop's Down TN4 . . . . . . .7 F3
Bishop's Down
  Cty Prim Sch TN4 . . . .7 E5
Bishop's Down Park Rd
  TN4 . . . . .7 F4
Bishop's Down Rd TN4 . . .7 F4
Bishop's La Ringmer BN8 .124 D6
  Robertsbridge TN32 . . . .64 A3
Bishop's Wlk TN40 . . . . . .157 F6
Bishops Cl BN25 . . . . .180 C4
Bishops Ct TN4 . . . . .7 F3
Bishops Dr BN7 . . . . .146 A8
Bishops Rd BN3 . . . . .142 C1
Bishopstone Dr BN2 . . . .177 B6
Bishopstone La BN6,RH17 .72 A7
Bishopstone Rd BN25 . . .180 C6
Bishopstone Sta BN25 . .180 B4
Bittern Ct BN27 . . . . . . .152 D7
Bixley La TN31 . . . . .68 B2
Black Hill RH16 . . . . .51 A7
Black Lion St BN1 . . . . .189 B1
Black Path BN26 . . . . . . .173 A6
Blackberry La RH7 . . . . .1 E8
Blackberry Rd RH19, RH7 . .1 D8
Blackbird Cl RH15 . . . . .72 D3
Blackboys CE Prim Sch
  TN22 . . . . .80 A6
Blackboys YH TN22 . . . . .80 A8
Blackbrook La BN8,RH17 .52 E2
Blackdon Hill TN3 . . . . .27 B6
Blackdown BN2 . . . . .164 F7
Blackdown Rd TN21 . . . . .83 D6
Blackfields Ave TN39 . . . .156 F5
Blackhouse La RH15 . . . .73 B4
Blackhurst La TN2 . . . . .8 F6
Blacklands TN33 . . . . . . .88 F1
Blacklands Cres RH18 . .11 F2
Blacklands Cty Prim Sch
  TN34 . . . . .136 E2
Blacklands Dr TN34 . . . .136 F2
Blackman Ave TN38 . . . . .136 A3
Blackman St BN1 . . . . . . .189 B3
Blackmill Cl TN39 . . . . .157 A8
Blackmores RH17 . . . . . . .74 A5
Blackness Rd TN6 . . . . . .38 A8
Blackness Villas TN6 . .38 A8
Blacksmith's Field TN33 .135 A4
Blacksmith's La TN5 . . .30 A5
Blacksmiths Copse BN27 152 A6
Blacksmiths Field TN32 . .46 C1
Blacksmiths La TN33 . . .133 C8
Blackstone Way RH15 . . .73 A5
Blackthorn Cl
  Brighton BN1 . . . . .142 D3
  Eastbourne BN23 . . . . .173 E2
  Portslade-by-Sea BN41 .141 B2
  St Leonards TN37 . . . .136 C4
Blackthorn Way TN35 . . .138 F4
Blackthorns RH16 . . . . . .51 A7
Blackthorns Cl RH16 . . .51 A6
Blackthorns Cty Prim Sch
  RH16 . . . . .51 A6
Blackthorns The RH15 . .73 B5
Blackwater Rd
  BN20, BN21 . . . . .184 F1
Blackwell Cty Prim Sch
  RH19 . . . . .1 E3
Blackwell Farm Rd RH19 . .1 F3
Blackwell Hollow RH19 . .1 F2
Blackwell Rd RH19 . . . . .1 F2
Blake Ct 2 BN2 . . . . .189 C3
Blake Way TN2 . . . . .8 D7
Blakeney Ave BN10, BN9 . .179 A6
Blaker St BN2 . . . . .189 C2
Blakes Way BN23 . . . . . . .185 F6
Blatchington Cl BN25 . .180 F4
Blatchington Hill BN25 .180 E4
Blatchington Mill Dr
  BN24 . . . . .174 C5
Blatchington Mill Sch
  BN3 . . . . .141 F2
Blatchington Rd
  Hove BN3 . . . . .163 B7
  Royal Tunbridge Wells TN1 . .8 B1
  Seaford BN25 . . . . . . .180 E3
Blenheim Cl RH19 . . . . . .2 A3
Blenheim Cl 1 Hove BN3 .163 A6
  Robertsbridge TN32 . . . .64 F3
Blenheim Fields RH18 . .11 E3
Blenheim Pl 3 BN1 . . . . .189 B3
Blenheim Way
  Flimwell TN5 . . . . .32 C3
  Polegate BN26 . . . . . . .173 D6
Bletchinglye La TN6 . . .27 E1
Bletchley Ct BN1 . . . . . .164 A8
Blind La BN8 . . . . .76 E6
Blois Rd BN7 . . . . .123 B2
Blomfield Rd TN37 . . . . .159 D8
Bloomsbury Pl 17 BN2 . .164 C4
Bloomsbury St 16 BN2 . .164 C4
Blossom Wlk BN27 . . . . . .129 B1
Blount Ave RH19 . . . . . . .1 C1
Blowers Hill Cowden TN8 . .4 D8

Blowers Hill continued
  Speldhurst TN3 . . . . . . .7 B8
Blue Haze Ave BN25 . . . .181 B6
Bluebell Cl
  East Grinstead RH19 . . .1 B1
  Haywards Heath RH16 . .50 F4
Bluebell Rly
  RH17, RH19, TN22 . . . .21 A5
Bluebell Rly Mus TN22 . .53 A4
Bluebell Way RH15 . . . . .72 D4
Bluebird Ct 11 BN3 . . . .163 A6
Bluemans La TN33 . . . . . .114 A4
Bluestone Cl TN38 . . . . .135 F2
Blunts Wood Cres RH17 . .50 B6
Blunts Wood Rd RH17 . . .50 C6
Blytons The RH19 . . . . . .1 B1
Boarders La TN5 . . . . . . .31 C3
Boast La BN8 . . . . .101 F5
Bocking Cl TN5 . . . . .29 C4
Boddingtons La BN6 . . . .98 D3
Bodiam Ave
  Bevendean BN2 . . . . . . .144 B1
  Bexhill TN40 . . . . .157 D6
Bodiam Castle (NT) TN32 .65 F8
Bodiam CE Prim Sch TN32 65 E8
Bodiam Cl Bevendean BN2 144 B2
  Seaford BN25 . . . . . . .181 C4
Bodiam Cres BN22 . . . . .174 A2
Bodiam Ct RH16 . . . . . . .50 E5
Bodiam Dr TN38 . . . . . . .135 D2
Bodiam Manor Sch TN32 .65 E8
Bodiam Rd TN18, TN32 . .46 F3
Bodiam Sta TN32 . . . . . .65 E6
Bodle Cres TN39 . . . . . .157 B7
Bodmin Cl BN20 . . . . . . .184 C3
Bohemia Rd TN34,TN37 . .159 D8
Boiler House Hill BN1 . .144 B7
Bolding Way RH16 . . . . .50 E2
Bolebrooke Rd TN40 . . .157 D3
Bolney Ave BN10 . . . . . .178 C6
Bolney Rd BN2 . . . . .143 F4
Bolnore RH16 . . . . .50 B4
Bolnore Rd RH16 . . . . . .50 C4
Bolsover Ct BN20 . . . . .188 F8
Bolsover Rd
  Eastbourne BN20 . . . . .188 F8
  Hove BN3 . . . . .162 E8
Bolton Cl TN22 . . . . . . .78 A6
Bolton Rd BN21 . . . . . . .185 A2
Boltro Rd RH16 . . . . . . .50 D5
Bonchurch Rd BN2 . . . . .164 C7
Bond St BN1 . . . . .189 B2
Bonfire La RH17 . . . . . .33 D5
Boniface Cl BN24 . . . . .174 C6
Bonny Wood Rd BN6 . . . .97 E3
Booker Cl TN6 . . . . .26 A1
Booth Mus of Natural
  History BN1 . . . . .163 E8
Bopeep Bostal BN26 . . .170 B2
Bopeep La BN26 . . . . . . .170 B8
Border Ct RH19 . . . . . . .1 F4
Borders La TN19 . . . . . .62 F7
Boreham Hill BN27,TN33 .132 A4
Boreham La BN27 . . . . . .131 C2
Borodales TN39 . . . . . . .156 E4
Borough La BN20 . . . . . .184 D3
Borough St BN1 . . . . . . .163 E6
Borrow King Cl BN2 . . .164 D8
Borrowdale Cl BN23 . . .174 C4
Boscawen Ct TN38 . . . . .185 F7
Boscobel Ct TN38 . . . . .159 B4
Boscobel Lodge TN38 . .159 B7
Boscobel Rd TN38 . . . . .159 A4
Boscobel Rd N TN38 . . .159 A4
Boship Cl BN23 . . . . . . .174 A4
Bostal Rd BN8 . . . . .148 B4
Boston Cl BN23 . . . . . . .185 F7
Boston Ct RH16 . . . . . . .51 A6
Boston Rd RH16 . . . . . . .51 A5
Boston St BN1 . . . . .189 B4
Boswell Wlk 8 BN23 . . .174 E2
Bough Beeches RH15 . . .73 C1
Boughey Pl BN7 . . . . . . .123 C3
Boulevard The BN24 . . .175 F6
Boundary Pas 10 BN3 . .163 E6
Boundary Rd Brighton BN2 164 F4
  Portslade-by-Sea
  BN3, BN41 . . . . .162 C7
  Royal Tunbridge Wells TN2 . .8 B1
Boundary The
  Langton Green TN3, TN4 . .7 B3
  2 Seaford BN25 . . . . .180 E2
Bourg-de-Peage Ave RH19 2 A1
Bourne Cty Prim Sch
  BN22 . . . . .185 B3
Bourne La TN3 . . . . .64 F7
Bourne Pas 12 TN34 . . .160 B4
Bourne St BN21 . . . . . . .185 B3
Bourne The Hassocks BN6 .97 E5
  Hastings TN34 . . . . . .160 B4
Bourneside Ct 12 BN22 .185 B3
Bowden House Sch BN25 180 F6
Bowden Rise BN25 . . . . .180 E6
Bowen Ct 11 BN3 . . . . . .163 C6
Bowen Rd TN4 . . . . .7 B4
Bower Cl TN37 . . . . .136 B4
Bower The RH16 . . . . . . .50 D5
Bowerhill Cotts RH19 . .21 F6
Bowlers Town TN31 . . . .70 A2
Bowles Outdoor Ctr TN6 .26 E6
Bowley Rd BN27 . . . . . . .152 C7
Bowlings The TN33 . . . .113 D8
Bowmans Dr TN33 . . . . .112 D6
Bowood Ave BN22 . . . . .185 B6
Bowrey Pl TN40 . . . . . . .157 C5
Bowring Way BN2 . . . . .164 D4

Bowsprit Mews TN38 . . .135 E7
Box La RH19 . . . . .11 E6
Box's La RH17 . . . . .34 C6
Boxes La RH17 . . . . .33 C5
Boxgrove Cl TN40 . . . . .157 F4
Boyce's St BN1 . . . . . . .189 A2
Boyne Pk TN4 . . . . .7 F4
Boyne Rd TN35 . . . . .160 C5
Bracken Cl
  Crowborough TN6 . . . . .26 C1
  Royal Tunbridge Wells TN2 . .8 E5
Bracken Rd
  Eastbourne BN20 . . . . .184 B5
  Royal Tunbridge Wells TN2 . .8 E5
  Seaford BN25 . . . . . . .181 A2
Bracken Way TN21 . . . . .59 E1
Brackenbury Cl BN41 . .141 B2
Brackendale TN35 . . . . .160 D6
Brackenhill TN7 . . . . . .13 A1
Brackerne Cl TN39 . . . .156 C2
Bradford Cl 9 BN2 . . . .185 B4
Bradford Rd BN7 . . . . . .123 B1
Bradford St BN21 . . . . .184 D3
Brading Cl
  Eastbourne BN23 . . . . .174 B4
  Hastings TN34 . . . . . .136 E2
Brading Rd BN2 . . . . . . .164 C7
Bradley Rd Wartling BN27 .131 C1
  White Post TN3 . . . . . .5 D5
Braemar Ho 11 BN1 . . . .163 E6
Braemore Cl BN2 . . . . . .162 E6
Braemore Rd BN3 . . . . .162 E6
Braeside Ave BN1 . . . . .143 A7
Bramber Ave Hove BN3 .141 F3
  Peacehaven BN10 . . . .178 C7
Bramber Ave N BN10 . .178 C8
Bramber Cl
  Haywards Heath RH16 . .50 D4
  Peacehaven BN10 . . . .178 C8
  3 Seaford BN25 . . . . .180 F2
Bramber Ct 8 Hove BN3 .163 B7
  2 Shoreham-by-Sea BN43 .161 B8
Bramber La BN25 . . . . . .180 F2
Bramber Rd BN25 . . . . . .180 F2
Bramber Way RH15 . . . .73 A4
Bramble Cl BN23 . . . . . .174 B3
Bramble Croft TN6 . . . .26 A2
Bramble Dr BN27 . . . . . .152 A7
Bramble Gdns RH15 . . .72 D4
Bramble Rise BN1 . . . . .142 C5
Bramble Twitten RH19 . .2 A1
Bramble Way
  Brighton BN1 . . . . .143 C6
  Fairlight Cove TN35 . .138 F4
Bramble Wlk TN2 . . . . . .8 D7
Brambledean Rd BN41 . .162 B7
Brambles BN6 . . . . .97 F5
Brambles The RH17 . . . .50 A6
Brambleside TN38 . . . . .78 A6
Brambletye La RH18 . . .11 C4
Brambletye Sch RH18 . .11 C5
Brambletyne Ave BN2 . .177 D5
Bramley Rd BN26 . . . . .173 D6
Bramleys BN7 . . . . .145 E5
Brampton Ave TN39 . . .156 F4
Brampton Ct TN39 . . . .156 F4
Brampton Rd BN22 . . . .184 F8
Brampton Road Trad Est
  BN22 . . . . .185 A8
Brand Rd BN22 . . . . . . .173 E1
Brands Cl BN9 . . . . .168 E2
Brangwyn Ave BN1 . . . .142 E5
Brangwyn Cres BN1 . . .142 E5
Brangwyn Ct BN1 . . . . .142 E6
Brangwyn Dr BN1 . . . . .142 E5
Brangwyn Way BN1 . . . .142 E5
Branksome Rd TN38 . . .159 A8
Branston Rd BN22 . . . .173 D1
Brassey Ave BN22 . . . .173 E1
Brassey Par BN22 . . . .173 F1
Brasslands Dr BN41 . . .140 F1
Braybon Ave BN1 . . . . .142 F4
Braybon Bsns Pk BN1 . .72 E2
Braybrooke Cl TN34 . . .159 E8
Braybrooke Rd TN34 . .159 F8
Braybrooke Terr TN34 .159 E8
Braypool La BN1 . . . . . .142 D7
Brazen Cl BN9 . . . . .179 B7
Bread St BN1 . . . . .189 B3
Breadsell La TN38 . . . .135 D6
Brecon Cotts TN6 . . . . .39 A8
Brecon Ct 6 BN3 . . . . . .163 C7
Brede Cl Brighton BN2 . .164 F5
  Eastbourne BN22 . . . .185 D6
  St Leonards TN37 . . . .135 F7
Brede Cty Prim Sch TN31 90 B4
Brede Hill TN31 . . . . . .115 B8
Brede La Cackle Street TN31 89 F2
  Sedlescombe TN31, TN33 .89 B2
Brede Valley View TN36 .116 E5
Breeds Pl TN34 . . . . . . .159 F7
Brendon Cl
  Eastbourne BN23 . . . . .174 E4
  Royal Tunbridge Wells TN2 . .8 D5
Brendon Rise TN34 . . . .137 B3
Brentor Ct TN2 . . . . . . .8 D6
Brentwood Cl BN1 . . . .143 B3
Brentwood Cres BN1 . .143 B3
Brentwood Rd BN1 . . . .143 B3
Bretland Ct TN4 . . . . . .7 D4
Bretland Rd TN4 . . . . . .7 D4
Brett Dr TN40 . . . . . . .157 F4
Bretton RH15 . . . . .72 E5
Bretts Field BN10 . . . .167 C2
Brewer St Brighton BN2 .164 C8
Brewers Gr TN20 . . . . . .40 B2

Brian Cres TN4 . . . . . . .8 B8
Briar Cl
  Fairlight Cove TN35 .139 A5
  Woodingdean BN2 . . . .165 D7
Briar Pl BN23 . . . . .174 B3
Briarcroft Rd BN2 . . . .165 D7
Briary The TN40 . . . . . .157 D5
Brick Kiln La TN20,TN22 .57 E6
Brickfield TN31 . . . . . .69 B2
Brickfields 9 E8
Brickhurst La BN8 . . . .126 C8
Brickmead TN6 . . . . . . .26 A1
Bricky The BN10 . . . . . .178 D8
Brickyard Cotts TN6 . .28 A4
Brickyard La
  Mark Cross TN6 . . . . .27 E5
  South Chailey BN8 . .100 E7
Bridge Cl Burgess Hill RH15 .72 F4
  Horam TN21 . . . . .107 A7
Bridge Ct BN9 . . . . . . .179 D7
Bridge End BN24 . . . . .175 B7
Bridge Farm Rd TN22 . .78 C6
Bridge Ho TN4 . . . . . . .8 B5
Bridge Pl TN31 . . . . . .93 C6
Bridge Rd RH16 . . . . . .50 F6
Bridge Road Bsns Pk
  RH16 . . . . .50 F7
Bridge St BN9 . . . . . . .179 D7
Bridge Way TN38 . . . . .158 C6
Bridgelands BN8 . . . . .101 D4
Bridgemere Rd BN22 . .185 B6
Bridger Way TN6 . . . . .26 A1
Bridgersmill RH16 . . . .50 D6
Bridgewick Cl BN7 . . .123 D3
Bridle Way BN10 . . . . .167 A1
Briers Ave TN34 . . . . .136 C3
Briers Gdns TN34 . . . .136 C3
Briers The TN37 . . . . .136 C4
Brigden St BN1 . . . . . .189 A4
Brigdens Hill BN8 . . .147 E6
Bright Ridge TN4 . . . .7 E8
Brighthelm BN1 . . . . . .144 B8
Brightland Rd BN20 . .184 D3
Brightling Ave TN35 . .137 E4
Brightling Rd
  Polegate BN26 . . . . . .173 B5
  Robertsbridge TN32 . .63 D2
Brighton & Hove
  High Sch for Girls BN3 .163 E6
Brighton & Hove Stad
  BN3 . . . . .142 B1
Brighton Coll BN2 . . .164 C5
Brighton Coll of Tech
  Brighton BN1 . . . . .189 A5
  Brighton BN1 . . . . .189 B3
  Brighton BN1 . . . . .189 C4
Brighton College
  Pre-Prep Sch BN2 . . .164 C5
Brighton Ctr The BN1 .189 A2
Brighton Fishing Mus
  BN1 . . . . .189 A1
Brighton General Hospl
  BN2 . . . . .164 D7
Brighton Marina BN2 . .164 F2
Brighton Marina Village
  BN2 . . . . .164 F3
Brighton Mus & Art Gall
  BN1 . . . . .189 B2
Brighton Pl BN1 . . . . .189 B2
Brighton Race Course
  BN2 . . . . .165 A8
Brighton Rd Hassocks BN6 .97 D2
  Lewes BN7 . . . . .146 A8
  Newhaven BN9 . . . . . . .179 B7
  Shoreham-by-Sea BN43 .161 B7
Brighton Sea Life Ctr
  BN1 . . . . .189 B1
Brighton Sq BN1 . . . . .189 B2
Brighton Sta BN1 . . . .189 B3
Brighton Steiner Sch
  (John Howard Ho) BN2 .164 F4
Brighton, Hove & Sussex
  Sixth Form Coll
  BN3 . . . . .163 E8
Brightwell Ind Est BN9 .179 E7
Brills La BN1, BN2 . . . .189 B1
Brincliffe TN6 . . . . . . .25 E3
Brinkers La TN6 . . . . . .30 A2
Bristol Gate BN2 . . . .164 D4
Bristol Gdns BN2 . . . .164 E4
Bristol Mews 3 BN2 . .164 E4
Bristol Pl BN2 . . . . . .164 E4
Bristol Rd Brighton BN2 .164 C4
  St Leonards TN38 . . .136 A3
Bristol St BN2 . . . . . .164 E4
Bristol Way TN38 . . . .136 A3
Britannia Cl BN2 . . . .165 A3
British Engineerium (Mus)
  BN3 . . . . .142 B2
Britland Est BN22 . . .185 C6
Brittany Ct 3
  Bexhill TN39 . . . . . . .157 A4
  Hove BN3 . . . . .162 D7
Brittany Ho TN6 . . . . .37 C3
Brittany Mews TN38 . .159 B7
Brittany Rd Hove BN3 . .162 D6
  St Leonards TN37,TN38 .159 B8
Britten Cl BN23 . . . . .174 D3
Brittenden La TN11 . .80 E5
Britts Farm Rd TN22 . .56 C3
Britts Orch TN22 . . . .56 C3
Broad Gn BN2 . . . . .165 E6
Broad Gr TN2 . . . . .8 A1
Broad Green Ave RH15 .73 C2
Broad La TN3 . . . . .4 A4
Broad Oak TN3 . . . . . . .15 C6
Broad Oak Cl
  Broad Oak TN31 . . . . .90 B5

Broad Oak Cl continued
  Eastbourne BN23 . . . .174 A4
  Royal Tunbridge Wells TN2 . . .7 F1
Broad Oak Cty Prim Sch
  TN21 . . . . .59 F2
Broad Rd BN20 . . . . . . .173 A4
Broad Rig Ave BN3 . . .141 D3
Broad St Brighton BN2 .189 B1
  Cuckfield RH17 . . . . .50 A6
  Icklesham TN36 . . . . .116 C6
  Seaford BN25 . . . . . . .180 E3
Broad View Bexhill TN39 .156 F6
  Broad Oak TN21 . . . . .59 E1
Broad Way TN35 . . . . . .138 F5
Broadcroft TN2 . . . . . .16 F8
Broadfields BN2 . . . . .143 E3
Broadfields Rd BN2 . .143 E3
Broadhill Cl TN21 . . . .59 E1
Broadlands
  Burgess Hill RH15 . . .98 B8
  Hastings TN35 . . . . . .137 D4
Broadley View TN33 . .133 E8
Broadmead TN2 . . . . . .16 E8
Broadmead Ave TN2 . . .16 E8
Broadoak La Bexhill TN39 .156 E5
  Bexhill TN39 . . . . . . .156 E5
Broads Cotts TN19 . . .62 B6
Broadstone RH18 . . . . .12 A2
Broadview Ct BN20 . . .172 F4
Broadwalk The TN39 . .156 B4
Broadwater Ct TN2 . . .16 E8
Broadwater Down TN2 .16 F8
Broadwater Down
  Cty Prim Sch TN4 . . .7 F1
Broadwater La
  Royal Tunbridge Wells TN2 .16 F8
  Royal Tunbridge Wells
  TN2, TN4 . . . . .7 F1
Broadwater Mews BN26 .172 E3
Broadwater Rise TN2 . .7 F1
Broadwater Way TN2 . .184 F8
Broadway Ct 11 BN43 . .161 C8
Broadway The
  Alfriston BN26 . . . . .170 F3
  Crowborough TN6 . . .25 F3
  Eastbourne BN22 . . .173 D1
  Hastings TN35 . . . . . .137 D4
  Haywards Heath RH16 .50 E5
  Lamberhurst TN3 . . .20 B5
Brockhurst BN2 . . . . .164 F7
Brockhurst Gate TN40 .157 F5
Brockley Rd TN39 . . . .157 A3
Brocks Gyhll BN20 . . .173 A3
Brodie Pl BN21 . . . . . .184 C4
Brodrick Cl BN22 . . . .173 F1
Brodrick Rd BN22 . . . .173 E2
Brokes Way TN4 . . . . .8 B8
Bromley Cl
  Eastbourne BN23 . . . .174 C2
  Keymer BN6 . . . . .98 A4
Bromley Rd Brighton BN2 .189 C5
  Seaford BN25 . . . . . . .181 A4
Brompton Cl BN1 . . . . .142 E6
Brontes The RH19 . . . .1 D1
Brook Ave BN6 . . . . . . .97 F3
Brook Cl Crowborough TN6 .26 D1
  East Grinstead RH19 . .2 B1
Brook Ho TN39 . . . . . .157 C6
Brook La Beddingham BN8 .147 A6
  Lindfield RH16 . . . . . .50 F8
Brook Rd TN2 . . . . .8 D7
Brook St Hastings TN34 .159 F8
  Lewes BN7 . . . . .123 D1
  Polegate BN26 . . . . . .172 F6
Brook Terr TN6 . . . . . .25 D4
Brook View TN6 . . . . . .25 D4
Brook Way TN35 . . . . . .137 B4
Brooker Pl BN3 . . . . . .163 A7
Brooker St BN3 . . . . . .163 B7
Brookfield TN18 . . . . .47 B5
Brookfield Ct 2 TN40 .157 E4
Brookfield Rd TN40 . .157 E4
Brookhouse Bottom TN34 34 D4
Brookhouse Rd TN22 . .79 A4
Brookland Cl
  Beachlands BN24 . . . .175 E6
  Hastings TN34 . . . . . .136 F2
Brooklands TN2 . . . . . .8 D7
Brooklands Ave TN6 . .37 C3
Brooklands Farm Cl TN3 . .6 A6
Brooklands Terr BN27 .128 C2
Brooklands Way RH19 . .10 D8
Brooklyn Rd BN25 . . .180 E3
Brookmead Cl BN22 . .185 B5
Brooks Cl Lewes BN7 . .123 C1
  Newhaven BN9 . . . . . .179 D6
Brooks Gdns BN8 . . . .76 D6
Brooks Rd BN7 . . . . . .123 D2
Brooks The RH15 . . . .72 E5
Brookside Piddinghoe BN9 .168 B2
  Uckfield TN22 . . . . . .78 A6
Brookside Ave BN26 . .172 F4
Brookside Cotts TN19 . .63 B8
Brookway Burgess Hill RH15 .51 A8
  Lindfield RH16 . . . . . .51 A8
Broom Cl BN22 . . . . . .173 D2
Broom La TN3 . . . . . . .6 E3
Broom Pk TN3 . . . . . . .6 E3
Brooman's Ct 16 BN7 . .123 D1
Broomans La BN7 . . . .123 D1
Broomfield Ave BN10 . .177 F4
Broomfield Dr BN41 . .141 A3
Broomfield St
  BN20, BN21 . . . . .184 C4
Broomgrove Rd TN34 . .160 B6

Broomham La BN8 ....127 B7
Broomham Sch TN35 ....116 A3
Broomhill Bank Sch TN3 ..7 C6
Broomhill Park Rd TN4 ....7 F8
Broomhill Rd TN3 ....7 D7
Bross Est BN9 ....179 D8
Brow The Burgess Hill RH15 .73 A2
  Friston BN20 ....183 B2
  Woodingdean BN2 ....165 D8
Brown Jack Ave BN26 ....172 F6
Brown's La TN22 ....78 D8
Browning Rd 2 TN21 ......82 A7
Browning Wlk 5 BN23 ...174 E2
Brownings The 1 RH19 ...1 C1
Brownleaf Rd BN2 ....165 E6
Browns Cl TN22 ....78 D8
Browns La TN21 ....81 B6
Browns Wood RH19 ....1 E4
Broyle Cl BN8 ....125 A8
Broyle La BN8 ....124 F8
Broyle Paddock BN8 ....124 F7
Broyle Side BN8 ....125 A7
Broyle The BN8 ....125 B7
Bruce Cl RH16 ....50 E3
Brunel Rd TN38 ....135 E4
Brunswick Mews 3 BN3 .163 D5
Brunswick Pl BN3 ....163 D6
Brunswick Rd BN3 ....163 D6
Brunswick Row BN1 ....189 B4
Brunswick Sq BN3 ....163 D5
Brunswick St E BN3 ....163 D5
Brunswick St W BN3 ......163 D5
Brunswick Terr
  Hove BN1, BN3 ....163 D5
  Royal Tunbridge Wells TN1 ...8 A2
Brushes La RH16 ....51 B8
Bryants Field TN6 ....25 E3
Brydges Cl BN22 ....185 C6
Buci Cres BN43 ....140 C1
Buckholt Ave TN40 ....158 A7
Buckholt La TN39 ....157 C8
Buckhurst Cl
  East Grinstead RH19 ....1 C3
  Eastbourne BN20 ....184 B8
  Lewes BN7 ....123 C3
Buckhurst La TN5 ....29 A6
Buckhurst Mead RH19 .....1 C4
Buckhurst Pl TN39 ....157 C4
Buckhurst Rd
  Bexhill TN40 ....157 C4
  Telscombe Cliffs BN10 ...177 F3
Buckhurst Way RH19 ....1 C3
Buckingham Cl 4
  Brighton BN1 ....189 A4
  Seaford BN25 ....180 C4
  Shoreham-by-Sea BN43 ...161 A8
Buckingham Dr RH19 ......11 A8
Buckingham Heights 1
BN22 ....185 A4
Buckingham Lodge BN1 ...189 A4
Buckingham Pl BN1 ....189 A4
Buckingham Rd
  Brighton BN1 ....189 A3
  Royal Tunbridge Wells TN1 ...8 B2
  St Leonards TN38 ....136 A4
Buckingham St BN1 ....189 A3
Buckland Rd BN25 ....180 F5
Buckle By-Pass BN25 .....180 C4
Buckle Cl BN25 ....180 C4
Buckle Dr BN25 ....180 C4
Buckle Rise BN25 ....180 C4
Buckler St BN41 ....162 B8
Bucklers Ct TN2 ....8 C3
Buckley Cl BN3 ....141 E4
Buckswood Grange Sch
TN22 ....78 B8
Buckthorn Cl BN25 ....181 C3
Buckwell Ct BN7 ....123 A3
Buckwell Rise BN27 ......130 E5
Buddens Gn TN31 ....68 B5
Bugsell La TN32 ....63 F4
Bulbeck Cl RH15 ....72 E1
Bull La 2 BN7 ....146 C8
Bull Lane Cotts TN3 ......19 C4
Bull Ring TN33 ....112 D4
Buller Cl TN6 ....26 A1
Buller Rd BN2 ....143 D1
Bullfinch Gdns BN22 ......78 E4
Bullingstone Cotts TN3 ....6 E7
Bullingstone La TN3 ....6 F7
Bulls Pl TN2 ....9 D6
Bulrush Pl TN38 ....135 E1
Bulverhythe Rd TN38 .....158 D6
Bungalows The TN22 ......79 B5
Bunny La TN3 ....16 E5
Bunting Cl TN38 ....158 E8
Burchetts Cl RH16 ....50 E2
Burden Pl TN38 ....136 A3
Burdett Pl 2 TN34 ....160 A3
Burdett Rd
  Crowborough TN6 ....26 C1
  Rusthall TN4 ....7 B4
Burdocks Dr RH15 ....73 D1
Burfield Park Ind Est
BN27 ....152 B6
Burfield Rd BN22 ....185 B3
Burgess Hill Sch RH15 ...73 B2
Burgess Hill Sta RH15 ...73 B2
Burgess Rd TN35 ....137 C5
Burgh Hill TN19 ....44 E2
Burgh La BN8 ....148 E8
Burgundy Ho 3 BN23 ....185 F8
Burhill Way TN38 ....158 F7
Burleigh Pl BN22 ....185 C6

Burlington Gdns BN41 ....141 C1
Burlington Pl BN21 ....185 A2
Burlington Rd BN21 ....185 B2
Burlington St BN2 ....164 C4
Burlow Cl Brighton BN2 ..164 E5
  Lower Willingdon BN22 ...173 C3
Burma Cl RH16 ....51 C4
Burners Cl RH15 ....73 D1
Burnham Cl BN2 ....165 F7
Burns Way RH19 ....1 C1
Burnside BN26 ....173 A6
Burnside Ct BN26 ....173 A6
Burnt House La TN3 ....7 A5
Burnt Lodge La TN5 ....31 B2
Burnt Oak Rd TN22, TN6 ...37 C2
Burnthouse Bostall BN6 ..120 C8
Burrell Rd RH16 ....50 D6
Burrells La TN22 ....55 A7
Burrells The BN43 ....161 B6
Burrow Down BN20 ....184 B5
Burrow Down Ct BN20 ....184 A5
Burrswood Villas TN3 ......15 B7
Burry Rd TN37 ....136 C3
Burstead Cl BN1 ....143 B3
Burston Gdns RH19 ....1 D4
Burton Rd BN21 ....184 E5
Burton Villas BN3 ....163 D8
Burton Way TN38 ....159 B6
Burton Wlk BN27 ....152 B7
Burwash CE Prim Sch
TN19 ....62 B6
Burwash Cl
  Eastbourne BN23 ....174 B4
  Hastings TN34 ....137 A5
Burwash Lodge BN1 ......143 C1
Burwash Rd
  Broad Oak TN21 ....82 C8
  Hove BN3 ....141 F3
Burwood Ho TN2 ....8 E5
Bush Cl
  Telscombe Cliffs BN10 ...167 A1
  Woodingdean BN2 ....165 D8
Bush Farm Dr BN41 ......141 C3
Bush Rd BN9 ....179 B8
Bushbury La TN22 ....80 A3
Busheyfields BN27 ....152 A8
Bushy Croft TN39 ....156 F5
Bushy Gill TN3 ....7 A3
Butcher's Cross TN7 ......13 B7
Butcher's La TN35 ....115 E2
Butcherfield La TN7 ....13 B6
Bute St BN2 ....164 D5
Butler's Green Ho RH16 ...50 B5
Butler's Green Rd RH16 ...50 C4
Butler's La BN27 ....130 E3
Butlers Way BN8 ....124 C5
Butterbox La RH17 ....52 D4
Buttercup Wlk BN1 ......143 B7
Butterfield RH19 ....1 B3
Butterfly Ctr BN22 ....185 D4
Buttermere Way BN23 ...174 C4
Button Ct BN2 ....189 C4
Butts Field BN27 ....152 C6
Butts La BN20 ....173 A1
Butts Rd BN42 ....161 E7
Buttsfield La BN8 ....105 A5
Buxted CE Prim Sch TN22 .55 F3
Buxted Ct TN22 ....56 C3
Buxted Rise BN1 ....143 B5
Buxted Wood La TN22 ....56 E5
Buxton Dr TN39 ....157 B6
Buxton Rd Brighton BN1 .163 E7
  Eastbourne BN20 ....188 E8
By Sunte RH16 ....50 F8
Bydown BN20 ....181 A4
Bye-law Cotts BN8 ....101 E6
Byeway The Bexhill TN39 .156 D5
  Hastings TN34 ....137 A4
Byeways The BN25 ....180 F4
Byfields Croft TN39 ......156 F5
Byland Cl BN22 ....173 E3
Bylands 3 BN2 ....164 F5
Byng Rd TN4 ....7 F5
Byre Cotts BN2 ....165 D4
Byron Ct 1 RH16 ....50 D5
Byron Gr 2 RH19 ....1 C1
Byron St BN3 ....163 A7
Byron Wlk BN23 ....174 E3
Byway The BN1 ....143 E5
Byways BN24 ....136 D6
Byworth Cl Bexhill TN39 ..156 C6
  Brighton BN2 ....164 F6

C

Cabbage Stalk La TN4 ....7 E2
Cabot Cl BN23 ....185 G7
Caburn Cres BN7 ....123 A2
Caburn Cres BN3 ....174 A4
Caburn Rd BN3 ....163 E7
Caburn View Bungalows
BN8 ....148 B3
Caburn View Cotts BN8 ..148 B3
Caburn Way BN27 ....152 B6
Cackle St
  Cackle Street TN31 ....90 A2
  Nutley TN22 ....35 E2
Cacklebury Cl BN27 ......152 A6
Cadborough Cliff TN31 ...93 A4
Cade St BN22 ....173 F2
Cadogan Ct
  Pevensey Bay BN24 ......175 C4
  3 Brighton BN1 ....163 E7
Cadogan Gdns 6 TN1 .....8 B4
Cairngorm Cl BN23 ......174 D3

Cairo Ave BN10 ....178 A8
Cairo Ave S BN10 ....178 A7
Caister's Cl BN3 ....163 C8
Caius Ct 16 BN43 ....161 C8
Calbourne RH16 ....50 D5
Caldbec Ct TN33 ....112 A5
Caldbec Hill TN33 ....112 D5
Caldicotts La BN27 ......128 C4
Caledonian Rd BN2 ......189 C5
Caley Rd TN2 ....8 A7
Calgary Rd TN39 ....157 B7
Callums Wlk TN40 ....157 E5
Calverley Ct TN1 ....8 C3
Calverley Park Cres 1 TN1 ..8 B3
Calverley Park Gdns TN1 ..8 C4
Calverley Pk TN1 ....8 B3
Calverley Rd
  Eastbourne BN21 ....184 F2
  Royal Tunbridge Wells TN1 ...8 B3
Calverley St TN1 ....8 B4
Calverley Wlk BN21 ......184 F2
Calvert Cl TN22 ....78 A7
Calvert Rd Hastings TN34 .160 A6
  Uckfield TN22 ....78 A7
Camber Cl
  Beachlands BN24 ....175 F6
  Bexhill TN40 ....157 E6
  Brighton BN2 ....164 F5
Camber Dr BN24 ....175 F6
Camber Rd TN31 ....94 B3
Camber Way BN24 ....175 F6
Camberlot Rd BN27 ......128 A2
Cambrian Rd TN4 ....8 C7
Cambridge Gdns
  Hastings TN34 ....159 E7
  Royal Tunbridge Wells TN2 ...8 B2
Cambridge Gr BN3 ....163 C7
Cambridge La TN21 ....81 C2
Cambridge Rd
  Bexhill TN40 ....157 C6
  Eastbourne BN22 ....185 C4
  Hastings TN34 ....159 E7
  Hove BN3 ....163 C6
Cambridge St TN2 ....8 C3
Cambridge Way TN22 .....55 C5
Camden Ave TN2 ....9 C6
Camden Ct Pembury TN2 ...9 D6
  2 Royal Tunbridge Wells TN1 ..8 B4
Camden Hill TN2 ....8 B3
Camden Pk TN2 ....8 C2
Camden Rd
  Eastbourne BN21 ....184 F2
  Royal Tunbridge Wells TN1 ...8 B4
Camden St BN41 ....162 C6
Camden Terr BN1 ....189 A3
Camelford St BN2 ....189 C1
Cameron Cl BN27 ....152 A8
Campbell Cl TN22 ....55 C1
Campbell Cres RH19 ....1 B1
Campbell Ct TN38 ....159 A8
Campbell Rd
  Brighton BN1 ....189 A5
  Royal Tunbridge Wells TN4 ...8 A6
Camperdown St TN39 ....157 B7
Canada Cl BN10 ....167 B1
Canada Way TN39 ....157 B7
Canadia Rd TN33 ....112 D8
Canal Bank TN35 ....139 B7
Canfield Cl BN2 ....143 D1
Canfield Rd BN2 ....143 D1
Canning St BN2 ....164 D5
Cannon Pl BN1 ....189 A2
Cansiron La
  Ashurst Wood RH19 ......11 F6
  Holtye TN7, TN8 ....3 C2
Cantelupe Mews 4 RH19 ..1 E1
Cantelupe Rd
  Bexhill TN40 ....157 D3
  East Grinstead RH19 ......1 F1
Canterbury Cl BN22 ......173 C2
Canterbury Dr 5 BN2 ....189 C4
Canterbury Rd TN2 ....9 E6
Canterbury Rise TN34 ....136 E3
Cantercrow Hill BN9 .....168 F2
Canton 3 RH16 ....50 D6
Cants Cl RH15 ....73 C3
Cants La RH15 ....73 C3
Canute Cl BN23 ....185 F8
Canute Rd TN35 ....137 D3
Capel Ave BN10 ....178 D7
Capello Path BN27 ....152 D7
Capenors RH15 ....72 F1
Caple Ct TN38 ....159 B8
Caple Gdns TN38 ....159 B7
Card Hill RH18 ....11 F1
Carden Ave BN1 ....143 B6
Carden Cl BN1 ....143 A6
Carden Cres BN1 ....143 A6
Carden Cty Inf Sch BN1 .143 B6
Carden Cty Jun Sch
BN1 ....143 B6
Carden Hill BN1 ....143 B5
Cardiff Rd TN38 ....159 C2
Cardinal Newman Sch
BN3 ....163 B6
Cardinals Cl TN40 ....157 F6
Carew Ct 8 BN21 ....184 E4
Carew Lodge 1 BN21 ....184 F4
Carew Rd BN21 ....184 E4
Carew Views 2 BN21 ....184 E4
Carey Down BN10 ....167 B1
Carfax TN39 ....157 B8
Carinus Gdns TN37 ......136 A6
Carisbrooke Ct BN23 ....174 B4
Carisbrooke Rd
  Brighton BN2 ....164 D7
  St Leonards TN38 ....159 C7
Carlisle Par TN34 ....159 F7

Carlisle Rd
  Eastbourne BN20, BN21 ..184 F1
  Hove BN3 ....162 F6
Carlton Cres BN25 ....180 E4
Carlton Cres TN1 ....8 C4
Carlton Ct 1 Bexhill TN40 .157 D3
  Portslade-by-Sea BN41 ...162 C8
Carlton Hill BN2 ....189 C2
Carlton Hill Cty Prim Sch
BN2 ....189 C2
Carlton Ho BN1 ....142 E2
Carlton Pl 5 BN2 ....189 C2
Carlton Rd
  Eastbourne BN22 ....185 C4
  Royal Tunbridge Wells TN1 ...8 C4
  Seaford BN25 ....180 D4
Carlton Terr
  Portslade-by-Sea BN3, BN41 162 C8
  Whitehill TN6 ....37 F8
Carlyle Ave BN2 ....143 D1
Carlyle St BN2 ....164 C7
Carmel TN39 ....156 D3
Carmen Ct BN20 ....173 B3
Carn Ct 7 BN2 ....164 C6
Carnoustie Ct TN38 ......158 F7
Carnoustie Ct 18 RH16 ...50 F4
Carol Cl BN1 ....142 F6
Caroline Ct BN25 ....180 D5
Carpenter Dr TN38 ......135 F4
Carpenters Croft BN8 ....105 A5
Carpenters Way BN27 ....152 A6
Carrier's Path BN27 .....152 B8
Carriers Pl TN3 ....5 B4
Carroll Wlk BN23 ....174 E2
Cashman Lodge BN1 .....143 A5
Caspian Ct 8 BN1 ....189 A4
Caspian Sq BN2 ....165 F1
Castle Banks 4 BN7 ....123 C1
Castle Bolton BN23 ......174 C4
Castle Ct BN7 ....123 D2
Castle Ditch La BN7 .....123 C1
Castle Dr BN24 ....175 C4
Castle Farm Cotts TN7 ...13 E4
Castle Gate 7 BN7 ......123 C1
Castle Gdns 10 TN34 ....159 F7
Castle Hill TN6 ....39 A5
Castle Hill Pas TN34 ....159 F8
Castle Hill Rd TN34 .....159 F7
Castle Hurst TN32 ....65 B8
Castle Mount BN20 ......184 D1
Castle Prec BN7 ....123 C1
Castle Rd Pevensey BN24 .175 A6
  Royal Tunbridge Wells TN4 ...8 A3
Castle Rise 8 Lewes BN7 .123 C1
  Uckfield TN22 ....78 D4
Castle Sq BN1 ....189 B2
Castle St Brighton BN1 ..163 E5
  9 Hastings TN34 ....159 F7
  2 Royal Tunbridge Wells TN1 ..8 A2
  Winchelsea TN36 ....117 F7
Castle Terr BN24 ....175 B6
Castle View Gdns BN24 ..174 E6
Castle Way TN22 ....78 D4
Castle Wlk TN5 ....29 E4
Castledean BN25 ....143 C2
Castledown Ave TN34 ....160 A4
Castledown Cty Prim Sch
TN34 ....160 A5
Castledown Terr 7 TN34 .160 A4
Castlefields TN7 ....13 E4
Castleham Rd TN38 ......135 F5
Castleross Rd BN24 .....175 C4
Cat St TN7 ....12 F1
Catherine Pl 7 TN1 ....8 A4
Catherine Vale BN2 ......165 E8
Catkin Way RH16 ....51 B4
Catley Ct 2 TN39 ....157 A4
Cats Field BN23 ....173 F4
Catsfield CE Prim Sch
TN33 ....133 F8
Catsfield Cl TN38 ....135 D2
Catsfield Rd TN33 ....111 C2
Catt's Corner Cotts TN6 ..27 D1
Catt's Hill TN6 ....27 E1
Causeway Sch The BN23 .174 A3
Causeway The
  Brighton BN2 ....164 D6
  7 Seaford BN25 ....180 E2
Cavalier Way RH19 ....10 F7
Cavalry Cres BN20 ......184 B5
Cavendish Mews 12 BN1 .163 D5
Cavell Ave BN10 ....178 B7
Cavell Ave N BN10 ....178 C8
Cavendish Ave
  Eastbourne BN22 ....185 B4
  St Leonards TN38 ....159 A7
Cavendish Cl BN10 ......167 B1
Cavendish Ct 9 TN40 ....157 D3
Cavendish Dr TN2 ....8 B1
Cavendish Ho 8
  Brighton BN1 ....163 E5
  Peacehaven BN10 ....167 C1
  9 St Leonards TN37 .....159 C7
Cavendish Hse RH16 ......50 F2
Cavendish Pl
  Brighton BN1 ....163 E5
  Eastbourne BN21 ....185 B3
  4 Hastings TN34 ....160 A4
Cavendish Sch BN21 .....184 C5
Cavendish St 11 BN2 ....189 C2
Caveridge La BN8 ....100 E8
Caverley Rd TN1 ....8 B4
Caves Rd TN38 ....159 A6
Cavix Field 1 TN31 ......67 B7
Caxton Way 15 RH16 .....50 F4
Cedar Cl Burgess Hill RH15 73 B5
  Eastbourne BN20 ....173 D2
  St Leonards TN37 ....136 D5

Cedar Ct TN4 ....8 A5
Cedar Lodge TN4 ....7 F3
Cedar Ridge TN2 ....8 D5
Cedar Way RH16 ....51 B4
Cedars Cl TN22 ....78 C8
Cedars Gdns BN1 ....142 E3
Cedars The
  1 Brighton BN2 ....189 C5
  Brighton, Withdean BN1 ..142 E3
  Hailsham BN27 ....129 B1
  Haywards Heath RH16 ....50 D7
  Peacehaven BN10 ....167 C1
  Uckfield TN22 ....78 D8
Cedarwell Cl BN9 ....168 B2
Cedarwood 3 BN1 ....142 E3
Celandine Dr TN38 ......136 A1
Centenary Ho BN1 ......142 E2
Centenary Ind Est 6
BN2 ....164 B8
Central Ave
  Eastbourne BN20 ....184 B5
  Polegate BN26 ....173 B7
  Telscombe Cliffs BN10 ...178 A8
Central Sta TN1 ....8 A3
Centurion Rd BN1 ....189 A3
Centurion Rise TN34 ....137 A4
Ceylon Pl BN21,BN22 ....185 B3
Ceylon Wlk TN39 ....156 E3
Chadborn Cl BN2 ....164 D5
Chaffinch Cl RH15 ....72 D4
Chaffinch Rd BN23 ......174 C2
Chaffinch Wlk TN22 ......78 D5
Chafford Cotts TN3 ....5 F5
Chafford La TN3 ....5 F5
Chailey Ave BN2 ....177 A5
Chailey Cl
  Eastbourne BN23 ....174 E1
  Hastings TN34 ....136 F5
Chailey Common
  Nature Reserve BN8 .....75 D7
Chailey Cres BN2 ....177 E5
Chailey Ct 2
  Haywards Heath RH16 ....50 F3
  Hove BN1 ....142 E3
Chailey Cty Sec Sch BN8 100 D7
Chailey Heritage Craft
  Sch & Hospl
  (New Heritage) BN8 ......52 E1
Chailey Heritage Craft
  Sch & Hospl
  (Old Heritage) BN8 .....75 C7
Chailey La BN8 ....76 B5
Chailey Rd BN1 ....143 E4
Chailey St Peter's
  CE Prim Sch BN8 ....75 E4
Chailey Windmill
  Rural Life Mus BN8 ......75 D7
Chain La TN33 ....112 C5
Chalden Pl TN39 ....156 C6
Chalfont BN27 ....152 C2
Chalfont Dr BN3 ....142 C3
Chalk Farm Cl BN20 ....173 B1
Chalkers La BN6 ....97 B8
Chalket La TN2 ....9 C5
Chalkland Rise BN2 .....165 E8
Chalky Rd BN41 ....141 A3
Challoners RH17 ....33 C4
Challoners Cl BN2 ....177 A6
Challoners Mews BN2 ...165 F2
Challow Cl BN6 ....97 E4
Chaloner Cl RH16 ....51 B7
Chaloner Rd RH16 ....51 B7
Chalvington Cl
  Brighton BN1 ....143 E6
  Seaford BN25 ....180 F6
Chalvington Dr TN37 ....136 C6
Chalvington Ho 8 BN21 .184 D4
Chalvington Rd BN21 ....184 C7
Chamberlain Rd BN21 ...184 C4
Chamberlaines La BN8 ...124 F6
Chambers Cres TN38 ....135 F3
Chambers Rd TN38 ......135 F3
Champions Row BN3 ....163 C8
Chancellor Ho TN4 ....7 F3
Chancellors Pk BN6 ......97 F4
Chanctonbury Dr TN34 ..136 F3
Chanctonbury Rd
  Burgess Hill RH15 ....73 A1
  Hove BN3 ....163 E7
Chandler Rd TN39 ....157 A4
Chandler's Mead BN8 ...123 A7
Chandos Ct 1 TN40 .....157 C3
Chandos Rd TN1 ....8 C5
Channel View
  Bexhill TN40 ....157 C3
  13 Southwick BN42 .....161 E7
Channel View E TN40 ....157 C3
Channel View Rd
  Eastbourne BN22 ....185 D5
  Pevensey Bay BN24 .....175 C5
  Woodingdean BN2 ....165 B8
Channel View W 5 TN40 .157 C2
Channel Way TN35 ....138 E3
Channers La BN8 ....126 D1
Chant La TN6 ....27 B1
Chantlers Cl RH19 ....1 C2
Chantlers Mead TN8 ......4 A5
Chantry Ave TN40 ....157 D6
Chantry Cty Inf Sch TN40 157 C5
Chantry La TN40 ....157 C5
Chantry The 12 BN21 ...184 E4
Chapel Barn Cl BN27 ...152 C7
Chapel Cl Burgess Hill RH15 72 F4
  Seaford BN25 ....180 E4
Chapel Cotts Battle TN33 .112 C4
  Mayfield TN20 ....40 B2
Chapel Field TN31 ....67 A7
Chapel Gn TN6 ....25 F2

Cha–Coa 197

Chapel Hill
Crowhurst TN33 134 F4
Lewes BN7 123 E1
Sedlescombe TN33 113 E7
Chapel La
Ashurst Wood RH19 11 D6
Blackboys TN22 80 B7
East Chiltington BN7 100 A3
Forest Row RH18 11 F2
Guestling Green TN35 138 A8
Horsted Keynes RH17 33 C5
Chapel Mews [8] BN3 163 D5
Chapel Park Rd TN37 159 C8
Chapel Pl
Portslade-by-Sea BN41 162 B7
[8] Royal Tunbridge Wells TN1 8 A2
Ticehurst TN5 31 E1
Chapel Rd
Plumpton Green BN7 99 E7
Southwick BN41 162 A7
Chapel St Brighton BN2 189 C2
Newhaven BN9 179 D7
Chapel Terr [2] BN2 164 D4
Chapman Way TN2 8 C8
Chapman's La
East Grinstead RH19 1 B1
East Grinstead RH19 1 D1
Chapman's Town La TN21 83 B2
Charis Ct [18] BN3 163 C7
Charity Farm Way TN6 26 A3
Charles Ave RH15 72 D2
Charles Bennett Ct RH16 51 A4
Charles Cl Hove BN3 142 A3
Seaford BN25 180 D5
Charles Ct TN2 8 C3
Charles Kingston Gdns
BN1 142 E4
Charles Moore Ct BN26 173 A7
Charles Rd TN38 159 C8
Charles Rd W TN38 159 B8
Charles St Brighton BN2 189 B1
Royal Tunbridge Wells TN4 8 A8
Charleston Farmhouse
BN8 149 A2
Charleston Manor Gdns
BN25 182 A6
Charleston Rd BN21 184 D4
Charlesworth Pk RH16 51 C4
Charlotte St BN2 189 C1
Charlston Ave BN9 179 A5
Charlton Gdns BN6 98 D3
Charlton's Way TN4 7 E1
Charltons The BN1 143 D6
Charlwood Gdns RH15 73 C5
Charlwood Rd RH15 73 D6
Charlwoods Bsns Ctr RH19 1 D2
Charlwoods Pl RH19 1 E3
Charlwoods Rd RH19 1 E3
Charters Ancaster Sch
TN40 157 F5
Charters Ancaster Sch
(Jun Dept) TN40 157 E5
Chartfield BN3 142 A2
Chartfield Way BN3 142 B2
Chartres TN40 157 D6
Chartres Cl TN40 157 D6
Chartwell Cl BN25 180 E6
Chartwell Ct BN1 189 A2
Chates Farm Ct BN2 189 C3
Chatfield Cres BN22 173 C1
Chatfield Rd RH17 50 A6
Chatham Pl Brighton BN1 189 A4
[14] Seaford BN25 180 E2
Chatham Rd [3] TN37 136 B2
Chatsfield Cl TN38 135 F4
Chatsworth Ave BN10 167 A1
Chatsworth Cl BN10 178 A8
Chatsworth Ct BN1 163 E8
Chatsworth Gdns BN20 188 F8
Chatsworth Pk BN10 167 B1
Chatsworth Rd
Brighton BN1 163 E8
Hove BN3 163 D7
Chaucer Ave [3] RH19 1 C1
Chaucer Ct [2] RH16 50 D5
Chaucer Ind Est BN26 173 D6
Chaucer Wlk BN23 174 E3
Chawbrook Rd BN22 185 B4
Cheal Cl BN43 161 A6
Cheapside BN1 189 B3
Cheeleys RH17 33 C5
Chelgates TN39 156 C2
Chelmsford Ct [3] BN20 184 F1
Chelsea Arc RH16 50 E4
Chelsea Cl TN40 157 D4
Chelston Ave BN3 162 D7
Cheltenham Pl BN1 189 B3
Chelwood Cl BN1 143 C6
Chelwood Ct RH15 73 A4
Chelwood Gate Rd
RH17,TN22 34 F7
Chelworth Rd BN22 173 D2
Chene Rd BN10 178 F6
Chenies Cl TN2 17 A8
Chepbourne Rd TN40 157 C4
Chepstow Ct BN1 143 F5
Chequer Grange RH18 11 E1
Chequer Mead Arts Ctr
RH19 1 F1
Chequer Rd RH19 1 F1
Chequers Cl TN6 26 A2
Chequers Way TN6 26 A2
Cherington Cl BN6 97 B5
Cherith Cotts [3] TN21 82 A6
Cheriton Ct BN20 184 C4
Cherry Cl RH15 72 E3
Cherry Clack TN21 83 D6
Cherry Cotts Fletching TN22 54 A4
Cherry Cotts *continued*
Hastings TN35 137 C3
Cherry Garden Rd BN20 184 B3
Cherry Gdns
Heathfield TN21 82 B5
High Hurstwood TN22 56 B8
Cherry Side BN27 152 A7
Cherry Tree Cl TN37 159 D8
Cherry Tree Ct TN21 106 F7
Cherry Tree Gdns TN40 157 F6
Cherry Tree Rd TN2 7 E1
Cherrywood [2] BN1 142 E3
Cherwell Cl BN24 173 F5
Cherwell Ct TN21 82 A8
Cherwell Rd TN21 82 A8
Chesham Pl BN2 164 D4
Chesham Rd BN2 164 D4
Chesham St BN2 164 D4
Cheshire Ct [6] BN22 185 B4
Chesnut Cl BN27 129 A1
Chester Ave TN2 8 D2
Chester Ct [12] BN3 163 E7
Chester Terr BN1 143 A1
Chesterfield Gdns BN20 188 E8
Chesterfield Rd BN20 188 E8
Chesterton Ave BN25 181 B3
Chesterton Cl RH19 10 F7
Chesterton Dr BN25 181 B3
Chestnut Ave TN4 8 B8
Chestnut Cl Broad Oak TN31 90 B5
Burgess Hill RH15 73 B5
East Grinstead RH19 2 A1
Eastbourne BN22 173 E2
Herstmonceux BN27 130 E6
Royal Tunbridge Wells TN4 8 B8
Chestnut Cotts
Fletching TN22 53 F3
[1] Heathfield TN21 82 A7
Chestnut Dr BN26 173 A6
Chestnut Pl TN8 4 A5
Chestnut Way BN9 179 B7
Chestnut Wlk
Bexhill TN39 156 C5
Felcourt RH19 1 C8
Chestnuts Cl RH16 51 A7
Chestnuts The
Lindfield RH16 50 F7
The Moor TN18 45 F8
Chet Nole RH19 1 D2
Cheviot Cl BN23 174 C3
Cheviots The TN34 137 C4
Cheyne Ct BN43 161 C7
Chichester Cl Bexhill TN39 157 B6
[15] Brighton BN2 164 D4
Eastbourne BN22 173 B2
Hove BN3 141 E4
Peacehaven BN10 178 F7
Saltdean BN2 177 C5
Seaford BN25 180 E3
Chichester Ct TN39 156 C3
Chichester Dr E BN2 177 C5
Chichester Dr W BN2 177 B5
Chichester Ho [6] TN40 157 D4
Chichester Lodge BN25 180 E3
Chichester Pl BN2 164 D4
Chichester Rd
Seaford BN25 180 E3
St Leonards TN38 136 B2
Chichester Terr [19] BN2 164 D4
Chichester Way RH15 73 C5
Chick Hill TN35 139 B8
Chicks La TN17 20 F2
Chiddingley Cl BN2 164 F5
Chiddingley Cty Prim Sch
BN8 127 E7
Chieveley Cotts TN38 136 B1
Chieveley Dr TN2 8 D1
Chilcomb RH15 73 C1
Chilham Cl BN23 174 D2
Chillies La TN22, TN6 37 B3
Chilling St RH19 21 D3
Chillis Wood Rd RH16 50 C5
Chilsham La BN27 130 E7
Chilston Cl TN4 8 A5
Chilston Rd TN4 8 A5
Chiltern Cl
Eastbourne BN23 174 D3
Shoreham-by-Sea BN43 161 C8
Chiltern Ct BN26 173 A7
Chiltern Dr TN34 137 B3
Chiltern Wlk TN2 8 D4
Chiltington Cl
Burgess Hill RH15 72 F5
Saltdean BN2 177 C6
Chiltington La BN7 100 D3
Chiltington Way BN2 177 C6
Chiswick Pl BN21 185 A2
Chitcombe Rd TN31 89 E5
Chitcombe Wlk TN34 137 A5
Chorley Ave BN2 177 B6
Chown's Hill TN35 137 A6
Chownes Mead La RH16 50 B4
Chrisdory Rd BN41 140 F3
Christ Church Ave [1] TN1 8 A2
Christ Church
CE Prim Sch TN37 136 C1
Christchurch Ct BN9 179 D7
Christie Ave BN8 124 D6
Christie Rd BN7 123 A2
Christies RH19 10 D8
Christine Cl TN40 158 A7
Christopher Rd RH19 1 E1
Church App TN22 79 B5
Church Ave
Haywards Heath RH16 50 E6
Westham BN24 175 A6
Church Bailey BN24 175 A5
Church Bailey Ct BN24 175 A5
Church Cl Brighton BN1 142 F5
Burgess Hill RH15 73 A3
Lower Willingdon BN20 173 A4
Church Ct
[3] Haywards Heath RH16 50 E4
Hove BN3 141 F1
Church Farm Cl TN19 44 C1
Church Gn BN43 161 C7
Church Hill Bexhill TN39 156 D4
Brighton BN1 142 E7
Etchingham TN19 44 B2
Newhaven BN9 179 C7
Pyecombe BN45 119 C6
Ringmer BN8 124 D6
Church Hill Ave TN39 156 D4
Church House Cl BN42 140 F1
Church in the Wood La
TN38 135 F3
Church La Burgess Hill RH17 73 F6
Buxted TN22 56 C5
Catsfield TN33 133 E8
Clayhill TN31 67 E4
Danehill RH17 34 A3
Ditchling BN6 98 D3
East Grinstead RH19 1 F1
[1] Eastbourne BN21 184 D3
Etchingham TN19 44 C1
Frant TN3 17 B4
Guestling Green TN35 116 B1
Hellingly BN27 129 A6
Hooe TN33 155 C7
Horsted Keynes RH17 33 C5
Jevington BN26 183 C7
Kingston near Lewes BN7 145 D5
Laughton BN8 126 C5
Lewes, South Malling BN7 123 D3
Lewes, St Anne's BN7 146 B8
Ninfield TN33 133 B5
Northbridge Street TN32 64 C5
Northiam TN31 67 C6
Peasmarsh TN31 92 B8
Pevensey BN24 175 B6
Pyecombe BN45 119 C6
Ripe BN27,BN8 149 E8
Seaford BN25 180 E2
Southwick BN42 161 D7
Westfield TN35 114 E3
Church Marks La BN8 104 F5
Church Mead BN6 98 B3
Church Mews BN20 173 B1
Church Pas [5] TN34 160 A4
Church Path BN27 129 A5
Church Pl BN2 164 E4
Church Rd Barcombe BN8 101 E2
Burgess Hill RH15 73 A3
Buxted TN22 56 B4
Catsfield TN33 133 F7
Crowborough TN6 25 F2
Flowers Green BN27 131 A1
Haywards Heath RH16 50 E4
Hove BN3 163 B6
Kilndown TN17 20 F3
Lamberhurst TN3 20 C6
Lewes BN7 123 C1
Mountfield TN32 87 B5
Newick BN8 76 E6
Polegate BN26 173 A6
Portslade-by-Sea BN41 162 B7
Royal Tunbridge Wells TN1 8 A3
Sandhurst Cross TN18 46 F4
Scaynes Hill RH17 51 F3
St Leonards TN37 159 D7
Church Sq TN31 93 C5
Church St Bexhill TN40 157 D5
Brighton BN1 189 B2
Cowden TN8 4 A5
Eastbourne BN20, BN21 184 D3
Hartfield TN7 13 D4
Hastings TN35 137 C3
Old Heathfield TN21 82 D5
Portslade-by-Sea BN41 162 B7
Rotherfield TN6 39 A8
Seaford BN25 180 E2
Ticehurst TN5 31 D1
Uckfield TN22 78 C7
Willingdon BN20,BN22 173 C2
Church Twitten [15] BN7 123 D1
Church Vale Rd TN40 157 D5
Church Way [5] BN2 189 C3
Church Wlk RH15 73 A3
Church Wood Cty
Prim Sch TN38 135 F3
Church Wood Dr TN38 135 E4
Church Wood Way TN38 135 F2
Churchdale Ave BN22 185 C6
Churchdale Pl BN22 185 B6
Churchdale Rd BN22 185 C6
Churchfield
East Dean BN20 187 B8
Westfield TN35 114 D3
Churchfields TN22 35 C4
Churchill Ave TN35 137 D5
Churchill Cl BN20 184 D3
Churchill Ct TN38 136 B2
Churchill Ho BN3 141 E2
Churchill Rd
Heathfield TN21 82 B6
Lewes BN7 123 B3
Seaford BN25 180 D5
Churchill Sq BN1 189 A2
Churchill Way RH15 73 C2
Churchland La TN33 88 E3
Churchsettle La TN5 42 B7
Churchyard Cotts TN3 7 A8
Chyngton Ave BN25 181 B4
Chyngton Cl BN23 174 A4
Chyngton Cty Prim Sch
BN25 181 B4
Chyngton Gdns BN25 181 B4
Chyngton Ho BN25 181 C2
Chyngton La BN25 181 C3
Chyngton La N BN25 181 C3
Chyngton Pl BN25 181 B2
Chyngton Rd BN25 181 A2
Chyngton Way BN25 181 C2
Cider House Wlk BN8 105 A5
Cinder Hill Chailey BN8 75 F3
Cinder Hill RH19 21 B1
Cinderford La BN27 129 F8
Cinque Ports St TN31 93 B5
Cinque Ports Way
Seaford BN25 181 C4
St Leonards TN38 158 E6
Cinquefoil BN10 178 C8
Circus Par BN1 189 B4
Circus St BN2 189 B2
Circus The BN23 185 D8
Cissbury Ave BN10 178 E7
Cissbury Cres BN2 177 E5
Cissbury Rd
Burgess Hill RH15 72 E4
Hove BN3 163 E7
Civic App TN22 78 C7
Civic Way Burgess Hill RH15 73 A3
Royal Tunbridge Wells TN1 8 A3
CJ Gallards Almshouses
TN4 8 A8
Clackhams La TN6 38 D7
Clair Ct RH16 50 E5
Clair Rd RH16 50 E5
Clanricarde Gdns [1] TN1 8 A3
Clanricarde Rd [2] TN1 8 A3
Clapham La BN26 182 A8
Claphatch La TN5 31 A5
Clappers The TN32 64 B4
Clare Rd BN7 123 A2
Clare Wlk BN2 164 D5
Claremont [9] TN34 159 E7
Claremont Ct BN25 180 D3
Claremont Cty Prim Sch
TN2 8 B2
Claremont Gdns TN2 8 B2
Claremont Rd
Bexhill TN39 157 B7
Newhaven BN9 168 F1
Royal Tunbridge Wells TN1 8 B2
Seaford BN25 180 D3
Claremont Rise TN22 55 C1
Claremont Sch TN33 114 B1
Clarence Ct BN24 175 C3
Clarence Dr [2] RH19 10 F7
Clarence Rd
Eastbourne BN22 185 B4
Royal Tunbridge Wells TN1 8 A3
St Leonards TN37 136 C1
Clarence Row TN1 8 A3
Clarence Sq BN1 189 A2
Clarendon Cl TN37 136 B4
Clarendon Gdns TN2 8 A1
Clarendon Ho [2] BN3 163 B7
Clarendon Pl
[16] Brighton BN2 164 C4
Portslade-by-Sea BN41 162 C6
Clarendon Rd Hove BN3 163 B7
Shoreham-by-Sea
BN42, BN43 161 D8
Clarendon Terr [16] BN2 164 D4
Clarendon Villas BN3 163 B7
Clarendon Way TN2 8 A1
Claridge TN1 8 B6
Clarke Ave BN3 141 F3
Clarke Ct BN3 162 F6
Clarks Ind Est BN3 163 B8
Claverham Cl TN33 112 B4
Claverham Com Coll
TN33 112 A4
Claverham Way TN33 112 B4
Clavering Wlk TN39 156 B2
Claxton Cl BN21 184 D5
Claxton Rd TN40 158 A5
Clay Corner BN8 101 F6
Clay Hill Rd TN3 19 D6
Clayfields BN10 178 B7
Clays Cl RH19 10 E8
Clayton Ave BN6 97 F3
Clayton Dr RH15 72 F1
Clayton Hill BN6,BN45 119 D7
Clayton Mill Rd BN24 174 B5
Clayton Pk BN6 97 E4
Clayton Rd Brighton BN2 164 D7
Ditchling BN6 98 C3
Clayton Way BN3 141 F3
Clayton Windmills BN6 119 E7
Clayton's La TN3 5 E2
Clearwater La RH17 52 A3
Clearwaters La RH16 73 D8
Cleeve Ave TN2 8 D2
Cleevelands BN22 173 B2
Clement Hill Rd TN34 137 B3
Clement La BN26 173 A5
Clementine Ave BN25 180 D5
Clerks Acre Keymer BN6 98 A3
Keymer BN6 98 A4
Clermont Ct BN1 142 E2
Clermont Rd BN1 142 E2
Clermont Terr BN1 142 E2
Cleve Cl TN22 79 B5
Cleve Terr BN7 146 B8
Clevedon Rd TN39 157 A6
Clevedown BN7 146 A8
Cleveland TN2 8 D4
Cleveland Cl BN23 174 C3
Cleveland Gdns RH15 73 B2
Cleveland Rd BN1 143 A1
Clevelands RH16 50 E6
Cliff App BN2 164 F4
Cliff Ave BN10 178 E5
Cliff Cl BN25 180 F1
Cliff Ct TN38 158 D6
Cliff End La TN35 139 B7
Cliff Gdns Seaford BN25 180 F1
Telscombe Cliffs BN10 177 F4
Cliff Park Cl BN10 178 F7
Cliff Rd Brighton BN2 164 F4
Eastbourne BN20 188 E7
Seaford BN25 180 F1
Cliff The BN2 164 F4
Cliff Way TN35 138 F5
Cliffe High St BN7 123 D1
Cliffe Ind Est BN8 146 F8
Clifford Ave BN21 184 C6
Clifford Ct [9] Bexhill TN40 157 C4
Crowborough TN6 25 F2
Clifford Rd [10] TN40 157 C4
Clifton Cl BN22 184 D8
Clifton Cotts TN2 8 D8
Clifton Ct TN34 159 E8
Clifton Hill BN1 189 A3
Clifton Ho BN22 184 D8
Clifton Mews BN1 189 A3
Clifton Pl Brighton BN1 163 E6
Royal Tunbridge Wells TN1 8 B2
Clifton Rd Brighton BN1 189 A3
Burgess Hill RH15 72 D5
Hastings TN35 137 C3
Newhaven BN9 179 D7
Royal Tunbridge Wells TN2 8 C7
Clifton Rise TN40 157 F5
Clifton St BN1 189 A4
Clifton Terr BN1 189 A3
Clifton Way BN10 178 A8
Cliftonville Ct [6] BN3 163 B7
Cliftonville Rd TN38 158 D6
Cliftonville Way TN38 158 D6
Climping Cl RH16 50 D3
Clinch Green Ave TN39 156 F7
Clinton Cres TN38 136 B1
Clinton Hill RH7 2 A8
Clinton La [2] BN25 180 E3
Clinton Pl BN25 180 E3
Clinton Way TN35 138 F5
Clive Ave TN35 160 C6
Clive Villas TN33 112 E3
Cliveden Ct BN1 142 E3
Clock House La TN22 35 C4
Clock Tower Ct [5] TN39 157 B3
Clockhouse TN2 8 F6
Cloisters BN9 179 C7
Cloisters The Battle TN33 112 D6
Eastbourne BN22 173 C2
St Leonards TN37 159 D7
Close Eight BN23 174 E3
Close Eighteen BN23 174 E2
Close Eleven BN23 174 E3
Close Fifteen [6] BN23 174 E2
Close Five BN23 174 E3
Close Four BN23 174 E2
Close Fourteen BN23 174 E3
Close Nine BN23 174 E2
Close Nineteen BN23 174 E2
Close One BN23 174 D2
Close Seven BN23 174 E3
Close Seventeen BN23 174 E2
Close Six BN23 174 E3
Close Sixteen BN23 174 E2
Close Ten BN23 174 E2
Close The Blackboys TN22 80 B6
Brighton BN1 142 E5
Burgess Hill RH15 73 C4
Crowborough TN6 25 E3
East Grinstead RH19 10 D8
Eastbourne BN20 184 B8
Fairlight TN35 138 C4
Friston BN20 183 A1
Groombridge TN3 15 C6
Hassocks BN6 97 F4
Lower Willingdon BN22 173 C3
Newhaven BN9 168 F2
Royal Tunbridge Wells TN2 8 C8
Rye TN31 93 A6
Seaford BN25 180 F2
Close Three BN23 174 D2
Close Twelve BN23 174 E2
Close Twenty BN23 174 E2
Close Twentyfive BN23 174 D2
Close Twentyfour [4]
BN23 174 E2
Close Two BN23 174 D2
Cloudesley Rd TN37 159 C8
Clovelly Ho BN26 173 A7
Clover Ct [2] RH16 50 E4
Clover Way BN41 141 B2
Cloverlea TN34 136 E5
Clovers End BN1 143 B7
Cluny St BN7 146 C8
Clyde Pk BN27 152 C7
Clyde Rd Brighton BN1 189 B5
St Leonards TN37, TN38 159 C7
Coach & Horses La RH17 34 C6
Coach & Horses Pas [15] TN2 8 A2
Coach House Cotts TN31 94 F2
Coach La RH17 34 C6
Coach Rd TN4 7 C3
Coast Rd BN24 176 B7
Coastal Counties Ho [18]
BN2 189 C3
Coastguard Cl BN24 176 D8
Coastguard Cotts
Camber TN31 94 D2
Normans' Bay BN24 176 D8
Coastguard La TN35 138 C4

Coastguard Sq
- 3 Eastbourne BN22 ....185 C4
- Rye Harbour TN31 ....94 A3

Coastguards TN35 ....139 C8
Coates Ct 11 BN42 ....161 E7
Cobald Rd BN24 ....175 E5
Cobbett's Ride TN19 ....7 F1
Cobbetts Mead RH16 .....51 B3
Cobblers Field TN19 .....61 A3
Cobbold Ave BN21 ....184 C5
Cobden Pl 5 BN27 .....152 C7
Cobden Rd BN2 ....164 C7
Cobdown La TN22 ....55 C5
Cobham Twrs 2 TN40 ...157 F4
Cobhams TN3 ....7 A8
Cobourg Pl 6 TN34 .....160 A4
Cobton Dr BN3 ....142 A3
Coburn Ct 12 BN7 ....123 D1
Cochrane Cl BN23 ....185 E7
Cockcrow Wood TN37 ...136 D5
Cockfield La BN8 ....76 B3
Cockhaise Cotts RH16 ...52 A8
Cockmount La TN5 ....29 F5
Cockshut Rd BN7 ....146 C6
Cogger's Cross TN21 ....106 F3
Cogger's La TN21 ....106 F4
Coggins Mill La TN20 .....40 D4
Coghurst Rd TN35 ....137 C4
Colbourne Ave BN2 .....143 D2
Colbourne Rd BN3 ....163 E7
Colchester Vale RH18 .....11 C2
Colchins RH17 ....72 F1
Coldean Cty Inf Sch BN1 143 D6
Coldean Cty Jun Sch BN1 143 D6
Coldean La BN1 ....143 E6
Coldharbour La
- Newick BN8 ....76 A7
- Rye Harbour TN31 ....69 E3

Coldharbour Rd
- Lower Dicker BN27 ....128 B2
- White Post TN8, TN11 .....5 E8

Coldthorn La BN26,BN27 .152 A4
Coldwaltham La RH15 ....73 D2
Colebrook Rd
- Brighton BN1 ....142 D4
- Royal Tunbridge Wells TN4 ..8 D4
- Southwick BN42 ....161 F7

Colebrooke Rd TN39 .....157 A4
Coleman Ave BN3 ....162 E7
Coleman St BN2 ....189 C4
Colemans Hatch Rd
- RH18,TN7 ....23 C6

Coleridge St BN3 ....163 A8
Coleridge Wlk 7 BN23 ..174 E2
Coles Ct TN5 ....8 C3
Colgate Cl BN2 ....164 F6
Coll of the Holy Child
- Jesus TN37 ....159 D7

College Cl
- East Grinstead RH19 ....1 F1
- Portslade-by-Sea BN41 ...140 F3

College Dr TN2 ....8 D4
College Gdns BN2 ....164 C4
College Gn BN21 ....184 E4
College La
- East Grinstead RH19 ....1 F1
- Hurst Wickham BN6 ....97 C6

College Pl Brighton BN2 .164 C4
- Hurst Wickham BN6 ....97 C6

College Rd Bexhill TN40 .157 F5
- Brighton BN2 ....164 C4
- Eastbourne BN21 ....184 F2
- Haywards Heath RH16 .....50 E7
- Seaford BN25 ....180 F2

College St 11 BN2 ....164 C4
College Terr BN2 ....164 D5
Collett Cl TN38 ....135 F5
Collier Cl BN22 ....185 B3
Collier Rd Hastings TN34 .160 A5
- Pevensey Bay BN24 ....175 D4

Collier's Gn TN21 ....83 F3
Collingford La RH17 ......34 B4
Collington Ave TN39 ....156 F3
Collington Cl BN20 ......184 E1
Collington Gr TN39 ......156 E4
Collington La E TN39 ....156 F4
Collington La W TN39 ...156 D3
Collington Man TN39 ....157 B3
Collington Park Cres
- TN39 ....156 F4

Collington Rise TN39 ....156 E4
Collington Sta TN39 .....157 A3
Collingwood Ave TN21 ...82 B7
Collingwood Cl
- 4 East Grinstead RH19 ....10 F7
- Eastbourne BN23 ....185 E6
- Peacehaven BN10 ....167 D1

Collingwood Ct BN2 .....165 A3
Collingwood Rise TN21 ...82 A7
Collinstone Rd TN38 .....159 A7
Collinswood Dr TN38 .....159 A7
Colmer Ct RH15 ....72 E3
Colmer Pl RH15 ....72 E3
Colonnade Gdns 13 BN21 185 B3
Colonnade Rd 14 BN21 .185 B3
Coltstocks Rd BN20 .....188 D8
Columbus Dr BN23 ......185 G7
Colville Ct 2 BN21 ....184 E4
Colwell Cl BN26 ....50 F3
Colwell Gdns RH16 ......50 F3
Colwell La
- Haywards Heath RH17 51
- B3 Haywards Heath, Fox Hill
- RH16, RH17 ....50 F1

Colwell Rd RH16 ....50 F2
Colwood Cres BN20 .....184 B6
Colwood Hospl RH17 .....51 A3
Combe End TN6 ....37 E8
Combe La
- Eastbourne BN20 ....188 D7
- Ninfield TN33 ....132 F6

Combe Rise BN20 ....173 A2
Combe The BN20 ....184 A4
Combermere Rd TN38 ...136 B1
Command Rd BN20 ......184 B5
Commanders Wlk TN35 .138 E4
Commercial Mews N 7
- BN21 ....185 A4

Commercial Rd
- Burgess Hill RH15 ....72 F3
- Eastbourne BN21 ....185 A3
- Royal Tunbridge Wells TN1 ..8 B5

Commercial Sq RH16 .....50 E6
Common La Ditchling BN6 .98 D6
- Selmeston BN26 ....149 E1

Common View TN4 ....7 C4
Common Wood Rise TN6 .25 F4
Compass Ct BN41 ....140 E3
Comphurst La BN27 ....131 B4
Compton Ave BN1 ....189 A4
Compton Cl 11 TN40 ....157 E4
Compton Dr BN20 ....184 C2
Compton Lodge BN21 ...184 E1
Compton Place Rd
- BN20, BN21 ....184 E2
- Compton Rd Brighton BN1 142 D1
- Lindfield RH16 ....51 B8

Compton St BN21 ....185 A1
Compton Terr BN27 .....152 C6
Compts The BN10 ....167 B1
Conan Doyle Ct TN6 .....25 E2
Concord Cl TN2 ....8 C4
Concorde Ct TN39 ....156 F6
Condor Way RH15 ....72 F6
Conduit Hill TN31 ....93 C6
Coney Furlong BN10 ....167 D1
Coneyburrow Gdns TN38 135 E4
Coneyburrow La TN39 ...155 F5
Coneyburrow Rd TN2 ......8 E5
Conghurst La TN18 ....46 B6
Conifer TN34 ....136 F3
Conifers The 6 BN21 ....184 F4
Coniston Ave TN4 ....7 E5
Coniston Ct 9 BN3 ......163 D7
Coniston Rd BN23 ......174 C4
Connaught Ctr Brighton
- Coll of Tech & F Ed
- BN3 ....163 A6

Connaught Rd
- 1 Eastbourne BN21 ......185 A2
- Hove BN3 ....163 A6
- Seaford BN25 ....180 C3

Connaught Terr BN3 .....163 B7
Connaught Way TN4 ......7 F5
Connell Dr BN2 ....165 E2
Conqueror Ind Est TN38 .135 F6
Conqueror Rd TN38 .....158 E7
Conqueror Terr TN33 ....88 F1
Conquest Hospl TN37 ...136 D6
Consort Way RH15 ......72 E2
Constable Rd BN23 .....174 D1
Constable Way TN40 ....157 E4
Convent of the Holy
- Child Jesus TN20 ....40 A3

Conway Ct 1 Hove BN3 .163 B7
- 9 St Leonards TN38 ......159 B6

Conway Pl BN3 ....163 B7
Conway St BN3 ....163 B8
Cooden Beach Sta TN39 .156 F2
Cooden Cl TN39 ....156 C3
Cooden Dr TN39 ....156 E2
Cooden Sea Rd
- Bexhill TN39 ....156 B2
- Bexhill TN39 ....156 C3

Cook Ave BN23 ....185 E6
Cookham Dene TN40 ....157 C4
Cooksbridge Rd BN2 ...164 E6
Cookson Gdns TN35 ....137 C3
Cookstown Cl TN33 .....132 F6
Coolham Dr BN2 ....164 E7
Coombe Cl BN27 ....131 B5
Coombe Hall Sch RH19 ..10 D6
Coombe Hill Rd RH19 ....10 D6
Coombe La TN5 ....41 C7
Coombe Lea 5 BN3 .....163 C6
Coombe Mdw BN2 ....166 E3
Coombe Rd Brighton BN2 .143 D1
- Eastbourne BN20 ....184 C4
- Lewes BN7 ....123 D2

Coombe Rise BN2 ....166 D3
Coombe Road
- Cty Prim Sch BN2 ....143 D1
Coombe Shaw TN33 .....133 A6
Coombe Terr BN2 ....143 C1
Coombe Vale BN2 ....166 D3
Coombers La RH16 ....51 B5
Coombs Cl TN31 ....68 C5
Coombs Cotts TN31 ......68 C5
Cooper Dr TN39 ....157 B8
Cooper Rd TN31 ....93 A3
Cooper Rise TN37 ....136 A5
Coopers Cl RH15 ....73 B5
Coopers Hill BN20 ....173 B2
Coopers La
- Crowborough TN6 ....25 D4
- Poundsbridge TN11, TN3 ...6 B7

Coopers Row TN22 ....55 D4
Coopers Way BN27 .....152 A6
Coopers Wood TN6 ....25 D4
Copestake Dr RH15 ......73 D3

Coplands Plot 3 TN31 ...67 B7
Coplands Rise TN31 ......67 B7
Coppards Cl RH17 ....74 C4
Coppards La TN31 ....67 C8
Copper Beeches
- Hove BN1 ....142 E1
- St Leonards TN37 ....136 C4

Copper Cl RH15 ....72 C4
Copper's Hill TN19 ....61 E4
Coppice Ave BN20 ....173 A4
Coppice Cl BN20 ....173 A4
Coppice The Battle TN33 .113 A3
- Hastings TN34 ....136 E1
- Pembury TN2 ....9 D7
- Scaynes Hill RH17 ....51 F3

Coppice View TN21 ......82 B6
Coppice Way RH16 ....50 D3
Copse Cl East Grinstead RH19 2 A3
- St Leonards TN38 ....135 D3

Copse Hill BN1 ....142 D5
Copse Rd TN39 ....156 E4
Copse The RH16 ....51 B5
Copt Hall TN18 ....48 D3
Copthorne Ct 2 BN3 ....163 C6
Copthorne Rd RH19 ....1 A4
Copwood Ave TN22 ....78 B7
Copyhold La RH17 ....50 A4
Copyhold Rd RH19 ....10 D8
Copythorne Ho RH16 ....50 E6
Coral Reef Cl BN23 .....175 A1
Corbyn Cres BN43 ......161 A7
Cordons BN7 ....145 D5
Cormorant Ct BN23 .....174 C2
Cornelius Ave BN9 ......179 A5
Corner Gn BN8 ....124 D5
Cornfield Cl BN25 ....180 F3
Cornfield Gn BN27 ......129 C1
Cornfield La BN21 ....185 A2
Cornfield Rd
- Eastbourne BN21 ....185 A2
- Seaford BN25 ....180 F3

Cornfield Terr
- 11 Eastbourne BN21 ......185 A2
- St Leonards TN37 ....136 C1

Cornford Cl
- Burgess Hill RH15 ....72 E5
- Crowborough TN6 ....26 A1
- Pembury TN2 ....9 B6
- Portslade-by-Sea BN41 ...141 B2

Cornford La TN2 ....9 B5
Cornford Pk TN2 ....9 C6
Cornish Cl BN23 ....174 B4
Cornmill Gdns BN26 ....172 E4
Cornwall Ave BN10 .....178 E6
Cornwall Ct
- Eastbourne BN20 ....184 C5
- 2 Hove BN3 ....163 C7

Cornwall Gdns
- Brighton BN1 ....142 E2
- 6 East Grinstead RH19 ....10 F7

Cornwall Ho BN1 ....142 E2
Cornwall Rd TN39 ....157 B3
Cornwallis Cl BN23 .....185 F7
Cornwallis Gdns TN34 ..159 E8
Cornwallis St 5 TN34 ...159 F8
Cornwallis Terr TN34 ...159 E8
Coronation Cotts
- Berner's Hill TN5 ....31 C2
- Burwash TN19 ....62 A6
- Northbridge Street TN32 ...64 C5

Coronation Gdns
- Battle TN33 ....112 F5
- Hurst Green TN19 ....44 F3

Coronation Rd RH19 .....10 E7
Coronation St 7 BN2 ....164 C7
Corseley Rd TN3 ....15 B5
Corsica Cl BN25 ....180 F2
Corsica Rd BN25 ....180 F1
Costells Edge RH17 ......51 F3
Costume Mus TN40 .....157 D4
Cotchford Hill TN7 ....13 D1
Cotchford La TN7 ....13 C1
Cotswold Cl
- Eastbourne BN23 ....174 C4
- Hastings TN34 ....137 B4

Cotswold Pl 7 BN2 ......164 F5
Cotswolds The BN42 ....161 E7
Cottage Bush Cl BN41 ...141 C2
Cottage Cl BN3 ....168 D2
Cottage Homes BN6 .....98 E6
Cottage La Hankham BN24 152 E1
- Westfield TN33, TN35 .....114 D7

Cottenden Rd TN5 ....43 A6
Cottesmore St Mary's
- RC Prim Sch BN3 ....163 D8

Coulstock Rd RH15 ......72 C3
Council Cotts
- Crowborough TN6 ....38 A8
- Robertsbridge TN32 ....63 F3

Council Hos
- Ginger's Green BN27 .....130 C6
- Rushlake Green TN21 ......83 D1

Countess of Thanet's
- Almshouses TN8 ....3 F3
County Oak Ave BN1 ....143 B6
Courcels BN2 ....164 E3
Course The BN7 ....146 B8
Court Cl Brighton BN1 ...142 E7
- East Grinstead RH19 ....1 F1

Court Cres RH19 ....1 F1
Court Farm Cl BN9 ......168 A2
Court Farm Rd Hove BN3 142 A2
- Newhaven BN9 ....179 C5
- Rottingdean BN2 ....165 F3

Court House Mus The
- BN24 ....175 B6
Court Mdw TN6 ....39 B8
Court Meadow Cl TN6 ....39 B7

Court Meadow Specl Sch
- RH17 ....50 A8

Court Ord Cotts BN2 ....165 F3
Court Ord Rd BN2 ....165 F3
Court Rd Eastbourne BN22 .173 F2
- Lewes BN7 ....123 D1
- Royal Tunbridge Wells TN4 ..7 F4

Court The BN20 ....173 B1
Courtenay Terr 7 BN3 ..163 B5
Courtenwell TN3 ....6 E4
Courthope Ave TN5 ......29 F4
Courthope Dr TN39 .....156 F5
Courthouse St TN34 ....160 B4
Courtland Rd BN26 .....173 A5
Courtlands
- 12 Brighton BN2 ....189 C3
- Dodd's Hill TN22 ....173 A5
- Haywards Heath RH16 .....50 E3
- Newhaven BN9 ....179 C7
- 5 St Leonards TN38 ......159 B6

Courtlands Pl TN6 ....25 C1
Courtlands Rd BN22 ....185 A5
Courtney Gate BN3 .....163 B5
Courtney King Ct 8 BN2 .164 C5
Courtney King Ho 1
- BN2 ....164 D4
Courtyard The
- East Grinstead RH19 ....2 B1
- Falmer BN1 ....144 D6
- Hastings TN34 ....136 E1

Cousley Wood Rd TN5 ...30 C7
Coventry Ct BN22 ....185 D6
Coventry Rd TN38 ......136 B3
Coventry St BN1 ....163 E8
Coverdale Ave TN39 ....156 C3
Coverdale Ct RH19 ....1 C3
Covers The BN25 ....180 F2
Covert The TN39 ....156 C2
Cow La BN20 ....181 F8
Cowden Cl TN18 ....45 E8
Cowden Cross TN8 ......4 C7
Cowden Hall La TN21 ...107 D5
Cowden La TN18 ....45 E7
Cowden Mews TN8 ....4 A5
Cowden Rd BN2 ....177 D4
Cowden Sta TN8 ....4 D8
Cowden Wlk TN38 ......136 A2
Cowdens Cl BN3 ....141 D4
Cowdray Cl TN39 ....156 D6
Cowdray Ct 1 BN3 ......163 D7
Cowdray Park Rd TN39 .156 C6
Cowfold Rd BN2 ....164 E5
Cowley Dr BN2 ....165 F7
Cownwy Ct BN2 ....165 F1
Cowper St BN3 ....163 A7
Cox Gr RH15 ....72 E5
Cox's Cotts BN7 ....99 E7
Coxheath Cl TN38 ....135 E7
Crabtree Ave BN1 ....143 B5
Crabtree Ho 1 TN38 ....159 B6
Crackendale Field BN8 ..124 E6
Cradle Hill Cty Prim Sch
- BN25 ....181 A5

Cradle Hill Ind Est BN25 .181 B5
Cradle Hill Rd BN25 .....181 B5
Craig Cl TN33 ....135 A6
Craigmore Hall TN6 ......26 A1
Craignair Ave BN1 ....142 F7
Cranborne Ave BN20 ...188 C3
Cranbourne St BN1 .....189 A2
Cranbrook 13 BN2 ....189 C3
Cranbrook Rd TN37 .....136 C1
Cranedown BN7 ....146 B7
Cranfield Rd TN40 ......157 C4
Cranleigh Ave BN2 ......177 B5
Cranleigh Cl TN39 ......154 A4
Cranley Ct BN3 ....162 D7
Cranmer Ave BN3 ....141 F1
Cranmer Cl BN7 ....123 D2
Cranston Ave TN39 .....157 A4
Cranston Cl TN39 ....156 F4
Cranston Rd RH19 ....1 F2
Cranston Rise TN39 .....156 F4
Cranwell Rd TN4 ....7 C4
Craven Rd BN2 ....164 D6
Crawford Way RH11 ......1 E3
Crawley Cres BN22 .....173 E2
Crawley Rd BN1 ....143 D6
Crayford Rd BN2 ....143 D1
Crazy La TN33 ....113 E7
Crecy Cl TN37 ....135 F7
Creek The 11 TN34 .....160 B4
Crendon Pk TN4 ....8 A8
Crescent Cl
- Burgess Hill RH15 ....73 B3
- Woodingdean BN2 ....165 E8

Crescent Dr N BN2 ......165 E8
Crescent Dr S BN2 ......165 E7
Crescent Mans BN2 .....189 C5
Crescent Pl BN2 ....164 C4
Crescent Rd Brighton BN2 .164 B8
- Burgess Hill RH15 ....73 A3
- East Grinstead RH19 ....1 D1
- Royal Tunbridge Wells TN1 ..8 B3

Crescent The
- Brighton BN2 ....143 E2
- Eastbourne BN20 ....184 B5
- Felcourt RH19 ....1 C8
- Groombridge TN3 ....15 C7
- Hastings TN34 ....136 C3
- Keymer BN6 ....98 B3
- Lower Willingdon BN20 ...173 A3
- Southwick BN42 ....161 F8

Crescent Way RH15 ......72 B3
Crespin Way BN1 ....143 C2
Crest Rd BN9 ....168 F1
Crest Way BN41 ....141 B3

Cresta Cl BN26 ....173 A7
Cresta Rd BN9 ....179 A6
Crestway Par BN1 ....143 C2
Crestway The BN1 ....143 C2
Cricket Ct RH19 ....1 E3
Cricketers Cl TN3 ....18 A5
Cricketers Field TN32 ...65 E1
Cricketfield BN8 ....76 D8
Cricketfield CT 6 BN25 .180 F2
Cricketfield Rd BN25 ...180 F2
Cricketing La BN27 .....130 C4
Criers La TN20,TN22 .....57 F7
Crink Hill BN8 ....101 F3
Cripland Cl RH16 ....51 B6
Cripps Ave BN10 ....167 D1
Crisp Rd BN7 ....123 A3
Crittle's Ct TN5 ....29 F4
Crockers Hatch Cnr TN3 ..6 D2
Crockers La TN31 ....67 B8
Crocks Dean BN10 ......167 D2
Croft Ave BN42 ....161 F7
Croft Cl BN26 ....173 A4
Croft Ct
- 2 Eastbourne BN21 ......185 B3
- 6 Seaford BN25 ....180 E3

Croft Dr BN41 ....141 A3
Croft La BN25 ....180 E3
Croft Rd Brighton BN1 ...142 D4
- Crowborough TN6 ....25 F2
- Hastings TN34 ....160 A4

Croft Terr 2 TN34 ....160 A4
Croft The Bexhill TN39 ..157 A4
- Hassocks BN6 ....97 F5
- Hastings TN34 ....160 A4
- Lower Dicker BN27 ....128 B4
- Southwick BN42 ....161 E8
- Willingdon BN20 ....173 B1

Croft Works TN37 ....152 B7
Crofton Park Ave TN39 .156 E3
Croham Rd TN6 ....25 F3
Cromarty Wlk 8 BN23 ..185 F8
Cromer Way BN27 ....129 A1
Cromer Wlk 3 TN34 ....136 F1
Cromleigh Way BN42 ...140 E2
Cromwell Ct 3 BN3 .....163 D7
Cromwell Pl 1 RH19 .....10 F7
Cromwell Rd
- Burgess Hill RH15 ....72 F3
- Hove BN3 ....163 C2
- Royal Tunbridge Wells TN2 ..8 C3

Cromwell St BN2 ....164 C7
Crooked La BN25 ....180 F2
Cross La TN5 ....31 D2
Cross Lane Gdns TN5 ....31 D1
Cross Levels Way
- BN21, BN22 ....184 E7

Cross Rd BN42 ....161 D8
Cross St Brighton BN1 ...189 B4
- 14 Hove BN1, BN3 ....163 D5
- Polegate BN26 ....173 A6
- St Leonards TN37 ....159 C2

Cross Way BN7 ....123 A2
Cross-in-Hand CE
- Prim Sch TN21 ....81 F7

Crossbush Rd BN2 ......164 E6
Crossroad Cl BN42 ......161 D8
Crossway The
- Brighton BN1 ....143 B2
- Portslade-by-Sea BN41 ...141 A4
- Royal Tunbridge Wells TN4 ..7 D2

Crossways Ave RH19 ......1 C1
Crossways The
- Broad Oak TN31 ....90 B4
- Hassocks BN6 ....97 C4
- Stone Cross BN24 ....174 A6

Crouch Cl BN20 ....173 B1
Crouch La Linkhill TN18 ...47 D6
- Lower Street TN33 ....133 B3
- Seaford BN25 ....180 E2

Crouchfield Cl 2 BN25 ..180 F2
Crowborough Hill TN6 ...26 B1
Crowborough Mews TN6 .25 E2
Crowborough Rd
- Hastings TN35 ....137 E4
- Marlpits TN22 ....35 E6
- Saltdean BN2 ....177 D4

Crowders La TN33 ......111 D3
Crowhurst CE Prim Sch
- TN33 ....134 F5

Crowhurst Cl BN23 ......174 A4
Crowhurst La TN39 ......157 C7
Crowhurst Rd
- Brighton BN1 ....143 C7
- Green Street TN38 ....135 B3
- St Leonards TN38 ....135 E2

Crowhurst Sta TN33 .....135 A6
Crowlink Cotts BN20 ....186 E2
Crowmere Ave TN40 ....157 C5
Crowmere Terr TN40 ....157 C5
Crown Cl Hailsham BN27 .152 A7
- 1 Hove BN3 ....163 D6
- Uckfield TN22 ....78 C8

Crown Ct 28 TN34 ......160 B4
Crown Gdns BN1 ....189 A2
Crown Hill
- 4 Brighton BN2 ....164 C6
- Seaford BN25 ....180 E2

Crown La TN34 ....160 B4
Crown Point Ho BN6 .....97 F4
Crown Rd
- Portslade-by-Sea BN41 ...162 A8
- Shoreham-by-Sea BN43 ...161 B8

Crown St Brighton BN1 ..189 A2
- 11 Eastbourne BN21 .....184 D4

Crowne Ho 8 BN21 .....184 E4
Croxden Way BN22 .....173 D3
Croxton La RH16 ....51 B6
Crump's Cnr TN22 .....103 D6

Crunden Rd BN20 . . . . . . .184 C4
Cubitt Way TN38 . . . . .135 E4
Cuckfield Cl TN40 . . . . . . .158 A5
Cuckfield Rd
  Burgess Hill RH15 . . . . . . .72 E7
  Goddards' Green BN6,RH17 .72 A4
Cuckmere Ct BN26 . . . . . . .170 F3
Cuckmere Dr BN24 . . . . . .174 A5
Cuckmere Ho BN24 . . . . . .175 E5
Cuckmere House Sch
  BN25 . . . . .181 C3
Cuckmere Path TN22 . . . .55 E1
Cuckmere Rd
  Newhaven BN9 . . . . .179 A5
  Seaford BN25 . . . . .181 B2
Cuckmere Rise TN21 . . . . .82 B8
Cuckmere Way BN1 . . . . . .143 C5
Cuckmere Wlk BN22 . . . . .173 D1
Cuckoo Dr TN21 . . . . .82 A6
Culpepper RH15 . . . . .72 E4
Culpepper Cl BN2 . . . . . . .143 D2
Culross Ave RH16 . . . . .50 D5
Culver Cl BN23 . . . . .174 B4
Culverden Ave TN4 . . . . . . .8 A6
Culverden Down TN4 . . . . .7 F5
Culverden Park Rd TN4 . . .7 F5
Culverden Pk TN4 . . . . .7 F5
Culverden Sq TN4 . . . . .8 A5
Culverden St TN1 . . . . .8 A4
Cumballa Ct BN20 . . . . . .188 F8
Cumberland Ct
  [3] Bexhill TN40 . . . . .157 D4
  Eastbourne BN20 . . . . . . .184 B6
Cumberland Dr BN1 . . . . .142 E2
Cumberland Gdns
  [10] Royal Tunbridge Wells TN1 . .8 A2
  St Leonards TN38 . . . . . . .159 B8
Cumberland Lodge [3]
  BN1 . . . . .142 E2
Cumberland Mews [12] TN1 .8 A2
Cumberland Rd
  Bexhill TN39 . . . . .157 B7
  Brighton BN1 . . . . .142 E2
Cumberland Wlk TN1 . . . . .8 A2
Cumberland Wlk [11] TN1 . . .8 A2
Cumnor House Sch RH17 .34 B5
Cunningham Cl TN4 . . . . . . .8 B7
Cunningham Ct [3] BN25 .180 E2
Cunningham Dr BN23 . . . .185 E7
Cunningham Ho [6] TN39 .157 B3
Cunningham Rd TN4 . . . . . .8 B7
Curlew Ct Hailsham BN27 .152 D7
  St Leonards TN38 . . . . . . .135 E3
Curlews The BN43 . . . . . . .161 A8
Currie Rd TN4 . . . . .8 A5
Curwen Pl BN1 . . . . .142 E3
Curzon Ho BN2 . . . . .177 C4
Cuthbert Cl TN39 . . . . . . .157 A7
Cuthbert Rd BN2 . . . . .164 C5
Cutter La [7] TN34 . . . . . . .160 A3
Cypress Cl
  Shoreham-by-Sea BN43 . . .140 A1
  St Leonards TN38 . . . . . . .159 A4
Cypress Gr TN2 . . . . .17 C8
Cyprus Mews RH15 . . . . . .73 B3
Cyprus Pl TN31 . . . . .93 B5
Cyprus Rd RH15 . . . . .73 A3

D

D'aubigny Rd BN2 . . . . . . .164 B8
Dacre Pk BN27 . . . . .152 D7
Dacre Rd
  Eastbourne BN20, BN21 . .184 C4
  Herstmonceux BN27 . . . . .130 C4
  Newhaven BN9 . . . . .179 D7
Dagg La TN32 . . . . .65 F5
Dakins The RH19 . . . . .10 E8
Dale Ave Brighton BN1 . . .142 F5
  Keymer BN6 . . . . .98 A3
Dale Cres BN1 . . . . .142 F6
Dale Dr BN1 . . . . .143 A6
Dale Hill BN45 . . . . .119 A6
Dale Rd Forest Row RH18 . .11 F1
  Lewes BN7 . . . . .146 A8
Dale St TN1 . . . . .8 A4
Dale View BN3 . . . . .141 D2
Dale View Gdns BN3 . . . .141 D2
Dalehurst TN6 . . . . .38 C7
Dalehurst Rd TN39 . . . . . .157 B7
Dales Cl BN27 . . . . .131 B5
Dalewood Gdns RH15 . . . .73 C2
Dallas La BN8 . . . . .101 F6
Dallaway Dr BN24 . . . . . . .174 A5
Dallington CE Prim Sch
  TN21 . . . . .84 D3
Dallington Cl TN40 . . . . . .158 A6
Dallington Rd
  Eastbourne BN22 . . . . . . .174 A1
  Hove BN3 . . . . .162 F8
Dalmeny Rd TN39 . . . . . . .157 A5
Dalmore Ct [3] TN40 . . . .157 C3
Dalton Rd BN20 . . . . .188 E8
Damian Way BN6 . . . . .98 B4
Damon Cl BN10 . . . . .178 C7
Dana Lodge BN10 . . . . . . .178 A7
Dane Cl BN25 . . . . .180 D2
Dane Court Ct TN39 . . . . .157 B6
Dane Hts [12] BN25 . . . . . .180 E2
Dane Rd Seaford BN25 . . .180 E3
  St Leonards TN38 . . . . . . .159 B8
Danehill CE Prim Sch
  RH17 . . . . .34 B4
Danehill La RH17 . . . . .33 E5
Danehill Rd BN2 . . . . .164 F5
Daniel Way TN31 . . . . .94 F2

Dannfields Ho BN25 . . . . .180 E3
Danny Sheldon Ho [14]
  BN2 . . . . .164 C4
Danum Cl BN27 . . . . .129 C3
Danworth La BN6 . . . . .72 B2
Darby's La TN5 . . . . .30 B2
Darcey Dr BN1 . . . . .143 A6
Darent Cl BN24 . . . . .173 F5
Daresbury Cl TN39 . . . . . .157 B6
Darley Rd BN20 . . . . .188 D7
Dart Ct RH19 . . . . .2 A3
Dartmouth Cl BN2 . . . . . .143 F1
Dartmouth Cres BN2 . . . .143 F1
Darvel Down TN33 . . . . . . .86 B2
Darwall Dr BN25 . . . . .181 A3
Darwall Cl
  Robertsbridge TN32 . . . . . .64 B3
  St Leonards TN38 . . . . . . .135 E1
Darwell Dr BN24 . . . . .174 A5
Davey Dr BN1 . . . . .143 B1
Davey's La BN7 . . . . .123 E2
David Lloyd Club The
  BN22 . . . . .184 F8
David Saloman's Ho
  TN3 .7 D8
Davids Hts BN21 . . . . .184 E5
Davigdor Cty Inf Sch
  BN3 . . . . .163 D6
Davigdor Rd BN3 . . . . . . .163 E7
Davis Cl TN39 . . . . .157 A7
Dawber Bldgs BN27 . . . . .152 B7
Dawlish Cl BN2 . . . . .143 F1
Dawson Terr BN1 . . . . . . .164 C6
Daynes Way RH15 . . . . . . .72 E1
De Cham Ave TN37 . . . . . .159 D8
De Cham Rd TN37 . . . . . .159 C8
De Chardin Dr TN34 . . . . .137 A5
De Courcel Rd BN2 . . . . . .164 E3
De Grey Cl BN1 . . . . .123 D2
De La Warr Gn BN7 . . . . .123 B3
De La Warr Par TN40 . . . .157 C3
De La Warr Pav TN40 . . . .157 C3
De La Warr Rd
  Bexhill TN40 . . . . .157 E5
  East Grinstead RH19 . . . . . .1 F1
De Moleyns Cl [1] TN40 . .157 D4
De Montfort Rd
  Brighton BN2 . . . . .164 C7
  Lewes BN7 . . . . .123 B1
De Roos Rd BN21 . . . . . . .184 E4
De Walden Mews BN20 . .188 E8
De Warrenne Rd BN7 . . . .123 B1
Deacons Dr BN41 . . . . . . .141 C2
Deadman's Cross TN21 . . .83 B5
Deadmans La TN31 . . . . . .93 C6
Deadmantree Hill BN8 . .101 B3
Deal Ave TN31 . . . . .93 B5
Dean Cl BN41 . . . . .141 C2
Dean Court Rd BN2 . . . . .177 A6
Dean Gdns BN41 . . . . . . .141 C2
Dean Rd BN25 . . . . .180 F2
Dean St BN1 . . . . .163 E5
Dean Wood Cl BN23 . . . .174 A4
Deanery Cl BN7 . . . . .123 D3
Deans Cl Bexhill TN39 . . .157 B6
  Woodingdean BN2 . . . . . .165 E8
Deans Dr TN39 . . . . .157 A6
Deans Mdw BN8 . . . . .101 B5
Deans Rd BN26 . . . . .170 F3
Deanway BN3 . . . . .142 B3
Decimus Burton Way
  TN37 . . . . .159 C7
Decoy Dr BN22 . . . . .173 D3
Deepdene TN5 . . . . .30 A6
Deepdene Gdns TN35 . . .137 C3
Deepdene Sch BN3 . . . . .162 D7
Deer Paddock La [7]
  BN27 . . . . .152 C7
Deerswood La TN39 . . . . .156 E5
Deeside The BN1 . . . . . . .143 A4
Delavall Wlk BN23 . . . . . .185 F6
Delaware Dr TN37 . . . . . .135 F6
Delaware Rd BN7 . . . . . . .146 A8
Delfryn BN41 . . . . .140 F3
Dell Cl TN38 . . . . .136 A1
Dell Dr TN2 . . . . .8 D4
Dell The
  East Grinstead RH19 . . . . . .2 B1
  Haywards Heath RH16 . . . .50 C5
Dellney Ave RH16 . . . . . . .50 F3
Dellsfoot Cotts TN6 . . . . . .28 A3
Delmonden Rd TN18 . . . . .45 C8
Delves Ave TN2 . . . . .8 C1
Delves Cl BN8 . . . . .124 C6
Delves Ho BN8 . . . . .124 D6
Delves Way BN8 . . . . .124 D6
Den Hill BN20 . . . . .184 A4
Denbigh Cl TN39 . . . . . . .156 E4
Denbigh Rd TN4 . . . . .8 C7
Dencher Rd BN7 . . . . .145 E3
Dene Cl BN20 . . . . .183 B1
Dene Dr BN22 . . . . .173 C1
Dene Path TN22 . . . . .55 D1
Dene Side BN20 . . . . .183 B1
Dene The Hastings TN35 . .137 A5
  Hove BN3 . . . . .141 D5
  Lower Willingdon BN20 . .173 A3
  Uckfield TN22 . . . . .55 D1
Dene Vale BN1 . . . . .142 D5
Dene Way TN3 . . . . .7 A7
Denecroft BN1 . . . . .142 D5
Denehurst Gdns TN35 . . .137 A5
Deneside BN1 . . . . .142 D5
Deneway The BN1 . . . . . .142 D4
Denham Cl TN38 . . . . . . .135 F4
Denham Ct RH15 . . . . .72 D3
Denham Rd RH15 . . . . . . .72 D3

Denham Way TN31 . . . . . . .94 E2
Denman's Cl RH16 . . . . . . .51 A8
Denman's La Lindfield RH16 51 A7
  Lindfield RH16 . . . . .51 B7
Denmark Pl TN34 . . . . . . .159 F7
Denmark Rd BN41 . . . . . .162 C7
Denmark Terr BN1 . . . . . .163 E6
Denmark Villas BN3 . . . . .163 E6
Dennis Hobden Cl BN2 . .143 E1
Denton Cl TN31 . . . . .93 A6
Denton Cty Prim Sch
  BN9 . . . . .168 E1
Denton Dr Brighton BN1 . .143 A6
  Newhaven BN9 . . . . .168 E1
Denton Rd
  Eastbourne BN20 . . . . . . .188 D8
  Newhaven BN9 . . . . .168 E1
Denton Rise BN9 . . . . . . .168 E2
Denton Terr BN9 . . . . .188 D8
Derby Ct [7] BN3 . . . . . . .163 E7
Derby Pl [6] BN2 . . . . . . .189 C2
Derek Ave BN3 . . . . .162 D6
Derek Ho BN3 . . . . .162 F6
Den La TN21 . . . . .106 B7
Dervia Ho BN3 . . . . .163 C7
Derwent Cl BN27 . . . . . . .129 A1
Derwent Ct BN1 . . . . .189 A3
Derwent Dr TN4 . . . . .7 E5
Derwent Lodge Sch TN1 . .8 A4
Derwent Rd BN20 . . . . . . .188 E8
Desmond Rd BN22 . . . . . .185 D5
Desmond Way BN2 . . . . . .164 F6
Devil's Dyke Rd BN1,BN3 .141 E7
Devon Villas RH16 . . . . . . .50 F4
Devonian Ct BN2 . . . . . . .189 C4
Devonport Ho TN31 . . . . . .93 C6
Devonshire Cl TN2 . . . . . . .16 F8
Devonshire Ct [1] BN3 . . .163 C7
Devonshire Lodge [1]
  BN22 . . . . .185 C5
Devonshire Pl
  Brighton BN2 . . . . .189 C2
  Eastbourne BN21 . . . . . . .185 A2
Devonshire Rd
  Bexhill TN40 . . . . .157 C3
  Hastings TN34 . . . . .159 F8
Devonshire Sq TN40 . . . .157 C3
Dew La TN31 . . . . .92 A8
Dewe Rd BN2 . . . . .143 C1
Dewhurst Cotts TN5 . . . . . .29 A7
Dewhurst La TN5 . . . . .29 B8
Dewlands Hill TN20 . . . . . .38 D2
Dewpond The BN10 . . . . .167 B1
Dexter Dr RH19 . . . . .10 E8
Diamond Cotts RH17 . . . . .74 A5
Diana Cl TN40 . . . . .158 A6
Dickens Cl RH19 . . . . .1 C1
Dickens Way BN23 . . . . . .174 E3
Dicklands The BN7 . . . . . .167 D8
Diggers The BN1 . . . . . . .143 B3
Dillingburgh Rd BN20 . . .184 C4
Dillon Way TN2 . . . . .8 D6
Dinapore Ho [10] BN2 . . .189 C3
Diplock Cl BN26 . . . . .172 F6
Diplocks Bldgs BN27 . . . .152 A7
Diplocks The BN27 . . . . . .152 A8
Diplocks Way BN27 . . . . .152 A7
Diplocks Wlk BN27 . . . . . .152 A8
Dirty La RH19 . . . . .11 E7
Ditchling Beacon
  Nature Reserve BN6 . . . .120 D7
Ditchling Bostall BN6 . . .120 D7
Ditchling Cl BN23 . . . . . . .173 F4
Ditchling Common Ctry Pk
  BN6 . . . . .73 F1
Ditchling Cres BN1 . . . . . .143 C5
Ditchling Ct [4] BN1 . . . .164 B8
Ditchling Dr TN35 . . . . . . .137 E4
Ditchling Gdns BN1 . . . . .143 B1
Ditchling Mus BN6 . . . . . . .98 C3
Ditchling Rd
  Brighton BN1,BN2 . . . . . .143 B4
  Westmeston BN1,BN6 . . .120 D4
Ditchling Rise BN1 . . . . . .164 A8
Ditchling Way BN27 . . . . .152 B6
Ditton's Cnr BN26 . . . . . . .173 C6
Ditton's Rd BN26 . . . . . . .173 D6
Dittons BN26 . . . . .173 C6
Dittons Mews TN38 . . . . . .135 E2
Dittons Rd BN21 . . . . .184 E3
Dixter La TN31 . . . . .67 B8
Dixter Rd TN31 . . . . .67 A6
Dock The BN8 . . . . .148 C3
Dodshill TN6 . . . . .26 A1
Dog Cotts RH19 . . . . .3 B1
Dog Kennel La TN20 . . . . .27 C6
Dogs Hill Rd TN36 . . . . . .118 B5
Doleham Cotts TN35 . . . .115 D5
Doleham Hill TN35 . . . . . .115 D5
Doleham La TN35 . . . . . . .115 B6
Doleham Sta TN35 . . . . . .115 D5
Dolphin Ct
  Eastbourne BN20 . . . . . . .188 E4
  [5] Hove BN3 . . . . .163 A6
Dolphin Ind Est BN43 . . .161 B7
Dolphin L Ctr The RH16 . .50 D6
Dolphin Mews BN43 . . . . .161 A7
Dolphin Rd
  Haywards Heath RH16 . . . .50 D4
  Shoreham-by-Sea BN43 . .161 B7
Dolphin Way BN43 . . . . . .161 B7
Donald Hall Rd BN2 . . . . .164 D5
Donald Way TN36 . . . . . . .118 A5
Donkey Mews [4] BN3 . . .163 D5
Donnington Rd BN2 . . . . .165 E6
Dorchester TN1 . . . . .8 B6
Dorchester Ct [2]
  Brighton BN1 . . . . .143 E1

Dorchester Ct continued
  [3] Eastbourne BN21 . . . .184 E4
Dordrecht Way TN34 . . . .136 E1
Dorin Ct TN2 . . . . .8 C3
Dorking Rd TN1 . . . . .8 C6
Dorman's Cl RH7 . . . . .2 A8
Dormans Gdns RH19 . . . . . .1 E6
Dormans High St RH7 . . . . .2 A8
Dormans Park Rd
  Dormans Park RH19 . . . . . .1 E6
  East Grinstead RH19 . . . . . .1 D3
Dormans Sta RH7 . . . . . . .1 F8
Dormans Station Rd RH7 . .1 F7
Dormansland Prim Sch
  RH7 . . . . .2 A8
Dornden Dr TN3 . . . . .7 A4
Dorothy Ave BN10 . . . . . .178 C7
Dorothy Ave N BN10 . . . .178 C8
Dorothy Rd BN3 . . . . .162 D8
Dorothy Stringer Sch
  BN1 . . . . .142 F3
Dorset Ave RH19 . . . . .1 C5
Dorset Cotts TN7 . . . . .14 B4
Dorset Ct [6]
  Eastbourne BN22 . . . . . . .185 B3
  Hove BN3 . . . . .162 F6
Dorset Gdns Brighton BN2 189 C2
  East Grinstead RH19 . . . . . .1 C3
Dorset Mews BN2 . . . . . . .189 C2
Dorset Pl Brighton BN2 . .189 C2
  Hastings TN34 . . . . .159 F7
Dorset Rd Bexhill TN40 . . .157 D4
  Bexhill TN40 . . . . .157 E5
  Lewes BN7 . . . . .146 D8
  Royal Tunbridge Wells TN2 . .8 D2
Dorset Rd S TN40 . . . . . . .157 D4
Dorset St BN2 . . . . .189 B2
Doubledays RH15 . . . . .73 B2
Doucegrove TN38 . . . . . . .136 A1
Douglas Cl BN27 . . . . .129 B2
Douglas Rd TN6 . . . . .27 D1
Douro Stables TN4 . . . . . . .8 A4
Dove Ct TN2 . . . . .78 C8
Dovedale Gdns BN22 . . . .173 F2
Dover Cl BN25 . . . . .181 C5
Dover Rd Brighton BN1 . . .143 C4
  Polegate BN26 . . . . .173 B7
Dower Cl BN2 . . . . .165 D3
Down Ave TN3 . . . . .20 C4
Down La TN3 . . . . .28 C8
Down Rd TN39 . . . . .157 A5
Down St TN22 . . . . .54 C5
Down Terr BN2 . . . . .164 C6
Down The BN3 . . . . .141 D4
Down's Rd TN34 . . . . .136 F3
Downash Cl BN2 . . . . .164 E6
Downash Ct TN5 . . . . .32 A3
Downash Ho TN5 . . . . .32 A3
Downes Ct [9] BN43 . . . . .161 C8
Downey Cl TN37 . . . . .136 B6
Downland Ave
  Peacehaven BN10 . . . . . . .178 E6
  Southwick BN42 . . . . .140 E1
Downland Cl
  Southwick BN42 . . . . .140 D1
  Woodingdean BN2 . . . . . .165 B8
Downland Copse TN22 . . .78 C8
Downland Cres BN3 . . . . .141 F3
Downland Ct BN41 . . . . . .141 A2
Downland Dr BN3 . . . . . . .141 F3
Downland Rd BN2 . . . . . . .165 B8
Downlands Ave TN39 . . . .157 B4
Downlands Cl TN39 . . . . . .157 A4
Downlands Sch BN6 . . . . .97 F3
Downlands Way BN20 . . . .183 B1
Downline Cl TN21 . . . . . . .106 F7
Downs Ave BN20 . . . . .184 B6
Downs Cl BN7 . . . . .123 A2
Downs Cty Inf Sch BN2 .164 B8
Downs Cty Jun Sch BN2 .143 A1
Downs Park Sch BN41 . . .141 D2
Downs Rd Burgess Hill RH15 72 E4
  Seaford BN25 . . . . .181 A3
  Willingdon BN22 . . . . .173 B2
Downs Sch The BN20 . . . .184 B4
Downs Valley Rd BN2 . . . .165 E8
Downs View Ninfield TN33 .133 B5
  North Chailey BN8 . . . . . . .75 E7
  Peacehaven BN10 . . . . . . .167 D2
Downs View Cl
  East Dean BN20 . . . . .183 C1
  North Chailey BN8 . . . . . . .75 E7
Downs View La BN20 . . . .183 C1
Downs View Rd BN2 . . . . . .97 F3
Downs View Sch BN2 . . . .165 C8
Downs Villas BN9 . . . . . . .168 E3
Downs Wlk BN10 . . . . .167 B2
Downscroft RH15 . . . . .73 D6
Downside Brighton BN1 . . .142 D5
  Hove BN3 . . . . .142 B3
  Lewes BN7 . . . . .146 A8
  Shoreham-by-Sea BN43 . .140 A1
Downside Cl
  Eastbourne BN20 . . . . . . .184 B4
  Shoreham-by-Sea BN43 . .140 A1
Downsmeade BN21 . . . . . .184 E3
Downsvalley Rd BN20 . . . .173 A4
Downsview Heathfield TN21 .82 B2
  Hove BN3 . . . . .141 D3
  Hurstpierpoint BN6 . . . . . . .97 A5
  Lower Willingdon BN20 . .173 A3
Downsview Ave BN2 . . . . .165 C8
Downsview Cotts BN8 . . .123 A7
Downsview Cres TN22 . . . .78 D8
Downsview Dr RH17 . . . . . .74 C4
Downsview Rd
  Lower Willingdon BN20 . .173 A3
  Portslade-by-Sea BN41 . .141 A2

Downsview Rd continued
  Seaford BN25 . . . . .181 A3
Downsview Way BN27 . . . .152 B7
Downsway Berwick BN26 . .150 B3
  Southwick BN42 . . . . .140 F1
  Woodingdean BN2 . . . . . .144 D1
Draffin La TN31 . . . . .94 D3
Drake Ave BN23 . . . . .185 E7
Drake Ct BN25 . . . . .180 E2
Drake Ho TN39 . . . . .156 E4
Drapers Way TN38 . . . . . .136 B2
Draxmont Way BN1 . . . . . .142 F3
Drayton Rise TN39 . . . . . .156 D4
Drive End [10] BN3 . . . . . .163 C7
Drive The Burgess Hill RH15 .73 B4
  Crowborough TN6 . . . . . . .25 D2
  Hailsham BN27 . . . . .152 B6
  Hove BN3 . . . . .163 C7
  Maresfield TN22 . . . . .55 A5
  Maresfield Park TN22 . . . . .55 A7
  Newhaven BN9 . . . . .179 C5
  Royal Tunbridge Wells TN2 . .8 B1
  Southwick BN42 . . . . .140 E1
  St Leonards TN38 . . . . . . .158 F8
  Uckfield TN22 . . . . .78 C8
Drockmill Ct BN26 . . . . . . .173 C6
Drove Ave BN2 . . . . .144 D2
Drove Cres BN41 . . . . .141 A2
Drove Rd Newhaven BN9 . .179 D8
  Portslade-by-Sea BN41 . .141 A2
  Woodingdean BN2 . . . . . .165 B8
Drove The Brighton BN1 . .142 D1
  Falmer BN1 . . . . .144 C5
  Newhaven BN9 . . . . .179 E8
  Offham BN7,BN8 . . . . . . .123 A5
Drovers Cl BN41 . . . . .141 C2
Drovers Way RH15 . . . . . . .73 C1
Droveway The
  Haywards Heath RH16 . . . .50 C6
  Hove BN3 . . . . .142 B2
  Hove BN3 . . . . .142 C1
  Lewes BN7 . . . . .146 A5
Drummond Cl RH16 . . . . . .50 D4
Drummond Ct RH16 . . . . . .50 D4
Drury La TN38 . . . . .136 A2
Drusilla's Zoo Park BN26 171 B6
Dryden Wlk BN1 . . . . .174 E3
Duchess Dr BN25 . . . . . . .180 E6
Dudeney Lodge BN1 . . . . .143 B1
Dudley Inf Sch TN35 . . . .160 C5
Dudley Lodge TN2 . . . . . . .8 C4
Dudley Rd Brighton BN1 . .143 B1
  Eastbourne BN22 . . . . . . .185 B4
  Hastings TN35 . . . . .160 C5
  Royal Tunbridge Wells TN1 . .8 A4
Dudwell Rd BN2 . . . . .165 E7
Duke Bernard Ct [7]
  BN22 . . . . .185 C5
Duke Mews [2] TN37 . . . .136 B2
Duke Rd TN37 . . . . .136 B2
Duke St Bexhill TN39 . . . .156 F5
  Brighton BN1 . . . . .189 A2
  St Leonards TN38 . . . . . . .136 B2
Duke Terr TN37 . . . . .136 B2
Duke's Dr BN20 . . . . .188 E7
Duke's Mound BN2 . . . . . .164 D4
Dukes Barn Ct RH16 . . . . .51 B7
Dukes Cl BN25 . . . . .180 D5
Dukes Hill TN33 . . . . .112 D6
Dukes La BN1 . . . . .189 A2
Dukes Rd Lindfield RH16 . .51 B8
  Royal Tunbridge Wells TN1 . .8 C5
Dulwich Cl BN25 . . . . .181 C5
Dumb Woman's La TN31 . .92 D3
Dumbrell Ct TN20 . . . . .27 B7
Dumbrells Court Rd BN6 . .98 D4
Dumbrells Ct BN6 . . . . .98 D4
Dumbrills Cl RH15 . . . . . . .73 A5
Dunbar Dr BN27 . . . . .129 A1
Duncan Ho BN10 . . . . .167 D1
Dunclutha Rd TN34 . . . . .136 F4
Duncton Cl RH16 . . . . .50 D4
Duncton Ho BN6 . . . . .97 E4
Dundale Rd TN3 . . . . .9 E1
Dunes Ave TN31 . . . . .94 F2
Dunning's Rd RH19 . . . . . .10 F5
Dunnings Mill L Complex
  RH19 . . . . .10 E6
Dunorlan Farm Cotts TN2 . .8 E4
Dunstall Ave RH15 . . . . . . .72 F4
Dunstall Farm Rd RH15 . .72 F4
Dunstan Gr TN4 . . . . .8 B6
Dunstan Rd TN4 . . . . .8 B6
Dunstans Croft TN20 . . . . .40 C3
Dunster Cl BN1 . . . . .143 B1
Dunvan Cl BN7 . . . . .123 C3
Durham Cl BN2 . . . . .144 A1
Durham Ct
  Eastbourne BN20 . . . . . . .184 B6
  [4] Hove BN3 . . . . .163 B6
Durkins Rd RH19 . . . . .1 D1
Durrell Cl BN23 . . . . .174 F2
Durrington Ct BN1 . . . . . .142 D5
Dursley Rd BN22 . . . . .185 A4
Dutchells Way BN22 . . . . .173 E4
Dyall Cl RH15 . . . . .72 E4
Dyke Cl BN3 . . . . .142 B4
Dyke Rd BN1,BN3 . . . . . . .163 C4
Dyke Road Ave BN1,BN3 .142 C3
Dyke Road Pl BN1 . . . . . .142 A4
Dyke Road Mews BN1,BN3 .189 A3
Dyke Rd [3] BN1 . . . . . . .142 C3
Dymchurch Cl
  Polegate BN26 . . . . .173 C7
  Seaford BN25 . . . . .181 C5

Dymock Cl BN25 . . . . .181 C4
Dymock's The BN6 . . . . . .98 D3
Dymond Rd TN38 . . . . . . .136 A3
Dynevor Rd TN4 . . . . .8 C7

E

Eagle Cl TN22 . . . . .78 E5
Eagle Rd TN31 . . . . .93 C6
Earl St TN34 . . . . .159 F8
Earl's Rd TN4 . . . . .7 F4
Earls Cl BN25 . . . . .180 C5
Earls Gdn 6 BN7 . . . . .123 D1
Earwig Cnr BN8 . . . . .123 E3
East Albany Rd BN25 . . . . .180 F3
East Ascent TN38 . . . . .159 C6
East Beach St TN34 . . . . . .160 B3
East Beeches Rd TN6 . . . . . .26 B2
East Bourne St 22 TN34 . . .160 B4
East Brighton Coll of
  Media Arts (Sch) BN2 . .164 F5
East Cl BN26 . . . . .173 B6
East Cliff TN31 . . . . .93 C6
East Cliff Rd TN4 . . . . .8 A6
East Dean Rd BN20 . . . . . .184 B2
East Dean Rise BN25 . . . . .181 A4
East Dr BN2 . . . . .164 C5
East Gdns BN6 . . . . .98 D3
East Grinstead Sta RH19 . . .1 D1
East Grinstead Town Mus
  RH19 .1 F2
East Hill RH19 . . . . .1 E6
East Hill Cliff Rly TN34 . . .160 B4
East Hill Pas 7 TN34 . . . . .160 B4
East Hoathly CE Prim Sch
  BN8 . . . . .104 F5
East Mascalls Rd RH16 . . . .51 C6
East Meadway BN43 . . . . . .161 A6
East Par TN34 . . . . .160 A3
East Point 6 BN43 . . . . . . .161 A6
East St Brighton BN1 . . . . .189 B1
  Coggins Mill TN20 . . . . . . .40 D3
  Falmer BN1 . . . . .144 C6
  Hastings TN34 . . . . .160 A4
  Lewes BN7 . . . . .123 D1
  Portslade-by-Sea BN41 . . .162 C7
  Rye TN31 . . . . .93 C5
  Seaford BN25 . . . . .180 E3
East Sussex F HQ BN7 . . . .123 B2
East Sussex Music Sch
  BN7 . . . . .146 C8
East Sussex Music Sch
  (Annexe) BN7 . . . . .123 D1
East Sussex National
  Golf Club TN22 . . . . .103 C7
East View TN21 . . . . .82 B6
East View Fields BN7 . . . . . .99 E5
East View Terr TN33 . . . . . . .88 F1
East Way BN7 . . . . .122 F2
East Wick RH16 . . . . .51 C7
Eastbank BN42 . . . . .140 F1
Eastbourne Ave BN24 . . . .175 D5
Eastbourne Coll BN21 . . . .184 F1
Eastbourne Coll of Arts
  & Tech Eastbourne BN21 .184 E7
  Eastbourne, Upperton BN21 .184 E4
  Eastbourne, Upperton BN21 .184 F4
Eastbourne Coll of
  Food & Fashion BN20 . .185 A1
Eastbourne District
  General Hospl BN21 . . . .184 E7
Eastbourne Miniature
  Steam Rly Pk BN23 . . . .185 A7
Eastbourne Rd
  Brighton BN2 . . . . .143 D1
  Felbridge RH19 . . . . .1 A5
  Halland BN8 . . . . .104 C6
  Lower Willingdon BN20 . . .173 B4
  Pevensey Bay BN24 . . . . .175 C4
  Seaford BN25 . . . . .181 C3
  Uckfield TN22 . . . . .78 F3
  Westham BN23,BN24 . . . .174 F4
Eastbourne Sta BN21 . . . .184 F3
Eastbridge Rd BN9 . . . . . .179 E7
Eastbrook Rd BN41 . . . . . .162 B7
Eastbrook Way BN42 . . . . .162 A7
Eastdale Rd RH15 . . . . .73 D4
Eastend La BN6 . . . . .98 D3
Eastergate TN39 . . . . .156 D6
Eastergate Rd BN2 . . . . . . .143 F4
Eastern Ave
  Polegate BN26 . . . . .173 B7
  Shoreham-by-Sea BN43 . .161 A7
Eastern Cl BN43 . . . . .161 A7
Eastern Cotts RH16 . . . . . . .51 B7
Eastern Pl BN2 . . . . .164 E4
Eastern Rd Brighton BN2 .164 E4
  Haywards Heath RH16 . . . .50 F3
  Lindfield RH16 . . . . .51 C7
  Wivelsfield RH17 . . . . .74 B4
Eastern Ring Rd BN1 . . . . .144 C7
Eastern Terr 10 BN2 . . . . . .164 D4
Eastern Terrace Mews
  BN2 . . . . .164 D4
Eastfield Cres BN1 . . . . . . .143 A4
Eastgate St BN7 . . . . .123 D1
Eastgate Wharf 9 BN7 . . .123 D1
Easthill Dr BN41 . . . . .141 B2
Easthill Way BN41 . . . . . . .141 B1
Eastlands Cl TN4 . . . . .16 E8
Eastlands Rd TN4 . . . . .7 C2
Eastport La BN7 . . . . .146 C8
Eastview Cotts BN8 . . . . . .124 E5
Eastway TN39 . . . . .156 D4

Eastwell Pl BN27 . . . . .152 B8
Eastwick Bottom BN1 . . . .143 B7
Eastwick Cl BN1 . . . . .143 B7
Eastwood Rd TN39 . . . . . . .157 A4
Eatenden La TN32,TN33 . . .87 B3
Eaton Ct 9 BN3 . . . . .163 B7
Eaton Gardens Mans 20
  BN3 . . . . .163 C7
Eaton Gate 17 BN3 . . . . . .163 C7
Eaton Gdns BN3 . . . . .163 C7
Eaton Gr BN3 . . . . .163 C7
Eaton Hall 19 BN3 . . . . . . .163 C7
Eaton Manor 11 BN3 . . . . .163 C7
Eaton Pl BN2 . . . . .164 D4
Eaton Rd BN3 . . . . .163 C7
Eaton Villas BN3 . . . . .163 B7
Eaton Wlk TN33 . . . . .88 D1
Ebden's Hill TN37 . . . . .136 B8
Ebenezer Rd TN34 . . . . . . .160 B4
Ecclesden 6 BN2 . . . . .189 C3
Ecmod Rd BN22 . . . . .185 C6
Edburton Ave BN1 . . . . . . .143 A1
Eden Cl BN24 . . . . .174 A5
Eden Dr TN39 . . . . .156 F4
Eden Rd TN1 . . . . .8 A2
Eden Vale
  Dormans Park RH19 . . . . . . .1 F5
  East Grinstead RH19 . . . . . .1 D4
Edenbridge Rd TN7 . . . . . . .13 E6
Edensor Rd BN20 . . . . .188 D7
Edgar Rd TN35 . . . . .160 C6
Edgehill Cl TN21 . . . . .81 F7
Edgehill Way BN41 . . . . . . .140 F2
Edgeland Terr BN22 . . . . . .173 F1
Edinburgh Ct
  Eastbourne BN20 . . . . . . .184 C5
  Seaford BN25 . . . . .180 D3
Edinburgh Rd
  Bexhill TN40 . . . . .157 C5
  8 Brighton BN2 . . . . .164 B8
  Seaford BN25 . . . . .180 D3
  St Leonards TN38 . . . . . . .158 E7
Edinburgh Way RH19 . . . . . .10 F7
Edison Rd BN23 . . . . .174 A1
Edith Ave BN10 . . . . .178 B7
Edith Ave N BN10 . . . . .178 C8
Edith Rd TN35 . . . . .137 D3
Edmond Cl BN23 . . . . .185 E8
Edmonton Rd TN39 . . . . . .157 B7
Edmund Rd TN35 . . . . .160 C6
Edward Ave Hove BN3 . . . .142 A3
  Saltdean BN2 . . . . .166 D3
Edward Cl Hove BN3 . . . . .142 A3
  Seaford BN25 . . . . .180 A6
Edward Ho BN3 . . . . .162 F6
Edward Rd
  Haywards Heath RH16 . . . .50 E2
  St Leonards TN37 . . . . . . .159 D7
Edward St Brighton BN2 . .189 C2
  6 Lewes BN7 . . . . .123 C1
  Royal Tunbridge Wells TN4 . . .7 F8
  Rusthall TN4 . . . . .7 C4
Edward Terr TN38 . . . . .136 A4
Edward Way RH15 . . . . .72 D2
Edwin Rd TN35 . . . . .160 C6
Effingham Cl BN2 . . . . .177 C6
Effingham Dr TN39 . . . . . .156 D3
Egbert Cl BN23 . . . . .185 E8
Egerton Ho BN20 . . . . .188 E8
Egerton Rd TN39 . . . . .157 B3
Egginton Cl BN1 . . . . .144 A5
Egginton Rd BN2 . . . . .144 A5
Egles Gr TN22 . . . . .78 B8
Egmont Rd BN3 . . . . .141 D1
Egremont Pl Brighton BN2 189 C2
  Hastings TN34 . . . . .160 B6
Eight Acre La TN35 . . . . . . .115 D1
Eight Bells Cl TN22 . . . . . . .56 C4
Eileen Ave BN2 . . . . .177 B5
Eisenhower Dr TN37 . . . . . .135 F6
Elder Cl BN41 . . . . .141 B2
Elder Pl BN1 . . . . .189 B4
Elderwood Cl
  Bexhill TN39 . . . . .157 C7
  Eastbourne BN22 . . . . . . .173 D2
Eldon Rd BN21 . . . . .184 C5
Eldred Ave BN1 . . . . .142 D5
Eleanor Cl Lewes BN7 . . . .123 B2
  Seaford BN25 . . . . .180 D5
Eleanor Terr TN35 . . . . . . .137 D4
Eley Cres BN2 . . . . .165 E3
Eley Dr BN2 . . . . .165 E3
Elford St 3 TN34 . . . . .159 F8
Elgar Way BN23 . . . . .174 E3
Elgin Gdns BN25 . . . . .181 C3
Elim Court Gdns TN6 . . . . . .25 E4
Elim Wlk TN34 . . . . .136 F2
Eliot Ho 4 RH16 . . . . .50 E3
Elizabeth Ave BN3 . . . . . . .142 A3
Elizabeth Cl Hove BN3 . . . .142 A3
  Seaford BN25 . . . . .180 A6
Elizabeth Cres RH19 . . . . . . .1 F3
Elizabeth Ct
  Eastbourne BN20 . . . . . . .184 C5
  2 Hailsham BN27 . . . . . . .152 C7
  7 Hove BN3 . . . . .163 C7
  Polegate BN26 . . . . .173 A6
Elizabeth Garlick Ct 1 TN1 .8 A4
Elizabeth Rd
  Shoreham-by-Sea BN43 . . .161 C8
  St Leonards TN37 . . . . . . .136 A2
Elizabethan Cl TN33 . . . . . .132 F2
Ellen Ho 3 BN3 . . . . .163 B7
Ellen St Hove BN3 . . . . . . .163 B7
  Portslade-by-Sea BN41 . .162 C7
Ellenslea Rd TN37 . . . . . . .159 C7
Ellenwhorne La TN32 . . . . . .89 A7
Ellerslie La TN39 . . . . .156 F6

Elliots Way TN21 . . . . .82 A8
Ellis Cl TN34 . . . . .159 E7
Ellis Gordon Ct BN9 . . . . . .179 B7
Ellis Way TN22 . . . . .78 A7
Ellison Cl TN6 . . . . .25 E4
Elm Cl Hove BN3 . . . . .142 C2
  Laughton BN8 . . . . .126 C7
  Seaford BN25 . . . . .181 C3
Elm Cotts Hailsham BN27 .151 A8
  Laughton BN8 . . . . .126 C7
Elm Ct Brighton BN1 . . . . .163 B8
  4 East Grinstead RH19 . . . . .1 D2
  Newhaven BN9 . . . . .179 B7
  Polegate BN26 . . . . .173 A6
Elm Dr East Grinstead RH19 . .2 A1
  Hove BN3 . . . . .141 E1
Elm Gn 4 BN27 . . . . .129 B1
Elm Gr Brighton BN2 . . . . .164 C7
  Eastbourne BN22 . . . . . . .173 F1
  5 Lewes BN7 . . . . .146 C8
Elm Grove Cty Prim Sch
  . . . . .164 C7
Elm Rd BN41 . . . . .162 B8
Elm Way TN21 . . . . .82 B6
Elmhurst Ave TN2 . . . . .9 D8
Elmore Rd BN2 . . . . .189 C3
Elms Ave BN21 . . . . .185 B2
Elms La TN35 . . . . .116 F1
Elms Lea Ave BN1 . . . . .142 E3
Elms Rd BN21 . . . . .185 B2
Elms The BN8 . . . . .124 C5
Elmsdown Pl BN27 . . . . . . .152 C7
Elmsmead TN31 . . . . .70 B4
Elmstead RH19 . . . . .10 E8
Elmstead Rd TN40 . . . . . . .157 E5
Elmwood 9 BN21 . . . . .184 F4
Elmwood Cl BN23 . . . . .174 C4
Elmwood Gdns BN23 . . . . .174 C4
Elphick Pl TN6 . . . . .25 F3
Elphick Rd
  Broyle Side BN8 . . . . .124 F7
  Newhaven BN9 . . . . .179 C8
Elphick's Pl TN2 . . . . .17 B8
Elphinstone Cty Prim Sch
  TN34 . . . . .160 A6
Elphinstone Gdns TN34 . .136 F3
Elphinstone Inf Sch TN34 136 F2
Elphinstone Rd TN34 . . . . .136 F2
Elrington Rd BN3 . . . . .142 C1
Elsted Cl BN22 . . . . .174 A1
Elsted Cres BN1 . . . . .143 C6
Elsted Rd TN39 . . . . .156 C2
Elven Cl BN20 . . . . .183 C1
Elven La BN20 . . . . .183 C1
Elven Cres BN2 . . . . .165 E4
Elwood Cl RH15 . . . . .72 F1
Elwyn Jones Ct BN1 . . . . . .142 E4
Ely Cl TN1 . . . . .8 A7
Embassy Ct
  10 Brighton BN1 . . . . .163 D5
  Haywards Heath RH16 . . . .50 E6
Emerald Quay BN43 . . . . . .161 A6
Emerson Coll RH18 . . . . . . .12 B3
Emmanuel Rd TN34 . . . . . .160 A5
Encore Ho TN21 . . . . .81 F8
Endcliffe Ct BN20 . . . . .188 E8
Endwell Rd TN40 . . . . .157 C3
Engalee RH19 . . . . .1 C2
English Cl BN3 . . . . .162 E8
English's Pas 10 BN7 . . . . .123 D1
Enterprise Est BN1 . . . . . . .143 C7
Enys Rd BN21 . . . . .184 F4
Epsom Cl TN38 . . . . .159 A8
Epsom Ct 6 TN40 . . . . .157 E4
Erica Cl BN23 . . . . .174 B2
Eridge Cl TN39 . . . . .157 A4
Eridge Dr TN6 . . . . .26 A3
Eridge Gdns TN6 . . . . .26 A3
Eridge Gn BN7 . . . . .123 B2
Eridge La TN3,TN6 . . . . .27 B2
Eridge Rd
  Boarshead TN3, TN6 . . . . . .26 D7
  Crowborough TN6 . . . . .26 A3
  Eastbourne BN21 . . . . .184 D7
  Hove BN3 . . . . .142 A2
  Royal Tunbridge Wells
    TN2,TN4 . . . . .7 E1
  Steel Cross TN6 . . . . .26 C4
Eridge Sta TN3 . . . . .15 E2
Erin Way RH15 . . . . .72 E3
Erroll Rd BN3 . . . . .162 C6
Ersham Rd BN27 . . . . .152 B5
Ersham Way BN27 . . . . . . .152 B6
Erskine Park Rd TN4 . . . . . . .7 C4
Esher Cl BN25 . . . . .180 F4
Eshton Rd BN22 . . . . .185 C5
Eskbank Ave BN1 . . . . .143 A7
Eskdale Cl BN23 . . . . .174 C4
Esplanade BN25 . . . . .180 E2
Esplanade Mews 4
  BN25 . . . . .180 E2
Esplanade The BN10 . . . . . .177 F3
Essenden Rd TN38 . . . . . . .159 A7
Essex Cl TN2 . . . . .16 F8
Essex Cl BN20 . . . . .184 B6
Essex Pl 3 Brighton BN2 . .164 C4
  Newhaven BN9 . . . . .179 C7
Essex Rd TN38 . . . . .136 A4
Essex St BN2 . . . . .164 C4
Estate Rd BN9 . . . . .179 E7
Estcots Cty Prim Sch RH19 .2 A1
Estcots Dr RH19 . . . . .2 A1
Etchingham CE Prim Sch
  TN19 . . . . .44 D2
Etchingham Rd BN23 . . . . .174 E1
Etchingham Sta TN19 . . . . .44 C1

Ethel St BN3 . . . . .163 B7
Ethelred Cl BN23 . . . . .185 E8
Etherington Hill TN3 . . . . . . .7 C8
Etherton Way BN25 . . . . . .181 A4
Ethnam La TN18 . . . . .47 E4
Eton Cl BN25 . . . . .181 A4
Eton Mews 3 BN21 . . . . . .185 A3
Eurythmy Sch RH19 . . . . . . .10 E6
Evelyn Ave BN9 . . . . .179 C7
Evelyn Ct BN41 . . . . .162 A8
Evelyn Glennie Ct 7
  BN2 . . . . .164 C5
Evelyn Rd BN7 . . . . .123 B2
Evelyn Terr BN2 . . . . .164 C5
Everest Ho 2 BN3 . . . . .162 F7
Eversfield Ct TN37 . . . . . . .159 D7
Eversfield Hospl TN38 . . . .159 A6
Eversfield Mews N 5
  TN37 . . . . .159 C7
Eversfield Pl TN37 . . . . . . .159 D7
Eversfield Rd BN21 . . . . . . .184 F4
Evershed Way BN43 . . . . . .161 B7
Eversley Cl TN37 . . . . .136 C2
Eversley Cres TN37 . . . . . . .136 C2
Eversley Rd Bexhill BN40 . .157 C3
  St Leonards TN37 . . . . . . .136 C2
Evesham Cl BN20 . . . . .184 B6
Evesham TN38 . . . . .136 A3
Ewart St BN2 . . . . .189 C3
Ewbank Ho BN3 . . . . .163 D7
Ewehurst La TN31 . . . . .6 F6
Ewell Ct 5 TN40 . . . . .157 E4
Ewhurst Cl TN34 . . . . .136 F4
Ewhurst La TN31 . . . . .66 F4
Ewhurst Rd BN2 . . . . .143 C1
Excelsior The BN1 . . . . .142 D4
Exeat Cl Brighton BN2 . . . .164 E6
  Eastbourne BN23 . . . . .174 B4
Exeter Cl BN22 . . . . .173 B2
Exeter St BN1 . . . . .163 E8
Exmouth Pl TN34 . . . . .160 A4

F

Factory La BN27 . . . . .152 A6
Fair Isle Cl BN23 . . . . .185 E8
Fair La
  Robertsbridge TN32 . . . . . .64 B4
  Robertsbridge TN32 . . . . . .64 C4
Fair Mdw TN31 . . . . .93 C7
Fair Oak Cl TN21 . . . . .82 A7
Fair View TN5 . . . . .30 A6
Fairbanks RH16 . . . . .50 E4
Fairbridge Rd RH15 . . . . . . .72 F5
Faircrouch La TN5 . . . . .29 B5
Fairdene BN42 . . . . .140 F1
Fairfax Ave TN37 . . . . .135 F7
Fairfield
  Herstmonceux BN27 . . . . .130 E6
  Peacehaven BN10 . . . . . . .178 B7
Fairfield Ave TN2 . . . . .9 D7
Fairfield Chase TN39 . . . . .156 F4
Fairfield Cl
  Burgess Hill RH15 . . . . . . .72 F4
  Shoreham-by-Sea BN43 . .140 C1
Fairfield Cotts BN26 . . . . . .149 D2
Fairfield Cres BN6 . . . . .97 A6
Fairfield Gdns
  Burgess Hill RH15 . . . . . . .72 F4
  Portslade-by-Sea BN41 . .141 B1
Fairfield Lodge BN20 . . . . .188 E8
Fairfield Rd
  Burgess Hill RH15 . . . . . . .72 F4
  East Grinstead RH19 . . . . .10 F8
  Eastbourne BN20 . . . . . . .184 E1
  St Leonards TN37 . . . . . . .136 C6
Fairfield Way RH16 . . . . .50 D8
Fairford Cl RH16 . . . . .50 E5
Fairglen Cotts TN5 . . . . .29 B3
Fairglen Rd TN5 . . . . .29 B4
Fairhaven BN7 . . . . .99 E1
Fairholme 8 BN3 . . . . .146 C8
Fairholme Ct TN6 . . . . .25 F1
Fairholme Rd BN9 . . . . .168 F1
Fairhurst BN10 . . . . .177 F3
Fairisle Cl BN27 . . . . .129 A2
Fairlawn 1 RH16 . . . . .50 E4
Fairlawn Cres RH19 . . . . .1 B2
Fairlawn Rd RH19 . . . . .1 B2
Fairlawns 9 Hove BN3 . . . .163 A6
  Shoreham-by-Sea BN43 . .161 A8
Fairlawns Dr BN27 . . . . . . .130 E6
Fairlea Cl RH15 . . . . .72 F4
Fairlie Gdns BN1 . . . . .142 E3
Fairlight TN22 . . . . .55 E1
Fairlight Ave
  Hastings TN35 . . . . .137 D3
  Telscombe Cliffs BN10 . . .177 F3
Fairlight Cl Bexhill TN40 . .158 A5
  Polegate BN26 . . . . .173 A6
Fairlight Ct BN10 . . . . .177 F4
Fairlight Cty Prim Sch
  BN2 . . . . .164 C8
Fairlight Field BN8 . . . . . . .124 D5
Fairlight Gdns TN35 . . . . . .138 F4
Fairlight Pl 8 BN2 . . . . . . .164 C8
Fairlight Rd
  Eastbourne BN22 . . . . . . .185 C5
  Fairlight TN35 . . . . .138 A4
Fairmile Rd TN35 . . . . .8 E5
Fairmount Rd TN40 . . . . . .157 D5
Fairoak BN26 . . . . .173 C6
Fairplace RH17 . . . . .74 C4
Fairview Cotts TN6 . . . . .25 E4
Fairview La TN6 . . . . .25 E4
Fairview Rise BN1 . . . . .142 D5

Fairway Cl BN20 . . . . .184 C2
Fairway Cres BN41 . . . . . . .141 C2
Fairway The Bexhill TN39 . .156 F6
  Newhaven BN9 . . . . .179 A7
  St Leonards TN38 . . . . . . .158 F8
Fairway Trad Est BN2 . . . . .143 E8
Fairways BN1 . . . . .163 E8
Fairways Cl BN25 . . . . .181 C2
Fairways Rd BN25 . . . . .181 B2
Fairways The TN4 . . . . .8 A7
Falaise Rd Hastings TN34 .159 D7
  Newhaven BN9 . . . . .168 F1
Falcon Cl BN43 . . . . .161 C6
Falcon Way BN27 . . . . .129 B3
Falconbury Dr TN39 . . . . . .156 D3
Falconer Dr TN33 . . . . .112 F4
Fallowfield Cl BN3 . . . . . . .141 F2
Fallowfield Cres BN3 . . . . .141 F2
Falmer Ave BN2 . . . . .177 B6
Falmer Cl BN20 . . . . .184 B7
Falmer Gdns BN2 . . . . .165 D8
Falmer Hill BN1 . . . . .144 B6
Falmer House Rd BN1 . . . .144 B6
Falmer Rd BN2 . . . . .165 E5
Falmer Sch BN1 . . . . .144 A5
Falmer Sta BN1 . . . . .144 B6
Falmouth Cl BN23 . . . . .185 F8
Faraday Ave RH19 . . . . .10 F6
Faraday Cl BN22 . . . . .173 F1
Faraday Lodge TN2 . . . . .8 E5
Farlaine Rd BN21 . . . . .184 C6
Farley Bank TN35 . . . . .160 B6
Farley Way TN35 . . . . .138 E5
Farleys Way TN35 . . . . .69 B2
Farlington Ave RH16 . . . . . .50 F5
Farlington Ct RH16 . . . . .50 F5
Farm Cl East Grinstead RH19 11 B8
  Hassocks BN6 . . . . .97 E4
  Portslade-by-Sea BN41 . .141 A2
  Seaford BN25 . . . . .181 B4
Farm Gdns TN31 . . . . .69 C2
Farm Hill BN2 . . . . .165 C8
Farm La Camber TN31 . . . . .94 D3
  Ditchling BN6 . . . . .98 E3
Farm Mews BN3 . . . . .163 D6
Farm Rd BN3 . . . . .163 D6
Farm Trail BN26 . . . . .151 A4
Farm Way Burgess Hill RH15 73 D1
  Southwick BN42 . . . . .162 A7
Farman St 13 BN3 . . . . . . .163 D5
Farmcombe Cl TN2 . . . . .8 B2
Farmcombe La TN2 . . . . .8 B2
Farmcombe Rd TN2 . . . . .8 C2
Farmet Ct RH19 . . . . .1 C3
Farmland Way TN29 . . . . . .129 C1
Farmlands Ave BN26 . . . . . .172 F4
Farmlands Cl
  Lower Willingdon BN26 . . .173 A4
  St Leonards TN37 . . . . . . .136 C5
Farmlands Ct BN26 . . . . . .173 A4
Farmlands Way BN26 . . . . .172 F5
Farmway Cl BN3 . . . . .141 D2
Farncombe Cl RH17 . . . . . . .74 D4
Farncombe Rd 6 BN7 . . . .123 C1
Farne Cl BN23 . . . . .129 A2
Farnham Ave BN6 . . . . .98 A5
Farnham Beeches TN3 . . . . .7 A3
Farnham Cl TN3 . . . . .7 A3
Farnham La TN3 . . . . .7 A3
Farnham Pl TN3 . . . . .7 A3
Farningham Rd TN6 . . . . . . .38 C8
Farnlea RH15 . . . . .73 D5
Farnol Ho 4 BN21 . . . . .184 D4
Farrance Ct TN1 . . . . .8 B4
Farriers Way TN22 . . . . .78 C6
Farthing Hill TN5 . . . . .31 E1
Farthing La BN27,TN33 . . .109 E4
Farthings The TN6 . . . . .26 A3
Fastnet Cl BN23 . . . . .185 E8
Faulkners Way RH15 . . . . . .73 A5
Faversham Rd BN23 . . . . . .174 D2
Faygate Cl TN39 . . . . .157 B8
Faygate Ct BN2 . . . . .164 E6
Faygate Rd BN22 . . . . .173 E2
Fayre Mdw TN32 . . . . .64 C4
Fazan Ct TN5 . . . . .29 F4
Fearon Rd TN34 . . . . .136 F2
Felbridge Cl RH19 . . . . .1 C3
Felbridge Ct RH19 . . . . .1 A4
Felbridge Ctr The RH19 . . . .1 A3
Felbridge Pl RH19 . . . . .1 A4
Felcourt Cotts RH19 . . . . . . .1 C8
Felcourt La RH19, RH7 . . . . .1 C8
Felcourt Rd RH19, RH7 . . . . .1 C7
Feld The RH19 . . . . .1 A3
Fellows Rd TN34 . . . . .137 B3
Felride RH16 . . . . .50 E3
Felwater Ct RH19 . . . . .1 A3
Fen Ct TN38 . . . . .135 E1
Fennel Wlk BN43 . . . . .140 B1
Fennell's Cl BN21 . . . . .184 E5
Ferbies TN3 . . . . .7 A7
Ferbies Cl TN3 . . . . .7 A7
Ferdinand Terr TN35 . . . . . .15 C7
Ferguson Rd TN29 . . . . .96 D2
Fermor Rd TN6 . . . . .38 A7
Fermor Row TN6 . . . . .37 F8
Fermor Way TN6 . . . . .38 A8
Fern Cl BN23 . . . . .174 C3
Fern Gn 1 BN27 . . . . .129 B1
Fern Rd TN38 . . . . .158 F8
Fernbank Sh Ctr TN6 . . . . .25 F3
Ferndale Ct TN2 . . . . .8 C5
Ferndale Cl TN2 . . . . .8 C5
Ferndale Point TN2 . . . . .8 C4
Ferndale Rd
  Burgess Hill RH15 . . . . . . .73 C2
  Hove BN3 . . . . .163 D7

Fernhurst Cl BN1 . . . . . . .143 B6
Fernhurst Cres BN1 . . . . . .143 B5
Fernlea Cl TN35 . . . . .114 E4
Ferns The TN1 . . . . .8 C4
Fernside **5** RH19 . . . . .1 D2
Fernside Ave TN38 . . . . . .135 F1
Fernwood Rise BN1 . . . . . .142 D6
Ferrers Rd BN7 . . . . .123 B1
Ferring Cl TN31 . . . . .93 A6
Ferring Ct BN1 . . . . .143 F5
Ferringham TN4 . . . . .7 F4
Ferry Hill TN36 . . . . .117 E8
Ferry Rd TN31 . . . . .93 B5
Festival Gdns TN39 . . . . . .157 C7
Feversham Cl BN43 . . . . . .161 B6
Field Cl Burgess Hill RH15 . .72 E4
Seaford BN25 . . . . .181 B2
Field Cotts RH15 . . . . .73 B4
Field End TN22 . . . . .55 A4
Field View TN32 . . . . .64 B3
Field Way TN38 . . . . .158 E8
Fielden La TN6 . . . . .25 D1
Fielden Rd TN6 . . . . .25 D2
Fieldfare Ct BN22 . . . . . . .152 D7
Fields End Cl RH16 . . . . . . .50 F4
Fieldway Broad Oak TN31 . . .90 C5
Ditchling BN6 . . . . .98 D3
Lindfield RH16 . . . . .50 F8
Fiennes Rd BN27 . . . . .130 E6
Figg La TN6 . . . . .37 F8
Filching Cl BN26 . . . . .172 E3
Filching Ct BN20 . . . . .184 B5
Filching Manor
Motor Mus BN26 . . . . . . .172 D2
Filching Rd BN20 . . . . .184 B5
Filder Cl BN22 . . . . .185 A6
Filsham Dr TN40 . . . . .158 A6
Filsham Rd TN38 . . . . .159 A8
Filsham Valley TN38 . . . . . .158 F7
Filsham Valley Sch TN38 . .158 F7
Finches Gdns RH16 . . . . . . .51 A8
Finches La RH16 . . . . .51 A8
Finches Park Rd RH16 . . . . .51 A8
Finches The Bexhill TN40 . .157 F4
Shoreham-by-Sea BN43 . . .161 A8
2 St Leonards TN38 . . . . . .136 A5
Findon Ave BN2 . . . . .177 E6
Findon Cl Bexhill TN39 . . . .156 E3
Hove BN3 . . . . .141 F3
Seaford BN25 . . . . .181 C3
Findon Rd BN2 . . . . .164 F5
Finistere Ave BN23 . . . . . .185 E8
Finley Ct TN38 . . . . .158 F6
Finmere Cl BN22 . . . . .185 C6
Finmere Ct BN22 . . . . .185 C6
Finmere Rd BN22 . . . . .185 C6
Finsbury Lodge **1** BN2 . .164 C6
Finsbury Rd BN2 . . . . .164 C6
Fir Cl BN2 . . . . .165 F7
Fir Grove Rd TN21 . . . . . . .81 B6
Fir Toll Cl TN20 . . . . .39 F2
Fir Toll Rd Woolbridge TN20 .39 C2
Woolbridge TN20 . . . . .39 E2
Fir Tree Cl Bexhill TN39 . . .156 C3
Hailsham BN27 . . . . .129 C2
Fir Tree Rd TN4 . . . . .7 F3
Fir Tree Way BN6 . . . . .98 A4
Fircroft Cl BN1 . . . . .142 E3
Firehills Cotts TN35 . . . . . .138 C3
Firlands RH16 . . . . .50 F4
Firle Bostal BN8 . . . . .148 A2
Firle CE Prim Sch BN8 . . .148 B4
Firle Cl Hastings TN35 . . . .137 E4
Seaford BN25 . . . . .180 E5
Firle Cres BN7 . . . . .122 F2
Firle Dr BN25 . . . . .180 E5
Firle Gn TN22 . . . . .55 E1
Firle Grange BN25 . . . . . . .180 E5
Firle Place BN8 . . . . .148 C3
Firle Rd Brighton TN39 . . . .156 D4
Brighton BN2 . . . . .164 D6
Eastbourne BN22 . . . . . . .185 B4
Peacehaven BN10 . . . . . . .178 C8
Seaford BN25 . . . . .180 E6
Firle Terr BN9 . . . . .168 D2
Firs Ct TN4 . . . . .7 F6
Firs The TN35 . . . . .160 C5
First Ave Bexhill TN40 . . . .157 F5
Camber TN31 . . . . .94 F2
Hove BN3 . . . . .163 C6
Newhaven BN9 . . . . .179 C7
First St TN3 . . . . .6 F3
Firtoft Cl RH15 . . . . .73 B3
Firtree Rd TN34 . . . . .160 A6
Firwood Cl
Eastbourne BN22 . . . . . . .173 E1
Heathfield TN21 . . . . .82 A8
Firwood Rise TN21 . . . . . . .82 A8
Fisher Cl BN23 . . . . .185 F7
Fisher St BN7 . . . . .123 C1
Fisher's Gate Cotts TN7 . . . .14 A1
Fishermen's Mus TN34 . . . .160 B3
Fishergate Cl BN41 . . . . . .162 A7
Fishersgate Cty Fst Sch
BN41 . . . . .162 A7
Fishersgate Sta BN41 . . . .162 B7
Fishersgate Terr BN41 . . . .162 A7
Fishmarket Rd TN31 . . . . . .93 C6
Fishponds La TN35 . . . . . .114 E3
Fitch Dr BN2 . . . . .143 F1
Fitzalan Ho **7** BN21 . . . .184 F4
Fitzgerald Ave BN25 . . . . .180 F2
Fitzgerald Cl BN20 . . . . . .184 F1
Fitzgerald Ho **5** BN25 . .180 E3
Fitzgerald Pk BN25 . . . . . .180 F2
Fitzgerald Rd BN7 . . . . . . .123 D3
Fitzherbert Dr BN2 . . . . . .164 D8
Fitzjohn Cl BN6 . . . . .97 F3

Fitzjohns Rd BN7 . . . . .123 B2
Fitzmaurice Ave BN22 . . . .185 B5
Fitzroy Rd BN7 . . . . .123 B2
Five Acre Wlk TN34 . . . . . .136 E1
Five Ashes CE Prim Sch
TN20 . . . . .58 B6
Five Chys La TN22 . . . . . . .57 A6
Five Hos The TN36 . . . . . . .117 E8
Five Villages Ho TN36 . . . .116 F6
Fiveways TN1 . . . . .8 A4
Flag Ct BN3 . . . . .163 B5
Flamsteed Rd BN27 . . . . . .131 A1
Fleetway Ct TN31 . . . . .94 F2
Fleming Ct BN23 . . . . .174 F2
Fletcher Ave TN37 . . . . . . .135 F7
Fletching CE Prim Sch
TN22 . . . . .53 F5
Fletching Cl BN2 . . . . .164 F6
Fletching Rd BN22 . . . . . . .174 A2
Fletching St TN20 . . . . .40 B3
Flimwell Bird Pk TN5 . . . . .32 E2
Flimwell Cl Brighton BN2 . .164 E5
Eastbourne BN23 . . . . . . .174 A4
Flimwell TN5 . . . . .32 D4
St Leonards TN38 . . . . . . .135 D3
Flint Cl
Portslade-by-Sea BN41 . . . .141 B2
Seaford BN25 . . . . .180 E6
Flints The BN7 . . . . .145 E5
Flitterbrook La TN21 . . . . . .83 C4
Florance La TN3 . . . . .15 B6
Florence Ave BN3 . . . . . . .162 D8
Florence Ct BN1 . . . . .142 F2
Florence Pl BN1 . . . . .143 B1
Florence Rd BN1 . . . . .164 A8
Florida Ct TN38 . . . . .158 F6
Fold Sch The BN3 . . . . . . .162 D7
Folders Cl RH15 . . . . .73 D1
Folders La RH15 . . . . .73 D1
Foley Cl BN23 . . . . .185 E7
Folkestone Cl BN25 . . . . . .181 C5
Folkestone Rd TN31 . . . . . .93 F8
Folkington Gdns TN37 . . . .136 C5
Folkington Rd BN26 . . . . . .172 D5
Follett Holt Ho BN8 . . . . . .100 E7
Folly Field BN9 . . . . .179 C7
Fonthill Rd BN3 . . . . .163 B8
Fontridge La TN19 . . . . .62 E3
Fontwell Ave TN39 . . . . . . .156 C5
Foords La BN24 . . . . .174 C7
Foot's La TN19 . . . . .61 B3
Ford Rd TN38 . . . . .135 F2
Fordbrook Hill TN6 . . . . . . .37 F2
Fordcombe CE Prim Sch
TN3 . . . . .6 B5
Fordcombe Rd TN3 . . . . .6 C4
Foredown Cl
Eastbourne BN20 . . . . . . .184 C2
Portslade-by-Sea BN41 . . . .141 B2
Foredown Dr BN41 . . . . . . .141 C1
Foredown Rd
Portslade Village BN41 . . . .141 B4
Portslade-by-Sea BN41 . . . .141 B2
Forest Dene
Crowborough TN6 . . . . . . .26 D1
Royal Tunbridge Wells TN2 . .8 C1
Forest Fold Cotts TN6 . . . . .25 D5
Forest La TN21 . . . . .83 D6
Forest Lodge
Crowborough Warren TN6 . . .37 D8
2 East Grinstead RH19 . . . .10 F8
Forest Pk
Crowborough TN6 . . . . . . .25 D2
Maresfield TN22 . . . . .54 F5
Forest Pl TN21 . . . . .80 F6
Forest Rd Brighton BN1 . . .143 E6
Forest Row RH18 . . . . .12 B2
Royal Tunbridge Wells TN2 . .8 C1
Forest Ridge RH19 . . . . . . .21 A5
Forest Rise TN6 . . . . .26 D1
Forest Row Bsns Pk RH18 .11 F4
Forest Row CE Inf Sch
RH18 . . . . .11 F2
Forest View
Hailsham BN27 . . . . .152 A8
Nutley TN22 . . . . .35 C3
Forest View Rd RH19 . . . . . .10 E6
Forest Way Hastings TN34 .136 E1
Pembury TN2 . . . . .9 D8
Royal Tunbridge Wells TN2 . .8 D1
Forewood La TN33 . . . . . . .135 A7
Forewood Rise TN33 . . . . .134 F6
Forge Cl
Portslade-by-Sea BN41 . . . .141 B2
Staplecross TN32 . . . . .65 E1
Uckfield TN22 . . . . .78 C6
Forge Field TN5 . . . . .42 F6
Forge La TN32 . . . . .65 E1
Forge Lane Cotts TN22 . . . .55 A8
Forge Rd TN3 . . . . .15 C2
Forge Rise TN22 . . . . .78 C6
Forge Way
Burgess Hill RH15 . . . . . . .73 A4
St Leonards TN37 . . . . . . .136 C5
Forgefield Cotts TN18 . . . . .47 A4
Forstal The Cobbarn TN3 . . .15 F3
Pembury TN2 . . . . .9 E8
Forstall TN3 . . . . .7 A4
Fort Gate BN9 . . . . .179 E5
Fort Haven BN43 . . . . .161 C6
Fort La BN22 . . . . .185 D6
Fort Newhaven BN9 . . . . . .179 D5
Fort Rd Eastbourne BN22 . .185 D6
Newhaven BN9 . . . . .179 D6
Fort Rise BN9 . . . . .179 D5
Forward Cl BN9 . . . . .168 E2
Foster Cl BN25 . . . . .180 E4
Foster Ct BN3 . . . . .163 E6

Foundry Ct RH15 . . . . .73 B3
Foundry La BN7 . . . . .123 C1
Foundry St BN1 . . . . .189 B3
Fountains Cl Brighton BN1 143 B2
Eastbourne BN22 . . . . . . .173 E3
Founthill Ave BN2 . . . . . . .177 B5
Founthill Rd BN2 . . . . .177 B5
Fourteen Acre La TN35 . . . .115 D4
Fourth Ave BN3 . . . . .163 B6
Fowey Rd BN43 . . . . .161 B6
Fowlers Cl TN39 . . . . .156 E5
Fowly La TN22 . . . . .56 C7
Fox Cl RH15 . . . . .72 F1
Fox Hill RH16 . . . . .50 E1
Fox Hill Cl RH16 . . . . .50 F1
Fox Hill Village RH16 . . . . .50 F1
Fox in the Wood TN5 . . . . . .29 C6
Fox Way BN41 . . . . .141 B2
Foxcote TN37 . . . . .136 D5
Foxdown Rd BN2 . . . . .165 F7
Foxglove Cl
Broyle Side BN8 . . . . .125 A7
Burgess Hill RH15 . . . . . . .72 D4
Foxglove Rd BN23 . . . . . . .174 B3
Foxhill Bexhill TN39 . . . . . .156 E5
Peacehaven BN10 . . . . . . .167 B1
Foxhill Ct **3** RH16 . . . . . . .50 E3
Foxhole La
Four Throws TN18 . . . . . . .46 D8
Wadhurst TN5 . . . . .30 B4
Foxhunters Rd BN41 . . . . . .140 F3
Foxwarren RH16 . . . . .50 C5
Framelle Mount TN22 . . . . .79 B6
Framfield **11** BN2 . . . . . .164 F5
Framfield CE Prim Sch
TN22 . . . . .79 B6
Framfield Cl BN1 . . . . .143 B6
Framfield Rd Buxted TN22 . .56 B3
Uckfield TN22 . . . . .78 D6
Framfield Way BN21 . . . . . .184 D6
Francis Rd RH16 . . . . .51 B8
Francis St BN1, BN2 . . . . . .189 B4
Francislea RH16 . . . . .50 E2
Frankfield Rise TN2 . . . . .8 A1
Franklands Cl RH15 . . . . . . .73 B1
Franklands Gdns RH15 . . . .98 A8
Franklin Rd Brighton BN2 . .164 C7
Portslade-by-Sea BN41 . . . .162 C7
Shoreham-by-Sea BN43 . . .140 D1
Franklin St BN2 . . . . .164 C8
Franklynn Ct RH16 . . . . . . .50 F3
Franklynn Rd RH16 . . . . . . .50 F3
Franshaven RH16 . . . . .51 A3
Frant Ave TN39 . . . . .156 C5
Frant CE Prim Sch TN3 . . . .17 B4
Frant Cl TN39 . . . . .156 C5
Frant Rd Hove BN3 . . . . . . .142 A2
Royal Tunbridge
Wells TN2,TN3 . . . . .17 A7
Frant Sta TN3 . . . . .17 A7
Frary Wlk TN21 . . . . .82 A3
Fraser Ave BN21 . . . . .185 E7
Fraser Ct **2** BN43 . . . . . .161 C8
Freckley Hollow TN33 . . . .111 C1
Fred Emery Ct **16** BN1 . .163 E5
Freda Gardham
Cty Prim Sch TN31 . . . . . .93 D6
Frederic Ho BN2 . . . . .177 B5
Frederic Cotts RH16 . . . . . .51 B7
Frederick Gdns BN1 . . . . . .189 B3
Frederick Pl BN1 . . . . .189 B3
Frederick Rd TN35 . . . . . . .137 C3
Frederick St BN1 . . . . .189 B3
Frederick Thatcher Place
TN33 . . . . .112 A4
Free Heath Rd TN3,TN5 . . . .19 D3
Freehold Terr **1** BN2 . . . .164 C8
Freek's La RH15 . . . . .73 A5
Freeland Ct BN25 . . . . . . .180 A6
Freeman Ave BN22 . . . . . .173 E1
Freemans Rd BN41 . . . . . .162 A8
Freezeland La TN39 . . . . . .134 A2
Fremlin Ct TN4 . . . . .7 B4
French Gdns RH16 . . . . . . .51 A6
Frenches Farm Dr TN21 . . . .82 A5
Frenchgate Cl BN22 . . . . . .173 F2
Frenchgate Rd BN22 . . . . . .173 F2
Freshfield Bank RH18 . . . . .11 F2
Freshfield Cl BN27 . . . . . . .152 B6
Freshfield Halt RH17 . . . . . .52 B8
Freshfield La RH17 . . . . . . .33 C2
Freshfield Pl BN2 . . . . .164 C5
Freshfield Rd BN2 . . . . . . .164 D6
Freshfield St BN2 . . . . .164 C6
Freshfield Way BN2 . . . . . .164 C5
Freshford Cl BN23 . . . . . . .174 D2
Freshwater Ave TN34 . . . . .136 E2
Freshwater Sq BN22 . . . . .173 B3
Freshway BN22 . . . . .173 C3
Frewen Cl TN31 . . . . .67 B7
Frewen Coll TN31 . . . . .67 C5
Frewen Ct TN38 . . . . .135 F4
Friar Cl BN1 . . . . .143 A4
Friar Cres BN1 . . . . .143 A3
Friar Rd BN1 . . . . .143 A3
Friar Wlk BN1 . . . . .142 F4
Friar's Cres TN35 . . . . .138 B7
Friar's Hill Terr TN35 . . . . .138 A7
Friar's Way TN34 . . . . .136 F4
Friars Bank TN35 . . . . .138 B7
Friars Cl BN6 . . . . .97 E4
Friars Hill TN35 . . . . .137 F7
Friars Oak Rd BN6 . . . . . . .97 E5
Friars Rd TN36 . . . . .117 F7
Friars Way TN2 . . . . .8 D6
Friars' Ave BN10 . . . . .178 E6
Friars' Wlk BN7 . . . . .123 D1

Fer–Gle **201**

Gattons Cty Inf Sch The
RH15 . . . . .72 E3
Gattons The RH15 . . . . .72 E3
Gatwick Farm Cotts RH19 . .3 A4
Gaudick Cl BN20 . . . . .184 E1
Gaudick Rd BN20 . . . . .184 E1
Gavin Astor Cl TN40 . . . . . .158 A6
Geary Pl TN35 . . . . .114 E3
Geering Pk BN27 . . . . .152 D7
Geering Rd BN24 . . . . .174 B5
Geers Wood TN21 . . . . .81 F6
Geerswood Cotts **2** TN21 .82 A6
Gemma Cl BN27 . . . . .152 E7
Geneva Rd BN9 . . . . .179 D6
Genistos The BN6 . . . . .97 E4
Gensing Rd TN38 . . . . .159 C7
George Hill TN32 . . . . .64 B3
George Rainey Sch TN38 159 C7
George St Brighton BN2 . . .189 B2
Hailsham BN27 . . . . .152 C7
Hastings TN34 . . . . .160 A3
Hove BN3 . . . . .163 B6
Portslade-by-Sea BN41 . . . .162 C7
Royal Tunbridge Wells TN2 . . .8 C3
Southwick BN41 . . . . .162 A7
Sparrow's Green TN5 . . . . .29 F5
Georgian Cl TN40 . . . . . . .157 E5
Georgian Wlk TN38 . . . . . .158 F5
Gerald Cl RH15 . . . . .73 D3
Gerald Rd BN25 . . . . .180 F1
Gerard St BN1 . . . . .189 B5
German St TN36 . . . . .117 E7
Ghyll Rd Crowborough TN6 . .25 E4
Heathfield TN21 . . . . .82 A6
Ghyll Side Rd TN31 . . . . . . .67 B7
Ghyllside BN2 . . . . .143 E1
Ghyllside Ave TN34 . . . . . .136 D4
Ghyllside Dr TN34 . . . . . . .136 D4
Ghyllside Way TN34 . . . . . .136 D4
Gibb Cl TN40 . . . . .158 A5
Gibbetts TN3 . . . . .6 F3
Gibbon Rd BN9 . . . . .179 C6
Gibraltar Rise TN21 . . . . . . .82 A7
Gibson Ct BN7 . . . . .123 D2
Giffards Cl RH19 . . . . .1 F1
Gilbert Rd
Eastbourne BN22 . . . . . . .185 B4
St Leonards TN37,TN38 . . .159 B8
Gilbert Way BN27 . . . . . . .152 B5
Gilberts Dr BN20 . . . . .187 B8
Gilda Cres BN26 . . . . .173 A6
Gildredge Rd
Eastbourne BN21 . . . . . . .184 F2
Seaford BN25 . . . . .180 F3
Gilham La RH18 . . . . .11 E2
Gill The TN2 . . . . .9 E8
Gillham Wood Ave TN39 . . .156 D3
Gillham Wood Rd TN39 . . .156 D3
Gilligans The RH15 . . . . . . .72 F5
Gillridge Gn TN6 . . . . .25 F4
Gillman's Dr TN38 . . . . . . .135 F4
Gillman's Hill TN38 . . . . . .136 A1
Gillman's Pk TN38 . . . . . . .135 F5
Gimble Way TN2 . . . . .9 D8
Gingerbread La TN18 . . . . . .32 F2
Gipps Cross La TN3 . . . . .6 F3
Girton Ho BN3 . . . . .162 F6
Githa Rd TN35 . . . . .160 C4
Glade The Hailsham BN27 .151 F6
Mayfield TN20 . . . . .40 A3
Uckfield TN22 . . . . .78 D7
Gladepoint RH16 . . . . .50 E5
Glades The Bexhill TN40 . .157 E5
East Grinstead RH19 . . . . . . .2 B1
Gladstone Bldgs BN8 . . . .101 E4
Gladstone Cl BN22 . . . . . .173 F1
Gladstone Pl BN2 . . . . . . .164 C8
Gladstone Rd
Burgess Hill RH15 . . . . . . .73 C4
Crowborough TN6 . . . . . . .25 F1
Hastings TN34 . . . . .160 A5
Portslade-by-Sea BN41 . . . .162 C8
Rusthall TN4 . . . . .7 B4
Gladstone Terr BN2 . . . . . .189 C4
Gladys Ave BN10 . . . . .178 D6
Gladys Rd BN3 . . . . .162 D8
Glanfield Ct TN1 . . . . .8 C5
Glassenbury Dr TN40 . . . . .157 F5
Glastonbury Rd BN3 . . . . .162 D6
Gleave Ct TN1 . . . . .2 A2
Glebe Cl Bexhill TN39 . . . .156 D3
Eastbourne BN20 . . . . . . .184 D3
Lewes BN7 . . . . .146 A3
Southwick BN42 . . . . .161 F4
Glebe Cotts TN33 . . . . . . .134 A7
Glebe Dr BN25 . . . . .180 E3
Glebe The Felbridge RH19 . . .1 A4
Hastings TN34 . . . . .160 B5
Hurstpierpoint BN6 . . . . . . .97 A6
Lindfield RH16 . . . . .51 B8
Pembury TN2 . . . . .9 D8
Pett TN35 . . . . .116 F3
Glebe Villas BN3 . . . . .162 D7
Glebelands Cl BN43 . . . . . .161 B8
Glebelands The TN6 . . . . . .25 F2
Glen Cl BN26 . . . . .172 F4
Glen Cotts BN26 . . . . .172 F3
Glen Rise BN1 . . . . .142 B5
Glen Rise Cl BN1 . . . . .142 B5
Glen The TN22 . . . . .55 D1
Glen Vue RH19 . . . . .1 E6
Glenburn Ct TN39 . . . . . . .157 C2
Glencoe TN6 . . . . .25 F2
Glendale Ave BN21 . . . . . .184 C5

Glendale Ct TN2 . . . . .8 D6
Glendale Rd
Burgess Hill RH15 . . . . .73 B2
Hove BN3 . . . . .163 D7
Glendor Rd BN3 . . . . .162 E6
Glendyne Cl RH19 . . . . .11 A8
Glendyne Way RH19 . . . . . . .11 A8
Gleneagles Cl
Bexhill TN40 . . . . .157 E5
Seaford BN25 . . . . .180 A6
Gleneagles Ct 13 RH16 . . . . .50 E4
Gleneagles Dr
Hailsham BN27 . . . . .152 A8
St Leonards TN38 . . . . .158 F7
Glenfalls Ave BN1 . . . . .143 A7
Glenfergus RH16 . . . . .50 E6
Glengorse TN33 . . . . .112 F3
Glengorse Ct TN33 . . . . . . .112 F3
Glenham Pl RH19 . . . . .21 A5
Glenleigh Ave TN39 . . . . . . .156 F6
Glenleigh Park Rd TN39 . . .157 A6
Glenleigh Wlk TN32 . . . . . .64 A4
Glenmore Mews 4 BN21 . .185 A3
Glenmore Pk TN6 . . . . .16 F8
Glenmore Rd TN6 . . . . .25 C3
Glenmore Rd E TN6 . . . . . . .25 D3
Glenside 1 RH19 . . . . .1 E1
Glenthorn Rd TN39 . . . . . . .157 A4
Glenthorne Ho 11 BN21 . . .184 F4
Glenview Cl TN35 . . . . .160 D5
Glessing Rd BN24 . . . . .174 B6
Gleton Ave BN3 . . . . .141 D2
Gloucester Ave TN40 . . . . . .158 A5
Gloucester Cl
East Grinstead RH19 . . . . . . .11 A8
Eastbourne BN22 . . . . .173 C2
Gloucester Cotts 13 TN34 .160 A4
Gloucester Ct BN23 . . . . . .174 E1
Gloucester Pas 2 BN1 . . . .189 B3
Gloucester Pl BN1, BN2 . . .189 B3
Gloucester Rd
Brighton BN1 . . . . .189 B3
Burgess Hill RH15 . . . . .72 F3
Sparrow's Green TN5 . . . . . . .29 F6
Gloucester St BN1, BN2 . . .189 B3
Glovers La TN39 . . . . .157 C7
Glynde Ave
Eastbourne BN22 . . . . .173 E1
Saltdean BN2 . . . . .177 D6
Glynde Cl BN9 . . . . .168 D2
Glynde Ct Bexhill TN39 . . .156 C3
Polegate BN26 . . . . .173 A6
Glynde Ho BN3 . . . . .163 D6
Glynde Rd BN2 . . . . .164 D6
Glynde Sta BN8 . . . . .147 F6
Glyndebourne Ave BN2 . . .177 C6
Glyndebourne Gdns
TN37 . . . . .136 C6
Glyndley Manor
Cottage Est BN24 . . . . . . .152 F2
Glyne Ascent TN40 . . . . . . .157 F5
Glyne Barn Cl TN40 . . . . . .158 A5
Glyne Dr TN40 . . . . .158 A5
Glyne Gap Sch TN40 . . . . .158 A5
Glyne Hall TN40 . . . . .157 D3
Glynleigh 17 BN2 . . . . .189 C3
Glynleigh Dr BN26 . . . . . . .173 C6
Glynleigh Rd BN24 . . . . . . .153 A1
Glynn Rd BN10 . . . . .167 C1
Glynn Rd W BN10 . . . . .167 C1
Glynn Rise BN10 . . . . .167 B1
Goatham La TN31 . . . . .89 E5
Godden Cl TN31 . . . . .67 B7
Godden Rd BN8 . . . . .76 C7
Goddens Gill TN31 . . . . .67 B7
Godfrey Cl TN7 . . . . .23 C3
Godwin Rd Hastings TN35 .160 C5
Hove BN3 . . . . .141 D1
Goffs The BN21 . . . . .184 E3
Golby Ct BN10 . . . . .178 A7
Gold La BN10 . . . . .167 C2
Goldbridge Rd BN8, TN22 . .76 E7
Goldcrest Dr TN22 . . . . .78 D5
Golden Hill RH15 . . . . .73 D3
Golden La 11 BN1 . . . . . . .163 D5
Golden Miller La BN26 . . . .172 F6
Goldhurst Gn TN36 . . . . . . .116 E5
Golding Rd BN23 . . . . .174 F2
Goldsmid Rd BN1, BN3 . . .163 E7
Goldsmith Cl BN23 . . . . . . .174 E3
Goldsmiths Ave TN6 . . . . . . .25 D3
Goldsmiths L Ctr TN6 . . . . .25 F4
Goldstone Cl BN3 . . . . .142 A2
Goldstone Cres BN3 . . . . . .142 B2
Goldstone Ct BN3 . . . . .142 A3
Goldstone Cty Jun Sch
BN3 . . . . .141 E1
Goldstone Ho 4 BN3 . . . . .163 B7
Goldstone La BN3 . . . . .163 B8
Goldstone Rd BN3 . . . . .163 B7
Goldstone Ret Pk BN3 . . . .163 B8
Goldstone St BN3 . . . . .163 B7
Goldstone Villas BN3 . . . . .163 B7
Goldstone Way BN3 . . . . . .142 A2
Golf Dr BN1 . . . . .143 B3
Goods Station Rd TN1 . . . . . .8 B4
Goodtrees La TN8 . . . . .4 B2
Goodwin Cl BN27 . . . . .129 A2
Goodwins Cl RH19 . . . . .1 D3
Goodwins The TN2 . . . . .7 F1
Goodwood Cl
Bexhill TN40 . . . . .157 D6
Willingdon BN20 . . . . .173 B2
Goodwood Ct 2 BN3 . . . . .163 D7
Goodwood Way BN2 . . . . . .143 F3

Gooseberry La TN31 . . . . . .67 A3
Gordon Ave BN43 . . . . .161 A7
Gordon Cl RH16 . . . . .50 E6
Gordon Ho RH15 . . . . .73 C4
Gordon Pl TN39 . . . . .157 B6
Gordon Rd Brighton BN1 . .142 F2
Burgess Hill RH15 . . . . .73 C4
Buxted TN22 . . . . .56 C3
Crowborough TN6 . . . . .25 F2
Hailsham BN27 . . . . .152 B7
Hastings TN34 . . . . .160 A4
Haywards Heath RH16 . . . . .50 E6
Portslade-by-Sea BN41 . . . .162 C7
Royal Tunbridge Wells TN4 . . .8 E7
Shoreham-by-Sea BN43 . . . .161 A7
Southwick BN41 . . . . .162 A7
Gore Park Ave BN21 . . . . . .184 D4
Gore Park Rd BN21 . . . . . . .184 D4
Gorham Ave BN2 . . . . .177 A6
Gorham Cl BN2 . . . . .177 A6
Gorham Ct BN10 . . . . .177 A6
Gorham Way BN10 . . . . . . .177 A6
Goring Ct BN1 . . . . .143 F5
Gorringe Cl
Lower Willingdon BN20 . . . .173 A3
Shoreham-by-Sea BN43 . . . .161 D7
Gorringe Dr BN20 . . . . .173 A3
Gorringe Rd BN22 . . . . .185 A4
Gorringe Valley Rd BN20 . .173 A3
Gorse Cl Eastbourne BN20 .184 B5
Portslade-by-Sea BN41 . . . .140 F4
Gorse Dr BN25 . . . . .180 F6
Gorse Hill TN21 . . . . .59 F1
Gorse Rd TN2 . . . . .8 E5
Gorselands TN33 . . . . .88 E1
Gorses The TN39 . . . . .156 C2
Gorsethorn Way TN35 . . . .138 E4
Gorseway The TN39 . . . . . .156 C5
Gosford Way BN26 . . . . . . .172 F6
Gote La BN8 . . . . .124 D4
Goudhurst Cl BN23 . . . . . . .174 D1
Gower Rd RH16 . . . . .50 E3
Gows Croft BN7 . . . . .145 E5
Grace Ct BN6 . . . . .97 E5
Gradwell End BN8 . . . . .100 D7
Graffham Cl BN2 . . . . .164 E6
Grafton St BN2 . . . . .189 C1
Graham Ave Brighton BN1 .142 F5
Portslade-by-Sea BN41 . . . .140 F4
Graham Cl BN41 . . . . .140 F4
Graham Cres BN41 . . . . . . .140 F4
Grammer Ct BN8 . . . . .75 D7
Grampian Cl
Eastbourne BN23 . . . . .174 C3
Royal Tunbridge Wells TN2 . . .8 D5
Granary Cotts TN33 . . . . . .112 E4
Grand Ave Bexhill TN40 . . .158 A5
Hassocks BN6 . . . . .97 F4
Hove BN3 . . . . .163 C6
Seaford BN25 . . . . .180 D6
Grand Avenue Mans 4
BN3 . . . . .163 C6
Grand Cres BN2 . . . . .177 A5
Grand Ct Eastbourne BN21 .185 A1
10 St Leonards TN37 . . . . .159 C6
Grand Hotel Bldgs BN21 .185 A1
Grand Junction Rd
BN1, BN2 . . . . .189 B1
Grand Par Brighton BN2 . . .189 B2
Eastbourne BN21 . . . . .185 B2
Polegate BN26 . . . . .172 F6
St Leonards TN37, TN38 . . .159 C6
Grand Parade Mews BN2 189 B2
Grange Ave TN34 . . . . .136 D4
Grange Cl Brighton BN1 . . .142 E1
Burgess Hill RH15 . . . . .73 C5
Crowborough TN6 . . . . .25 D1
Horam TN21 . . . . .106 F6
Grange Court Dr TN39 . . . .157 B6
Grange Ct
Eastbourne BN20 . . . . .184 F2
Lewes BN7 . . . . .146 C8
9 Southwick BN42 . . . . . . .161 E7
Grange End BN20 . . . . .184 F1
Grange Gdns
Eastbourne BN20 . . . . .184 F2
Rusthall TN4 . . . . .7 D4
Grange Ind Est The
BN42 . . . . .161 D7
Grange Mus & Art Gallery
BN2 . . . . .165 F2
Grange Rd
Barcombe Cross BN8 . . . . .101 D4
Eastbourne BN21 . . . . .184 F1
Hastings TN34 . . . . .136 E5
Hove BN3 . . . . .162 E8
Lewes BN7 . . . . .146 C8
Rusthall TN4 . . . . .7 D4
Southwick BN42 . . . . .161 E7
Uckfield TN22 . . . . .78 C7
Grange The
Barcombe Cross BN8 . . . . .101 D4
Saltdean BN2 . . . . .177 D4
Uckfield TN22 . . . . .78 C7
Grangeways BN1 . . . . .142 E5
Granoon Cotts BN20 . . . . . .187 A4
Grant St BN2 . . . . .189 C4
Grantham Bank BN8 . . . . . .101 E4
Grantham Cl BN8 . . . . .100 E7
Grantham Rd BN1 . . . . .143 A1
Grants Hill Ho TN22 . . . . . . .78 C7
Granville Ct 2
Eastbourne BN20 . . . . .184 F1
10 Hove BN3 . . . . .163 B7
2 Seaford BN25 . . . . .180 E2
Granville Rd
Eastbourne BN20 . . . . .184 F1
Hove BN3 . . . . .163 E7

Granville Rd continued
Royal Tunbridge Wells TN1 . . .8 C5
Graperies The 3 BN2 . . . .164 C5
Grasmere Cl BN23 . . . . . . .174 B4
Grassington Rd BN20 . . . . .184 F1
Grassmere Ave BN10 . . . . .177 F4
Grassmere Ct BN10 . . . . . .178 A8
Gratton Ct TN39 . . . . .157 A3
Gravelye Cl RH16 . . . . .51 B5
Gravelye La
Haywards Heath RH16 . . . . .51 A4
Haywards Heath RH16 . . . . .51 B6
Gravett Ct RH15 . . . . .72 F2
Graycoats Dr TN6 . . . . .25 F2
Grays Cotts TN33 . . . . .112 F3
Grays Cty Inf Sch BN9 . . . .179 D6
Graystone La TN35 . . . . . . .137 D3
Grazebrook Cl TN39 . . . . . .156 D3
Great Brooms Rd TN4 . . . . . .8 C8
Great Cliffe Rd BN23 . . . . .174 E1
Great College St BN2 . . . . .164 C4
Great Courtlands TN3 . . . . . .7 A3
Great Dixter TN31 . . . . .66 F7
Great Footway TN3 . . . . .6 F3
Great Hall Arc 3 TN1 . . . . .8 B3
Great Heathmead RH16 . . . .50 D6
Great House Ct 4 RH19 . . .10 F8
Great Knelle Farm
(Childrens Farm) TN31 . .68 A8
Great Oak TN19 . . . . .45 A3
Great Rough BN8 . . . . .76 A6
Great Sanders Ho TN33 . . .88 D4
Great Walstead Sch RH16 .51 F6
Great Wilkins BN1 . . . . .144 B5
Greater Paddock BN8 . . . . .124 E6
Greatham Ct BN1 . . . . .142 E6
Grecian Rd TN1 . . . . .8 B2
Greeba Ct 8 TN38 . . . . . . .159 B6
Green Cl Ringmer BN8 . . . .124 C6
4 Southwick BN42 . . . . . . .161 E7
Green Ct 3 BN42 . . . . .161 E7
Green Field Cl BN42 . . . . . .161 E8
Green Gate BN10 . . . . .167 C1
Green Gr BN27 . . . . .152 B8
Green Hedges TN32 . . . . . . .63 E4
Green Hedges Ave RH19 . . .1 D2
Green Hedges Cl RH19 . . . .1 D2
Green La Bexhill TN39 . . . .156 D5
Broyle Side BN8 . . . . .103 B1
Crowborough TN6 . . . . .26 B2
Heathfield TN21 . . . . .82 B6
Jevington BN26 . . . . .172 C1
Lewes BN7 . . . . .146 C8
Seaford BN25 . . . . .180 E2
South Chailey BN8 . . . . . . .100 E7
South Street BN8 . . . . .75 E1
Wivelsfield RH17 . . . . .74 B5
Woodingdean BN2 . . . . . . .165 E6
Green Mdws RH16 . . . . .51 B8
Green Park Cnr RH17 . . . . . .74 B4
Green Rd RH17 . . . . .74 B5
Green Ridge BN1 . . . . .142 B5
Green Sq TN5 . . . . .29 F5
Green St BN21 . . . . .184 C4
Green The Blackboys TN22 .80 A6
Bodiam TN32 . . . . .65 E7
Catsfield TN33 . . . . .133 E8
Ewhurst Green TN32 . . . . . . .66 B5
Frant TN3 . . . . .17 B3
Hailsham BN27 . . . . .129 C2
Hove BN3 . . . . .142 C2
Langton Green TN3 . . . . .6 E3
Newick BN8 . . . . .76 D7
Ninfield TN33 . . . . .133 B5
Ringmer BN8 . . . . .124 D5
Rottingdean BN2 . . . . .165 F2
Sedlescombe TN33 . . . . . . .113 E8
Southwick BN42 . . . . .161 E7
St Leonards TN38 . . . . .159 B8
Green View RH15 . . . . .72 E3
Green Way TN2 . . . . .8 E8
Green Wlk Hailsham BN27 .129 C1
Seaford BN25 . . . . .181 B2
Green Wlk The BN2 . . . . . .173 B3
Greenacres Brighton BN1 . .142 F1
Peacehaven BN10 . . . . .167 D2
Telscombe Cliffs BN10 . . . .178 A7
Westfield TN35 . . . . .114 E3
Greenacres Dr
Hailsham BN27 . . . . .152 C7
Ringmer BN8 . . . . .124 D4
Greenacres Way BN27 . . . .152 C8
Greenbank Ave BN2 . . . . . .177 D6
Greene Ct BN7 . . . . .146 B8
Greenfield Cl
Brighton BN1 . . . . .143 A5
Rusthall TN4 . . . . .7 C5
Greenfield Cres BN1 . . . . . .142 F5
Greenfield Dr TN22 . . . . . . .78 D4
Greenfield Rd
Burwash TN19 . . . . .62 C7
Eastbourne BN21 . . . . .184 D4
Greenfields BN27 . . . . .129 A1
Greenfields Cl TN37 . . . . . .136 B6
Greenfields Sch RH18 . . . .11 C1
Greenhill Pk RH17 . . . . .51 A2
Greenhill Way
Haywards Heath RH17 . . . . .51 A2
Peacehaven BN10 . . . . .167 C2
Greenlands Cl RH15 . . . . . . .98 B8
Greenlands Dr RH15 . . . . . .98 B8
Greenleaf Gdns BN26 . . . .173 A8
Greenleas Hove BN3 . . . . . .141 D2
Pembury TN2 . . . . .9 C6
Greenstede Ave RH19 . . . . .1 F2
Greenway BN20 . . . . .184 B6
Greenway Ct BN2 . . . . .177 A5
Greenways Bexhill TN39 . . .156 F7

Greenways continued
Haywards Heath RH16 . . . . .50 F6
Ovingdean BN2 . . . . .165 D3
Portslade-by-Sea BN41 . . . .141 B1
Southwick BN42 . . . . .140 F1
Greenways Cnr BN2 . . . . . .165 D4
Greenways Cres BN43 . . . .140 A1
Greenwell Ct BN25 . . . . . . .181 B4
Greenwich Rd BN27 . . . . . .152 D7
Greenwoods La TN21 . . . . . .83 D7
Greggs Wood Rd TN2 . . . . . .8 E7
Gregory Ct 2 RH19 . . . . . . .1 E1
Gregory La BN24 . . . . .174 F5
Gregory Wlk TN33 . . . . . . .113 E8
Grenada 4 TN39 . . . . .157 A2
Grenada Cl TN39 . . . . .156 D4
Grenham Ct TN35 . . . . .137 C3
Grenville Ho BN10 . . . . . . .167 D1
Grenville Rd BN24 . . . . .175 C4
Grenville St BN1 . . . . .189 A2
Gresham Cl BN24 . . . . .175 B6
Gresham Cl BN21 . . . . .184 C6
Gresham Way TN38 . . . . . . .159 A8
Gresley Dr TN38 . . . . .135 F5
Greville Rd TN35 . . . . .137 C3
Grey Alders RH16 . . . . .51 B6
Grey Tower Bglws BN24 . . .175 C2
Greyfriars BN3 . . . . .163 D8
Greyfriars Ct BN7 . . . . .123 D1
Greyfriars Pl TN36 . . . . . . .118 B6
Greyhorses TN39 . . . . .156 B4
Greys Rd BN20 . . . . .184 D3
Greystones Ct TN6 . . . . .25 D4
Grinley Ct 8 TN40 . . . . . . .157 C4
Grinstead La RH19 . . . . .21 C7
Grinstead Mount 4
BN2 . . . . .164 F5
Gromenfield TN3 . . . . .15 C7
Groombridge Hill TN3 . . . . .6 D1
Groombridge Pl TN3 . . . . . .15 C8
Groombridge Place Gdns
TN3 .15 C8
Groombridge Rd TN3 . . . . . .6 A1
Groombridge Sta TN3 . . . . .15 C7
Grosvenor Bridge TN1 . . . . .8 B5
Grosvenor Cl BN26 . . . . . . .172 F5
Grosvenor Cres TN38 . . . . .159 A6
Grosvenor Gdns TN38 . . . .158 F6
Grosvenor Mans 1
BN3 . . . . .163 B6
Grosvenor Pk TN1 . . . . .8 A4
Grosvenor Rd
East Grinstead RH19 . . . . . . .1 D1
Royal Tunbridge Wells TN1 . . .8 A4
Seaford BN25 . . . . .180 E4
Grosvenor St BN2 . . . . .189 C2
Grosvenor Wlk TN1 . . . . . . .8 A4
Grove Ave TN1 . . . . .8 A2
Grove Bank 8 BN2 . . . . . . .189 C3
Grove Ct 12 BN3 . . . . .163 C6
Grove Hill Brighton BN2 . . .189 C3
Grove Hill BN27 . . . . .129 D7
Grove Hill Gdns TN1 . . . . . .8 B2
Grove Hill Rd TN1 . . . . .8 B3
Grove La TN31 . . . . .70 C4
Grove Park Sch TN6 . . . . . .25 E1
Grove Rd
Burgess Hill RH15 . . . . .73 B3
Eastbourne BN21 . . . . .184 F2
Hastings TN35 . . . . .137 D4
Seaford BN25 . . . . .180 F3
Grove Sch The TN38 . . . . . .135 F2
Grove St BN2 . . . . .189 C3
Grove The Battle TN33 . . . .112 F3
Bexhill TN39 . . . . .156 E5
Crowborough TN6 . . . . .25 E1
Eastbourne BN20 . . . . .184 B7
Hailsham BN27 . . . . .152 B6
Haywards Heath RH16 . . . . .51 B3
Mayfield TN20 . . . . .40 A2
Newhaven BN9 . . . . .168 E2
Pembury TN2 . . . . .9 D8
Rye TN31 . . . . .93 C6
Willingdon BN20 . . . . .172 F3
Grove Villa 3 BN1 . . . . . . .189 A4
Groveburry BN27 . . . . .152 C7
Grovelands Cl RH15 . . . . . . .72 F1
Grovelands Cty Prim Sch
BN27 . . . . .129 A1
Grovelands Rd BN27 . . . . . .129 A1
Grovely La TN21 . . . . .84 B1
Grover St 3 TN1 . . . . .8 B4
Growers End BN8 . . . . .76 D7
Guardian Ct BN26 . . . . .172 F7
Guardswell Pl BN25 . . . . . .180 F3
Guestling Rd BN2 . . . . .185 D5
Guestling-Bradshaw
Prim Sch TN35 . . . . .138 A8
Guildford Rd 7 TN1 . . . . . .8 B3
Guildford St BN1 . . . . .189 A3
Guilford Rd BN1 . . . . .189 A3
Guinness St BN9 . . . . .168 E1
Guinness Trust Bglws
BN9 . . . . .168 E2
Guldeford La TN29, TN31 . .71 F3
Guldeford Lane Cnr
TN31 . . . . .71 D2
Guldeford Rd TN31 . . . . . . .93 E7
Gun Rd TN22 . . . . .80 A6
Gundreda Rd BN7 . . . . .123 B2
Gunter's La TN39 . . . . .157 A6
Gurth Rd TN35 . . . . .160 C5
Gwent Ct 8 BN2 . . . . .185 C4
Gwydyr Mans 3 BN3 . . . . .163 C6
Gwyneth Gr TN40 . . . . .157 F7
Gwynne Gdns RH19 . . . . . . .1 C2

H

Hackenden Cl RH19 . . . . . . .1 E3
Hackenden Cotts RH19 . . . .1 E3
Hackenden La RH19 . . . . . . .1 E3
Hackhurst La BN27 . . . . . . .128 B4
Hackhurst Lane Ind Est
BN27 . . . . .128 B4
Hackwood TN32 . . . . .63 E4
Haddington Cl BN3 . . . . . . .163 B6
Haddington St 11 BN3 . . . .163 B7
Hadley Ct Polegate BN26 . .173 A6
Royal Tunbridge Wells TN4 . . .7 F6
Hadley Ho 4 BN21 . . . . . . .184 F3
Hadlow Ave BN23 . . . . .174 B4
Hadlow Cl BN2 . . . . .164 D6
Hadlow Down Rd TN6 . . . . .38 D3
Hadrian Ave BN2 . . . . .162 A8
Hadrian Gdns TN37 . . . . . . .136 A6
Haig Ave BN1 . . . . .143 D6
Hailsham Ave BN2 . . . . . . .166 D3
Hailsham Com Coll BN27 . .152 B8
Hailsham Ct 2 TN40 . . . . . .157 C3
Hailsham Rd
Heathfield TN21 . . . . .82 A6
Herstmonceux BN27 . . . . . .130 E5
Polegate BN26 . . . . .172 F7
Stone Cross BN24, BN26 . . .173 F8
Hairpin Croft BN10 . . . . . . .167 C1
Half Mile Dro BN8 . . . . . . .125 B7
Hall La TN22 . . . . .57 C5
Hall's Grove Rd TN2 . . . . . . .8 D2
Hall's Hole Rd TN2 . . . . .8 E4
Halland Cl BN22 . . . . .173 D1
Halland Rd BN2 . . . . .143 F4
Hallands The RH15 . . . . .73 C4
Hallett Rd BN2 . . . . .164 D7
Halley Pk BN27 . . . . .152 D7
Halley Rd Cade Street TN21 .82 E8
Wartling BN27 . . . . .131 B1
Halls Cotts TN5 . . . . .29 F5
Hallyburton Rd BN3 . . . . . .162 D8
Halsford Croft RH19 . . . . . . .1 B3
Halsford Gn RH19 . . . . .1 B3
Halsford La RH19 . . . . .1 C3
Halsford Park Cty Prim Sch
RH19 .1 C2
Halsford Park Rd RH19 . . . .1 C2
Halton Cres TN34 . . . . .160 B6
Halton Hts TN34 . . . . .160 B6
Halton Pl TN34 . . . . .160 B6
Halton Rd BN22 . . . . .185 C4
Halton Shaws BN6 . . . . .97 B5
Halton Terr TN34 . . . . .160 B6
Ham Bsns Ctr BN43 . . . . . .161 A7
Ham La Burwash TN19 . . . . .62 B1
Lewes BN7 . . . . .146 D8
Ringmer BN8 . . . . .124 C6
Scaynes Hill RH17 . . . . .51 E3
Ham Rd BN43 . . . . .161 A7
Hamble Rd BN24 . . . . .173 F5
Hambleton Cl BN23 . . . . . .174 D3
Hambrook RH15 . . . . .73 C1
Hamelsham Ct BN27 . . . . . .152 A8
Hamilton Cl BN41 . . . . .141 A3
Hamilton Ct Brighton BN2 .165 A3
Royal Tunbridge Wells TN4 . . .8 A5
Hamilton Gdns TN35 . . . . . .137 D3
Hamilton Ho
13 Eastbourne BN21 . . . . . .184 E4
Royal Tunbridge Wells TN4 . . .8 A5
Seaford BN25 . . . . .180 E4
Hamilton Lodge Sch
BN2 . . . . .164 D5
Hamilton Mans 8 BN3 . . . .163 B5
Hamilton Rd BN1 . . . . .189 A4
Hamilton Terr TN39 . . . . . . .157 A4
Hamlands La BN22 . . . . . . .173 B3
Hamlin's Cnr BN6 . . . . .72 A6
Hammer La BN27, TN21 . . .107 F5
Hammerwood Pk TN19 . . . .3 C2
Hammerwood Rd RH19 . . . .11 E6
Hammonds Dr BN23 . . . . . .185 C2
Hammonds Gardens RH15 .72 F1
Hammonds Ridge RH15 . . . .72 F1
Hammy Cl BN43 . . . . .161 C8
Hammy La BN43 . . . . .161 B8
Hammy Way BN43 . . . . .161 B8
Hampden Ave BN22 . . . . . .173 F1
Hampden Cl TN33 . . . . .112 B4
Hampden Gdns BN9 . . . . . .168 D2
Hampden Park
Cty Inf Sch BN22 . . . . .173 F2
Hampden Park Dr BN22 . . .184 E8
Hampden Park Sch BN22 . .173 E2
Hampden Park Sports Ctr
BN22 . . . . .173 D2
Hampden Park Sta BN22 . .173 F1
Hampden Rd BN2 . . . . .164 C7
Hampden Terr 8 BN22 . . . .185 C4
Hampshire Ct
Brighton BN2 . . . . .189 C1
6 Eastbourne BN23 . . . . . .174 E1
Hampstead Rd BN1 . . . . . . .142 D1
Hampton Pl BN1 . . . . .163 E5
Hampton St 24 BN1 . . . . . .163 E5
Hampton Terr 7 RH19 . . . . .163 E6
Hampton Way RH19 . . . . . . .10 F7
Hamsey Cl Brighton BN2 . .164 F5
Eastbourne BN20 . . . . .184 B6
Hamsey Cres BN7 . . . . .123 A2
Hamsey Cty Prim Sch
BN8 . . . . .123 A8
Hamsey La
Cooksbridge BN8 . . . . .123 B7
Seaford BN25 . . . . .181 C2
Hamsey Rd Saltdean BN2 . .177 D4

Hamsey Rd *continued*
Sharpthorne RH19 . . . . .21 A6
Hamshaw Ct BN22 . . . . . . .184 F8
Hamsland RH17 . . . . .33 C4
Hanbury La RH16 . . . . .51 A5
Hanbury Park Sports Stad
RH16 . . . . .51 A5
Hanging Birch La TN21 . . .81 D1
Hangleton Cl BN3 . . . . . . .141 D2
Hangleton City
Inf & Jun Sch BN3 . . . . .141 E2
Hangleton Gdns BN3 . . . .141 D1
Hangleton La
Hove BN3, BN41 . . . . . . .141 C2
Portslade-by-Sea BN41 . .141 B2
Hangleton Manor Cl
BN3 . . . . .141 D2
Hangleton Rd BN3 . . . . . .141 E2
Hangleton Valley Dr
BN3 . . . . .141 D4
Hangleton Way BN3 . . . . .141 D3
Hankham Cty Prim Sch
BN24 . . . . .174 B8
Hankham Hall Rd BN24 . .174 D7
Hankham Rd BN24 . . . . . .174 B6
Hankham St BN24 . . . . . .174 B8
Hanlye La RH17 . . . . .50 B8
Hannington Pl BN6 . . . . . . .97 A7
Hanover Cl Bexhill TN40 .157 C5
Seaford BN25 . . . . .180 B6
Hanover Cres BN2 . . . . . .189 C4
Hanover Ct Brighton BN2 .189 C4
Eastbourne BN21 . . . . . .184 D5
Haywards Heath RH16 . . .50 D4
Hanover Mews BN2 . . . . .189 C4
Hanover Rd
Eastbourne BN22 . . . . . .185 C4
Royal Tunbridge Wells TN1 . .8 A4
Hanover St BN2 . . . . .189 C4
Hanover Terr BN2 . . . . . .189 C4
Hanson Rd BN9 . . . . .179 C6
Harbour Barn TN36 . . . . .118 B6
Harbour Ct BN42 . . . . . . .161 F7
Harbour Farm TN36 . . . . .118 B6
Harbour Rd TN31 . . . . .93 D4
Harbour View Cl BN25 . . .180 B6
Harbour View Rd BN9 . . .179 B5
Harbour Way
Shoreham-by-Sea BN43 . .161 B6
St Leonards TN38 . . . . . .135 C4
Harbour's Yd TN33 . . . . . .112 A2
Harcourt Cl TN22 . . . . .78 C6
Harcourt Rd TN22 . . . . . . .78 D6
Harding Ave BN22 . . . . . .185 B6
Hardrada Rise TN34 . . . .136 E3
Hardwick Rd
Eastbourne BN21 . . . . . .185 A2
Hove BN3 . . . . .141 E3
Hardwick Way BN3 . . . . . .141 E3
Hardwicke Rd TN34 . . . . .160 B6
Hardy Dr BN23 . . . . .185 F6
Hare Way TN37 . . . . .136 C5
Harebeating Cl BN27 . . . .129 C2
Harebeating Cres BN27 . .129 C2
Harebeating Dr BN27 . . . .129 C2
Harebeating Gdns BN27 . .129 C2
Harebeating La BN27 . . . .129 C2
Harebell Cl BN23 . . . . . . .174 C3
Harebell Dr BN41 . . . . . . .141 A3
Harecombe Rd TN6 . . . . . .37 F8
Harecombe Rise TN6 . . . . .37 F8
Haremere Hall Gdns TN19 44 E2
Haremere Hill TN19 . . . . . .44 D2
Harescroft TN2 . . . . .16 F7
Harewood Cl TN39 . . . . . .157 A3
Harewood Ct **8** BN3 . . . .163 C6
Harfield Cl BN9 . . . . .168 F2
Hargate Cl TN2 . . . . .16 F8
Hargreaves Rd BN23 . . . .174 A1
Harison Rd TN38 . . . . . . .181 A4
Harkness Dr TN34 . . . . . .137 B5
Harlands Cl RH16 . . . . .50 C6
Harlands Cty Prim Sch
Haywards Heath RH16 . . .50 D7
Uckfield TN22 . . . . .78 D5
Harlands Rd RH16 . . . . . . .50 D6
Harlequin Gdns TN37 . . . .136 A6
Harlequin La TN6 . . . . .37 E8
Harlequin Pl TN6 . . . . .37 E8
Harley La TN21 . . . . .82 A6
Harley Shute Rd TN38 . . .158 E7
Harley Way TN38 . . . . . . .158 E6
Harmans Dr RH19 . . . . .2 B1
Harmans Mead RH19 . . . . .2 B1
Harmers Hay Rd BN27 . . .129 B1
Harmers Hill BN8 . . . . .76 C7
Harmony St TN4 . . . . .7 D4
Harmony Wood TN34 . . . .136 F5
Harmsworth Cres BN3 . . .141 E3
Harold Cl BN24 . . . . .175 F7
Harold Dr BN23 . . . . .185 F8
Harold Ho TN2 . . . . .8 C7
Harold Mews **2** TN38 . . .159 C6
Harold Pl TN34 . . . . .159 F7
Harold Rd TN35 . . . . .160 C5
Harold Terr TN33 . . . . . . .112 F3
Harpers Rd BN9 . . . . .179 C7
Harrier La TN33 . . . . .112 F4
Harriers Ct BN27 . . . . . . .152 E7
Harries Rd TN2 . . . . .8 E7
Harrington Ct BN1 . . . . . .142 E2
Harrington Mans BN1 . . . .142 E2
Harrington Pl BN1 . . . . . .143 B2
Harrington Rd BN1 . . . . . .142 E2
Harrington Villas BN1 . . . .142 F2
Harris Ct BN21 . . . . .185 A3
Harrisons La BN8 . . . . . . .124 E5
Harrow Cl BN25 . . . . .181 A4

Harrow La TN37 . . . . .136 B5
Hart Cl TN22 . . . . .78 A7
Hartfield Ave BN1 . . . . . .143 A5
Hartfield La BN21 . . . . . . .184 F4
Hartfield Mdw TN38 . . . . .135 D3
Hartfield Rd Bexhill TN39 .156 E2
Cowden TN8 . . . . .4 C6
Eastbourne BN21 . . . . . .184 F3
Forest Row RH18 . . . . . . .12 B2
Saltdean BN2 . . . . .177 D5
Seaford BN25 . . . . .181 A3
Harting Combe TN38 . . . .159 B8
Hartington Mansions
BN21 . . . . .185 A2
Hartington Pl
Brighton BN2 . . . . .164 C8
Eastbourne BN21 . . . . . .185 A2
Hartington Rd BN2 . . . . . .164 C8
Hartington Terr BN2 . . . . .164 C8
Hartington Villas BN3 . . . .163 B8
Hartwood Lodge **6**
TN40 . . . . .157 C4
Harvard Cl BN7 . . . . .123 C3
Harvard Rd BN8 . . . . .124 D5
Harvest Cl Lindfield RH16 . .51 B7
Telscombe Cliffs BN10 . . .167 B2
Harvest Hill RH19 . . . . . . .10 E8
Harvest Way TN37 . . . . . .136 C5
Harvesters RH16 . . . . .50 D2
Harvey Cl TN38 . . . . .135 F4
Harvey's La BN8,TN22 . . .103 D4
Harveys Way BN1 . . . . . .123 E1
Harvington Bsns Pk
BN22 . . . . .184 F8
Harwood Cl BN23 . . . . . . .185 E7
Harwoods Cl **3** RH19 . . . .10 F7
Harwoods La RH19 . . . . . .10 F7
Haslam Cres TN40 . . . . . .157 F6
Hassock Cl BN23 . . . . . . .173 F4
Hassocks Cty Inf Sch BN6 .97 F4
Hassocks Lodge BN6 . . . . .97 B5
Hassocks Sta BN6 . . . . . . .97 C4
Hastings Ave BN25 . . . . . .181 C5
Hastings Castle TN34 . . . .160 A4
Hastings Ct BN26 . . . . . . .173 B7
Hastings Coll of Arts &
Tech TN38 . . . . .159 B6
Hastings Mus & Art
Gall TN34 . . . . .159 E7
Hastings Mus of Local
History TN34 . . . . .160 A4
Hastings Rd Battle TN33 . .113 B2
Bexhill TN40 . . . . .157 E5
Bexhill TN40 . . . . .157 F5
Brighton BN2 . . . . .164 C8
Newenden TN17,TN18 . . . .48 C6
Pembury TN2 . . . . .9 D6
Pembury TN2 . . . . .9 F5
The Moor TN18 . . . . .45 F6
Hastings Sea Life Ctr
TN34 . . . . .160 B3
Hastings Sports Ctr
TN34 . . . . .159 D8
Hastings Sta TN34 . . . . . .159 E8
Hatch End RH18 . . . . .11 F2
Hatchgate Cl RH17 . . . . . .50 A6
Hatchgate La RH17 . . . . . .50 A6
Hatfield Ct **18** BN3 . . . . . .163 C6
Hatherley Rd TN37 . . . . . .159 C7
Havana Ct **10** BN23 . . . . .185 F8
Havelock Rd Bexhill TN40 .157 C6
Brighton BN1 . . . . .142 F1
Eastbourne BN22 . . . . . .185 B4
Hastings TN34 . . . . .159 F7
Haven Brow BN25 . . . . . .181 A4
Haven Cl Beachlands BN24 175 E6
Lower Willingdon BN22 . . .173 B3
Haven Rd TN38 . . . . .158 D6
Havering Cl TN2 . . . . .8 F4
Hawkenbury Cl TN2 . . . . . .8 D2
Hawkenbury Mead TN2 . . .8 D1
Hawkenbury Rd TN2,TN3 . . .8 E1
Hawkenbury Way BN7 . . .123 A1
Hawkes Farm
Cty Prim Sch BN27 . . . .129 B3
Hawkhurst CE Prim Sch
TN18 . . . . .45 F8
Hawkhurst Cl BN23 . . . . . .174 D2
Hawkhurst Pl BN1 . . . . . .143 D6
Hawkhurst Rd
Brighton BN1 . . . . .143 D6
Flimwell TN5,TN18 . . . . . .32 E2
Hawkhurst Way TN39 . . . .156 E3
Hawkins Cl BN43 . . . . . . .140 D1
Hawkins Cres BN43 . . . . . .140 D2
Hawkins Rd BN43 . . . . . .140 D1
Hawkins Way BN27 . . . . . .152 B8
Hawks Farm Cl BN27 . . . .129 B2
Hawks Rd BN27 . . . . .129 B2
Hawks Town Cres BN27 . .129 C2
Hawksbridge Cl BN22 . . . .173 C3
Hawkstown Cl BN27 . . . . .129 B3
Hawkstown Gdns BN27 . . .129 B3
Hawkstown View BN27 . . .129 B3
Hawkswood Dr BN27 . . . . .129 C3
Hawkswood Rd BN27 . . . . .129 C3
Hawth Cl BN25 . . . . .180 C4
Hawth Cres BN25 . . . . . . .180 C4
Hawth Gr BN25 . . . . .180 C4
Hawth Hill BN25 . . . . . . .180 C5
Hawth Park Rd BN25 . . . .180 C4
Hawth Pl BN25 . . . . .180 C4
Hawth Rise BN25 . . . . . . .180 C5
Hawth Valley Ct **1** BN25 .180 C4
Hawth Way BN25 . . . . . . .180 D4
Hawthorn Ave TN39 . . . . .156 D3

Hawthorn Bank BN2 . . . . .143 F4
Hawthorn Cl
Burgess Hill RH15 . . . . . .73 D5
Saltdean BN2 . . . . .177 C6
Hawthorn Ct BN26 . . . . . .173 B6
Hawthorn Rd
Eastbourne BN23 . . . . . .185 C7
Hastings TN35 . . . . .160 D6
Hawthorn Rise BN9 . . . . .179 B7
Hawthorn Way BN41 . . . . .141 A3
Hawthorne Cl TN21 . . . . . .82 B6
Hawthornes The TN31 . . . .90 B4
Hawthorns The
Burgess Hill RH15 . . . . . .73 A5
Hailsham BN27 . . . . .152 A7
Hawthylands Cres BN27 . .129 B2
Hawthylands Dr BN27 . . . .129 B2
Hawthylands Rd BN27 . . . .129 B2
Haybourne Cl BN2 . . . . . .164 E7
Haybourne Rd BN2 . . . . . .164 E7
Hayes Cl
Portslade-by-Sea BN41 . .162 C8
Ringmer BN2 . . . . .124 D5
Hayes La TN31 . . . . .91 C5
Hayes Plat TN31 . . . . .67 C5
Hayland Gn BN27 . . . . . . .129 C1
Haylind Rd RH16 . . . . .51 B5
Haystoun Cl BN22 . . . . . .173 C2
Haystoun Pk BN22 . . . . . .173 C2
Hayward Rd BN7 . . . . . . .123 A4
Haywards Heath Coll
RH16 . . . . .50 A4
Haywards Heath Sta RH16 50 E6
Haywards Rd
Brighton BN1 . . . . .143 A6
Haywards Heath RH16 . . .50 E3
Haywood Way TN35 . . . . .137 C4
Hazel Bank **3** BN2 . . . . . .189 C4
Hazel Cl Newhaven BN9 . .179 B7
Portslade-by-Sea BN41 . .141 C5
Hazel Court Sch BN23 . . .174 B3
Hazel Court Sec Sch
BN23 . . . . .174 A3
Hazel Ct TN35 . . . . .136 F6
Hazel Gr Burgess Hill RH15 .73 B1
Lower Willingdon BN20 . . .173 A3
Hazelbank TN3 . . . . .6 F3
Hazeldene BN25 . . . . .181 B3
Hazeldene Meads BN1 . . .142 D3
Hazeledene La BN8 . . . . . .75 F7
Hazelgrove Gdns **8** RH16 .50 E4
Hazelgrove Rd RH16 . . . . .50 E4
Hazelholt BN41 . . . . .140 F3
Hazelwood Ave BN22 . . . .173 D4
Hazelwood Cl
Bexhill TN39 . . . . .156 C3
Royal Tunbridge Wells TN2 . . .8 B7
Hazelwood Cotts TN5 . . . .31 D1
Hazelwood Rd TN35 . . . . .136 D5
Hazleden Cross RH19 . . . .10 B6
Headland Ave BN25 . . . . .181 A3
Headlands Cl BN10 . . . . . .178 E7
Headway Ct TN4 . . . . .7 B4
Heansill La TN18 . . . . .45 E8
Heath Cl **9** RH16 . . . . . . .50 E4
Heath Ct RH16 . . . . .50 E5
Heath Hill Ave BN2 . . . . . .144 A4
Heath Rd RH16 . . . . .50 E5
Heath Sq RH16 . . . . .50 D5
Heathcote Dr RH19 . . . . . . .1 C2
Heathdown Cl BN10 . . . . .167 D2
Heather Bank RH16 . . . . . .50 D5
Heather Cl BN23 . . . . .174 B3
Heather Ct **6** BN1 . . . . . .163 E6
Heather Way TN35 . . . . . .138 F4
Heather Wlk TN6 . . . . .26 D1
Heatherdune Rd TN39 . . . .157 A5
Heathfield Ave BN2 . . . . . .177 D6
Heathfield CE Prim Sch
TN21 . . . . .82 D6
Heathfield Cl TN34 . . . . . .136 F5
Heathfield Cres TN39 . . . .140 F3
Heathfield Dr BN41 . . . . . .140 F4
Heathfield Gdns TN32 . . . .64 B3
Heathfield L Ctr TN21 . . . .82 D7
Heathfield Rd BN25 . . . . . .180 D7
Heathfield Sch & Com Coll
TN21 . . . . .82 E7
Heathfields TN2 . . . . .8 D4
Heathlands TN35 . . . . . . .114 C9
Heathy Brow BN10 . . . . . .167 B1
Heavegate Rd TN6 . . . . . . .37 C8
Heaven Farm RH17 . . . . . .34 B1
Hectors La RH19 . . . . .11 C7
Heighton Cl TN39 . . . . . . .156 D3
Heighton Cres BN9 . . . . . .168 D2
Heighton Rd BN9 . . . . . . .168 E2
Heights The Brighton BN1 .142 B5
Hastings TN35 . . . . .136 F6
6 Haywards Heath RH16 . .50 E4
Helena Cl BN41 . . . . .141 C2
Helena Ct TN38 . . . . .159 B7
Helena Rd BN2 . . . . .144 C1
Helensdene Wlk TN37 . . . .159 D8
Hellingly Cl BN2 . . . . .164 F5
Hellingly Cty Prim Sch
BN27 . . . . .128 F5
Helvellyn Dr BN23 . . . . . .174 C4
Hempstead Gdns TN22 . . . .78 D7
Hempstead La
Hailsham BN27 . . . . .128 F1
Uckfield TN22 . . . . .78 D7

Hempstead La *continued*
Uckfield TN22 . . . . .78 E8
Hempstead Rd
Saltdean BN2 . . . . .166 D3
Uckfield TN22 . . . . .78 C7
Hempstead Rise TN22 . . . .78 C7
Hemsley Ho TN21 . . . . . . .81 F8
Henderson Cl TN34 . . . . . .136 F3
Hendon St BN2 . . . . .164 D5
Henfield Cl BN2 . . . . .164 F5
Henfield Rd BN22 . . . . . . .173 E2
Henfield Way BN3 . . . . . . .141 F3
Henge Way BN41 . . . . . . .141 B2
Hengist Dr BN23 . . . . .185 F8
Henleaze BN21 . . . . .184 E3
Henley Cl
Royal Tunbridge Wells TN2 . . .8 C4
Rye TN31 . . . . .93 A6
Henley Ct BN2 . . . . .164 F4
Henley Rd BN2 . . . . .164 F4
Henley's Hill BN27 . . . . . .131 F7
Henry Burt Way RH15 . . . .72 C1
Henry Terr **3** TN34 . . . . . .160 B4
Henwood Green Rd
TN12, TN2 . . . . .9 E6
Henwoods Cres TN2 . . . . . .9 D6
Henwoods Mount TN2 . . . . .9 C6
Herbert Rd BN1 . . . . .142 F2
Herbrand Wlk TN39 . . . . .156 A1
Hereford Ct **15**
Brighton BN2 . . . . .189 C2
1 Eastbourne BN23 . . . .174 E1
15 Hove BN3 . . . . .163 C7
Hereford St BN2 . . . . .164 C5
Hereward Rd BN23 . . . . . .185 F8
Hereward Way BN7 . . . . . .123 D3
Hermitage La RH19 . . . . . .10 F8
Hermitage Rd RH19 . . . . . . .1 D3
Hermitage The TN34 . . . . .159 E8
Herne Down TN6 . . . . .38 A7
Herne Jun Sch TN6 . . . . . .37 F7
Herne Rd TN6 . . . . .37 F8
Heron Cl Eastbourne BN23 174 C2
St Leonards TN38 . . . . . .158 E8
Uckfield TN22 . . . . .78 D5
Heron Cotts TN18 . . . . . . .48 D3
Heron Ct BN27 . . . . .152 D7
Heron Pl RH19 . . . . .10 F8
Heron Ridge BN26 . . . . . .173 B6
Heron's Tye BN6 . . . . .97 F3
Herons The BN43 . . . . . . .161 A8
Herons Way TN9 . . . . .9 B2
Heronsdale Rd BN2 . . . . . .165 F8
Herontye Dr RH19 . . . . . . .11 A8
Herring's Rd TN21,TN33 . .109 F8
Herstmonceux
Castle Gdns BN27 . . . . .131 A1
Herstmonceux
CE Prim Sch BN27 . . . . .130 E6
Hertford Cl TN38 . . . . . . .119 B4
Hertford Cty Inf Sch BN1 143 B2
Hertford Cty Jun Sch
BN1 . . . . .143 B2
Hertford Rd BN1 . . . . .143 B2
Heskett Pk TN2 . . . . .9 E6
Hestings Plat **2** TN34 . . . .160 B4
Heston Ave BN1 . . . . .142 F7
Hever Cl BN23 . . . . .174 D2
Hever Cres TN39 . . . . .156 F5
Heyworth Cl BN2 . . . . . . .165 F8
Heyworth Cty Prim Sch
RH16 . . . . .50 F4
Hickling Cl BN23 . . . . . . .174 B4
Hickman Way TN34 . . . . . .136 D4
Hickman's Cl RH16 . . . . . . .51 B8
Hickman's La RH16 . . . . . .51 A8
Hidden Spring Vineyard
TN21 . . . . .107 B3
Hide Hollow BN23 . . . . . .174 D3
Higglers Cl TN22 . . . . .56 C3
High Bank TN35 . . . . .137 C3
High Bank TN35 . . . . .160 C6
High Beach Ho BN25 . . . . .180 C3
High Beech Cl TN37 . . . . .135 F4
High Beech Country
Club The TN37 . . . . .135 F6
High Beech La RH16 . . . . . .50 E4
High Beeches TN2 . . . . .8 D6
High Branches TN39 . . . . .156 E4
High Broom Ind Pk TN2 . . .8 C7
High Broom La TN6 . . . . . . .37 E7
High Broom Rd TN6 . . . . . .37 F7
High Brooms Rd TN4 . . . . .8 C7
High Brooms Sta TN4 . . . . .8 C7
High Cl **1** East Dean BN20 .183 C2
Portslade-by-Sea BN41 . .141 A1
High Cross Fields TN6 . . . .25 F3
High Fords TN36 . . . . .116 E5
High Fords Cl TN36 . . . . . .116 E5
High Heath La BN6 . . . . . .72 B4
High Hurst Cl BN8 . . . . . . .76 D7
High Hurstwood
CE Prim Sch TN22 . . . . .37 A1
High Mdw TN31 . . . . .67 B7
High Park Ave BN3 . . . . . .141 E3
High Pk TN31 . . . . .67 A7
High Point RH16 . . . . .51 A3
High Rocks La TN3, TN4 . . . .7 C1
High Rocks TN3 . . . . .7 B1
High Sh Hall The **15**
BN25 . . . . .180 E2
High St Alfriston BN26 . . . .171 A2
Barcombe Cross BN8 . . . .101 A3
Battle TN33 . . . . .113 D4
Bexhill TN40 . . . . .157 D5
Brighton BN2 . . . . .189 C2
Burwash TN19 . . . . .62 A6

High St *continued*
Buxted TN22 . . . . .56 C3
Cowden TN8 . . . . .4 B5
Crowborough TN6 . . . . . . .25 F3
Ditchling BN6 . . . . .98 D3
East Grinstead RH19 . . . .10 F8
East Hoathly BN8 . . . . . .105 A5
Eastbourne BN21 . . . . . .184 E3
Etchingham TN19 . . . . . . .44 C1
Flimwell TN5 . . . . .32 C3
Frant TN3 . . . . .17 C4
Hailsham BN27 . . . . .152 C8
Hartfield TN7 . . . . .13 D4
Hastings TN34 . . . . .160 B4
Heathfield TN21 . . . . .82 A8
Hurstpierpoint BN6 . . . . . .97 A5
Lamberhurst TN3 . . . . . . .20 B5
Lewes BN7 . . . . .123 C1
Lindfield RH16 . . . . .51 B8
Maresfield TN22 . . . . .55 B4
Mayfield TN20 . . . . .40 B2
Newhaven BN9 . . . . .179 C7
Newick BN8 . . . . .76 D7
Ninfield TN33 . . . . .133 A6
Nutley TN22 . . . . .35 C3
Pembury TN2 . . . . .9 C6
Pevensey BN24 . . . . .175 B6
Polegate BN26 . . . . .173 A6
Portslade-by-Sea BN41 . .141 A1
Robertsbridge TN32 . . . . .64 B4
Rotherfield TN6 . . . . .39 B8
Rottingdean BN2 . . . . . . .165 F1
Royal Tunbridge Wells TN1 . .8 A2
Rye TN31 . . . . .93 C5
Seaford BN25 . . . . .180 E2
Ticehurst TN5 . . . . .31 C1
Uckfield TN22 . . . . .78 C6
Wadhurst TN5 . . . . .29 F4
Westham BN24 . . . . .175 A6
Winchelsea TN36 . . . . . . .117 F7
High St (School Hill) TN22 55 B4
High Trees
3 Eastbourne BN21 . . . .184 F4
Haywards Heath RH16 . . .50 F5
Uckfield TN22 . . . . .78 C5
High View TN21 . . . . .82 B8
High View Rd TN21 . . . . . .59 E1
High Wickham TN35 . . . . .160 B5
High Woods La TN2 . . . . . . .9 B3
Higham Gdns TN35 . . . . . .138 A8
Higham La TN31 . . . . .67 A7
Highbank BN1 . . . . .142 C5
Highbridge La BN7 . . . . . .100 B4
Highbrook Cl BN2 . . . . . . .143 D3
Highcliff Ct BN2 . . . . .177 A5
Highcombe BN20 . . . . . . .188 D7
Highcroft Cres TN21 . . . . .82 A7
Highcroft Lodge BN1 . . . . .163 E8
Highcroft RH19 . . . . .21 A6
Highcroft Villas BN1, BN3 .163 E8
Highden **2** BN2 . . . . .164 C6
Highdown BN41, BN42 . . .140 F1
Highdown Cl BN42 . . . . . .140 F1
Highdown Cotts TN17 . . . .20 F3
Highdown Ct BN1 . . . . . . .142 E3
Highdown Rd
Hove BN1, BN3 . . . . .163 C7
Lewes BN7 . . . . .123 A2
Highfield RH17 . . . . .33 C4
Highfield Cl TN6 . . . . .9 D6
Highfield Cres BN1 . . . . . .143 A5
Highfield Ct **7** RH16 . . . . .50 E4
Highfield Cty Jun Sch
BN22 . . . . .174 A1
Highfield Dr
Hurstpierpoint BN6 . . . . . .97 C5
St Leonards TN38 . . . . . .135 D3
Highfield Gdns TN39 . . . . .157 C7
Highfield Ind Est N BN23 174 A1
Highfield Ind Est S BN23 174 A1
Highfield Rd
East Grinstead RH19 . . . . .1 D3
Horam TN21 . . . . .106 F7
Royal Tunbridge Wells TN4 . .8 C7
Highfields Brighton BN1 . .143 E5
Burwash TN19 . . . . .62 A6
Forest Row RH18 . . . . . . .11 F2
Rye TN31 . . . . .93 B7
Highgate Flats TN6 . . . . . .27 B1
Highgate Rd RH18 . . . . . . .11 F1
Highgrove Battle TN33 . . . .112 B4
Royal Tunbridge Wells TN2 . .17 A8
Highland Ct RH16 . . . . . . .50 E4
Highland Grange TN6 . . . . .25 E3
Highland Lodge BN21 . . . .184 F4
Highland Rd RH16 . . . . . . .50 D7
Highlands TN2 . . . . .8 D7
Highlands Ave TN22 . . . . . .78 A4
Highlands Cl Bexhill TN39 .156 F7
Crowborough TN6 . . . . . . .25 E3
Keymer BN6 . . . . .98 A3
Highlands Ct TN6 . . . . .25 E3
Highlands Dr
Burgess Hill RH15 . . . . . .73 A4
St Leonards TN38 . . . . . .159 A7
Highlands Gdns TN38 . . . .159 B7
Highlands Mews **2** TN38 159 B6
Highlands Rd
Portslade-by-Sea BN41 . .141 B1
Seaford BN25 . . . . .180 B1
Highlands The
Bexhill TN39 . . . . .156 F7
Cuckfield RH17 . . . . .50 A8
Highlea Cl TN37 . . . . .136 C5
Highleigh **7** BN2 . . . . . . .189 C3

Highsted Pk BN10 . . . . . .167 D2
Highview Ave N BN1 . . . .142 E6
Highview Ave S BN1 . . . .142 E6
Highview Cl
   St Leonards TN37 . . . . . . .136 D5
   Windmill Hill BN27 . . . . . .131 B5
Highview Ct BN20 . . . . . .184 F1
Highview La TN22 . . . . . . .78 C4
Highview Rd Brighton BN1 142 E6
   Telscombe Cliffs BN10 . . . .177 F4
Highview Way BN1 . . . . . .142 E6
Highwater View TN37 . . . .135 F7
Highway Cl BN2 . . . . .143 D2
Highway The
   Brighton BN2 . . . . .143 D2
   Brighton BN2 . . . . .143 D3
   Newhaven BN10, BN9 . . . . .179 A6
Highways BN41 . . . . .141 B2
Highwoods Ave TN39 . . . .156 C6
Highwoods Ct TN39 . . . . .156 E5
Hiham Bglws TN36 . . . . . .117 E7
Hiham Gn TN36 . . . . .117 E7
Hilary Cl BN26 . . . . .172 F5
Hilary Lodge 2 BN2 . . . .164 C5
Hilbert Cl TN2 . . . . .8 C5
Hilders Farm Cl TN6 . . . . .26 B1
Hilgrove Rd BN2 . . . . . . .166 D3
Hill Brow BN3 . . . . .142 B3
Hill Cl TN6 . . . . .25 E1
Hill Crest Dormans Park RH19 1 E6
   Royal Tunbridge Wells TN4 . . . .8 B8
Hill Crest Ct BN9 . . . . . .179 C6
Hill Crest Rd BN9 . . . . . .179 D6
Hill Dr BN3 . . . . .142 B3
Hill Farm Way
BN42, BN43 . . . . .140 E2
Hill Mead TN22 . . . . .35 C4
Hill Rd Eastbourne BN20 . .184 E5
   Fairlight TN35 . . . . .138 C4
   Lewes BN7 . . . . .123 A4
   Newhaven BN9 . . . . .168 F2
   Saltdean BN2 . . . . .177 B5
Hill Rise Newhaven BN9 . .168 F2
   Seaford BN25 . . . . .180 C5
Hill Side BN9 . . . . .179 D7
Hill St Hastings TN34 . . . .160 A4
   Royal Tunbridge Wells TN1 . . .8 B5
Hill Top BN1 . . . . .142 B5
Hill Top Cl BN41 . . . . . . .140 F2
Hill View Rd TN4 . . . . .7 C4
Hillary Cl RH19 . . . . .2 A3
Hillbank BN41 . . . . .140 F3
Hillbert Rd TN2 . . . . .8 C5
Hillborough Cl TN39 . . . .156 D4
Hillbrow (Brighton Univ)
BN20 . . . . .184 E1
Hillbrow Rd BN1 . . . . . . .142 D4
Hillbury Gdns TN5 . . . . . .31 D1
Hillcrest Brighton BN1 . . .142 C5
   Rye TN31 . . . . .93 B7
Hillcrest Ave TN39 . . . . . .157 A6
Hillcrest Cl BN1 . . . . .142 C5
Hillcrest Ct BN1 . . . . . . .142 C5
Hillcrest Dr TN2 . . . . .8 D7
Hillcrest La RH17 . . . . . . .51 F3
Hillcrest Sch TN35 . . . . . .137 E5
Hillcroft BN41 . . . . .140 F2
Hillgarth TN4 . . . . .8 A8
Hillman Cl BN7 . . . . .123 E1
Hillrise TN6 . . . . .26 B2
Hillside Brighton BN2 . . . .143 E2
   Forest Row RH18 . . . . .11 E3
   Friston BN20 . . . . .183 B1
   Mayfield TN20 . . . . .40 B2
   Portslade-by-Sea BN41 . . . .141 C1
   Southwick BN42 . . . . .140 F1
Hillside Ave BN25 . . . . . .181 C5
Hillside Cl RH19 . . . . .1 E3
Hillside Cotts TN5 . . . . . . .30 B8
Hillside Dr TN21 . . . . . . .106 F7
Hillside Rd Bexhill TN40 . .157 C5
   Hastings, Silverhill
   Park TN34 . . . . .136 E5
   Hastings, St Helen's
   Wood TN34 . . . . .136 E3
Hillside Sch BN41 . . . . . .141 B2
Hillside Way Brighton,
   Moulsecoomb BN2 . . . . . .143 E2
   Brighton, Westdene BN1 . . .142 C4
Hilltop Dr TN31 . . . . .93 B7
Hillview Rd BN2 . . . . .165 B8
Hillyfield BN7 . . . . .146 B8
Hillyglen Cl TN34 . . . . . .159 E8
Hindleap Warren
   Activity Ctr RH18 . . . . . . .22 D5
Hindover Cres BN25 . . . . .181 A4
Hindover Rd BN25 . . . . . .181 A4
Hinton Cl BN1 . . . . .143 C2
Hither Chantlers TN3 . . . . .7 A2
Hoad Rd BN22 . . . . .185 B4
Hoad's Wood Rd TN34 . . .137 A3
Hoadleys La TN6 . . . . .25 D5
Hoath Hill TN32 . . . . .87 C5
Hoathdown Ave BN9 . . . .179 A7
Hobbs La TN31 . . . . .68 D6
Hoblands RH16 . . . . .51 B4
Hobney Rise BN24 . . . . . .174 F5
Hockington La BN20 . . . . .173 B1
Hodcombe Cl BN23 . . . . .174 B4
Hoddern Ave BN10 . . . . . .178 B8
Hoddern Cty Jun Sch
BN10 . . . . .178 B8
Hodshrove La BN2 . . . . . .143 E3

Hodshrove Pl BN2 . . . . . .143 E3
Hodshrove Rd BN2 . . . . . .143 E3
Hoe The TN37 . . . . .136 B6
Hogarth Ho TN38 . . . . . . .159 A8
Hogarth Rd
   Eastbourne BN23 . . . . . . .174 D1
   Hove BN3 . . . . .162 F7
Hoghole La TN3 . . . . .19 F2
Hogs Edge BN2 . . . . .144 A2
Hogtrough La TN36 . . . . . .117 E7
Holbrook Cl BN20 . . . . . .188 E8
Holden Park Rd TN4 . . . . . .8 A8
Holdings The
   Kingston near Lewes BN7 . . .145 F5
   Upper Wellingham BN8 . . . .124 B7
Hole Farm Cl TN34 . . . . . .136 E2
Hollamby Pk BN27 . . . . . .152 D7
Holland Ave TN39 . . . . . .156 C4
Holland Mews BN3 . . . . . .163 D5
Holland Rd BN3 . . . . .163 D6
Holland St BN2 . . . . .189 C3
Hollands Way RH19 . . . . . .2 A4
Hollier's Hill TN40 . . . . . .157 C6
Hollies The TN20 . . . . . . .40 A2
Hollin Cl TN4 . . . . .7 F4
Hollingbourne Ct 8 BN2 .164 B4
Hollingbury Copse BN1 . .143 A4
Hollingbury Cres BN1 . . .143 B2
Hollingbury Ind Est BN1 .143 C7
Hollingbury Park Ave
BN1 . . . . .143 A2
Hollingbury Pl BN1 . . . . .143 B3
Hollingbury Rd BN1 . . . . .143 B1
Hollingbury Rise BN1 . . .143 A3
Hollingbury Rise W BN1 .143 A3
Hollingbury Terr BN1 . . .143 A2
Hollingdean La BN1 . . . . .164 B8
Hollingdean Rd BN2 . . . . .164 B8
Hollingdean St BN1 . . . . .143 B1
Hollingdean Terr BN1 . . .143 B2
Hollinghurst Cl TN37 . . . .136 B5
Hollinghurst Rd TN37 . . . .136 B4
Hollington Ct TN38 . . . . . .159 A8
Hollington Cty Inf Sch
TN38 . . . . .136 A4
Hollington Cty Jun Sch
TN38 . . . . .136 A4
Hollington Old La TN38 . .136 A4
Hollington Park Cl TN38 .136 A1
Hollington Park Rd TN38 136 A1
Hollow La Blackboys BN22 . .80 B4
   Dormansland RH19, RH7 . . . .2 D6
Hollow The RH16 . . . . .51 B5
Holly Bank 3 BN2 . . . . . .189 C5
Holly Bank Ct TN6 . . . . . . .26 B2
Holly Cl Bexhill TN39 . . . .156 C6
   Brighton BN1 . . . . .142 E3
   Hailsham BN27 . . . . .152 B6
   Heathfield TN21 . . . . .82 A6
Holly Ct TN6 . . . . .25 E2
Holly Dr TN21 . . . . .82 A6
Holly Pl BN22 . . . . .173 E3
Holly Rd RH16 . . . . .51 A3
Hollybank Gdns TN38 . . . .136 B1
Hollycroft BN7 . . . . .100 A3
Hollydene Rd TN5 . . . . . . .29 F6
Hollyshaw Cl TN2 . . . . .8 C2
Hollywood Ct RH16 . . . . . .50 E5
Holm Oak Cl TN39 . . . . . .156 E3
Holmbush Cl
   Haywards Heath RH16 . . . . .50 E2
   Shoreham-by-Sea BN43 . . . .140 D2
Holmbush Ct 8 BN43 . . . .161 C8
Holmbush Cty Fst Sch
BN43 . . . . .140 D1
Holmbush Way
BN42, BN43 . . . . .140 E1
Holmdale Rd BN9 . . . . . . .169 A1
Holmebury Ho 1 TN34 . . .159 E7
Holmes Ave BN3 . . . . . . .141 F1
Holmes Cl BN25 . . . . .180 A6
Holmes Farm Cotts TN39 156 A8
Holmes Hill Cotts BN8 . . .127 C6
Holmesdale Cl TN5 . . . . . .29 E5
Holmesdale Ct TN34 . . . . .159 E8
Holmesdale Gdns TN34 . .159 E7
Holmesdale Rd
   Bexhill TN39 . . . . .157 A4
   Burgess Hill RH15 . . . . . . .73 A1
Holmewood Ho TN3 . . . . . .7 A2
Holmewood Rd TN4 . . . . . .8 C7
Holmewood Ridge TN3 . . . .6 F3
Holmhurst Cl TN4 . . . . .7 F4
Holmhurst La TN37 . . . . . .136 B5
Holmstead BN2 . . . . .189 C4
Holmwood Ct BN6 . . . . . . .97 F4
Holt Lodge 1 BN2 . . . . . .189 C4
Holt The Burgess Hill RH15 .72 F7
   Hailsham BN27 . . . . .152 A6
   Seaford BN25 . . . . .180 F5
Holters Way BN25 . . . . . .180 F5
Holton Hill BN2 . . . . .165 E7
Holtview Rd BN2 . . . . . . .165 B8
Holtye Ave RH19 . . . . .2 A3
Holtye Golf Club TN8 . . . . .3 F3
Holtye Rd RH19 . . . . .2 B3
Holy Cross CE Prim Sch
TN22 . . . . .78 C7
Holyhead Cl BN27 . . . . . .129 A1
Holyrood RH19 . . . . .11 A8
Holywell Cl BN20 . . . . . . .188 E7
Holywell Rd BN20 . . . . . .188 E7
Holywell Wlk BN27 . . . . .152 B7
Home Farm Bsns Ctr
BN1 . . . . .143 D3
Home Farm Ct Frant TN3 . .17 C4
   Horsted Keynes RH17 . . . . .33 C5
Home Farm La TN2 . . . . . . .8 E8

Home Farm Rd BN1 BN2 .143 D3
Home Platt RH19 . . . . .21 A6
Home Rd BN1 . . . . .142 E1
Homebush Ave
   Saltdean BN2 . . . . .177 D5
   Telscombe BN7 . . . . .166 F3
Homecoast Ho BN10 . . . . .178 B7
Homedane Ho 8 TN34 . . .159 F7
Homedrive Ho BN3 . . . . . .163 C8
Homefield Cl BN25 . . . . . .180 F4
Homefield Rd BN25 . . . . .180 F4
Homegate Ho 3 BN21 . . .184 F3
Homeglade Ho BN20 . . . . .188 E8
Homehill Ho 7 TN40 . . . .157 C4
Homelands Cl TN39 . . . . .157 A6
Homelatch Ho 1 BN21 . . .185 A4
Homelawn Ho 3 TN40 . . .157 E4
Homeleigh BN1 . . . . .142 E5
Homeridge Ho BN2 . . . . .177 D5
Homestall Rd RH19 . . . . . .11 E8
Homestead La RH15 . . . . . .73 C6
Homestead The TN3 . . . . .15 C7
Hometye Ho BN25 . . . . . .180 D3
Homewarr Ho 4 TN40 . . .157 E4
Homewood Cl BN22 . . . . .185 B6
Homewood Rd TN3 . . . . . . .6 F3
Homoepathic Hospl TN1 . . .8 A3
Honey Croft BN3 . . . . . . .141 D4
Honey La BN8 . . . . .149 D7
Honeycrag Cl BN26 . . . . .173 A7
Honeypot La BN7, BN8 . . .100 B7
Honeysuckle Cl
   Eastbourne BN23 . . . . . . .174 B3
   Hailsham BN27 . . . . .152 B5
   St Leonards TN37 . . . . . . .136 D5
Honeyway Cl BN26 . . . . . .172 F3
Honies St TN39 . . . . .157 C6
Hoo Gdns BN20 . . . . .173 B1
Hoo The BN20 . . . . .173 B1
Hood Cl BN23 . . . . .185 E7
Hooe Rd TN33 . . . . .133 A3
Hook Hill TN5 . . . . .31 A6
Hookswood Cl TN6 . . . . . .26 A3
Hoopers Cl BN7 . . . . .123 C3
Hope Cl TN37 . . . . .135 F7
Hop Gdn TN22 . . . . .36 C2
Hope Cotts BN42 . . . . . . .161 E8
Hopehouse La TN17,TN18 . .47 C7
Hopfield Gdns TN22 . . . . . .78 E8
Hopgarden Cl TN34 . . . . .159 E8
Hoppers Croft La TN19 . . . .62 B6
Hopwood Gdns TN4 . . . . . .8 A6
Horam Park Cl TN21 . . . . .106 F7
Horebeech La TN21 . . . . .107 A6
Horizon Cl TN4 . . . . .8 B7
Horleigh Green Rd TN20 . .39 C1
Horley Pl BN2 . . . . .164 E6
Hornbeam TN19 . . . . .62 B7
Hornbeams The RH15 . . . . .72 D4
Hornblower Cotts TN19 . . .44 C1
Hornbuckles Cl BN8 . . . . .100 E7
Hornby Pl BN2 . . . . .144 A1
Hornby Rd BN2 . . . . .144 A1
Horning Cl BN23 . . . . . . .174 B4
Horns Rd TN18 . . . . .45 D8
Horntye Pk TN37,TN38 . . .159 D8
Horntye Rd TN37 . . . . . . .136 C1
Horsa Cl BN23 . . . . .185 E8
Horsegrove Ave TN5 . . . . .31 F1
Horsegrove La TN6 . . . . . .39 B8
Horseshoe Cl TN38 . . . . .136 B2
Horseshoe La TN31 . . . . . .68 A1
Horsewalk BN27,TN33 . . .154 E7
Horsfield Rd BN7 . . . . . . .123 B3
Horsgate Ho RH17 . . . . . . .50 A8
Horsgate La RH17 . . . . . . .50 A6
Horsham Ave BN10 . . . . . .178 C7
Horsham Ave N BN10 . . . .178 C8
Horsham Rd BN2 . . . . . . .164 F6
Horsham Rise 1 TN4 . . . . .50 F3
Horsted Keynes Ind Est
RH17 . . . . .33 B7
Horsted Keynes Sta RH17 .33 A7
Horsted La Danehill RH17 . .34 A4
   Isfield TN22 . . . . .102 F7
   Sharpthorne RH19 . . . . . . .21 B3
Horsted Pond La TN22 . . . .78 A3
Horsted Sq TN22 . . . . .78 A6
Horsye Rd BN22 . . . . .185 B7
Horton Rd BN1 . . . . .143 B1
Hoskins Pl RH19 . . . . .2 A4
Hosmers Field TN6 . . . . . .39 D8
Hospital Villas RH16 . . . . .50 F7
Houghton Green La TN31 . .70 C2
Houghton La TN31 . . . . . . .70 C3
Houndean Cl BN7 . . . . . . .146 A8
Houndean Rise BN7 . . . . .145 F7
Hova Villas BN3 . . . . .163 B6
Hove Bsns Ctr BN3 . . . . .163 B8
Hove Ent Ctr BN41 . . . . .162 C6
Hove General Hospl BN3 163 A7
Hove Manor 8 BN3 . . . . .163 A6
Hove Mus & Art Gall
BN3 . . . . .163 A6
Hove Park Gdns
   Hove BN3 . . . . .142 B1
   Hove BN3 . . . . .163 B8
Hove Park Rd BN3 . . . . . .142 C1
Hove Park Sch (Lower)
BN3 . . . . .141 D2
Hove Park Sch (Upper)
BN3 . . . . .142 A1
Hove Park Villas BN3 . . . .163 B8
Hove Park Way BN3 . . . . .142 C1
Hove Pl BN3 . . . . .163 B5
Hove Sta BN3 . . . . .163 B8
Hovedene BN3 . . . . .163 C7

How's Cl TN31 . . . . .90 B5
Howard Ave RH15 . . . . . . .72 E4
Howard Cl BN27 . . . . .152 D6
Howard Ct Hove BN3 . . . .142 A2
   Peacehaven BN10 . . . . . . .178 B7
Howard Gdns TN2 . . . . . . .8 A1
Howard Ho Bexhill TN39 . .156 E4
   Peacehaven BN10 . . . . . . .167 D1
Howard Pl BN1 . . . . .189 A4
Howard Rd BN2 . . . . .164 C7
Howard Sq BN21 . . . . . . .185 A4
Howard Terr BN1 . . . . . . .189 A4
Howards Cres TN39 . . . . .156 C4
Howbourne La TN22 . . . . . .56 E5
Howes Cotts TN18 . . . . . . .45 F8
Howey Cl BN9 . . . . .168 F1
Howlett Cl TN38 . . . . .135 F4
Howlett Dr BN27 . . . . . . .129 B2
Howletts Cl BN22 . . . . . . .173 F1
Hoyle Rd BN10 . . . . .178 C7
Hudson Cl BN23 . . . . .185 G7
Hudson Ct BN22 . . . . .185 C6
Huggett's La BN22 . . . . . .173 B3
Hughenden Ct 2 TN34 . . .136 F2
Hughenden Pl 1 TN34 . . .136 F2
Hughenden Rd TN34 . . . . .160 A6
Hughes Rd BN2 . . . . .164 B8
Hughes Way TN22 . . . . . . .78 C8
Hugletts La TN21 . . . . .83 A7
Humboldt Cl TN2 . . . . .8 D5
Humphrey Lodge RH15 . . .73 D3
Humphrey's Gap BN43 . . .161 A7
Hundred Acre La
   BN6, RH17 . . . . .74 B2
Hundredhouse La TN31 . . .90 F4
Hungershall Park Cl TN4 . .7 E1
Hungershall Pk TN4 . . . . . .7 E2
Hunloke Ave BN22 . . . . . .185 B6
Hunston Cl BN2 . . . . .165 F7
Hunt's Gate RH17 . . . . . . .52 E3
Hunters Way
   Royal Tunbridge Wells TN2 . . .7 F1
   Uckfield TN22 . . . . .78 B8
Hunting Cl TN40 . . . . .157 C5
Huntingdon Rd TN6 . . . . . .25 F1
Huntingdon Way RH15 . . . .73 D5
Huntington Cl 1 BN2 . . . .123 E1
Huntley Mill Rd TN5 . . . . .31 E3
Huntleys Pk TN4 . . . . .7 F5
Hurdis Rd BN25 . . . . .180 A6
Hurrell Rd TN34 . . . . .160 B6
Hurst Cres BN41 . . . . . . .162 B8
Hurst Farm Rd RH19 . . . . .10 D7
Hurst Green CE Sch TN19 . .45 A2
Hurst Hill BN1 . . . . .143 C5
Hurst La Eastbourne BN21 .184 D4
   Sedlescombe TN33 . . . . . . .88 F3
   Windmill Hill BN27 . . . . . .131 B5
Hurst Rd Eastbourne BN21 184 D5
   Hassocks BN6 . . . . .97 D4
Hurst Shaw TN21 . . . . . . .107 C8
Hurst The TN2 . . . . .8 E7
Hurst Way TN35 . . . . .137 A6
Hurst Wickham Cl BN6 . . .97 C5
Hurstfield Cl RH17 . . . . . . .51 A4
Hurstwood 6 BN2 . . . . . .164 F5
Hurstwood Cl TN40 . . . . .158 B5
Hurstwood La
   Haywards Heath RH17 . . . . .51 A2
   Royal Tunbridge Wells TN4 . . .7 F3
   Sharpthorne RH17, RH19 . . .21 D1
Hurstwood Pk TN4 . . . . . . .7 F3
Hurstwood Rd TN22 . . . . . .56 A6
Hurtis Hill TN6 . . . . .37 E7
Hutton Rd BN1 . . . . .143 B3
Hyde Cl BN7 . . . . .145 E5
Hyde Gdns BN21 . . . . . . .185 A4
Hyde Rd BN21 . . . . .184 F2
Hyde The BN2 . . . . .164 F8
Hyde Tynings Cl BN20 . . .188 D8
Hydehurst Cl TN6 . . . . . . .25 F1
Hydney St BN22 . . . . .185 C5
Hydneye The BN22 . . . . . .173 F1
Hylden Cl BN2 . . . . .165 B8
Hyperion Ave BN26 . . . . .172 E6
Hythe Ave BN25 . . . . .181 C4
Hythe Cl Polegate BN26 . .173 C7
   Seaford BN25 . . . . .181 C5
Hythe Cres BN25 . . . . . . .181 C4
Hythe Rd BN1 . . . . .143 A2
Hythe View BN25 . . . . . . .181 C4

I

Ian Cl TN40 . . . . .157 F7
Icklesham CE Prim Sch
TN36 . . . . .116 E6
Icklesham Dr TN38 . . . . . .135 D3
Iden Cl BN2 . . . . .164 E5
Iden Ct TN34 . . . . .136 D3
Iden Hurst BN6 . . . . .97 A7
Iden Rd TN31 . . . . .70 D7
Iden St BN22 . . . . .174 A2
Iden's La TN21 . . . . .82 D8
Ifield Cl BN2 . . . . .177 E6
Ifield Mill Ct BN24 . . . . . .174 B5
Iford & Kingston
   CE Prim Sch BN7 . . . . . . .145 F5
Iford Cl BN9 . . . . .168 D1
Ilex Ct BN42 . . . . .141 A1
Ilex Gn 6 BN27 . . . . .129 B1
Image Cross Flats RH19 . .21 A5
Imberhorne Bsns Ctr RH19 .1 B2
Imberhorne La RH19 . . . . . .1 B2
Imberhorne Lower Sch
RH19 . . . . .1 D1

Imberhorne Sch RH19 . . . .1 B3
Imberhorne Way RH19 . . . .1 B3
Impala Gdns TN4 . . . . .8 B6
Imperial Arc BN1 . . . . . . .189 A2
Independent Bsns Pk The
RH19 . . . . .1 A3
Ingham Dr BN1 . . . . .143 D6
Inglesea Sch TN38 . . . . . .135 F4
Ingleside TN38 . . . . .135 E4
Ingleside Dr TN38 . . . . . .25 E2
Inglewood Gdns TN38 . . .135 E4
Ingram Cres E BN3 . . . . .162 E8
Ingram Cres W BN3 . . . . .162 E8
Ingram Ct BN3 . . . . .162 E7
Ingrams Ave TN39 . . . . . .157 C7
Ingrams Way BN27 . . . . . .152 A6
Inholmes Cl RH15 . . . . . . .73 B3
Inholmes Park Rd RH15 . . .73 B3
Inkerman Terr TN31 . . . . . .94 A3
Innham's Wood TN6 . . . . . .25 C4
Innings Dr BN24 . . . . .175 C4
Innovation Dr RH15 . . . . . .72 D2
Insley Ct TN39 . . . . .156 F3
Inverness Rd 4 BN2 . . . . .164 C8
Inwood Cres BN1 . . . . . . .142 E1
Iona Cl BN27 . . . . .129 A3
Iona Way 12 RH16 . . . . . . .50 E4
Irelands La BN7 . . . . .123 B1
Ironlatch Ave TN38 . . . . . .135 F2
Ironlatch Cl TN38 . . . . . . .135 F2
Ironstone Way TN22 . . . . . .78 E7
Ironstones TN3 . . . . .7 B3
Irving Ho TN1 . . . . .8 B5
Isaac's La RH16, RH15 . . . .50 A2
Isabel Cl BN25 . . . . .180 E5
Isabel Cres BN3 . . . . .162 E8
Isfield Rd Brighton BN1 . .143 C2
   Isfield BN8,TN22 . . . . .102 E5
Isherwood TN33 . . . . .112 B5
Isle of Thorns
   (Univ of Sussex) RH17 . . .22 D1
Islingword Pl BN2 . . . . . . .164 C6
Islingword Rd BN2 . . . . . .164 C7
Islingword St BN2 . . . . . .189 C3
Ismay Lodge TN39 . . . . . .156 D3
Ive Grange TN33 . . . . .132 F5
Iveagh Cres BN9 . . . . .168 D2
Ivor Rd BN2 . . . . .144 C1
Ivors La BN8 . . . . .123 B5
Ivory Pl BN2 . . . . .189 C3
Ivy Cotts BN8 . . . . .104 C5
Ivy Dene La RH19 . . . . . . .11 D6
Ivy Mews 15 BN3 . . . . . . .163 D5
Ivy Pl BN1, BN3 . . . . .163 D5
Ivy Terr BN21 . . . . .184 F3
Ivyhouse Employment Area
TN35 . . . . .137 B4
Ivyhouse La TN35 . . . . . . .137 B6
Ivylands Yd TN31 . . . . .93 B5

J

Jack O'Dandy Cl BN21 . . .184 C7
Jackdaws The TN22 . . . . . .78 E4
Jackies La BN8 . . . . .76 B7
Jacks Hill TN7 . . . . .13 D2
Jackson Mews BN9 . . . . . .179 C7
Jackson St BN2 . . . . .189 C4
Jacobs Acre TN40 . . . . . . .157 C5
Jacqueline Du Pre Ct
BN2 . . . . .164 C5
Jamaica Way BN23 . . . . . .185 F8
James Ave BN27 . . . . .130 E6
Jameson Cres TN38 . . . . .136 A3
Jameson Rd TN40 . . . . . . .157 D4
Jane Murray Way
BN6,RH15 . . . . .72 C3
Janes Cl RH15 . . . . .73 C5
Janes La RH15 . . . . .73 D4
Janeston Ct 4 BN3 . . . . .163 C7
Japonica Cl BN43 . . . . . . .140 B1
Jardine Ct TN6 . . . . .25 F2
Jarretts Cl TN31 . . . . .93 B5
Jarvis Brook Ctry Pk TN6 .38 B8
Jarvis Brook Sta TN6 . . . . .38 C7
Jarvisbrook Cl TN39 . . . . .156 D3
Jasmine Cotts TN3 . . . . . .15 C7
Jasmine Ct Brighton BN1 . .142 F5
   Hove BN3 . . . . .163 D7
Jasmine Gn 2 BN27 . . . . .129 B1
Jason Cl BN10 . . . . .178 C7
Jay Cl BN23 . . . . .174 C2
Jay Rd BN10 . . . . .178 C7
Jays The Burgess Hill RH15 .72 E4
   Uckfield TN22 . . . . .78 D4
Jefferies RH17 . . . . .33 C4
Jefferies Way TN6 . . . . . . .25 F4
Jefferson Way TN37 . . . . .135 F6
Jeffreys Way TN22 . . . . . . .55 D1
Jellicoe Cl BN23 . . . . .185 F7
Jenner's La TN35 . . . . . . .137 E6
Jephson Cl BN20 . . . . . . .188 F8
Jerome Cl BN23 . . . . .174 E2
Jersey St BN2 . . . . .189 C3
Jervis Ave BN23 . . . . .185 E6
Jesmond Cl BN3 . . . . .162 E7
Jesmond Rd BN3 . . . . . . .162 E7
Jesters RH16 . . . . .73 C7
Jevington Cl TN39 . . . . . .156 D2
Jevington Ct BN43 . . . . . .161 D6
Jevington Dr
   Brighton BN2 . . . . .143 D1
   Seaford BN25 . . . . .180 D5
Jevington Gdns BN21 . . . .185 A1
Jevington Ho 7 BN21 . . . .184 D4
Jevington Rd BN26 . . . . . .172 D2
Jew St BN1 . . . . .189 B2

Jireh Ct RH16 . . . . .50 E5
Joan Hughes Ct BN26 . . .173 A6
Joan Nightingale Ho
  RH16 . . . . .50 C4
Job's La BN6 . . . . .72 A6
Joe's La BN27 . . . . .131 B5
John Dann Cl TN22 . . . . . . .80 A6
John Macadam Way
  TN37 . . . . .136 A6
John Spare Ct TN4 . . . . .8 A6
John St Brighton BN2 . . . . .189 C4
  Royal Tunbridge Wells TN4 . . .8 A4
John Whittle Lodge BN2 143 C1
John's Cross Rd TN32 . . . .87 C8
Johns Cl BN10 . . . . .167 C2
Johnson Bank 4 BN2 . . . .164 C7
Johnson Cl TN37 . . . . .135 F6
Johnson Dr RH15 . . . . .73 D3
Jonas Dr TN5 . . . . .29 C5
Jonas La TN5 . . . . .29 C5
Jordan Ct BN3 . . . . .162 E8
Jordans La BN22 . . . . .173 D3
Jordans La E BN22 . . . . . . .173 D3
Jordans La W BN22 . . . . . .173 C3
Jordans The RH19 . . . . .10 E8
Joyce Villas TN21 . . . . . . .106 E5
Jubilee Cl RH16 . . . . .51 A4
Jubilee Ct BN2 . . . . .143 E2
Jubilee Gdns BN25 . . . . . . .181 A5
Jubilee Ho BN9 . . . . .179 C7
Jubilee Rd Bexhill TN39 . . .157 A7
  Burgess Hill RH15 . . . . .72 E2
  Portslade-by-Sea BN41 . . . .162 A8
Jubilee St BN1 . . . . .189 B3
Judge's Terr RH19 . . . . .10 E8
Jugg's Rd BN7 . . . . .146 B7
Juggs Cl BN7 . . . . .146 B8
Juggs Rd BN7 . . . . .146 A7
Julian 5 BN43 . . . . .161 C8
Julian Rd BN3 . . . . .163 E7
Junction Cl RH15 . . . . .73 C4
Junction Rd
  Bodiam TN18, TN32 . . . . . .46 A3
  Brighton BN1 . . . . .189 B4
  Burgess Hill RH15 . . . . .73 B3
  Cripp's Corner TN32 . . . . . .65 C5
  Cripp's Corner TN32,TN33 . .88 D5
  Eastbourne BN21 . . . . .185 A3
  St Leonards TN37 . . . . . . .136 B7
Junction St BN26 . . . . .173 B6
Juniper Cl
  Portslade-by-Sea BN41 . . . .141 B3
  Seaford BN25 . . . . .181 C3
  St Leonards TN38 . . . . . . .135 E3
Juniper Wlk BN43 . . . . . . .140 C1
Jury's Gap
  Coastguard Cotts TN31 . . .95 E1
Jury's Gap Rd TN29 . . . . . .96 F1

K

Kammond Ave BN25 . . . . . .181 B5
Kane Hythe Rd TN33 . . . . .111 D6
Karenza Ct BN1 . . . . .164 A8
Katherine Way BN25 . . . . .180 D5
Keaton Ho RH16 . . . . .50 E6
Keats Cl TN38 . . . . .158 F6
Keats Pl RH19 . . . . .1 D1
Keats Wlk BN23 . . . . .174 C3
Kebbell Lodge 12 BN2 . . . .189 C2
Kedale Rd BN25 . . . . .180 E4
Keel Gdns TN4 . . . . .7 E8
Keere St BN7 . . . . .146 C8
Keith Wlk BN23 . . . . .185 F6
Keld Ave TN22 . . . . .78 D6
Keld Cl TN22 . . . . .78 D6
Keld Dr TN22 . . . . .78 D6
Kelly Rd BN3 . . . . .142 D1
Kelsey Cotts BN8 . . . . .124 E6
Kelsey Ct RH15 . . . . .73 D3
Kemble Cl TN2 . . . . .8 E7
Kemp Ct BN2 . . . . .164 E4
Kemp St BN1 . . . . .189 B3
Kemp Town Pl 18 BN2 . . . .164 D4
Kemps Farm Rd TN6 . . . . .26 B1
Kemps Way TN32 . . . . .64 C5
Kemptown Mews 11 BN2 .164 E4
Kendal Cl BN9 . . . . .179 E7
Kendal Pk TN4 . . . . .7 E5
Kendal Rd BN3 . . . . .162 F8
Kenilworth Cl BN2 . . . . . . .144 A2
Kenilworth Rd TN38 . . . . .159 B7
Kenmure Ave BN1 . . . . . . .143 A7
Kennard Ct RH18 . . . . .11 E3
Kennedy Ave RH19 . . . . .1 D3
Kennedy Cl TN21 . . . . .82 B6
Kennedy Ct TN38 . . . . .136 B3
Kennedy Rd TN40 . . . . .157 E4
Kennedy Way BN9 . . . . . . .179 B8
Kennel Cnr BN8 . . . . .124 F6
Kennel La TN39 . . . . .156 C4
Kennett Cl BN24 . . . . .173 F5
Kenrith Ct TN34 . . . . .136 E2
Kensington Cl TN38 . . . . . .135 D3
Kensington Gdns BN1 . . . .189 B3
Kensington Pl BN1 . . . . . . .189 B3
Kensington St BN1 . . . . . . .189 B3
Kent & East Sussex
  Steam Rly TN17 . . . . .49 C5
Kent & Sussex Hospl TN4 . .8 A4
Kent Cl Bexhill TN40 . . . . . .158 A5
  Shoreham-by-Sea BN43 . . .161 C7
  Winchelsea TN36 . . . . .117 C7
Kent Ct BN20 . . . . .184 B6
Kent Fields BN7 . . . . .145 E5
Kent Ho TN1 . . . . .8 C6
Kent La TN32 . . . . .85 F6

Kent Rd
  Royal Tunbridge Wells TN4 . .8 A6
  St Leonards TN38 . . . . . . .135 F4
Kent St TN33 . . . . .114 A3
Kent's La BN6 . . . . .99 C7
Kentish Gdns TN2 . . . . .16 E8
Kenton Cl TN39 . . . . .157 A5
Kenton Ct BN21 . . . . .185 A1
Kenton Rd BN3 . . . . .162 D7
Kents Rd RH16 . . . . .50 F3
Kenwards BN1 . . . . .143 D7
Kenwood Cl TN34 . . . . .137 B4
Kenya Ct 2 BN1 . . . . .163 E6
Keppel Rd TN34 . . . . .136 F2
Kepplestone BN20 . . . . . . .188 E8
Kerrara Terr BN22 . . . . . . .185 B5
Kerrison Mews 7 BN3 . . . .163 D5
Kestrel Cl Bexhill TN40 . . . .157 E4
  Hove BN3 . . . . .163 D8
Kestrel Ct BN27 . . . . .152 D7
Kestrels The
  Shoreham-by-Sea BN43 . . .161 A8
  St Leonards TN38 . . . . . . .135 F5
Ketcham Cnr BN24 . . . . . . .174 E6
Ketche's La RH17,TN22 . . . .52 E7
Kevin Gdns BN2 . . . . .165 E8
Kew St BN1 . . . . .189 A3
Kewhurst Ave TN39 . . . . . .156 D3
Key West BN23 . . . . .185 G8
Keymer Ave BN10 . . . . . . .178 D7
Keymer Cl
  Eastbourne BN23 . . . . .174 E1
  St Leonards TN38 . . . . . . .158 E6
Keymer Ct RH15 . . . . .73 B2
Keymer End RH16 . . . . .50 D3
Keymer Gdns RH15 . . . . . . .73 B1
Keymer Par RH15 . . . . .73 B2
Keymer Pk BN6 . . . . .98 B3
Keymer Rd Brighton BN1 . .143 B6
  Burgess Hill RH15 . . . . .98 B8
  Hassocks BN6 . . . . .97 F3
Kibbles La TN4 . . . . .7 E8
Kidbrook RH16 . . . . .51 B6
Kidbrooke Park
  (Michael Hall Sch) RH18 11 D1
Kidbrooke Rise RH18 . . . . .11 E2
Kidd's Hill TN7 . . . . .24 A4
Kilburn Terr 6 BN25 . . . . .185 A3
Kilda St 1 BN22 . . . . .185 B4
Kildare Cl TN34 . . . . .137 B4
Kildare Ct BN20 . . . . .184 C3
Kiln Cl TN22 . . . . .78 D4
Kiln Dr TN31 . . . . .93 B8
Kiln La
  Haywards Heath RH16 . . . . .51 B5
  Hooe TN33 . . . . .155 B7
  Isfield TN22 . . . . .102 E5
Kiln Rd BN8 . . . . .125 A8
Kiln The RH15 . . . . .73 C3
Kilnbank TN2 . . . . .8 C7
Kilnbarn Ct RH16 . . . . .50 D2
Kilnbarn Way RH16 . . . . . . .50 D2
Kilnwood La BN8 . . . . .100 E7
Kilpatrick Cl BN23 . . . . . . .174 D3
Kimberley Ct TN39 . . . . . . .157 C6
Kimberley Rd
  Brighton BN2 . . . . .143 D1
  Seaford BN25 . . . . .180 C4
Kindersley Cl RH19 . . . . .2 B3
Kinfauns Ave BN22 . . . . . .185 B6
King Alfred (Swimming
  Pool & Sports Ctr) BN3 163 A5
King Charles Pl 8 BN43 . .161 A6
King Edward Ave TN34 . . .136 C3
King Edward Cl TN34 . . . . .136 C3
King Edward's Par BN20 . .188 F8
King George Ave RH19 . . . . .1 C3
King George Rd BN43 . . . . .161 D8
King George V Hill TN1 . . . .8 C5
King George VI Ave
  BN1, BN3 . . . . .142 A3
King George VI Dr BN3 . . .142 A4
King George VI Mans
  BN3 . . . . .141 F2
King Henry's Rd BN7 . . . . .123 B2
King John Ct 4 BN43 . . . . .161 A6
King Offa Cty Prim Sch
  TN39 . . . . .157 B5
King Offa Way TN40 . . . . .157 C5
King St Brighton BN1 . . . . .189 B2
  East Grinstead RH19 . . . . . . .1 E1
King Wood Hill TN31 . . . . .90 A3
King's Ave
  Eastbourne BN21 . . . . .184 E5
  Newhaven BN9 . . . . .168 E1
  Rye TN31 . . . . .93 C6
King's Bank La TN31 . . . . .68 A3
King's Cl BN21 . . . . .184 E5
King's Dr BN21 . . . . .184 D7
King's Espl BN3 . . . . .163 A5
King's Gdns BN3 . . . . .163 B5
King's Hill Rd TN19 . . . . . . .62 B3
King's Manor Sch BN43 . .161 D8
King's Mead La BN25 . . . .180 D4
King's Rd
  Brighton BN1, BN3 . . . . . . .163 E5
  Haywards Heath RH16 . . . . .50 F3
  St Leonards TN37 . . . . . . .159 C4
Kingfisher Cl TN22 . . . . . . .78 E5
Kingfisher Ct BN27 . . . . . . .152 D7
Kingfisher Dr BN23 . . . . . .174 C2
Kingfisher Rise RH19 . . . . . .10 F8
Kings Chase TN6 . . . . .25 D3
Kings Cl Bexhill TN40 . . . . .157 C4
  Eastbourne BN21 . . . . .184 F5
Kings Copse 9 RH19 . . . . .10 F8

Kings Ct TN6 . . . . .25 E2
Kings Ct E 4 BN23 . . . . . . .185 F8
Kings Ct S 6 BN23 . . . . . . .185 F8
Kings Ct W 5 BN23 . . . . . .185 F8
Kings Dr BN6 . . . . .97 F4
Kings Gate BN3 . . . . .163 C8
Kings Mead St BN20 . . . . .188 D7
Kings Mews BN3 . . . . .163 B6
Kings Par BN1 . . . . .143 A2
Kings Pk TN2 . . . . .8 D3
Kings Rd BN42 . . . . .140 E1
Kings Ride Alfriston BN26 .170 F1
  Burgess Hill RH15 . . . . .73 D1
  Seaford BN25 . . . . .180 D4
Kings Toll Rd TN2 . . . . .9 F6
Kings Way RH15 . . . . .73 D2
Kings Wlk 10 TN34 . . . . . .159 F8
Kingsbury Rd BN1 . . . . . . .189 B4
Kingsbury St BN1, BN2 . . .189 B4
Kingscote Lodge BN1 . . . .143 F5
Kingscott TN39 . . . . .157 B8
Kingsdale Cl Battle TN33 . .112 F3
  St Leonards TN37 . . . . . . .136 C6
Kingsfield Cl BN42 . . . . . . .161 E8
Kingsfield Cotts BN8 . . . . .149 E8
Kingsfold 2 BN2 . . . . .164 F5
Kingsfold Cl 1 BN25 . . . . .180 F2
Kingsford BN23 . . . . .185 D7
Kingsland BN43 . . . . .161 C7
Kingsley Cl TN37 . . . . .136 A5
Kingsley Ct
  7 Brighton BN1 . . . . .163 E5
  Wadhurst TN5 . . . . .30 A4
Kingsley Rd Brighton BN1 .142 D1
  Lewes BN7 . . . . .123 B2
Kingsmarsh Cotts TN20 . . .58 B6
Kingsmead BN25 . . . . .180 E5
Kingsmead Cl BN25 . . . . . .180 E4
Kingsmead Way BN25 . . . .180 E4
Kingsmead Wlk BN25 . . . .180 E4
Kingsmere BN1 . . . . .142 E2
Kingsmere Ct 2 BN21 . . . .184 D4
Kingsmere Way BN23 . . . .185 F8
Kingsthorpe Rd BN3 . . . . .162 F8
Kingston Ave BN25 . . . . . .181 B3
Kingston Bay Rd BN43 . . .161 C6
Kingston
  Broadway BN42, BN43 . . .140 D1
Kingston Buci Cty Fst Sch
  BN43 . . . . .161 B8
Kingston Cl Brighton BN1 . .143 E6
  Hove BN3 . . . . .141 E2
  Seaford BN25 . . . . .181 B3
  Shoreham-by-Sea BN43 . . .161 C8
Kingston Ct 17 BN43 . . . . .161 C8
Kingston Gn BN25 . . . . . . .181 B3
Kingston La BN42,BN43 . . .161 D7
Kingston Quay 9 BN23 . . .185 F8
Kingston Rd
  Eastbourne BN22 . . . . .173 F2
  Lewes BN7 . . . . .146 B7
Kingston Ridge BN7 . . . . . .145 D6
Kingston Villas TN21 . . . . .106 E5
Kingston Way
  Seaford BN25 . . . . .181 B3
  Shoreham-by-Sea
  BN42, BN43 . . . . .140 D1
Kingsway Hove BN3, BN41 .163 B5
  Seaford BN25 . . . . .180 D4
Kingsway Ct Hove BN3 . . . .163 C5
  Seaford BN25 . . . . .180 C4
Kingswood Ave TN39 . . . . .156 F6
Kingswood Cl TN2 . . . . .8 C3
Kingswood Flats BN2 . . . .189 C2
Kingswood Rd TN2 . . . . .8 C3
Kingswood St BN2 . . . . . . .189 B2
Kinross Ct 4 BN21 . . . . . .185 A4
Kinsale St 5 BN23 . . . . . . .163 D7
Kinver La TN40 . . . . .158 A6
Kipling Ave BN2 . . . . .165 E7
Kipling Ct Bexhill TN40 . . . .157 C6
  3 Haywards Heath RH16 . . .50 D7
  Rottingdean BN2 . . . . .177 A5
Kipling Way RH19 . . . . .1 C1
Kipling Wlk 1 BN23 . . . . . .174 C3
Kirby Dr BN10 . . . . .167 A1
Kirdford Cl RH15 . . . . .73 C1
Kirk Way BN20 . . . . .184 B5
Kirkdale Rd TN1 . . . . .8 A4
Kirkstall Cl BN22 . . . . .173 E3
Kitchenour La TN31 . . . . . .68 E5
Kite Cl TN38 . . . . .158 E8
Kites Nest Wlk TN39 . . . . .156 B4
Kitilear Ct TN3 . . . . .6 D6
Knebworth Rd TN39 . . . . . .156 F5
Knelle Rd TN32 . . . . .64 A4
Knelle View 2 TN31 . . . . . .67 B7
Knepp Cl BN2 . . . . .143 F2
Knight's Ridge TN2 . . . . .9 D7
Knights Cl TN2 . . . . .9 D7
Knights Gate Rd BN1 . . . .144 C7
Knights Gdn BN27 . . . . . . .152 B6
Knights Mdw TN22 . . . . . . .78 E8
Knightsbridge Cl TN4 . . . . . .7 E5
Knole Cl 4 TN40 . . . . .157 C4
Knole Gr RH19 . . . . .1 C3
Knole Rd Bexhill TN40 . . . . .157 D3
  Rottingdean BN2 . . . . .177 A4
Knoll Bsns Ctr The BN3 . .162 D8
Knoll Cl BN13 . . . . .141 D1
Knoll Cres BN22 . . . . .174 A1
Knoll Cty Inf Sch BN13 . . .141 D1
Knoll Rd BN22 . . . . .174 A2
Knoll Rise TN38 . . . . .159 A7
Knowle Cl
  Crowborough TN6 . . . . .38 C8
  Langton Green TN3 . . . . .6 F3
Knowle Cotts TN3 . . . . .17 E1

Knowle Ct TN38 . . . . .136 B1
Knowle Hill Bodiam TN32 . .65 D8
  Mayfield TN20 . . . . .40 A1
Knowle Pk
  Crowborough TN6 . . . . .25 D2
  Mayfield TN20 . . . . .40 A1
Knowle Rd TN35 . . . . .138 E5
Knoyle Rd BN1 . . . . .142 E5
Knyveton Ct RH15 . . . . .73 B3
Kylemore BN24 . . . . .175 B6
Kymer Gdns BN6 . . . . .98 A3

L

La Marne Ct TN34 . . . . . . .136 E2
Laburnam Wlk BN22 . . . .173 D3
Laburnham Gn 5 BN27 . .129 B1
Laburnum Ave BN3 . . . . . .141 E5
Laburnum Ct TN2 . . . . .8 C7
Laburnum Gdns TN40 . . . .157 F6
Laburnum Gr BN1 . . . . . . .143 B3
Laburnum Way RH16 . . . . . .51 B4
Lacys Hill BN8 . . . . .147 F8
Ladies Mile Brighton BN1 .143 B7
  Withyham TN3 . . . . .14 C7
Ladies' Mile Cl BN1 . . . . .142 F6
Ladies' Mile Rd BN1 . . . .142 F6
Lady Bee Ind Est BN42 . .161 E6
Lady Oak La TN5,TN17 . . . .32 C7
Lady's Gift Rd TN4 . . . . .7 F8
Ladycross Cl BN25 . . . . . . .181 C3
Ladyfern Ct TN2 . . . . .8 C4
Ladymead RH15 . . . . .73 C5
Ladysmith Rd BN2 . . . . . . .164 D8
Lagwood Cl BN6 . . . . .97 F3
Laine Cl BN1 . . . . .142 E3
Laines The BN26 . . . . .170 F3
Lake Dr BN10 . . . . .178 B8
Lake House Cl TN39 . . . . . .156 D4
Lake Rd TN4 . . . . .7 E4
Lake St TN20,TN6 . . . . .40 D7
Lake View 1 BN2 . . . . .164 C5
Lake View Rd RH19 . . . . .1 F5
Lakehurst La TN33 . . . . . . .110 B8
Lakelands Cl BN22 . . . . . . .174 A1
Lakelands Dr TN39 . . . . . .156 D4
Lakeman Way TN4 . . . . .8 B7
Lakeside TN2 . . . . .8 E6
Lakeside Ct BN22 . . . . .174 A1
Laleham Cl
  Eastbourne BN21 . . . . .184 E4
  St Leonards TN37 . . . . . . .136 C5
Lamberhurst CE Prim Sch
  TN3 . . . . .20 B6
Lamberhurst Rd TN3, TN12 20 C8
Lamberhurst Vineyard
  TN3 . . . . .20 A4
Lambert Pl BN7 . . . . .123 C3
Lambert Rd BN23 . . . . .174 E3
Lamberts Cotts TN33 . . . . .112 E3
Lamberts Rd TN2 . . . . .8 D8
Lambourn Ave BN24 . . . . .174 A5
Lambourn Cl RH19 . . . . .1 E3
Lambourn Way TN2 . . . . . . .8 D1
Lambourne Cl BN1 . . . . . . .143 C2
Lambourne Rd BN1 . . . . . .143 C2
Lampington Row TN3 . . . . . .6 E3
Lampool Cnr TN22 . . . . . . .55 A7
Lanark Ct BN20 . . . . .184 B6
Lancaster Ct
  16 Eastbourne BN22 . . . . .185 B3
  12 Hove BN3 . . . . .163 A6
Lancaster Dr RH19 . . . . .2 A3
Lancaster House Rd BN1 144 B7
Lancaster Rd
  Brighton BN1 . . . . .189 A4
  St Leonards TN38 . . . . . . .135 F5
Lancaster St BN7 . . . . .123 D1
Lancing Cl TN34 . . . . .136 D3
Lancing Ct 6 BN2 . . . . . . .164 F5
Lancing Way BN26 . . . . . . .172 F4
Landgate TN31 . . . . .93 C6
Landport Farm Rd BN7 . . .123 A3
Landport Rd Lewes BN7 . . .123 B3
  Lewes BN7 . . . . .123 C2
Landsdown Rd BN25 . . . . .181 C5
Landsdowne Way TN40 . . .157 C5
Landseer Rd BN3 . . . . .163 A8
Lane The TN3 . . . . .6 C5
Langdale Cl BN23 . . . . .174 C4
Langdale Cl BN3 . . . . .162 F6
Langdale Gdns BN3 . . . . . .162 F6
Langdale Rd BN3 . . . . .162 F6
Langham Cl Hastings TN34 136 F4
  Ringmer BN8 . . . . .124 D5
Langham Rd
  Hastings TN34 . . . . .136 F4
  Robertsbridge TN32 . . . . . .63 F4
Langholm Rd TN3 . . . . .6 F3
Langhurst 9 BN2 . . . . .164 E4
Langley Cl TN39 . . . . .157 B8
Langley Cres BN2 . . . . .144 E1
Langney Cty Prim Sch
  BN23 . . . . .174 E1
Langney Gn BN23 . . . . . . .185 E8
Langney Rd BN21,BN22 . . .185 B3
Langney Rise BN23 . . . . . .174 D2
Langney Sh Ctr BN23 . . . .174 C2
Langridge Dr
  East Grinstead RH19 . . . . . .10 E8
  Portslade-by-Sea BN41 . . . .141 B3
Langridge La RH16 . . . . . . .51 A5
Langridge Way RH15 . . . . . .72 E5
Langridges Cl BN8 . . . . . . .76 C7
Langton TN33 . . . . .112 E4

Jir-Lee 205

Langton Green
  Cty Prim Sch TN3 . . . . .6 E4
Langton Rd Rusthall TN3, TN4 7 C3
  Speldhurst TN3 . . . . .7 A7
Langton Ridge TN3 . . . . . . .7 B3
Lansdown Pl BN7 . . . . .146 D8
Lansdown Terr TN21 . . . . . .82 B6
Lansdowne Cres BN27 . . . .129 B2
Lansdowne Dr BN27 . . . . . .129 A2
Lansdowne Gdns BN27 . . .129 B2
Lansdowne Mews 7
  BN3 . . . . .163 D6
Lansdowne Pl BN3 . . . . . . .163 D6
Lansdowne Rd
  Hailsham BN27 . . . . .129 B2
  Hove BN1, BN3 . . . . .163 D6
  Royal Tunbridge Wells TN1 . .8 B4
Lansdowne Sq
  1 Hove BN3 . . . . .163 D5
  8 Royal Tunbridge Wells TN1 . .8 B4
Lansdowne St BN3 . . . . . . .163 D6
Lansdowne Way BN27 . . . .129 B2
Lapierre Rd BN9 . . . . .179 B7
Lapwing Cl BN23 . . . . .174 C2
Lapwing Ct BN27 . . . . .152 D7
Larch Cl Heathfield TN21 . . .82 B5
  St Leonards TN38 . . . . . . .136 A1
  Woodingdean BN2 . . . . . . .165 F7
Larch Gdns BN22 . . . . .173 D3
Larch Way RH16 . . . . .51 B4
Lark Hill BN3 . . . . .141 E3
Larke Cl BN43 . . . . .161 C7
Larkfield Cl TN38 . . . . .136 A3
Larkfield Way BN1 . . . . . . .143 A4
Larkhill TN40 . . . . .157 C4
Larkspur Dr BN23 . . . . .174 B3
Larnach Cl TN22 . . . . .78 D8
Lascelles Terr BN21 . . . . . .185 A1
Lashbrooks Rd TN22 . . . . . .78 B7
Latimer Rd BN22 . . . . .185 C4
Laton Rd TN34 . . . . .136 F2
Laughton Cl BN23 . . . . . . .174 A4
Laughton Cty Prim Sch
  BN8 . . . . .126 C6
Laughton Lodge BN8 . . . . .126 A8
Laughton Rd
  Broyle Side BN8 . . . . .125 D6
  Woodingdean BN2 . . . . . . .165 F8
Laundry La RH17 . . . . .22 D1
Laurel 2 RH16 . . . . .50 D6
  Royal Tunbridge Wells TN4 . . .8 B8
Laurel Bank Bexhill TN40 . .157 C4
  Wadhurst TN5 . . . . .30 A4
Laurel Cl RH15 . . . . .73 D5
Laurel Dene RH19 . . . . .1 F1
Laurel Rd TN2 . . . . .8 D7
Laurel La TN36 . . . . .116 F3
Laurel Way TN2 . . . . .8 D7
Laurel Wlk TN38 . . . . .135 E3
Laurels The
  4 Brighton BN2 . . . . .189 C5
  Uckfield TN22 . . . . .78 E8
Lauren Ct TN38 . . . . .158 F7
Lauriston Rd BN1 . . . . .142 E2
Lavant Cl TN39 . . . . .156 C6
Lavant Rd BN24 . . . . .174 B5
Lavender Cl BN23 . . . . .174 A3
Lavender Gdns TN5 . . . . . . .31 C1
Lavender Hill BN43 . . . . . .140 B1
Lavender Ho BN2 . . . . .189 C1
Lavender Line TN22 . . . . .102 E8
Lavender St 2 BN2 . . . . . .189 C1
Lawes Ave BN9 . . . . .179 C7
Lawn The TN38 . . . . .159 C7
Lawns Ave BN21 . . . . .184 D4
Lawns The
  Eastbourne BN22 . . . . .185 C5
  Hailsham BN27 . . . . .152 C6
  Willingdon BN20 . . . . .173 B1
  Willingdon BN20 . . . . .173 B2
Lawrence Cl BN23 . . . . .174 D1
Lawrence Ho TN22 . . . . . . .78 C7
Lawrence Rd BN3 . . . . .162 F7
Lawrie La RH16 . . . . .51 B5
Laylands Cl BN41 . . . . .162 A7
Laylands Rd BN41 . . . . .162 A7
Lazanby Ct TN38 . . . . .159 B8
Le Brun Rd BN21 . . . . .184 F5
Lea Ave TN31 . . . . .93 A6
Lea Ct BN9 . . . . .179 C8
Lea Rd BN10 . . . . .178 B8
Leach Ct BN22 . . . . .164 C5
Leaf Hall Rd 10 BN22 . . . .185 B3
Leaf Hospl
  (Univ of Brighton) BN21 184 F4
Leaf Rd BN21 . . . . .185 A3
Leahurst Court Rd BN1 . . .142 E3
Leahurst Ct 1 BN1 . . . . . .142 E3
Lealands Cl TN3 . . . . .15 C6
Lealands Dr TN22 . . . . .55 C1
Leamland Wlk TN22 . . . . .152 B7
Leap Cross Small Bsns Ctr
  BN27 . . . . .129 A1
Leas The Burgess Hill RH15 . .72 F4
  Peacehaven Heights BN10 . .178 F6
  St Leonards TN37 . . . . . . .159 A6
  Turner's Green TN5 . . . . . . .30 A6
Leasam La TN31 . . . . .93 B8
Leasingham Gdns TN39 . . .157 A5
Ledsham Ave TN37 . . . . . .136 B5
Ledsham Cl TN37 . . . . .136 B5
Ledsham Pk TN37 . . . . .136 B5
Ledsham Way TN37 . . . . . .136 B5
Lee Rd BN7 . . . . .123 B2

Lee Way BN9 . . . . .179 C8
Leeds Ave BN23 . . . . .185 D7
Leeds Cl TN35 . . . . .137 D4
Leeds La TN20 . . . . .58 D6
Leeford Cotts TN33 . . . . . . .88 A1
Leeves Cl TN21 . . . . .82 A6
Leeves Way TN21 . . . . .82 A6
Leeward Quay BN23 . . . . . .185 F8
Leggs' La TN3 . . . . .6 E5
Legsheath La RH18, RH19 . .21 F8
Leicester Cl **5** BN22 . . . . . .185 B4
Leicester Dr TN3 . . . . .16 F8
Leicester Rd BN7 . . . . .123 B1
Leicester St BN2 . . . . .189 C2
Leicester Villas BN3 . . . . . .162 D7
Leighton Cl TN4 . . . . .8 A7
Leighton Rd
  Horsted Keynes RH17 . . . . .33 C5
  Hove BN3 . . . . .163 A8
Leighton Villas RH17 . . . . . .33 C5
Leneda Dr TN2 . . . . .16 E8
Lenham Ave BN2 . . . . .177 B5
Lenham Rd E BN2 . . . . . . .177 B5
Lenham Rd W BN2 . . . . . . .177 A5
Lennox Cl BN20 . . . . .184 B5
Lennox Ct TN21 . . . . .82 B8
Lennox Rd Hove BN3 . . . . . .162 F8
  Shoreham-by-Sea BN43 . . .161 B8
Lennox St BN2 . . . . .189 C2
Leopold Rd Bexhill TN39 . .157 B4
  Brighton BN1 . . . . .189 A3
Lepeland BN27 . . . . .129 A1
Lesley Cl TN40 . . . . .157 F7
Leslie St BN22 . . . . .185 B4
Letheren Pl BN1 . . . . .184 D3
Leveller End BN8 . . . . .76 D7
Leveller Rd BN8 . . . . .76 D7
Levett Ave BN26 . . . . .173 C6
Levett Cl BN26 . . . . .173 C6
Levett Rd BN26 . . . . .173 C6
Levett Way BN26 . . . . .173 C6
Levetts La TN32 . . . . .46 D1
Lewes Bsns Ctr BN7 . . . . . .123 C2
Lewes Cl Bexhill TN39 . . . .157 A6
  Saltdean BN2 . . . . .177 E5
Lewes Cres BN2 . . . . .164 C4
Lewes Ct BN1 . . . . .144 A8
Lewes High Sch BN7 . . . . . .123 B1
Lewes Ho BN2 . . . . .184 F4
Lewes Mews **12** BN2 . . . . .164 E4
Lewes Rd
  Brighton BN1, BN2 . . . . . . .143 E3
  Chelwood Gate RH17, RH18 . .22 C1
  Danehill RH17 . . . . .34 B3
  Ditchling BN6 . . . . .98 E2
  Eastbourne BN21 . . . . .184 F5
  Forest Row RH18 . . . . .11 E2
  Haywards Heath RH16,RH17 .51 D4
  Horsted Keynes RH17 . . . . .33 C5
  Isfield TN22 . . . . .102 E6
  Lindfield RH16 . . . . .51 B7
  Newhaven BN9 . . . . .179 C8
  Polegate BN26 . . . . .172 C6
  Ringmer BN8 . . . . .124 D6
  Scaynes Hill RH17 . . . . . . .51 D4
  Uckfield TN22 . . . . .78 D4
Lewes St BN2 . . . . .189 C3
Lewes Sta BN7 . . . . .146 D8
Lewes Tertiary Coll
  Lewes BN7 . . . . .123 B1
  Lewes BN7 . . . . .146 D8
Lewes Tertiary Coll
  (S Bldg) BN7 . . . . .146 D8
Lewinscourt TN33 . . . . . . .112 D5
Lewis Ave TN40 . . . . .158 A5
Lewis Cl BN9 . . . . .168 F2
Lewis Ct **6** BN2 . . . . .164 C8
Lewis Rd TN38 . . . . .136 A3
Lewry Cl BN9 . . . . .179 B7
Lexden Ct BN25 . . . . .181 A4
Lexden Dr BN25 . . . . .181 A5
Lexden Lodge Ind Est TN6 .38 D8
Lexden Rd BN25 . . . . .180 F6
Leybourne Cl BN2 . . . . . . .144 A1
Leybourne Gdns TN37 . . . .136 C4
Leybourne Par BN2 . . . . . .144 A1
Leybourne Rd BN2 . . . . . . .144 A1
Leyland Rd BN24 . . . . .175 D4
Leylands Pk RH15 . . . . . . .73 B5
Leylands Rd RH15 . . . . . . .73 B4
Library Way TN2 . . . . .78 C7
Lichfield Ct **10** BN2 . . . . . .164 F5
Lifeboat Mus BN21 . . . . . . .185 A1
Lilac Cl BN22 . . . . .173 D3
Lillesden Cotts TN18 . . . . . .45 E7
Lillywhite Cl RH15 . . . . . . .72 F5
Limden Cl TN5 . . . . .42 F6
Lime Cl Frant TN3 . . . . .17 B3
  St Leonards TN38 . . . . . . .136 B1
  Uckfield TN22 . . . . .78 D8
Lime Cross BN27 . . . . .130 F5
Lime Hill Rd TN1 . . . . .8 A4
Lime Tree Ave TN22 . . . . . . .78 D7
Lime Tree Gr RH16 . . . . . . .51 C7
Lime Tree Terr TN19 . . . . . .62 A6
Lime Way TN21 . . . . .82 B6
Limekiln Ct TN6 . . . . .26 C3
Limes La TN22 . . . . .56 D3
Limes The
  Dormans Park RH19 . . . . . . .1 A5
  14 Eastbourne BN21 . . . .184 E4
Limetree Ave TN22 . . . . . .173 D3
Limney Rd BN2 . . . . .164 E7
Linchmere BN2 . . . . .164 F7
Linchmere Ave BN2 . . . . . .177 C5

Lincoln Ave BN10 . . . . . . .178 A7
Lincoln Ave S BN10 . . . . . .178 A7
Lincoln Cl
  Eastbourne BN20 . . . . .188 C8
  2 St Leonards TN38 . . . .136 A4
Lincoln Cotts BN2 . . . . . . .189 C3
Lincoln Ct
  Eastbourne BN20 . . . . .184 B7
  Hove BN3 . . . . .163 C8
  Peacehaven BN10 . . . . . . .178 A7
Lincoln Rd BN41 . . . . .162 B7
Lincoln St BN2 . . . . .189 C4
Lincoln Way TN6 . . . . .38 A8
Lincoln Wood RH16 . . . . . . .50 C5
Linden Ave RH19 . . . . .1 C2
Linden Chase TN22 . . . . . . .78 D7
Linden Cl Eastbourne BN22 .173 E2
  Royal Tunbridge Wells TN4 . . .8 A2
Linden Ct TN2 . . . . .78 C7
Linden Gdns TN2 . . . . .7 F1
Linden Gr Hailsham BN27 . .129 C3
  Lindfield RH16 . . . . .51 B7
Linden Park Rd TN2 . . . . . . .8 A2
Linden Rd TN40 . . . . .157 C3
Lindens The **4** BN2 . . . . .189 C4
Lindfield BN41 . . . . .141 A1
Lindfield Ave BN25 . . . . . . .181 C2
Lindfield Cl BN2 . . . . .177 B6
Lindfield Ct BN1 . . . . .143 C2
Lindfield Cty Inf Sch RH16 .51 A7
Lindfield Cty Jun Sch
  RH16 . . . . .51 B7
Lindfield Dr BN27 . . . . . . .152 B7
Lindfield Ent Pk RH16 . . . . .51 C6
Lindfield Rd BN20 . . . . . . .173 D1
Lindfield Sch The BN22 . . .173 D2
Lindon Cl BN20 . . . . .183 B1
Lindsay Cl BN20 . . . . .184 C2
Lingfield Rd RH19 . . . . .1 D3
Link Rd BN20 . . . . .184 D1
Link The Friston BN20 . . . .183 C2
  Rye TN31 . . . . .93 A5
Link Way TN2 . . . . .8 E8
Linkden Cotts TN18 . . . . . . .47 E5
Links Ave BN10, BN9 . . . . .179 A7
Links Cl Crowborough TN6 . .25 D2
  Portslade-by-Sea BN41 . . . .162 C8
  Seaford BN25 . . . . .181 A2
Links Dr TN40 . . . . .157 E4
Links Rd
  Portslade-by-Sea BN41 . . . .162 C8
  Seaford BN25 . . . . .181 A2
Links The **6** Bexhill TN40 .157 D3
  St Leonards TN38 . . . . . . .158 F8
Links Way TN31 . . . . .94 E2
Linkswood BN21 . . . . .184 E2
Linkway Eastbourne BN20 . .184 B7
  Westham BN24 . . . . .174 A6
Linkway The BN1 . . . . .143 B1
Linley Cl Bexhill TN40 . . . .157 D4
  Hastings TN34 . . . . .137 A3
Linley Dr TN34 . . . . .137 A3
Linnet Cl BN23 . . . . .174 C2
Linnet Gn TN22 . . . . .78 D5
Linosa Ct **17** BN22 . . . . . .185 B3
Linthouse Cl BN10 . . . . . . .167 D2
Linton Cres TN34 . . . . .159 E8
Linton Ct TN34 . . . . .159 E8
Linton Rd Hastings TN34 . . .159 E8
  Hove BN3 . . . . .162 F8
Lion Hill BN23,BN24 . . . . .174 B5
Lion Hill Cotts BN24 . . . . .174 B5
Lion La BN21 . . . . .185 B3
Lion Mews **4** BN3 . . . . . .162 F7
Lion St TN31 . . . . .93 C5
Lionel Rd TN40 . . . . .157 E3
Lions Ct BN2 . . . . .164 E5
Lions Dene BN1 . . . . .142 D4
Lions Gdns BN1 . . . . .142 D4
Lions Pl BN25 . . . . .180 F2
Liphook Cl BN1 . . . . .143 C1
Lipscombe Rd TN2 . . . . .8 D6
Liptraps La TN2 . . . . .8 D7
Lismore Rd BN21 . . . . .185 A2
Lister Ave RH19 . . . . .10 F6
Lister Rd BN23 . . . . .174 A1
Litlington Ct **4** BN25 . . . .180 C4
Little Bayham Cotts TN3 . . .18 F4
Little Bentswood RH16 . . . .50 F5
Little Bentswood Cl RH16 . .50 F5
Little Black Hill RH16 . . . . .51 B7
Little Common
  Cty Prim Sch TN39 . . . . . .156 D4
Little Common Rd TN39 . . .156 E5
Little Copse Rd BN6 . . . . . .97 E4
Little Cranfield Ct RH19 . . . .1 D1
Little Cres BN2 . . . . .177 B5
Little East St Brighton BN2 189 B1
  Lewes BN7 . . . . .123 D1
Little Footway TN3 . . . . .6 F3
Little George St BN2 . . . . .189 B1
Little Horsted
  CE Prim Sch TN22 . . . . . . .78 C1
Little Iridge Farm Cotts
  TN19 . . . . .45 C1
Little King St RH19 . . . . .1 E1
Little London Rd TN21 . . .106 F8
Little Mallett TN38 . . . . .6 F3
Little Mead BN8 . . . . .123 A4
Little Mount Sion TN1 . . . . .8 A2
Little Paddock
  Crowborough TN6 . . . . .25 E1
  Heathfield TN21 . . . . .82 A7
  Ringmer BN8 . . . . .124 E6
Little Park Cotts TN33 . . . .112 E5
Little Pk TN5 . . . . .29 E4
Little Preston St BN1 . . . . .163 E5
Little Ridge Ave TN37 . . . .136 C5

Little Ridge Cty Prim Sch
  TN37 . . . . .136 C5
Little Sherwood Ind Pk
  TN36 . . . . .116 D5
Little Sunnyside TN6 . . . . . .25 F1
Little Trogers La TN20 . . . . .40 B4
Little Twitten TN39 . . . . . .156 C3
Little Western St **1** BN1 . .163 E5
Littlemead TN22 . . . . .35 C3
Littlewood La TN22 . . . . . . .56 C4
Littleworth Cl BN2 . . . . . . .165 F4
Living World The BN25 . . . .181 F4
Livingstone Ho **5** BN3 . . .163 B7
Livingstone Rd
  Burgess Hill RH15 . . . . .72 F3
  Hove BN3 . . . . .163 B7
Livingstone St BN2 . . . . . .164 D5
Lloyd Cl BN3 . . . . .163 C8
Lloyd Rd BN3 . . . . .163 C8
Lockhart Ct RH16 . . . . .50 F2
Lockitt Way BN7 . . . . .145 E5
Locks Cres BN41 . . . . .141 B1
Locks Ct **10** BN42 . . . . . .161 E7
Locks Hill BN41 . . . . .141 B1
Lockwood Cl BN2 . . . . .165 E7
Lockwood Cres BN2 . . . . . .165 E7
Loder Pl BN1 . . . . .142 F2
Loder Rd BN1 . . . . .142 F2
Lodge Ave BN26 . . . . .173 C1
Lodge Cl East Grinstead RH19 1 D1
  Lewes BN7 . . . . .146 A8
  Portslade-by-Sea BN41 . . . .140 F2
Lodge Hill La BN6 . . . . .98 C4
Lodge La BN6 . . . . .98 A2
Lodge Rd TN35 . . . . .160 C5
Lodge The Brighton BN2 . . .189 C1
  14 Eastbourne BN21 . . . .185 A2
Lodsworth BN2 . . . . .164 F7
Lodsworth Cl BN2 . . . . . . .164 F7
Lomaria Ct TN2 . . . . .8 C4
Lomas La TN18 . . . . .47 F5
Lomond Ave BN1 . . . . .143 B7
London Meed Cty
  Prim Sch RH15 . . . . .73 A1
London Rd Bexhill TN39 . . .157 B5
  Brighton BN1 . . . . .189 B4
  Brighton, Withdene BN1 . . .142 D4
  Burgess Hill RH15 . . . . .72 F5
  Crowborough TN6 . . . . .25 E4
  Danehill RH17 . . . . .34 A4
  East Grinstead RH19 . . . . . . .1 C1
  East Hoathly BN8 . . . . . . .105 A5
  Flimwell TN5 . . . . .32 D3
  Forest Row RH18 . . . . .11 E4
  Hailsham BN27 . . . . .129 A2
  Hassocks BN6, RH15 . . . . . .97 E6
  Hurst Green TN19 . . . . .45 A3
  John's Cross TN32,TN33 . . . .87 D3
  Maresfield TN22 . . . . .55 B4
  Pyecombe BN1,BN45 . . . . .119 C4
  Royal Tunbridge Wells TN4 . . .8 A8
  Royal Tunbridge Wells,Mount
    Sion TN1 . . . . .8 A3
  St Leonards TN37, TN38 . . .159 C8
  Uckfield TN22 . . . . .55 D2
London Road Sta BN1 . . . .164 A8
London Terr BN1 . . . . .189 B4
Loney Ct **1** BN43 . . . . . .161 C8
Long Acre Cl BN21 . . . . . .184 D5
Long La TN40 . . . . .158 A6
Long Man The BN26 . . . . .171 E3
Long Meads TN3, TN4 . . . . . .7 B4
Long Park Cnr BN6 . . . . . . .98 D2
Long Slip TN3 . . . . .7 A3
Long Wlk RH16 . . . . .51 B4
Longacre Cl TN37 . . . . . . .136 C6
Longbury TN22 . . . . .78 C5
Longfield Rd TN2 . . . . .8 D8
Longhill Cl BN2 . . . . .165 E4
Longhill Rd BN2 . . . . .165 E4
Longhill Sch BN2 . . . . .165 E4
Longhurst RH15 . . . . .73 D2
Longhurst Cotts BN8 . . . . . .75 D7
Longland Rd BN20 . . . . . . .184 C4
Longridge Ave BN2 . . . . . .177 D5
Longstone Rd BN21 . . . . . .185 A3
Longview TN21 . . . . .82 A5
Longview Way TN2 . . . . .8 D7
Lonsdale Gdns TN1 . . . . .8 A3
Lookout The BN10 . . . . . . .167 D3
Loose Farm Barns TN33 . . .113 A2
Loose Farm Cotts TN33 . . .113 A2
Lordine La TN32 . . . . .66 B4
Lords La TN35 . . . . .137 D3
Lords The BN25 . . . . .180 E6
Lordslaine Cl BN20 . . . . . .188 D8
Lordswell La TN6 . . . . .37 E8
Loriners Ct BN3 . . . . .162 D8
Lorna Rd BN3 . . . . .163 D7
Lorne Rd BN1 . . . . .189 B5
Lorraine Ct **2** Hove BN3 . .163 B6
  11 Hove BN3 . . . . .163 E7
Lorraine Rd BN9 . . . . .179 D7
Lossenham La TN18 . . . . . . .48 D3
Lottbridge Dr BN22 . . . . . .173 F1
Lottbridge Dro
  Eastbourne BN23 . . . . .185 B7
  Eastbourne BN23 . . . . .185 D7
Lottbridge Rdbt BN23 . . . .185 A8
Lovat Mead TN38 . . . . .158 E6
Love La Eastbourne BN20 . .184 D3
  Mayfield TN20 . . . . .39 F2

Love La continued
  Rye TN31 . . . . .93 B6
Lovegrove Ct BN3 . . . . . . .162 E8
Lovell Ct BN21 . . . . .184 D5
Lover's Wlk BN1 . . . . .163 F8
Lover's Wlk Cotts BN1 . . . .163 F8
Lowdells Cl RH19 . . . . .1 C4
Lowdells Dr RH19 . . . . .1 C4
Lowdells La RH19 . . . . .1 C3
Lower Bevendean Ave
  BN2 . . . . .143 E1
Lower Chalvington Pl
  BN2 . . . . .164 E5
Lower Church Rd RH15 . . . .72 F3
Lower Cross Cotts TN31 . . . .91 E2
Lower Dene RH19 . . . . .2 A1
Lower Dicker BN27 . . . . . . .128 C3
Lower Glen Rd TN37 . . . . . .136 B4
Lower Green Rd
  Pembury TN2 . . . . .9 D7
  Rusthall TN3, TN4 . . . . .7 C6
Lower Hazelhurst TN5 . . . . .31 A4
Lower High St TN5 . . . . .30 A4
Lower Lake TN33 . . . . .112 C4
Lower Market St **6** BN3 .163 D5
Lower Mere RH19 . . . . .10 F8
Lower Park Rd TN34 . . . . . .136 C1
Lower Pl BN9 . . . . .179 C7
Lower Platts TN5 . . . . .31 F1
Lower Rd
  Eastbourne BN21 . . . . .184 D4
  Forest Row RH18 . . . . .11 C3
  Golden Cross BN27 . . . . . .130 E3
Lower Rock Gdns BN2 . . . .189 C1
Lower Roedale Cotts
  BN1 . . . . .143 B3
Lower Saxonbury TN6 . . . . .25 B3
Lower South Rd TN37 . . . . .136 C1
Lower Sq RH18 . . . . .11 E3
Lower St East Dean BN20 . .187 B8
  Lower Street TN33 . . . . . . .133 B5
Lower Station Rd BN8 . . . . .76 A6
Lower Waites La TN35 . . . . .138 F4
Lowfield Rd RH16 . . . . .50 F3
Lowlands Rd RH15 . . . . . . .73 B5
Lowlands The BN27 . . . . . .129 A1
Lowther Cl BN23 . . . . .174 D3
Lowther Rd BN1 . . . . .143 A2
Loxdale (The Swedish
  Folk High Sch) BN41 . . . .141 B1
Loxfield Cl TN20 . . . . .40 A2
Loxfield Gdns TN6 . . . . .26 B1
Loxwood Cl Bexhill TN39 . .156 D5
  Eastbourne BN22 . . . . .173 C1
Loyal Par BN1 . . . . .142 C5
Lucas Rd TN35 . . . . .160 C5
Lucas Cl RH19 . . . . .2 A1
Lucas Grange RH16 . . . . . . .50 D5
Lucas Shadwell Way TN31 93 F12
Lucas Way RH16 . . . . .50 C5
Lucastes Ave RH16 . . . . . . .50 C6
Lucastes La RH16 . . . . .50 C6
Lucastes Rd RH16 . . . . .50 C5
Lucerne Cl BN41 . . . . .141 B1
Lucerne Rd BN1 . . . . .143 A1
Lucinda Way BN25 . . . . . . .180 F6
Lucraft Rd BN1, BN2 . . . . .144 A5
Ludley Hill TN31 . . . . .91 A6
Ludlow Rise BN2 . . . . .144 A1
Ludpit La TN19, TN32 . . . . .63 C6
Luke Lade Ct BN27 . . . . . .152 C7
Lulham Cl BN10 . . . . .167 B2
Lullington Ave BN3 . . . . . .162 F8
Lullington Cl
  Bexhill TN40 . . . . .158 A6
  Eastbourne BN21 . . . . .184 C7
  Seaford BN25 . . . . .181 B2
Lullington Gdns TN37 . . . .136 C5
Lullington Ho **4** BN21 . . .184 E4
Lunce's Hill RH16, RH17 . . .73 F7
Lundy Wlk
  7 Eastbourne BN23 . . . .185 F8
  Hailsham BN27 . . . . .129 A2
Lureland Ct BN10 . . . . . . .178 C6
Lurgashall RH15 . . . . .73 C1
Lushington La BN21 . . . . . .185 A2
Lushington Rd BN21 . . . . . .185 A2
Lustrells Cl BN2 . . . . .177 B6
Lustrells Cres BN2 . . . . . . .177 C6
Lustrells Rd BN2 . . . . .177 A6
Lustrells Vale BN2 . . . . . . .177 C6
Luther St BN2 . . . . .164 C7
Luton Cl BN21 . . . . .184 C6
Luxford Cl TN22 . . . . .78 C7
Luxford Cotts TN6 . . . . .38 A8
Luxford Dr TN6 . . . . .38 A8
Luxford La TN6 . . . . .38 A8
Luxford Rd
  Crowborough TN6 . . . . .38 A8
  Lindfield RH16 . . . . .51 B7
Luxford's La RH19 . . . . .11 B6
Lychgates Cl TN40 . . . . . . .157 D5
Lydd Cl BN23 . . . . .174 D2
Lydd Rd TN31 . . . . .94 F2
Lymden La TN5 . . . . .43 A7
Lyminster Ave BN1 . . . . . . .143 A5
Lynchet Cl BN1 . . . . .143 C3
Lynchet Down BN1 . . . . . . .143 C2
Lynchet Wlk BN1 . . . . .143 C2
Lynchets Cres BN3 . . . . . . .141 D3
Lynchets The BN7 . . . . . . .123 E3
Lynden Ct **1** BN1 . . . . . .142 E2
Lyndhurst Ave TN34 . . . . . .137 A4
Lyndhurst Cl BN3 . . . . . . .163 D7
Lyndhurst Rd BN3 . . . . . . .163 D7
Lynholm Rd BN26 . . . . . . .173 C6

Lynton Cl
  East Grinstead RH19 . . . . . . .2 A2
  Hurstpierpoint BN6 . . . . . . .97 B5
Lynton Park Ave RH19 . . . . .2 A2
Lynton St BN2 . . . . .164 C7
Lynwood TN3 . . . . .15 C5
Lynwood Cl TN37 . . . . . . .136 D5
Lynwood Rd BN2 . . . . .177 C4
Lyon Cl BN3 . . . . .163 D7
Lyoth La RH16 . . . . .51 C4
Lyoth Villas RH16 . . . . .51 C4
Lytham Cl TN38 . . . . .158 F8

M

Mabb's Hill TN5 . . . . .42 F7
Maberley Rd TN40 . . . . . . .157 C6
Mackenzie Ho RH19 . . . . . . .1 A4
Mackerel Hill TN31 . . . . . . .68 F4
Mackerel's Rocks BN8 . . . . .76 F3
Mackie Ave Brighton BN1 . .143 A7
  Keymer BN6 . . . . .98 A5
Macmillan Dr BN21 . . . . . .184 C5
Madehurst Cl BN2 . . . . . . .164 D5
Madeira Dr BN2 . . . . .164 C4
Madeira Pk TN2 . . . . .8 B2
Madeira Pl BN2 . . . . .189 C1
Madeira Way BN23 . . . . . . .185 F8
Maderia Dr TN34 . . . . .136 C3
Mafeking Rd BN2 . . . . .143 D1
Magdalen Cl BN23 . . . . . . .174 C3
Magdalen Ct **5** TN40 . . . .157 D4
Magdalen Rd Bexhill TN40 157 D4
  St Leonards TN37 . . . . . . .159 D7
Magellan Way BN23 . . . . . .185 G7
Magna Ct TN40 . . . . .157 B4
Magnolia Cl TN21 . . . . .82 B5
Magnolia Dr BN22 . . . . . . .173 D2
Magnolia Wlk BN22 . . . . . .173 D2
Magpie Cl Bexhill TN39 . . .156 C6
  St Leonards TN38 . . . . . . .158 E8
Magpie Rd BN23 . . . . .174 C3
Magreed La TN21 . . . . .59 E2
Maidstone Rd TN2 . . . . .9 E8
Main Rd
  Icklesham TN35,TN36 . . . .116 D5
  Westfield TN35 . . . . .114 C4
Main St Iden TN31 . . . . .70 B4
  Northiam TN31 . . . . .67 B5
  Peasmarsh TN31 . . . . .69 B2
Mainstone Rd **1** BN3 . . . .162 F7
Maitland Cl TN34 . . . . .136 E6
Major Cl BN1 . . . . .143 B1
Major York's Rd TN4 . . . . . . .7 F2
Malcolm Gdns BN26 . . . . . .173 A7
Maldon Rd BN1 . . . . .142 D2
Malines Ave BN10 . . . . . . .178 B8
Malines Ave S BN10 . . . . . .178 A7
Mallard Cl BN22 . . . . .184 F8
Mallard Dr TN22 . . . . .78 E5
Mallard Pl RH19 . . . . .10 F8
Mallett Cl **5** BN25 . . . . . .180 E2
Malling Cl BN7 . . . . .123 D3
Malling Down BN7,BN8 . . .123 E3
Malling Hill BN7 . . . . .123 E2
Malling House
  (Sussex Pol HQ) BN7 . . . .123 D3
Malling St **2** Lewes BN7 . .123 E1
  Lewes BN7 . . . . .123 E2
Mallory Rd BN3 . . . . .142 C2
Malt House Trad Est
  BN43 . . . . .161 B7
Malthouse Bsns Pk The
  TN31 . . . . .69 C2
Malthouse Ct **14** BN2 . . .189 C2
Malthouse La
  Brighton BN2 . . . . .189 C3
  Burgess Hill BN6,RH15 . . . .72 C2
  Peasmarsh TN31 . . . . .69 B2
  Peasmarsh TN31 . . . . .69 D2
  St John's Common RH15 . . . .72 D4
Malthouse Trad Est
  BN43 . . . . .161 B7
Malthouse Way BN7,BN8 . .123 A7
Maltings Barn The **7**
  BN7 . . . . .123 E1
Maltings The
  Burgess Hill RH15 . . . . .72 D4
  Peasmarsh TN31 . . . . .69 B2
Malton Way TN2 . . . . .8 F7
Malvern Cl BN22 . . . . .173 E4
Malvern Ho **11** TN39 . . . .157 B3
Malvern St **12** BN3 . . . . . .163 B7
Malvern Way TN34 . . . . . . .137 B4
Manaton Cl RH16 . . . . .50 F4
Manchester Rd TN33 . . . . .133 A6
Manchester St BN2 . . . . . .189 B1
Mandalay Ct BN1 . . . . .142 D4
Manhattan Ct BN1 . . . . . . .142 D3
Manhattan Gdns TN35 . . . .137 D4
Manifold Rd BN22 . . . . . . .185 B4
Mann St TN34 . . . . .159 F8
Manner Ct BN8 . . . . .75 D7
Manning Ct RH19 . . . . .1 D2
Manor Ave BN6 . . . . .98 A5
Manor Cl Brighton BN2 . . . .164 E5
  Broyle Side BN8 . . . . .124 F7
  Burgess Hill RH15 . . . . .73 D4
  Horam TN21 . . . . .106 F7
  Icklesham TN36 . . . . .116 F5
  Royal Tunbridge Wells TN4 . . .7 E3
  Seaford BN25 . . . . .181 G3
  Southwick BN42 . . . . .162 A8
  Uckfield TN22 . . . . .78 C8
  Willingdon BN20 . . . . .173 B2
Manor Cotts TN3 . . . . .20 B5

Manor Cres BN2 ....164 E5
Manor Ct Seaford BN25 ...181 B3
Southwick BN42 ....162 A7
Manor Cty Prim Sch TN22 78 D8
Manor Dr BN10 ....167 B1
Manor End TN22 ....78 C8
Manor Field Cty Prim Sch
RH15 ....73 C4
Manor Gdns BN2 ....164 E5
Manor Gn BN2 ....164 E5
Manor Hall Cty Fst Sch
BN42 ....161 F7
Manor Hall Cty Mid Sch
BN42 ....161 F8
Manor Hall Rd BN42 ....161 F8
Manor Hill BN2 ....164 E6
Manor House Ct TN22 ...78 C8
Manor Paddock BN2 ....164 E4
Manor Park Cl BN27 ....129 A3
Manor Park Ct BN26 ....173 A6
Manor Park Rd BN27 ....129 A3
Manor Pk TN4 ....7 E3
Manor Pl BN2 ....164 E4
Manor Rd Bexhill TN40 ...157 D4
Brighton BN2 ....164 E5
Burgess Hill RH15 ....73 D3
East Grinstead RH19 ......1 C2
Eastbourne BN22 ....174 A2
Hastings TN34 ....160 A5
Horam TN21 ....106 F8
Portslade-by-Sea BN41 ...141 B1
Rusthall TN4 ....7 C4
Seaford BN25 ....181 B3
Manor Rd N BN25 ....181 B3
Manor Terr 9 BN7 ......146 C8
Manor The TN2 ....8 E5
Manor Way Brighton BN2 ..164 E5
Crowborough TN6 ....37 E8
Eastbourne BN20 ....184 B8
Polegate BN26 ....173 B6
Uckfield TN22 ....78 C8
Mansell Cl TN39 ....156 C4
Mansell Ct RH15 ....73 B3
Mansell Rd BN43 ....161 B8
Mansers La BN27 ....128 C3
Mansfield Rd BN3 ......162 E7
Mansion Cl RH15 ....73 D3
Manston Way TN34 .....136 E2
Mantell Cl BN7 ....123 C4
Mantell Ho 2 BN2 .....189 C2
Manton Ct BN23 ....185 D8
Manton Rd BN2 ....143 E1
Manvers Rd BN20 ......184 B3
Maple Ave TN39 ....156 C3
Maple Cl Bexhill TN39 ...156 C3
Burgess Hill RH15 ....73 B5
Haywards Heath RH16 ...51 B3
Maresfield TN22 ....55 A4
Royal Tunbridge Wells TN2 ...8 A1
Woodingdean BN2 .....165 E7
Maple Ct Hailsham BN27 ..152 A8
St John's Common RH15 ..72 D3
Maple Dr
Burgess Hill RH15 ....73 A5
East Grinstead RH19 ......2 A1
Maple Gdns BN3 ....141 F1
Maple Hts TN37 ....136 B7
Maple Leaf Cl BN9 .....179 B7
Maple Rd
Eastbourne BN23 ....185 D7
Peacehaven Heights BN10 ..178 F6
Maple Wlk TN39 ....156 C3
Maplehurst Cl TN37 ....136 B7
Maplehurst Dr TN37 ...136 C8
Maplehurst Rd
Eastbourne BN22 ....173 D2
Portslade-by-Sea BN41 ...141 A1
St Leonards TN37 ......136 B7
Maplehurst Rise TN37 ...136 B7
Mapleleaf Gdns BN26 ..173 A8
Maples Cotts TN22 .....80 A6
Maplewood 4 BN1 .....142 E3
Marbles Cl BN8 ....76 D7
Marchants Cl BN6 ......97 A6
Marchants Dr TN31 ....94 E2
Marchants Rd BN6 .....97 A6
Marchants Way RH15 ...72 F5
Marcia Cl BN20 ....184 A8
Marcus Gdns TN37 .....136 A5
Mardan Cl TN38 ....159 B7
Marden Cl BN2 ....144 E1
Marden Ct TN39 ....157 A3
Marden's Hill TN6 ......25 B6
Mare Bay Cl TN38 ......135 E7
Maresfield Bonners
CE Prim Sch TN22 ......55 B4
Maresfield Dr BN24 ....175 E6
Maresfield Rd BN2 .....164 E5
Margaret Ct BN10 .....178 B7
Margaret St BN2 ....189 C1
Margery Rd BN3 ....162 D8
Marianne Pk TN35 .....160 B5
Marina Bexhill TN40 ...157 C3
St Leonards TN38 ......159 B6
Marina Court Ave 4
TN40 ....157 C3
Marina Ct BN9 ....179 D6
Marina Heights TN38 ...159 A6
Marina Way BN2 ....164 F3
Marina Wlk BN23 ......185 E8
Marine Ave
Beachlands BN24 ......175 F6
Hove BN3 ....162 E6
Marine Cl
Beachlands BN24 ......175 F6
Saltdean BN2 ....177 B5
Marine Cotts TN31 .....94 E2
Marine Cres BN25 .....180 F2

Marine Ct
Rottingdean BN2 ....177 A5
Seaford BN25 ....180 C3
4 St Leonards TN38 ...159 C6
Telscombe Cliffs BN10 ..177 F3
Marine Dr
Rottingdean BN2 ....165 C2
Seaford BN25 ....180 B5
Marine Gdns BN2 ......189 C1
Marine Par Brighton BN2 ..164 C4
Eastbourne BN21,BN22 ..185 B3
Hastings TN34 ....160 A3
Seaford BN25 ....180 C3
Marine Parade Rd 15
BN21 ....185 B3
Marine Rd
Eastbourne BN22 ......185 B3
Pevensey Bay BN24 ....175 D5
Marine Sq BN2 ....164 C4
Marine Terr BN24 .....175 D5
Marine Terrace Mews
BN2 ....164 C4
Marine View 3 BN2 ....189 C2
Mariners Quay BN2 ....164 F3
Mariteau Ho TN36 ....117 E7
Marjoram Pl BN43 .....140 B1
Mark Cl BN25 ....181 C2
Mark Cross BN38 .....126 B2
Mark Cross CE Prim Sch
TN6 ....28 A3
Mark La BN21 ....185 A2
Market La 7 BN7 .....123 D1
Market Pas
6 Hastings TN34 .....160 A3
9 St Leonards TN38 ...159 C6
Market Pl
Burgess Hill RH15 .....73 A2
Hailsham BN27 ....152 C7
Haywards Heath RH16 ...50 D6
14 Royal Tunbridge Wells TN2 ...8 A2
Market Rd Battle TN33 ..112 C5
Rye TN31 ....93 C5
Market Sq Battle TN33 ..112 D5
1 Hailsham BN27 ....152 C7
Royal Tunbridge Wells TN1 ...8 B4
Market St Brighton BN1 ..189 B2
Hailsham BN27 ....152 C7
Lewes BN7 ....123 D1
15 Royal Tunbridge Wells TN2 ...8 A2
Rye TN31 ....93 C5
St Leonards TN38 ......159 C6
Market Terr 8 TN38 ...159 C6
Markland Way TN22 ...78 A7
Marklye La Heathfield TN21 ..59 B2
Rushlake Green TN21 ...83 C3
Markstakes Cnr BN8 ...75 E1
Markstakes La BN8 ....76 C2
Markwick Terr TN38 ...159 B8
Marlborough Cl
Eastbourne BN23 ......174 D3
Royal Tunbridge Wells TN4 ...7 E4
St Leonards TN38 ......136 A1
Marlborough Ct
Burgess Hill RH15 .....72 E3
Eastbourne BN21 .....184 F3
1 Hove BN3 ....163 C6
Marlborough Dr RH15 ..73 C2
Marlborough Mews BN1 ..189 A2
Marlborough Pl BN1,BN2 ..189 B3
Marlborough St BN1 ...189 A2
Marle Ave RH15 ....73 A4
Marle Green Cotts TN21 ..107 B6
Marley Cl TN33 ....112 F4
Marley Gdns TN33 ....112 F4
Marley La TN33 ....113 B6
Marley Lodge BN2 ....189 C4
Marley Rd TN31 ....93 A6
Marley Rise TN33 .....112 F4
Marline Ave TN38 .....136 A4
Marline Rd TN38 ......136 A4
Marlinspike The BN43 ..161 A6
Marlow Ave BN22 .....185 B6
Marlow Ct BN2 ....189 C4
Marlow Dr
Haywards Heath RH16 ..51 C4
St Leonards TN37 ......136 C5
Marlow Rd BN26 ......164 F4
Marlowes The TN40 ...157 E5
Marlpit Cl RH19 ....1 E4
Marlpit Gdns TN5 .....31 E1
Marlpit Rd RH19 ......21 A6
Marlpit The TN5 ....29 E5
Marlpits La TN33 ......133 A7
Marmion Rd BN3 .....162 F7
Marsden Rd TN23 .....174 E1
Marsh Ho 3 BN42 ....161 D7
Marsh Quarter La TN18 ..47 C3
Marshall Cl BN22 .....173 D1
Marshall La BN9 ......179 C2
Marshall Rd BN23 ....185 A8
Marshall Rdbt BN23 ..174 A1
Marshall Way BN3 ....141 F1
Marshalls Row BN1 ...189 B4
Marshfoot La BN27 ...152 D8
Marshlands Cty Prim Sch
BN27 ....152 D8
Marshlands La TN21 ...82 A7
Marston Rd 10 BN3 ...163 E7
Martello Cl TN31 ......93 B4
Martello Ct
Pevensey Bay BN24 ...175 C3
South Heighton BN9 ...168 D2
Martello Mews 1 BN25 ..180 E2
Martello Rd
Eastbourne BN22 .....185 D6
Seaford BN25 ....180 E2
Martello Tower Mus
BN25 ....180 E1

Martens Field BN7 ....146 E1
Martha Gunn Cl BN2 ..143 E1
Martin Ct BN22 ....173 D1
Martin Rd BN3 ....141 D1
Martineau La TN35 ....137 F5
Martins The BN10 .....167 B1
Martlet Ho Brighton BN1 ..164 A8
Saltdean BN2 ....177 D4
Martlet The BN3 ......142 D1
Martlets Bexhill TN40 ..157 E5
Lower Willingdon BN22 ..173 B3
Martlets The
Broad Oak TN31 ....90 C4
Burgess Hill RH15 .....73 A3
Crowborough TN6 .....25 F1
Hailsham BN27 ....152 A7
Hastings TN34 ....136 C4
Lewes BN7 ....123 D3
South Chailey BN8 ...100 D7
Martletts The
Burwash Common TN19 ..60 F3
Ringmer BN8 ....124 E6
Martyn's Cl BN2 ......165 E4
Martyns Pl RH19 ......11 A8
Martyns Way TN40 ...158 A5
Marwick Ct TN38 .....159 B8
Mary Burfield Ct 3 TN21 ..82 A7
Mary Stamford Gn TN31 ..94 A3
Maryan Ct BN27 .....152 B8
Maryland Rd TN2 ......8 D1
Marylands RH16 ....50 F5
Maskelyne Rd BN27 ...131 A1
Mason Cl RH11 ....1 E2
Mason Rd Rye TN31 ...93 A5
Seaford BN25 ....180 F4
Matlock Rd Brighton BN1 ..142 D2
Eastbourne BN20 .....188 B8
Maudlin Ct TN37 ......159 C8
Maunsell Ct RH16 .....50 F3
Maunsell Rd TN38 ....135 F5
Maurice Rd BN25 .....180 F1
Maxfield Cl BN20 .....184 B5
Maxfield La TN35 .....115 D2
May Ave BN25 ....181 B3
May Rd BN2 ....164 D7
May Tree Gdns TN40 ..157 F6
Mayfair Cl BN26 ......172 F4
Mayfair Ct BN20 .....173 B1
Mayfair Rd BN10 .....178 D6
Mayfield CE Prim Sch
TN20 ....39 E3
Mayfield Cl Brighton BN1 ..143 A5
Mayfield TN20 ....39 F2
Mayfield Cres BN1 ....142 F5
Mayfield Ct Broad Oak TN21 59 E1
Burgess Hill RH15 .....73 B3
Saltdean BN2 ....177 C6
Mayfield Flat TN21,TN22 ..81 A8
Mayfield La Durgates TN5 ..29 D4
St Leonards TN38 .....135 D2
Mayfield Pk TN5 ......29 E5
Mayfield Pl BN22 .....185 A4
Mayfield Rd
Mark Cross TN6 ....28 A2
Rotherfield TN6 ....39 A7
Royal Tunbridge Wells TN4 ...7 F4
Mayfield Way TN40 ...157 E5
Mayflower Ct
Haywards Heath RH16 ..50 F4
9 Shoreham-by-Sea BN43 ..161 A6
Mayflower Rd RH16 ...50 F4
Mayflower Sq BN1 ....189 B4
Mayhew Way BN7 ....123 D2
Mayhouse Rd RH15 ...72 F1
Maynard's Green
Cty Prim Sch TN21 ....82 A2
Mayne Waye TN34 ....137 B4
Mayo Cl 5 BN2 ....164 B8
Mayo La TN39 ....157 A8
Mayo Rd BN2 ....164 B8
Mayo Rise TN39 ......157 A8
Maypole Cotts TN22 ..56 B8
Maypole Rd
Ashurst Wood RH19 ...11 E6
East Grinstead RH19 ....1 F4
Maytham Rd TN17 ....49 C7
Maytree Cotts BN8 ...100 C7
Maytree Wlk BN3 .....141 E1
Mayvern Ct TN6 ....25 F3
Mayview TN21 ....59 E1
Maywood Ave BN22 ..173 A7
Maze Hill TN38 ....159 B7
Maze Hill Terr TN38 ..159 B7
Mcbechie Ho RH19 .....1 B1
McIndoe Rd RH19 ......1 D1
McMichael Way TN19 ..45 A3
McWilliam Rd BN2 ....144 C1
Meachants Cl BN20 ...173 B2
Meachants La BN20 ...173 B2
Mead The TN39 ......156 D4
Meadow Bank TN33 ..112 E4
Meadow Cl Hailsham BN27 129 B1
Hove BN3 ....142 B3
Portslade-by-Sea BN41 ..141 B2
Rottingdean BN2 .....165 F3
Southwick BN42 ......162 A8
St Leonards TN38 .....136 A4
Meadow Cres TN39 ...157 A8
Meadow Dr RH16 .....51 B6
Meadow Hill Rd 6 TN1 ..8 B3
Meadow Ho BN8 .....100 E7
Meadow La
Burgess Hill RH15 .....72 F1
Lindfield RH16 ....51 B6
Meadow Par BN2 .....165 F3
Meadow Pl TN22 ......78 C6

Meadow Rd
Groombridge TN3 ....15 C7
Hailsham BN27 ....152 A6
Royal Tunbridge Wells TN1 ...8 A4
Rusthall TN4 ....7 C4
Meadow Rise TN21 ...106 F7
Meadow The TN2 ......9 E8
Meadow Vale BN2 ....165 E5
Meadow View
Rotherfield TN6 ....39 C7
Westfield TN35 ....114 E4
Meadow View Cotts .45 A3
Meadow Way
Fairlight Cove TN35 ...138 E4
Heathfield TN21 ......82 A6
Seaford BN25 ....181 B3
Meadowcroft Cl RH19 ....1 C2
Meadowlands Ave BN22 .173 D1
Meadows BN6 ....97 F5
Meadows Rd BN22 ...173 B2
Meadows The
Crowborough TN6 .....25 F2
Hove BN3 ....141 C3
Lewes BN7 ....123 E3
St Leonards TN37 ....136 C5
Meadowside TN33 ....88 E1
Meadowside Cotts TN5 ..31 F1
Meadowview
Brighton BN2 ....143 E1
Lower Street TN33 ...133 B5
Meads Ave Bexhill TN39 .156 C4
Hove BN3 ....141 C3
Meads Brow BN20 ...188 D8
Meads CE Prim Sch
BN20 ....188 D7
Meads Cl BN3 ....141 C3
Meads Ct BN20 ....184 E1
Meads Cty Prim Sch The
RH19 ....10 E7
Meads Gate BN20 ....188 E8
Meads Rd Bexhill TN39 ..156 C4
Eastbourne BN20 .....184 E1
Seaford BN25 ....180 E3
Meads St BN20 ....188 E8
Meads The Brighton BN1 ..143 D5
East Grinstead RH19 ...10 E7
Royal Tunbridge Wells TN1 ...8 C2
Meadsway BN20 ......188 E8
Meadway Cres BN20 ..141 F2
Meadway Ct BN42 ...161 D8
Meadway The
Brighton BN2 ....164 F5
Shoreham-by-Sea BN43 ..161 A6
Mealla Cl BN3 ....123 C3
Medina Dr BN24 .....174 B5
Medina Pl BN3 ....163 B6
Medina Terr Hove BN3 ..163 B5
St Leonards TN38 .....159 A6
Medina Villas BN3 ...163 B6
Medmerry Hill BN2 ..143 E2
Medway Crowborough TN6 ..26 C1
Hailsham BN27 ....129 A2
Medway Dr
East Grinstead RH19 ...10 D6
Forest Row RH18 ......12 A2
Medway La BN24 .....174 A5
Medway Rd TN1 ....8 B5
Medway View RH18 ...12 A2
Meeching Ct BN9 .....179 C7
Meeching Pl BN9 .....179 C7
Meeching Rd BN9 ....179 C7
Meeching Rise BN9 ...179 C7
Meeching Valley
Cty Prim Sch BN9 ....179 B7
Meeds Rd RH15 ....73 A2
Meeting House La BN1 ..189 B2
Megrims Hill TN18 ....47 A6
Melbourne Rd BN22 ..185 B4
Melbourne St BN2 ...164 C8
Melfort Rd TN6 ....25 D1
Melrose Ave BN41 ...141 A1
Melrose Cl Brighton BN1 ..143 C2
Hailsham BN27 ....152 A8
Melvill La BN20 ......173 B1
Melville Rd BN3 ......163 E7
Mendip Ave BN23 ....174 D3
Mendip Gdns TN34 ...137 B3
Mendip Wlk TN2 ....8 D5
Menzies Rd TN38 .....136 B2
Meon Cl BN24 ....174 A5
Mercatoria TN38 .....159 C6
Mercer St TN1 ....8 B5
Mercers TN3 ....7 A3
Mercia Ct 1 TN40 ...157 C4
Mercread Rd BN25 ...180 F3
Meres La TN20 ....58 D7
Merevale BN1 ....143 B2
Merewood Ct BN21 ..184 E4
Mereworth Rd TN4 .....8 A6
Meridian Ctr BN10 ...178 C7
Meridian Cty Prim Sch
BN10 ....167 C1
Meridian Ind Est The
BN10 ....178 C7
Meridian L Ctr BN10 ..178 C7
Meridian Rd BN7 .....123 B2
Meridian Way
East Grinstead RH19 ....1 F3
Peacehaven BN10 ....178 C7
Merivale TN35 ....137 A6
Merlin Cl BN3 ....163 D8
Merlin Ct BN27 ....152 E7
Merlin Way RH19 ....2 A3
Merlynn 12 BN2 .....185 A2
Mermaid Pas TN31 ...93 B5
Mermaid St TN31 .....93 B5
Merrimac Ho 1 TN40 ..157 E4
Merrimede Cl TN38 ..159 A7

Merriments La TN18, TN19 .45 D5
Merrion Cl TN4 ....8 B7
Merrion Way TN4 ......8 B7
Merston Cl BN2 ....165 E6
Merston Ct RH19 ......93 C5
Merton Ct 7 TN40 ....157 E4
Meryon Ct TN31 ......93 C5
Metcalfe Ave BN9 ....179 B8
Metropole Ct
12 Brighton BN1 .....163 E5
11 Eastbourne BN22 ..185 B3
Mewetts Ct BN20 ....173 B3
Mews RH19 ....10 F6
Mews Rd TN39 ....159 C6
Mews The Brighton BN1 ..142 E2
East Hoathly BN8 .....105 A5
Pembury TN2 ....9 C6
5 Royal Tunbridge Wells TN1 ...8 B3
Seaford BN25 ....181 B4
Meyners Cl BN3 ......141 C4
Michael Fields RH18 ..11 E2
Michael Tetley Hall
(Nursery Trng Coll,
Dr Barnardo's Home) TN2 8 D6
Michel Cl BN20 ......183 C1
Michel Dene Cl BN20 ..183 C1
Michel Dene Rd BN20 ..183 C1
Michel Gr BN21 ......184 E4
Michelbourne Cl RH15 ..72 E1
Michele Cl 1 TN38 ...136 B1
Michelham BN23 .....174 A4
Michelham Priory BN27 ..151 B7
Michelham Rd BN22 ...55 E1
Michelson Cl TN38 ...135 F4
Micklefield Sch BN25 ..181 B3
Middle Dr BN25 ......55 A6
Middle Field TN2 ......9 E8
Middle Furlong BN25 ..180 F3
Middle La TN21 ......83 E3
Middle Rd
Bells Yew Green TN3 ...18 A5
Brighton BN1 ....142 E1
Hastings TN35 ....137 D4
Shoreham-by-Sea BN43 ..161 B7
Middle Row 1 RH19 ...10 F8
Middle St Brighton BN1 ..189 A2
Falmer BN1 ....144 C6
9 Hastings TN34 .....159 F8
Portslade-by-Sea BN41 ..162 B6
Middle Street
Cty Prim Sch BN1 ....189 A2
Middle Way
Burgess Hill RH15 .....73 B3
Lewes BN7 ....123 A1
Middle Wlk TN2 ....8 E8
Middleham Cl BN8 ...124 C4
Middleham Way BN23 ..174 C4
Middlesex Ct 4 BN22 ..185 B4
Middlesex Rd TN40 ..157 D3
Middleton Ave BN3 ...162 D6
Middleton Dr BN23 ..185 E7
Middleton Rise BN1 ..143 E5
Middleway BN27 .....131 B5
Midfields Cl RH15 ....73 B3
Midfields Dr RH15 ...73 B3
Midfields Wlk RH15 ...73 B4
Midhurst Rd BN22 ...173 F2
Midhurst Rise BN1 ...143 B6
Midhurst Wlk BN3 ...141 F3
Midway Rd BN2 ......165 C8
Midway The TN4 ......7 D2
Mighell St BN2 ....189 C2
Milchester Ho BN20 ..188 B4
Milcote Ave BN3 .....162 F8
Mildenhall Dr TN37 ..136 B3
Mildmay Cl BN8 .....124 D6
Mildmay Rd BN7 .....123 A1
Mile End Cotts BN1 ..142 E4
Mile Oak Cres BN42 ..140 F1
Mile Oak Cty Prim Sch
BN41 ....140 F3
Mile Oak Gdns BN41 ..141 A1
Mile Oak Rd
Portslade-by-Sea BN41 ..140 F3
Southwick BN42 ......140 F1
Milestones TN21 ......82 B8
Milfoil Dr BN23 ......174 B3
Military Rd TN30,TN31 ..70 F3
Mill Brooks BN8 .....100 D7
Mill Cl East Grinstead RH19 ..10 E7
Friston BN20 ....183 A1
Hastings TN35 ....137 E4
Heathfield TN21 ......81 F7
Portslade-by-Sea BN41 ..141 C1
Ringmer BN8 ....124 E5
South Chailey BN8 ...100 D4
Staplecross TN32 .....65 E2
Wannock BN26 ....172 F4
Westfield TN35 ....114 E5
Mill Cnr TN31 ....67 A3
Mill Cotts RH19 ....10 E7
Mill Cres TN6 ....25 F3
Mill Dr Crowborough TN6 ..25 F3
Hove BN3 ....142 A3
Seaford BN25 ....181 A3
Mill Dro Seaford BN25 ..180 A5
Uckfield TN22 ....78 C6
Mill Gap Rd BN21 ...184 F4
Mill Gdns Heathfield TN21 ..82 A5
Ringmer BN8 ....124 D5
Mill Green Rd RH16 ..50 E7
Mill Hill Cl RH16 .....50 E7
Mill Ho BN26 ....173 A4
Mill La Barcombe BN8 ..101 D2
Clayton BN6,BN45 ...119 C2
Crowborough TN6 ....25 E2

Mill La continued
Dormansland RH7 . . . .**1** F8
East Hoathly BN8 . . . .**105** A5
Flackley Ash TN31 . . . .**68** F3
Goddards' Green BN6 . . . . . .**72** A3
Hastings TN35 . . . .**137** E5
Hellingly BN27 . . . .**129** A6
Hooe Common TN33 . . . . . .**132** F2
Mark Cross TN6 . . . .**28** A3
Portslade-by-Sea BN41 . . . . .**141** B1
Punnett's Town TN21 . . . . . .**83** D6
Rodmell BN7 . . . .**167** D8
Uckfield TN22 . . . .**78** C6
Westfield TN35 . . . .**114** E5
Mill Mead BN8 . . . .**124** E5
Mill Path BN8 . . . .**124** E5
Mill Pk RH15 . . . .**73** B3
Mill Race BN27 . . . .**97** E8
Mill Rd Brighton BN1 . . . . .**142** C6
Burgess Hill RH15 . . . .**73** B3
Eastbourne BN21 . . . .**184** E5
Hailsham BN27 . . . .**152** D6
Heathfield TN21 . . . .**81** F7
Lewes BN7 . . . .**123** E3
Ringmer BN8 . . . .**124** D5
Rye TN31 . . . .**93** C7
Southwick BN41 . . . .**162** B7
Winchelsea TN36 . . . .**117** E8
Mill Rd Ind Est BN41 . . . . . .**162** B7
Mill Rise Brighton BN1 . . . .**142** C5
Heathfield TN21 . . . .**82** A8
Robertsbridge TN32 . . . .**64** A3
Mill St BN1 . . . .**144** C7
Mill Stream Mdw RH16 . . . . .**50** D7
Mill View BN8 . . . .**124** C4
Mill View Cl BN24 . . . .**174** D6
Mill View Hospl BN3 . . . . . .**141** E1
Mill View Rd TN39 . . . .**157** B7
Mill Way
East Grinstead RH19 . . . . . .**10** E7
Wannock BN26 . . . .**172** E4
Mill Wood RH15 . . . .**73** B3
Milland Cl TN40 . . . .**157** E6
Milland Rd BN27 . . . .**129** B1
Millbank RH15 . . . .**73** B4
Millberg Rd BN25 . . . .**181** C4
Millbrook Bsns Pk TN6 . . . . .**38** D8
Millbrook Cl TN21 . . . .**107** A7
Millbrook Gdns BN20 . . . . .**184** B6
Millbrook Ind Est TN6 . . . . . .**38** D8
Millbrook Rd TN6 . . . .**26** A3
Millcroft BN1 . . . .**142** C5
Millcroft Ave BN42 . . . . . .**140** E1
Millcroft Gdns BN42 . . . . . .**140** E1
Millcross Rd BN41 . . . .**141** B1
Milldown Rd BN25 . . . .**180** F3
Miller's Hill TN35 . . . .**114** E6
Miller's Rd BN1 . . . .**142** E1
Millers Rd BN27 . . . .**152** A6
Millers Way RH15 . . . .**73** B4
Millfield Bexhill TN40 . . . . .**157** C4
Ninfield TN33 . . . .**133** A6
Millfield Cl Newick BN8 . . . . .**76** C7
Seaford BN25 . . . .**181** B4
Millfield Cotts BN2 . . . . . .**164** D4
Millfield Ct TN40 . . . .**157** C4
Millfield Rise TN40 . . . . . .**157** C4
Millfields BN26 . . . .**173** A7
Millfields Ct BN26 . . . .**173** A7
Milham Cl TN39 . . . .**156** F5
Millington Ct TN22 . . . .**78** C6
Millrace The BN26 . . . .**172** F4
Millstream Cl TN3 . . . .**5** D2
Millstream Gdns BN26 . . . .**172** F4
Milward Rd BN24 . . . .**175** C3
Millwood Cl TN22 . . . .**55** D4
Millwood La TN22 . . . .**55** C4
Millwood Rd TN39 . . . .**157** A8
Millyard Cres BN2 . . . .**165** D7
Milner Flats BN2 . . . .**189** C2
Milner Rd BN2 . . . .**143** D1
Milnthorpe Gdns BN20 . . . .**188** E8
Milnthorpe Rd
Eastbourne BN20 . . . .**188** E8
Hove BN3 . . . .**162** F8
Milton Cres
East Grinstead RH19 . . . . . .**10** C8
Eastbourne BN21 . . . .**184** C4
Milton Ct RH16 . . . .**50** D5
Milton Dr
Royal Tunbridge Wells TN2 . . . .**8** D7
Southwick BN42 . . . .**161** F8
Milton Rd Brighton BN2 . . .**189** C4
Eastbourne BN21 . . . .**184** C4
Haywards Heath RH16 . . . . . .**50** D6
Milton St BN24 . . . .**174** B7
Milward Cres TN34 . . . .**160** A4
Milward Ct BN43 . . . .**161** C4
Milward Rd TN34 . . . .**160** A5
Mimosa Cl BN26 . . . .**173** A7
Mimosa St BN1 . . . .**143** B3
Mimram Rd BN24 . . . .**174** A5
Mindleheim Ave RH19 . . . . . .**2** B2
Minnels The BN6 . . . .**98** A3
Minsted Sq TN39 . . . .**156** C2
Minster Cl BN26 . . . .**173** A4
Mint The TN31 . . . .**93** B5
Mistley Cl TN40 . . . .**158** A6
Mitchelldean BN10 . . . .**167** C1
Mitre Ho BN1 . . . .**163** E5
Mitten Rd TN40 . . . .**157** C4
Moat Croft Ct BN21 . . . . . .**184** E3
Moat Croft Rd BN21 . . . . . .**184** E4
Moat Farm TN2 . . . .**17** A7
Moat La Cowden TN8 . . . .**4** E7

Moat La continued
Waldron TN21 . . . .**80** D2
Westfield TN33 . . . .**114** B3
Moat Rd RH19 . . . .**1** E2
Mocatta Way RH15 . . . .**72** D5
Modena Rd BN3 . . . .**162** F7
Moira House Sch BN20 . . . .**188** D8
Molesey Ct TN22 . . . .**78** C7
Molesworth St BN3 . . . .**162** F8
Molyneux Almshouses TN4 . . .**7** B4
Molyneux Ct TN4 . . . .**7** F4
Molyneux Park Gdns TN4 . . . .**7** F4
Molyneux Park Rd TN4 . . . . . .**7** F4
Mona Rd BN22 . . . .**185** B5
Monarch Gdns
Eastbourne BN23 . . . .**174** F1
Seaford BN25 . . . .**181** A5
St Leonards TN37 . . . .**136** A5
Monarch Ho BN22 . . . .**185** E5
Monastery Gdns TN6 . . . . . .**39** B8
Monceux Rd
Eastbourne BN21 . . . .**184** C4
Herstmonceux BN27 . . . . . .**130** E6
Monckton Way BN7 . . . . . .**145** E6
Monger's Mead BN8 . . . . . .**101** E4
Monk Cl BN1 . . . .**143** E6
Monks La BN11 Lewes BN7 . .**146** C8
Newbury's TN5 . . . .**30** B8
Monks Way Lewes BN7 . . . .**123** C3
Northiam TN31 . . . .**67** B8
Monks' Wlk TN36 . . . .**117** E7
Monmouth St BN3 . . . .**163** B7
Monson Rd TN1 . . . .**8** B4
Monson Way TN1 . . . .**8** B4
Montacute Gdns TN2 . . . .**7** F2
Montacute Rd Lewes BN7 . .**146** A8
Royal Tunbridge Wells TN2 . . . .**8** A1
Montacute Way TN22 . . . . . .**78** D8
Montague Cl BN43 . . . .**161** D7
Montague Ct
Brighton BN2 . . . .**164** C4
Shoreham-by-Sea BN43 . . . .**161** D7
Montague Pl BN2 . . . .**164** C4
Montague St BN2 . . . .**164** C4
Montague Way BN24 . . . . . .**174** F5
Montana Ct TN38 . . . .**135** E6
Montargis Way TN6 . . . .**26** A1
Montefiore Rd BN3 . . . .**163** E7
Monteith Cl TN3 . . . .**7** A3
Monterey Cl TN39 . . . .**156** E3
Monterey Ct BN1 . . . .**142** E3
Monterey Gdns TN39 . . . . .**156** E3
Montes Hill RH16 . . . .**51** F8
Monteswood La
RH16,RH17 . . . .**52** B8
Montford Cl BN43 . . . .**161** D8
Montford Ct BN24 . . . .**174** F6
Montford Rd BN24 . . . .**174** F6
Montgomery Rd
Hastings TN35 . . . .**137** D5
Royal Tunbridge Wells TN4 . . . .**8** B7
Montgomery St BN3 . . . . . .**163** A7
Montpelier Cres BN1 . . . . . .**163** E6
Montpelier Lodge BN1 . . . .**163** E6
Montpelier Pl BN1 . . . .**163** E5
Montpelier St BN1 . . . .**163** E6
Montpelier Villas BN1 . . . . .**163** E6
Montreal Rd BN2 . . . .**189** C3
Montserrat TN39 . . . .**157** A2
Monument View BN2 . . . . . .**164** D4
Moon's La RH19, RH7, TN8 . . . .**2** E8
Moons Hill TN33 . . . .**133** B6
Moor Hall Dr TN33 . . . .**132** F6
Moor Hill TN18 . . . .**45** F8
Moor La Ashton Green BN8 **125** B3
Westfield TN35 . . . .**114** E3
Moor Pl RH19 . . . .**1** D2
Moor Rd TN35 . . . .**114** E3
Moor The TN18 . . . .**45** F8
Moore Pk BN27 . . . .**152** D7
Moore's La TN31 . . . .**90** E8
Moorhen Cl TN38 . . . .**158** E8
Moorhurst Rd TN38 . . . .**135** F5
Moorings The
East Grinstead RH19 . . . .**1** A3
Eastbourne BN20 . . . .**188** E8
Lewes BN7 . . . .**123** E1
Shoreham-by-Sea BN43 . . . .**161** C6
Moray Wlk BN27 . . . .**129** A2
Morecambe Rd BN1 . . . . . .**143** A6
Morestead BN10 . . . .**167** D1
Morgan Cl TN39 . . . .**157** B8
Morgay Wood La TN35 . . . .**115** C2
Morlais Pl TN36 . . . .**118** B6
Morlais Ridge TN36 . . . . . .**118** B6
Morland Dr TN3 . . . .**20** B5
Morlands Cl TN33 . . . .**133** B5
Morley Cl BN7 . . . .**146** B7
Morley St BN2 . . . .**189** C3
Morningside Cl BN25 . . . . .**180** F4
Mornington Cres BN2 . . . . .**162** D7
Mornington Mansions
BN3 . . . .**162** D7
Morris Rd BN7 . . . .**123** C4
Mortain Pk BN27 . . . .**152** D7
Mortain Rd BN24 . . . .**174** F4
Mortimer Gdns BN26 . . . . .**172** F4
Mortimer Rd
Eastbourne BN22 . . . .**185** A6
Hove BN3 . . . .**163** A8
Morton Rd RH19 . . . .**10** E7
Moscow Rd TN35 . . . .**137** C3
Motcombe Ct TN40 . . . .**157** D3
Motcombe Cty Inf Sch
BN21 . . . .**184** C5
Motcombe La BN21 . . . .**184** D4

Motcombe Rd BN21 . . . . . .**184** D4
Motte Field TN7 . . . .**13** E4
Mottins Hill TN6 . . . .**38** D8
Moulsecoomb
Cty Inf Sch BN2 . . . .**143** E3
Moulsecoomb
Cty Jun Sch BN2 . . . .**143** E3
Moulsecoomb Sta BN2 . . . .**143** D2
Moulsecoomb Way BN2 . . .**143** F4
Mount Caburn Cres
BN10 . . . .**167** C2
Mount Cl BN9 . . . .**179** F8
Mount Dr BN2 . . . .**177** D6
Mount Edgcumbe Rd TN4 . . .**8** A3
Mount Ephraim TN4 . . . .**8** A4
Mount Ephraim Ct TN4 . . . . .**7** F4
Mount Ephraim Rd TN1 . . . . .**8** A4
Mount Harry Rd BN7 . . . . .**123** A2
Mount Idol View TN39 . . . .**157** A8
Mount Joy TN33 . . . .**112** D5
Mount Pl BN7 . . . .**123** C1
Mount Pleasant
Blackboys TN22 . . . .**80** A6
Brighton BN2 . . . .**189** C2
Crowborough TN6 . . . .**38** B7
Hook Green TN3 . . . .**19** E6
Mount Pleasant BN8 . . . . . .**101** E6
Sparrow's Green TN5 . . . . . .**29** C5
St Leonards TN38 . . . .**159** C6
The Moor TN18 . . . .**45** F8
Uckfield TN22 . . . .**78** C6
Mount Pleasant Ave TN1 . . .**8** B3
Mount Pleasant Cres
TN34 . . . .**136** F1
Mount Pleasant La TN34 . . .**160** A6
Mount Pleasant La TN3 . . . . .**20** C4
Mount Pleasant Rd
Hastings TN34 . . . .**160** A6
Royal Tunbridge Wells TN1 . . . .**8** A3
Mount Rd
Eastbourne BN20 . . . .**188** F8
Hastings TN35 . . . .**160** C6
Newhaven BN9 . . . .**179** F8
Mount Sion TN1 . . . .**8** A2
Mount St Battle TN33 . . . . . .**112** D5
Lewes BN7 . . . .**146** C8
Mount The Hailsham BN27 . .**152** C6
St Leonards TN38 . . . .**159** B7
Mount View Terr BN27 . . . .**152** C6
Mount Zion Pl BN1 . . . .**189** A3
Mountain Ash Cl BN27 . . . .**152** A8
Mountbatten Cl TN35 . . . . .**137** D5
Mountbatten Ct BN3 . . . . . .**162** E8
Mountbatten Dr BN23 . . . . .**185** F7
Mountfield & Whatlington
CE Prim Sch
TN32 . . . .**87** D7
Mountfield Ct TN1 . . . .**8** B3
Mountfield Gdns TN1 . . . .**8** B3
Mountfield La TN32 . . . .**86** C8
Mountfield Rd
Eastbourne BN22 . . . .**173** F1
Lewes BN7 . . . .**146** D8
Royal Tunbridge Wells TN1 . . . .**8** B3
Mountfield Villas TN32 . . . . .**87** C5
Mountfields BN1 . . . .**143** C2
Mountney Bridge Bsns Pk
BN24 . . . .**174** F4
Mountney Dr BN24 . . . .**175** F7
Mountney Rd BN21 . . . .**184** C4
Mountreed TN20 . . . .**58** B7
Mowden Sch BN1 . . . .**142** D1
Moy Ave BN22 . . . .**185** B5
Moyne Cl BN3 . . . .**141** E1
Muirfield Ct RH16 . . . .**50** E4
Muirfield Rise TN38 . . . . . .**158** F8
Mulberry Cl Bexhill TN39 . . .**156** C4
Brighton BN1 . . . .**142** F3
Eastbourne BN22 . . . .**173** E3
Shoreham-by-Sea BN43 . . . .**140** D1
Mulberry Ct BN26 . . . .**173** A6
Mulberry La BN6 . . . .**98** D3
Mulberry Way TN21 . . . .**82** B5
Mulberry Wlk TN37 . . . .**136** D5
Munns Dr RH15 . . . .**73** B4
Munster Cotts BN8 . . . .**101** E4
Munster Gn BN8 . . . .**101** E4
Murray Ave BN9 . . . .**179** C7
Museum of Rural Life
TN32 . . . .**64** B4
Museum of Shops BN21 . . . .**185** A2
Musgrave Ave RH19 . . . .**10** E8
Mushroom Field RH17 . . . . .**145** E5
Muster Cl RH16 . . . .**50** D4
Muster Gn N RH16 . . . .**50** D4
Muster Gn S RH16 . . . .**50** D4
Mutton Hall Hill TN21 . . . . . .**82** B8
Mutton Hall La TN21 . . . .**82** B8
Mutton Hill RH7 . . . .**2** F7
Myrtle Cotts TN6 . . . .**25** F3
Myrtle Rd Crowborough TN6 **25** F1
Eastbourne BN22 . . . .**185** D6

N

Namrik Mews BN3 . . . .**163** A6
Nan Kemp's Grave BN7 . . . .**145** E6
Nan Tucks La TN22 . . . .**56** C2
Nanson Rd BN1 . . . .**143** D6
Naomi Cl BN20 . . . .**184** E1
Napier Ho BN2 . . . .**164** C7
Napier Rd
Royal Tunbridge Wells TN2 . . . .**8** D2
St Leonards TN38 . . . .**135** E4
Nash La RH17 . . . .**52** B4
Natal Rd BN2 . . . .**143** D1

Neale Cl RH19 . . . .**1** B3
Neath Rd TN29 . . . .**96** A2
Neaves La BN8 . . . .**125** A5
Neill's Cl BN9 . . . .**179** C7
Neills Rd BN3 . . . .**19** D2
Neilson Ct TN34 . . . .**136** D1
Nellington Ct TN4 . . . .**7** B4
Nellington Rd TN3, TN4 . . . . .**7** B4
Nelson Dr BN23 . . . .**185** E6
Nelson Ho TN39 . . . .**156** E4
Nelson Pl BN2 . . . .**189** C3
Nelson Rd Hastings TN35 . .**160** A5
Nelson Row BN2 . . . .**189** C2
Neptune Ct BN2 . . . .**164** F3
Nesbitt Rd BN2 . . . .**143** D1
Nestor Ct BN1 . . . .**163** E8
Nether La TN22 . . . .**35** C3
Netherfield Ave BN23 . . . . .**174** F2
Netherfield CE Prim Sch
TN33 . . . .**86** C2
Netherfield Gn BN2 . . . . . .**165** F8
Netherfield Hill TN33 . . . . .**112** B7
Netherfield Hill Cotts
TN33 . . . .**112** B7
Netherfield Rd TN33 . . . . . .**111** F8
Netherfield Way TN33 . . . . . .**86** D2
Netherwood Cl TN33 . . . . .**136** F5
Nettleton Cl BN1 . . . .**143** B1
Nevill Ave
Eastbourne BN22 . . . .**173** E1
Hove BN3 . . . .**141** F1
Nevill Cl
Crowborough Warren TN6 . . .**37** C8
Hove BN3 . . . .**142** A2
Nevill Cotts BN6 . . . .**98** D2
Nevill Cres BN7 . . . .**123** A1
Nevill Ct
Crowborough Warren TN6 . . .**37** C8
Hove BN3 . . . .**142** A1
Nevill Gate TN2 . . . .**8** B1
Nevill Gdns BN3 . . . .**142** A2
Nevill Gn BN22 . . . .**55** D1
Nevill Lodge TN2 . . . .**8** C4
Nevill Pk TN4 . . . .**7** E3
Nevill Pl BN3 . . . .**142** A2
Nevill Rd
Crowborough TN6 . . . .**25** F3
Hove BN3 . . . .**142** A2
Lewes BN7 . . . .**123** A2
Rottingdean BN2 . . . .**165** F1
Uckfield TN22 . . . .**55** D1
Nevill Ridge TN4 . . . .**7** D3
Nevill St TN2 . . . .**8** A2
Nevill Terr
Crowborough TN6 . . . .**25** F3
Royal Tunbridge Wells TN2 . . . .**7** F2
Nevill Way BN3 . . . .**142** A2
Neville Rd
Eastbourne BN22 . . . .**185** B4
Peacehaven BN10 . . . .**178** D6
New Barn Cl
Hailsham BN27 . . . .**152** C6
Portslade-by-Sea BN41 . . . .**141** B4
Shoreham-by-Sea BN43 . . . .**140** B1
New Barn La BN2 . . . .**78** C5
New Barn Rd
Rottingdean BN2 . . . .**165** F3
Shoreham-by-Sea BN43 . . . .**140** B1
New Church Rd BN3 . . . . . .**162** E7
New Coastguards Cotts
BN25 . . . .**180** C4
New College Cl BN23 . . . . .**174** C4
New Cotts
Crowborough TN6 . . . .**38** C8
Eastbourne BN20 . . . .**188** D8
Five Ashes TN20 . . . .**58** B6
Scaynes Hill RH17 . . . .**51** F1
New Cut Mountfield TN32 . . . .**87** C5
Westfield TN35 . . . .**114** E4
New Dorset St BN1 . . . .**189** A3
New England Ho BN1 . . . . .**189** B4
New England La Rye TN31 . .**93** C8
Sedlescombe TN33 . . . .**113** F6
New England Rd
Brighton BN1 . . . .**189** A4
Haywards Heath RH16 . . . . . .**50** F4
Royal Tunbridge Wells TN4 . . . .**8** A7
New England Rise BN1 . . . .**141** A4
New England St BN1 . . . . . .**189** B4
New Farthingdale RH7 . . . . . .**2** B8
New Forest Lodge TN6 . . . . .**37** C8
New Langney Ct BN23 . . . . .**174** E1
New Lydd Rd TN31 . . . .**94** E2
New Moorsite TN35 . . . .**114** F3
New Park Ave TN40 . . . .**157** C4
New Pl Eastbourne BN21 . . .**184** D3
Uckfield TN22 . . . .**78** C5
New Pond Hill TN21 . . . .**81** D6
New Rd Brighton BN1 . . . . .**189** B2
Crowborough TN6 . . . .**25** F3
Eastbourne BN22 . . . .**185** B4
Fairlight TN35 . . . .**138** C4
Hailsham BN27 . . . .**129** C4
Hastings TN35 . . . .**160** D6
Keymer BN6 . . . .**98** B2
Lewes BN7 . . . .**123** C1
Mill Corner TN31 . . . .**67** B3
Polegate BN26 . . . .**173** B6
Ringmer BN8 . . . .**124** D3
Rotherfield TN6 . . . .**39** C8
Rye TN31 . . . .**93** D6
Saint's Hill TN11 . . . .**6** A8
South Heighton BN9 . . . . . .**168** D1
Uckfield TN22 . . . .**78** D3
New Steine BN2 . . . .**189** C1
New Steine Mews BN2 . . . .**189** C2
New Sussex Hospl BN3 . . . .**163** E6

New Upperton Rd
BN21 . . . .**184** E4
New Way La BN6 . . . .**97** B2
New Winchelsea Rd
TN31, TN36 . . . .**93** B3
Newark Pl BN2 . . . .**189** C3
Newbury Cotts TN5 . . . .**30** B8
Newbury La TN5 . . . .**30** C8
Newcomen Rd TN4 . . . .**8** A5
Newdigate Rd TN40 . . . . . .**157** D3
Newells Cl BN2 . . . .**144** E1
Newfield La BN9 . . . .**179** C7
Newfield Rd BN9 . . . .**179** C7
Newgate Rd TN37 . . . .**136** C1
Newhaven Harbour Sta
BN9 . . . .**179** D6
Newhaven Hts BN9 . . . .**179** C5
Newhaven Local &
Maritime Mus BN9 . . . . . .**168** D1
Newhaven Marine Sta
BN9 . . . .**179** E6
Newhaven Rd BN25 . . . . . .**180** B5
Newhaven Sq BN9 . . . .**179** D7
Newhaven St BN2 . . . .**189** C3
Newhaven Town Sta
BN9 . . . .**179** D8
Newhaven Wlk TN38 . . . . . .**136** A3
Newick CE Prim Sch BN8 . . .**76** C6
Newick Cl BN25 . . . .**181** C2
Newick Dr BN8 . . . .**76** C7
Newick Hill BN8 . . . .**76** C7
Newick House Sch RH15 . . . .**73** C1
Newick La TN20, TN21 . . . . .**59** C5
Newick Rd Brighton BN1 . . .**143** E4
Eastbourne BN20 . . . .**184** C6
Newington Ct TN5 . . . .**31** E1
Newlands TN3 . . . .**7** A3
Newlands Ave TN39 . . . . . .**157** B5
Newlands Cl
Hastings TN34 . . . .**136** C5
Keymer BN6 . . . .**98** B3
Newlands Cres RH19 . . . .**1** D2
Newlands Manor Sch
(Senior) BN25 . . . .**181** A4
Newlands Park Way BN26 . . .**76** C2
Newlands Pl RH18 . . . .**11** F3
Newlands Rd
Rottingdean BN2 . . . .**177** A5
Royal Tunbridge Wells TN4 . . . .**8** B7
Newlands Rise TN4 . . . .**8** A6
Newlands Sch BN25 . . . . . .**181** A4
Newlands Way TN4 . . . .**8** B7
Newmans Way TN35 . . . . . .**137** C6
Newmarket Rd BN2 . . . . . .**164** C8
Newmarket Terr BN2 . . . . .**164** C8
Newnham Rd TN21 . . . .**82** A6
Newnham Way TN21 . . . . . .**82** A7
Newport Rd RH15 . . . .**72** F3
Newport St BN2 . . . .**189** C4
Newstead BN1 . . . .**189** A4
Newtimber Dr BN41 . . . . . .**141** A1
Newton Ave RH19 . . . .**10** F6
Newton Cl RH16 . . . .**51** B7
Newton Pk BN27 . . . .**152** D7
Newton Rd Lewes BN7 . . . .**123** B2
Lindfield RH16 . . . .**51** C7
Peacehaven BN10 . . . .**178** C7
Royal Tunbridge Wells TN1 . . . .**8** A4
Newton Willows TN3 . . . . . .**15** C7
Newton's Hill TN7 . . . .**13** D3
Newtown Rd BN3 . . . .**163** B8
Nicholson Cl
East Grinstead RH19 . . . . . .**10** F6
Eastbourne BN23 . . . .**174** C2
Nicolson Dr BN43 . . . .**161** A8
Nightingale Cl
East Grinstead RH19 . . . . . .**10** F6
Eastbourne BN23 . . . .**174** C2
Nightingale Cotts TN35 . . . .**114** F4
Nightingale La RH15 . . . . . .**97** F8
Nightingale Rise TN22 . . . . . .**78** D4
Nightingales The
Royal Tunbridge Wells TN4 . . . .**8** A5
Uckfield TN22 . . . .**78** E5
Nile St BN1 . . . .**189** B2
Ninfield CE Prim Sch
TN33 . . . .**133** B5
Ninfield Pl BN2 . . . .**164** C2
Ninfield Rd TN39 . . . .**157** B7
Nizells Ave BN3 . . . .**163** E7
Noahs Ark La RH16 . . . .**51** C7
Noble Ct BN3 . . . .**162** E7
Nodes La BN27 . . . .**129** F4
Noel Gn RH15 . . . .**73** B4
Noel Rise RH15 . . . .**73** B4
Nolan Rd BN2 . . . .**165** C7
Nook Cl TN35 . . . .**137** D3
Nook The TN22 . . . .**78** D4
Norbury Cl TN6 . . . .**25** E4
Nore Rd BN9 . . . .**179** B6
Norfolk Bldgs BN1 . . . .**163** E5
Norfolk Cl TN39 . . . .**157** B7
Norfolk Ct
Brighton BN1 . . . .**163** E5
Eastbourne BN22 . . . .**185** C4
Norfolk Dr TN38 . . . .**135** F5
Norfolk Ho BN2 . . . .**159** C7
Norfolk Mews BN1 . . . .**163** E5
Norfolk Pl BN1 . . . .**163** E5
Norfolk Rd Hove BN1 . . . . .**163** E5
Royal Tunbridge Wells TN1 . . . .**8** B2
Norfolk Sq BN1 . . . .**163** E5
Norfolk St BN1 . . . .**163** E5
Norfolk Terr BN1 . . . .**163** E6
Norfolk Way TN22 . . . .**78** C8
Norlington Ct BN8 . . . .**124** D6
Norlington Fields BN8 . . . . .**124** D6
Norlington La BN8 . . . .**124** D7
Norman Cl Battle TN33 . . . .**112** F4

Norman Cl *continued*
Seaford BN25 . . . .**180** B6
Norman Ct 6 TN34 . . . .**159** E7
Norman Rd
Burgess Hill RH15 . . . .**73** A3
Hove BN3 . . . .**162** E6
Newhaven BN9 . . . .**179** C7
Pevensey Bay BN24 . . . . . .**175** D4
Royal Tunbridge Wells TN1 . . . .**8** B5
St Leonards TN37 . . . .**159** C6
Normandale TN39 . . . .**156** F3
Normandale Ho TN39 . . . . .**156** F3
Normandy Cl 7 RH19 . . . . . .**10** F8
Normandy Ct 2 TN39 . . . . .**157** B3
Normandy Ho 3 BN3 . . . . .**163** C6
Normandy Rd TN34 . . . . . .**136** C3
Normanhurst 9 BN2 . . . . .**189** C3
Normans TN39 . . . .**156** F3
Normans' Bay Sta BN24 . .**176** C8
Normansal Cl BN25 . . . . . .**181** A6
Normansal Park Ave
BN25 . . . .**181** A6
Normansland TN22 . . . .**36** B2
Normanton St 2 BN2 . . . . .**164** C7
Norstead Gdns TN4 . . . .**8** B7
North Ave BN20 . . . .**184** B5
North Bank BN6 . . . .**97** E4
North Barnes La BN7 . . . . .**100** A5
North Beeches Rd TN6 . . . . .**26** A2
North Camp La BN25 . . . . .**180** F5
North Cl Polegate BN26 . . . .**173** B7
Portslade-by-Sea BN41 . . . .**141** A2
North Cnr TN21 . . . .**107** C4
North Common Rd
BN8, RH17 . . . .**74** E5
North Crescent Ind Est
BN27 . . . .**152** A7
North Ct Hassocks BN6 . . . . .**97** E4
Lewes BN7 . . . .**123** E1
North Dr BN2 . . . .**164** C6
North End BN6 . . . .**98** D4
North Farm Cotts BN41 . . .**141** A2
North Farm Rd TN2 . . . .**8** C8
North Gdns BN1 . . . .**189** A3
North Heath Cl BN27 . . . . .**129** C2
North La Lidham Hill TN35 . .**115** F1
Portslade-by-Sea BN41 . . . .**141** A3
North Pl BN1 . . . .**189** B2
North Point 1 BN43 . . . . . .**161** A6
North Quay BN9 . . . .**179** D8
North Rd Alfriston BN26 . . .**170** F3
Bexhill TN39 . . . .**157** C7
Bodle Street Green BN27 . . .**109** C2
Brighton BN1 . . . .**189** B3
Brighton, Preston BN1 . . . . .**142** E1
Haywards Heath RH16 . . . . .**51** A4
Pevensey Bay BN24 . . . . . .**175** D5
Portslade-by-Sea BN41 . . . .**141** A2
Ringmer BN8 . . . .**124** D6
St Leonards TN37 . . . .**136** C1
North Road Cotts BN8 . . . .**124** D6
North Row TN22 . . . .**78** C6
North Salts TN31 . . . .**93** C6
North St Alfriston BN26 . . . .**171** A3
Brighton BN1 . . . .**189** B2
Cowden TN8 . . . .**4** A6
Eastbourne BN21 . . . .**185** B3
Hailsham BN27 . . . .**152** B8
Hellingly BN27 . . . .**129** A7
Lewes BN7 . . . .**123** D2
Lower Horsebridge BN27 . . .**107** A2
Lower Horsebridge BN27 . . .**128** F4
Mayfield TN20 . . . .**40** B3
Portslade-by-Sea BN41 . . . .**162** C7
Punnett's Town TN21 . . . . . .**83** D6
Roser's Cross TN21 . . . .**80** F5
Rotherfield TN6 . . . .**39** B8
Royal Tunbridge Wells TN2 . . . .**8** C1
St Leonards TN38 . . . .**159** C7
Winchelsea TN36 . . . .**117** E8
North Terr TN34 . . . .**160** C6
North Trade Rd TN33 . . . . .**112** B4
North Way Lewes BN7 . . . . .**123** A4
Newhaven BN9 . . . .**179** C8
Seaford BN25 . . . .**180** F5
North–South Rd BN1 . . . . .**144** B7
Northampton Way 1
TN38 . . . .**136** A4
Northbourne Rd BN22 . . . .**185** C6
Northbridge St TN32 . . . . . .**64** B5
Northcliffe Cl BN25 . . . . . .**180** F4
Northcote La BN10 . . . .**167** A1
Northdown Cl BN9 . . . .**179** C6
Northdown Rd BN9 . . . . . .**179** B6
Northdown Terr RH19 . . . . . .**1** D3
Northease Cl BN3 . . . .**141** D2
Northease Dr BN3 . . . .**141** E3
Northease Gdns BN3 . . . . .**141** E3
Northease Wall BN7 . . . . . .**146** D3
Northerlea BN41 . . . .**141** A1
Northern Ave BN26 . . . . . .**173** B7
Northfield BN26 . . . .**172** F5
Northfield Cl BN25 . . . .**180** F5
Northfield Cotts TN22 . . . .**102** D8
Northfield Rise Hove BN3 **141** D4
Rottingdean BN2 . . . .**177** A6
Northfield Way BN1 . . . . . .**143** A4
Northfields TN3 . . . .**7** A8
Northfields Bsns Pk
BN27 . . . .**128** A4
Northgate Cl BN2 . . . .**165** F2
Northiam CE Prim Sch
TN31 . . . .**87** B5
Northiam Rd
Broad Oak TN31 . . . .**90** A6
Eastbourne BN20, BN21 . . .**184** C4
Northiam Rise TN38 . . . . . .**135** D2
Northiam Sta TN31 . . . .**48** C2

Northlands Ave RH16 . . . . . .**51** B4
Northlands Cotts TN32 . . . .**46** C1
Northlands Wood
Cty Prim Sch RH16 . . . . . .**51** B4
Northridge TN31 . . . .**67** A7
Northumberland Ct
BN22 . . . .**174** A2
Northway RH15 . . . .**73** C4
Northwood Ave BN2 . . . . . .**177** E5
Norton Cl BN3 . . . .**163** B6
Norton Dr BN2 . . . .**144** E1
Norton Rd Hove BN3 . . . . . .**163** B6
Newhaven BN9 . . . .**179** E7
Norton Terr BN9 . . . .**179** E7
Norton Wall BN7 . . . .**146** C4
Norway Rd BN22 . . . .**185** D6
Norway St BN41 . . . .**162** C7
Norwich Cl BN2 . . . .**144** A4
Norwich Cres BN2 . . . .**143** F2
Norwich Dr BN2 . . . .**144** A2
Norwich House Rd BN1 . . .**144** B7
Norwood BN1 . . . .**143** A4
Nottidge Rd TN4 . . . .**7** D1
Novington La BN7 . . . .**100** A3
Nunnery La TN11 . . . .**5** F8
Nunnery Stables BN7 . . . .**123** B1
Nursery Cl Hailsham BN27 **152** C8
Haywards Heath RH16 . . . . .**50** D5
Polegate BN26 . . . .**173** B6
Portslade-by-Sea BN41 . . . .**162** A6
Shoreham-by-Sea BN43 . . .**161** B8
Union Street TN5 . . . .**32** B3
Nursery Field TN22 . . . .**56** C4
Nursery La
Maresfield Park TN22 . . . . . .**55** B7
Nutley TN22 . . . .**35** C4
Uckfield TN22 . . . .**78** D4
Waldron Down TN21, TN22 . .**80** E8
Windmill Hill BN27 . . . .**131** B5
Nursery Path BN27 . . . . . .**152** B6
Nursery Rd TN4 . . . .**8** B8
Nursery The RH15 . . . .**73** C4
Nursery Way TN21 . . . .**81** E7
Nutbourne Cl BN23 . . . . . .**174** E2
Nuthatch Rd BN23 . . . .**174** C2
Nuthurst Cl BN2 . . . .**164** F6
Nuthurst Pl BN2 . . . .**164** F5
Nutley Ave BN2 . . . .**164** F6
Nutley CE Prim Sch TN22 **35** C5
Nutley Cl Hove BN3 . . . .**141** F3
Rye TN31 . . . .**93** A6
Nutley Mill Rd BN24 . . . . . .**174** B5
Nye Cl TN6 . . . .**25** F1
Nye La Ditchling BN6 . . . . . .**98** D1
Westmeston BN6 . . . .**120** D8
Nye Rd RH15 . . . .**73** C3
Nyetimber Hill BN2 . . . . . .**143** E2
Nym Cl BN8 . . . .**100** E7

O

Oak Bank RH16 . . . .**50** F7
Oak Cl BN1 . . . .**142** E3
Oak Croft RH19 . . . .**11** A8
Oak Field The TN35 . . . . . .**116** F1
Oak Hall Pk RH15 . . . .**73** B1
Oak Ho TN2 . . . .**8** C7
Oak Pas 8 TN34 . . . .**160** A4
Oak Rd Bexhill TN40 . . . . . .**157** C5
Royal Tunbridge Wells TN2 . . . .**8** D7
Oak Terr TN31 . . . .**67** B6
Oak Tree Cl
Eastbourne BN23 . . . .**174** C4
Royal Tunbridge Wells TN1 . . . .**8** A1
Oak Tree Cotts
Burgess Hill RH15 . . . .**73** B3
Danehill RH17 . . . .**34** A4
Oak Tree Ct TN22 . . . .**78** D8
Oak Tree La BN23 . . . .**174** C4
Oak Tree Way BN27 . . . . . .**129** C2
Oakapple Rd BN42 . . . .**140** E1
Oakdale Rd TN4 . . . .**7** F4
Oakdene Brighton BN2 . . . .**143** F4
Haywards Heath RH16 . . . . .**50** D5
Oakdene Ave BN41 . . . . . .**140** E3
Oakdene Cl BN41 . . . .**140** E3
Oakdene Cres BN41 . . . . . .**140** E3
Oakdene Gdns BN41 . . . . .**140** E3
Oakdene Rise BN41 . . . . . .**140** E4
Oakdene Way BN41 . . . . . .**140** E4
Oakdown Ct TN19 . . . .**61** A4
Oakenfield RH15 . . . .**73** A5
Oakfield Cl RH16 . . . .**51** A7
Oakfield Court Rd TN2 . . . . .**8** C3
Oakfield Rd TN35 . . . .**137** C3
Oakfield The TN31 . . . .**90** B5
Oakfield Way Bexhill TN39 **156** C6
East Grinstead RH19 . . . .**1** F3
Oakhill Cotts TN31 . . . .**68** C4
Oakhill Dr TN31 . . . .**90** B5
Oakhurst RH16 . . . .**50** D8
Oakhurst Cl TN34 . . . .**136** E5
Oakhurst Dr TN6 . . . .**26** A3
Oakhurst Gdns RH19 . . . . . .**1** C2
Oakhurst La RH16 . . . .**50** D8
Oakhurst Rd TN33 . . . .**112** D7
Oakland Dr TN32 . . . .**63** D4
Oakland Villas TN3 . . . .**7** F4
Oaklands Crowborough TN6 **26** B1
 5 Eastbourne BN21 . . . . .**185** A4
South Chailey BN8 . . . .**100** C7
Westham BN24 . . . .**174** D6
Oaklands Ave BN2 . . . .**177** D5
Oaklands Cl BN26 . . . .**173** B6
Oaklands Rd
Groombridge TN3 . . . .**15** B6

Oaklands Rd *continued*
Haywards Heath RH16 . . . . .**50** D5
Oaklands Way BN27 . . . . . .**152** A6
Oaklea Cl TN37 . . . .**136** C4
Oaklea Ct TN7 . . . .**13** D4
Oaklea Way TN22 . . . .**78** C7
Oakleaf Cl BN26 . . . .**173** A7
Oakleaf Dr BN26 . . . .**173** A7
Oakleigh Dr TN21 . . . .**82** B6
Oakleigh Rd TN39 . . . .**156** C4
Oakley Cl RH19 . . . .**11** B7
Oakley Cotts RH19 . . . .**11** C7
Oakley Ct TN22 . . . .**78** D6
Oakmead Rd RH15 . . . .**72** F1
Oakmede Way BN8 . . . .**124** D5
Oakroyd Cl RH15 . . . .**73** D5
Oaks Forstal TN18 . . . .**47** C5
Oaks The Burgess Hill RH15 **72** D4
East Grinstead RH19 . . . . . .**11** B8
Haywards Heath RH16 . . . . .**51** A4
Haywards Heath RH16 . . . . .**51** C4
Heathfield TN21 . . . .**82** B6
St Leonards TN37 . . . .**136** D5
Oaktree BN8 . . . .**101** E4
Oakwood RH16 . . . .**50** D4
Oakwood Ave TN39 . . . .**157** B7
Oakwood Cl
Burgess Hill RH15 . . . .**73** B2
Hastings TN34 . . . .**136** F3
Oakwood Dr TN22 . . . .**78** E8
Oakwood Pk
Forest Row RH18 . . . .**11** F2
Nutley TN22 . . . .**35** C4
Oakwood Rd
Burgess Hill RH15 . . . .**73** B2
Haywards Heath RH16 . . . . .**50** D4
Oakwood Rise TN2 . . . .**8** E7
Oast Cl TN2 . . . .**8** D7
Oast House Dr TN31 . . . .**92** F4
Oast House Field TN36 . . . .**116** F6
Oast House Rd TN36 . . . . . .**116** F6
Oasthouse Cl TN37 . . . .**136** D5
Oathall Ave RH16 . . . .**50** F6
Oathall Com Coll RH16 . . . .**50** F6
Oathall Rd RH16 . . . .**50** E5
Oban Rd TN37 . . . .**136** B3
Observatory View BN27 . . .**152** D7
Oceania 4 TN39 . . . .**157** B3
Ochiltree Cl TN34 . . . .**137** A4
Ochiltree Rd TN34 . . . .**137** A4
Ockenden Way BN6 . . . .**97** E3
Ockley Hill BN6, RH15 . . . . .**98** B6
Ockley La Burgess Hill RH15 **98** B3
Keymer BN6 . . . .**98** B4
Ockley Way BN6 . . . .**98** A5
Ocklynge Ave 1 BN21 . . . .**184** D4
Ocklynge Cl TN39 . . . .**156** C5
Ocklynge Cty Jun Sch
BN21 . . . .**184** C6
Ocklynge Rd BN21 . . . .**184** D4
Ockman La TN31 . . . .**93** C5
Octagon The BN2 . . . .**164** F3
Offa Ct TN40 . . . .**157** C4
Offa Rd TN35 . . . .**137** D3
Offham Cl
Eastbourne BN23 . . . .**173** F4
Seaford BN25 . . . .**180** F5
Offham Ct 3 BN25 . . . .**180** C4
Offham Rd BN7 . . . .**123** B2
Okehurst Rd BN21 . . . .**184** C3
Old Barn Cl BN20 . . . .**173** B1
Old Barn Ct RH16 . . . .**50** D2
Old Barn Way BN42 . . . . . .**162** A7
Old Ben Homes BN25 . . . . .**180** F4
Old Boat Cnr BN1 . . . .**143** D8
Old Boat Wlk BN1 . . . .**143** B7
Old Brickyard TN31 . . . .**93** A5
Old Camp Rd BN20 . . . .**184** C2
Old Church Rd Pembury TN2 **9** D8
St Leonards TN38 . . . .**159** D7
Old Clergy Ho (NT) BN26 **171** A2
Old Coastguard Cotts
BN9 . . . .**179** D6
Old Coastguards TN35 . . . .**139** C7
Old Convent The RH19 . . . . .**1** E2
Old Court Cl BN1 . . . .**142** F4
Old Dr BN26 . . . .**172** F6
Old Drove BN23 . . . .**174** C3
Old Farm Rd Bexhill TN39 **157** B6
Brighton BN1 . . . .**142** F5
Old Fire Station The 5
BN22 . . . .**185** A3
Old Foord Cl BN8 . . . .**100** D7
Old Forest La TN36 . . . .**38** E8
Old Forewood La TN33 . . . .**134** F7
Old Forge La TN22 . . . .**36** A1
Old Fort Rd BN43 . . . .**161** B6
Old Gardens Cl TN2 . . . .**17** B8
Old Ghyll Rd TN21 . . . .**82** A5
Old Harrow Rd TN37 . . . . .**136** B4
Old Heath Cl BN4 . . . .**50** D8
Old Hop Garden The TN31 **69** C2
Old House Gdns TN34 . . . .**136** F4
Old House La TN3 . . . .**6** C7
Old Humphrey Ave 1
TN34 . . . .**160** B4
Old La Crowborough,
Crowborough Warren TN6 . . .**25** D3
Crowborough,
Poundfield TN6 . . . .**26** B1
Mayfield TN20 . . . .**40** A2
Old London Rd
Brighton BN1 . . . .**142** E6
Hastings TN34, TN35 . . . . .**160** C6
Old Lydd Rd TN31 . . . .**94** E2
Old Malling Way BN7 . . . . .**123** C3

Old Manor Cl TN40 . . . .**157** D4
Old Mansion Cl BN20 . . . . .**184** A8
Old Mill Cl Brighton BN1 . . .**142** E5
Hailsham BN27 . . . .**129** A3
Southwick BN41 . . . .**162** A7
Old Mill Ct TN6 . . . .**25** E2
Old Mill La BN26 . . . .**172** F4
Old Mill Pk TN39 . . . .**157** A6
Old Mill Wlk TN33 . . . .**112** C5
Old Mint House BN24 . . . . .**175** B6
Old Motcombe Mews
BN21 . . . .**184** D4
Old Orch TN18 . . . .**47** B5
Old Orchard Pl BN27 . . . . .**152** B7
Old Orchard Rd BN21 . . . . .**184** F2
Old Parish La BN2 . . . .**165** B2
Old Park Cl TN17 . . . .**50** A6
Old Patcham Mews BN1 . . .**142** E6
Old Place Ct BN2 . . . .**165** F1
Old Rd East Grinstead RH19 . . .**1** F1
Magham Down BN27 . . . . .**130** A4
Old Rectory Gdns BN42 . . .**161** D8
Old Riding School The
TN3 . . . .**15** B2
Old River Way TN36 . . . . . .**118** B7
Old Roar Rd TN37 . . . .**136** C5
Old School Cl BN8 . . . .**124** E6
Old School Cotts BN7 . . . . . .**99** E5
Old School Ho BN20 . . . . . .**131** B5
Old School La BN26 . . . . . .**173** A4
Old School Pl RH15 . . . .**72** F2
Old Shoreham Rd
Portslade-by-Sea
BN3, BN41 . . . .**162** C8
Southwick BN42 . . . .**140** E1
Old Station Rd TN5 . . . .**29** E6
Old Steine BN1, BN2 . . . . . .**189** B2
Old Swan La BN27 . . . .**152** D6
Old Timbers La TN22 . . . . . .**78** C6
Old Top Rd TN35 . . . .**137** D4
Old Viaduct Ct 10 BN2 . . . .**164** C8
Old Wardsdown TN5 . . . . . .**32** B3
Old Wickham La RH16 . . . . .**50** E7
Old Willingdon Rd BN20 .**183** B2
Old Wish Rd BN21 . . . .**184** F1
Old World Cotts TN31 . . . . .**94** D2
Oldaker Rd BN8 . . . .**76** D7
Olde Place Mews BN2 . . . . .**165** F1
Oldfield Ave BN20 . . . .**173** A4
Oldfield Cres
Hailsham BN27 . . . .**129** B1
Southwick BN42 . . . .**161** E8
Oldfield Rd BN20 . . . .**173** A4
Oldlands Ave BN6 . . . .**98** A4
Oldlands Hall TN22 . . . .**36** D4
Oldlands Hill TN22 . . . .**36** C2
Olive Rd BN3 . . . .**162** D8
Oliver Cl Brighton BN2 . . . .**164** C5
Crowborough TN6 . . . .**26** A1
Hastings TN34 . . . .**159** E7
Oliver Ho 9 BN3 . . . .**163** B5
Olives Mdw TN22 . . . .**78** D9
Onslow Rd BN3 . . . .**142** C2
Open Mkt The BN1 . . . .**189** A1
Orange Row BN1 . . . .**189** B2
Orchard Bsns Ctr TN2 . . . . . .**8** D8
Orchard Cl Fairwarp TN22 . .**36** B2
Hastings TN34 . . . .**136** F2
Haywards Heath RH16 . . . . .**50** D8
Royal Tunbridge Wells TN2 . . . .**8** D6
Scaynes Hill RH17 . . . .**51** F3
Southwick BN42 . . . .**161** F8
Orchard Cnr RH16 . . . .**51** B5
Orchard Cotts TN6 . . . .**39** B8
Orchard Gdns BN3 . . . .**142** B1
Orchard Gr TN1 . . . .**8** B5
Orchard La Ditchling BN6 . . .**98** D4
Hassocks BN6 . . . .**97** F3
Nutley TN22 . . . .**35** C4
Orchard Mews 2 BN9 . . . .**168** E2
Orchard Par BN20 . . . .**173** A3
Orchard Rd Bexhill TN40 . . .**157** C6
Burgess Hill RH15 . . . .**72** E3
Hove BN3 . . . .**142** B1
Lewes BN7 . . . .**123** E2
Orchard Rise TN3 . . . .**15** B7
Orchard The
Broad Oak TN31 . . . .**90** B4
Etchingham TN19 . . . .**44** C1
Hassocks BN6 . . . .**97** F3
Nutley TN22 . . . .**35** C4
Orchard Way
Burgess Hill RH15 . . . .**72** F3
East Grinstead RH19 . . . .**1** E1
Haywards Heath RH16 . . . . .**50** D8
Peasmarsh TN31 . . . .**69** C1
Sedlescombe TN33 . . . .**88** E1
Orchards Sh Ctr 11 RH16 . .**50** E4
Orchards The BN23 . . . .**143** E3
Orchid Cl BN23 . . . .**174** B3
Orchid Pk RH16 . . . .**51** C4
Orchid View BN1 . . . .**143** C6
Orchidhurst TN2 . . . .**8** D7
Ore Pl TN34 . . . .**137** A5
Ore Sta TN34 . . . .**160** A6
Oriental Pl BN1 . . . .**163** E5
Orion Cl BN27 . . . .**152** D7
Orion Par BN6 . . . .**97** F3
Orkney Cl BN20 . . . .**184** B6
Ormerod Ave TN38 . . . .**136** A4
Ormerod Ct RH16 . . . .**50** E5
Orpen Rd BN3 . . . .**142** D1
Orwell Cl BN24 . . . .**174** B5
Osbern Cl TN39 . . . .**156** C3
Osborne Ct TN34 . . . .**136** E2
Osborne Ct 7 BN43 . . . . . .**161** C4
Osborne Hill TN6 . . . .**38** C8
Osborne Rd Brighton BN1 . .**143** A2

Osborne Rd *continued*
Crowborough TN6 . . . .**38** C8
Eastbourne BN20 . . . .**184** B4
Osborne Villas BN3 . . . .**163** B6
Osbourne Ct BN26 . . . .**173** A7
Osmers Hill TN5 . . . .**29** C7
Osmond Gdns BN3 . . . .**163** E7
Osmond Rd BN3 . . . .**163** E7
Osmunda Bank RH19 . . . .**1** E6
Osmunda Ct BN3 . . . .**8** C4
Osprey Dr TN22 . . . .**78** E5
Osprey Ho 13 BN1 . . . .**163** E5
Ospringe Pl TN2 . . . .**8** F6
Oswald Ct TN40 . . . .**157** C4
Otham Court La BN26 . . . . .**173** B8
Otham Pk BN27 . . . .**152** D7
Otham Rd BN22 . . . .**174** A2
Ottafield Ct RH16 . . . .**50** F6
Otteham Ct BN26 . . . .**173** B6
Otterbourne Pl RH19 . . . .**1** B1
Oulton Cl BN23 . . . .**174** B4
Our Lady of Lourdes
RC Prim Sch BN2 . . . .**165** F1
Ousedale Cl BN7 . . . .**123** C1
Outlook Ave BN10 . . . .**178** F6
Outlook The BN20 . . . .**183** A1
Oval Cl BN10 . . . .**167** C2
Over St BN1 . . . .**189** B3
Overdown Rise BN41 . . . . .**140** F4
Overhill BN42 . . . .**140** E1
Overhill Dr BN1 . . . .**142** E5
Overhill Gdns BN1 . . . .**142** E5
Overhill Way BN1 . . . .**142** E6
Overton Shaw RH19 . . . .**1** E4
Ovingdean Cl BN2 . . . .**165** D5
Ovingdean Grange Cotts
BN2 . . . .**165** D4
Ovingdean Hall Sch BN2 **165** D4
Ovingdean Rd BN2 . . . .**165** D5
Owen Cl RH15 . . . .**72** F1
Owl House Gdns TN3 . . . . . .**19** E7
Owls Gdns TN5 . . . .**42** F5
Owlsbury Cross TN21 . . . . . .**83** B5
Ox Lea TN3 . . . .**7** A3
Oxbottom Cl BN8 . . . .**76** B6
Oxenbridge Row TN19 . . . . .**63** C8
Oxendean Gdns BN22 . . . . .**173** B4
Oxford Cl BN1 . . . .**189** B4
Oxford Mews BN3 . . . .**163** C7
Oxford Pl BN1 . . . .**189** B4
Oxford Rd 8
Eastbourne BN22 . . . .**185** B4
St Leonards TN38 . . . .**136** A3
Oxford St BN1, BN2 . . . . . .**189** B4
Oxford Terr 9 TN34 . . . . . .**160** B4
Oxshott Cl TN40 . . . .**157** F4
Oyster Creek TN31 . . . .**94** A3

P

Pacific Dr BN23 . . . .**175** B2
Packer Cl RH19 . . . .**2** A3
Packham Way RH15 . . . .**72** F4
Paddock Cl Bexhill TN40 . . .**157** D6
Fordcombe TN3 . . . .**6** B5
Paddock Cotts BN24 . . . . . .**175** A6
Paddock Ct BN41 . . . .**140** F3
Paddock Field BN1 . . . .**144** B5
Paddock Gdns
East Grinstead RH19 . . . . . .**10** E7
Polegate BN26 . . . .**172** F4
Paddock La BN7 . . . .**123** C1
Paddock Rd Lewes BN7 . . . .**123** C1
St Leonards TN37 . . . .**136** C5
Paddock The
Eastbourne BN22 . . . .**173** F2
Hove BN3 . . . .**142** C1
Maresfield TN22 . . . .**55** A4
 4 Northiam TN31 . . . .**67** B7
Pembury TN2 . . . .**9** C6
Paddockhall Rd RH16 . . . . . .**50** D5
Paddocks The Cowden TN8 . . .**4** B7
Hailsham BN27 . . . .**129** A2
Plumpton Green BN7 . . . . . .**99** E6
Rodmell BN7 . . . .**167** D8
Padgham Cnr TN21 . . . .**109** D8
Padgham La TN21 . . . .**109** D8
Padua Ho BN2 . . . .**165** F8
Padua House Flats BN2 . . .**165** F8
Page's Cotts TN21 . . . .**82** B8
Pages Ave TN39 . . . .**156** F2
Pages Cl TN21 . . . .**81** E7
Pages Hill TN21 . . . .**81** E7
Pages La TN39 . . . .**156** F3
Pagets The BN8 . . . .**76** D7
Pagham Ct BN23 . . . .**174** B4
Pain's Flat RH15, RH17 . . . . .**72** D8
Paine's Cnr TN21 . . . .**60** C4
Paines Cotts TN31 . . . .**94** A3
Palace Ct TN34 . . . .**159** E7
Palace Pier BN2 . . . .**189** B1
Palace Pl BN1 . . . .**189** B2
Palesgate La TN6 . . . .**26** C2
Palliser Cl BN23 . . . .**185** E6
Palm Ct 2 BN3 . . . .**163** D6
Palma Cl BN26 . . . .**173** A7
Palmeira Ave BN3 . . . .**163** D6
Palmeira Ct BN3 . . . .**163** C6
Palmeira Ho 6 BN3 . . . . . .**163** D7
Palmeira Mans 21 BN3 . . . .**163** C6
Palmeira Pl BN3 . . . .**163** D7
Palmeira Sq BN3 . . . .**163** C6
Palmer Ho BN8 . . . .**100** E7

Palmers Row BN27 ......152 B7
Palmerston Rd BN9 .....168 F1
Pangdean La BN6 ....72 C4
Pangdene Cl RH15 ....72 E1
Pankhurst Ave BN2 ......164 D6
Pankhurst Rise TN39 ....157 A8
Pankhurst Rise TN39 ....157 A8
Pannel La TN35,TN36 ....116 E2
Pannell Cl RH19 ....1 D1
Pannett RH15 ....72 E4
Pantiles The
  17 Royal Tunbridge Wells TN2 ..8 A2
  Royal Tunbridge Wells TN4 ...7 F2
Parade The
  Beachlands BN24 ....175 F6
  Brighton BN1 ....142 B4
  East Grinstead RH19 ......1 B3
  Hove BN3 ....141 E2
  Pevensey Bay BN24 .....175 E5
Paradise Cl BN20 ....184 D2
Paradise Dr BN20 ....184 D2
Paradise Family L Pk
  BN9 ....168 D1
Paragon The BN20 ....172 F3
Parham Cl BN2 ....164 D5
Parham Ho **12** BN3 ....163 D7
Park Ave Bexhill TN39 ...157 B3
  Eastbourne BN21,BN22 ..184 D7
  Hastings TN34 ....136 C4
  Hove BN3 ....162 E7
  Keymer BN6 ....98 A2
  Shoreham-by-Sea BN43 ..161 A8
  Telscombe Cliffs BN10 ..178 A8
Park Cl Brighton BN1 ...143 E5
  Burgess Hill RH15 ......72 F4
  Eastbourne BN20 ....184 D3
  Hailsham BN27 ....152 B6
  Hastings TN34 ....136 D3
  Hove BN3 ....141 E3
  Hurstpierpoint BN6 .....97 A6
  Portslade-by-Sea BN41 ..141 B1
Park Cnr BN8 ....104 F2
Park Cres Brighton BN2 .189 C4
  Crowborough TN6 ....25 F3
  Forest Row RH18 ....12 A4
  Hastings TN34 ....136 D2
  Portslade-by-Sea BN41 ..162 A8
  Rottingdean BN2 ....165 F1
Park Crescent Pl BN2 ...189 C4
Park Crescent Rd BN2 ..189 C4
Park Crescent Terr BN2 .189 C4
Park Croft BN26 ....173 A5
Park Ct
  Brighton, Patcham BN1 ..142 E6
  Brighton, Preston BN1 ..142 F1
  Burgess Hill RH15 ......73 A3
  4 Haywards Heath RH16 ..50 E4
  Hove BN3 ....163 D7
Park Dr TN34 ....136 D2
Park Drive Cl BN9 ......168 F2
Park Farm Ct TN19 ......63 B8
Park Gate Brighton BN1 .163 F8
  Hailsham BN27 ....129 D3
  Hove BN3 ....163 D6
Park Gates **16** BN21 ...185 A2
Park Hill BN2 ....189 C2
Park La Ashurst Wood RH19 .11 D6
  Battle TN33 ....112 D4
  Bexhill TN39 ....157 A6
  Crowborough TN6 ....25 F3
  Eastbourne BN21 ....184 C8
  Laughton BN8 ....126 E7
  Southwick BN42 ....161 D7
  Whatlington TN32 ......88 A5
Park Lodge
  10 Eastbourne BN21 ...185 A2
  Hove BN3 ....163 D8
Park Lodge Ct TN38 .....159 B7
Park Manor BN1 ....142 D3
Park Mead Cty Prim
  Sch BN27 ....151 A7
Park Par RH16 ....50 E4
Park Rd Bexhill TN39 ...157 B3
  Brighton BN1 ....143 E5
  Burgess Hill RH15 ......73 A3
  Crowborough TN6 ....25 F3
  Dormans Park RH19 ......1 F6
  East Grinstead RH19 .....1 D1
  Forest Row RH18 ....12 A2
  Hailsham BN27 ....129 B4
  Haywards Heath RH16 ...50 E4
  Heathfield TN21 ....82 B7
  Heathfield TN21 ....82 C6
  Lewes BN7 ....123 C1
  Peacehaven Heights BN10 .178 F6
  Rottingdean BN2 ....165 F1
  Royal Tunbridge Wells TN4 ...8 B5
  Seaford BN25 ....180 D3
  Shoreham-by-Sea BN43 ..161 A8
Park Rise BN3 ....141 E3
Park Road Terr **4** BN2 .189 C2
Park Royal BN1 ....163 E6
Park Shaw TN33 ....88 E1
Park St Brighton BN2 ...189 C2
  Falmer BN1 ....144 C6
  Royal Tunbridge Wells TN2 ..8 C3
Park Terr BN2 ....165 F1
  8 Brighton BN2 ....189 C2
Park The Crowborough TN6 .25 F3
  Rottingdean BN2 ....177 A5
Park View Brighton BN1 .163 E8
  Brighton BN2 ....164 C6
  Buxted TN22 ....56 C4
  Hastings TN34 ....136 D2
  Haywards Heath RH16 ...50 E6
  Northiam TN31 ....67 A6

Park View continued
  Peasmarsh TN31 ....69 B2
Park View Dr BN10 .....167 A1
Park View Rd BN3 ......142 B1
Park View Rise BN10 ...178 A8
Park View Terr
  Brighton BN1 ....163 E8
  Westfield TN35 ....114 E4
Park Village Rd BN1 ...144 B8
Park Village The BN1 ..144 A8
Park Villas TN21 ....82 B6
Park Way Hastings TN34 .136 D3
  Southwick BN42 ....161 E8
Park Way Cl BN42 ......161 F8
Park Wood Rd BN34 ....136 F6
Parker BN21 ....184 E5
Parker Ct BN41 ....141 B2
Parker Rd TN34 ....137 A3
Parkfield Ave BN22 ....173 E1
Parkhurst Rd TN40 .....157 C3
Parkland Cty Inf Sch
  BN22 ....173 E1
Parkland Cty Jun Sch
  BN22 ....173 D1
Parklands Maresfield TN22 .55 A5
  Royal Tunbridge Wells TN4 ...7 F8
  Shoreham-by-Sea BN43 ..161 C8
Parklands Rd BN6 ....97 F3
Parkmead BN2 ....189 C4
Parkmore Terr BN1 .....189 A5
Parks The BN41 ....141 B3
Parks Yd TN33 ....112 D4
Parkside Burgess Hill RH15 .72 F3
  East Grinstead RH19 .....1 C1
  Heathfield TN21 ....82 B6
  Keymer BN6 ....98 A4
  Portslade-by-Sea BN43 ..140 A1
Parkside Cty Prim Sch
  TN21 ....82 C5
Parkside Rd BN25 ......180 F4
Parkstone Par TN34 ....136 D4
Parkstone Rd TN34 .....136 D4
Parkstone Terr TN34 ...136 D4
Parkview
  Hurstpierpoint BN6 .....97 A5
  Royal Tunbridge Wells TN2 ..8 D4
Parkview Rd TN22 ......55 D1
Parkway BN20 ....184 B8
Parkwood TN31 ....70 B4
Parkwood Cf TN34 ......8 C6
Parnell Ct **3** BN3 ....163 B6
Parochial Terr BN2 ....189 C2
Parrock Ct TN7 ....12 E2
Parry Cl BN23 ....174 E3
Parsonage Cl TN4 ......7 B5
Parsonage La
  Icklesham TN36 ....116 F6
  Lamberhurst TN3 ......20 B6
  Westfield TN33,TN35 ...114 C4
Parsonage Rd
  Eastbourne BN21 ....184 D4
  Rusthall TN4 ....7 B5
Parsons Cl TN38 ....135 F4
Partridges La TN5 ......28 E6
Pashley Down Cty Inf Sch
  BN20 ....184 B4
Pashley Manor Gdns TN5 .44 B7
Pashley Rd BN20 ....184 C2
Paston Ho BN1 ....163 F8
Paston Pl BN2 ....164 D4
Pasture Hill Rd RH16 ...50 D6
Patagonia Ho TN2 ......8 C3
Patcham By-Pass BN1 ..142 E6
Patcham Cty Inf Sch BN1 142 E6
Patcham Cty Jun Sch
  BN1 ....142 F6
Patcham Grange BN1 ...142 E5
Patcham High Sch BN1 .142 F6
Patcham House Sch BN1 142 E6
Patcham Mill Rd BN24 ..174 B5
Patchdean BN1 ....142 F5
Patching Lodge **5** BN2 .164 C5
Paton Rd TN39 ....157 A8
Paul Cl BN27 ....129 A3
Pavilion Bldgs BN1 ....189 B2
Pavilion Cl BN6 ....97 E5
Pavilion Ct **15** BN1 ..163 E7
Pavilion Par BN2 ......189 B2
Pavilion Ret Pk BN2 ...143 C1
Pavilion St BN2 ....189 B2
Pavilion Way RH19 ....10 E8
Paxhill Cl TN38 ....135 E4
Paygate Rd TN33 ......113 E7
Payne Ave BN3 ....162 F4
Payne Terr BN1 ....143 B1
Paynsbridge Way TN34 .107 A7
Paynters Way BN8 .....76 C7
Paynton Rd TN37 ......136 B3
Paythorne Cl BN42 ....140 D1
Payton Dr RH15 ....72 F2
Payton Ho RH15 ....73 D3
Peace Cl BN1 ....143 C1
Peacehaven Cty Inf Sch
  BN10 ....178 B7
Peacock Ind Est BN3 ..163 D7
Peacock La BN1 ....142 E4
Peakdean Cl BN20 .....183 B2
Peakdean La BN20 .....183 B2
Pearl Ct **3** BN21 ....185 A2
Pearse Pl TN3 ....20 B5
Peartree Cl RH15 .....72 E3
Peartree Field TN36 ..116 F6
Peartree Hill TN5 ....42 E4
Peartree La TN39 .....156 D6
Peasmarsh CE Prim Sch
  TN31 ....69 B1
Pebble Rd BN24 ....175 E5

Pebsham Cty Prim Sch
  TN40 ....158 A5
Pebsham Dr TN40 .....158 A6
Pebsham La TN38,TN40 .158 A6
Peckham Cl BN7 ....123 C3
Peel Rd BN2 ....164 F4
Peelings La BN24 .....174 D6
Peeps La TN6 ....39 A6
Pegasus Way RH19 .....2 B3
Pegler Ave BN9 ....179 B6
Pegwell Cl BN34 ......136 E2
Pelham Arc **1** TN34 ...160 A3
Pelham Cl
  Peacehaven BN10 ......167 D1
  Westham BN24 ....174 F5
Pelham Cres
  Hailsham BN27 ....152 C6
  Hastings TN34 ....160 A3
Pelham Ct **15** BN25 ...180 E2
Pelham Pl TN34 ....160 A3
Pelham Place Cotts BN27 .152 C6
  Seaford BN25 ....180 E2
Pelham Rd Lindfield RH16 .51 A6
  Seaford BN25 ....180 E2
Pelham Rise BN10 .....167 D1
Pelham Sq BN1 ....189 B3
Pelham St Brighton BN1 .189 B3
  Hastings TN34 ....159 F7
Pelham Terr Brighton BN2 .143 C1
  Lewes BN7 ....123 C2
Pelham Yd **18** BN25 ..180 E2
Pell Cl TN5 ....30 A6
Pellbrook Rd BN7 .....123 B3
Pellings Farm Cl TN6 ..26 B2
Pellings Rise TN6 ....26 B3
Pelwood Rd TN31 ......95 A2
Pembroke Ave BN3 ....163 A7
Pembroke Cl BN27 ....129 C3
Pembroke Cres BN3 ...163 A7
Pembroke Ct **2** BN3 ..163 A6
Pembroke Gdns BN3 ..163 A6
Pembury Cl
  Haywards Heath RH16 ..51 B3
  Pembury TN2 ....9 D7
Pembury Cty Prim Sch TN2 9 D8
Pembury Gr TN39 .....157 A7
Pembury Grange TN2 ...9 A6
Pembury Hospl TN2 ....9 B7
Pembury Rd
  Eastbourne BN23 .....174 D1
  Royal Tunbridge Wells TN2 ..8 E4
Pendean RH15 ....73 C1
Pendragon Ct BN3 ....163 A8
Pendrill Pl TN5 ......29 F5
Penhale Rd BN2 ......185 D5
Penhurst Cl
  Eastbourne BN22 .....174 A1
  St Leonards TN37 ....136 D5
Penhurst Dr TN40 ....158 A6
Penhurst La TN33 ....110 E6
Penhurst Pl BN2 .....164 F6
Penland Cl RH16 .....50 D7
Penland Ct **9** TN40 ..157 E4
Penland Rd Bexhill TN40 .157 E5
  Haywards Heath RH16 ..50 D7
Penn Cres
  Haywards Heath RH16 ..51 A5
  Ringmer BN8 ....124 D5
Penn Yd TN2 ....9 C6
Pennine Rise TN34 ...137 B4
Pennine Way BN23 ....174 D3
Pennine Wlk TN2 .....8 D5
Pennington Ho RH16 ..51 A3
Penny La TN40 ....158 A5
Pennybridge La TN20 ..40 D5
Penrith Way BN23 ....174 C4
Pensford Dr BN23 ....174 D3
Penshurst Rd TN1,TN3 ..6 E8
Penstock Terr TN31 ..93 F3
Penstone Ct **4** BN43 ..161 C8
Pentland Cl
  Eastbourne BN23 .....174 E3
  St Leonards TN37 ....136 C5
Pentlands BN26 ......183 C7
Pepper Dr RH15 ......72 F1
Pepper Hall Cotts RH17 .74 B5
Peppercombe Rd BN20 .184 B4
Pepys Wlk BN23 ......174 E3
Percival Cres BN22 ..173 F3
Percival Rd BN22 ....173 F3
Percival Terr **14** BN2 .164 D4
Percy Rd TN35 ....137 C3
Percy Terr TN4 ......8 A6
Perry Ave RH19 ......1 E3
Perry Hill BN2 ......166 C3
Perryfields RH15 ....72 E4
Perryhill Cotts TN7 ..13 E8
Perryhill La TN7 ....13 E8
Perryman's La RH17 ..34 D3
Perrymans Ct TN2 ....36 F1
Perrymount Rd RH16 ..50 E5
Perth Cl BN25 ....181 C3
Perth Ct **3** BN21 ...185 A4
Perth Rd TN37 ....136 B3
Peter Gladwin
  Cty Prim Sch BN41 ..141 B2
Peter James Cl TN31 ..94 E2
Peter James La TN35 ..138 C6
Petersfield TN2 .....9 E7
Petland Gdns RH16 ...50 F3
Petlands Rd RH16 ....50 E3
Pett Cl BN2 ....164 F6
Pett La TN36 ....117 A4
Pett Level Rd TN35 ..139 B7
Pett Rd TN35 ....138 C8
Petworth Dr RH15 ....73 A4

Petworth Ho **13** BN3 ..163 D7
Petworth Pl BN22 ....173 E2
Petworth Rd BN1 .....143 B6
Pevensey & Westham
  CE Prim Sch BN24 ....175 A6
Pevensey & Westham Sta
  BN24 ....175 A6
Pevensey Bay Rd BN23 .175 A2
Pevensey Bay Sta BN24 .175 C6
Pevensey Castle BN24 ..175 A6
Pevensey Cl BN25 ....181 B4
Pevensey Ct **3**
  Bexhill TN39 ....157 B3
  Pevensey Bay BN24 ...175 D4
Pevensey Park Rd BN24 .174 F6
Pevensey Rd **7**
  Brighton BN2 ....164 C8
  Eastbourne BN21,BN22 .185 B3
  Newhaven BN9 ....179 B5
  Polegate BN26 ....173 C6
  St Leonards TN38 ....159 B7
Peverells The BN25 ...181 A5
Peyton Cl BN23 ......185 F7
Philip Cole Cl **16** TN34 .160 B4
Philip Ct **8** BN3 ....163 C7
Phoenix Brewery Halls
  BN2 ....189 C4
Phoenix Cl
  Eastbourne BN23 .....185 G8
  Hailsham BN27 ....152 E7
Phoenix Cres BN2 ....161 D8
Phoenix Cswy BN7 ....123 D1
Phoenix Ct **3** BN2 ..185 B3
Phoenix La RH19 .....11 E6
Phoenix Pl Brighton BN2 .189 C3
  Lewes BN7 ....123 D1
Phoenix Rise BN2 ....189 C3
Phoenix Way BN42 ....161 D8
Phyllis Ave BN10 ....178 B8
Piazza The BN2 ......185 F8
Picardy Cl TN33 .....112 E4
Piccadilly La TN20 ...40 C1
Pickers Gn RH16 .....51 A8
Picketts La TN22 ....54 D8
Pickforde La TN5 ....31 D1
Picton St BN2 ....164 C7
Piddinghoe Ave BN10 .178 D6
Piddinghoe Cl BN10 ..178 D7
Piddinghoe Mead BN9 .168 B1
Pilgrim Ct RH16 .....51 A5
Pilgrims Old Sch BN7 .146 A7
Pilgrims Way TN34 ...136 F4
Pilmer Rd TN6 ....25 F4
Pilot Ho **1** BN2 ....189 C2
Pilot Rd TN34 ....137 B4
Piltdown Cl Bexhill TN39 .157 B4
  Hastings TN34 ....136 E1
Piltdown Rd BN2 .....164 F6
Piltdown Rise TN22 ..78 D8
Piltdown Way BN22 ..174 A4
Pinders Rd TN35 .....160 D6
Pine Ave TN34 ......137 B4
Pine Gr Crowborough TN6 .25 E3
  East Grinstead RH19 ...1 B3
Pine Tree Cl
  Hurstpierpoint BN6 ...97 B5
  Newhaven BN9 ....179 C7
Pine Tree Rd TN21 ...82 A6
Pine Trees BN6 ......97 D4
Pine Trees Ct BN6 ...97 D4
Pine Way BN27 ......152 A7
Pine Way Cl RH19 ...10 E7
Pine Wlk TN22 ......78 D8
Pineham Copse RH16 ..50 F4
Pinehurst RH15 .....73 A1
Pinehurst Wlk TN34 ..137 B3
Pines The **2** Brighton BN2 .189 C4
  Hastings TN34 ....137 B3
  Haywards Heath RH16 ..51 B4
  Hove BN3 ....163 B6
Pinewood **5** BN1 ...142 E3
Pinewood Chase TN6 ..25 D3
Pinewood Cl
  Eastbourne BN22 ....173 D2
  Hove BN1 ....142 D2
  Seaford BN25 ....180 F4
Pinewood Ct RH16 ...50 D2
Pinewood Rd TN3 ....8 D5
Pinewood Way
  Haywards Heath RH16 ..50 D2
  St Leonards TN38 ...135 E3
Pinewoods BN25 .....156 E4
Pinewoods Ct TN39 ..156 E4
Pinfold **4** RH16 ....50 D6
Pinfold Cl BN2 ......165 E6
Pinton Hill TN5 ....31 B3
Pinwell Rd BN7 .....146 D8
Pipe Pas **6** BN7 ...123 C1
Piper's Gate TN22 ..78 D4
Pipers Cl Bexhill TN40 .157 C5
  Hove BN3 ....141 C2
  Wadhurst TN5 ....30 A4
Pipers Field TN22 ..78 D4
Pipers La TN32 .....64 B3
Pipit Mdw TN22 ....78 D5
Pit La BN6 ....97 A5
Pitcairn Ave BN25 ..175 B2
Pitreavie Dr BN27 ..152 A8
Pitt Dr BN25 ......181 A5
Pitt Gdns BN2 .....165 D3
Place La BN25 ......180 E3
Plainfields Ave BN1 ..143 A7
Plaistow Cl BN2 ....164 F6
Plashett Park Gates
  TN22 ....102 F5
Plat The TN31 ......67 B6
Platt The Dormansland RH7 ..2 A8

Platt The continued
  Frant TN3 ....17 B1
  Haywards Heath RH16 ..17 B1
Plaw Hatch La RH18, RH19 .21 E5
Playden Cl **1** BN2 ..164 E4
Playden Gdns TN34 ...137 B4
Playden La TN31 ....70 C3
Playden St Michael's
  CE Prim Sch TN31 ...70 C2
Pleasant View Cotts TN6 ..25 F4
Pleasant View Rd TN6 ..25 F4
Pleasure Island TN34 ..160 B4
Plemont Gdns TN39 ..157 A6
Pleyden Rise TN39 ...155 F4
Plough La TN37 .....136 B5
Plover Cl BN23 .....174 C2
Plover Ct Hailsham BN27 .152 D7
  St Leonards TN38 ...135 E3
Plum Tree Cotts TN18 ..45 E8
Plumey Feather Cotts TN3 14 E3
Plumpton Agricultural
  Coll BN6 ....121 D8
Plumpton Bostall BN7 .121 E6
Plumpton Cl Bexhill TN40 .157 F5
  Eastbourne BN23 ....174 A4
Plumpton Cross BN7 ..99 E3
Plumpton Crossways
  BN7, BN8 ....74 F1
Plumpton Cty Prim Sch
  BN7 ....99 F5
Plumpton La BN7 ....99 E3
Plumpton Race Course
  BN7 ....99 E4
Plumpton Rd BN2 ....164 D6
Plumpton Sta BN7 ...99 F5
Plymouth Ave BN2 ...143 F1
Plymouth Cl BN23 ...185 F8
Plynlimmon Rd TN34 ..160 A4
Pocock's Rd BN21 ...184 D5
Polegate By-Pass BN26 .172 F7
Polegate Cty Prim Sch
  BN26 ....173 A7
Polegate Sta BN26 ..173 A6
Polesden Rd TN2 ....8 D2
Polley Cl TN2 ......9 D7
Pollington Pl TN6 ..25 F2
Pomper La BN8 .....72 A2
Pond Cl TN31 ......90 B5
Pond Way RH19 .....2 B1
Pondcroft Rd RH16 ..51 B7
Pondsyde Ct BN25 ..180 F4
Ponswood Rd TN38 ..136 B2
Pont Cl TN21 ......83 C6
Pook Reed Cl TN21 ..81 F6
Pook Reed La TN21 ..81 F6
Pool Valley BN2 ...189 B1
Poona Rd TN1 ......8 B2
Popes Cott TN17 ...20 F2
Poplar Ave BN3 ....141 E3
Poplar Cl Brighton BN1 .142 F2
  Hove BN3 ....141 E3
Poplar Wlk BN22 ...173 D3
Poplars The BN2 ...98 A3
Poppinghole La TN32 ..87 E8
Popps La TN39 .....156 C3
Poppyfield TN31 ...70 C1
Port Hall Ave BN1 ..163 E8
Port Hall Mews BN1 .163 E8
Port Hall Pl BN1 ...163 E8
Port Hall Rd BN1 ..163 E8
Port Hall St BN1 ..163 E8
Port Rd BN22 .....174 A1
Port View BN9 ....168 E2
Porters Way BN26 ..173 B6
Portfield Ave BN1 ..143 A6
Portfield Cl TN40 ..157 D5
Portland Ave BN3 ..162 E7
Portland Cl BN27 ..129 A1
Portland Cotts **11** TN34 .159 F8
Portland Gate BN3 ..162 E7
Portland Ho **5** RH19 ..10 F8
Portland Mews **19** BN2 .164 C4
Portland Pl
  11 Brighton BN2 ...164 C4
  18 Hastings TN34 ..159 F8
Portland Rd
  Burgess Hill RH15 ..72 F3
  East Grinstead RH19 ..10 F8
  Hove BN3 ....162 E7
Portland Road Trad Est
  BN3 ....162 D8
Portland Sq TN21 ...82 D7
Portland St BN1 ....189 A2
Portland Terr **15**
  Hastings TN34 ......159 F8
  South Heighton BN9 ..168 D2
Portland Villas **16**
  Hastings TN34 ......159 F8
  Hove BN3 ....162 D7
Portlands BN23 .....185 G7
Portsdown Way BN20 .173 B2
Portside BN2 ......164 F3
Portslade Com Coll
  (Lower) BN41 ....141 A3
Portslade Com Coll
  (sixth Form)
  Portslade-by-Sea BN41 .140 F2
  Portslade-by-Sea BN41 .141 A1
Portslade Cty Inf Sch
  BN41 ....162 B8
Portslade Sta BN3 ..162 C8
Portsmouth Rd RH16 ..50 F8
Portsmouth Wood RH16 .50 F8
Portsmouth Wood Cl
  RH16 ....50 F8
Portsmouth Wood Dr
  RH16 ....50 F8
Posey Cotts BN27 ...131 B5

Possingworth Cl TN21 ....80 F8
Post Horn Cl RH18 ....12 B1
Post Horn La RH18 ....12 B2
Post Office Pas 10 TN34 .160 A4
Potato La BN8 ....124 F5
Potman's La TN33, TN39 .133 F4
Pottens Mill La TN21 .....59 F4
Potter's La BN7 ....146 C8
Potteries Cotts BN27 .....128 D3
Potteries The TN22 ......78 D4
Potters Field BN8 .....124 D6
Potters La RH15 ....72 F1
Pottery Cl TN31 ....90 A2
Pottery Cotts BN6 ......74 A1
Pottery La TN31 ....90 A2
Pottingfield Rd TN31 .....93 A6
Potts Marsh Ind Est
  BN24 ....174 F4
Pouchlands Dr BN8 .....100 C7
Pound Cl BN23 ....185 F6
Pound Cnr BN8 ....101 D3
Pound Gate BN6 ....97 D3
Pound La Framefield TN22 ..79 E7
  Laughton BN8 ......126 C7
Pound The RH15 ....72 F4
Poundfield Farm TN6 ....26 B2
Poundfield Rd
  Crowborough TN6 ......26 B2
  Sandhurst TN18 ....47 B5
Poundsbridge Hill
  TN11, TN3 ....6 D7
Poveys Cl RH15 ....72 D4
Powder Mill La TN4 ....8 B8
Powdermill Cl TN4 ......8 C8
Powdermill La
  Battle TN33 ....112 C1
  Goatham Green TN31, TN33 ..89 D3
Powell Gdns BN9 ......168 D1
Powell Rd BN8 ....76 D7
Powis Gr BN1 ....189 A3
Powis Rd BN1 ....163 E6
Powis Sq BN1 ....163 E6
Powis Villas BN1 ......189 A3
Poynings Cl BN25 .....181 C2
Poynings Dr BN3 ......141 F3
Poynter Rd BN3 ....163 A8
Pratt's Folly La TN6 .....25 E1
Prescott Gdns RH15 ......73 A3
Preston Cir BN1 ....189 B4
Preston Dro BN1 ......142 F2
Preston Gr TN22 ....79 B6
Preston Grange BN1 ...142 E1
Preston Manor (Mus)
  BN1 ....142 E1
Preston Park Ave BN1 ...142 F1
Preston Park Sta BN1 ..142 D2
Preston Rd Bexhill TN39 ..157 B7
  Brighton BN1 ....163 F8
Preston St BN1 ....163 E5
Preston Village Mews
  BN1 ....142 E1
Prestonville Ct
  2 Brighton BN1 ......163 E7
  1 Brighton BN1 ......189 A4
Prestonville Rd BN1, BN3 189 A4
Prideaux Rd BN21 .....184 E5
Primrose Cl
  Burgess Hill RH15 .....72 D4
  Eastbourne BN23 ....174 B3
Primrose Hill Bexhill TN39 156 F6
  Fairlight Cove TN35 ...138 F5
Primrose La RH18 ....12 A1
Prince Albert St BN1 ...189 B2
Prince Charles Cl
  BN41, BN42 ....141 A1
Prince Charles Rd BN7 .123 E3
Prince Edward's Rd BN7 .123 B1
Prince Of Wales Ct BN1 162 F6
Prince Regent's Cl BN2 .164 E4
Prince Regent's Ct 2
  BN2 ....164 E4
Prince William Par BN23 185 F6
Prince's Cres BN2 ......189 C5
Prince's Pl BN1 ....189 B2
Prince's Rd Brighton BN2 .164 B8
  St Leonards TN37 .....159 D7
Prince's St Brighton BN2 .189 B2
  Royal Tunbridge Wells TN2 ..8 C3
Prince's Terr BN2 .....164 E4
Princes Ave BN3 ......163 A6
Princes Cl Seaford BN25 ..180 E5
  Uckfield TN22 ....78 A7
Princes Cres BN3 .....163 A6
Princes Ct 6 BN3 .....163 A6
Princes Field BN26 ....150 B3
Princes Rd BN23 ......185 E4
Princes Sq BN3 ....163 A6
Princess Dr BN25 .....180 D5
Prinkle La BN27 ....109 C1
Prinsep Rd BN3 ....163 A8
Prior's Way TN8 ....4 A6
Priory Ave TN34 ......136 E1
Priory Cl Hastings TN34 .136 E1
  Pevensey Bay BN24 ...175 D5
Priory Cres BN7 ......146 C8
Priory Ct Brighton BN1 ..163 F8
  1 Eastbourne BN20 ...184 F1
  Lewes BN7 ....146 D8
Priory Ct CT TN40 ....157 E5
Priory Flats 7 BN7 ...146 C8
Priory Ho BN7 ....146 D8
Priory Hts BN20 ......184 A5
Priory Meadow Sh Ctr
  TN34 ....159 F8
Priory Orch 8 BN23 ..174 E1
Priory Rd Burgess Hill RH15 73 A1
  Eastbourne BN23 ....174 E2

Priory Rd continued
  Forest Row RH18 ......11 D2
  Hassocks BN6 ....97 E5
  Hastings TN34 ......160 B5
Priory Sch BN7 ....146 E8
Priory St Hastings TN34 .159 F7
  Lewes BN7 ....146 C8
Priory The Brighton BN1 .142 D5
  5 Hove BN3 ....163 B5
Priory Way RH16 ......50 F4
Promenade BN10 .....178 C6
Promenade The BN24 ..175 D4
Prospect Cotts
  Crowborough TN6 ......25 E3
  Lamberhurst TN3 ......20 A3
Prospect Gdns 10 BN21 .184 D4
Prospect Pl TN34 .....159 E7
Prospect Rd
  Heathfield TN21 ....82 B6
  Royal Tunbridge Wells TN2 ..8 C3
  Royal Tunbridge Wells TN4 ...7 F8
Prospect Terr TN21 .....82 A7
Providence Cotts
  Crowborough TN6 ......25 D4
  Groombridge TN3 ......15 C7
Providence Pl BN1 ....189 B4
Prowting Mead TN39 ...156 C4
Pudding Cake La TN22 ...78 C7
Pulborough Ave BN22 ...173 E2
Pulborough Cl BN2 ....164 F7
Pump Ho The BN3 .....162 D8
Pump La TN22 ....79 D4
Punnetts Town
  Cty Prim Sch TN21 ...83 B6
Purbeck Cl BN23 ......174 C4
Putlands Cres TN39 ...157 A8
Pyecombe St BN45 ....119 A6

Q

Quadrangle The BN8 ...105 C5
Quadrant BN1 ....189 A2
Quadrant The
  Eastbourne BN21 ....184 E4
  Keymer BN6 ....98 A4
Quail Ct BN27 ....152 D7
Quakers La RH16 ....51 A5
Quantock Cl
  Eastbourne BN23 ....174 D3
  Royal Tunbridge Wells TN2 ...8 D5
Quantock Gdns TN34 ..137 B3
Quarry Bank Rd BN1 ..143 B2
Quarry Cotts TN5 ......29 D7
Quarry Cres TN34 ....160 A5
Quarry Hill
  Hayward's Heath RH17 ..50 C6
  St Leonards TN38 ....159 B7
Quarry Ho TN38 ......159 B6
Quarry La BN25 ......181 A5
Quarry Rd
  Hastings TN34 ......160 A5
  Newhaven BN9 ......179 D5
  Royal Tunbridge Wells TN1 ...8 B5
Quarry Rise RH19 ....2 A3
Quarry Terr TN34 .....136 F1
Quay Ct BN43 ....161 B6
Quay The 5 BN43 ....161 A6
Quebec Cl Bexhill TN39 .157 A5
  Eastbourne BN23 ....185 F7
Quebec Mans TN38 ...159 A8
Quebec Rd TN38 .....136 A4
Quebec St BN2 ....189 C3
Queen Alexandra Ave
  BN3 ....142 A3
Queen Anne's Cl BN7 .123 C1
Queen Caroline Cl BN3 .142 A3
Queen Elizabeth Ave
  RH15 ....73 A2
Queen Mary Ave BN3 .142 A3
Queen Sq BN1 ....189 A2
Queen St TN18 ....47 B5
Queen Victoria Ave BN3 .142 A3
Queen Victoria Hospl The
  RH19 ....1 F3
Queen's Ave 4 TN34 .159 F7
Queen's Cres BN23 ...185 E7
Queen's Ct RH16 ......50 F6
Queen's Gdns
  Brighton BN1 ....189 B3
  Eastbourne BN21 ....185 B3
  Hove BN3 ....163 C5
  Royal Tunbridge Wells TN4 ..8 B6
Queen's Par
  Eastbourne BN22 ....173 F1
  Hove BN3 ....141 E2
Queen's Park
  Cty Prim Sch BN2 ...164 C5
Queen's Park Rd BN2 ..164 C6
Queen's Park Rise BN2 .164 C6
Queen's Park Terr BN2 .164 C6
Queen's Pl Brighton BN1 .189 B4
  Shoreham-by-Sea BN43 ..161 D7
Queen's Rd Brighton BN1 .189 A3
  East Grinstead RH19 ....1 E1
  Eastbourne BN23 ....185 D7
  Hastings TN34 ......159 F8
  Lewes BN7 ....123 D3
  Royal Tunbridge Wells TN4 ..8 B6
Queen's Wlk RH19 .....1 E1
Queens App TN22 .....55 D1
Queens Cotts TN5 .....29 E6
Queens Cres RH15 .....73 A2
Queens Dr Hassocks BN6 ..97 F4
  Maresfield TN22 ......54 F4
Queens Park Gdns BN25 .180 C4

Queens Rd
  Crowborough TN6 .....25 F1
  Haywards Heath RH16 ..50 E6
  Herstmonceux BN27 ..130 E5
  Southwick BN42 .....140 E1
Queens Sq TN34 .....159 F8
Queensbury Mews BN1 .163 E5
Queensdown Sch BN1 .143 C3
Queensdown School Rd
  BN1, BN2 ....143 D2
Queensmount TN20 .....58 B7
Queensway Brighton BN2 .164 D6
  East Grinstead RH19 ....1 E1
  Seaford BN25 ......181 A6
  St Leonards TN37, TN38 .135 E5
Querneby Cl BN43 ....161 D7
Quickbourne La TN31 ...67 C7
Quinnell Dr BN23 .....129 B2
Quintin Cl BN27 ......152 A5
Quintins The BN27 ...152 C8

R

Radcliffe Cl TN37 .....136 C3
Radinden Dr BN3 .....142 D1
Radinden Manor Rd BN3 163 D8
Radnor Mews TN38 ...135 E2
Ragged Dog La TN21 ....81 B3
Raglan Ct Brighton BN1 .189 A2
  Pevensey Bay BN24 ...175 C3
Railway App
  East Grinstead RH19 ....1 E1
  Newhaven BN9 ......179 C7
Railway Cotts Cowden TN8 ..4 D8
  Horsted Keynes RH17 ...33 A8
  Ripe BN8 ....149 A6
  St Leonards TN38 ....158 F6
Railway La BN7 ......123 D1
Railway Rd BN9 .....179 D7
Railway St BN1 ......189 A3
Railway View TN6 .....38 C8
Raleigh Cl BN23 .....185 E7
Ramsay Way BN23 ...185 F7
Ramslye Cotts TN3 .....16 D8
Ramslye Rd TN4 ....16 E8
Ranalah Est BN9 .....179 D8
Randiddles Cl BN6 .....97 B4
Randolph La TN31 ......70 B3
Ranelagh Ct BN23 ....185 E6
Ranelagh Villas BN3 ..163 B8
Rangemore Dr BN21 ..184 D6
Rankine Rd TN2 ....8 D7
Rannoch Rd TN6 ......25 D2
Rannoch Rd W TN6 .....25 D2
Ranscombe Hill BN8 ..147 A6
Ranscombe La BN8 ...147 D6
Ranworth Cl BN23 ....174 B4
Raphael Rd BN3 .....162 F7
Rapson's Rd BN20 ...173 A3
Rastrick Cl RH15 ......72 F1
Rattle Rd BN24 ......174 D6
Ratton Dr BN20 ......184 B7
Ratton Gdn BN20 ....184 B7
Ratton Rd BN21 ......184 E4
Ratton Sch BN21 .....184 C7
Ratton Village BN20 ..184 B8
Raven Ct Battle TN33 ..112 F4
  St Leonards TN38 ....135 E3
Ravens Cl TN39 ......156 C3
Ravens Croft BN20 ...188 F8
Ravens Ct BN20 .....188 F8
Ravenside Ret & L Pk
  TN40 ....158 A4
Ravenswood BN6 ......97 E4
Ravenswood Ave TN2 ....8 D6
Ravenswood Dr BN2 ..165 F6
Ravenswood Rd RH15 ..73 B3
Ravine Cl TN34 ......137 A3
Rayford Cl BN10 .....178 C2
Rayford Ct
  2 Bexhill TN40 ......157 D4
  8 Seaford BN25 .....180 E2
Raymond Cl BN25 ....181 A5
Rayner Cl TN6 ....25 F3
Raystede Ctr for Animal
  Welfare BN8 ....103 D1
Readers La TN31 ......69 F5
Reading Rd BN2 ......164 F4
Reba Ct BN2 ....177 D4
Rectory Cl Burwash TN19 ..62 B6
  East Hoathly BN8 ....105 A5
  Eastbourne BN20 ....184 D3
  Hove BN3 ....162 D7
  Newhaven BN9 ......179 C6
  Shoreham-by-Sea BN43 ..161 D7
  St Leonards TN38 ....136 B2
Rectory Ct 15 BN43 ..161 C8
Rectory Field TN7 .....13 E4
Rectory La Beckley TN31 ..67 F4
  Iden TN31 ....70 B4
  Rye TN31 ....93 C8
  Winchelsea TN36 ....117 E7
Rectory Rd Newhaven BN9 168 E2
  Shoreham-by-Sea BN43 ..161 D7
Rectory Way TN40 ...157 D5
Red Dyke Cotts BN24 ..173 F6
Red Lake Cty Prim Sch
  TN35 ....137 D4
Red Lake Terr TN35 ..137 D4
Red Oak TN18 ....45 E8
Red Oast Cotts TN5 ...32 C3
Redbridge La TN6 .....37 D5
Redbrook La TN22 .....56 D4
Redford Cl BN23 .....174 E1
Redgarth Ct RH19 ......1 B3
Redgeland Rise TN38 .135 C2

Redgill Cl BN8 ....53 B1
Redhill Cl BN1 ....142 C5
Redhill Dr BN1 ......142 C5
Redleaf Cl TN2 ....8 D6
Redman King Ho BN20 .184 F2
Redmayne Dr TN34 ...159 E7
Redoubt Fortress & Mus
  BN22 ....185 C2
Redoubt Rd BN22 ....185 C4
Redshank Cl BN27 ...152 D7
Redvers Rd BN2 ......143 D1
Redwell Ave TN39 ...157 B8
Redwood Dr RH16 .....50 D3
Reed Ct BN7 ....123 D3
Reed Ho BN8 ....100 E7
Reed Pond Wlk RH16 ..51 A4
Reedham Rd BN23 ...174 B4
Reedswood Rd
  Broad Oak TN31 ......90 B4
  St Leonards TN38 ....158 E8
Reeves Ct TN3 ....6 B5
Reeves Hill BN1 .....143 D5
Reeves Terr TN5 ......31 E1
Refectory Rd BN1 ....144 B7
Regal Dr 10 RH19 ......10 F8
Regency Cl TN22 ......78 C8
Regency Ct BN1 .....142 D3
Regency Gdns TN38 ..159 A8
Regency Hall 10 TN2 ....8 A2
Regency Ho TN2 ....8 B2
Regency Mews
  15 Brighton BN1 ....163 E5
  Eastbourne BN20 ....185 A1
Regency Rd BN1 .....189 A2
Regency Sq BN1 .....163 E5
Regent Arc BN1 .....189 B2
Regent Bsns Pk RH15 ..72 E2
Regent Hill BN1 .....189 A2
Regent Pl
  Royal Tunbridge Wells TN2 ..8 D3
  St Leonards TN37 ...135 F7
Regent Row BN1 .....189 A2
Regent Sq TN31 ......93 C6
Regent St BN1 ......189 B2
Regents Cl BN25 ....180 E5
Regina Ct TN4 ....7 F4
Reginald Rd TN39 ....157 B4
Regnum Cl BN22 ....173 E4
Reigate Rd BN1 .....142 D1
Renascent Ho 18 BN21 .185 B3
Renfrew Cl BN2 .....185 A1
Resting Oak Hill BN8 .100 F3
Reynolds Dr TN40 ...157 E5
Reynolds La TN4 ....7 F6
Reynolds Rd
  Eastbourne BN23 ....174 E1
  Hove BN3 ....162 F7
Reynoldstown La BN26 .172 F6
Ribbetts Cotts BN6 ....97 A5
Ribbetts Ho BN6 ......97 A5
Riccards La TN33 .....88 A2
Rices Hill RH19 ....1 E1
Richard Allen Ct BN2 .143 C1
Richardson Ct 5 BN3 .162 F7
Richardson Rd Hove BN3 .162 F7
  Royal Tunbridge Wells TN4 ...8 A3
Richborough Cl TN34 .136 D4
Richington Way BN25 .181 B5
Richland Cl TN35 ....137 E4
Richmead Gdns TN20 ..40 B2
Richmond Ave TN39 ..156 F3
Richmond Cl TN39 ...157 A3
Richmond Ct 9 BN3 .163 E7
Richmond Gr BN3 ....157 A2
Richmond Hts 11 BN2 .189 C3
Richmond Par BN2 ...189 C3
Richmond Pl
  Brighton BN2 ....189 B3
  Eastbourne BN21 ....184 F4
  Royal Tunbridge Wells TN2 ..8 B1
Richmond Rd
  Bexhill TN39 ....157 A3
  Brighton BN2 ....164 B8
  Pevensey Bay BN24 ..175 D5
  Seaford BN25 ......180 E3
Richmond Sq RH19 .....1 D1
Richmond St
  Brighton BN2 ....189 C3
  Hastings TN35 ......160 C6
Richmond Terr
  Brighton BN2 ....189 C4
  1 Seaford BN25 .....180 E3
Richmond Way RH19 ..10 F8
Riddens Cl BN7 ....99 E5
Riddens La BN7 ....99 E6
Riddens The BN7 .....99 E5
Riddlesdale Ave TN4 ....8 A6
Ride The BN1 ....142 F1
Riders Bolt TN39 ....156 E5
Ridge Cl Nutley TN22 ..35 C5
  Portslade-by-Sea BN41 ..141 A4
Ridge Rd BN1 ....144 C7
Ridge The Groombridge TN3 15 A4
  Hastings TN34,TN37 ..136 D6
  Winchelsea Beach TN36 .118 C6
Ridge View BN1 .....143 E5
Ridge W The TN37 ...136 A7
Ridge Way RH17 ......51 B2
Ridgelands Cl BN20 ..184 C3
Ridgeside Ave BN1 ..142 E5
Ridgeway
  East Grinstead RH19 ..10 E7
  Hurst Green TN19 ....45 A3
  Pembury TN2 ....9 D7
  Southwick BN41, BN42 ..140 F1
  The Moor TN18 ......45 E8
Ridgeway Cl
  Heathfield TN21 ......82 A8

Pos-Roc 211

Ridgeway Cl continued
  Southwick BN42 .....140 F1
Ripsley Gdns BN2 ....165 E7
Ridgeway The
  Burgess Hill RH15 ....73 B4
  Friston BN20 ....183 B1
  Herstmonceux BN27 ..130 E6
  Seaford BN25 ......180 F4
Ridgewood Ave BN2 ..166 C3
Ridgewood Cl TN22 ...78 D4
Ridgewood Gdns
  Bexhill TN39 ....157 F4
  Hastings TN34 ......136 E5
Ridgewood Ind Pk TN22 .78 E4
Ridgway Cl BN2 .....165 D8
Ridgway The BN2 ....165 D8
Ridings The Bexhill TN39 .156 F8
  Burgess Hill RH15 ....73 C2
  Newick BN8 ....76 C7
  Ovingdean BN2 .....165 C4
  Royal Tunbridge Wells TN2 ...8 F6
  Seaford BN25 ......180 F5
  St Leonards TN37 ...136 C5
  Telscombe Cliffs BN10 .167 B2
Rigden Rd BN3 ......142 C1
Riley Rd BN2 ....143 C1
Rill Wlk RH19 ....2 B1
Ringle Gn TN18 ....47 C5
Ringmer Bsns Pk BN8 .124 F6
Ringmer Cl BN1 .....143 E4
Ringmer Com Coll BN8 .124 E6
Ringmer Cty Prim Sch
  BN8 ....124 E5
Ringmer Rd Brighton BN1 .143 E4
  Brighton BN1 ....143 F4
  Newhaven BN9 ......179 B6
  Seaford BN25 ......180 E2
Ringmer Way BN23 ..174 A4
Ringwood Cl BN2 ....185 B5
Ringwood Ct 5 BN22 .185 C5
Ringwood Rd
  Bexhill TN39 ....157 C7
  Eastbourne BN22 ....185 B5
Ripe La BN8 ....126 E2
Ripley Chase BN21 ..184 E3
Ripsley Cl BN23 .....174 E2
Risden La TN18 ....46 D7
Rise Park Gdns BN23 .174 E2
Rise The
  East Grinstead RH19 ..10 F8
  Haywards Heath RH16 ..51 B5
  Horam TN21 ....106 F7
  Portslade-by-Sea BN41 ..140 F2
Riseden Rd TN5 ......29 C1
Rising The BN23 ....174 E2
Rissom Ct BN1 .....142 E2
River La BN26 ....171 A3
River Way TN22 ......78 C6
Riverbourne Ho 10 BN2 .185 B4
Riverbridge Cotts TN33 .113 E8
Riverdale TN2 ....123 C2
Riverhall Hill TN5 .....28 F8
Riverside Forest Row RH18 11 E3
  Hadlow Down TN22 ...57 D1
  Newhaven BN9 ......179 D6
  Southwick BN42 ....161 E7
Riverside Bsns Ctr BN43 .161 A7
Riverside Gdns TN6 ...38 C8
Riverside Ind Est BN7 .123 D2
Riverside Rd BN43 ...161 A6
Rixons Cl RH17 ......33 C5
Rixons Orch RH17 ....33 C5
Roadean Cl BN25 ....181 A4
Robert Lodge BN2 ...164 F4
Robert Mitchell Sch
  TN39 ....157 B7
Robert St BN1 ......189 B3
Robert Tressell Cl TN34 .136 E1
Robert Tressell
  Workshops 7 TN34 .159 F8
Robert's Hill TN36 ...117 E8
Roberts Row TN31 ....68 C5
Robertsbridge Com Coll
  TN32 ....63 F4
Robertson Pas TN34 .159 F7
Robertson Rd BN1 ...142 D1
Robertson St TN34 ..159 F7
Robertson Terr 1 TN34 .159 F7
Robertsons Hill TN34 .160 B6
Robian Cl TN22 ....55 A4
Robin Cl East Grinstead RH19 .1 F2
  Eastbourne BN23 ....174 C2
Robin Ct TN39 ......157 A3
Robin Davis Cl BN2 ..143 E1
Robin Dene BN2 .....164 E4
Robin Hill TN39 .....156 D4
Robin Post La BN26 ..151 B1
Robin Rd RH15 ....72 D2
Robinia Lodge BN1 ..142 E2
Robins Row BN41 ....141 A1
Robinson Rd BN9 ...179 C8
Robinsons Ct BN22 ..185 C6
Roborough Cl BN21 ..185 A4
Robsack Ave TN38 ...135 C4
Robsack Wood
  Cty Prim Sch TN38 .135 E2
Rochdale Ho TN1 ......8 C5
Rochdale Rd TN1 ......8 C6
Rochester Cl
  Eastbourne BN20 ....188 C8
  5 Hove BN3 ....163 D6
Rochester Ct 4 BN3 .163 D6
Rochester Gdns BN3 .163 D6
Rochester Ho TN6 ....26 C1

Rochester Rd 4 TN37 . . .136 B2
Rochester St BN2 . . . . . . .164 D5
Rochester Way TN6 . . . . . .26 B1
Rochford Way BN25 . . . . .180 B6
Rochmans Way TN6 . . . . .38 A8
Rock Channel TN31 . . . . .93 C5
Rock Channel Quay TN31 .93 C5
Rock Cl Hastings TN35 . . . .137 D4
  12 Southwick BN42 . . . . .161 E7
Rock Cotts TN3 . . . . .17 B1
Rock Gr BN2 . . . . .164 E4
Rock Hall Cotts TN22 . . . .78 D8
Rock La TN35 . . . . .137 D7
Rock Lodge Vineyard
  RH17 . . . . .52 A2
Rock Pl BN2 . . . . .189 C1
Rock St BN2 . . . . .164 E4
Rock Villa Rd TN1 . . . . . . .8 A4
Rock's Hill TN35 . . . . . . .114 E7
Rock-a-Nore Par TN34 . .160 B4
Rock-a-Nore Rd TN34 . . .160 B3
Rockall Ave BN23 . . . . . .185 F8
Rockall Dr BN27 . . . . . . .129 A2
Rockhurst Dr BN20 . . . . .184 B6
Rockington Way TN6 . . . .38 B8
Rocklands Cotts BN27 . .131 B5
Rocklands La TN35 . . . . .160 C5
Rockmead Rd TN35 . . . . .138 F4
Rocks Hill TN32 . . . . .64 E6
Rocks La TN22 . . . . .55 F7
Rocks Park Cty Prim Sch
  TN22 . . . . .78 B8
Rocks Park Rd TN22 . . . . .78 B7
Rocks The RH19 . . . . .11 D6
Rocky La RH16, RH15 . . .50 D1
Roderick Ave
  Peacehaven BN10 . . . . .178 D8
  Peacehaven BN10 . . . . .178 C8
Roderick Ave N BN10 . . .167 C2
Rodmell Ave BN2 . . . . . .177 D5
Rodmell CE Prim Sch
  BN7 . . . . .146 E1
Rodmell Ct 5 BN25 . . . . .180 C4
Rodmell Ho BN9 . . . . . . .168 D3
Rodmell Pl BN1 . . . . .143 A6
Rodmell Rd
  Royal Tunbridge Wells TN2 . . .8 A2
  Seaford BN25 . . . . .181 B2
Rodmill Dr BN21 . . . . . . .184 D6
Rodmill Rd BN21 . . . . . . .184 D5
Rodney Cl BN23 . . . . . . .185 F7
Rodwell TN6 . . . . .26 C1
Roebuck St 18 TN34 . . . .160 B4
Roedale Rd BN1 . . . . .143 B1
Roedean Cl TN39 . . . . . . .157 A4
Roedean Cres BN2 . . . . .165 A4
Roedean Hts BN2 . . . . . .165 A4
Roedean Path BN2 . . . . .165 A4
Roedean Rd Brighton BN2 .164 F4
  Royal Tunbridge Wells TN2 . .8 A1
Roedean Sch BN2 . . . . . . .165 C3
Roedean Terr BN2 . . . . . .165 B3
Roedean Vale BN2 . . . . . .165 B3
Roedean Way BN2 . . . . . .165 B3
Roeheath BN8 . . . . .75 F4
Roffrey Ave BN22 . . . . . .173 D1
Rolfe Dr RH15 . . . . .73 D3
Romaine Cl RH15 . . . . . . .73 D5
Roman Cl BN25 . . . . .180 B6
Roman Cres BN42 . . . . . .161 E8
Roman Croft BN21 . . . . .184 E4
Roman Rd Hove BN3 . . . .162 D6
  Southwick BN42 . . . . . .161 E8
Roman Way
  Southwick BN42 . . . . . .161 E8
  Uckfield TN22 . . . . .78 E7
Romans Way BN24 . . . . .174 E6
Romany Cl BN41 . . . . . . .162 B8
Romford Rd TN2, TN12 . . .9 F7
Romney Cl BN25 . . . . . . .181 C4
Romney Rd Polegate BN26 173 B7
  Rottingdean BN2 . . . . . .177 A5
Romney St BN22 . . . . . . .185 C5
Romsey Cl BN1 . . . . .143 C2
Rookery Cl Hove BN1 . . . .142 E1
  South Heighton BN9 . . . .168 E2
Rookery La
  Rushlake Green TN21 . . . .83 C2
  Winchelsea TN36 . . . . . .117 F7
Rookery The BN23 . . . . . .174 C4
Rookery Way
  Haywards Heath RH16 . . . .50 E1
  Newhaven BN9 . . . . . . .168 C2
  Seaford BN25 . . . . .180 B5
Rookhurst Rd TN40 . . . . .157 F5
Rookley Cl TN2 . . . . .8 D2
Rookwood Cl TN22 . . . . .78 E8
Roopers TN3 . . . . .7 A7
Roosevelt Ct TN38 . . . . .136 B3
Rope Wlk Hailsham TN27 .152 B8
  Rye TN31 . . . . .93 C6
Rope Wlk The TN18 . . . . .47 B5
Roper's Gate TN2 . . . . . . .7 E1
Rosary Ct RH15 . . . . .73 B2
Rose Cotts RH17 . . . . . . .34 A4
Rose Ct BN6 . . . . .97 E4
Rose Hill BN2 . . . . .189 C4
Rose Hill Cl BN1, BN2 . . .189 B4
Rose Hill Ct BN2 . . . . . . .189 B4
Rose Hill Ho TN1 . . . . .8 A3
Rose Hill Sch TN4 . . . . .7 E5
Rose Hill Terr BN1 . . . . . .189 B4
Rose Walk Cl BN9 . . . . . .179 C7
Rose Wlk BN25 . . . . .180 F4
Rose Wlk The BN9 . . . . .179 C7

Rosebarn Cl RH15 . . . . . . .73 C1
Rosebery Ave
  Eastbourne BN22 . . . . . .173 E1
  Woodingdean BN2 . . . . .165 C8
Rosedale Pl BN22 . . . . . .173 D3
Rosedene Cl BN2 . . . . . . .165 E6
Rosefield Cotts TN32 . . . . .65 F1
Rosehill Gdns TN6 . . . . . .26 C1
Rosehill Wlk TN1 . . . . .8 A3
Roselands Bexhill TN39 . .156 F6
  Sedlescombe TN33 . . . . . .88 E1
Roselands Ave
  Eastbourne BN22 . . . . . .185 C5
  Wellbrook TN20 . . . . .39 C1
Roselands Cl BN22 . . . . .185 C5
Roselands Cty Inf Sch
  BN22 . . . . .185 B5
Roseleigh Gdns RH17 . . . .51 F3
Rosemary Cl
  Haywards Heath RH17 . . . .50 B6
  Peacehaven BN10 . . . . .167 C1
Rosemary Dr BN43 . . . . .140 C1
Rosemary La
  Shellies Green TN35 . . . .138 D6
  Stonecrouch TN5 . . . . . . .32 A5
Rosemount Cl BN25 . . . . .180 A6
Rosetti Rd BN2 . . . . .175 D4
Roseveare Rd BN22 . . . . .185 C6
Rossdale TN2 . . . . .8 D5
Rosslyn Ave BN43 . . . . . .161 A7
Rosslyn Rd BN43 . . . . . . .161 A7
Rotary Lodge BN1 . . . . . .143 E6
Rotary Point BN41 . . . . . .141 B1
Rothbury Rd BN3 . . . . . . .162 D7
Rother Ave BN24 . . . . . . .173 F5
Rother Cl Burwash TN19 . . .62 B6
  Crowborough TN6 . . . . . .38 A7
Rother Ct TN39 . . . . .157 B6
Rother Rd BN25 . . . . .181 A2
Rother Valley Railway Mus
  TN32 . . . . .64 A4
Rother View TN19 . . . . . . .62 B7
Rotherfield Ave
  Bexhill TN40 . . . . .157 D4
  Eastbourne BN23 . . . . . .174 A4
  Hastings TN34 . . . . .160 B5
Rotherfield Cl BN1 . . . . . .143 B6
Rotherfield Cres BN1 . . .143 B5
Rotherfield Cty Prim Sch
  TN6 . . . . .39 B8
Rotherfield La TN20 . . . . .39 F4
Rotherfield Rd TN6 . . . . . .38 E8
Rotherhurst La TN6 . . . . .39 B6
Rothermead TN20 . . . . . . .39 F1
Rotherview TN32 . . . . . . .64 C5
Rothley Chase RH16 . . . . .50 F4
Rothsay Rd TN38 . . . . . . .159 B7
Rothwell Ct BN9 . . . . . . .179 A7
Rotten Row RH7 . . . . .146 B8
Rottingdean
CE Prim Sch BN2 . . . . . .177 A6
Rottingdean Pl BN2 . . . . .165 C4
Rotunda Rd BN23 . . . . . .185 D8
Rotyngs The BN2 . . . . . . .165 F2
Rough Brow BN25 . . . . . .181 A4
Rough Field RH19 . . . . .1 D4
Rough The BN8 . . . . .76 C7
Round Hill Rd 2 BN2 . . . .164 B8
Round Hill St 3 BN2 . . . .164 B8
Roundacres Way TN40 . . .157 E6
Roundel The TN37 . . . . . .136 D5
Roundhay Ave BN10 . . . .178 E6
Roundhill Cres BN2 . . . . .164 B8
Roundhill Rd TN2 . . . . .8 D1
Roundhouse Cotts TN21 . .82 D7
Roundway BN1 . . . . .143 E5
Roundwood La RH16 . . . . .50 F8
Roundwood Rd TN37 . . . .136 B5
Rowan Ave
  Eastbourne BN22 . . . . . .173 D3
  Hove BN3 . . . . .141 E1
Rowan Cl
  Haywards Heath RH16 . . . .51 B4
  Heathfield TN21 . . . . .82 A5
  Portslade-by-Sea BN41 . .141 A1
  Seaford BN25 . . . . .181 C3
  St Leonards TN37 . . . . . .136 D6
Rowan Ct Hove BN1 . . . . .142 E1
  Polegate BN26 . . . . .173 A6
Rowan Gdns TN40 . . . . . .157 F6
Rowan Tree Rd TN2 . . . . . .7 E1
Rowan Way BN2 . . . . . . .165 E4
Rowan's Ct 1 BN7 . . . . . .123 C1
Rowanden Ct BN2 . . . . . .177 C4
Rowans The RH15 . . . . . . .72 D4
Rowbarns TN33 . . . . .112 C6
Rowe Ave BN10 . . . . .178 B7
Rowe Ave N BN10 . . . . . .178 B8
Rowsley Rd BN20 . . . . . .188 D7
Royal Alexandra Hospl
for Sick Children The
  BN1 . . . . .189 A3
Royal Chase TN4, TN1 . . . .7 F4
Royal Cres BN2 . . . . .164 C4
Royal Crescent Mans
  BN2 . . . . .164 C4
Royal Crescent Mews
  BN2 . . . . .164 C4
Royal Dr BN25 . . . . .180 E6
Royal George Par BN43 . .140 C1
Royal George Rd RH15 . . .72 E3
Royal Mews TN38 . . . . . .159 B4
Royal Military Rd TN36 . .118 A8
Royal Oak La TN22 . . . . . .56 B8
Royal Par
  Eastbourne BN22 . . . . . .185 C4
  Eastbourne BN22 . . . . . .185 D5

Rosebarn Cl RH15 . . . . . . .73 C1
Royal Pavilion BN1 . . . . .189 B2
Royal Sovereign View
  BN23 . . . . .185 F6
Royal Sussex Cres BN20 .184 B5
Royal Sussex Ct BN7 . . . .146 D8
Royal Sussex Cty Hospl
  (General) BN2 . . . . .164 D4
Royal Terr 4 TN37 . . . . . .159 B2
Royal Victoria Place Sh Ctr
  TN1 . . . . .8 B4
Royles Cl BN2 . . . . .177 A6
Royston Cl BN20 . . . . . . .183 A1
Royston Gdns TN40 . . . . .157 F6
Rudyard Cl BN2 . . . . .165 E8
Rudyard Kipling
Cty Prim Sch BN2 . . . . . .165 E7
Rudyard Rd BN2 . . . . .165 E8
Rue De Bayeux TN33 . . . .112 D5
Ruffet Ct TN2 . . . . .7 E1
Rufus Ct BN2 . . . . .123 C1
Rugby Cl BN25 . . . . .181 B4
Rugby Ct 5 BN2 . . . . . . .164 E4
Rugby Pl BN2 . . . . .164 E4
Rugby Rd BN1 . . . . .143 A1
Rumbolds La RH16 . . . . . .50 D2
Rumsey Ct TN6 . . . . .25 F1
Rusbridge La 4 BN7 . . . .123 E1
Rush Ct 4 BN2 . . . . .185 B3
Rushers Cross TN20 . . . . .40 E5
Rushes The RH16 . . . . .51 C4
Rushetts TN3 . . . . .6 F4
Rushey Cl BN8 . . . . .124 E5
Rushey Rd RH15 . . . . .73 C4
Rushlake Cl BN1 . . . . .143 E5
Rushlake Cres BN21 . . . .184 D6
Rushlake Rd BN1 . . . . . . .143 E5
Rushlye Cl TN3 . . . . .17 F5
Rushmere Rise TN38 . . . .135 E1
Rushwood Cl RH16 . . . . . .51 B4
Ruskin Rd Hove BN3 . . . . .162 F8
  Willingdon BN20 . . . . . .173 B1
Rusper Rd Brighton BN1 .143 D6
  Eastbourne BN20 . . . . . .184 B6
Ruspers BN1 . . . . .73 D2
Russell Cotts 5 BN21 . . .184 E4
Russell Cres 2 BN1, BN3 .189 A4
Russell Ct 9 TN34 . . . . . .160 A3
Russell Mews 14 BN1 . . .163 E5
Russell Pl BN1 . . . . .189 A2
Russell Rd BN1 . . . . .189 A2
Russell Row BN7 . . . . . . .123 C3
Russell Sq BN1 . . . . .189 A2
Russell St TN34 . . . . .159 F8
Russet Cl BN26 . . . . .173 C6
Rusthall Grange TN4 . . . . .7 D4
Rusthall High St TN4 . . . . .7 C4
Rusthall Pk TN4 . . . . .7 D4
Rusthall Rd TN4 . . . . .7 D4
Rustic Cl BN10 . . . . .167 B1
Rustic Rd BN10 . . . . .167 B2
Rustington Dr BN20 . . . . .188 F8
Rustington Rd BN1 . . . . . .143 A5
Rustlings Cl RH16 . . . . . . .51 B5
Rustwick TN4 . . . . .7 D4
Rutherfords Bsns Pk
  TN33 . . . . .113 B7
Rutland Cl BN21 . . . . . . .184 D6
Rutland Ct
  3 Eastbourne BN23 . . . .174 E1
  Hove BN3 . . . . .162 F6
Rutland Gdns BN3 . . . . . .162 F7
Rutland Rd BN3 . . . . .163 A7
Rutley Cl TN32 . . . . .64 C5
Ruxley Ct BN23 . . . . .174 D2
Rydal Cl TN4 . . . . .7 E5
Rydal Dr TN4 . . . . .7 E5
Rydal Way BN23 . . . . . . .174 C4
Ryde Ct BN3 . . . . .141 D1
Ryde Rd BN2 . . . . .164 D7
Ryders TN3 . . . . .7 A3
Rye Cl Polegate BN26 . . .173 C7
  Saltdean BN2 . . . . .177 F6
  Seaford BN25 . . . . .181 C4
Rye Harbour
Nature Reserve TN31 . . . .94 B1
Rye Ind Est TN31 . . . . .93 D4
Rye Rd Four Throws TN18 . .46 D8
  Hastings TN35 . . . . .137 D5
  Iden TN30, TN31 . . . . . . .70 A8
  Rye Foreign TN31 . . . . . . .69 E2
Rye St BN22 . . . . .185 D6
Rye Sta TN31 . . . . .93 B6
Ryecroft 1 Brighton BN2 .164 F5
  Haywards Heath RH16 . . . .50 E3
Ryefield Cl BN21 . . . . . . .184 C7
Ryelands Dr BN2 . . . . . . .143 D3
Rylstone Rd BN22 . . . . . .185 C4
Rymers Cl TN2 . . . . .8 D7
Rymill Rd TN38 . . . . .136 A3
Ryst Wood Rd RH18 . . . . .12 B1

S

Sackville Cl
  East Grinstead RH19 . . . . . .1 C3
  Lewes BN7 . . . . .123 C1
Sackville Coll RH19 . . . . . . .1 F1
Sackville Ct Bexhill TN40 .157 D5
  3 East Grinstead RH19 . . .10 F8
Sackville Gdns
  East Grinstead RH19 . . . . . .1 C4
  Hove BN3 . . . . .162 F6
Sackville La RH19 . . . . .1 C2
Sackville Rd Bexhill TN39 .157 B3
  Eastbourne BN22 . . . . . .173 F2
  Hailsham BN27 . . . . . . .152 C6
  Hove BN3 . . . . .163 A7
Sackville Sch RH19 . . . . .2 A1

Sackville Trad Est BN3 . .163 B8
Sacred Heart RC Prim Sch
  TN35 . . . . .160 B5
Sacred Heart Sch TN5 . . . .29 D5
Saddler's Ct 6 TN38 . . . . .159 B6
Saddlers Cl RH15 . . . . . . .73 D1
Sadler Way BN2 . . . . .164 F6
Sadlers Way BN8 . . . . . . .124 D4
Saffreys Ct TN38 . . . . . . .159 B7
Saffron Cl BN43 . . . . .140 C1
Saffron Gate BN21 . . . . . .184 D6
Saffron Gdns BN26 . . . . .170 F3
Saffrons Ct BN21 . . . . . . .184 E2
Saffrons Mead BN20 . . . .184 E2
Saffrons Pk BN20 . . . . . . .184 E1
Saffrons Rd BN21 . . . . . . .184 F2
Saffrons The RH15 . . . . . . .72 F5
St Agnes Rd RH19 . . . . .1 E2
St Andrew's CE Inf Sch
  BN3 . . . . .185 D6
St Andrew's CE Prim Sch
  BN3 . . . . .163 B6
St Andrew's Ct BN9 . . . . .179 B7
St Andrew's Dr BN25 . . . .180 B6
St Andrew's La 11 BN7 . .123 C1
St Andrew's Rd
  Bexhill TN40 . . . . .157 C5
  Brighton BN1 . . . . .143 A1
  Portslade-by-Sea BN41 . .162 C7
St Andrew's Sq 6 TN34 . .159 F8
St Andrews Cl BN27 . . . . .129 A1
St Ann's Ct BN3 . . . . .163 D7
St Anne's Cl TN40 . . . . . .157 C3
St Anne's Cres BN7 . . . . .123 B1
St Anne's Ct
  6 Brighton BN1 . . . . . . .189 A4
  9 Brighton BN2 . . . . . . .164 C4
St Anne's Gdns BN6 . . . . .98 A3
St Anne's Ho 7 BN1 . . . . .189 A4
St Anne's Rd BN21 . . . . . .184 F4
St Anne's Sch BN7 . . . . . . .146 B8
St Annes Gn TN19 . . . . . . .62 A6
St Annes Rd BN20 . . . . . .173 B3
St Annes Well Ho 6
  . . . . .163 D6
St Anns Mans 8 BN1 . . . .163 E7
St Anthony's Ave BN23 . .185 E8
St Anthonys BN8 . . . . . . .124 E6
St Aubyn's Cres BN41 . . .162 B7
St Aubyn's Gdns 13 BN3 .163 A6
St Aubyn's Mead BN2 . . .177 A5
St Aubyn's Rd
  Eastbourne BN22 . . . . . .185 B3
  Portslade-by-Sea BN41 . .162 C7
  Southwick BN41 . . . . . . .162 A7
St Aubyns BN3 . . . . .163 B6
St Aubyns Mans BN3 . . . .163 A5
St Aubyns S BN3 . . . . . . .163 A5
St Aubyns Sch BN2 . . . . . .165 F1
St Augustine Cl RH17 . . . .51 F3
St Augustine's Cl TN39 . .156 F3
St Augustine's
RC Prim Sch TN4 . . . . .8 A7
St Barnabas CE Prim Sch
  TN1 . . . . .8 B5
St Barnabas' Cl TN1 . . . . . .8 B5
St Bartholomew's
CE Prim Sch BN1 . . . . . .189 B4
St Bede's Prep Sch BN20 188 B7
St Bernadette's
RC Prim Sch BN1 . . . . . .142 E2
St Boswells Cl BN27 . . . . .152 A8
St Brelades BN21 . . . . . . .185 B2
St Catherine's Cl TN37 . . .159 D8
St Catherine's Terr 6
  BN3 . . . . .163 B5
St Christopher's
(Trng Coll, Dr Barnardo's
Home) TN2 . . . . .8 B4
St Christopher's Rd BN6 . .97 A6
St Christopher's Sch
  BN3 . . . . .163 A6
St Clement's Caves TN34 160 A4
St Clement's Ct BN21 . . . .184 D6
St Clements Pl 5 TN38 . .159 C6
St Crispians BN25 . . . . . .180 D3
St Crispians Ct BN25 . . . .180 D3
St Cuthmans Cl BN2 . . . .164 F6
St David's Ave TN40 . . . . .157 C5
St David's Cl BN10 . . . . . .178 B8
St David's Rd TN4 . . . . .8 B6
St Davids Cl BN22 . . . . . .173 D4
St Dominic Cl TN38 . . . . .159 A8
St Edmund's Rd RH16 . . . .50 F3
St Edward's Cl RH19 . . . . . .1 C1
St Elizabeth's BN25 . . . . .180 F4
St Francis Chase TN39 . . .157 A5
St Francis Cl RH16 . . . . . . .50 F2
St George's La BN6 . . . . . .97 B5
St George's Mews BN1 . . .189 B3
St George's Pk TN2 . . . . . .16 F8
St George's Pl
  Brighton BN1 . . . . .189 B3
  Hurstpierpoint BN6 . . . . . .97 B5
St George's Rd
  Bexhill TN40 . . . . .157 C5
  Brighton BN2 . . . . .164 D4
  Eastbourne BN22 . . . . . .185 B4
  Hastings TN34 . . . . .160 A5
St George's Sch 9 A5
St George's Terr 5 BN2 . .164 C4
St Georges St BN2 . . . . . . .1 D1
St Giles CE Prim Sch
  RH17 . . . . .33 C6
St Giles Cl
  Shoreham-by-Sea BN43 . .161 B8
  Winchelsea TN36 . . . . . .117 E7

St Gregory Cl BN20 . . . . .188 E8
St Gregory's
Catholic Comp Sch TN4 . . .8 A7
St Helen's Ave TN34 . . . . .136 E2
St Helen's Cres
  Hastings TN34 . . . . .136 E2
  Hove BN3 . . . . .141 D3
St Helen's Ct TN34 . . . . . .136 E2
St Helen's Down TN34 . . .137 A3
St Helen's Dr BN3 . . . . . . .141 D3
St Helen's Hospl TN35 . . . .137 C3
St Helen's Park Rd TN34 136 E3
St Helen's Rd
  Brighton BN2 . . . . .164 D7
  Hastings TN34 . . . . .136 D2
St Helena's Ct 1 BN21 . .184 E4
St Helens's Wood Rd
  TN34 . . . . .136 E5
St Heliers Ave BN3 . . . . . .162 E7
St James La TN22 . . . . . . .35 C4
St James Rd BN25 . . . . . .185 C4
St James St BN7 . . . . .146 C8
St James Wlk BN25 . . . . . .75 E1
St James' Ave TN40 . . . . .157 D6
St James' CE Inf Sch TN2 . .8 C4
St James' CE Jun Sch TN2 . .8 C4
St James' Cl TN40 . . . . . .157 C7
St James' Cres TN40 . . . .157 D7
St James' Ho 18 BN2 . . . .189 C2
St James' Pk TN1 . . . . .8 C5
St James' Rd Bexhill TN40 157 C6
  Royal Tunbridge Wells TN1 . .8 C5
St James's Ave BN2 . . . . .189 C2
St James's Ct TN1 . . . . .8 B4
St James's Rd
  East Grinstead RH19 . . . . . .1 D1
  Hastings TN34 . . . . .136 F1
St James's St BN2 . . . . . .189 C2
St James's Street Mews
  BN2 . . . . .189 C2
St John Bank BN8 . . . . . .100 D8
St John St BN7 . . . . .123 D1
St John the Baptist RC
Prim Sch BN2 . . . . .164 D5
St John's Ave RH15 . . . . . .72 F7
St John's CE Prim Sch
  Crowborough TN6 . . . . . .25 C4
  Royal Tunbridge Wells TN4 . .8 A5
St John's Cl
  Crowborough TN6 . . . . . .25 E3
  East Grinstead RH19 . . . . . .1 E2
  South Chailey BN8 . . . . .100 D7
St John's Dr BN24 . . . . . .174 E6
St John's Hill 2 BN7 . . . .123 C1
St John's Ho BN20 . . . . . .188 F8
St John's Mount 8 BN2 . .189 C2
St John's Pk 8 A8
St John's Pl Brighton BN2 189 C2
  22 Hove BN3 . . . . .163 C6
St John's Rd Bexhill TN40 157 D6
  Crowborough TN6 . . . . . .25 D4
  East Grinstead RH19 . . . . . .1 E2
  Eastbourne BN20 . . . . . .188 F8
  Haywards Heath RH16 . . . .50 E2
  Hove BN3 . . . . .163 C6
  Polegate BN26 . . . . .173 A6
  Royal Tunbridge Wells TN4 . .8 A6
  Seaford BN25 . . . . .180 E2
  St Leonards TN37 . . . . . .159 C7
St John's Sch
  Brighton BN2 . . . . .164 D5
  Seaford BN25 . . . . .180 E6
St John's Terr 3 BN2 . . . .123 C1
St Johns CE Prim Sch TN4 . .8 B7
St Johns Cl RH15 . . . . .73 A3
St Johns Rd RH15 . . . . . . .73 A3
St Joseph's Cl BN3 . . . . . .163 C6
St Joseph's
RC Cty Prim Sch BN2 . . .143 C1
St Joseph's
RC Prim Sch RH16 . . . . . .50 E4
St Joseph's Trad Est
  BN3 . . . . .163 A8
St Josephs Way RH16 . . . .50 E4
St Julian's La BN43 . . . . . .161 D7
St Julians Cl BN43 . . . . . .161 C7
St Keyna Ave BN3 . . . . . . .162 D6
St Kitts 3 TN39 . . . . .157 A2
St Laurence Cl BN10 . . . .167 A4
St Lawrence CE Prim Sch
  BN6 . . . . .97 A6
St Lawrence Mews BN23 175 A1
St Lawrence Pl BN23 . . . .175 A1
St Lawrence Rd TN39 . . . .157 B7
St Lawrence Way
  Hurstpierpoint BN6 . . . . . .97 A7
  Pevensey Bay BN23 . . . . .175 A1
St Leonard's Ave BN3 . . . .162 D7
St Leonard's Gdns BN3 . .162 D7
St Leonard's Pl BN20 . . . .184 C3
St Leonard's Rd 9
  Brighton BN2 . . . . .164 C8
  Eastbourne BN21 . . . . . .185 A3
  Hove BN3 . . . . .162 C7
  Newhaven BN9 . . . . . . .168 F2
St Leonards CE Prim Sch
  TN38 . . . . .159 A7
St Leonards Cl BN9 . . . . .168 F2
St Leonards Ct TN38 . . . .159 A6
St Leonards Pk RH19 . . . . .1 E2
St Leonards Rd TN40 . . . .157 C3
St Leonards Terr BN26 . . .172 F7
St Leonards Warrior
Square Sta TN38 . . . . . . .159 C7
St Louie Cl BN42 . . . . . . .162 A8
St Lucia 1 TN39 . . . . .157 A2
St Lucia Wlk BN23 . . . . . .185 F8

St Luke's CE Inf Sch TN4 ..8 C7
St Luke's Cty Inf Sch
BN2 ....164 C6
St Luke's Cty Jun Sch
BN2 ....164 C6
St Luke's La BN9 ....179 C7
St Luke's Rd Brighton BN2 164 C6
Royal Tunbridge Wells TN4 ...8 B6
St Luke's Terr BN2 .....164 C6
St Lukes Ct RH15 ....73 A3
St Margaret CE Prim Sch
BN6 ....98 D3
St Margaret's Ave RH19 ...1 F6
St Margaret's Pl BN1 ...189 C7
St Margaret's Rd
East Grinstead RH19 ......1 F3
St Leonards TN37 ....159 D7
St Margaret's Rise BN25 .180 A6
St Margaret's Terr TN37 .159 D7
St Margarets BN2 ....177 A5
St Margarets Cres TN39 .156 B8
St Margarets Terr TN31 ..93 C5
St Mark's CE Prim Sch
Brighton BN2 ....164 E5
Hadlow Down TN22 ......57 C5
Royal Tunbridge Wells TN4 ...7 D1
St Mark's Rd TN2 ....16 F7
St Mark's St BN2 ....164 E4
St Marks Cl TN39 ....156 D5
St Marks Field TN22 .....57 B5
St Martin's Flats 6 BN2 .164 C7
St Martin's La 8 BN7 ...146 C8
St Martin's Pl BN2 .....164 C7
St Martin's St BN2 .....189 C5
St Martins TN33 ....112 C5
St Martins CE Prim Sch
BN2 ....164 C8
St Martins Cres BN9 ....168 D1
St Martins Ho BN8 .....124 E6
St Martins Rd BN22 ....173 D3
St Mary Magdalen
RC Prim Sch BN1 ....163 C6
St Mary Magdalen's
RC Prim Sch TN40 ...157 F6
St Mary Magdalene St
BN2 ....189 C5
St Mary Star of the Sea
RC Prim Sch TN37 ...159 D8
St Mary the Virgin
CE Prim Sch TN7 .....13 D4
St Mary's CE Sch RH19 ...1 D2
St Mary's Cl
Cackle Street TN31 ......90 A2
Ticehurst TN5 ....31 D1
Willingdon BN22 ....173 B2
St Mary's Cnr 3 BN21 ..184 D3
St Mary's Cotts
Battle TN33 ....112 E3
Bexhill TN39 ....156 F8
4 Eastbourne BN20 ....184 D3
St Mary's Ct
2 Eastbourne BN21 ....184 D3
8 St Leonards TN37 ...159 C7
St Mary's Farmhouse
TN33 ....112 E3
St Mary's Gdns TN33 ...112 E3
St Mary's La Bexhill TN39 .156 F8
Speldhurst TN3 ....7 A8
Ticehurst TN5 ....31 D1
St Mary's Pl BN2 ....189 C2
St Mary's RC Prim Sch
Crowborough TN6 ....26 A2
Portslade-by-Sea BN41 ..162 B7
St Mary's Rd
Burgess Hill RH15 ....72 F4
Eastbourne BN21 ....184 D4
Hastings TN34 ....160 A5
St Mary's Rd W RH15 ...72 E4
St Mary's Sch
Bexhill TN40 ....157 E6
Maynard's Green TN21 ...82 A1
St Mary's Sq 17 BN2 ...164 D4
St Mary's Terr
Battle TN33 ....112 F3
Hastings TN34 ....160 A5
St Mary's Villas TN33 ..112 F3
St Mary's Wlk BN27 ....152 C7
St Mary-in-the-Fields
TN20 ....40 B2
St Marys TN21 ....80 E7
St Marys Ave BN27 .....152 C7
St Marys Garth TN2 .....56 C4
St Marys Pl 3 BN43 ....161 A6
St Matthew's Dr TN38 ..136 C1
St Matthew's Gdns
TN38 ....136 B1
St Matthew's High Brooms
CE Prim Sch TN4 ....8 B8
St Matthew's Rd TN38 ..136 B1
St Matthews Ct BN2 ...164 C5
St Mellion Cl BN27 ....151 F6
St Michael's Cty Prim Sch
TN7 ....14 B5
St Michael's Pl
Brighton BN1 ....163 E6
8 Hastings TN34 ......159 E7
St Michael's Rd
Portslade-by-Sea BN41 ..162 B7
Royal Tunbridge Wells TN4 ...8 B7
St Michael's Terr BN7 ..123 D3
St Michaels Cl
Crowborough TN6 ......38 B8
Stone Cross BN24 .....174 A6
St Michaels Rd RH19 .....1 E2
St Nicholas CE Inf Sch .51 A6
St Nicholas La 13 BN7 .123 D1
St Nicholas Lodge BN1 .189 A2
St Nicholas Pl 2 BN43 .161 A6

St Nicholas Rd
Brighton BN1 ....189 A3
Portslade-by-Sea BN41 ..162 B7
St Nicholas' CE Jun Sch
BN41 ....162 B8
St Nicolas & St Mary
CE Sch BN43 ....161 A8
St Nicolas Cl BN24 ....175 B6
St Olive's Cl TN21 ....81 C7
St Pancras Gdns BN7 ...146 B8
St Pancras Gn BN7 .....145 E5
St Pancras RC Prim Sch
BN7 ....123 B1
St Pancras RC Prim Sch
BN7 ....146 B1
St Patrick's Cres TN40 .157 C5
St Patrick's Rd BN3 ....163 A7
St Paul's CE Prim Sch
BN1 ....189 A3
St Paul's CE Prim Sch
TN37 ....136 D1
St Paul's Cl RH16 ....50 F5
St Paul's Ct Rusthall TN4 ...7 C4
St Leonards TN37 ......159 D8
St Paul's Pl TN37 ......159 D8
St Paul's RC Sec Sch
RH16 ....50 F5
St Paul's Rd TN37 .....136 C1
St Paul's St Brighton BN2 189 C5
Rusthall TN4 ....7 C4
St Pauls CE Inf Sch TN4 ...7 B4
St Pauls CE Jun Sch TN4 ...7 B4
St Pauls Cl BN22 ......173 D3
St Peter & St Paul
CE Prim Sch TN40 ...157 C4
St Peter's Ave BN10 ...178 A8
St Peter's CE Prim Sch TN28 C3
St Peter's Cl Hove BN3 .141 E7
Seaford BN25 ....180 E5
St Peter's Cres TN40 ..157 C5
St Peter's Cty Inf Sch
BN41 ....162 B7
St Peter's Mews TN40 ..157 D5
St Peter's Pl BN1, BN2 .189 B3
St Peter's RC Prim Sch
BN43 ....161 A8
St Peter's RC Sch RH19 ...1 C1
St Peter's Rd
Portslade-by-Sea BN41 ..162 B7
Seaford BN25 ....180 E5
St Leonards TN37 ......159 C8
St Peter's St Brighton BN1 189 B4
Royal Tunbridge Wells TN2 ...8 C3
St Peters Mdw TN2 ......39 A7
St Peters Pl BN7 ....123 C1
St Peters Rd RH15 ......73 A4
St Peters Row TN3 ......6 A5
St Philip's Ave BN22 ...185 B5
St Philip's RC Prim Sch
TN22 ....78 C5
St Philips Ct TN2 ....8 D6
St Philips Mews 3 BN3 .162 F7
St Richard's Ct BN3 ....141 D1
St Richard's Flats BN41 .162 B7
St Richard's RC Sch
TN40 ....157 E4
St Richard's Rd Bexhill TN40 .162 B7
St Richards Ho 3 TN38 .159 C7
St Richards Rd TN6 ......38 A7
St Saviour's Rd TN38 ..158 F6
St Saviours Ct 1 BN1 ..164 B8
St Stephens Ct TN1 ......8 B5
St Swithun's Cl RH19 ....1 F1
St Swithun's La 1 BN7 .146 C8
St Swithun's Terr 6 BN7 .146 C8
St Thomas 5 TN39 .....157 A2
St Thomas a' Becket
RC Inf Sch BN21 .....184 F5
St Thomas a' Becket
RC Jun Sch BN21 ....184 F5
St Thomas CE Prim Sch
TN36 ....117 F7
St Thomas Ct 3 BN7 ...123 E1
St Thomas of Canterbury
Ct TN20 ....40 A2
St Thomas' CE Prim Sch
TN3 ....15 C6
St Thomas's Rd TN34 ..160 A5
St Thomas's St TN36 ...117 F7
St Vincent's Ct BN2 ...165 A3
St Vincent's Sch TN38 ..158 F7
St Vincents Flats TN37 .136 B4
St Vincents Pl BN20 ...184 E1
St Vincents Rd TN38 ...158 F7
St Wilfred's 5 RH16 ....50 E4
St Wilfred's Pl BN25 ...181 B3
St Wilfreds Rd RH15 ....73 B4
St Wilfrid's CE Prim Sch
RH16 ....50 F3
St Wilfrid's Ct TN37 ...152 B8
St Wilfrid's Gn BN27 ...152 C8
St Wilfrid's Way RH16 ..50 E4
St Wilfrids RC Prim Sch
RH15 ....72 F2
Saint Hill Manor RH19 ...10 C4
Saint Hill Rd RH19 ......10 C5
Saints Hill TN11 ....6 A8
Salcey Cl TN38 ....135 E2
Salehurst CE Prim Sch
TN32 ....64 B4
Salehurst Gdns TN38 ...135 D2
Salehurst Rd BN21 ....184 C4
Salisbury Cl BN22 .....173 C2
Salisbury Ct BN25 .....180 E4
Salisbury Rd Bexhill TN40 .157 D5
Eastbourne BN20 ......188 C8
Hove BN3 ....163 C6
Langton Green TN3 ......6 F3
Royal Tunbridge Wells TN4 ...8 C8

Salisbury Rd continued
Seaford BN25 ....180 E3
St Leonards TN37 ......136 C1
Salisbury Terr TN21 ....81 B8
Salisbury Yd TN37 .....136 C1
Sally Ct 3 BN22 ....185 B3
Salomons Rd TN4 ....7 C4
Saltcote La TN31 ....93 C7
Saltcote Mews TN31 ....93 C7
Saltdean Cl TN39 ......156 E3
Saltdean Cty Prim Sch
BN2 ....177 C6
Saltdean Dr BN2 ....177 B5
Saltdean Park Rd BN2 ..177 C5
Saltdean Vale BN2 .....177 D6
Saltdean Way TN39 ....156 D3
Salters La TN34 ....160 B4
Saltwood Rd BN25 .....181 C4
Salvador BN23 ....185 F7
Salvington Cres TN39 ..156 F4
Samoa Way BN23 ......175 B2
San Feliu Ct RH19 ....2 B2
San Jose Ct TN35 .....160 C6
Sancroft Rd BN20 .....184 B3
Sanctuary The BN20 ...184 B4
Sand Hill La BN8,TN22 ..104 B8
Sand Rd TN3 ....20 A4
Sandbanks Cl BN27 ....152 A5
Sandbanks Gdns BN27 ..152 B5
Sandbanks Gr BN27 ....152 B6
Sandbanks Rd BN27 ...152 A5
Sandbanks Way BN27 ..152 B6
Sandbrook BN6 ....97 F3
Sanders Ho BN3 ....162 E8
Sandfield Rd TN11 ......6 A7
Sandgate Cl BN25 .....181 C5
Sandgate Rd BN1 .....143 A2
Sandhawes Hill BN19 ....2 A4
Sandhill La Boarshead TN6 ..26 E7
Churches Green BN27 ...109 B6
Sandhurst Ave Pembury TN2 ..9 E6
Woodingdean BN2 .....144 D1
Sandhurst Cl
Royal Tunbridge Wells TN2 ...8 C6
Sandhurst Cross TN18 ...47 A4
Sandhurst Cty Prim Sch
TN18 ....47 C5
Sandhurst Ho TN2 ....8 D5
Sandhurst La TN39 ....156 B6
Sandhurst Pk TN2 ....8 D6
Sandhurst Rd TN2 ....8 D6
Sandhurst Vineyards TN18 47 E5
Sandore Cl BN25 ....181 A4
Sandore Rd BN25 ......181 A4
Sandown Cl
Eastbourne BN23 .....174 B4
Royal Tunbridge Wells TN2 ...8 F6
Sandown Court Com Coll
TN2 ....8 F5
Sandown Ct BN23 .....141 D1
Sandown Cty Prim Sch
TN34 ....137 C4
Sandown Gr TN2 ....8 F6
Sandown Pk TN2 ....8 F6
Sandown Rd Brighton BN2 164 D7
Hastings TN35 ....137 C3
Southwick BN42 ....161 E8
Sandown Way TN40 ....157 E6
Sandpiper Wlk BN23 ...174 C2
Sandridge TN6 ....25 F1
Sandringham Cl
East Grinstead RH19 .....11 A8
Hove BN3 ....142 A3
Seaford BN25 ....181 A6
Sandringham Dr BN3 ..142 A3
Sandringham Hts TN38 .135 D3
Sandringham Lodge 17
BN3 ....163 C6
Sandrock Hall TN34 ....136 F5
Sandrock Hill TN33,TN38 .135 A4
Sandrock Ho TN2 ....8 D4
Sandrock Pk TN34 .....136 F5
Sandrock Rd TN2 ....8 C4
Sandrocks Way RH16 ...50 E2
Sandwich Dr TN38 .....158 F8
Sandwich St BN22 .....185 C6
Sandy Cl TN37 ....136 B5
Sandy Cross Cotts TN21 .82 A5
Sandy Cross La TN21 ...82 B5
Sandy La
Chelwood Gate RH17 ....34 C8
Coleman's Hatch TN7 ...23 D6
East Grinstead RH19 .....1 F1
Framefield TN22 ....79 A7
Lions Green TN21 ......81 E2
Sandy Vale RH16 ....50 E2
Sanshaw Ct BN21 .....184 E3
Santa Cruz Dr BN23 ...185 F7
Santer Ho TN18 ....45 E8
Sanyhils Ave BN1 .....142 F7
Saunders Cl
Hastings TN34 ....160 A5
Uckfield TN22 ....78 A8
Saunders Mill BN1 ....143 D7
Saunders Park Ho 2
BN2 ....164 C8
Saunders Park Rise BN2 143 C1
Saunders Park View BN2 143 C1
Saunders Rd TN4 ....7 E1
Saunders Way TN31 ....95 A2
Savill Rd RH16 ....51 A8
Sawyard Cotts TN22 ....53 C5
Sawyers Ct RH15 ....73 D1
Saxby Cl BN23 ....174 E1
Saxby Rd Bexhill TN39 ...157 A5
Burgess Hill RH15 ......72 D4

Saxon Cl BN2 ....177 C6
Saxon Ct Hove BN3 ....162 D6
St Leonards TN37 ......159 C8
Saxon Ground BN21 ...184 E4
Saxon La BN25 ....180 E2
Saxon Mount Sch TN38 .158 E7
Saxon Pl BN21 ....184 C6
Saxon Rd Hastings TN35 .137 D3
Hove BN3 ....162 D6
Newhaven BN9 ....179 C7
Saxon Rise TN40 ......157 E4
Saxon St TN37 ....159 C6
Saxonbury 15 BN2 ....189 C3
Saxonbury Cl TN6 ......25 F2
Saxonhurst Ct TN37 ...136 B4
Saxons TN39 ....156 F2
Saxonwood Rd TN33 ...112 C5
Sayerland La BN26 ....173 A8
Sayerland Rd BN26 ...173 A8
Sayers The 5 RH19 .....1 C1
Scamps Hill RH16 ......51 C5
Scanlon Cl BN20 ......173 A3
Scarborough Rd BN1 ..142 C5
Scarletts Cl TN22 ....78 B7
Scaynes Hill CE Prim Sch
RH17 ....51 F3
Sceptre BN1 ....142 E2
Schofield Way BN23 ...185 F7
School Cl Burgess Hill RH15 .72 F2
1 Southwick BN42 ....161 E7
School Cotts
East Chiltington BN7 ...100 B3
Maresfield TN22 ....55 B3
School Field BN8 ......101 E5
School Hill
Barcombe Cross BN8 ...101 E4
Lamberhurst TN3 ....20 B6
Old Heathfield TN21 ....82 D5
Winchelsea TN36 ......117 E8
School La
Ashurst Wood RH19 ....11 E6
Blackboys TN22 ....80 A6
Crowborough, Blackness TN6 .25 F1
Crowborough, St John's TN6 .25 D4
Danehill RH17 ....34 B5
Forest Row RH18 ....11 F2
Hadlow Down TN22 .....57 B5
Nutley TN22 ....35 C5
Peasmarsh TN31 ....69 B2
Polegate BN26 ....173 A7
Pyecombe BN45 ....119 C6
Saltdean BN2 ....177 C6
School Path BN8 ......101 D4
School Pl TN40 ....158 A5
School Rd Hastings TN35 .137 C3
Hove BN3 ....162 F8
School Rise Brighton BN2 .164 E6
Royal Tunbridge Wells TN2 ...7 F1
School Terr TN32 ....64 C5
Schwerte Way 5 TN37 .159 E7
Science Park Rd BN1 ..144 B7
Science Park Sq BN1 ...144 B6
Scotland St BN2 ....189 C3
Scotney Castle TN3 .....20 D3
Scotney Castle Gdns TN3 20 D3
Scotsford Cl TN21 ......59 F1
Scotsford Hill TN20 .....40 E1
Scotsford Rd TN21 .....59 F2
Scott Rd BN3 ....162 F7
Scotts Acre TN31 ......94 E2
Scotts Way TN2 ....16 E8
Scrace Hill Terr RH16 ...73 F8
Scraper's Hill BN8 .....128 A8
Scrase Lodge RH15 .....73 D3
Scutes Ct TN34 ....137 A3
Sea Cotts 5 BN25 .....180 F2
Sea Ho 14 BN42 ......161 E7
Sea Rd Bexhill TN40 ...157 D3
Camber TN31 ....94 F2
Fairlight Cove TN35 ...139 A5
Hastings TN38 ....158 F6
Pevensey Bay BN24 ...175 D5
Winchelsea Beach TN36 .118 B7
Seabeach La BN22 ....185 C5
Seabourne Rd
Bexhill TN40 ....158 A6
Bexhill TN40 ....158 A5
Seacliffe BN10 ....177 F3
Seafield Cl BN25 ......181 B5
Seafield Rd BN3 ......163 B6
Seaford Cty Prim Sch
BN25 ....180 E4
Seaford Head Com Coll
(Lower) BN25 ....180 F2
Seaford Head Com Coll
(Upper) BN25 ....181 A2
Seaford Rd
Eastbourne BN22 .....185 C5
Hove BN3 ....162 C6
Newhaven BN9 ....179 F8
Seaford Sta BN25 .....180 E3
Seagrave Cl BN25 .....180 A6
Seagrove Way BN25 ...180 D5
Searle Ave BN10 ......178 E6
Seasaw Way BN2 .....164 F7
Seaside BN22,BN23 ...185 C5
Seaside Rd
Eastbourne BN21 .....185 B3
Eastbourne TN38 .....158 F6
Seaside Way TN38 ....158 F6
Seaview Ave BN10 ....178 E6
Seaview Cotts
Hailsham BN27 ....129 D3
Icklesham TN36 ....116 E5
Seaview Est BN42 ....161 F7
Seaview Rd
Newhaven BN9 ....168 F1

Seaview Rd continued
Peacehaven BN10 .....178 E6
Woodingdean BN2 .....165 B8
Seaview Terr
Icklesham TN36 ....116 E5
Rye TN31 ....93 C5
Seaville Dr
Eastbourne BN23 .....185 D5
Pevensey Bay BN24 ...175 D5
Second Ave Bexhill TN40 .157 F5
Camber TN31 ....94 F7
Hove BN3 ....163 C6
Newhaven BN9 ....179 C6
Second Rd BN10 ......178 A7
Sedgebrook Gdns TN34 .136 E2
Sedges The TN38 ......135 E1
Sedgewick Rd TN40 ...157 C6
Sedlescombe CE Prim Sch
TN33 ....88 E1
Sedlescombe Gdns TN38 136 B2
Sedlescombe Rd N TN37 136 B4
Sedlescombe Rd S TN38 136 B1
Sedlescombe Vineyard
TN32 ....88 D5
Sefton Chase TN6 ......26 A3
Sefton Rd BN41 ....140 F3
Sefton Way TN6 ....26 A3
Segrave Cl BN7 ....123 B2
Selba Dr BN2 ....143 E3
Selborne Pl BN3 ......163 C7
Selborne Rd BN3 .....163 C6
Selby Cl TN22 ....78 D5
Selby Ct RH16 ....50 E3
Selby Gdns TN22 ....78 D5
Selby Rd Eastbourne BN21 184 D5
Uckfield TN22 ....78 D6
Selby Rise TN22 ....78 D5
Selham Cl BN1 ....143 D6
Selham Dr BN1 ....143 D6
Selham Ho 6 BN21 ...184 D4
Selhurst Rd BN2 ......165 E6
Sellbourne Pk TN3 .....17 C4
Selmeston Cl TN34 ...136 D1
Selmeston Ct 2 BN25 .180 C4
Selmeston Ho 6 BN21 .184 D4
Selmeston Pl BN2 ....164 F6
Selmeston Rd BN21 ..184 C7
Selmestone Rd BN2 ..164 F5
Selsey Cl BN1 ....143 E6
Selsfield Cl BN21 .....184 D6
Selsfield Dr BN2 ......143 D3
Selwyn Dr BN21 ......184 E4
Selwyn Ho 10 BN21 ..184 E4
Selwyn Park Ct 9 BN21 184 E4
Selwyn Rd BN21 .....184 E4
Semley Lodge BN6 ....97 E4
Semley Rd Brighton BN1 .143 A1
Hassocks BN6 ....97 E4
Sempstead La TN31,TN32 ..66 C6
Senlac Gdns TN33 ....112 E4
Senlac Ct TN33 ....112 D5
Senlac Green TN22 ....78 E8
Senlac Pl TN3 ....15 C7
Senlac Rd BN9 ....179 D7
Senlac Way TN37 .....136 C5
Sergison Cl RH16 ......50 C5
Sergison Rd RH16 .....50 D5
Setfords Field BN8 .....75 E1
Sevelands Cl BN2 ....164 F7
Seven Acre Cl TN37 ...136 A5
Seven Dials BN1 ......189 A4
Seven Sisters Ctry Pk
BN25 ....182 A2
Seven Sisters Rd BN22 .173 C3
Sevenfields RH15 ......72 D4
Sevenoaks Rd BN23 ..174 D2
Seville St BN2 ....164 C7
Sewell Ave TN40 ......157 C5
Seymour Ho 5 BN2 ...164 D4
Seymour Sq 3 BN2 ...164 D4
Seymour St 4 BN2 ....164 D4
Seymour Villas TN37 ..137 A3
Shaftesbury Ct TN22 ...78 C8
Shaftesbury Pl BN1 ...164 A8
Shaftesbury Rd
Brighton BN1 ....189 B5
Royal Tunbridge Wells TN4 ...8 A5
Shakespeare St BN3 ..163 A8
Shakespeare Wlk BN23 .174 D2
Shalesbrook La RH18 ...12 A1
Shalfleet Cl BN23 .....174 B3
Shandon Cl TN2 ....8 C4
Shands BN6 ....97 F3
Shanklin Cl BN23 .....174 B4
Shanklin Ct 11
Brighton BN2 ....164 C8
Hove BN3 ....141 D1
Shanklin Rd BN2 .....164 C8
Shannon Cl BN10 .....167 B1
Shannon Way BN23 ...185 F8
Sharp's Cnr TN21 .....116 B8
Sharpthorne Cres BN41 .141 C1
Sharrow Ct RH16 ......50 E5
Shaw The TN2 ....8 C2
Shawcross Ho BN1 ...142 E2
Shawfield TN6 ....26 B2
Shaws Cnr 5 TN31 ....67 B7
Shearwater Terr TN34 .136 D4
Shedden Ct TN21 ......82 A8
Sheddingdean Bsns Ctr
RH15 ....72 F5
Sheddingdean Cl RH15 .73 A4
Sheddingdean Cty Inf Sch
RH15 ....73 A5

Sheddingdean Neighbourhood Ctr
RH15 . . . . .73 A5
Sheen Rd BN22 . . . . .185 B4
Sheep Pen La 3 BN25 . .181 A3
Sheep Plain TN6 . . . . .37 D8
Sheep Wlk BN2 . . . . .165 F1
Sheepbell Cl BN41 . . . . . .141 B3
Sheepfair BN7 . . . . .123 A2
Sheepfold The BN10 . . . . .167 C1
Sheepsetting La TN21 . . . . .81 E7
Sheepstreet La TN19,TN5 . .43 E5
Sheepwash La TN22 . . . . . .80 C8
Sheerwater Cres TN34 . .136 D4
Sheffield Mill La TN22 . . . .53 C8
Sheffield Park Gdns TN22 53 D5
Sheffield Park Sta TN22 . .53 A4
Sheffield Park Way BN23 174 A4
Sheiling Rd TN6 . . . . .25 E3
Shell La 9 TN34 . . . . . . .160 A3
Shelldale Ave BN41 . . . . .162 B7
Shelldale Cres BN41 . . . . .162 B7
Shelldale Rd BN41 . . . . . .162 B8
Shelley Cl BN7 . . . . .123 B1
Shelley Ct 4 RH16 . . . . . .50 D5
Shelley Pk 4 TN21 . . . . . .82 A7
Shelley Rd
East Grinstead RH19 . . . . . .1 D1
Hove BN3 . . . . .162 F7
Ringmer BN8 . . . . .124 D5
Shelley Wood RH15 . . . . . .72 D4
Shelly Wlk 3 BN23 . . . . .174 E2
Shenfield Way BN1 . . . . .143 B3
Shenstone RH16 . . . . .51 B8
Shepham Ave BN2 . . . . . .177 D6
Shepham La BN26 . . . . . .173 C8
Shepherd St 3 TN38 . . . . .159 C6
Shepherd's Cl TN35 . . . . .156 D4
Shepherd's Hill TN7 . . . . . .23 D4
Shepherd's Way TN35 . . . .138 E4
Shepherds Cl
Eastbourne BN22 . . . . . . .173 F3
Piddinghoe BN9 . . . . . . .168 B2
Ringmer BN8 . . . . .124 C5
Shepherds Cot BN10 . . . .167 D2
Shepherds Croft BN1 . . . .142 C4
Shepherds Ct TN35 . . . . .138 E4
Shepherds Mead RH15 . . . .72 F4
Shepherds Way
Ringmer BN8 . . . . .124 C5
South Chailey BN8 . . . . . .100 C5
Uckfield TN22 . . . . .78 C5
Shepherds Wlk
Crowborough TN6 . . . . . . .26 C1
Hassocks BN6 . . . . .97 F5
Royal Tunbridge Wells TN2 . . .8 D4
Shepherdsgrove La RH19 . . .3 A4
Sheppard Way BN41 . . . . .141 B1
Sheppey Wlk BN27 . . . . . .129 A3
Sheppeys RH16 . . . . .50 D2
Shepway The BN25 . . . . . .181 B4
Sheraton Cl BN21 . . . . . .184 F2
Sherborne Ct 3 BN21 . . . .184 D4
Sherbourne Cl Hove BN3 .141 D3
Royal Tunbridge Wells TN2 . . .8 D2
Sherbourne Rd BN3 . . . . .141 D3
Sherbourne Way BN3 . . . .141 D3
Sheridan Cl RH19 . . . . .1 C1
Sheridan Mans BN3 . . . . .163 A4
Sheridan Terr BN3 . . . . . .163 A4
Sheriff's La TN6 . . . . .39 D7
Sheringham Cl TN32 . . . . .65 E2
Sherrington Rd BN2 . . . . .165 F8
Sherwood Cl TN34 . . . . . .136 F1
Sherwood Dr RH16 . . . . . .50 C5
Sherwood Gn BN27 . . . . .152 B6
Sherwood Park
Cty Prim Sch TN2 . . . . . . .8 D6
Sherwood Pl TN3 . . . . .6 C7
Sherwood Rd
Royal Tunbridge Wells TN2 . . .8 D5
Seaford BN25 . . . . .180 F4
Sherwood Rise BN25 . . . .180 F4
Sherwood Way 8 D6
Shinewater Ct BN23 . . . . .174 B3
Shinewater
Cty Prim Sch BN23 . . . . .174 B4
Shinewater La BN23 . . . . .174 B4
Shinewater Rdbt BN23 . .174 B1
Shingle Ct TN38 . . . . . . .135 E7
Shingle Rd BN43 . . . . . . .161 A6
Ship St Brighton BN1 . . . .189 A2
East Grinstead RH19 . . . . .10 E8
Newhaven BN9 . . . . .179 C8
Ship Street Gdns BN1 . . .189 A2
Shipley La TN39 . . . . .156 D3
Shipley Mill Cl BN24 . . . .174 B5
Shipley Rd BN2 . . . . .165 E7
Shipwreck Heritage Ctr
(Mus) TN34 . . . . .160 B3
Shipyard La TN31 . . . . . . .93 C5
Shirlea View TN33 . . . . . .112 E4
Shirley Ave BN3 . . . . .142 B2
Shirley Cl RH43 . . . . .161 D8
Shirley Dr Hove BN3 . . . . .142 C2
St Leonards TN37 . . . . . . .136 B4
Shirley Gdns TN4 . . . . .7 C5
Shirley Gr TN4 . . . . .7 C5
Shirley Rd BN3 . . . . .163 C8
Shirley St BN3 . . . . .163 B7
Shirleys BN6 . . . . .98 C2
Shoreham Beach
Cty Fst Sch BN43 . . . . . .161 A6
Shoreham By-Pass
BN41,BN43 . . . . .140 D2

Shoreham Coll BN43 . . . .161 D7
Short Brow BN25 . . . . . . .181 A4
Short Brow Cl BN22 . . . . .173 B3
Shortdean Pl BN21 . . . . . .184 D4
Shortgate La
Laughton BN8 . . . . .126 B8
Shortgate BN8 . . . . .104 B2
Shortgate Rd BN2 . . . . . .143 F4
Shorts Cl RH16 . . . . .50 E3
Shotters RH15 . . . . .72 E1
Shovelstrode La RH19 . . . .11 D8
Showfields Rd TN2 . . . . . . .7 F1
Shropshire Ct BN20 . . . . .184 B7
Shrub La TN19 . . . . .62 C7
Shrublands The TN39 . . . .156 E3
Sicklehatch La TN21 . . . . . .82 B2
Sidcup Cl BN23 . . . . .174 D2
Sidehill Dr BN41 . . . . .140 F2
Sidley Cty Prim Sch
TN39 . . . . .157 C7
Sidley Gn TN39 . . . . .157 C7
Sidley Rd BN22 . . . . .185 C5
Sidley St TN39 . . . . .157 C7
Sidney Cl TN2 . . . . .16 F8
Silchester Rd TN38 . . . . . .159 C7
Sillwood Ct 16 BN1 . . . . . .163 E5
Sillwood Hall 2 BN1 . . . . .163 E5
Sillwood Pl 17 BN1 . . . . . .163 E5
Sillwood Rd BN1 . . . . .163 E5
Sillwood St BN1 . . . . .163 E5
Sillwood Terr 22 BN1 . . . .163 E5
Silva Cl TN40 . . . . .158 A6
Silvan Rd TN38 . . . . .135 E4
Silver Bank Cotts TN19 . . .64 B8
Silver Birches
Haywards Heath RH16 . . . .51 A4
Hove BN1 . . . . .142 E1
Silver Hill TN19 . . . . .45 B1
Silverdale BN6 . . . . .98 B3
Silverdale Ave BN3 . . . . . .163 D7
Silverdale Ct BN27 . . . . . .152 B8
Silverdale Cty Prim Sch
TN38 . . . . .136 B3
Silverdale La
Royal Tunbridge Wells TN4 . . .8 B6
Sandhurst Cross TN18 . . . .46 F5
Silverdale Rd
Burgess Hill RH15 . . . . . . .73 B2
Eastbourne BN20 . . . . . . .184 F1
Hove BN3 . . . . .163 D7
Royal Tunbridge Wells TN4 . . .8 B6
Silverden Cotts TN18 . . . . .46 F4
Silverhill Ave TN37 . . . . . .136 C4
Silverlands Rd 1 TN37 . . .136 B2
Silvester Rd TN40 . . . . . . .157 C5
Simmonds Ct TN2 . . . . . . .8 E7
Simmons Ct TN4 . . . . .7 B4
Simons Cl TN6 . . . . .26 A1
Singleton Mill Rd BN24 . . .174 C5
Singleton Rd BN1 . . . . . . .143 A6
Singleton Way RH15 . . . . .73 C1
Sinnock Sq 17 TN34 . . . . .160 B4
Sir Henry Fermor
CE Prim Sch TN6 . . . . . . .26 A2
Six Bells Mews TN31 . . . . .67 C5
Skinner's La TN33 . . . . . . .133 D8
Skinners' Sch The TN4 . . . .8 A6
Skippers Hill Manor
Prep Sch TN20 . . . . .58 B7
Skyline View BN10 . . . . . .167 D1
Slade The TN3 . . . . .20 A3
Sleeches Cross TN3 . . . . . .17 B2
Sleepers Stile Rd TN5 . . . .19 B1
Slider's La TN22 . . . . .53 A7
Slides The TN38 . . . . .135 F3
Slimbridge Rd RH15 . . . . . .72 F3
Slindon Ave BN10 . . . . . .178 D6
Slindon Cres BN23 . . . . . .174 E1
Slinford Cl BN2 . . . . .164 D5
Sliverick's La TN33 . . . . . .109 F7
Sloane Ct 4 BN2 . . . . . . .164 C5
Sloe La BN26 . . . . .171 A3
Slonk Hill Rd BN43 . . . . . .140 A1
Sloop La RH17 . . . . .52 D5
Slugwash La RH17 . . . . . . .74 B7
Smeatons La TN36 . . . . . .118 B5
Smith Cl TN33 . . . . .133 B5
Smithy The Durgates TN5 . .29 A3
Uckfield TN22 . . . . .78 B6
Smithy's Cl TN37 . . . . . . .136 C5
Smolletts RH19 . . . . .10 C8
Smugglers Cl BN26 . . . . .170 F3
Smugglers La TN6 . . . . . . .25 D5
Smugglers Way TN35 . . . .138 F4
Snape La TN5 . . . . .29 D1
Snape View TN5 . . . . .29 F4
Snatt's Rd TN22 . . . . .55 C1
Snednore BN7 . . . . .145 F5
Snipe Cl TN2 . . . . .9 E8
Snowdon Cl BN23 . . . . . .174 D3
Snowdrop La RH16 . . . . . .51 C4
Snowflakes La RH16 . . . . .51 D6
Soames Ct RH15 . . . . .72 F4
Solomon's La TN32 . . . . . .87 C4
Solomons Cl BN23 . . . . . .175 B2
Solway BN27 . . . . .129 A2
Solway Ave BN1 . . . . .142 F7
Somerhill Ave BN3 . . . . . .163 D7
Somerhill Ct 8 BN3 . . . . .163 D7
Somerhill Cty Jun Sch
BN3 . . . . .163 D6
Somerhill Lodge BN3 . . . .163 D6
Somerhill Rd BN3 . . . . . .163 D6
Somerset Ct
Eastbourne BN23 . . . . . . .174 E1
3 Hove BN3 . . . . .163 C7

Somerset Point 1 BN2 . .164 C4
Somerset Rd TN4 . . . . .8 A6
Somerset St BN2 . . . . . . .164 C5
Somerset Villas TN3 . . . . .15 C7
Somerville Gdns TN4 . . . . .7 F4
Sompting Cl BN2 . . . . . . .164 F7
Sompting Ct 3 BN43 . . . .161 B8
Sorrel Cl BN23 . . . . .174 C3
Sorrel Dr BN23 . . . . .174 C3
South Ave Brighton BN2 .164 C5
Eastbourne BN20 . . . . . . .184 B5
Hurstpierpoint BN6 . . . . . .97 A5
South Bank BN6 . . . . . . .97 E3
South Brooks Rd TN29 . . . .96 F2
South Cl Beachlands BN24 .175 F6
Burgess Hill RH15 . . . . . . .72 E3
Hailsham BN27 . . . . .152 B6
South Cliff Bexhill TN39 . .156 F2
Eastbourne BN20 . . . . . . .188 F8
South Cliff Ave
Bexhill TN39 . . . . .156 E2
Eastbourne BN20 . . . . . . .184 F1
South Cliff Tower BN20 . .188 F8
South Cliffe 8 BN7 . . . . . .123 E1
South Coast Rd
Peacehaven BN10 . . . . . .178 D6
Telscombe Cliffs BN2,BN10 .177 E4
South Ct 5 Lewes BN7 . . .123 E1
Royal Tunbridge Wells TN4 . . .8 A6
South Downs BN7 . . . . . .99 E5
South Downs Bsns Pk
BN7 . . . . .123 E2
South Downs Rd BN7 . . . .123 D2
South Dr RH15 . . . . .72 E3
South Gr TN1 . . . . .8 A2
South La Newhaven BN9 .179 D7
Wood's Corner TN21 . . . . .84 E2
South Lodge 6 BN2 . . . . .164 F5
South Lodge Cl RH15 . . . . .72 F4
South Lynn Dr BN21 . . . . .184 F4
South Malling
CE Prim Sch BN7 . . . . . . .123 E2
South Pl 3 BN7 . . . . .123 D1
South Point 7 BN43 . . . . .161 A6
South Rd Brighton BN1 . . .142 E1
Hailsham BN27 . . . . .152 B6
Haywards Heath RH16 . . . .50 E4
Newhaven BN9 . . . . .179 D7
Wivelsfield Green RH17 . . . .74 D4
South Rough BN8 . . . . . . .76 C7
South Side TN21 . . . . . . .59 E1
South St Brighton BN1 . . .189 A2
Crowborough TN6 . . . . . . .25 F1
Ditchling BN6 . . . . .98 D3
East Hoathly BN8 . . . . . . .104 F4
Eastbourne BN21 . . . . . . .185 A2
Falmer BN1 . . . . .144 C6
Lewes BN7 . . . . .123 E1
Mayfield TN20 . . . . .40 B2
Portslade-by-Sea BN41 . . .141 A1
Rotherfield TN6 . . . . .39 B8
Seaford BN25 . . . . .180 E2
St Leonards TN37 . . . . . . .159 C7
South Terr Broad Oak TN21 .59 E1
Hastings TN34 . . . . .159 F8
Westfield TN35 . . . . .114 E3
South Undercliff TN31 . . . .93 C5
South View Ditchling BN6 . .98 E5
11 Eastbourne BN21 . . . . .184 E4
Hastings TN34 . . . . .160 B4
1 South Heighton BN9 . . .168 B2
South View Cl TN19 . . . . .44 F3
South View Rd
Crowborough TN6 . . . . . . .25 E1
Royal Tunbridge Wells TN4 . . .8 B8
Turner's Green TN5 . . . . . .29 F6
South Way Lewes BN7 . . .123 A1
Newhaven BN9 . . . . .179 D7
Seaford BN25 . . . . .181 C1
South Woodlands BN1 . . .142 E5
Southall Ave BN2 . . . . . . .143 D2
Southampton Cl BN23 . . .185 F8
Southampton St BN2 . . . .189 C3
Southborough
CE Prim Schs TN4 . . . . . . .7 F8
Southbourne Rd BN22 . . .185 C6
Southcourt Ave TN39 . . . .156 F2
Southdown Ave
Brighton BN1 . . . . .143 A1
Hastings TN34 . . . . .137 B3
Lewes BN7 . . . . .146 A8
Lower Willingdon BN20 . . .173 A3
Peacehaven BN10 . . . . . .178 E6
Portslade-by-Sea BN41 . . .162 C8
Southdown Cl
Haywards Heath RH16 . . . .50 D2
Newhaven BN9 . . . . .179 B6
Southdown Cotts BN20 . .173 B3
Southdown Ct
3 Hailsham BN27 . . . . . .152 C7
Polegate BN26 . . . . .172 F6
Southdown
Cty Jun Sch BN9 . . . . . . .179 C7
Southdown Ho 4 BN20 . .184 F1
Southdown Pl
Brighton BN1 . . . . .143 A1
Lewes BN7 . . . . .123 E2
Southdown Rd
Brighton BN1 . . . . .143 A1
Eastbourne BN20 . . . . . . .184 C2
Newhaven BN9 . . . . .179 B6
Portslade-by-Sea BN41 . . .141 A2
Seaford BN25 . . . . .181 A2
Southwick BN42 . . . . .161 E7
Southease Sta BN8 . . . . . .168 A7
Southerden Cl BN27 . . . . .152 C7
Southern Ave BN26 . . . . .173 B6

Southern Rd BN22 . . . . . .173 F2
Southern Ring Rd BN1 . . .144 B6
Southfield BN26 . . . . .172 F5
Southfield Rd TN4 . . . . . . .8 A6
Southfields
Sparrow's Green TN5 . . . . .29 F6
Speldhurst TN3 . . . . .7 A7
Southfields Ct 6 BN21 . . .184 F3
Southfields Rd BN21 . . . . .184 F3
Southfields Way TN4 . . . . .8 B8
Southgate TN4 . . . . .7 F3
Southlands RH19 . . . . .10 E7
Southlands Ave TN39 . . . .157 A7
Southlands Ct 1 BN43 . . .161 B8
Southlands General Hospl
BN43 . . . . .161 B8
Southlands Rd TN39 . . . . .157 A7
Southmead Cl TN20 . . . . .40 D3
Southmount BN1 . . . . . . .143 B1
Southon Cl BN41 . . . . . . .140 F3
Southover CE Prim Sch
BN7 . . . . .146 C8
Southover High St BN7 . .146 C8
Southover Manor Ho 10
BN7 . . . . .146 C8
Southover Pl BN2 . . . . . . .189 C4
Southover Rd BN7 . . . . . .146 C8
Southover St BN2 . . . . . . .189 C3
Southridge Rd TN6 . . . . . .37 E8
Southridge Rise TN6 . . . . .37 E8
Southview RH17 . . . . .51 F3
Southview Cl
Crowborough TN6 . . . . . . .25 E1
Southwick BN42 . . . . .140 E1
Southview Dr TN22 . . . . . .78 B8
Southview Rd
Peacehaven BN10 . . . . . .178 C8
Southwick BN42 . . . . .161 E8
Southwater Cl BN2 . . . . . .164 D6
Southwater Rd TN37 . . . . .159 C8
Southway RH15 . . . . .72 D3
Southway Cty Jun Sch
RH15 . . . . .72 D3
Southwick Cl RH19 . . . . . . .1 D1
Southwick Ho 6 RH19 . . . .1 D2
Southwick Sq BN42 . . . . .161 E7
Southwick St BN42 . . . . . .161 E8
Southwick Sta BN42 . . . .161 E7
Southwood Ave TN4 . . . . . .8 A6
Southwood Cl TN38 . . . . .136 A1
Southwood Rd TN4 . . . . . .7 B5
Sovereign Cl
Hastings TN34 . . . . .137 A4
Seaford BN25 . . . . .181 A5
Sovereign Ct
Brighton BN2 . . . . .165 A3
Eastbourne BN22 . . . . . . .185 C5
Sovereign Ctr
Burgess Hill RH15 . . . . . . .72 E2
Eastbourne BN22 . . . . . . .185 E6
Spa Ct 4 BN3 . . . . .163 E6
Spa Ind Est TN2 . . . . .8 E8
Spa Valley Rly TN4 . . . . . . .7 E1
Spaldings The TN38 . . . . .135 E1
Spanish Ct RH15 . . . . .73 B4
Sparks Gdns TN33 . . . . . .133 A6
Sparrow Way RH15 . . . . . .72 D3
Sparrows Green Rd TN5 . . .29 C5
Sparrows The BN10 . . . . .167 D1
Spatham La BN6 . . . . .98 F4
Speldhurst CE Prim Sch
TN3 . . . . .7 A7
Speldhurst Hill TN3 . . . . . .7 B8
Speldhurst Rd
Langton Green TN3 . . . . . . .6 F4
Royal Tunbridge Wells
TN3,TN4 . . . . .7 E8
Spencer Ave BN3 . . . . . . .141 D3
Spencer Mews 6 TN1 . . . .8 A2
Spencer Rd BN21 . . . . . . .185 A2
Spencer's Mews 4 TN1 . . .8 A2
Spences Field BN7 . . . . . .123 E2
Spences La BN7 . . . . .123 E2
Spicers Cl RH15 . . . . .72 F5
Spindlewood Dr TN39 . . .156 C4
Spinnals Gr BN42 . . . . . . .161 D7
Spinney Cl BN6 . . . . .97 C5
Spinney The Battle TN33 . .112 F3
Bexhill TN39 . . . . .156 D3
Burgess Hill RH15 . . . . . . .73 B5
Hassocks BN6 . . . . .97 F5
Hastings TN34 . . . . .136 E1
Haywards Heath RH16 . . . .50 D8
Haywards Heath RH16 . . . .50 F3
Hove BN3 . . . . .142 C3
Robertsbridge TN32 . . . . . .63 F3
Spinneys The
Heathfield TN21 . . . . .82 B6
Lewes BN7 . . . . .123 E2
Spital Rd BN7 . . . . .123 B1
Spithurst Rd BN8 . . . . . . .101 E6
Spode La TN8 . . . . .4 A7
Sponden La TN18 . . . . .47 A3
Sportcentre Rd BN1 . . . . .144 A6
Spotted Cow La TN22 . . . .56 C5
Spout Hill TN6 . . . . .27 D1
Spray Hill TN3 . . . . .20 B4
Spray's La TN33,TN35 . . . .114 B4
Spring Cl BN20 . . . . .173 B1
Spring Copse RH19 . . . . . . .1 D1
Spring Gdns
Brighton BN1 . . . . .189 B2
Glynde BN8 . . . . .147 F5
Lewes BN7 . . . . .123 D1
Rusthall TN4 . . . . .7 D3
6 Royal Tunbridge Wells TN4 . .8 A2
Spring Hill Northiam TN31 . .67 B7
Saint's Hill TN11, TN3 . . . . .6 A7

Spring Hill Wildfowl Pk
RH18 . . . . .11 A1
Spring La Bexhill TN39 . . .156 C5
Burwash TN19 . . . . .61 F6
Clayton BN6 . . . . .119 E8
Five Ashes TN20 . . . . .58 A5
Spring Lodge Cl BN23 . . .174 E2
Spring Mdw RH18 . . . . . . .11 F1
Spring Park TN21 . . . . . . .82 A8
Spring St Brighton BN1 . . .163 E5
St Leonards TN37 . . . . . . .136 C1
Spring Steps TN36 . . . . . .117 F8
Spring Way RH19 . . . . .2 A4
Springate Rd BN42 . . . . . .161 F8
Springett Almshouses
TN18 . . . . .45 E8
Springett Ave BN8 . . . . . .124 D5
Springett Cotts BN8 . . . . .124 D5
Springfield RH19 . . . . .1 D4
Springfield Ave BN10 . . . .177 F4
Springfield Cl
Crowborough TN6 . . . . . . .26 B2
Westham BN24 . . . . .174 F6
Springfield Cotts
Cackle Street TN31 . . . . . .90 A2
Rotherfield TN6 . . . . .39 B8
Springfield Rd
Bexhill TN40 . . . . .157 C6
Brighton BN1 . . . . .164 A8
Eastbourne BN22 . . . . . . .185 B4
Groombridge TN3 . . . . .15 C7
St Leonards TN38 . . . . . . .136 B1
Springfield Valley Rd
TN38 . . . . .136 B1
Springfields TN5 . . . . .31 E1
Springfields Farm Ind Est
RH17 . . . . .73 F2
Springhead TN2 . . . . .8 D5
Springhead Way TN6 . . . . .37 E8
Springside Wlk TN38 . . . .135 F1
Springview Apartments
TN2 . . . . .8 D6
Springwood Rd TN21 . . . . .82 A8
Spruce Cl BN22 . . . . .173 D2
Spur Rd BN26 . . . . .173 B5
Spurway Pk BN26 . . . . . . .173 B5
Squab La BN27 . . . . .130 A5
Square The
Beachlands BN24 . . . . . . .175 F6
Brighton BN1 . . . . .142 E6
Cowden TN8 . . . . .4 B6
Hailsham BN27 . . . . .152 A7
Wadhurst TN5 . . . . .30 A4
Squirrel Cl Bexhill TN39 . .156 E5
St Leonards TN38 . . . . . . .135 F3
Squirrel Way TN2 . . . . .8 E5
Stable Ctyd TN22 . . . . . . .23 A1
Stable Mews TN37 . . . . . .136 C5
Stabledene Way TN2 . . . . .9 D6
Stablefield TN35 . . . . .114 E4
Stables La 9 BN21 . . . . . .185 A3
Stacey's Cnr TN21 . . . . . . .85 A5
Stafford Ct 2 BN23 . . . . .174 E1
Stafford Cty Jun Sch
BN22 . . . . .185 A6
Stafford Ho 6 BN21 . . . .184 F3
Stafford House F Ed Ctr
BN6 . . . . .98 A3
Stafford Rd Brighton BN1 .163 E8
Royal Tunbridge Wells TN2 . . .8 E4
Seaford BN25 . . . . .180 F3
Stafford Way BN6 . . . . . . .98 A3
Stag Rd TN2 . . . . .8 D8
Stainsby St 1 TN37 . . . . .159 C7
Stalkers La TN38 . . . . . . .105 E5
Stamford 6 RH16 . . . . . . .50 D6
Stamford Ct TN35 . . . . . . .160 D6
Stamford Lodge 2 BN1 . .142 E2
Stanam Rd TN2 . . . . .9 E6
Standard Hill Cl TN33 . . . .132 F6
Standean Cl BN1 . . . . .143 D6
Standen Cl RH19 . . . . .1 A4
Standen (NT) RH19 . . . . . .10 D4
Standen St
Royal Tunbridge Wells TN4 . . .8 A5
Standen Street TN17,TN18 . . .47 E8
Stanford Ave
Brighton BN1 . . . . .143 A1
Hassocks BN6 . . . . .97 E4
Stanford Cl Hassocks BN6 . .97 E4
Hove BN3 . . . . .142 C1
Stanford Cty Inf Sch BN1 163 E8
Stanford Cty Jun Sch
BN1 . . . . .163 F8
Stanford Rd BN1 . . . . . . .163 F8
Stanford Terr BN6 . . . . . . .97 E4
Stanhope Pl 1 TN38 . . . . .159 C6
Stanhope Rd TN1 . . . . .8 C5
Stanier Rd TN38 . . . . .135 F5
Stanley Ave BN41 . . . . . . .140 F3
Stanley Ave S BN41 . . . . .140 F3
Stanley Ct 3 BN2 . . . . . . .164 C8
Stanley Deason L Ctr
BN2 . . . . .164 F5
Stanley Rd Brighton BN1 . .189 B4
2 Eastbourne BN22 . . . . .185 B4
Hastings TN34 . . . . .159 E8
Peacehaven BN10 . . . . . .167 B1
Portslade-by-Sea BN41 . . .162 A8
Royal Tunbridge Wells TN1 . . .8 B6
Stanley St BN2 . . . . .189 C3
Stanmer BN1 . . . . .143 F8
Stanmer Ave BN2 . . . . . . .166 D3
Stanmer Cl BN1 . . . . .143 A2
Stanmer Dr BN22 . . . . . . .173 D1
Stanmer Ho BN1 . . . . . . .143 B2
Stanmer Park Rd BN1 . . . .143 B2

Stanmer St BN1 . . . . .143 B2
Stanmer Villas BN1 . . . . . .143 B2
Stansfield Rd BN7 . . . . . . .123 B2
Stanstead Cres BN2 . . . . . .165 F6
Stansted Rd BN22 . . . . . . .185 A4
Staplecross Methodist
    Prim Sch TN32 . . . . .65 E2
Staplefield Dr BN2 . . . . . . .143 F3
Stapley Ct BN3 . . . . .162 D8
Stapley Rd BN3 . . . . .141 D1
Star La Alfriston BN26 . . . .171 A3
  Blackboys BN22 . . . . .80 B6
  Mayfield TN20 . . . . .40 B2
Star Mews TN20 . . . . .40 B2
Star Rd 6 BN21 . . . . .184 E4
Starboard Ct BN2 . . . . . . .164 F3
Starborough Cotts RH7 . . . .1 F7
Starfield TN6 . . . . .25 E1
Starling Cl RH15 . . . . .72 C3
Starr's Cotts 10 TN34 . . . . .160 B4
Starr's Green La TN33 . . . .113 A3
Starrs Mead TN33 . . . . . . .113 A3
Starvecrow La TN31 . . . . . .91 D6
Starwell Cl TN34 . . . . .136 D3
Station App Battle TN33 . . .112 E3
  Eastbourne BN22 . . . . .173 F1
  Etchingham TN19 . . . . .44 C1
  Falmer BN1 . . . . .144 B6
  Hassocks BN6 . . . . .97 F4
  Hastings TN34 . . . . .159 E8
  Heathfield TN21 . . . . .82 A7
  Horsted Keynes RH17 . . . . . .33 A7
  Hove BN3 . . . . .163 B8
  Mayfield TN20 . . . . .39 F2
  Seaford BN25 . . . . .180 E3
  St Leonards TN37 . . . . . . .159 C7
Station Cl
  Plumpton Green BN7 . . . . . . .99 E5
  Town Row TN6 . . . . .27 D1
Station Cotts
  Crowhurst TN33 . . . . .135 A6
  Hassocks BN6 . . . . .97 E4
  Winchelsea TN36 . . . . .92 D1
Station Par 7 BN21 . . . . . .184 F3
Station Rd Bexhill TN40 . . .157 C4
  Brighton BN1 . . . . .142 D3
  Burgess Hill RH15 . . . . .73 B2
  Crowhurst TN33 . . . . .134 F5
  East Grinstead RH19 . . . . . . .1 D1
  Forest Row RH18 . . . . .11 F3
  Groombridge TN3 . . . . .15 C7
  Hailsham BN27 . . . . .152 C6
  Hastings TN34 . . . . .159 F8
  Heathfield TN21 . . . . .82 A7
  Hellingly BN27 . . . . .129 A5
  Horsted Keynes RH17 . . . . . .33 C5
  Hurst Green TN19 . . . . .45 A3
  Isfield TN22 . . . . .102 D8
  Lewes BN7 . . . . .146 D8
  Mayfield TN20 . . . . .40 A2
  Newhaven BN9 . . . . .168 F1
  North Chailey BN8 . . . . .75 F7
  Northiam TN31 . . . . .67 B8
  Plumpton Green BN7 . . . . . . .99 E6
  Polegate BN26 . . . . .173 A6
Portslade-by-Sea
    BN3, BN41 . . . . .162 C7
  Robertsbridge TN32 . . . . . . .64 B4
  Rockrobin TN5 . . . . .29 C6
  Seaford BN25 . . . . .180 B5
  Sharpthorne RH19 . . . . .21 A6
  7 Southwick BN42 . . . . . . .161 E7
  Stonegate TN5 . . . . .42 E5
  Town Row TN6 . . . . .27 C1
  Winchelsea TN36 . . . . .92 E1
  Withyham TN7 . . . . .14 B5
Station Road Ind Est
    BN27 . . . . .152 C6
Station St Brighton BN1 . . .189 B2
  8 Eastbourne BN21 . . . . . .185 A4
  Lewes BN7 . . . . .123 D1
Staveley Rd BN20 . . . . . . .188 E8
Steellands Rise TN5 . . . . . .31 F1
Steep Hill Brede La TN31 . .89 E2
Steep Rd TN20, TN6 . . . . . .38 D3
Steine Gdns BN2 . . . . .189 B2
Steine La BN1, BN2 . . . . . .189 B2
Steine St BN2 . . . . .189 B1
Stennings The RH19 . . . . . . .1 C3
Stephen's Rd TN4 . . . . .8 B6
Stephens Cl BN8 . . . . .124 D5
Stephens Rd BN1 . . . . . . .143 B2
Stephenson Dr RH19 . . . . . .10 F7
Stevens Cl TN39 . . . . .157 C7
Stevens Ct BN3 . . . . .162 E7
Stevenson Cl BN23 . . . . . .174 E3
Stevenson Rd
  Brighton BN2 . . . . .164 C5
  1 St Leonards TN37 . . . . . .136 B3
Stewards Inn La 3 BN7 . . .146 C8
Stewart Rd TN4 . . . . .8 C7
Steyne Cl 4 BN25 . . . . . . .180 F2
Steyne Ct 11 BN25 . . . . . .180 E2
Steyne Rd BN25 . . . . .180 F2
Steyne The BN25 . . . . . . .180 E2
Steyning Ave Hove BN3 . . .141 F3
  Peacehaven BN10 . . . . .178 C7
Steyning Cl BN25 . . . . . . .181 C2
Steyning Ct 7 BN3 . . . . . .163 B7
Steyning Rd
  Rottingdean BN2 . . . . .177 A5
  Seaford BN25 . . . . .181 C2
Stiles The BN2 . . . . .152 C7
Stirling Ave BN25 . . . . . . .181 C4
Stirling Cl
  Burgess Hill RH15 . . . . .73 C4
  Seaford BN25 . . . . .181 C4
Stirling Court Rd RH15 . . .73 C4

Stirling Ct 5 BN3 . . . . . . .163 C7
Stirling Pl BN3 . . . . .163 A6
Stirling Rd TN38 . . . . .135 F5
Stirling Way RH19 . . . . .2 B3
Stock Dale TN35 . . . . .138 F4
Stockland Green Rd TN3 . . .7 B8
Stockland La TN22 . . . . . . .57 B6
Stockleigh Rd TN38 . . . . . .159 C7
Stocks Mdw TN33 . . . . . . .133 B5
Stockwell Ct
  Burgess Hill RH15 . . . . .72 F3
  1 Haywards Heath RH16 . . . .50 E3
Stockwell Rd RH19 . . . . . . .10 E6
Stoddards La TN31 . . . . . . .67 F6
Stoke Brunswick Sch
    RH19 . . . . .11 E7
Stoke Cl BN25 . . . . .181 B3
Stoke Manor Cl BN25 . . . .181 B4
Stokes Cotts TN19 . . . . . . .60 F3
Stokes Ho 4 TN39 . . . . . .157 A4
Stone Cotts TN3 . . . . .19 F4
Stone Court La TN2 . . . . . . .9 E8
Stone Cross
  Eastbourne BN24 . . . . .174 B5
  Mayfield TN20 . . . . .39 F2
Stone Cross Cty Prim Sch
    BN24 . . . . .174 A5
Stone Cross Rd
  Crowborough TN6 . . . . .38 A7
  Wadhurst TN5 . . . . .30 A4
Stone Pit La TN18 . . . . . . .47 E5
Stone Quarry Rd RH17 . . . .34 D7
Stone Row TN3 . . . . .6 B5
Stone Row Cotts TN3 . . . . .6 D1
Stone St Brighton BN1 . . . .163 E5
  12 Hastings TN34 . . . . . . .159 F8
  Royal Tunbridge Wells TN1 . . .8 B4
Stone Works Cotts TN1 . . .93 F3
Stonebeach Rise TN38 . . . .135 E7
Stonebridge La TN22 . . . . . .79 F5
Stonecott Cl TN6 . . . . .37 F8
Stonecroft Cl BN3 . . . . . . .141 E4
Stonecross Rd BN2 . . . . . .143 F4
Stonedene Cl RH18 . . . . . . .12 B2
Stonefield Pl 2 TN34 . . . . .159 F8
Stonefield Rd TN34 . . . . . .159 F8
Stonefield Way RH15 . . . . . .72 F5
Stonegate CE Prim Sch
    TN5 . . . . .42 F5
Stonegate Cl BN23 . . . . . .174 A4
Stonegate Ct TN5 . . . . .42 F5
Stonegate La TN5 . . . . .30 C1
Stonegate Sta TN5 . . . . . . .42 D3
Stonegate Way TN21 . . . . . .82 B8
Stoneham Cl BN7 . . . . . . .123 C3
Stoneham Rd BN3 . . . . . . .162 F7
Stonehaven Ct 5 TN40 . . .157 D3
Stonehouse Dr Hastings,
  Beauport Park TN33,TN38 . .113 F1
  St Leonards TN38 . . . . . . .136 A2
Stonehurst Ct 10 BN2 . . . .164 C6
Stonehurst La TN20,TN22 . .57 D7
Stoneleigh Ave BN1 . . . . . .142 F6
Stoneleigh Cl
  Brighton BN1 . . . . .142 F6
  East Grinstead RH19 . . . . . . .1 F1
Stonelink Ct TN37 . . . . . . .135 F7
Stonepark Dr RH18 . . . . . . .12 A2
Stonepound Crossroads
    BN6 . . . . .97 D4
Stonepound Rd BN6 . . . . . .97 E4
Stonery Cl BN41 . . . . .141 A2
Stonery Rd BN41 . . . . .141 A2
Stonestile La TN35 . . . . . . .136 F8
Stonewall Park Rd TN3 . . . .6 F3
Stonewood Cl
  Royal Tunbridge Wells TN4 . . .8 A8
  Seaford BN25 . . . . .181 C4
Stoney La Hailsham BN27 . .152 C7
  Shoreham-by-Sea BN43 . . . .161 C8
Stoneywish Ctry Pk BN6 . . .98 E3
Storrington Cl BN3 . . . . . . .141 E2
Straight Half Mile TN22 . . .55 B5
Strand TN31 . . . . .93 B5
Strand Ct TN31 . . . . .93 B5
Strand Hill TN36 . . . . .117 F7
Strand Mdw TN19 . . . . .62 B7
Strand The BN2 . . . . .165 A3
Stratford St TN1 . . . . .8 C5
Strathenden Ct 9 BN25 . . .180 E2
Strathfield Cl RH16 . . . . . . .50 F4
Stratton Ct 6 BN21 . . . . . .162 F7
Strawberry Cl TN2 . . . . . . .16 E7
Strawberry Fields TN31 . . .67 A7
Strawlands BN7 . . . . .99 E6
Stream La
  Fairlight Cove TN35 . . . . . . .139 A5
  Sedlescombe TN33 . . . . .88 C2
  The Moor TN18 . . . . .46 A7
Stream Lane Cotts TN18 . .46 A7
Stream Pit La TN18 . . . . . . .47 B5
Stream Pk RH19 . . . . .1 A3
Streamside Cl TN34 . . . . . .136 E3
Streat Bostall BN6 . . . . . . .121 C6
Streat La BN6 . . . . .99 C4
Streatfield Gdns TN21 . . . .81 F8
Streatfield Ho TN22 . . . . . .78 C8
Streatfield Rd
  Heathfield TN21 . . . . .81 F8
  Uckfield TN22 . . . . .78 B7
Streele La TN22 . . . . .56 D1
Streele View TN22 . . . . . . .78 E8
Street End La
  Broad Oak TN21 . . . . .59 E1
  Broad Oak TN21 . . . . .59 E5
Street The Framefield TN22 .79 B6
  Kingston near Lewes BN7 . . .145 E5
  Sedlescombe TN33 . . . . .88 E1

Street The continued
  West Firle BN8 . . . . .148 B3
  Westmeston BN6 . . . . .120 F8
Streetlands TN33 . . . . .88 E1
Stringer Way BN1 . . . . . . .142 F3
Stringwalk The BN27 . . . . .152 C7
Stroma Gdns BN27 . . . . . .128 F2
Strome Ho TN3 . . . . .157 C7
Strongs Pas 5 TN34 . . . . .160 B4
Strood Gate RH17 . . . . . . .74 C5
Strood Rd TN37 . . . . .136 C2
Stuart Ave BN21 . . . . .184 C6
Stuart Cl TN2 . . . . .16 F8
Stuart Way RH19 . . . . .10 F7
Stubb La TN31 . . . . .90 D2
Stubbygrove Cotts TN3 . . . .17 E4
Stud Cotts BN27 . . . . .151 A8
Studdens La BN27 . . . . . . .108 D1
Sturdee Cl BN23 . . . . .185 F7
Sturdee Pl BN2 . . . . .160 A3
Sturton Pl BN27 . . . . .152 B7
Sudeley Pl BN2 . . . . .164 D4
Sudeley St BN2 . . . . .164 D4
Sudeley Terr 6 BN2 . . . . . .164 D4
Suffolk Cl 5 BN22 . . . . . . .185 C4
Suffolk Rd TN39 . . . . .157 C2
Suffolk St BN3 . . . . .162 F8
Sugar La RH17 . . . . .33 C4
Sugworth Cl RH16 . . . . . . .50 D7
Sullington Cl BN2 . . . . . . .143 F4
Sullington Way BN43 . . . . .161 A8
Sumach Cl BN22 . . . . .173 E2
Summer Cl BN41 . . . . .162 A7
Summer Ct BN20 . . . . .188 D7
Summer Hill TN38 . . . . . . .159 A8
Summer Hill Rd TN39 . . . .156 F6
Summercourt BN27 . . . . . .152 B8
Summerdale Rd BN3 . . . . .141 D2
Summerdown Cl BN20 . . . .184 D3
Summerdown La BN20 . . . .183 C1
Summerdown Rd BN20 . . . .184 D3
Summerfields Ave BN27 . . .152 A8
Summerheath Rd BN27 . . .152 B8
Summerhill Cl RH16 . . . . . .50 F7
Summerhill Dr RH16 . . . . . .51 A7
Summerhill Grange RH16 . .50 F7
Summerhill La RH16 . . . . . .50 F7
Summerlands Rd BN22 . . . .173 C2
Summersdeane BN42 . . . . .140 F1
Summervale Rd TN2, TN4 . . .7 E1
Sun La 8 TN34 . . . . .160 A3
Sun St BN7 . . . . .123 C1
Sunhill Ct TN2 . . . . .9 C6
Sunningdale Cl
  10 Bexhill TN40 . . . . .157 E4
  Hailsham BN27 . . . . .129 A1
  Seaford BN25 . . . . .181 A2
Sunningdale Dr TN38 . . . . .158 F7
Sunninghill Ave BN1 . . . . .141 F2
Sunninghill Cl BN3 . . . . . .141 E2
Sunnybank TN5 . . . . .32 E3
Sunnybank Cl TN20 . . . . . . .40 B2
Sunnybrooke Cl TN22 . . . . .78 D7
Sunnycroft Cl RH17 . . . . . .51 E2
Sunnydale Ave BN1 . . . . . .143 A6
Sunnydale Cl BN1 . . . . . . .143 A6
Sunnyside Rd TN4 . . . . .7 C4
Sunnywood Dr RH16 . . . . . .50 D3
Sunset Cl Beachlands BN24 .175 F6
  Telscombe Cliffs BN10 . . . . .167 B1
Sunstar La BN26 . . . . .172 E6
Sunte Ave RH16 . . . . .50 F7
Sunte Cl RH16 . . . . .50 E7
Sunview Ave BN10 . . . . . . .178 D6
Surrenden Cl BN1 . . . . . . .142 F4
Surrenden Cres BN1 . . . . . .142 E4
Surrenden Holt BN1 . . . . . .142 F3
Surrenden Lodge BN1 . . . .142 F2
Surrenden Pk BN1 . . . . . . .143 A4
Surrenden Rd BN1 . . . . . . .142 F3
Surrey Cl
  Royal Tunbridge Wells TN2 . . .16 F8
  Seaford BN25 . . . . .180 D4
Surrey Ho 12 BN2 . . . . . . .164 D4
Surrey Rd BN25 . . . . .180 C4
Surrey St BN1 . . . . .189 A3
Susan's Rd BN21 . . . . .185 A3
Susans Cl BN8 . . . . .105 A5
Sussex Ave BN27 . . . . .152 B8
Sussex Chambers 8
    TN34 . . . . .159 F8
Sussex Cl Bexhill TN39 . . .156 F5
  Hailsham BN27 . . . . .152 B8
  Royal Tunbridge Wells TN2 . . .8 C1
Sussex Ct
  Eastbourne BN22 . . . . .185 B5
  2 Haywards Heath RH16 . . . .50 E3
  15 Hove BN3 . . . . .163 C6
  Shoreham-by-Sea BN43 . . . .161 A6
Sussex Cty Cricket Gd
    BN3 . . . . .163 C7
Sussex Eye Hospl BN2 . . .164 D4
Sussex Gdns
  East Dean BN20 . . . . .183 C1
  Haywards Heath RH17 . . . . .51 B3
Sussex Ho
  6 Eastbourne BN21 . . . . . .185 A2
  Telscombe Cliffs BN10 . . . . .177 F3
Sussex House Bsns Pk
    BN3 . . . . .162 F8
Sussex Hts 13 BN1 . . . . . .163 E5
Sussex Mews
  4 Brighton BN2 . . . . .164 E4
  16 Royal Tunbridge Wells TN2 .8 A2
Sussex Nuffield Hospl
  Hove BN3 . . . . .162 F7
  Woodingdean BN2 . . . . .165 C8
Sussex Pl BN2 . . . . .189 C3

Sussex Rd
  Haywards Heath RH16 . . . . .50 E3
  Hove BN3 . . . . .163 B5
  St Leonards TN38 . . . . . . .159 A6
Sussex Sq Brighton BN2 . .164 E4
  17 Haywards Heath RH16 . . .50 E4
Sussex St BN2 . . . . .189 C2
Sussex Terr BN2 . . . . .189 C3
Sussex Toy & Model Mus
    BN1 . . . . .189 B3
Sussex Way
  Burgess Hill RH15 . . . . .72 E5
  Telscombe Cliffs BN10 . . . . .177 F3
Sutherland Ave TN39 . . . . .157 A4
Sutherland Cl 1 TN39 . . . .157 A4
Sutherland Rd
  Brighton BN2 . . . . .164 C5
  Royal Tunbridge Wells TN1 . . .8 B3
Sutton Ave
  Peacehaven BN10 . . . . .178 B7
  Seaford BN25 . . . . .181 A4
Sutton Ave N BN10 . . . . . .178 B8
Sutton Cl BN2 . . . . .144 E1
Sutton Cotts BN7 . . . . . . .146 B3
Sutton Croft La 4 BN25 . . .180 E3
Sutton Dro BN25 . . . . .180 F4
Sutton Park Rd BN25 . . . . .180 E3
Sutton Pl TN40 . . . . .157 E4
Sutton Rd
  Eastbourne BN21 . . . . .185 A4
  Seaford BN25 . . . . .181 A3
Sutton Wall BN7 . . . . .146 A4
Suttons Ind Pk TN36 . . . . .118 A7
Suttons The Camber TN31 . .95 A1
  St Leonards TN38 . . . . . . .135 F2
Swaine's Pas 6 TN34 . . . .160 B4
Swaines Way TN31 . . . . . . .82 A6
Swainham La TN38 . . . . . . .135 B4
Swainsthorpe Cl RH16 . . . .50 F3
Swale Dr BN24 . . . . .174 A5
Swallow Bank TN38 . . . . . .135 F2
Swallow Cl BN23 . . . . .174 C2
Swallow Ct TN22 . . . . .78 D5
Swallow Dr Battle TN33 . . .112 F4
  Royal Tunbridge Wells TN2 . . .8 F6
Swallow Rest RH15 . . . . . . .72 C3
Swallows The BN10 . . . . . .167 B1
Swan Ave 9 TN34 . . . . . . .160 A4
Swan Bsns Ctr BN27 . . . . .152 D6
Swan Cl BN8 . . . . .100 E7
Swan Rd BN27 . . . . .152 D6
Swan Terr TN34 . . . . .160 A4
Swanborough Dr BN2 . . . .164 F3
Swanborough Dro BN7 . . .145 B4
Swanborough Hollow
    BN7 . . . . .146 A4
Swanborough Pl BN2 . . . . .164 F7
Swanley Cl BN23 . . . . .174 D2
Swann Cl RH15 . . . . .73 D3
Swannee Ct BN10 . . . . . . .167 D1
Swans Ghyll RH18 . . . . . . .11 E3
Swansbrook La BN27 . . . . .106 E2
Swaylands Ave TN6 . . . . . . .37 F7
Sweda Ct 3 BN24 . . . . . . .164 D4
Sweeps Hill Cl TN2 . . . . . . .9 D7
Sweethaws La TN6 . . . . . . .37 C6
Sweetings La TN3,TN5 . . . .19 D1
Sweetlands BN6 . . . . .98 B5
Swife La TN21 . . . . .60 D5
Swift Cl Burgess Hill RH15 . .72 D3
  Crowborough TN6 . . . . .25 D1
  Uckfield TN22 . . . . .78 D5
Swiftsden Cotts TN19 . . . . .44 F6
Swinburne Ave BN22 . . . . .173 C3
Swingate Cross BN27 . . . . .129 C5
Swissland Hill RH19, RH7 . . .1 E7
Swynford Dr 1 TN38 . . . . .136 A5
Sybron Way TN6 . . . . .38 D8
Sycamore Cl Bexhill TN39 .156 C4
  Eastbourne BN22 . . . . .173 D3
  Heathfield TN21 . . . . .82 B6
  Portslade-by-Sea BN41 . . . .141 C3
  Seaford BN25 . . . . .181 C3
  St Leonards TN38 . . . . . . .136 A1
  Woodingdean BN2 . . . . .165 E8
Sycamore Cotts TN2 . . . . . .9 C6
Sycamore Ct TN22 . . . . . . .78 D8
Sycamore Dr
  East Grinstead RH19 . . . . . . .2 A1
  Hailsham BN27 . . . . .152 B5
Sycamores The BN10 . . . .167 D1
Sydenham Ct TN40 . . . . . .157 D3
Sydney Cl TN38 . . . . .136 B3
Sydney Little Rd TN38 . . . .135 D4
Sydney Rd
  Eastbourne BN22 . . . . .185 B4
  Haywards Heath RH16 . . . . .50 E6
Sydney St BN1 . . . . .189 B3
Sydney Tidy Ho 5 BN2 . . .164 C6
Sylvan Cl RH16 . . . . .51 B4
Sylvester Way BN3 . . . . . .141 C3
Symbister Rd BN41 . . . . . .162 C7
Syresham Gdns RH16 . . . . .50 F4

T

Tackleway TN34 . . . . .160 B4
Taddington Ho 2 BN22 . . .185 C4
Taddington Rd 1 BN22 . . .185 C4
Tainter's Brook TN22 . . . . .78 E8
Talbot Cres BN1 . . . . .143 D6
Talbot Pk TN2 . . . . .8 D5
Talbot Rd TN18 . . . . .45 F8
Talbot Terr BN7 . . . . .123 C1
Tall Ash Dr TN37 . . . . .136 C4
Talland Par 17 BN25 . . . . .180 E2
Tamar Cl BN24 . . . . .174 A5

Tamarack Cl BN22 . . . . . . .173 D2
Tamerisk Stps 24 TN34 . . .160 B4
Tamplin Terr BN2 . . . . . . .189 C3
Tamworth Rd BN3 . . . . . . .162 F7
Tan Yard Cotts TN30 . . . . .117 F8
Tanbridge Rd BN23 . . . . . .174 F2
Tandridge Rd BN3 . . . . . . .162 E6
Tangier La TN3 . . . . .17 B6
Tanglewood Coppice
    TN39 . . . . .156 E3
Tangmere Cl TN39 . . . . . . .156 E3
Tangmere Rd BN1 . . . . . . .143 A6
Tanhouse La TN31 . . . . . . .68 F2
Tanners Field RH17 . . . . . .74 A5
Tanners Way TN6 . . . . .26 A1
Tanners' Brook BN7 . . . . . .146 D8
Tanyard TN18 . . . . .47 B5
Tanyard Ave RH19 . . . . . . .11 A8
Tanyard Cotts Battle TN33 .112 E3
  Buxted TN22 . . . . .56 C1
Tanyard La Chelwood
    Common RH17,TN22 . . . . .34 C4
  Winchelsea TN36 . . . . .117 F8
Tapsell's La TN5 . . . . .29 D5
Tarland Ho TN2 . . . . .8 D3
Tarner Rd BN2 . . . . .189 C3
Tarragon Way BN43 . . . . . .140 C1
Tarring Cl RH19 . . . . .168 D2
Tas Combe Way BN20 . . . .173 B2
Tate Cres RH15 . . . . .72 F5
Taunton Gr BN2 . . . . .144 A1
Taunton Pl BN2 . . . . .144 A1
Taunton Rd BN2 . . . . .143 F1
Taunton Way BN2 . . . . . . .144 A1
Tavistock 8 BN21 . . . . . . .185 A2
Tavistock & Summerhill
    Sch RH16 . . . . .50 F7
Tavistock Down BN1 . . . . .143 C2
Taylor Cl TN38 . . . . .135 F4
Taylor Ct TN2 . . . . .8 C7
Taylor St TN4 . . . . .8 A8
Tea Garden La TN3, TN4 . . .7 C2
Teal Ct Hailsham BN27 . . . .152 D7
  St Leonards TN38 . . . . . . .135 E3
Teasley Mead TN3 . . . . .5 C4
Tedder Rd TN4 . . . . .8 B7
Tedder Terr TN35 . . . . . . .137 D5
Teg Cl BN41 . . . . .141 C2
Teise Cl TN2 . . . . .8 D2
Teknol Ho RH15 . . . . .72 E2
Telegraph St 12 BN2 . . . . .164 C4
Telford Rd TN38 . . . . .136 A5
Telham Cl TN34 . . . . .137 A5
Telham La TN33 . . . . .112 E1
Telscombe Cliffs
    Cty Prim Sch BN10 . . . . .178 A8
Telscombe Cliffs Way
    BN10 . . . . .178 A8
Telscombe Pk BN10 . . . . . .167 C2
Telscombe Rd
  Eastbourne BN23 . . . . .174 F2
  Peacehaven BN10 . . . . .167 D2
Temple Gdns BN1, BN3 . . .163 A5
Temple Gr RH15 . . . . .72 D4
Temple Grove Sch TN22 . . .36 E3
Tenantry Down Rd BN2 . . .164 C8
Tenantry Rd BN2 . . . . .164 D8
Tennis Cl BN27 . . . . .152 B7
Tennis Rd BN3 . . . . .162 E6
Tennyson Ct 5 RH16 . . . . .50 D5
Tennyson Rise RH19 . . . . .10 C8
Tennyson Wlk BN23 . . . . . .174 E3
Tenterden Cl BN23 . . . . . . .174 D2
Tenterden Rise TN34 . . . . .136 E2
Terminus Ave TN39 . . . . . .157 A3
Terminus Pl
  1 Brighton BN1 . . . . .189 A4
  6 Hailsham BN27 . . . . . . .152 C7
Terminus Rd Bexhill TN39 .157 B3
  Brighton BN1 . . . . .189 A4
  Eastbourne BN21 . . . . .185 A3
Terminus St BN1 . . . . .189 A3
Terrace Rd TN37 . . . . .159 C7
Tescombe Grange BN10 . . .177 F3
Teynham Ho BN2 . . . . .177 C4
Thackeray Cl BN23 . . . . . .174 E3
Thakeham Cl TN40 . . . . . .158 A6
Thalia Ho TN40 . . . . .157 B4
Thames Cl BN2 . . . . .189 C2
Thanet Way TN34 . . . . . . .136 E2
Thatchers Cl RH15 . . . . . . .73 D1
Thatchings The BN26 . . . . .173 A5
Theaklen Dr TN38 . . . . . . .136 B2
Theobalds Gn TN21 . . . . . .82 A5
Theobalds Rd RH15 . . . . . .73 D6
Theobold Ho 1 BN1 . . . . .189 B3
Theodore Cl TN2 . . . . .8 E7
Third Ave Bexhill TN40 . . . .157 F6
  Hove BN3 . . . . .163 B6
  Newhaven BN9 . . . . .179 C6
Third Rd BN10 . . . . .178 A7
Third St TN3 . . . . .6 F3
Thirlmere Rd TN4 . . . . .7 E5
Thomas Brassey Cl TN37 .136 B5
Thomas St Lewes BN7 . . . .123 C2
  Royal Tunbridge Wells TN4 . . .8 A5
Thomas Turner Dr BN8 . . .105 A5
Thompson Rd
  Brighton BN1 . . . . .143 C1
  Newhaven BN9 . . . . .168 F2

Thorn Cotts TN35 ....116 A4
Thornbank Cres TN39 ...156 F3
Thornbush Cres BN41 ...141 B3
Thornden Rd BN2 ....143 D3
Thornden Ct TN17 ....49 A8
Thornden La TN17 ....49 A8
Thorne Cres TN39 ....133 E1
Thornfield Gdns TN2 ....8 F5
Thornhill Ave BN1 ....143 A7
Thornhill Cl BN3 ....141 E2
Thornhill Rise BN41 ...141 A4
Thornhill Way BN41 ...141 A3
Thorns The TN35 ....138 A8
Thornsdale **4** BN2 ....189 C3
Thornton Ct **5** BN22 ...185 B3
Thornwell Rd BN26 ...171 F7
Thornwood Cl BN22 ...173 E2
Thorny Cl TN21 ....82 A7
Thorpe Works TN4 ....7 F8
Three Gables TN22 ....35 C4
Three Oaks La TN5 ....29 D7
Three Oaks Sta TN35 ...115 D2
Thurrock Cl BN20 ....173 B4
Thyme Cl BN43 ....140 C1
Thyssel La TN31 ....67 B6
Tibbs Mill La TN2,TN6 ...37 E2
Ticehurst Ave TN39 ...155 F5
Ticehurst CE Prim Sch
  TN5 ....43 D8
Ticehurst Cl Bexhill TN39 .155 F4
  Hastings TN35 ....137 C3
Ticehurst Ct TN38 ....159 B7
Ticehurst Rd BN2 ....164 F5
Tichborne Cotts RH16 ...51 C6
Tichborne St BN1 ....189 B2
Tickerage La TN22 ....79 F6
Tidebrook TN5,TN20 ....40 F7
Tidebrook Gdns BN23 ...174 F2
Tideswell Rd BN21 ....185 A3
Tideway Sch
  & Sixth Form Ctr BN9 .179 B6
Tidy St BN1 ....189 B3
Tilbury Pl BN2 ....189 C2
Tilbury Way BN2 ....189 C3
Tile Barn Cl TN22 ....102 D8
Tile Barn Rd TN38 ....135 F4
Tilebarn Ct RH16 ....50 E2
Tilehurst Dr BN27 ....152 A8
Tilekiln La TN35 ....137 E4
Tilers Cl RH15 ....73 D3
Tilford Ct **1** TN40 ....157 F4
Tilgate Cl Brighton BN2 .164 D6
  Eastbourne BN21 ....184 D7
Tilgate Dr TN39 ....156 D3
Tilley La BN27 ....131 E6
Tilling Green Cty Inf Sch
  TN31 ....93 A5
Tillingham Ave TN31 ...93 B6
Tillingham Cl BN24 ...174 A5
Tillingham La TN31 ....92 A6
Tillingham View TN31 ...90 B5
Tillingham Way BN2 ...174 A5
Tillington BN2 ....164 F7
Tillington Terr TN35 ...160 C6
Tillstone Cl BN2 ....143 D2
Tillstone St BN2 ....189 C2
Tilsmore Cnr TN21 ....81 F7
Tilsmore Rd TN21 ....81 F7
Timber Yard Cotts BN7 .123 E1
Timberlaine Rd BN24 ...175 C4
Timberley Rd BN22 ...173 D1
Timbers Ct BN27 ....152 C8
Tindal Ct RH15 ....73 D3
Tinker's La TN22 ....57 E3
Tinkers La TN5 ....31 E3
Tintagel Ct BN3 ....163 A8
Tintern Cl Brighton BN1 .143 B1
  Eastbourne BN23 ....173 E3
Tisbury Rd BN3 ....163 C6
Titchfield Cl RH15 ....73 D1
Tithe Barn Field TN36 .116 F5
Titian Rd BN3 ....162 F7
Tiverton Dr TN40 ....157 E5
Tivoli BN1 ....142 E2
Tivoli Cres BN1 ....142 D1
Tivoli Cres N BN1 ....142 D2
Tivoli Pl BN1 ....142 D2
Tivoli Rd BN1 ....142 D2
Tobago **6** TN39 ....157 A2
Tobias Sch of Art RH19 ..10 E6
Tolkien Rd BN2 ....174 F2
Toll La Fairwarp TN22 ...36 A1
  Nutley TN22 ....35 F1
Toll Wood Rd TN21 ....106 F7
Tollgate Lindfield RH16 ...51 B8
  Peacehaven BN10 ....167 B1
Tollgate Cty Jun Sch
  BN23 ....185 D7
Tollgate Gdns BN23 ...185 D7
Tollgate Lock TN31 ....93 B4
Tollgates TN33 ....112 B4
Tollwood Pk TN6 ....26 B1
Tollwood Rd TN6 ....38 B8
Tompset's Bank RH18 ...11 E1
Tomtits La RH18 ....11 E1
Tonbridge Rd TN2,TN11 ...9 A7
Tonbridge Way TN31 ....94 E2
Tongdean Ave BN3 ....142 C2
Tongdean Ct BN1 ....142 D4
Tongdean La
  Brighton BN1 ....142 C4
  Brighton BN1 ....142 D4
Tongdean Rd BN3 ....142 C3
Tongdean Rise BN1 ....142 C4
Top Cross Rd TN40 ....158 A7

Top Dr TN22 ....55 A6
Top Rd RH19 ....21 B5
Tor Rd BN10 ....167 C1
Tor Rd W BN10 ....167 C2
Torcross Cl BN2 ....143 E1
Torfield Cl TN34 ....160 B4
Torfield Cl BN21 ....184 E4
Torfield Ho TN34 ....160 B4
Torfield Rd BN21 ....184 E4
Torfield Sch TN34 ....160 B5
Toronto Terr
  Brighton BN2 ....164 C6
  Lewes BN7 ....123 C1
Torrance Cl BN3 ....141 F1
Totland Rd BN2 ....164 D7
Tott Hill BN6 ....97 B5
Tott Yew Rd BN20 ....173 A4
Tottington Way BN43 ...140 B1
Tovey Cl BN21 ....184 D6
Tower Cl
  Beachlands BN24 ....175 F7
  East Grinstead RH19 ....1 E2
Tower Ct RH19 ....1 E2
Tower Ho Brighton BN1 .142 E2
  Burgess Hill RH15 ....73 B2
Tower Mill Pl BN26 ....173 A5
Tower Rd Brighton BN2 .164 C6
  St Leonards TN37 ....136 C1
Tower Rd W TN37,TN38 .159 B8
Tower Ride Uckfield TN22 .55 D1
  Uckfield TN22 ....55 E1
Tower St Heathfield TN21 ..82 B8
  Rye TN31 ....93 C6
Tower View TN22 ....78 D8
Towergate BN1 ....142 E2
Towerscroft Ave TN37 .136 C5
Town Hill TN3 ....20 A4
Town Place Farm Cotts
  RH17 ....52 C7
Towner Art Gall & Mus
  BN21 ....184 D3
Townlands Rd TN5 ....29 F4
Tozer Ct BN41 ....162 B7
Traders Pas TN31 ....93 B5
Trafalgar Cl
  Peacehaven BN10 ....167 C1
  St Leonards TN37 ....135 F7
Trafalgar Cotts **8** TN34 .160 B4
Trafalgar Ct BN1 ....189 B3
Trafalgar Gate BN2 ....164 F3
Trafalgar La BN1 ....189 B3
Trafalgar Mews **9** BN22 .185 C4
Trafalgar Pl BN1 ....189 B3
Trafalgar Rd BN41 ....162 B8
Trafalgar St BN1 ....189 B3
Trafalgar Terr BN1 ....189 B3
Tram Rd TN31 ....94 A2
Transit Rd BN9 ....179 D7
Travellers La TN35 ....137 C4
Trebilco Cl TN2 ....8 D7
Treblers Rd TN20,TN6 ....38 E6
Tredcroft Rd BN3 ....142 C2
Tree Tops Cl BN2 ....165 E8
Treemaines Rd BN23 ...174 F2
Treemans Rd RH17 ....33 B2
Tremola Ave BN2 ....177 C6
Trenches Rd TN6 ....25 F1
Trevor Gdns BN8 ....147 F6
Treyford Cl BN2 ....144 E1
Triangle Ho **4** RH16 ....50 F3
Triangle L Ctr The RH15 ..72 D4
Triangle Rd RH16 ....50 E3
Triangle The BN20 ....173 B3
Triangle Way RH15 ....72 D5
Trickland Cotts TN22 ...53 C5
Trinity Cl TN2 ....8 D4
Trinity Field BN8 ....124 E6
Trinity Mews **3** TN34 ...159 E7
Trinity Pl BN21 ....185 B2
Trinity Rd BN6 ....97 A6
Trinity St Brighton BN2 ..189 C4
  10 Hastings TN34 ....159 E7
Trinity Trees BN21 ....185 A2
Trinity Villas **2** TN34 ...159 E7
Tristan Gdns TN4 ....7 D4
Trojans Platt TN36 ....117 E7
Troon Cl BN25 ....180 A6
Troon Ct RH16 ....50 E4
Trossachs Cl BN23 ....174 D3
Troy Cl TN6 ....26 A1
Truleigh Cl BN2 ....165 F7
Truleigh Dr BN41 ....141 A4
Truleigh Way BN43 ...140 A1
Truman Dr TN37 ....135 F6
Trumpet La BN27 ....109 C2
Tubwell La
  Crowborough TN6 ....38 D7
  Maynard's Green TN21 ...81 F2
Tudor Ave TN38 ....159 A7
Tudor Cl
  East Grinstead RH19 ....10 F8
  Hove BN3 ....141 F2
  Rottingdean BN2 ....177 A6
  Seaford BN25 ....180 D4
Tudor Ct TN2 ....7 E1
Tudor Gdns RH15 ....72 F4
Tudor Rose Pk Cvn Site
  BN10 ....178 F6
Tudor Wlk TN22 ....79 B5
Tugwell Rd BN2 ....173 F2
Tumulus Rd BN2 ....166 C3
Tunbridge Wells
  Gram Sch for Boys TN4 ..8 A7
Tunbridge Wells
  Gram Sch for Girls TN4 ..8 A6
Tunbridge Wells
  Ind Hospl The TN3 ....6 B3
Tunbridge Wells Mus TN1 .8 B4

Tunbridge Wells Rd
  Argos Hill TN20,TN6 ....39 E5
  Mark Cross TN3,TN6 ....28 A5
Tunbridge Wells Trade Pk
  TN2 ....8 D8
Tunnel Rd TN1 ....8 B4
Tuppen Ho BN7 ....145 E5
Tuppenney Cl TN35 ....137 C3
Turkey Cock La TN31 ....93 C6
Turkey La RH15 ....73 B3
Turkey Rd TN39 ....156 E7
Turley Cotts TN3 ....7 A8
Turnberry Cl TN38 ....158 F7
Turnberry Ct **14** RH16 ....50 E4
Turnberry Dr BN27 ....152 A8
Turner Ct Bexhill TN40 .157 E5
  Eastbourne BN23 ....174 D1
Turner Ct RH19 ....2 A3
Turner's Hill Rd RH19 ...10 B6
Turners Cotts TN31 ....68 C5
Turners Green La TN5 ....29 F6
Turners Green Rd TN5 ....29 F6
Turners Mill Cl RH16 ....50 D7
Turners Mill Rd RH16 ....50 D6
Turners Way RH15 ....72 F4
Turnpike Cl
  Broyle Side BN8 ....125 A8
  Peacehaven BN10 ....167 C1
Turnpike Piece BN1 ....144 B6
Turret Ct RH19 ....1 C3
Turton Cl BN2 ....164 D5
Tuscan Ct BN10 ....177 F3
Tutts Barn La BN22 ....185 A5
Tuxford Rd TN4 ....7 B5
Tweedsmuir Cl BN23 ...174 C3
Twineham Cl BN2 ....164 F7
Twineham Rd BN21 ....184 D7
Twitten Cl **2** BN42 ....161 E7
Twitten The Bexhill TN39 .156 D4
  Burgess Hill RH15 ....73 B4
  Crowborough TN6 ....25 E1
  Ditchling BN6 ....98 D3
  Southwick BN42 ....161 E7
Twyford Cres TN37 ....136 C4
Twyford Rd BN1 ....143 E6
Twyfords TN6 ....25 E1
Twyhurst Ct RH19 ....1 D3
Twysden Cotts TN18 ....47 A4
Tye Cl BN2 ....177 D4
Tye View BN10 ....167 A1
Tyedean Rd BN10 ....177 F4
Tyler's Gn RH16,RH17 ....50 E4
Tylers La TN22 ....35 E1
Tyndale Ave TN39 ....156 C3
Tyson Pl **9** BN2 ....189 C2

U

Uckfield Cl BN2 ....164 F6
Uckfield Com Coll TN22 .78 D8
Uckfield Com Hospl TN22 .78 D6
Uckfield Rd Poundgate TN6 .37 B7
  Upper Wellingham BN8 ...124 B7
Uckfield Sta TN22 ....78 C6
Uckham La TN33 ....112 E6
Udiam Cotts TN32 ....65 C5
Udimore Rd TN31 ....91 C3
Under Rd BN27 ....130 B3
Undercliff
  St Leonards TN38 ....159 B6
  St Leonards TN38 ....159 C6
Undercliff Terr **7** TN38 .159 C6
Underdown Rd BN42 ...161 E8
Underhill TN22 ....55 B5
Underhill La Clayton BN6 .119 E8
  Westmeston BN6 ....120 C8
Unicorn Ho **1** TN34 ....160 A4
Union Cl BN27 ....129 B3
Union Rd BN2 ....189 C4
Union Sq **18** TN2 ....8 A2
Union St Brighton BN1 ...189 B2
  11 St Leonards TN38 ....159 C7
  Union Street TN5 ....32 B3
Univ of Brighton
  Brighton BN1 ....189 B2
  Eastbourne BN20 ....188 D8
  Falmer BN1 ....144 B6
Univ of Brighton
  (Belgrave Street Annexe)
  BN2 ....189 C3
Univ of Brighton
  (Cockcroft/Watts Annexes)
  BN2 ....143 D2
Univ of Brighton
  (Finsbury Road Annexe)
  BN2 ....189 C3
Univ of Brighton
  (St Peter's Ho) BN2 ..189 B3
Univ of Sussex BN1 ...144 A7
Upland Rd BN20 ....184 C3
Uplands Cl Bexhill TN39 ..156 F6
  Uckfield TN22 ....55 C1
Uplands Com Coll TN5 ..30 A4
Uplands Pk TN21 ....59 E1
Uplands Rd BN1 ....143 C2
Uplands Sch BN1 ....143 C2
Uplands The TN38 ....159 B7
Upper Abbey Rd BN2 ...164 D4
Upper Ave BN21 ....185 A4
Upper Bedford St BN2 ..164 C4
Upper Belgrave Rd BN25 .180 F5
Upper Bevendean Ave
  BN2 ....143 E1
Upper Broomgrove Rd
  TN34 ....137 B3
Upper Carlisle Rd BN20 .188 D7

Upper Chalvington Pl
  BN2 ....164 E5
Upper Church Rd TN37 .136 B4
Upper Chyngton Gdns
  BN25 ....181 B4
Upper Cl RH18 ....11 F2
Upper Clarence Rd TN37 136 C1
Upper Cotts BN2 ....165 D4
Upper Cumberland Wlk
  TN1 ....8 B1
Upper Dr The BN3 ....163 D8
Upper Duke's Dr BN20 ..188 C7
Upper Dunstan Rd TN4 ...8 B6
Upper Gardner St BN1 ..189 B3
Upper Glen Rd TN37 ...136 A5
Upper Gloucester Rd
  BN1 ....189 A3
Upper Greenwoods La
  TN21 ....83 C6
Upper Grosvenor Rd
  TN1, TN4 ....8 B6
Upper Hamilton Rd BN1 .189 A5
Upper Hollingdean Rd
  BN1 ....143 B1
Upper Horsebridge Rd
  BN27 ....129 A3
Upper King's Dr BN20 ..173 B1
Upper Kingston La
  BN42, BN43 ....140 D1
Upper Lake TN33 ....112 E4
Upper Lewes Rd BN2 ...189 C4
Upper Lodges BN1 ....143 D8
Upper Market St **5** BN3 .163 D5
Upper Maze Hill TN38 ..159 B7
Upper Nellington TN3 ....7 B4
Upper North St BN1 ....189 A2
Upper Park Pl **7** BN2 ...189 C2
Upper Park Rd TN37 ...136 C1
Upper Platts TN5 ....31 F1
Upper Profit TN3 ....7 A3
Upper Ratton Dr BN20 ..184 B8
Upper Rock Gdns BN2 ..189 C2
Upper Roedale Cotts
  BN1 ....143 B4
Upper Sea Rd TN40 ....157 D4
Upper Sherwood Rd
  BN25 ....181 A4
Upper Shoreham Rd
  Shoreham-by-Sea
  BN42, BN43 ....140 D1
  Shoreham-by-Sea BN43 ..140 B1
Upper South Rd TN37 ..136 C1
Upper Sq RH18 ....11 E3
Upper St East Dean BN20 .187 B8
  Rusthall TN4 ....7 D4
Upper St James's St BN2 189 C1
Upper St Johns Rd RH15 .73 A4
Upper Station Rd TN21 ...82 A7
Upper Stephens TN3 ....7 A3
Upper Sudeley St **7**
  BN2 ....164 D4
Upper Valley Rd BN9 ...179 B6
Upper Wellington Rd
  BN2 ....164 C7
Upper Winfield Ave BN1 .142 F6
Upper Wish Hill BN20 ..184 B8
Upperton Gdns BN21 ...184 F3
Upperton La BN21 ....184 F3
Upperton Rd BN21 ....184 E4
Upton Ave BN42 ....140 E1
Upton Quarry TN3 ....6 F3
Upwick Rd BN20 ....184 C3

V

Val Mascal TN38 ....136 A1
Val Prinseps Rd BN24 ...175 C4
Vale Ave Brighton BN1 ..142 E7
  Royal Tunbridge Wells TN1 ...8 A3
Vale Cl BN25 ....181 B4
Vale Ct BN41 ....162 B7
Vale Gdns BN41 ....162 B7
Vale Rd Battle TN33 ....112 B5
  Haywards Heath RH16 ....50 B2
  Mayfield TN20 ....40 B2
  Portslade-by-Sea BN41 ..162 C7
  Royal Tunbridge Wells TN1 ...8 A3
  Saltdean BN2 ....166 D3
  Seaford BN25 ....181 A4
  St Leonards TN37 ....136 C2
Vale The BN2 ....165 E5
Vale View Rd TN21 ....82 B6
Valebridge Cl RH15 ....73 C6
Valebridge Dr RH15 ....73 C5
Valebridge Rd RH15 ....73 C6
Valence Rd BN7 ....123 B1
Valentine Ct
  2 Eastbourne BN21 ....185 A2
  14 Hove BN3 ....163 C7
Valentine Dr RH15 ....72 E4
Valerie Cl BN41 ....141 C2
Vallance Cl RH15 ....72 E4
Vallance Ct **7** BN3 ....163 A6
Vallance Gdns BN3 ....163 A6
Vallensdean Cotts BN41 .141 C2
Valley Cl Brighton BN1 ...142 C4
  Newhaven BN9 ....179 B8
Valley Dene BN9 ....179 B7
Valley Dr Brighton BN1 ..142 C4
  Seaford BN25 ....181 A5
Valley Rd Crowborough TN6 .25 F1
  Lewes BN7 ....146 A8
  Newhaven BN9 ....179 A7
  Newhaven BN9 ....179 B7
  Peacehaven BN10 ....167 C2
  Portslade-by-Sea BN41 ..141 A2

Valley Rd continued
  Rusthall TN4 ....7 D4
Valley Rise BN25 ....180 F4
Valley Side Rd TN35 ...137 C3
Valley View TN22 ....53 A8
Valley View Cl TN6 ....25 F1
Valverde Ho **18** BN3 ....163 C7
Vanbrugh Ct **21** BN3 ....163 C7
Vancouver Rd BN23 ....175 B2
Vantage Wlk TN38 ....136 B2
Varndean Cl BN1 ....142 E3
Varndean Coll BN1 ....142 F3
Varndean Dr BN1 ....142 E3
Varndean Gdns BN1 ....142 E3
Varndean Holt BN1 ....142 F3
Varndean Rd BN1 ....142 E3
Varndean Sch BN1 ....143 A3
Vega Cl BN27 ....152 D7
Ventnor Cl BN23 ....174 B4
Ventnor Villas BN3 ....163 B6
Venture Cl TN40 ....157 F4
Verbania Way RH19 ....2 B1
Verdant Cl TN34 ....159 D8
Vere Rd BN1, BN2 ....189 B5
Veric **12** BN3 ....163 C7
Vermont Rd TN4 ....7 C4
Vermont Way TN37 ....135 F6
Vernon Ave
  Peacehaven BN10 ....178 D6
  Woodingdean BN2 ....165 C8
Vernon Cl BN23 ....185 E7
Vernon Gdns **4** BN1 ....163 E6
Vernon Gdns **4** BN1 ....163 E6
Vernon Lodge **9** BN21 .185 A2
Vernon Rd
  Royal Tunbridge Wells TN1 ...8 C6
  Uckfield TN22 ....78 D6
Vernon Terr BN1 ....163 E7
Vernons Rd BN8 ....76 C7
Veronica Way BN2 ....189 C1
Verrall's Wlk **12** BN7 ...146 C8
Verulam Pl TN37 ....159 E7
Viaduct Rd BN1, BN2 ...189 B4
Vian Ave BN23 ....185 F7
Vicarage Cl
  Newhaven BN9 ....168 E2
  Ringmer BN8 ....124 D5
  Seaford BN25 ....180 F3
Vicarage Dr BN20 ....184 D3
Vicarage Field BN27 ...152 C8
Vicarage La
  Burwash Common TN19 ...61 A3
  Eastbourne BN20 ....184 D3
  Hailsham BN27 ....152 C8
  Hellingly BN27 ....129 A6
  Rottingdean BN2 ....165 F1
  Scaynes Hill RH17 ....51 F3
  Westfield TN35 ....114 D3
Vicarage Rd
  Burwash Common TN19 ...61 A3
  Eastbourne BN20 ....184 D3
  Hailsham BN27 ....152 C7
  Hastings TN34 ....160 A5
Vicarage Terr BN2 ....165 F1
Vicarage Way
  Hurst Green TN19 ....45 A3
  Ringmer BN8 ....124 D5
Viceroy Lodge **10** BN3 ..163 A6
Victor Cl BN23 ....180 E5
Victoria Ave
  Burgess Hill RH15 ....72 E3
  Hastings TN35 ....137 C4
  Peacehaven BN10 ....178 C7
Victoria Cl
  Burgess Hill RH15 ....72 E3
  Burgess Hill RH15 ....72 F2
  Polegate BN26 ....172 F7
Victoria Cotts
  High Cross TN6 ....39 C6
  2 Hove BN3 ....163 B5
  St Leonards TN37 ....136 A5
  Stone Cross BN24 ....174 B7
Victoria Ct **8** Hove BN3 .163 C6
  Portslade-by-Sea BN41 ..162 C8
  St Leonards TN38 ....159 B6
Victoria Dr BN20, BN21 ..184 C5
Victoria Gdns
  Burgess Hill RH15 ....72 F2
  Eastbourne BN20 ....184 C4
Victoria Gr **7** BN3 ....163 C6
Victoria Ind Est RH15 ...72 E2
Victoria Mews BN2 ....165 F1
Victoria Pl **6** BN1 ....163 E6
Victoria Rd Bexhill TN39 .157 B4
  Brighton BN1 ....163 E6
  Burgess Hill RH15 ....72 E2
  Crowborough TN6 ....38 C8
  Eastbourne BN20 ....184 C5
  Hailsham BN27 ....152 C7
  Haywards Heath RH16 ...51 A3
  Mayfield TN20 ....40 A3
  Polegate BN26 ....172 F7
  Portslade-by-Sea BN41 ..162 C8
  Royal Tunbridge Wells TN1 ...8 B4
  Southwick BN42 ....161 D7
  St Leonards TN37 ....159 D7
  Windmill Hill BN27 ....131 B5
Victoria St BN1 ....189 A3
Victoria Terr Burwash TN19 .62 A6
  1 Hove BN3 ....163 B5
Victoria Way
  Burgess Hill RH15 ....72 F2
  East Grinstead RH19 ....10 F7
  Winchelsea Beach TN36 ..118 A5
Victory Mews BN2 ....165 A3
View Bank TN35 ....160 D6
View Rd BN10 ....178 C8
View Terr RH7 ....2 A8

Views Path RH16 . . . . .51 B4
Views Wood Path TN22 . .55 D1
Viking Cl BN25 . . . . .180 B6
Viking Way BN23 . . . . .185 F8
Villa Rd TN37 . . . . .159 D7
Village Barn The BN1 . . .142 E7
Village Mews TN39 . . . . .156 C4
Village The BN20 . . . . .188 D8
Village Way BN1 . . . . .144 C6
Village Wks BN8 . . . . .105 A5
Villiers Cl BN2 . . . . .165 E8
Villiers Ct BN1 . . . . .189 B3
Vincent Cl BN23 . . . . .185 F7
Vine Cotts TN6 . . . . .38 C7
Vine Farm Cotts BN8 . . . .104 A5
Vine Pl BN1 . . . . .189 A3
Vine Sq BN22 . . . . .185 D6
Vine St BN1 . . . . .189 B3
Vinehall (Prep Sch for Boys)
    TN32 . . . . .87 E6
Vinehall Cl TN34 . . . . .137 A5
Vinehall Rd TN32 . . . . .87 E5
Vineries The
    Burgess Hill RH15 . . . . .73 D3
    Eastbourne BN23 . . . . .174 D2
    Hove BN3 . . . . .163 E6
Vines Cross Rd
    Brighton BN2 . . . . .164 F7
    Horam TN21 . . . . .107 B7
Vineyard La TN5 . . . . .31 C2
Vintry The
    Eastbourne BN21 . . . . .184 C7
    Nutley TN22 . . . . .35 C4
Virgin's Croft TN33 . . . . .112 D6
Virgin's La TN33 . . . . .112 D6
Volks Electric Rly
    BN1, BN2 . . . . .164 C4
Vue Gris Nez TN36 . . . . . .118 B5

W

Wade Cl BN23 . . . . .185 F7
Wadhurst Bsns Pk TN5 . . .29 B7
Wadhurst CE Prim Sch
    TN5 . . . . .29 F5
Wadhurst Cl
    Eastbourne BN22 . . . . .173 F2
    St Leonards TN37 . . . . .136 B5
Wadhurst La TN33 . . . . . . .111 E6
Wadhurst Par TN5 . . . . .29 F4
Wadhurst Rd TN6 . . . . .28 C3
Wadhurst Rise BN2 . . . . . .164 F5
Wadhurst Sta TN5 . . . . .29 C6
Wadlands Brook Rd RH19 . .1 D5
Wagg Cl RH19 . . . . .2 A1
Waghorns La TN22 . . . . . . .57 C6
Wainwright Cl TN38 . . . . .135 D3
Wainwright Rd TN39 . . . . .157 B4
Waite Cl BN7 . . . . .123 D2
Waites La TN35 . . . . .138 E5
Wakefield Rd BN2 . . . . . . .189 C5
Waldegrave Rd BN1 . . . . .143 A1
Waldegrave St TN4 . . . . . .159 F8
Waldene Cl TN34 . . . . .136 F2
Waldergrave Ct BN2 . . . . .166 D3
Waldron Ave BN1 . . . . . . .143 D6
Waldron Cl BN22 . . . . .184 D8
Waldron Pl BN1 . . . . .143 D6
Waldron Rd BN8 . . . . .105 A5
Waldron Thorns TN21 . . . . .82 A7
Waldshut Rd BN7 . . . . . . .123 A3
Wales Farm Cotts BN7 . . .121 C7
Walesbeech Rd BN2 . . . . .177 D4
Walker Cl BN23 . . . . .185 F7
Walks The TN3 . . . . .15 C8
Wall Hill Rd RH18, RH19 . .11 E5
Wallace Cl TN2 . . . . .17 A8
Wallands Cres BN7 . . . . . .123 C1
Wallands Cty Prim Sch
    BN7 . . . . .123 A2
Walled Garden The TN22 . .55 D4
Wallers TN3 . . . . .7 A8
Wallington Twrs TN40 .157 F4
Wallis Ave BN23 . . . . .185 E7
Wallis Cl TN6 . . . . .26 A1
Wallis Field TN3 . . . . .15 B6
Wallis Ho RH19 . . . . .1 E1
Wallis Pl BN23 . . . . .185 E8
Wallis Way RH15 . . . . .72 E4
Wallsend Rd BN24 . . . . . . .175 C6
Walmer Cres BN2 . . . . .144 B1
Walmer Rd BN25 . . . . .181 C4
Walnut Cl Brighton BN1 . .142 E3
    Heathfield TN21 . . . . .82 B6
Walnut Ct BN26 . . . . .173 A6
Walnut Pk RH16 . . . . .51 B4
Walnut Tree Wlk BN20 . . .184 B8
Walnut Wlk BN26 . . . . .173 A6
Walpole Rd BN2 . . . . .164 D5
Walpole Terr BN2 . . . . .164 D5
Walpole Wlk BN23 . . . . . . .174 E3
Walshes Rd TN6 . . . . .38 B7
Walsingham Cl BN22 . . . . .173 D3
Walsingham Rd BN3 . . . . .162 F6
Walter May Ho TN4 . . . . .159 E8
Walters Green Rd TN11 . . . .5 F6
Walton Bank BN1 . . . . .143 E5
Walton Cl
    Eastbourne BN23 . . . . .174 E3
    St Leonards TN37 . . . . .136 C5
Walton Pk TN39 . . . . .156 F4
Walwers La TN7 . . . . .123 D1
Wanderdown Cl BN2 . . . . .165 E4
Wanderdown Dr BN2 . . . . .165 E4
Wanderdown Rd BN2 . . . . .165 D4

Wanderdown Way BN2 . .165 E4
Wannock Ave BN20 . . . . .172 F3
Wannock Cl TN40 . . . . . . .158 A6
Wannock Dr BN26 . . . . . . .172 F5
Wannock Gdns BN26 . . . . .172 F3
Wannock La BN20, BN26 . .172 F3
Wannock Rd
    Eastbourne BN22 . . . . .185 D5
    Polegate BN26 . . . . .172 F5
War Meml Hospl TN6 . . . .25 E1
Warbleton Cl BN2 . . . . . . .164 E5
Warburton Cl
    East Grinstead RH19 . . . . . .11 A8
    Eastbourne BN21 . . . . .184 C8
    Uckfield TN22 . . . . .78 D8
Ward Cl TN5 . . . . .29 E5
Ward Way TN39 . . . . .157 A6
Ward's La TN5 . . . . .30 E4
Warden Ct RH17 . . . . .50 A6
Warden Park Sch RH17 . . .50 A5
Wardsbrook Rd TN5 . . . . . .43 D7
Ware Ct RH15 . . . . .73 D3
Warelands RH15 . . . . .72 F1
Warenne Rd BN3 . . . . .141 C4
Wares Field TN22 . . . . .78 D4
Wares Rd TN22 . . . . .78 D4
Warleigh Rd BN1, BN2 . . .189 B5
Warmdene Ave BN1 . . . . .142 F6
Warmdene Cl BN1 . . . . . . .142 F5
Warmdene Rd BN1 . . . . . .142 F6
Warmdene Way BN1 . . . . .142 F6
Warminster Rd BN24 . . . . .175 D5
Warner Ct RH15 . . . . .73 A3
Warnham Ct BN3 . . . . .163 C5
Warnham Gdns TN39 . . . . .156 C2
Warnham Rise BN1 . . . . . .143 A5
Warren Ave BN2 . . . . .165 C8
Warren Cl Crowborough TN6 .25 E2
    Eastbourne BN20 . . . . .188 C8
    Friston BN20 . . . . .183 B1
    Lewes BN7 . . . . .146 B8
    Roser's Cross TN21 . . . . . . .81 A6
    St Leonards TN38 . . . . .158 E8
    Woodingdean BN2 . . . . .165 B8
Warren Cnr TN21 . . . . .81 A8
Warren Cotts
    Mayfield TN20 . . . . .40 C3
    North Chailey BN8 . . . . .75 F7
Warren Ct Crowborough TN6 .25 D4
    Southwick BN42 . . . . .140 E1
Warren Dr BN7 . . . . .146 A8
Warren Farm La TN3 . . . . .16 B4
Warren Gdn TN6 . . . . .25 E2
Warren Hill BN20 . . . . .184 A1
Warren La
    Beacon Down TN21 . . . . .81 A7
    Friston BN20 . . . . .183 B1
    North Chailey BN8 . . . . .75 E8
Warren Lodge BN10 . . . . .167 A1
Warren Rd
    Crowborough TN6 . . . . .25 C1
    Fairlight TN35 . . . . .138 C4
    Woodingdean BN2 . . . . .165 B8
Warren Ridge
    Crowborough TN6 . . . . .25 D2
    Frant TN3 . . . . .17 C3
Warren Rise BN2 . . . . .165 B8
Warren The
    Burgess Hill RH15 . . . . .73 C1
    Mayfield TN20 . . . . .40 C2
    Ticehurst TN5 . . . . .31 E1
Warren Way
    North Chailey BN8 . . . . .75 F8
    Telscombe Cliffs BN10 . . . .167 A1
    Woodingdean BN2 . . . . .165 D8
Warren Wood TN6 . . . . .25 D1
Warrenwood BN8 . . . . .53 A1
Warrior Cl BN41 . . . . .141 B2
Warrior Ct TN37 . . . . .159 D7
Warrior Gdns TN37 . . . . . .159 C7
Warrior Ho BN20 . . . . .188 E8
Warrior Sq
    Eastbourne BN22 . . . . .185 C4
    St Leonards TN37 . . . . .159 D7
Warrs Hill La BN8 . . . . .75 E8
Wartling Cl TN38 . . . . .135 F3
Wartling Dr TN39 . . . . . . .155 F5
Wartling Rd
    Eastbourne BN22 . . . . .185 D6
    Wartling BN27 . . . . .131 C2
Warwick Cl BN27 . . . . .129 C3
Warwick Ct
    Eastbourne BN23 . . . . .174 E1
    Hove BN3 . . . . .163 E7
Warwick Mount BN2 . . . .164 C4
Warwick Pk TN2 . . . . .8 B1
Warwick Rd Bexhill TN39 . .156 F5
    Royal Tunbridge Wells TN1 . .8 A2
    Seaford BN25 . . . . .180 E3
Washington Ave TN37 . . . .135 F6
Washington Rd RH16 . . . . .51 A5
Washington St BN2 . . . . . .189 C4
Washwell La TN5 . . . . .29 F3
Wassall La TN17 . . . . .48 E7
Watchbell La TN31 . . . . . . .93 C5
Watchbell St TN31 . . . . . . .93 C5
Waterbury Hill RH17 . . . . .33 B5
Waterdown Rd TN4 . . . . . . .7 C1
Waterdyke Ave BN42 . . . . .161 C2
Waterfield TN2 . . . . .17 A7
Waterford Cl BN10 . . . . . .167 C2
Waterfrets Cotts TN3 . . . . . .6 F5
Watergate BN7 . . . . .159 B8
Watergate La BN7 . . . . . . .146 C8
Waterhall Rd BN1 . . . . . . .142 C6
Waterloo Cl TN37 . . . . . . .135 F7
Waterloo Ho BN3 . . . . . . .163 D5
Waterloo Pas TN34 . . . . . .160 B4

Waterloo Pl
    Brighton BN1 . . . . .189 C3
    Hastings TN34 . . . . .160 B4
    Lewes BN7 . . . . .123 D1
Waterloo Sq BN26 . . . . . .171 A3
Waterloo St BN3 . . . . .163 D5
Watermen's Cl TN34 . . . . .136 F3
Watermill Bexhill TN39 . .157 B7
    Lower Willingdon BN20 . . . .173 A5
Watermill Dr TN38 . . . . . .135 D3
Watermill La Clayhill TN31 .67 D2
    Icklesham TN35,TN36 . . . . .116 C3
    Watermill TN39 . . . . .134 B2
Waters Cotts TN5 . . . . .30 A4
Waterside RH19 . . . . .2 B1
Waterside Cl TN35 . . . . . . .137 C3
Waterworks Cotts
    Friston BN20 . . . . .183 A1
    Hastings TN34 . . . . .159 F8
Waterworks Rd
    Eastbourne BN22 . . . . .185 A4
    Hastings TN34 . . . . .136 F1
Watling Cl BN42 . . . . .161 E7
Watling Ct BN42 . . . . .161 E7
Watling Rd BN42 . . . . .161 E7
Wattle's Wish TN33 . . . . . .112 C6
Watts Cl TN5 . . . . .29 F4
Watts La BN21 . . . . .184 E4
Watts Lodge RH15 . . . . .73 D3
Watts' Palace La TN31 . . . .89 D7
Waverley Cres BN1 . . . . . .143 C1
Waverley Ct
    Hastings TN34 . . . . .159 E7
    Seaford BN25 . . . . .180 F2
Waverley Dr TN2 . . . . .8 F6
Waverley Gdns BN24 . . . . .175 D5
Wayfaring Down BN26 . . .172 D3
Wayfield Ave BN3 . . . . . . .141 F1
Wayfield Cl BN3 . . . . .141 F1
Wayford Cl BN23 . . . . .174 D2
Wayland Ave BN1 . . . . . . .142 C3
Wayland Hts BN1 . . . . . . .142 C4
Wayside Brighton BN1 . . . .142 D6
    East Dean BN20 . . . . .183 B1
Wayside Wlk TN21 . . . . . . .81 F6
Weald Ave BN3 . . . . .162 F8
Weald Cl
    Barcombe Cross BN8 . . . . .101 E4
    Lewes BN7 . . . . .123 C2
Weald Rd RH15 . . . . .72 E3
Weald Rise RH16 . . . . .50 E1
Weald The RH19 . . . . .1 F4
Weald View
    Barcombe Cross BN8 . . . . .101 E4
    Staplecross TN32 . . . . .65 E2
    Turner's Green TN5 . . . . . . .29 F6
Wealden Cl TN6 . . . . .25 F3
Wealden Cotts TN19 . . . . . .61 C3
Wealden Ind Est TN6 . . . . .38 F7
Wealden Pk BN22 . . . . . . .173 C1
Wealden View TN19 . . . . . .62 B7
Wealden Way
    Bexhill TN39 . . . . .156 C6
    Haywards Heath RH16 . . . . .50 D4
Wealdview Rd TN21 . . . . . .81 F7
Weare Rd TN4 . . . . .8 C8
Weatherby Cl BN21 . . . . . .184 C8
Weavers Cl RH15 . . . . .73 D1
Weavers La BN26 . . . . .170 F3
Weavers Rock La TN21 . . . .82 C5
Wedderburn Rd BN20 . . . .173 B1
Week La BN8 . . . . .124 D2
Weir Wood Resr
    (Nature Reserve) RH19 . . .10 D1
Welbeck Ave Hove BN3 . . .162 E6
    Royal Tunbridge Wells TN4 . .8 D8
    St Leonards TN38 . . . . .159 A7
Welbeck Cl
    Burgess Hill RH15 . . . . .73 D4
    Eastbourne BN22 . . . . .173 D3
Welbeck Cl BN25 . . . . .180 E3
Welbeck Dr RH15 . . . . .73 D4
Welesmere Rd TN34 . . . . . .166 A3
Welkin (Brighton Univ)
    BN20 . . . . .184 E1
Welkin The RH16 . . . . .51 B8
Well House Pl BN7 . . . . . . .123 C1
Welland Cl TN34 . . . . .38 A8
Wellcombe Cres BN20 . . .188 D7
Weller Rd TN4 . . . . .7 C4
Wellesley Cl Bexhill TN39 .156 D3
    Crowborough TN6 . . . . .25 D1
Wellesley Ct TN34 . . . . . . .160 B4
Wellesley Rd BN21 . . . . . .185 A3
Wellfield RH19 . . . . .11 C7
Wellgreen La BN7 . . . . . . .145 F5
Wellhouse La RH15 . . . . . . .98 C7
Wellingham La BN8 . . . . . .124 A7
Wellington Ct
    Brighton BN2 . . . . .165 A3
    Eastbourne BN22 . . . . .185 C5
Wellington Gdns TN33 . . .112 C5
Wellington Ho TN34 . . . . .159 F8
Wellington Lodge TN34 . .160 A4
Wellington Mews TN34 . .159 F8
Wellington Pk BN25 . . . . .181 A3
Wellington Pl
    Hastings TN34 . . . . .159 F7
    Sparrow's Green TN5 . . . . . .29 F5
Wellington Rd
    Brighton BN2 . . . . .189 C4
    Hastings TN34 . . . . .160 A4
    Newhaven BN9 . . . . .168 F2
    Peacehaven BN10 . . . . .178 E6
    Portslade-by-Sea BN41 . . . .162 B6
Wellington Sq TN34 . . . . .159 F8
Wellington St
    Brighton BN2 . . . . .164 C7

Wellington St continued
    Lewes BN7 . . . . .123 D1
Wellington Terr TN4 . . . . .159 F8
Wellington Town Rd RH19 . .1 D2
Wellingtonia Cl BN1 . . . . .142 E3
Wellis Ct TN38 . . . . .159 A8
Wellis Gdns TN38 . . . . . . .159 A8
Wellplace Cotts TN36 . . . .116 F5
Wells Chase BN7 . . . . .99 E6
Wells Cl Eastbourne BN20 .188 C8
    Plumpton Green BN7 . . . . . .99 C5
    Royal Tunbridge Wells TN1 . .8 A3
Wells Ho TN4 . . . . .7 F4
Wells Lea RH19 . . . . .1 D3
Wells Mdw RH19 . . . . .1 D4
Wellsbourne BN2 . . . . .164 F5
Wellsbourne Rd BN24 . . . .174 A5
Welsley Mews TN6 . . . . . . .25 F2
Wendale Dr BN10 . . . . .167 D2
Wendover Grange
    BN3 . . . . .163 A6
Went Hill Gdns BN20 . . . . .173 B3
Went Hill Pk BN25 . . . . . . .181 A3
Went La BN20 . . . . .183 C1
Went Way BN20 . . . . .187 B8
Wenthill Cl BN20 . . . . .187 B8
Wentworth Cl
    Bexhill TN40 . . . . .157 F5
    Hailsham BN27 . . . . .129 A1
Wentworth Ct BN23 . . . . . .185 E6
Wentworth St BN2 . . . . . . .189 C1
Wentworth Way TN38 . . . .158 F8
West Ascent TN38 . . . . . . .159 B6
West Beeches Rd TN6 . . . .26 B2
West Blatchington
    Inf Sch BN3 . . . . .141 E4
West Blatchington
    Jun Sch BN3 . . . . .141 E4
West Cl Alfriston BN26 . . .170 F3
    Polegate BN26 . . . . .173 B7
West Comm RH16 . . . . .50 F6
West Common Dr RH16 . . .51 A7
West Dean Rise BN25 . . . .181 A4
West Down Rd TN39 . . . . . .157 A5
West Dr BN2 . . . . .164 C6
West End BN27 . . . . .130 C6
West End Cotts TN19 . . . . .60 F3
West Furlong La BN6 . . . . .97 A5
West Furlong La BN6 . . . . .97 A5
West Gate BN7 . . . . .99 C6
West Hill Dormans Park RH19 . .1 E6
    East Grinstead RH19 . . . . . .10 D8
West Hill Arc TN34 . . . . .160 A3
West Hill Cliff Rly TN34 . .160 A4
West Hill Ct TN38 . . . . . . .159 B6
West Hill Mews TN38 . . . .158 F6
West Hill Pl BN1 . . . . .189 A3
West Hill Rd Brighton BN1 .189 A3
    St Leonards TN38 . . . . .159 A6
West Hill St BN1 . . . . .189 A4
West Ho BN21 . . . . .185 A2
West Hoathly Rd RH19 . . .10 D4
West Hove Cty Inf Sch
    BN3 . . . . .162 F7
West Hove Cty Jun Sch
    BN3 . . . . .162 F7
West Kent Coll of F Ed TN4 & A7
West La RH19 . . . . .10 D8
West Leigh RH19 . . . . .10 E7
West Mallion RH16 . . . . . . .50 F3
West Par TN39 . . . . .157 B2
West Park Cres RH15 . . . . .72 D4
West Point BN43 . . . . .161 A6
West Rd Kilndown TN17 . . . .20 F3
    Portslade-by-Sea BN41 . . . .162 A7
West Rise Cty Inf Sch
    BN23 . . . . .174 C2
West Rise Cty Jun Sch
    BN23 . . . . .174 C2
West St Alfriston BN26 . . .170 F3
    Brighton BN1 . . . . .189 A2
    Burgess Hill RH15 . . . . .72 E4
    Ditchling BN6 . . . . .98 D3
    Dormansland RH7 . . . . .2 A8
    East Grinstead RH19 . . . . . .10 E8
    Eastbourne BN21 . . . . .184 F2
    Hastings TN34 . . . . .160 A3
    Lewes BN7 . . . . .123 D1
    Mayfield TN20 . . . . .40 A2
    Portslade-by-Sea BN41 . . . .162 C7
    Rottingdean BN2 . . . . .165 F1
    Rye TN31 . . . . .93 C5
    Seaford BN25 . . . . .180 E2
West St Leonards
    Cty Prim Sch TN38 . . . .158 F8
West St Leonards Sta
    TN38 . . . . .158 F7
West Street La TN21 . . . . . .81 F2
West Terr
    Eastbourne BN21 . . . . .184 F2
    Herstmonceux BN27 . . . . . .130 E6
West Undercliff TN31 . . . . .93 A5
West View Hastings TN34 .160 B6
    Hove BN3 . . . . .163 C8
    Lindfield RH16 . . . . .51 B6
    Seaford BN25 . . . . .180 E2
    Uckfield TN22 . . . . .55 D1
West View Cotts RH16 . . . .51 B6
West View Ct BN25 . . . . . .180 E2
West View Gdns RH19 . . . .10 E8
West View Terr BN9 . . . . . .168 D2
West Way BN3 . . . . .141 D2
Westaway Dr TN39 . . . . . .157 A4
Westbourne Ct TN39 . . . . .156 C2
Westbourne Gdns BN3 . . .163 A7
Westbourne Gr BN3 . . . . . .163 A7
Westbourne Pl BN3 . . . . . .163 A6
Westbourne St BN3 . . . . . .163 A7

Westbourne Villas BN3 . .162 F6
Westbrook
    Forest Row RH18 . . . . .11 E3
    Saltdean BN2 . . . . .177 C6
Westbrook La TN35 . . . . . .114 E5
Westbrook Terr TN2 . . . . . . .8 D1
Westbrook Way BN42 . . . .161 F7
Westcliff Mansion BN20 . .188 F8
Westcombe BN1 . . . . .163 E7
Westcourt Dr TN39 . . . . . .156 F3
Westdean Ave BN9 . . . . . .179 A5
Westdene Cl TN37 . . . . . . .136 C6
Westdene Cty Prim Sch
    BN1 . . . . .142 C5
Westdene Dr BN1 . . . . .142 C5
Westdown Ho BN21 . . . . . .185 A2
Westdown La TN19 . . . . . . .61 A3
Westdown Rd BN25 . . . . . .180 D4
Westergate Rd BN2 . . . . . .143 E4
Westerham Rd BN23 . . . . .174 D1
Westerings The TN21 . . . . .82 A6
Westerleigh Cl TN38 . . . . .159 A8
Western Ave BN26 . . . . . . .173 B7
Western Espl BN3, BN41 . .162 D6
Western Gdns TN6 . . . . .38 D8
Western Rd Bexhill TN40 . .157 C3
    Burgess Hill RH15 . . . . .72 E3
    Crowborough TN6 . . . . .38 C7
    Eastbourne BN22 . . . . .185 B4
    Hailsham BN27 . . . . .152 B7
    Haywards Heath RH16 . . . . .50 F4
    Hove BN1, BN3 . . . . .163 E5
    Hurstpierpoint BN6 . . . . .97 A7
    Lewes BN7 . . . . .123 B1
    Newhaven BN9 . . . . .179 C6
    Newick BN8 . . . . .76 C7
    Pevensey Bay BN24 . . . . . .175 D4
    Royal Tunbridge Wells TN1 . . .8 C5
    St Leonards TN37 . . . . .159 C7
    Turner's Green TN5 . . . . . . .29 F6
Western Road
    Cty Prim Sch BN7 . . . . .146 C8
Western St BN1 . . . . .163 E5
Western Terr BN1 . . . . . . .163 E6
Westfield Ave BN2 . . . . . . .166 D3
Westfield Ave N BN2 . . . . .166 D3
Westfield Ave S BN2 . . . . .166 D3
Westfield Cl Brighton BN1 .143 A4
    Five Ashes TN20 . . . . .58 B6
    Polegate BN26 . . . . .173 A7
Westfield Cres BN1 . . . . . .143 A5
Westfield Ct BN26 . . . . . . .173 A6
Westfield Cty Prim Sch
    TN35 . . . . .114 E4
Westfield La TN35,TN37 . .136 C8
Westfield Rd BN21 . . . . . . .184 D6
Westfield Rise BN2 . . . . . .166 C3
Westgate St BN7 . . . . .123 C1
Westham BN26 . . . . .164 F5
Westham Cl TN39 . . . . .156 D3
Westham Dr BN24 . . . . . . .175 F6
Westhill Dr RH15 . . . . .72 E3
Westland Ct BN41 . . . . . . .162 A7
Westlands Rd RH16 . . . . . . .51 B5
Westlords BN21 . . . . .184 C8
Westmeston Ave BN2 . . . .177 B6
Westminster Cl BN22 . . . .173 D4
Westminster Cres TN34 . .137 A4
Westmoreland Cl TN38 . . .135 F3
Westmoreland Ct TN22 . . .78 C5
Westmorland Ct
    Eastbourne BN20 . . . . .184 B7
    Hove BN3 . . . . .163 E7
Westmount BN2 . . . . .164 C6
Westmount Cl BN42 . . . . . .161 D8
Westpoint BN8 . . . . .76 C7
Westville Rd TN39 . . . . . . .157 A4
Westway TN2 . . . . .9 D7
Westway Cl BN41 . . . . .140 E4
Westway Gdns BN41 . . . . .140 E4
Westwood Rd TN4 . . . . .7 C5
Wharf Rd
    Eastbourne BN21 . . . . .184 F3
    Hove BN3 . . . . .162 D6
Whatlington Rd TN33 . . . .112 E7
Whatlington Way TN38 . . .135 D2
Wheatfield Ct TN37 . . . . . .136 C5
Wheatfield Way BN2 . . . . .143 A3
Wheatland Cl BN10 . . . . . .167 B2
Wheatsheaf Cl RH15 . . . . . .72 E5
Wheatsheaf Gdns BN7 . . .123 E2
Wheatsheaf La RH17 . . . . . .50 A6
Wheel Farm Bsns Pk
    TN35 . . . . .114 D3
Wheel La TN35 . . . . .114 D3
Wheeler Ct RH16 . . . . .50 F2
Wheelers La TN22 . . . . .57 D6
Wheelers Lane Cotts
    TN22 . . . . .57 D5
Wheelwright Cl BN22 . . . .173 D4
Wheelwright La RH15 . . . . .73 D1
Whichelo Pl BN2 . . . . .164 C6
Whiffens Cl BN27 . . . . .152 A6
Whin Croft Pk TN6 . . . . .37 D8
Whipping Post La BN2 . . .165 F1
Whippingham Rd BN2 . . . .164 C7
Whippingham St BN2 . . . .164 C8
Whistler Cl BN1 . . . . .142 F1
Whitbread Cl BN23 . . . . . .174 B4
White Bear Pas BN1 . . . . . .8 A2
White Chys TN6 . . . . .26 A1
White Ct BN26 . . . . .170 F2
White Hill BN7 . . . . .123 C1
White Hill Ave TN39 . . . . .156 E4
White Hill Dr TN39 . . . . . .156 E4

White House
  Cty Prim Sch BN27 .....152 B8
White Lodge Hove BN3 . .163 C8
  Royal Tunbridge Wells TN1 . . .8 C4
White Rock TN34, TN37 . .159 E7
White Rock Gdns **7**
  TN34 . . . . .159 E7
White Rock
  Pleasure Grounds TN34 159 E7
White Rock Rd
  TN34, TN37 . . . . .159 E7
White St BN2 . . . . .189 C2
White Way Alfriston BN26 .170 F1
  Lewes BN7 . . . . .146 B1
White's Cl BN27 . . . . .97 A7
Whitebread La TN31 . . . . . . .67 E8
Whitecross St BN1 . . . . . .189 B3
Whitefield Rd TN4 . . . . .8 A6
Whitefriars Rd TN34 . . . .160 A5
Whitegate Cl TN4 . . . . .8 A8
Whitegates Cl BN8 . . . . . .100 E7
Whitegates La TN5 . . . . .29 D8
Whitegates Pk TN35 . . . . .114 D2
Whitehall Par **3** RH19 . . . . .1 E1
Whitehawk Cl BN2 . . . . . .164 E5
Whitehawk Cres BN2 . . . .164 E5
Whitehawk Cty Inf Sch
  BN2 . . . . .164 E6
Whitehawk Cty Jun Sch
  BN2 . . . . .164 E6
Whitehawk Hill Rd BN2 .164 D5
Whitehawk Rd
  Brighton BN2 . . . . .164 E6
  Brighton BN2 . . . . .164 E6
Whitehawk Way BN2 . . .164 F6
Whitehill Cl TN6 . . . . .25 F1
Whitehill Cty Inf Sch TN6 .26 A1
Whitehill Rd TN6 . . . . .37 F8
Whitehouse Ave TN39 . . .157 B7
Whitehouse La TN21 . . . . . .81 B4
Whitelot Cl BN42 . . . . .140 E2
Whitelot Way BN42 . . . . .140 E2
Whiterock Pl BN42 . . . . . .161 E7
Whitethorn Dr BN1 . . . . .142 B4
Whiteway Cl BN25 . . . . . .180 E6
Whiteway La BN2 . . . . . . .177 A6
Whiteways Cotts BN7 . . .146 D2
Whitfeld La BN8 . . . . .123 C6
Whitley Rd BN22 . . . . . . .185 B5
Whittingehame Gdns
  BN1 . . . . .142 F3
Whittington Coll RH19 . . . .1 A4
Whittington's Way TN34 .137 B4
Whittle Dr BN23 . . . . . . .174 A1
Whittlewood Cl TN38 . . . .135 E2
Whitworth Rd TN37 . . . . .136 B7
Whybourne Crest TN2 . . . . .8 D1
Whydown Hill TN33 . . . . .113 E6
Whydown Rd TN39 . . . . .156 B7
Wick Hall BN3 . . . . .163 D6
Wickets The RH15 . . . . . . .72 F5
Wickham Ave TN39 . . . . .157 B3
Wickham Cl RH16 . . . . . . .50 E7
Wickham Dr BN6 . . . . .97 C5
Wickham Gdns TN4 . . . . . . .7 D5
Wickham Hill BN6 . . . . . . .97 C4
Wickham La BN7, BN8 . . . .100 E3
Wickham Rock La TN36 . .117 C5
Wickham Way RH16 . . . . . .50 E7
Wickhurst Cl BN41 . . . . . .140 F2
Wickhurst Rd BN41 . . . . .141 A2
Wickhurst Rise BN41 . . . .140 F3
Wicklands Ave BN2 . . . . .177 D5
Widbury TN3 . . . . .6 F2
Widdicombe Way BN2 . . .143 E2
Wigmore Cl BN1 . . . . .143 B1
Wilbury Ave BN3 . . . . . . .163 C8
Wilbury Cres BN3 . . . . . .163 D7
Wilbury Gdns BN3 . . . . . .163 C8
Wilbury Gr BN3 . . . . .163 C7
Wilbury Grange **9** BN3 . .163 C6
Wilbury Lodge **13** BN3 . .163 C6
Wilbury Rd BN3 . . . . .163 C7
Wilbury Villas BN3 . . . . .163 C7
Wilby Ave BN42 . . . . .140 E1
Wild Park Cl BN2 . . . . . . .143 E3
Wild Park Nature Trail
  BN2 . . . . .143 D5
Wilderness Gdns TN31 . . . .67 B7
Wilderness La TN22 . . . . . .57 C3
Wilderness Pk TN6 . . . . . . .25 E2
Wilderness Rd BN6 . . . . . . .97 A6
Wilderness Rise RH19 . . . . .2 A6
Wilderness The RH15 . . . . .51 B8
Wilderness Wood
  (Adventure Pk) TN22 . . . .57 D4
Wilderwick Rd RH19, RH7 . . .2 A5
Wildwood BN23 . . . . .174 C4
Wilfrid Rd BN3 . . . . .141 D1
Wiliamson Cott Homes
  BN3 . . . . .163 A7
Wilkins Way TN40 . . . . . .157 F6
Wilkinson Cl BN2 . . . . . . .165 F3
Wilkinson Way BN25 . . . .180 E4
Willard Cl BN22 . . . . .185 A6
Willetts Cotts BN3 . . . . .5 C4
Willetts Field BN8 . . . . . .127 E8
Willetts La TN5 . . . . .5 C4
William Allen La RH16 . . . .51 B6
William Parker Sch TN36 . . . .92 D1
  (Lower) TN34 . . . . .136 D3
William Parker Sch
  (Upper) TN34 . . . . .136 D4
William Rd TN38 . . . . . . .158 E7
William St Brighton BN2 . .189 B2

William St continued
  Royal Tunbridge Wells TN4 . . . .8 A5
  Southwick BN42 . . . . .162 B7
William Sutton Ho BN1 . .189 B2
Williams Ct **7** BN23 . . . .174 E1
Williams Rd BN43 . . . . . .161 C8
Willicombe Pk TN2 . . . . .8 D4
Willie Cotts BN7 . . . . .123 E1
Willingdon Ave
  Bexhill TN39 . . . . .157 A4
  St Leonards TN38 . . . . . .136 A5
Willingdon Cl
  St Leonards TN38 . . . . . .136 A5
  Willingdon BN20 . . . . . . .173 B1
Willingdon Ct BN20 . . . .173 B3
Willingdon Cty Prim Sch
  BN20 . . . . .173 A3
Willingdon Dro BN23 . . . .174 B2
Willingdon La BN26 . . . . .183 C7
Willingdon Park
  Dr BN22 . . . . .173 D2
Willingdon Rd
  Brighton BN2 . . . . .143 E1
  Eastbourne BN20, BN21 . .184 C6
  Willingdon Sch BN20 . . . .172 F4
Willingdon Trees
  Cty Prim Sch BN22 . . . . .173 D3
Willingdon Way
  St Leonards TN38 . . . . . .136 A5
  Willingdon BN22 . . . . . . .173 B2
Willingford La TN19 . . . . .61 C2
Willoughby Cres BN22 . .185 C6
Willow Ave BN27 . . . . . . .129 B1
Willow Bank TN32 . . . . . . .64 B3
Willow Cl
  East Grinstead RH19 . . . . . .1 D3
  Etchingham TN19 . . . . . . .63 B8
  Heathfield TN21 . . . . .82 B8
  Uckfield TN22 . . . . .78 D8
  Woodingdean BN2 . . . . . .165 E8
Willow Ct **4** Hove BN3 . .163 D7
  Polegate BN26 . . . . .173 A6
Willow Dr Bexhill TN39 . .156 C5
  Polegate BN26 . . . . .173 A5
  Seaford BN25 . . . . .181 C3
Willow End TN34 . . . . . . .136 F4
Willow Est The BN9 . . . . .179 E8
Willow Gdns BN6 . . . . .97 A7
Willow Ho BN6 . . . . .97 E5
Willow La TN36 . . . . .118 B6
Willow Mead **8** RH19 . . . .10 F8
Willow Mews TN32 . . . . . .64 B3
Willow Pk RH16 . . . . .51 B4
Willow Stream Cl TN35 . .115 E3
Willow Tree Rd TN2 . . . . . . .7 F1
Willow Way BN6 . . . . .97 A8
Willow Wlk
  Eastbourne BN22 . . . . . . .173 D2
  Newhaven BN9 . . . . .179 C8
  Royal Tunbridge Wells TN2 . . . .8 E8
Willowbed Wlk TN34 . . . .136 E5
Willowbrook Way BN6 . . . .98 A3
Willowdowne Cl BN26 . . .173 A5
Willowfield Rd BN22 . . . .185 B4
Willowfield Sq **7** BN22 . .185 B3
Willowmead TN6 . . . . .37 E8
Willows Rise TN22 . . . . . . .79 B5
Willows The
  Barcombe Cross BN8 . . . . .101 E5
  2 Brighton BN2 . . . . . . .189 C5
  Burgess Hill RH15 . . . . . . .73 B5
  Hassocks BN6 . . . . .97 E4
  St Leonards TN37 . . . . . . .136 A6
Wilman Rd TN4 . . . . .8 B7
Wilmington Cl
  Brighton BN1 . . . . .143 A5
  Hassocks BN6 . . . . .97 F4
Wilmington Gdns BN21 . .185 A1
Wilmington Par BN1 . . . .142 F5
Wilmington Rd
  Hastings TN34 . . . . .137 A3
  Newhaven BN9 . . . . .179 B6
  Seaford BN25 . . . . .180 D4
Wilmington Sq BN21 . . . .185 A1
Wilmington St BN26 . . . .171 F6
Wilmington Way
  Brighton BN1 . . . . .143 A5
  Haywards Heath RH16 . . . .51 A5
Wilmot Ct **6** BN43 . . . . .161 C8
Wilmot Rd BN43 . . . . .161 C8
Wilson Ave BN2 . . . . .164 F6
Wilson Gr TN22 . . . . .78 A7
Wilson's Cross BN27 . . . .131 F7
Wilton **1** RH16 . . . . .50 D6
Wilton Ave BN22 . . . . . . .173 F2
Wilton Ho TN38 . . . . .158 F6
Wilton Rd TN40 . . . . .157 C3
Wiltshire Ct BN23 . . . . . .174 E1
Wiltshire Ho **16** BN2 . . . .189 C2
Wiltshire Way TN2 . . . . .8 D7
Winceby Cl TN39 . . . . . . .156 E2
Winchcombe Rd BN22 . . .185 A4
Winchelsea Cl BN25 . . . .181 C5
Winchelsea La
  Cock Marling TN31, TN36 . . .92 C1
  Hastings TN35 . . . . .137 E5
Winchelsea Mus TN36 . . .117 E7
Winchelsea Rd
  Eastbourne BN22 . . . . . . .185 D6
  Guestling Green TN35 . . . .137 F7
  Hastings TN35 . . . . .137 D4
  Rye TN31 . . . . .93 B5
Winchelsea Sta TN36 . . . . .92 D1
Winchester Ho BN22 . . . .173 E3
Winchester St BN1 . . . . . .189 B5
Winchester Way BN22 . . .173 C2
Wincombe Rd BN1 . . . . . .142 D1
Windermere Cres BN22 . .185 C5

Windermere Ct **9** BN2 . .164 C6
Windermere Rd RH16 . . . .50 F4
Windgrove Cotts TN33 . . .112 C6
Windgrove Ho TN33 . . . . .112 C6
Winding St **21** TN34 . . . . .160 B4
Windlesham Ave
  BN1, BN3 . . . . .163 E6
Windlesham Cl BN41 . . . .141 A1
Windlesham Ct **14** BN1 . .163 E7
Windlesham Gdns
  BN1, BN3 . . . . .163 E7
Windlesham Rd BN1 . . . .163 E6
  Shoreham-by-Sea BN43 . . . .163 E8
Windmill Ave BN6 . . . . . . .97 F3
Windmill Cl
  Eastbourne BN21 . . . . . . .184 D6
  Heathfield TN21 . . . . .82 B8
  Hove BN3 . . . . .141 F2
Windmill Ct
  Royal Tunbridge Wells TN2 . . . .8 C3
  Winchelsea Beach TN36 . . .118 B6
Windmill Dr Bexhill TN39 .157 B6
  Brighton BN1 . . . . .142 C6
  Burgess Hill RH15 . . . . . . .73 A4
Windmill Gn BN24 . . . . . .174 C5
Windmill La
  Ashurst Wood RH19 . . . . . .11 C7
  Cousley Wood TN5 . . . . . . .30 C8
  Durgates TN5 . . . . .29 E4
  East Grinstead RH19 . . . . . . .1 D3
  Friston BN20 . . . . .183 A1
Windmill Par BN42 . . . . . .140 E1
Windmill Pl BN26 . . . . . . .173 A5
Windmill Rd
  Polegate BN26 . . . . .173 A6
  Southwick BN42 . . . . .140 E1
  St Leonards TN38 . . . . . . .136 B2
Windmill St Brighton BN2 .189 C3
  Royal Tunbridge Wells TN2 . . . .8 C3
Windmill Terr **18** BN2 . . .189 C3
Windmill View BN1 . . . . .143 B7
Windmill Way TN36 . . . . .118 B7
Windmills Cty Jun Sch
  BN6 . . . . .98 A3
Windover Cres BN7 . . . . .123 A2
Windover Way BN22 . . . .173 B3
Windsor Cl
  Eastbourne BN23 . . . . . . .174 C3
  Haywards Heath RH16 . . . .50 E2
  Hove BN3 . . . . .142 A3
  Seaford BN25 . . . . .180 B6
Windsor Ct Brighton BN1 .189 A2
  Brighton, Withdean BN1 . . .142 D4
  Crowborough TN6 . . . . . . .38 C8
  8 Eastbourne BN22 . . . .185 B3
  Polegate BN26 . . . . .173 A7
Windsor Lodge **5** BN3 . .163 B6
Windsor Pl
  Crowborough TN6 . . . . . . .38 C8
  East Grinstead RH19 . . . . .11 A8
  Hastings TN34 . . . . .136 E2
Windsor Rd Bexhill TN39 .157 B4
  Crowborough TN6 . . . . . . .38 C8
  Hailsham BN27 . . . . .152 B6
  St Leonards TN37 . . . . . . .136 B3
Windsor St BN1 . . . . .189 A2
Windsor Way
  Polegate BN26 . . . . .173 A7
  Winchelsea Beach TN36 . . .118 A5
Windward Quay **11** BN23 .185 F8
Wineham Way TN40 . . . . .157 F4
Winfield Ave BN1 . . . . . . .142 F6
Winfield Cl Brighton BN1 .142 F5
  Portslade-by-Sea BN41 . . .141 A4
Wingate Cl TN38 . . . . . . .136 A1
Wingle Tye Rd RH15 . . . . .98 A8
Winkfield Ct RH16 . . . . . . .50 D5
Winkhurst Way RH15 . . . .73 D1
Winkney Rd BN22 . . . . . . .173 F3
Winnals Pk RH16 . . . . .50 D5
Winscote Cl TN6 . . . . .25 D1
Winston BN27 . . . . .152 B7
Winston Cres BN23 . . . . .185 D7
Winston Dr TN39 . . . . . . .156 F4
Winstone Scott Ave TN3 . . .6 C4
Winterbourne Cl
  Hastings TN34 . . . . .159 D8
  Lewes BN7 . . . . .146 A8
Winterbourne Hollow
  BN7 . . . . .146 B8
Winterbourne La BN7 . . .146 A8
Winterbourne Mews
  BN7 . . . . .146 B8
Winterton Way BN43 . . . .161 B6
Winton Ave BN2 . . . . .166 C3
Winton St BN26 . . . . .171 A4
Wisden Ave RH15 . . . . . . .72 E5
Wiseacre TN3 . . . . .20 A3
Wish Cl BN3 . . . . .162 E8
Wish Hill BN20 . . . . .173 B1
Wish Rd Eastbourne BN21 .185 A2
  Hove BN3 . . . . .162 E6
Wish St TN31 . . . . .93 B5
Wish Tower Mus BN21 . . .185 A1
Wish Ward TN31 . . . . .93 B5
Wishing Tree Cl TN38 . . .135 F2
Wishing Tree La TN38 . . .135 F1
Wishing Tree Rd TN38 . . .135 F2
Wishing Tree Rd N TN38 .136 A4
Wiston Ct **12** BN43 . . . . .161 C8
Wiston Rd BN2 . . . . .164 F6
Wiston Way BN2 . . . . .164 F7
Withdean Ave BN1 . . . . . .142 D2
Withdean Cl BN1 . . . . . . .142 D3
Withdean Court Ave BN1 142 D3
Withdean Cres BN1 . . . . .142 E3
Withdean Ct **7** BN1 . . . .142 E3
Withdean Hall BN1 . . . . .142 E3

Withdean Rd BN1 . . . . . . .142 D3
Withdean Rise BN1 . . . . .142 D3
Witherenden Rd TN20 . . . .41 A1
Withy Bush RH15 . . . . .72 E5
Withyham Ave BN2 . . . . . .177 C5
Withyham Cl BN22 . . . . . .173 F1
Withyham Rd
  Bexhill TN39 . . . . .156 C2
  Groombridge TN3 . . . . .15 B7
Wittersham Rd Iden TN31 . . .49 D4
  Potman's Heath TN17, TN30 . .49 D4
Wittersham Road Sta
  TN17 . . . . .49 D6
Wivelsfield Cty Prim Sch
  RH17 . . . . .73 F6
Wivelsfield Rd
  Haywards Heath RH16 . . . .50 E2
  Saltdean BN2 . . . . .166 C3
Wivelsfield Sta RH15 . . . .73 C4
Woburn Cl BN27 . . . . .129 A1
Woburn Pl BN1 . . . . .143 F5
Woburn Way BN22 . . . . . .173 D3
Wolfe Cl TN6 . . . . .38 A8
Wolseley Rd Brighton BN1 143 D6
  Portslade-by-Sea BN41 . . .162 A8
  Royal Tunbridge Wells TN4 . . . .8 C7
Wolstead Lodge **3** RH16 . .50 F3
Wolstonbury Cl BN6 . . . . .97 B4
Wolstonbury Ct RH15 . . . .73 B2
Wolstonbury Rd BN3 . . . .163 E7
Wolstonbury Way RH15 . . .73 B2
Wolverstone Dr BN1 . . . .143 C2
Wood La BN27 . . . . .131 D2
Wood Ride RH16 . . . . .50 D3
Wood St East Grinstead RH19 1 D1
  Royal Tunbridge Wells TN1 . . . .8 B4
Wood's Pas **4** TN34 . . . . .160 B4
Woodbourne Ave BN1 . . .143 A4
Woodbrook Rd TN34 . . . .136 F2
Woodbury Ave RH19 . . . . . .2 B1
Woodbury Cl
  East Grinstead RH19 . . . . .11 B8
  Royal Tunbridge Wells RH19 . . . .8 A5
Woodbury Park Gdns TN4 . .8 B5
Woodbury Park Rd TN4 . . . .8 B5
Woodcombe TN34 . . . . . .136 F4
Woodcote Rd RH18 . . . . . .11 F2
Woodcrest Rd RH15 . . . . .72 F1
Woodcroft RH15 . . . . .72 F5
Woodcroft Dr BN21 . . . . .184 C7
Woodcutters RH17 . . . . . .51 F3
Woodgate Mdw BN27 . . . .99 E2
Woodgate Rd BN22 . . . . .185 C5
Woodhams Cl TN33 . . . . .112 D5
Woodhill Pk TN2 . . . . .7 E5
Woodhouse Cl BN3 . . . . .162 E7
Woodhouse Rd BN3 . . . . .162 E7
Woodingdean
  Cty Prim Sch BN2 . . . . . .165 C8
Woodland Ave
  Burgess Hill RH15 . . . . . . .73 C4
  Eastbourne BN22 . . . . . . .173 C1
  Hove BN3 . . . . .142 B3
Woodland Cl
  Burgess Hill RH15 . . . . . . .73 C4
  Hove BN3 . . . . .142 B2
  Royal Tunbridge Wells TN4 . . . .8 C7
Woodland Cres RH15 . . . .73 C4
Woodland Ct
  Burgess Hill RH15 . . . . . . .73 B3
  Hove BN3 . . . . .142 B4
Woodland Dr BN3 . . . . . .142 B3
Woodland Mews TN21 . . . .82 B6
Woodland Par BN3 . . . . . .142 B3
Woodland Rd TN4 . . . . .8 C7
Woodland Rise TN40 . . . .157 E4
Woodland Vale Rd
  TN37, TN38 . . . . .159 C8
Woodland Walks TN33 . . .113 B5
Woodland Way
  Brighton BN1 . . . . .142 F4
  Crowborough TN6 . . . . . . .37 F8
  Crowhurst TN33 . . . . .134 F4
  Fairlight Cove TN35 . . . . .138 E4
  Heathfield TN21 . . . . .82 B6
Woodland Wlk BN2 . . . . .165 D4
Woodlands Hove BN3 . . . .142 C2
  Romford TN2 . . . . .9 F7
Woodlands Cl
  Hailsham BN27 . . . . .129 C2
  Heathfield TN21 . . . . .82 B5
  Peacehaven BN10 . . . . . . .167 B1
  Uckfield TN22 . . . . .78 D8
Woodlands Rd
  East Grinstead RH19 . . . . . .2 A4
  Haywards Heath RH16 . . . .50 F4
Woodlands The
  Brighton BN1 . . . . .142 E5
  Hastings TN34 . . . . .136 E5
Woodlands Way TN34 . . .136 E6
Woodleigh Rd RH15 . . . . .73 C4
Woodmans Oak TN33 . . . .88 A3
Woodpecker Cres RH15 . . .72 D3
Woodpecker Dr BN27 . . . .152 A8
Woodpecker Rd BN23 . . .174 B2
Woodpecker Way TN22 . . .78 D5
Woodridge Cl RH16 . . . . . .51 A3
Woodruff Ave BN3 . . . . . .142 C2
Woods Green Cotts TN5 . .29 F7
Woods Hill Cl RH19 . . . . . .11 D6
Woods Hill La RH19 . . . . . .11 D6
Woods Ho BN3 . . . . .163 A8
Woodsgate Ave TN40 . . . .157 C6
Woodsgate Pk TN39 . . . . .157 B6
Woodsgate Way TN2 . . . . . .9 B6
Woodside Crowborough TN6 25 E2
  Kilndown TN17 . . . . .20 F2
Woodside Ave BN1 . . . . . .142 D2

Woodside Cl TN2 . . . . .9 E6
Woodside Lodge BN1 . . .142 D2
Woodside Rd Pembury TN2 . .9 E6
  Rusthall TN4 . . . . .7 D4
Woodside Terr BN26 . . . .151 F4
Woodside Way TN27 . . . .152 A4
Woodslands Cl BN6 . . . . . .97 F4
Woodslands Rd BN6 . . . . . .97 F4
Woodspring CI TN37 . . . .136 B5
Woodstock RH19 . . . . .1 C2
Woodstock Rd TN39 . . . . .156 C6
Woodview Cl BN1 . . . . . . .143 D6
Woodville Ct **9** TN39 . . . .157 B3
Woodville Rd TN39 . . . . . .157 B3
Woodward Cl BN23 . . . . . .185 E2
Woodwards Cl RH15 . . . . .73 B1
Woolven Cl RH15 . . . . .72 C5
Worcester Ct
  5 Eastbourne BN23 . . . .174 E1
  1 Hove BN3 . . . . .163 C6
Worcester Villas BN3 . . .162 C7
Wordsworth Dr BN23 . . . .174 E2
Wordsworth Rise **6** RH19 . .1 C1
Wordsworth St BN3 . . . . .163 A7
Workhouse La TN36 . . . . .116 F5
Worsham La TN40 . . . . . . .157 F7
Worsted La RH19 . . . . .11 B8
Wray Cl RH19 . . . . .11 D6
Wren Cl Burgess Hill RH15 . .72 D3
  Heathfield TN21 . . . . .82 A7
Wren Ct Battle TN33 . . . . .112 F4
  St Leonards TN38 . . . . . . .135 E3
Wrentham Ho RH15 . . . . . .73 B3
Wrestwood Ave BN22 . . . .173 C1
Wrestwood Cl TN40 . . . . .157 D6
Wrestwood Rd TN40 . . . .157 D6
Wrotham Cl
  Eastbourne BN23 . . . . . . .174 D1
  Hastings TN34 . . . . .136 E5
Wroxham Rd BN23 . . . . . .174 B4
Wyatts La TN17 . . . . .33 D5
Wyberlye Rd RH15 . . . . . . .73 A4
Wybourne Rise TN2 . . . . . .17 B8
Wychperry Rd RH16 . . . . .50 D5
Wychurst Gdns TN40 . . . .157 D6
Wyck Ct BN41 . . . . .162 A7
Wykeham Ct TN34 . . . . . .159 E8
Wykeham Rd TN34 . . . . . .159 E8
Wykeham Terr BN1 . . . . . .189 A2
Wykeham Way RH15 . . . . .73 C2
Wynberg Cotts TN6 . . . . . .39 C6
Wyndham St BN2 . . . . . . .189 C1
Wynnes Mews BN3 . . . . .163 A7
Wynnstay RH15 . . . . .73 B2
Wyshe The BN45 . . . . . . .119 C6
Wythwood RH16 . . . . .50 E1

Y

Yardley St BN1 . . . . .189 B5
Yates Cl TN31 . . . . .95 A2
Yeomans BN8 . . . . .125 A7
Yew Ct **1** RH19 . . . . .1 D2
Yew La RH19 . . . . .1 B3
Yew Tree Cl
  Broyle Side BN8 . . . . .124 F7
  Hastings TN34 . . . . .136 E6
  Heathfield TN21 . . . . .82 A6
Yew Tree Cotts
  Burgess Hill RH15 . . . . . . .73 B3
  Groombridge TN3 . . . . .15 F8
Yew Tree Rd TN4 . . . . .8 B8
Yewtree La TN6 . . . . .39 E8
Yielding's Cl BN21 . . . . . .184 D5
York Ave
  East Grinstead RH19 . . . . .11 A8
  Hove BN3 . . . . .163 E6
York Bldgs **6** TN34 . . . . .159 F7
York Ct **18** BN3 . . . . .163 E7
York Gdns **5** TN34 . . . . .159 F7
York Gr BN1 . . . . .189 A4
York Hill BN1 . . . . .189 B4
York Ho BN41 . . . . .162 B8
York Pl Brighton BN1, BN2 .189 B3
  Hove BN3 . . . . .163 E6
York Rd Bexhill TN40 . . . .158 A5
  Burgess Hill RH15 . . . . . . .72 D2
  Eastbourne BN21 . . . . . . .184 F2
  Hove BN1, BN3 . . . . .163 E6
  Peacehaven BN10 . . . . . . .178 E6
  Royal Tunbridge Wells TN1 . . . .8 A4
  St Leonards TN37 . . . . . . .136 C2
York Villas BN1 . . . . .189 A4
Yorkshire Ct BN20 . . . . . .184 B7
Youl Grange BN20 . . . . . .184 D1
Youngsmere Cl BN1 . . . . .143 B6
Yvonne Robertson Ho
  TN40 . . . . .157 D5

Any feature in this atlas can be given a unique reference to help you find the same feature on other Ordnance Survey maps of the area, or to help someone else locate you if they do not have a Street Atlas.

The grid squares in this atlas match the Ordnance Survey National Grid and are at 500 metre intervals. The small figures at the bottom and sides of every other grid line are the National Grid kilometre values (**00** to **99** km) and are repeated across the country every 100 km (see left).

To give a unique National Grid reference you need to locate where in the country you are. The country is divided into 100 km squares with each square given a unique two-letter reference. Use the administrative map to determine in which 100 km square a particular page of this atlas falls.

The bold letters and numbers between each grid line (**A** to **F**, **1** to **8**) are for use within a specific Street Atlas only, and when used with the page number, are a convenient way of referencing these grid squares.

Example   The railway bridge over DARLEY GREEN RD in grid square B1

Step 1: Identify the two-letter reference, in this example the page is in **SP**

Step 2: Identify the 1 km square in which the railway bridge falls. Use the figures in the southwest corner of this square: Eastings **17**, Northings **74**. This gives a unique reference: **SP 17 74**, accurate to 1 km.

Step 3: To give a more precise reference accurate to 100 m you need to estimate how many tenths along and how many tenths up this 1 km square the feature is (to help with this the 1 km square is divided into four 500 m squares). This makes the bridge about **8** tenths along and about **1** tenth up from the southwest corner.

This gives a unique reference: **SP 178 741**, accurate to 100 m.

Eastings (read from left to right along the bottom) come before Northings (read from bottom to top). If you have trouble remembering say to yourself "Along the hall, THEN up the stairs"!

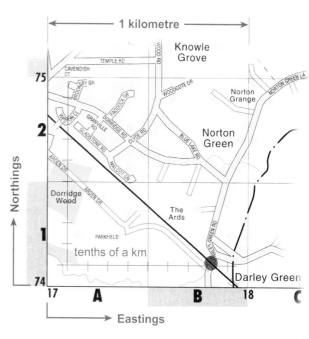

Addresses

Name and Address	Telephone	Page	Grid reference

Name and Address	Telephone	Page	Grid reference

Street Atlases from Philip's

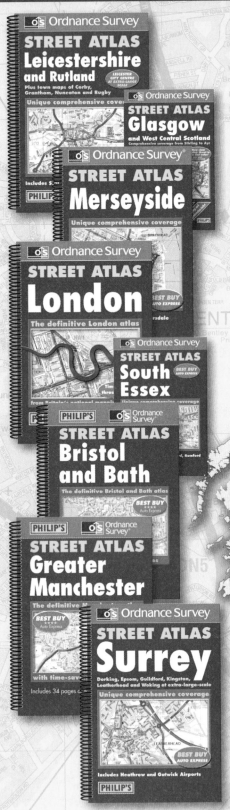

Philip's publish an extensive range of regional and local street atlases which are ideal for motoring, business and leisure use. They are widely used by the emergency services and local authorities throughout Britain.

Key features include:

◆ Superb county-wide mapping at an extra-large scale of 3½ inches to 1 mile, or 2½ inches to 1 mile in pocket editions

◆ Complete urban and rural coverage, detailing every named street in town and country

◆ Each atlas available in three handy formats – hardback, spiral, pocket paperback

'The mapping is very clear... great in scope and value'
★★★★ BEST BUY   AUTO EXPRESS

1 Bedfordshire
2 Berkshire
3 Birmingham and West Midlands
4 Bristol and Bath
5 Buckinghamshire
6 Cardiff, Swansea & The Valleys
7 Cheshire
8 Derbyshire
9 Durham
10 Edinburgh and East Central Scotland
11 North Essex
12 South Essex
13 Glasgow and West Central Scotland
14 North Hampshire
15 South Hampshire
16 Hertfordshire
17 East Kent
18 West Kent
19 Lancashire
20 Leicestershire and Rutland
21 London
22 Greater Manchester
23 Merseyside
24 Northamptonshire
25 Nottinghamshire
26 Oxfordshire
27 Staffordshire
28 Surrey
29 East Sussex
30 West Sussex
31 Tyne and Wear
32 Warwickshire
33 South Yorkshire
34 West Yorkshire

How to order

The Philip's range of street atlases is available from good retailers or directly from the publisher by phoning 01933 443863